## Major Formulas

Confidence Interval Around Mean for Large Samples $= \bar{x} \pm z_\alpha \left[ \dfrac{s}{\sqrt{n-1}} \right]$      (9.2)     p. 242

Confidence Interval Around Mean for Small Samples $= \bar{x} \pm t_\alpha \left[ \dfrac{s_x}{\sqrt{n-1}} \right]$      (9.3)     p. 248

Confidence Interval Around Proportions $= \hat{p} + z_\alpha(\sigma_p)$      (9.4)     p. 251
$$\text{where:}$$

$\hat{p}$ = sample proportion,

$$\sigma_p = \sqrt{\dfrac{P(1-P)}{n}}$$

$P$ - population proportion

Hypothesis Test For One Sample Mean $= z_{obt} = \dfrac{\bar{x} - \mu}{s/\sqrt{n-1}}$      (10.3)     p. 270

Hypothesis Test For One Mean Using Small Samples $= t_{obt} = \dfrac{\bar{X} - \mu}{s/\sqrt{n-1}}$      (10.4)     p. 279

Chi Square Test $= \chi^2 = \Sigma \dfrac{f_o^2}{f_e} - n$      (11.3)     p. 307

where:
$f_o$ is the observed cell frequency
$f_e$ is the expected cell frequency, and
$k$ is the number of cells in the table

Expected Cell Frequency $= f_{ij} = \dfrac{RM_i CM_j}{n}$      (11.2)     p. 305

where:
$RM$ = the row marginal for row $i$
$CM$ = the column marginal for column $j$

*Statistical Methods for Criminology and Criminal Justice*

# Statistical Methods for Criminology and Criminal Justice

Ronet Bachman

*Department of Sociology and Criminal Justice*
*University of Delaware*

Raymond Paternoster

*Department of Criminology and Criminal Justice*
*University of Maryland*

The McGraw-Hill Companies, Inc.

*New York   St. Louis   San Francisco   Auckland   Bogotá   Caracas*
*Lisbon   London   Madrid   Mexico City   Milan   Montreal   New Delhi*
*San Juan   Singapore   Sydney   Tokyo   Toronto*

# McGraw-Hill

A Division of The **McGraw·Hill** Companies

*Dedicated to the memory of John B. Paternoster,*
*beloved brother and dear friend*

*and, when he shall die,*
*Take him and cut him out in little stars,*
*And he will make the face of heaven so fine*
*That all the world will be in love with night*
*And pay no worship to the garish sun.*

SHAKESPEARE

*STATISTICAL METHODS FOR CRIMINOLOGY AND CRIMINAL JUSTICE*

This book was printed on acid-free paper.

2 3 4 5 6 7 8 9 0 DOC DOC 9 0 9 8 7

ISBN 0-07-003000-6

*This book was set in Times Roman by Graphic World, Inc.*
*The editor was Marjorie Byers; the production supervisor was Annette Mayeski.*
*The cover was designed by Farenga Design Group.*
*R. R. Donnelley & Sons Company was printer and binder.*

**Library of Congress Cataloging-in-Publication Data**

Bachman, Ronet.
    Statistical methods for criminology and criminal justice / Ronet
Bachman, Raymond Paternoster.
    p.    cm.
    Includes bibliographical references.
    ISBN 0-07-003000-6
    1.  Criminal statistics.    I.  Paternoster, Raymond.    II.  Title.
HV6208.B33   1997                              96-22514
3649.0195195 — dc20

# About the Authors

RONET BACHMAN received her Ph.D. from the University of New Hampshire in 1989 and worked as a postdoctoral fellow there at the Family Research Laboratory until 1991. For several years she worked at the U.S. Department of Justice as a statistician and research analyst. Currently, she is an assistant professor in the Department of Sociology and Criminal Justice at the University of Delaware. She is the author of many articles that explore the epidemiology and origins of violent victimization, with particular emphasis on victimization against women, the elderly, and minority populations. She also is the author of *Death and Violence on the Reservation: Homicide, Suicide, and Family Violence in Contemporary American Indian Populations* (Greenwood Press) and coauthored *Stress, Culture and Aggression in the United States* (Yale University Press).

RAYMOND PATERNOSTER is currently a professor in the Department of Criminology and Criminal Justice at the University of Maryland. His research interests include testing theories of crime and social control, particularly choice-based theories, and issues related to capital punishment. He is the author of *Capital Punishment in America* (Lexington Press).

# Contents

# Preface

*Statistical Methods for Criminology and Criminal Justice* was primarily written for undergraduate students taking their first statistics course. We have tried to present a discussion of basic statistical procedures that is comprehensive in its coverage, yet accessible and readable for the general undergraduate student. In view of this general goal, we have chosen to emphasize a practical approach to the use of statistics in research. We have stressed the interpretation and understanding of statistical operations in answering research questions, be they theoretical or more of a public policy nature. This approach is at the expense of a detailed theoretical or mathematical treatment of introductory statistics. As reflects our "statistics as a research tool" approach, we have not provided the derivations of formulas or presented proofs or the underlying statistical theory behind the operations. This does not mean, however, that we have ducked presenting the hard stuff or have sacrificed statistical rigor. We discuss some very complex statistical procedures in the course of the text, and in addition to presenting numerous statistical operations, we have given reasons why some things are done and others are not. We have done so, we hope, in a way that illustrates the usefulness of the procedure for answering research questions and that will help the undergraduate student understand *why* they are doing what they are doing.

Given the title, it is obvious that we had the student majoring in criminology and criminal justice particularly in mind as a reader of this text. This can easily be seen in the nature of the examples throughout the book. We have tried to take these examples and illustrations from the past and current literature in criminology and criminal justice. Given the broad nature of these two fields, we were able to couch our statistical lessons in a wide and diverse range of topics and issues, including gun control, prison overcrowding, theories of delinquency and adult criminality, and discrimination in the legal system.

Although we think that this book will be of particular interest and relevance for students of criminology and criminal justice, we would quickly add that it is of a much broader scope. We think that students of sociology, social work, political science, and psychology will also find the book quite illuminating. The statistical methods we present have wide interdisciplinary application, and we believe that we have written a very clear, concise, yet comprehensive, introductory statistics text that will be appropriate for students in all social and behavioral sciences. Even though each field has its own disciplinary interests and issues, students from different backgrounds should nonetheless find our examples interesting.

In addition, we have structured this book in such a way that it will have very diverse applications. It is, as we have noted, an introductory statistics book. Our intention was that it be used as the primary text in a one-semester course. Instructors will find that they can omit some chapters at their discretion (probability theory, nonparametric statistics, multiple ordinary least-squares regression, or logit and probit regression) with no loss of continuity. Because the text is very comprehensive in the kinds of statistical procedures it covers, from one-sample $z$ and $t$ tests to binary regression models, it also would fit very nicely in a two-semester statistics course. Finally, although we had the undergraduate student in mind with what we hope is a readable style, the book could easily be used as the primary statistics text in an introductory graduate-level course. Graduate students will especially benefit from the chapters on multivariate statistics, and we think that they will find their understanding and comprehension of $t$ tests, ANOVA, and the general linear model enhanced by a thorough reading of the chapters on these issues.

## Organization and Features

The book is organized sequentially. We begin with a basic understanding of research and data gathering in criminology and criminal justice. Chapters 1 and 2 discuss the research enterprise, sampling techniques, and levels of measurement. Chapters 2–5 describe basic descriptive statistics, such as rates, proportions, and measures of central tendency and dispersion. We also devote two chapters (3 and 6) to what we think is a particularly important topic in introductory statistics, the graphical display of data. A recurring theme throughout the text is that research can benefit by both a graphical understanding of one's own data (the shape and unique features of a data distribution) and a graphical presentation of one's findings.

From this discussion of descriptive statistics, we move in Chapter 7 to a presentation of the foundation of inferential statistics, probability theory and sampling distributions such as the normal distribution in Chapter 8. The remainder of the book concerns issues related to hypothesis testing and a search for relationships between one or more independent variables and a dependent variable. Chapters 9 and 10 present one sample estimation and hypothesis testing problems. Chapter 11 discusses the analysis of categorical variables with contingency tables. It also includes a discussion of the chi-square test of independence, and various measures of association with categorical variables. Chapters 12 and 13 return the reader to the problem of hypothesis testing with means. Chapter 12 presents the familiar dependent and independent samples $t$-test, and hypothesis tests with two population proportions. Chapter 13 is devoted to the analysis of variance, and hypothesis testing involving three or more population means.

Chapter 14 provides a detailed background to an important statistical tool in criminology and criminal justice—linear regression analysis. We discuss the essential framework of linear regression analysis: scatterplots, the notion of "least squares," the regression line, linear prediction, linear correlation, and hypothesis tests with slopes and correlation coefficients. This chapter is restricted to models with one independent variable. In Chapter 15, we extend this discussion to the two variable regression model.

Chapter 16 presents the use and usefulness of nonparametric statistics and the use of rank order analogs to parametric statistic tests such as the *t*-test, analysis of variance, and correlation coefficient.

Chapter 17 ends the book with a brief discussion of the essential components of logistic and probit regression models. A discussion of regression analysis with binary dependent variables is seldom included in an introductory statistics text, but these models have become so prominent in social science research that we felt their omission would have done a great disservice to those wanting some degree of comprehensiveness in their first statistics course.

Finally, the study of statistics cannot really be accomplished without an understanding of the use of statistical software programs. These software programs now do most, if not all, of the statistical "grunt work" for us. This has certainly not made the learning of statistics or the practice of hand-calculating statistics obsolete, because we still have to tell the software programs the right things to do at the right times, and we still have to interpret and understand what we get back from these programs. Nevertheless, the role of computers is an important component in any study of statistics.

We have decided against *directly* incorporating a particular statistical software program into our discussion of various statistical procedures. We emphasize that this was not because we thought the integration of computer work into statistics is not important—quite the contrary! We believe it is essential. Rather, our decision not to directly integrate a computer software component was based on the diversity of such software programs, and particular instructors' devotion to one or the other program. The list of computer software programs that can be used beneficially by introductory statistics classes only begins with SPSS, SAS, MINITAB, STATA, BMDP. We have chosen the path of presenting a generic approach to introductory statistics and let the individual instructor decide (1) if they want to incorporate a computer element into their course, and if so (2) which particular software program they want to use.

For those who have decided to integrate a computer component into their course, we have written a companion volume to this statistics text called ***Computer Applications in Criminology and Criminal Justice Using SPSS.*** This companion volume does integrate the chapters of this book into a discussion of the computer software program SPSS-PC. Our decision to write a companion volume to the primary text reflects the convergence of three lines of thought: (1) our desire to not directly incorporate one software program into the primary text, (2) our belief that statistical analysis by computer is an essential task to learn, and (3) our own prior training and weakly felt biases in favor of SPSS. This companion volume contains a brief introduction to SPSS commands and individual chapters that correspond to the inferential statistics chapters of the primary text.

In this companion workbook, we go through examples of data analysis with SPSS procedures. In addition, the workbook contains a disk with five data sets that we use in the volume to illustrate various statistical operations and that students can use on their own to explore the statistical procedures available in SPSS. These data sets include (1) robbery incidents from the National Crime Victimization Survey (NCVS) for 1991, (2) incidents involving violence against women from the NCVS for 1993, (3) attitude and perceptual information, including self-reported involvement in delinquency, for a sample of approximately 1200 students in the 10th and 11th grades, (4) a sample of approximately 1300 homicide defendants whose cases went to trial by jury or judge, (5) a state-level data set that includes homicide rates, rates of poverty, stress, social disorganization, and social indicators.

Again, we would emphasize the generality of our companion volume. Although the commands are written for a personal computer version of SPSS, they can easily be adapted to a mainframe version of SPSS, and the data sets themselves could be adapted to other software programs.

## *ACKNOWLEDGMENTS*

We are grateful to the Longman Group, Ltd. 1974, on behalf of the literary executor of the late Sir Ronald A. Fisher, F.R.S. and Dr. Frank Yates, F.R.S. for permission to reproduce Table III from *Statistical Tables for Biological, Agricultural, and Medical Research,* 6th edition, 1974.

No undertaking of this magnitude could have been accomplished without the assistance and support of numerous persons and organizations. We would both like to thank our three very careful and dedicated reviewers: Thomas Petee of Auburn University, Dan Powers of the University of Texas, and Leonore Simon of Temple University. They did Herculean work. Their suggestions were invaluable in improving the quality of this text. We were astonished at the care, attention to detail, and deliberateness with which they reviewed and commented on our work with an eye to improving it. Two things are true because of their efforts: (1) this is by now a far, far better book for students, and (2) any problems, omissions, misunderstandings, ambiguities, or errors that remain are attributable to us, and us alone.

We would also like to thank Alex Piquero, Mark "Doogie" Rizzo, Steve Tibbetts, and Bob Brame who read and reread each chapter and checked and rechecked the arithmetic throughout the book. They were very helpful in giving us the students' perspective. Although technically students of Ray's, they performed like colleagues. We know that they are as relieved as we are that the book is completed. We would like to extend a word of thanks to the many students who were subjected to early versions of each of these chapters. They were invaluable in letting us know what worked and especially what did not work in presenting sometimes confusing and always complex statistical topics. Finally, we would both also like to acknowledge our gratitude to McGraw-Hill for undertaking this project and for providing us with Phil Butcher who first accepted the idea and Hilary Jackson and Bridget Isacsen, editor and assistant editor, respectively, who nurtured it and provided support throughout the course of the project, and Marge Byers, who brought it to closure.

Ray would like to extend a deep sense of gratitude and thanks to two special people. One is Charles F. Wellford who was the chair of the Department of Criminology and Criminal Justice at the University of Maryland during the time the book was written. Charles has been and continues to be the absolute ideal person to work for. He has been unrelenting and generous in his encouragement and support, both emotional and material, for this project. I owe him much, and give him my deepest and most heartfelt "thank you." The second person is his coauthor and wife, Ronet Bachman. Both this book and she are a labor of love. She has been a continuous source of encouragement, support, wisdom, good cheer, and above all else love.

Ronet would like to acknowledge personally the statistical mentors she has had in her career, including James Rafferty, Sally Ward, and Larry Hamilton. Each has provided a model of uncompromising integrity and unrelenting enthusiasm for the teaching, study, and application of statistics in their own work and in the work of their students. She would also like to thank her parents, Ronald and Lois Bachman and Bill and Jan Vermilyea, for providing a safe haven from the storms of life, and give a special thanks to her mother, Jan, who is also her best friend and an ever-present source of encouragement, guidance, and love. Finally, she thanks Ray, her coauthor, husband, and traveling companion through this thing called life—I couldn't walk the planet without you!

Ronet Bachman
*University of Delaware*

Raymond Paternoster
*University of Maryland*

# CHAPTER 1

# Why Do I Need to Learn This Stuff?

## The Purpose of Statistics in Criminology and Criminal Justice

*Fear is the main source of superstition, and one of the main sources of cruelty. To conquer fear is the beginning of wisdom.*

—BERTRAND RUSSELL

## 1.1 INTRODUCTION

Most students reading this book are probably taking a course in statistics, primarily because it is required to graduate. You are not taking the course because you were seeking a little adventure and thought a statistics course would be fun. Nor are you taking the course because there is something missing in your life and, thus, you think that the study of statistics is necessary to make you intellectually "well rounded." At least this has been our experience when teaching an undergraduate statistics course. Perhaps it is universal that every statistics professor must hear the litany of sorrows expressed by their students at the beginning of the course. "Oh, I have been putting this off for so long—I dreaded having to take this," "I have a mental block about math," or, "Math was never my thing—I always hated it in high school!"

Except for those fortunate few for whom math comes easy, the rest of us experience apprehension and anxiety when approaching our first statistics course. Psychologists are quick to tell us that what we most often fear is not real—it is merely our mind imagining and exaggerating things. This is a comforting thought; however, these psychologists do not have to take our statistics course. An acronym, False Expectations Appearing Real or FEAR, has been developed. Long ago Aristotle said, "Fear is pain arising from anticipation." But his definition does not help us much either, because, again, Aristotle is not taking our statistics course.

Although it is impossible for us to allay all the fear and apprehension you may be experiencing right now, it may help you to know that virtually everyone can and will make it through this course, even those of you who have trouble making change or balancing your checkbooks. This is not, of course, a guarantee, and we are not saying it will be easy, but we have found that persistence and tenacity can overcome even the most extreme mathematical handicaps.

1

Those of you who are particularly rusty with your math, and also those who just want a quick confidence builder, should refer to Appendix A at the back of this book. Appendix A discusses some basic math lessons in detail. In fact, it reviews all the math you probably need to know to pass this course. It also includes practice problems and, more important, the answers to those problems. Perhaps by examining this appendix you will be more confident in your statistical and mathematical abilities.

We hope that after this course you will not only be able to understand and calculate various statistics for yourself but also that you will be a knowledgeable consumer of the statistical material that you are confronted with daily. Understanding how to interpret statistics will be a tremendous asset to you regardless of the direction you plan to take with your criminology degree. This book is meant to provide you with this understanding. In addition to the mathematical skills required to compute statistics, we also hope to leave you with an understanding of what different statistical tests or operations can and cannot do, and what they do and do not tell you about a given problem.

The foundations for the statistics presented in this book are derived from complicated mathematical theory. You will be glad to know, however, that we do not mean to provide you with the proofs necessary to substantiate this body of theory. In this book, we offer two very basic types of knowledge: (1) the ability to calculate and conduct statistical analyses for your own research, and (2) the ability to interpret the results of statistical analysis and to apply them to the real world.

We want you, then, to both calculate and comprehend social statistics. These two purposes are not mutually exclusive but are intimately related. We believe that the ability to carry out the mathematical operations of a statistical formula is almost worthless unless you also can interpret the result you have obtained and give it meaning. Therefore, information both about the mechanics of conducting statistical tests and about interpreting the results of these tests is equally emphasized throughout this text.

Furthermore, learning about statistics for perhaps the first time does not mean that you will always have to calculate your statistics by hand, with the assistance of only a calculator. Most, if not all, researchers do their statistical analyses with a computer and software programs. Many useful and "user-friendly" statistical software programs are available for the introductory statistics student. These statistical programs, such as SPSS, SAS, STATA, and MINITAB, have the capacity to do all the statistics discussed in this book.

You may be wondering why you have to learn statistics and how to hand-calculate them if you can avoid all of this by using a computer and some statistical software. First, we believe it is important for you to understand exactly what it is the computer is doing when it is calculating statistics. Without this knowledge, you will have no idea what is happening when your software does the analysis. You will get results, but with little comprehension as to how they were obtained. We believe that this is not a good way to learn statistics. Second, without a firm foundation in the basics of statistics, you will have no real knowledge of what to request of your computer. In spite of its talent for doing things, the computer is actually pretty dumb, as it will do only what it is told and your instructions usually have to be quite specific. The computer has no ability to determine if what it is told to do is correct; that is up to you. Neither will the computer make sense out of the results; that also is your responsibility.

## 1.2 SEARCHING FOR RELATIONSHIPS

One important purpose of statistics in the field of criminology is to help mathematically ascertain the extent to which phenomena are related. For example, is there a relationship between the availability of handguns in an area and the homicide rate? Do communities with more police officers on patrol have lower rates of crime than similar communities with fewer officers? Do defendants with their own lawyers fare better in court than those with appointed counsel or a public defender? With the help of causal reasoning, we entertain these relationships in our head every day. However, statistical theory allows us to make this reasoning more explicit and more exact.

As another example, each of you taking this course probably realizes that the amount of time you spend studying for this course will affect the grade you receive. This assumption is primarily based on your past experience or the vicarious experience of watching straight-A students labor for hours in the library. Generally speaking, by now, it probably has dawned on you that there is a positive relationship between the hours you study for a course and the grade you receive for that course. That is, you have a greater likelihood of receiving a good grade in a class if you spend more time studying. If you conducted a formal survey to explore this relationship and calculated statistics with those data, you would probably come to the same conclusion.

Criminologists use this same process to describe and establish the existence of relationships among more complex phenomena, for example, homicide. When you think of Washington, DC, you may think of the grandeur of the Smithsonian museums, the Capitol building, or the White House, but your mind might also flash to the images of death and violence that are too often played out there. When urban homicide rates are released every year, the District of Columbia is almost always at the top of the list. But how does the rate of homicide in Washington, DC, actually compare with that of other large metropolitan areas? Perhaps more important, why do some cities have such high rates of homicide whereas other similar-size cities have much lower rates?

Criminologists examining the differences in homicide rates in various areas of the United States have long struggled with the question, "What factors account for regional, state, and city variations in homicide rates?" That is, why do some regions, states, and cities have homicide rates that are so much higher than others? In answering this question, criminologists entertain what are called *hypotheses* about a phenomenon. Hypotheses are simply informed hunches about what explains homicide rates and the like. Hypotheses may be derived from an existing body of theoretical or empirical literature or from one's own personal experience.

In making hypotheses about the causes of homicide, some criminologists have relied on subcultural explanations (Wolfgang & Ferracuti, 1967). Researchers who advocate subcultural explanations speculate that certain population subgroups possess a culture that encourages, or at least fails to condemn, the use of violence to resolve interpersonal conflict.[1] This explanation of homicide, then, is based on the idea that people learn about or become socialized into a subculture that encourages or tolerates violence. People socialized into such a subculture would be expected to commit homicide and other acts of aggression more frequently than people socialized into a subculture that is less permissive of violence. Other criminologists have hypothesized that differences in homicide rates in various areas may be explained best by social conditions such as the levels of poverty, unemployment, or social disorganization that exist in those areas.[2] These hypotheses suggest that homicide is related to material deprivation and weak social relationships.

What is most likely the case, however, is that the rate of homicide is not influenced by only one of these factors, but that it is affected by several things, including cultural definitions of violence, poverty, unemployment, and disorganized social relationships. To see more easily the hypothesized relationships among several variables, criminologists often provide a visual or graphic description called a *model*. An example of such a model for the explanation of homicide is shown in Figure 1.1. This model illustrates that homicide rates are influenced by (1) cultural norms, (2) poverty and unemployment (material deprivation), (3) powerlessness, (4) social disorganization, and (5) drug and alcohol use.

Criminologists interested in homicide conduct research, gather data, and empirically test different ideas or hypotheses about the causes of homicide and violence. Empirical tests are done through various statistical analyses, and the researcher's study is often communicated with the assistance of statistical and

FIGURE 1.1. A model of homicide.
(*Adapted from Bachman, 1992.*)

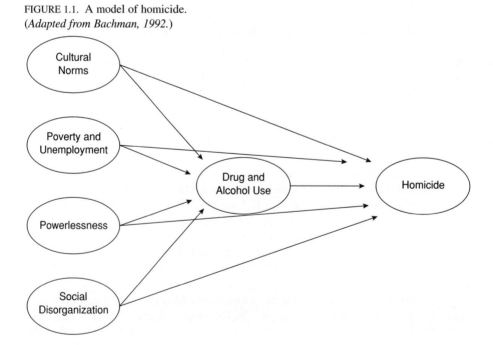

graphical procedures. A given hypothesis will sink or swim, so to speak, based on the results of these statistical analyses.

Another area of intense debate among criminologists is the extent to which the availability of guns, particularly handguns, increases homicide rates. In fact, this is a debate that triggers incensed emotion in most U.S. citizens. A billboard mounted above Times Square in New York City is vivid testimony to this emotion (Figure 1.2). The billboard keeps a tally of two numbers: the number of gun-related deaths (from street murders to hunting accidents) and the number of guns in circulation in the United States.

This societal debate, as well as the one being staged in the criminology literature, centers around the following question: "Would rates of homicide and other acts of violence involving firearms decline if the availability of guns was restricted?" To address this question in the criminology field, researchers have tracked homicide rates within a given location both before and after the implementation of specific gun control legislation. If they find significant decreases in rates of violent death after the implementation of gun control legislation, the new gun control statutes are assumed to be one factor responsible for the decrease in violent death.[3] Research investigating the effects of gun control legislation, however, remains somewhat equivocal. Although some researchers have found significant declines in the rates of violent death after gun control legislation has been implemented, others have found ambiguous effects or no significant effects at all.[4]

FIGURE 1.2. Gun fighters deathclock, Times Square, New York City.
(*Photo: Carol DeFrances and Chris Laskowski.*)

Keep in mind that these research topics have been presented in a very simplistic way. We include these discussions to demonstrate a few real-world issues investigated by criminologists with the assistance of statistical analyses. These discussions are not meant to give you an in-depth review of the comparative homicide or gun control literature. They are provided simply to illustrate the role of statistics in our field. Statistics are used as tools both to describe criminological phenomena and to examine relationships that may or may not exist among these phenomena.

Before we become more familiar with statistics in the upcoming chapters, we first want to set the stage for statistical inquiry. Virtually every statistic we examine in this text is based on central assumptions about the data being used. The data we utilize in criminology are derived from many different sources—from official government agency data, such as the Federal Bureau of Investigation's (FBI's) Uniform Crime Reports or the Bureau of Justice Statistics' National Crime Victimization Survey, to smaller data sources, such as surveys conducted independently by researchers themselves.

Because the data we use in criminology are most often obtained from samples, the remainder of this chapter covers some basic principles of sampling. We provide this discussion because issues of sampling are inextricably linked to the statistical process. We begin with a discussion of samples, populations, and sampling procedures and conclude by examining the differences between descriptive and inferential statistics.

## 1.3 POPULATIONS AND SAMPLES

The words "population" and "sample" should already have some meaning to you. When you think of a population, you probably think of the population of some locality such as the United States, the city or state in which you reside, or the university or college that you attend. Although we do not often encounter the concept of a sample in everyday life, you have probably heard of some instance in which samples were taken from a larger whole. For example, news stories related to physical conditions are often accompanied by references to samples, such as samples of paint in housing developments to detect the lead content, samples of blood to detect rates of HIV infection, samples of urine to detect drug or alcohol use, and samples of people to determine the potential winner of a political election. As with most social science research, samples in criminology most often consist of samples of people. Since it is too difficult, too costly, and sometimes impossible to get information on the entire population of interest, we must often solicit the information from samples. *Samples* are simply subsets of the larger *population.*

---

1. A **population** is the larger set of cases or aggregate number of people in which a researcher is actually interested or wishes to know something about.
2. A **sample** is a subset of the population that a researcher often must use to make generalizations about the larger population.

---

Most official statistics collected by the U.S. government are derived from information obtained from samples, not from the entire population. For example, the National Crime Victimization Survey (NCVS), a survey used to obtain information on the incidence and characteristics of crime in the United States, is based on a sample of the U.S. population. Every year, the NCVS interviews more than 100,000 individuals age 12 or older to solicit information on their experiences with victimization, both those that were reported and unreported to the police. Essentially, professional interviewers ask persons who are selected into the sample if they were the victim of a crime in the past 6 months and if they reported their victimization to the police. The purpose of the NCVS is to provide an estimate of the number of people in the United States who have experienced an act of violence or theft.

Other major "quality-of-life" indicators provided by the government also are derived from samples, not the entire U.S. population. When Tom Brokaw, Dan Rather, or Peter Jennings announce the unemployment rate released by the U.S. Department of Labor, Bureau of Labor Statistics, on the national news every month, what do you think this number is based on? It would be impossible to ask all people in the United States on a monthly basis whether they have recently lost their jobs. Instead, the Bureau of Labor solicits employment information from a sample of the U.S. population, calculates the percentage of this sample who are unemployed and/or looking for work, and then generalizes this percentage to the entire U.S. population.

You may be thinking right now, "What if I am only interested in a small population? What if I am not interested in the entire U.S. population, but a smaller population?" Good question! Let's say, for example, we were interested in all persons convicted of robbery who were incarcerated in state prisons. Although it would be easier to contact every individual in this population than every U.S. citizen, it would still be extremely difficult and costly to obtain information from every person convicted of robbery. In almost all instances, we have to settle on a sample derived from the overall population. For this reason, the "population" usually remains an unknown entity whose characteristics we only can estimate.

We make estimates about the unknown characteristics of the population by using the data we have from our sample. In essence, we use what we do know about the sample to understand what we do not know about the population. Although we discuss this in more detail in later chapters, it is important to have some idea now about the differences between sample and population information. Let's take as our example the previously mentioned practice of the U.S. Department of Labor to take a sample of persons' employment status to make an estimate of the level of unemployment in the entire U.S. population. The unemployment rate obtained from the sample is called a *sample estimate,* or *statistic.* If, for example, the U.S. Department of Labor obtains a sample of 2000 persons, interviews them, and finds that 7 percent of them reported being unemployed in the previous month, this 7 percent unemployment rate for the sample is a statistic. Notice that we know the actual value of the statistic (in this case, the sample unemployment rate) because it is derived from sample information or data. It is also important to see that our sample value of 7 percent is not fixed; rather, it varies across different samples. If we take another sample of 2000 persons, the percent unemployed will probably be different than 7 percent. Furthermore, if we took yet another sample, we would likely get another value. The sample statistic, then, varies from sample to sample.

This is not such a problem, however, because we are not really interested in the unemployment rate in our sample but in the United States as a whole. The unknown information that we want to know about is the overall level of unemployment in the United States. This unknown population characteristic is called a *parameter*. We do not know the "real" level of unemployment. We do know, however, that we could find out what it is by asking every person in the population. The population level of unemployment, then, is unknown but knowable. Moreover, unlike the sample estimate, the population level of unemployment is fixed. That does not mean that it does not change over time. By saying it is fixed, we only mean that, if it were possible to ask everyone in the population about their employment status again, the results would not change (assuming, of course, that their employment status did not change since we first asked them about it). The difference between a sample statistic and a population parameter, then, is that a sample statistic is known (because we gather data on sample characteristics) and varies across samples, whereas a population parameter is not known (but is knowable) and is fixed.

Our purpose in selecting a sample is to be able to make a generalization about some unknown population characteristic based on what we know about the sample. In other words, we use the known sample statistic to make an inference or generalization about the unknown population parameter. Because the purpose of sampling is to make these generalizations, we must be meticulous when selecting our sample. The primary goal of sampling is to make sure that the sample we select is representative of the population we are estimating.

Think about this goal for a minute. Suppose you were interested in the extent to which high school students were afraid of being attacked or otherwise victimized in their schools. It would be impossible (or at least very expensive and time consuming) to obtain questionnaires soliciting these perceptions of fear from every high school student in the United States (i.e., a population); therefore, you would have to collect questionnaires from a sample of students. Would you be comfortable obtaining this information from just any high school? For example, would it be a good idea to collect information on fearfulness from high school kids in Faith, South Dakota (population 565)? Would you be confident that the levels of fear the students from Faith High School perceived were representative of high school students across the United States? Would a sample from a rural school in South Dakota be similar to a sample from an inner-city or an affluent suburban school? Obviously it would not be similar.

When estimating or inferring information about a phenomenon from a sample to a population, whether it be attitudes or crime victimization rates, we must, therefore, be sure that our sample is representative of our target population. What do we mean by representative? Generally, if the characteristics (e.g., age, race/ethnicity, gender) of a sample are reasonably similar to those of the population, it is said to be representative. For example, if you were interested in estimating the proportion of the population that considers itself members of the Democratic Party, to be representative, your sample should contain about 50 percent men and 50 percent women because that is the makeup of the U.S. population. It also should contain about 85 percent whites and 15 percent nonwhites, because that is the makeup of the U.S. population. If you include a high proportion of males or nonwhites, your sample would be unrepresentative. If your sample is unrepresentative of the population you want to know about, the sample statistic will be an inaccurate estimate of the population parameter. If, for example, your sample was 50 percent nonwhite, you would get an inaccurate estimate of the proportion of the U.S. population that considers itself members of the Democratic Party, because racial minorities are more likely to be Democrats than racial majorities.

With a few special exceptions, therefore, a good sample should be representative of the larger population. If the goal of sampling is to obtain a representative sample, how does one achieve this goal (i.e., what are the means?)? There are various procedures to obtain a sample; these procedures range from the simple to the complex.

## *1.4 TECHNIQUES OF SAMPLING*

From the previous discussion, it should be apparent that accuracy is one of the primary problems we face when generalizing information obtained from a sample to a population. How accurately does our sample reflect the true population? This question is inherent in any inquiry because with any sample we only represent a part, and sometimes a small part, of the whole population. The goal in obtaining or selecting a sample, then, is to select it in a way that increases the chances of this sample being representative of the entire population.

When we select a sample, we select an *element* of the population to be included in that sample. An element simply is a single member of the population. If the population is made up of all persons tried in state courts in the year 1995, then an element of that population would be a person tried in the state of Florida in that year. If a population is made up of several hundred cities with populations of 250,000 or more, then an element is a city with 250,000 or more people. The question, then, is how do we select elements of the population in order to ensure that the sample is representative of it?

*Probability sampling* increases the likelihood of accomplishing this goal of representativeness. In probability sampling, each population element has a known and nonzero probability of being selected into the sample. The fundamental strategy in probability sampling is the *random selection* of elements into the sample. When a sample is randomly selected from the population, every element has a known, equal, and independent chance of being selected into the sample. What

---

A necessary and sufficient condition for probability sampling is that we know the probability that each element of the population will be selected into the sample, that this probability be nonzero, and that the selection of one element is independent of the selection of all other elements.

random selection adds is that each element of the population has an equal chance of being selected.

Flipping a coin or rolling a set of dice are typical examples used to characterize the process of random selection. When you flip a coin, you have the same chance of obtaining a head as you do of obtaining a tail: one out of two. Similarly, when rolling a die, you have the same probability of rolling a two as you do of rolling a six: one out of six. In criminology, researchers usually use random numbers tables, such as Table B.1 in Appendix B, or other computer-generated random selection programs to select a sample.

Using probability sampling techniques not only serves to minimize any potential bias we may have when selecting a sample, but also allow us to gain access to probability theory in our data analysis. This body of mathematical theory allows us to estimate more accurately the degree of error we have when generalizing results obtained from known sample statistics to unknown population parameters. But do not worry about probability theory now. We discuss probability issues in much greater detail in Chapter 7. For now, let's examine some of the most common types of probability samples used in criminological research.

## 1.5 PROBABILITY SAMPLING TECHNIQUES

### Simple Random Samples

Perhaps the most common type of probability sample to use when we want to generalize information obtained from the sample to a population is called a *simple random sample.* In a simple random sample, each element of the population has an equal, known, and independent chance of being selected into the sample. True simple random sampling is done by placing a selected element back into the population so that there continues to be an equal and independent chance of any given element being selected. This is referred to as sampling *"with replacement."* Let's go through an example of selecting a simple random sample from a population. Suppose we are interested in the attitudes that police officers have about gun control. The first step we must make is to specify our population. Because it is probably impossible to obtain a list of every police officer in the United States, let's say we specify our population based on a list of 100 enrolled members of the Police Officer's Association of America (POAA—the POAA does not really exist). The population of 100 police officers we are sampling from is represented in Figure 1.3. Our goal is to select a random sample of 10 individuals from this population. Yes, this is a very small sample, but remember, this is for illustration purposes only!

---

**Random selection** is the fundamental element of **probability samples.** The essential characteristic of random selection is that every element of the population has a **known, equal, and independent chance** of being selected into the sample.

FIGURE 1.3. Collecting a simple random sample of police officers using a random numbers table.

To obtain a simple random sample, we must first assign a number to every element in the population. In this case, our elements are police officers, so we will assign a number to each of the 100 officers. The first officer on the membership list will be assigned the number 0 and the last officer will be assigned the number 99. We can now begin the selection of our sample by using the random numbers table in Appendix B (Table B.1). Because Table B.1 contains random numbers, there is no ordering to them. By definition, then, it does not matter where we enter the table to begin our selection of numbers. Let's begin at the top of the sixth column. Because the numbers in our population go up only to two digits (remember the officers are numbered from 0 to 99), we are really concerned only with two-digit numbers. We decide to use only the two numbers at the left of the column. The first of these numbers is the number 77. Number 77 from our population list of police officers is then selected into the sample. The second step is to move to another set of two numbers. Because the numbers in this table are not ordered in any particular way, we can select the numbers immediately before 77, below 77, or even next to 77—it does not matter in which direction we go for this second move. Let's just move down to the first two numbers in the next row directly below 77. Here, we find the number 73. Therefore, the police officer who was assigned number 73 is selected into our sample. Moving down to the next row, we select number 03 and so on. We continue this process until we have the 10 police officers we need for our sample. This is an example of selecting a simple random sample.

## Systematic Random Samples

Simple random sampling is easy to do if your population is organized in a list, such as from a phone book, registered voters list, a court docket, or a membership list, such as the one we had in our POAA example. We can make the process of simple random selection a little less time-consuming by systematically sampling the cases. In systematic random sampling, we select the first element into the sample randomly, as we did in the POAA example. Instead of continuing with this random selection for every other element in the population, in a systematic random sample we systematically choose the rest of the sample. The general rule for systematic random sampling is to begin with the $k$th element (any number selected randomly) in the population and then proceed to select the sample by choosing every $k$th element thereafter. The $k$th element is the only element that is truly selected at random. The starting element can be selected from a random numbers table or by some other random method. Systematic random sampling eliminates the process of deriving a new random number for every element selected, thus saving time.

Figure 1.4 is an example of systematic random sampling for a sample of circles. If it helps, you can enhance this illustration by imagining these circles as a population of incarcerated felons who are being randomly selected for urinalysis to check them for drug use. Let's systematically select a sample of 10 from this list. We must begin by randomly selecting a number to represent our first element. For the sake of this example, let's say we choose the number 8. To begin sample selection, then, we select the eighth element from our list and every eighth element thereafter until we have selected our entire sample of ten as shown in Figure 1.4.

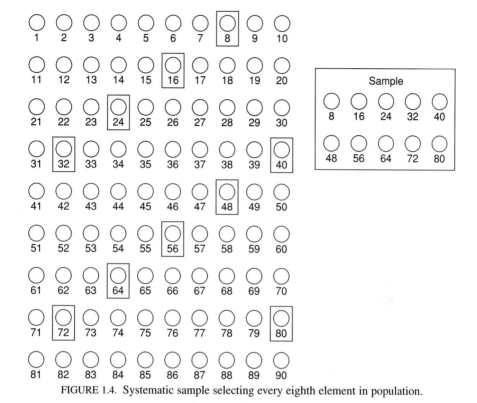

FIGURE 1.4. Systematic sample selecting every eighth element in population.

A sample obtained in this way is a *systematic random sample.* For systematic sampling procedures to approximate a simple random sample, the population list must be truly random, not ordered. For example, we could not have a list of convicted felons ordered by offense type, by age, or by some other characteristic. If the list is ordered in any meaningful way, this will introduce bias to the sampling process and the resulting sample is not likely to be representative of the population.

## Multistage Cluster Samples

So far, we have examined ways to obtain a sample when we have a population list available to us. There are often times, however, when we do not have the luxury of a population list. In fact, if we wanted to obtain a sample from the entire U.S. population, there would be no list available. Yes, there are telephone books that list residents in various places who have telephones, lists of those who have registered to vote, lists of those who hold driver's licenses, lists of those who pay taxes, and so on. However, all these lists are incomplete (e.g., some people do not list their phone number or do not have phones, some people do not register to vote or drive cars, the unemployed do not pay taxes). Using these incomplete lists would introduce bias into our sample.

In such cases, the sampling procedures become a little more complex. We usually end up working toward the sample we want through successive approximations: first, by extracting a random sample of groups, collectivities, or clusters of elements that are available; and then by random sampling the individual elements of interest from within these selected clusters. Samples of this nature are typically called *multistage cluster samples.*

The sampling design used to conduct the NCVS is an excellent example of a multistage cluster sample. Because the population of the NCVS is the entire U.S. population, the first stage of sampling requires selecting a first-order sample of counties and large metropolitan areas called primary sampling units (PSUs). From these PSUs, another stage of sampling involves the selection of geographic districts within each of the PSUs that have been listed by the 1990 population census. Finally, a probability sample of residential dwelling units is selected from these geographic districts. These dwelling units, or addresses, represent the final stage of the multistage sampling. Anyone who resides at a selected address who is older than the age of 12 and is a U.S. citizen is eligible for the NCVS sample. Approximately 50,500 housing units or other living quarters are designated for the survey each year and are selected in this manner.

## Weighted Samples

In some cases, the types of probability samples previously described do not actually serve our purposes. Sometimes, we may want to make sure that certain segments of the population of interest are represented within our sample, and we do not want to leave this to chance. For example, suppose that we are interested in incidents of personal larceny involving contact, such as purse snatching or pickpocketing. More specifically, we may be interested in whether there are differences in the victimization circumstances (e.g., place or time of occurrence, number of offenders, amount of personal injury) between two groups of persons; those under the age of 65 and those 65 years of age or older. To investigate this, we want to conduct a sample survey with the entire U.S. population. A simple random sample of this population, however, may not result in a sufficient number of individuals older than 65 to use for comparison purposes, because individuals older than 65 make up a relatively small proportion of the entire population (approximately 12 percent). Imagine a gum ball machine that has 88 percent red gum balls and only 12 percent green gum balls (which represent elderly Americans). You have 10 pennies to spend and you want to end up with five red and five green gum balls. Given the fact that there are far more red gum balls than green ones, unless you do something to increase the chance of getting a green ball, you will not end up with a 50/50 split. There are times, therefore, when we will want to "oversample" purposefully a particular group. In our previous crime example, we will want to oversample the age group older than 65 to obtain enough cases for us to compare their victimization experiences with those younger than 65 years of age.

One way to achieve this goal would be to weight disproportionately the elements in our population. These samples are referred to as *weighted samples.* Instead of having an equal chance of being selected, as in the case of random samples, individuals would have an unequal chance of being selected. That is, some elements would have a greater probability of being selected into the sample than others. This would be necessary in our example of the victimization of the elderly because, as noted, persons older than 65 represent only about 12 percent of the total U.S. population. Because we want to investigate differences between the victimizations of those younger than and older than 65, we want to have more than this 12 percent proportion represented in our sample. To do this, we would disproportionately weight our sample selection procedures to give persons older than 65 a better chance of being selected. An example may help you better understand the notion of a weighted sample.

Suppose there was a population of 1000 persons. We knew that in this population, 880 (88 percent) were younger than 65, while 120 (12 percent) were older than 65. Because we want to compare the victimization experiences of those older than 65 with those younger than 65 years of age, we want to select our sample so that we have roughly equal numbers in each group. Let's say we want to select 40 persons younger than 65 and 40 persons older than 65, so that we have a total sample size of 80. Because we are selecting 40 of the 120 elderly (those older than 65), the probability that any one will be selected is 40/120, or .333. However, as we are selecting 40 of the 880 nonelderly (those younger than 65), the probability that any one of them will be selected is only 40/880, or .045. We are giving those older than 65 more than a seven-fold greater probability of being selected into the sample than those younger than 65 (.333/.045 = 7.40). That essentially defines a weighted sample. If we then wish to make generalizations from our weighted sample of 80 (where 50 percent of the sample is elderly) to our population (where only 12 percent is elderly), we will have to make adjustments to our statistics that take this sample weighting into account.[5]

## *1.6 NONPROBABILITY SAMPLING TECHNIQUES*

Obtaining a sample using probability sampling techniques such as those described in Section 1.5, although the most reliable and trustworthy, can be laborious. The techniques we discuss in this section are less complicated in nature and are usually subsumed under the category of *nonprobability sampling techniques.* Unlike the samples we already have discussed, when collecting a sample using nonprobability sampling techniques, elements within the population *do not* have a known probability of being selected into the sample. Because the chance of any individual being selected is unknown, we cannot be certain the selected sample actually represents our population. This is a significant problem because we generally are interested in making inferences from a sample statistic to a population parameter.

Often, however, nonprobability sampling techniques are the only way of obtaining samples from particular populations or for certain types of research questions. Suppose, for example, that we are interested in the crime of shoplifting and, thus, want to investigate the various rationalizations and excuses used by shoplifters (e.g., they shoplifted for survival purposes, for thrills, to get even). It would be hard to define a population because we do not have a list of shoplifters from which to randomly select. We discuss three types of nonprobability samples in this section: quota samples, purposive or judgment samples, and availability samples.

## Quota Samples

One type of nonprobability sample that would serve our purposes well in a study of the victimization of elderly persons is called a *quota sample*. Quota samples are similar to the weighted samples we discussed in Section 1.5, but they are generally less rigorous and precise in their selection procedures. While quota sampling techniques range from the simple to the rigorous, all quota samples are still considered nonprobability samples. Simply, quota sampling involves designating the population into proportions of some group that you want to be represented in your sample. In some cases, these proportions may actually represent the true proportions observed in the population. For example, if the population you are interested in is 50 percent male, you will want to ensure that your sample is also 50 percent male. At other times, these quotas may represent predetermined proportions of subsets of people you deliberately want to oversample. Think back to our victimization example involving elderly and nonelderly persons. For a study such as this, we may decide that we want 50 percent of our sample to consist of individuals 65 years of age or older and 50 percent to consist of those younger than 65 years of age. When these proportions are decided, they represent quotas. Elements of the population are then collected until each quota is filled. In our example, we would select the sample until we have exactly 50 percent of the elements younger than 65 and 50 percent older than 65 years of age. Quota sampling may be more complex in that we can add additional quotas to fill. For example, we may want 80 percent of persons younger than 65 and persons older than 65 to be white and 20 percent to be nonwhite.

## Purposive, or Judgment, Samples

Another type of nonprobability sample often used in the field of criminology is called a *purposive, or judgment, sample.* In general, this type of sample is selected based on the specific purpose of a given study and the researcher's subjective judgment of the unique appropriateness of the sample for that purpose. It is called a "judgment sample," then, because the researcher uses his or her own judgment about whom to select into the sample, rather than drawing sample elements randomly. This type of sample does not provide the luxury of generalizability, but it can provide a wealth of information not otherwise or easily attainable from a typical random sample.

Many studies in criminology and criminal justice have been carried out using a purposive sample. For example, in their book, *Crimes of the Middle Class,* Weisburd and his colleagues (1991) examined a sample of white-collar criminal offenders convicted in seven federal judicial districts. These judicial districts were not randomly selected from an exhaustive list of all federal districts, but were instead deliberately selected by the researchers because the seven districts were judged by them to provide a suitable amount of geographical diversity. They were also selected because they were believed to have a substantial proportion of white-collar crime cases.

Judgment samples have also been employed to provide detailed examinations of the decision-making processes that lead to criminality. For example, in their study of residential burglary, *Burglars on the Job,* Wright and Decker (1994) interviewed 105 active burglars operating in St. Louis, Missouri. These burglars were not, of course, randomly selected from some known population of St. Louis burglars. Rather, they were selected by an ex-offender working for the two researchers. In this case, it was not the researchers' judgment that was critical but their ex-offender accomplice's, who was "in the know" about St. Louis street crime. This ex-offender used his "professional" judgment in selecting known burglars in given high-crime areas of St. Louis. Because of this judgment sample, Wright and Decker were able to obtain richly descriptive information about residential burglary in St. Louis. The cost of such nonprobability samples, however, is generalizability, and we do not know if their findings hold true for residential burglary committed in other areas.

## Availability Samples

The final type of sampling technique we discuss is one that is perhaps too frequently used and one that is based solely on the availability of respondents. This type of sample is appropriately termed an *availability sample.* We admit that in conducting our own research, we have used this type of sample once or twice. You have probably even been an element in one of these samples. Have you ever been asked to complete a questionnaire in one of your classes before? University researchers frequently conduct surveys by passing out questionnaires in their large lecture classes. Usually, the sample obtained from this method consists of those students who "voluntarily" agree to participate or those who receive course credit for doing so. It is not surprising that this type of sample is so popular; it is one of easiest and least expensive sampling techniques available. It is also, however, a technique that may produce the least representative and generalizable type of sample. Like most things in life, the price of ease is often precision and accuracy.

When such samples are used, it is necessary to describe explicitly the sampling procedures used in the methodology section of research reports to acknowledge the nonrepresentativeness of the sample. For example, in a study that we conducted to investigate factors affecting the probability that a man would force a woman to have sex against her will, we utilized a sample of male college students. In a paper published from this research, we stated:

> The respondents in this study consisted of 94 male undergraduate students enrolled in introductory social science courses at a state university in New England. The students were given extra credit for their participation in the study, and were administered the data collection instrument during nonclass hours. (Bachman, Paternoster, & Ward, 1992)

This sample was partially justified for two reasons: (1) because the study was exploratory in nature, and (2) because college women have been shown to be at extremely high risk of becoming the victims of sexual assault perpetrated by their male peers. However, it was still a large leap of faith to assume that the college males from the one university used in the sample were representative of males in general or of male college students in general. For example, the sample elements in this study were predominately white.

Another, more classic, example of an availability sample is found in John Irwin's *The Felon* (1970), a study of the postprison "careers" of a group of California criminal felons. To conduct his study of felons, Irwin did not take a simple or systematic random sample of all felons released from the California Department of Corrections. Instead, because he resided and worked in the San Francisco Bay area, Irwin studied offenders released on parole from California penal institutions in the San Francisco and Oakland parole districts.

Despite their limitations, however, availability samples still serve several purposes in criminological research. First, they are an excellent way to pretest and refine a questionnaire that will eventually be given to a more representative sample. They also are useful for obtaining data that can be used for other types of exploratory analyses before investing time and money into more elaborate and rigorous sampling methodologies. However, we hope that, if asked, you could outline the disadvantages of this type of sample. A good answer would be:

> As the goal of most research is to learn something about a population and not simply something about a sample from a population, the techniques used to obtain a sample are very important. The use of nonprobability samples like availability samples severely limits the ability we have to make inferences from what we observe in the sample to the larger population. Put another way, nonprobability samples limit our ability to generalize sample results to a population. Put yet another way, with nonprobability samples, we do not really know how precise an estimate of the population parameter our sample statistic is.

This disadvantage applies to all three types of nonprobability samples that we examined in this section.

As noted, we believe it is fundamental that you are aware of sampling issues before beginning a course in statistics. All inferential statistics we examine in this text assume that the data being examined were taken from some kind of probability sample, usually a simple random sample. What are inferential statistics, you ask? Good question. We answer this in Section 1.7.

## 1.7 DESCRIPTIVE AND INFERENTIAL STATISTICS

Traditionally, the study of statistics has been divided into two areas: descriptive statistics and inferential statistics. In large part, this distinction relies on the extent to which one is interested in simply describing some phenomenon or in "inferring" characteristics of some phenomenon from a sample to a population. As you can now surmise, the problem of using a known sample statistic to estimate an unknown population parameter is an inferential statistics problem. Therefore, as you can see, an understanding of sampling issues is already necessary.

*Descriptive statistics* are used to describe the characteristics of a sample or a population. The key point here is that you are using the statistics for description only. For example, if we wanted to describe the number of parking tickets given out by university police or the amount of revenues these parking tickets generated, we could utilize various statistics, including simple counts or averages.

If, however, we wanted to generalize this information to university police departments across the United States, we must move into the realm of *inferential statistics*. Inferential statistics allow us to take measurements from a sample (our sample statistic) and "infer," or use, this information to estimate the unknown characteristic of a larger population (the population parameter). Of course, before we are able to use inferential statistics, we must assume that our sample is actually representative of the population. To do this, we must obtain our sample by using appropriate probability sampling techniques. The larger picture is, we hope, beginning to emerge.

## *1.8 SUMMARY*

Our goal in this introductory chapter is to underscore the nature of the relationship between statistics and criminology and criminal justice. We have also set the stage to begin our exploration into the realm of statistics. Because it is almost never possible to obtain information on every individual or element in the population of interest, our investigations usually rely on data taken from samples of the population. Furthermore, as virtually all the statistics we examine in this text are based on assumptions about the origins of our data, we discuss the most common types of samples used in criminology and criminal justice. Samples generally fall into two types: those derived from probability sampling techniques and those derived from nonprobability sampling techniques.

In the best possible world, we would have the ability always to be certain that our research sample was truly representative of the population. However, we do not live in this world. Therefore, we rely on probability theory (discussed in greater detail in Chapter 7) to guide us in selecting a sample. Probability sampling increases the likelihood that our sample will reflect the population. The fundamental element in probability sampling is random selection. When a sample is randomly selected from the population, it means that every element (e.g., individual) has an equal and known chance of being selected into the sample.

We examine four types of probability samples: the simple random sample, the systematic random sample, the multistage cluster sample, and the weighted sample. In addition, we also provided a brief discussion of three types of nonprobability samples: quota samples, purposive, or judgment, samples, and availability samples. The chapter concluded with a brief discussion of descriptive and inferential statistics.

### *Key Terms*

| | |
|---|---|
| availability sample | probability sampling |
| descriptive statistics | purposive or judgment sample |
| element | quota sample |
| hypothesis | random selection |
| inferential statistics | sample |
| model | sample estimate |
| multistage cluster sample | simple random sample |
| nonprobability sampling | statistic |
| parameter | systematic random sample |
| population | weighted sample |

### *Problems*

1. Obtain a list of full-time university sophomores from the registrar's office at your university. Using this list and Table B.1 in Appendix B, select a simple random sample of 60 students. What are the steps you performed in doing this? Comment on the representativeness of this

sample to the entire sophomore class. Now, conduct a systematic random sample from the same list. Are there any differences?

2. How can you approximate a simple random sample when you do not have a list of the population?
3. Discuss the importance of probability sampling techniques.
4. How does random selection ensure that we are obtaining the most representative sample possible?
5. If we wanted to make sure that certain segments of the population were represented and/or over-represented within our sample, which two types of sampling techniques could we use?
6. What is the danger in using nonprobability samples in research?
7. In what types of situations would nonprobability samples be the most appropriate?

## Solutions to Problems

1. The first step we must take to obtain a simple random sample is to specify the population. In this case, the population is all full-time sophomore students enrolled at your university. If you were going to generalize to all sophomores attending all universities, you would have to obtain enrollment lists from other universities, select a sample of the lists, and then select a sample of sophomores from within each selected list. Quite time-consuming!

   The next step is to assign a number to every student on the population list. After all individuals are numbered, you can begin sample selection by entering a random numbers table at any place to make the first selection. By definition, it does not matter where you enter the table because it is a random numbers table; that is, there is no inherent order to the numbers. After you have entered the table, however, you should systematically move within the table, say, select every third number down from your original starting point, or every second number to the left, or whatever. You should continue this selection process until the entire sample of 60 students has been obtained.

   Using these random sampling techniques, every element in the population—that is, every student in the sophomore class—has an equal and known probability of being selected for the sample. By selecting a sample in this way, you have maximized the probability that your sample of 60 sophomores will be representative of the entire population of sophomores at your university.

   In systematic sampling, we begin with a random starting point but systematically select elements thereafter. The general rule for systematic sampling is to begin with the $k$th (any number selected randomly) element in the population, and select every $k$th element thereafter. The $k$th element is the only element that is truly selected at random; it can be selected from a random numbers table or by some other random method. Systematic sampling eliminates the process of deriving a new random number for every element selected. For example, if we selected the number 7 to begin systematic sampling from the list of sophomores, our first student selected would be number 7. We would continue to select every seventh student thereafter until we had the entire sample of 60 students selected.

2. When lists of a population are not complete or, more often, not available, we must utilize other sampling techniques. In such cases, the sampling procedures become more complex. We usually end up working toward the sample we want through successive approximations—first, by extracting a sample from lists of groups or clusters that are available, and then sampling the elements of interest from these selected clusters. Sampling procedures of this nature are typically called *multistage cluster sampling.*

3. One of the primary problems we face when generalizing information obtained from a sample to a population is uncertainty. How accurately does our sample reflect the true population?

This uncertainty is inherent in any sample because, by definition, we only have part of the population. The goal when obtaining a sample, then, is to select elements from the population in a way that increases the chances of this sample being representative. *Probability sampling techniques* increase the likelihood of accomplishing this goal. The fundamental element in probability sampling is *random selection.* When a sample is randomly selected from the population, this means every element (e.g., individual) has an equal and independent chance of being selected for the sample.

4. When a sample is randomly selected from the population, it means every element (e.g., individual) has a known and independent chance of being selected for the sample. The notion of randomness implies "no bias" within the selection process.
5. Weighted or quota sampling techniques.
6. Unlike probability samples, when we collect a sample using nonprobability sampling techniques, elements within the population *do not* have a known probability of being selected. Because the chance of one individual being selected versus another remains unknown, we cannot be certain that the selected sample actually represents our population. Because we are generally interested in making inferences to a population, this uncertainty can represent a major problem.
7. Nonprobability sampling techniques are often the only way of obtaining samples from particular populations or for certain types of research questions. The example used in the chapter of shoplifters is one example. It would be hard to define technically a population of shoplifters because we do not have a list of shoplifters from which to randomly select. In other cases, we may want to oversample certain subsets of the population. Nonprobability sampling techniques allow us the flexibility to obtain samples for these types of research problems.

## *Endnotes*

1. For example, see Doerner, 1978, 1983; Gastil, 1971, 1975; Hackney, 1969; Lundsguarde, 1977; Messner, 1982, 1983; Reed, 1971; Wolfgang & Ferracuti, 1967.
2. See Bachman, 1992; Bailey, 1984; Blau & Blau, 1982; Crutchfield, Geerken, & Gove, 1982; DeFronzo, 1983; Humphries & Wallace, 1980; Loftin & Hill, 1974; Smith & Parker, 1980; Wilkinson, 1984; Williams, 1984; Williams & Flewelling, 1988.
3. For a discussion of this issue, see Zimring, 1991, and Kleck & Patterson, 1993.
4. Of course, this is a simplistic discussion of the literature investigating the effects of gun control legislation. For research that documents significant declines in the rates of violence after gun control legislation, see Lester, 1988; Loftin et al., 1991; McPheters, Mann, & Schlapenhauf, 1984; Seitz, 1972. For studies that report equivocal or ambiguous findings, see Lester & Murrel, 1982; Nicholson & Garner, 1980; Pierce & Bowers, 1981. The following reports have found no significant effects of gun control whatsoever: Jung & Jason, 1988; Kleck & Patterson, 1993; Loftin, Heumann, & McDowall, 1983; Loftin & McDowall, 1984; Magaddino & Medoff, 1982, 1984; Murray, 1975.
5. For a detailed discussion of weighted samples, see H. W. Smith (1975), *Strategies of Social Research,* Englewood Cliffs, NJ: Prentice-Hall. For an example of a weighted sample used in criminological research, see M. Farnworth & M. J. Leiber (1989), "Strain theory revisited: Economic goals, educational means, and delinquency," *American Sociological Review,* 54(2):263–274. Farnworth and Leiber collected a weighted sample of adolescents to oversample the number of youths thought to be "at risk" for delinquency.

CHAPTER 2

# Levels of Measurement and Aggregation

*If you steal from one author, it's plagiarism; if you steal from many, it's research.*

—WILSON MIZNER

## 2.1 INTRODUCTION

In the preceding chapter, we examined various sampling techniques that can be used for selecting a sample from a given population. Once we have selected our sample, we can begin the process of gathering information. The information we gather is usually referred to as "data," and in its entirety it is called a "data set." The process of gathering a data set often is referred to as "data collection." In this chapter, we take a closer look at the types of variables that can make up a data set.

Even though this may be the first time you have been formally exposed to statistics, we are sure that each of you has some idea about what a variable is, even though you may not label it as such. A *variable* is any element to which different values can be attributed. Respondents' sex is a variable with two values, male and female. Race/ethnicity is a variable with many values, such as American Indian, African American, Asian, Hispanic, white. Age is another variable that can take on different values, such as 2, 16, or 55 years of age. The entire set of values a variable takes on is called a *frequency distribution,* or an *empirical distribution.* In a given data set, a frequency, or empirical distribution, is a *distribution* (a list) of outcomes or values for a variable. It is referred to as an *"empirical"* distribution because it is a distribution of empirical (i.e., actual) data, and a *"frequency"* distribution because it tells you how frequent each value or outcome is. For example, the age variable in a given data set may range from 18 to 38. There may be five persons 18 years of age, two persons 19 years of age, and so on. An empirical, or frequency, distribution would not only tell you what the different ages are but also how many 18-year-olds, how many 19-year-olds, how many 20-year-olds, and so on are represented.

In contrast, something that does not vary in a data set is called a *constant.* Unlike a variable, whose values vary or are different, a constant has only one value. For example, if you have a sample of inmates from a male correctional institution, respondent's sex would be considered a constant. Since all elements of the sample were male, respondents' sex would not vary in that data set. If you selected a sample of 20-year-old youths from the sophomore class at a state university, age would be a constant rather than a variable because the age of each person would be the same (20 years).

Notice that a given characteristic, such as respondents' sex or age, is not always a variable or a constant. Under different conditions, it may be one or the other. For example, in a sample of male prisoners, sex is a constant, but age would be a variable because the male inmates are likely to be different ages. In the sample of 20-year-old sophomore students from a state university, age is a constant, and respondents' sex is a variable because some persons in the sample would be male and some would be female.

We can classify variables in many different ways and make several distinctions among them. First, differing levels of measurement can be associated with variables. The first part of this chapter examines these measurement differences, beginning with the classification of variables as either *continuous* or *categorical variables.* We then examine the four *levels of measurement* within these two broad categories: *nominal, ordinal, interval,* and *ratio.* The second section addresses the difference between *independent* and *dependent variables* and the different ways of presenting variables. The final section discusses variations in the units of analysis of our data sets.

## 2.2 LEVELS OF MEASUREMENT

As noted, data generally come from one of three places: They are gathered by us personally, gathered by another criminologist, or gathered by a government agency. Doing research on a previously collected data set is often referred to as "secondary data analysis." No matter how they were collected, by definition, data sets are simply a collection of many variables and constants.

Imagine that we were interested in students' substance use (both alcohol and drug use) and their demographic characteristics, such as sex, age, religion, and year in college (freshman, sophomore, junior, or senior). Table 2.1 displays the small data set we may have obtained had we investigated this issue by collecting questionnaire surveys from a random sample of 20 college students.

To measure the extent to which each student used alcohol and drugs, let's say that we asked them these questions: "How often each month do you consume alcohol?" "When you do consume alcohol, how much do you usually consume?" Assume that we asked the same two questions about the consumption of other drugs. From the answers to these questions, we then compute what is termed in Table 2.1 a "Drink Index" and a "Drug Index." These two indices indicate the combined sum of the quantity and frequency of each student's consumption of alcohol and drugs on a 50-point scale. Each of the other variables in the table relates to other information about each student in the sample. Everything listed in this table, including the respondent's identification number, is a variable. All of these variables combined represent our data set.

The first thing you may notice about these variables is that some are represented by categories and some are represented by actual numbers. The variable

**TABLE 2.1. Example of the Format of a Data Set from a Survey Investigating the Relationship between Age, College Year, Sex, GPA, Religion, and Students' Use of Alcohol and Drugs**

| Respondent's Identification Number | Sex | Age | College Year | GPA | Score on Drink Index | Score on Drug Index | Religion |
|---|---|---|---|---|---|---|---|
| 1 | Female | 20 | Sophomore | 2.8 | 25 | 13 | Protestant |
| 2 | Female | 18 | Freshman | 2.1 | 47 | 21 | Catholic |
| 3 | Male | 21 | Senior | 2.9 | 20 | 15 | Catholic |
| 4 | Female | 20 | Freshman | 2.5 | 38 | 20 | Jewish |
| 5 | Male | 18 | Freshman | 1.9 | 48 | 50 | Protestant |
| 6 | Male | 19 | Sophomore | 2.8 | 39 | 24 | Protestant |
| 7 | Female | 38 | Senior | 3.8 | 4 | 0 | Catholic |
| 8 | Male | 19 | Sophomore | 2.9 | 39 | 21 | Protestant |
| 9 | Male | 20 | Junior | 3.3 | 10 | 0 | Jewish |
| 10 | Female | 20 | Junior | 3.4 | 20 | 5 | Protestant |
| 11 | Male | 44 | Freshman | 2.0 | 9 | 0 | Protestant |
| 12 | Female | 19 | Sophomore | 3.2 | 39 | 0 | Catholic |
| 13 | Female | 20 | Junior | 3.5 | 10 | 0 | Catholic |
| 14 | Male | 21 | Senior | 2.9 | 20 | 9 | Jewish |
| 15 | Male | 18 | Freshman | 2.1 | 49 | 27 | Protestant |
| 16 | Female | 24 | Senior | 3.2 | 20 | 2 | Jewish |
| 17 | Male | 20 | Sophomore | 2.7 | 33 | 30 | Catholic |
| 18 | Male | 28 | Freshman | 2.4 | 20 | 0 | Catholic |
| 19 | Female | 51 | Sophomore | 3.9 | 5 | 0 | Protestant |
| 20 | Female | 21 | Junior | 3.1 | 30 | 25 | Protestant |

Respondent's Sex, for example, is comprised of two categories, or values, female and male. This type of variable is often referred to as a *qualitative,* or *categorical,* variable, implying that the values represent qualities or categories only. Other examples of qualitative variables would include race or ethnicity, because the values would represent only distinct or different types of racial or ethnic groups, such as white, African American, Hispanic, Native American, and Asian. Year in School is another qualitative or categorical variable because the values represent distinct categories: freshman, sophomore, junior, or senior.

Some variables in our data set, however, do not have categories as values, but numbers or counts. The variable Drink Index, for example, is comprised of a range of numerical values. This type of variable is often referred to as a *quantitative,* or *continuous,* variable, implying that the values represent quantities or measurements that are continuous in nature. Age is another example of a continuous variable when it is measured in years. One's grade point average (GPA) in school is another example of a quantitative or continuous variable because the values may take on a very large number of possible values.

Whether a variable is categorical or continuous is not always a fixed or immutable characteristic of that variable. Age, for instance can be either a categorical or a continuous variable. When it is measured as the precise number of years a person is (20, 23, 28, or 30 years old, for example), it is a continuous variable because there are a very large number of different values. When it is measured in terms of the age interval or age category one falls into, however (10–15 years of age; 16–21 years of age; 22–27 years of age, and so on), it is a categorical variable. Therefore, variables measured at the continuous level can also be measured at the categorical level.

The converse is not, however, true. Variables measured at the categorical level cannot be measured at the continuous level. A person's sex (male/female), for instance, cannot be converted from a categorical to a continuous variable. If age is measured as a set of categories or intervals and we know what age category a person falls into, we still will not know his or her specific age. In this case, we would be unable to convert the categorical measurement to continuous measurement. For example, if a person fell into the age category 16 to 21 years of age, she or he may be 16, 17, 18, 19, 20, or 21 years old. In this case, we simply would not know the exact age; the only thing we know for sure is that she or he is 16 or older or 21 or younger.

Recall that any variable that tells us what type or what category a case falls into is a qualitative variable. Which variables in Table 2.1 are qualitative? There are three qualitative variables here. In this case, they are easy to identify because each of the three qualitative variables is represented by *alphanumeric data* (the data are represented by letters rather than numbers). The three qualitative variables, then, are respondent's sex, grade, and religion. Data that are represented by numbers are called *numeric data*. A good device to remember the distinction between these two types of data is to think that *alpha*numeric data consist of letters of the *alpha*bet, whereas *num*eric data consist of *num*bers.

It is certainly possible to include alphanumeric data in any data set, as we have done in Table 2.1, but most often alphanumeric data are converted to or represented by numeric data. For example, females may arbitrarily be given the score or numerical value of 1, rather than the word "Female," and males may arbitrarily be assigned a score or numerical value of 2, rather than the word "Male." Assigning numbers to categorical responses or answers (either alphanumeric or numeric) is called "coding" the data.

Which numbers get assigned to alphanumeric data (for example, 1 for females and 2 for males) is arbitrary because the numerical code (number) assigned has no real meaning. In the preceding example, males could have been coded or scored as 1 and females as 2. The numbers assigned could have been 5 for men and 10 for women; the values have no meaning because if women are coded with the value of 1 and men the value of 2, it does not mean that men have twice as much of the variable Sex as women. All we can say is that men are different from women and that

---

**Qualitative or categorical variables** refer to qualities or categories. They tell us what kind, what group, or what type a value is referring to.

**Quantitative or continuous variables** refer to quantities or different measurements. They tell us how much or how many of something a value has.

they, therefore, fall into different categories. It does not matter whether those categories are represented by letters (e.g., Male or Female) or numbers (e.g., 2 or 1). The only important thing is that they be assigned different combinations of letters or different numbers so we can tell them apart. Why convert the letters into numbers, then, if the numbers assigned have no real meaning? Numbers often are assigned because computer statistical programs find it easier to work with data in number form (numeric data) rather than in letter form (alphanumeric data).

Returning to our qualitative variables in the hypothetical data set of Table 2.1 (sex, year in school, religion), regardless of whether the values are alphanumeric or numeric data, each of the values that represent these three variables simply tells us what category a case falls into. For example, respondent 7 is a female, a senior, and classified herself as a Catholic. Again, because these are qualitative variables, none of these values implies any sort of quantity or numerical measurement.

A student's age, GPA, and scores on the drinking and drug indices are all quantitative variables. We know that student 15 is 18 years of age, has a GPA of 2.1, and scored 49 and 27 on the drinking and drug indices, respectively. Each of these values is quantitative; it gives numerical amounts of something. Unlike qualitative variables, quantitative variables have numerically meaningful values.

In addition to distinguishing between categorical and continuous variables, we can differentiate variables in terms of what is called their "level of measurement." The four levels of measurement are: (1) *nominal,* (2) *ordinal,* (3) *interval,* or (4) *ratio* level.

## Nominal Measurement

Variables measured at the nominal level are exclusively qualitative in nature. The values of nominal-level variables convey classification or categorization information *only.* Therefore, the only thing we can say about two or more nominal-level values of a variable is that they differ. We cannot say that one value reflects more or less of the variable than the other. The most common types of nominal-level variables are sex (male and female), religion (Protestant, Catholic, Jewish, Muslim, etc.), or political party (Democrat, Republican, Independent, etc.). These values are distinct from one another and can give us only descriptive information about the type or label attached to a value.

Because they only represent distinctions of kind (one is merely different from the other), the categories of a nominal-level variable are not related to one another in any meaningful numeric way. This is true even if the alphanumeric values are converted or coded into numbers. For example, let's take the variable Political Party and assign the value 1 to Democrats, 2 to Republicans, and 3 to Independents instead of their respective alphanumeric names. These assigned numbers on a nominal-level scale have no numerical meaning. The fact that Democrats are assigned the code of 1 and Republicans 2 does not mean that Republicans have a political party twice as large as Democrats. The only thing that the codes of 1 and 2 mean is that they refer to qualitatively different political parties. Because we cannot make distinctions of less than or more than with them, then, nominal-level variables do not allow us to rank-order people on that variable. In other words, nominal-level measurement does not have the property of order. There is no recognition of less than or more than, just the fact that some people are different from others on this variable (some are Democrats, some Republicans, some Independents). Reflecting this, mathematical operations cannot be performed with nominal-level data. With our political party data, for example, we cannot subtract a 2 (a Republican) from a 3 (an Independent) to get a 1 (a Democrat). Nor can we form a ratio of 3 (an Independent) to a 1 (a Democrat) and state that Independents have a political party three times (3/1 = 3) the size as Democrats do. See how meaningless mathematical operations are with nominal-level data!

## Ordinal Measurement

The values of ordinal-level variables not only are categorical in nature, but also the categories also have some type of relationship to each other. This relationship is one of order. That is, the categories of an ordinal variable can be rank-ordered from high (more of the variable) to low (less of the variable). In addition to the quality of a nominal-level variable, then the values of ordinal-level variables can be ordered. We can rank-order the categories of an ordinal-level variable, but we cannot know the precise difference among cases that fall into different categories. In other words, categories often reflect "more" or "less" of something, but we do not know exactly how much more or less. The properties of ordinal-level measurement are clearer with an example.

Let's say that we have the variable income and that we have two people, Joe and Moe. Let's say that Joe really earns $40,000 a year and Moe really earns $20,000 a year. When we measure their income, however, we do not ask them to tell us the exact amount they earn per year. We only ask them to tell us which income category they fall into:

*Category Code 1:*   more than $50,000

*Category Code 2:*   $45,001–$50,000

*Category Code 3:*   $35,001–$45,000

*Category Code 4:*   $25,001–$35,000

*Category Code 5:*   less than $25,000

Joe tells us that he falls into Category 3, and Moe tells us that he falls into Category 5. Because we have ordinal-level measurement, we can say not only that Joe and Moe have different incomes (the property of nominal measurement), but also that Joe has more income than Moe. What we do not know, however, is how much more money Joe makes than Moe. Had we measured income in terms of actual dollars earned per year rather than income category, we would be able to make more precise distinctions.

## Interval Measurement

In addition to enabling us to rank-order values, interval-level measurements allow us better to quantify the numeric relationship among them. To be classified as an interval-level variable, the categories of the variable must have an *equal* and *known* quantity. In other words, we have an interval scale of measurement if the difference between adjacent values along the measurement scale is the same at every two points. In addition to equal values between each set of adjacent points, another characteristic of interval-level measurement is that the zero point is arbitrary. An arbitrary zero means that, although a value of zero is possible, zero does not mean the absence of the phenomenon. A meaningless zero is an arbitrary zero. Another property is that scores on an interval scale can be added and subtracted, but meaningful multiplication and division cannot be performed. Sounds a little confusing, doesn't it. How about an example?

The classic example of interval-level measurement is the measurement of temperature with a Fahrenheit temperature scale. A temperature reading of 73 degrees is higher than a temperature reading of 63 degrees. Thus, Fahrenheit degrees can be rank-ordered in terms of higher or lower, just like an ordinal scale. Unlike an ordinal scale, however, we can say more if we have interval measurement. The temperature difference between 73° and 63° (10 degrees) is the same as the difference between 65° and 55°, or between 27° and 17°. In each case, the first temperature is exactly 10° warmer than the second. Similarly, the difference between 80° and 81° is the same as that between −20° and −21°, exactly 1°. A Fahrenheit temperature scale also has interval-level properties because the zero point is arbitrary. A temperature reading of 0° Fahrenheit does not mean that there is no temperature! It only means that it is colder than a temperature reading of, say, 20° and warmer than a reading of −20°.

In criminological research many attitude scales are presumed to be measured at the interval level. For example, if I wanted to measure attitudes toward the police, I might ask people the following question: "How satisfied are you with the police services in your community?" with the possible response options ranging from 0 ("very dissatisfied") to 10 ("very satisfied"). For interval-level measurement, I would have to *assume* that the difference between any two scores is the same. For example, that the difference between a score of 5 and 6 is the same as the difference between 10 and 9 or 1 and 2. The zero point is certainly arbitrary, because a score of zero does not mean that there is an absence of opinion about police services. We emphasize the word "assume" because with attitude scales such as this one, there is no way to be absolutely sure that differences between adjacent scores are the same. It is an assumption that researchers make about their data before performing their statistical operations. These assumptions may or may not be true. If the assumed properties of the data are not in fact the real properties, then the statistics performed on them are distorted.

A recent example of attitude questions in the criminological literature is provided by Alissa Pollitz Worden (1993). Using the Police Services Study, which surveyed police officers in 24 departments in three metropolitan areas (St. Louis, Tampa, and Rochester), Worden examined sex differences in police officers' attitudes on several issues, including their acceptance of rules and authority, their perceived level of citizen support, and their preparedness for routine encounters. The majority of these attitudes were measured using questions that required the respondent to make one of a limited number of responses. For example, to solicit information on an officer's acceptance of legal restrictions and using the response categories of strongly agree (1), agree (2), disagree (3), and strongly disagree (4), respondents were asked to respond to the following statements:

1. If police officers in tough neighborhoods had fewer restrictions on their use of force, many of the serious crime problems in those neighborhoods would be greatly reduced.
2. Police officers here would be more effective if they didn't have to worry about "probable cause" requirements for searching citizens.
3. When a police officer is accused of using too much force, only other officers are qualified to judge such a case.

The police officer's answers to these questions using the four-point response scale could be presumed to represent measurement at the interval level. We would have to make the assumption that the differences between adjacent responses are the same. For example, that the difference between strongly agree (scored as 1) and agree (scored as 2) is the same as that between disagree (scored as 3) and strongly disagree (scored as 4). If we are not comfortable making this assumption, we can only assume that we have ordinal-level measurement and can use the statistics appropriate for that level only.

## Ratio Measurement

Ratio-level variables have all of the qualities of interval-level variables, but in addition, the numerical difference between values is based on a natural, or true-zero point. A true-zero point means that a score of zero indicates that the phenomenon is absent. Ratio measurement allows meaningful use of multiplication and division, in addition to addition and subtraction. We can, therefore, divide one number by another to form a ratio—hence the name ratio measurement.

An example of ratio-level variable is the length of a prison sentence received by a convicted offender. Prison sentences are usually measured according to the number of years or months that someone is sentenced to prison. The U.S. Sentencing Commission, which monitors sentencing policies and practices for the federal court system, collects information on the sentencing outcomes of cases tried in federal courts. In 1992 the Commission reported that the average sentence (in months) received by primary offenders was as follows:[1]

| Primary Offense | Average Sentence (months) |
| --- | --- |
| Total | 66.1 |
| Robbery | 105.8 |
| Larceny | 13.5 |
| Embezzlement | 9.1 |
| Fraud | 17.1 |
| Drug trafficking | 89.6 |
| Simple possession | 10.2 |
| Counterfeiting | 17.0 |
| Firearms | 61.6 |
| Immigration | 15.3 |

We can identify two variables in this list: primary offense and sentence length in months received by those convicted. You should now be able to recognize the first variable, primary offense, as a nominal-level variable. Sentence length, however, is a ratio-level variable. As with an interval-level scale, the distance between adjacent values on a ratio scale is presumed to be the same. The difference in sentence length between a sentence of 12 months and one of 18 months (6 months) is the same as that between 24 and 30 months. Unlike an interval scale, however, there is an absolute zero point for ratio measurement. We can say that someone received zero months of imprisonment if, for example, they were given probation as a sentence or a fine. In the case of a ratio variable, then, zero does mean the absence of the variable. Because division is meaningful for variables measured at the ratio level, we can say, for example, that the ratio of months in prison is over 11 times greater for those convicted of robbery than for those convicted of embezzlement (105.8/9.1 = 11.6).

The Sentencing Commission provides other interesting information on sentencing practices. For example, we also know from some of the other variables this agency collects that these sentences were based on two possible modes of conviction: plea bargaining or trial. What type of variable is this? If you guessed nominal, you're right. The values indicate only the extent to which a defendant pleaded guilty or received his or her sentence after a jury trial.

Income, of course, is another variable that indisputably has a true zero point and equal distance between adjacent values so that it can be measured at the ratio level. A value of no income, "zero bucks," has inherent meaning to all of us, and the difference between $10 and $11 is the same as that between $1,000,000 and $1,000,001. Criminologists' interest in income takes many forms and does not reflect an interest merely in an individual's or family's income. Take the numbers presented in Table 2.2, for example. This table presents a list of U.S. senators according to two variables: their "Yes" or "No" vote on the Brady Bill and the contributions they received from the National Rifle Association (NRA) from January 1, 1987, to September 30, 1993. To refresh your memory, the Brady Bill requires a five-day waiting period and a background check for potential buyers of handguns. The variable Vote on the Brady Bill in this case represents the nominal level of measurement ("Yes" or "No"). The contribution variable is clearly measured at the ratio level because it reflects the actual dollar amount contributed by the NRA. More than 30 senators received no contributions from the NRA. The Senate voted 63 to 36 on November 20, 1993, to approve the Brady Bill. Table 2.2 presents a very

---

FOUR TYPES OF MEASUREMENT

**Nominal:** Values represent categories or qualities only.

**Ordinal:** Values not only represent categories, but they also can be rank-ordered.

**Interval:** In addition to an inherent rank order, a value's relationship to other values is known. There is an equal and constant distance between values.

**Ratio:** Not only can distances be determined between values, but these distances are based on a true-zero point.

**TABLE 2.2.** United States Senator's Votes on the Brady Bill and Previous Contributions ($) Received by Each Senator from the National Rifle Association

| | | | |
|---|---|---|---|
| **Paul Coverdell (R-Ga.)** | **$95,806** | *Byron L. Dorgan (D-N.D.)* | *4450* |
| **Alfonse M. D'Amato (R-N.Y.)** | **20,486** | **Mitch McConnell (R-Ky.)** | **3085** |
| Dan Coats (R-Ind.) | 19,800 | Mark O. Hatfield (R-Ore.) | 3000 |
| **Arlen Specter (R-Pa.)** | **18,072** | Bob Packwood (R-Ore.) | 2000 |
| **Lauch Faircloth (R-N.C.)** | **17,973** | Wendell H. Ford (D-Ky.) | 1568 |
| **Jesse Helms (R-N.C.)** | **17,957** | **Conrad Burns (R-Mont.)** | **1000** |
| Christopher S. Bond (R-Mo.) | 14,850 | Bob Kerrey (D-Neb.) | 1000 |
| Max Baucus (D-Mont.) | 14,639 | John D. Rockefeller IV (D-W.Va.) | 1000 |
| **Larry Pressler (R-S.D.)** | **14,400** | John W. Warner (R-Va.) | 1000 |
| Kay Bailey Hutchison (R-Tex.) | 11,509 | **Hank Brown (R-Colo.)** | **0** |
| **Larry E. Craig (R-Idaho)** | **11,286** | **Patrick J. Leahy (D-Vt.)** | **0** |
| **Robert C. Smith (R-N.H.)** | **11,000** | **Alan K. Simpson (R-Wyo.)** | **0** |
| Slade Gorton (R-Wash.) | 10,900 | Daniel K. Akaka (D-Hawaii) | 0 |
| **Howell T. Heflin (D-Ala.)** | **10,244** | Joseph R. Biden Jr. (D-Del.) | 0 |
| **Richard C. Shelby (D-Ala.)** | **10,226** | David L. Boren (D-Okla.) | 0 |
| **Ted Stevens (R-Alaska)** | **10,197** | Barbara Boxer (D-Calif.) | 0 |
| **Robert F. Bennett (R-Utah)** | **9900** | Bill Bradley (D-N.J.) | 0 |
| **John Breaux (D-La.)** | **9900** | Dale Bumpers (D-Ark.) | 0 |
| **Dirk Kempthorne (R-Idaho)** | **9900** | John H. Chafee (R-R.I.) | 0 |
| **Phil Gramm (R-Tex.)** | **9900** | Christopher J. Dodd (D-Conn.) | 0 |
| **Charles E. Grassley (R-Iowa)** | **9900** | Russell Feingold (D-Wis.) | 0 |
| **Ernest F. Hollings (D-S.C.)** | **9900** | Dianne Feinstein (D-Calif.) | 0 |
| **John McCain (R-Ariz.)** | **9900** | John Glenn (D-Ohio) | 0 |
| **Frank Murkowski (R-Alaska)** | **9900** | Bob Graham (D-Fla.) | 0 |
| **Don Nickles (R-Okla.)** | **9900** | Tom Harkin (D-Iowa) | 0 |
| J. James Exon (D-Neb.) | 9900 | Daniel K. Inouye (D-Hawaii) | 0 |
| Strom Thurmond (R-S.C.) | 9900 | James M. Jeffords (R-Vt.) | 0 |
| **J. Bennett Johnston (D-La.)** | **9508** | Nancy Landon Kassebaum (R-Kan.) | 0 |
| Harry M. Reid (D-Nev.) | 9450 | Edward M. Kennedy (D-Mass.) | 0 |
| Kent Conrad (D-N.D.) | 9450 | John F. Kerry (D-Mass.) | 0 |
| **Malcolm Wallop (R-Wyo.)** | **8764** | Herb Kohl (D-Wis.) | 0 |
| **Orrin G. Hatch (R-Utah)** | **7950** | Frank R. Lautenberg (D-N.J.) | 0 |
| **Connie Mack (R-Fla.)** | **6500** | Carl M. Levin (D-Mich.) | 0 |
| **Trent Lott (R-Miss.)** | **6000** | Joseph I. Lieberman (D-Conn.) | 0 |
| **Judd Gregg (R-N.H.)** | **5950** | Harlan Mathews (D-Tenn.) | 0 |
| Jeff Bingaman (D-N.M.) | 5950 | Howard M. Metzenbaum (D-Ohio) | 0 |
| Thomas A. Daschle (D-S.D.) | 5950 | Barbara A. Mikulski (D-Md.) | 0 |
| Dave Durenberger (R-Minn.) | 5900 | George J. Mitchell (D-Maine) | 0 |
| Jim Sasser (D-Tenn.) | 5450 | Carol Moseley-Braun (D-Ill.) | 0 |
| **Richard H. Bryan (D-Nev.)** | **4950** | Daniel Patrick Moynihan (D-N.Y.) | 0 |
| **Ben Nighthorse Campbell (D-Colo.)** | **4950** | Patty Murray (D-Wash.) | 0 |
| **Thad Cochran (R-Miss.)** | **4950** | Sam Nunn (D-Ga.) | 0 |
| **Robert J. Dole (R-Kan.)** | **4950** | Claiborne Pell (D-R.I.) | 0 |
| **Pete V. Domenici (R-N.M.)** | **4950** | David Pryor (D-Ark.) | 0 |
| Robert C. Byrd (D-W.Va.) | 4950 | Donald W. Riegle Jr. (D-Mich.) | 0 |
| Dennis DeConcini (D-Ariz.) | 4950 | Charles S. Robb (D-Va.) | 0 |
| Richard G. Lugar (R-Ind.) | 4950 | Paul S. Sarbanes (D-Md.) | 0 |
| William V. Roth Jr. (R-Del.) | 4950 | Paul Simon (D-Ill.) | 0 |
| William S. Cohen (R-Maine) | 4950 | Paul Wellstone (D-Minn.) | 0 |
| John C. Danforth (R-Mo.) | 4500 | Harris Wofford (D-Pa.) | 0 |
| | | Total | $576,72 |

*Key:* Boldface: voted "No." Lightface: voted "Yes." Italic: Did not vote.

*Source:* Adapted from *The Washington Post*, December 8, 1993, p. A21.

interesting picture of the relationship between NRA contributions and a senator's vote. We will leave you to ponder this relationship on your own!

Before we leave this section, we would be remiss if we did not tell you that the distinction between interval- and ratio-level measurement is at times a very subtle one, particularly in the social sciences. It also is true that the fine distinction between interval- and ratio-level measurement has limited practical significance. Most, if not all, of the statistical procedures that can be performed on ratio-level variables can also be confidently performed on variables measured at the interval level. In fact, many statistics books will simply note that a given statistical procedure requires data measured "at least at the interval level," implying that interval- and ratio-level variables are, for practical purposes, fairly comparable.

## 2.3 INDEPENDENT AND DEPENDENT VARIABLES

In addition to levels of measurement, researchers frequently distinguish between an *independent variable* and a *dependent variable*. In contrast to the levels of measurement associated with variables, which are governed by distinct numerical properties, defining a variable as independent or dependent relies solely on a researcher's assumptions about the causal relationship existing between two or more variables. The designation of a given variable as an independent variable or a dependent variable, therefore, may change according to the nature of the research problem.

In general, dependent variables in research are those variables that a researcher wishes to explain or predict. It is also sometimes referred to as the *outcome variable*. Independent variables are those variables that a researcher assumes will explain or predict the dependent variables. Stated another way, a researcher believes that the independent variable will somehow affect the dependent variable; the dependent variable, then, *depends* on the independent variable. In a causal relationship, the independent variable is the cause and the dependent variable is the effect.

For example, think about the crime rate in a given state as a dependent variable. What independent variables could explain this phenomenon? Different people believe that different factors influence the crime rate. Some have argued that unemployment is one of the leading contributors to crime. Higher unemployment, they believe, results in a higher crime rate. In this example, the phenomenon to be explained is the crime rate and the phenomenon doing the explaining is unemployment. Unemployment is the independent variable. You can also think of this in cause-and-effect terms. Which factor or condition is thought to be the cause and which is thought to be the effect? In this example, unemployment is thought to be at least one of the causes of crime.

Let's go through another example from the literature. For many reasons, women have often been found less likely to receive prison sentences when convicted of a

---

**Independent variables** are the variables thought to affect or in some way contribute to fluctuations or changes in **dependent variables.**

This simply involves multiplying the number obtained in our calculation by 100,000; this would result in a rate of murder of 9.6 per 100,000 population in the West (.000096 $\times$ 100,000 = 9.6). If we calculated rates per 100,000 population for the other three regions, we would obtain rates of 7.8, 8.4, and 12.1 for the Midwest, Northeast, and South, respectively. Notice that rates give us a somewhat different regional rank order for murder victimization than the frequency counts. After standardizing for the size of the population, we see that the South had the highest rate of murder in 1992 followed by the West. We also see that the Midwest, not the Northeast, had the lowest murder rate.

Here is another dramatic example about how a frequency count can mislead you, but a rate will not. In 1991 the number of murders in New York City was 2154 compared to 482 in the District of Columbia. This may make intuitive sense to you; the "Big Apple" is a very dangerous place, you may think, "my mother warned me about New York," you may exclaim! Before you pack your bags for Washington, DC, stop and think that maybe one reason New York has so many more murders than the District of Columbia is because there are many more people living there. In fact, the population of New York City in 1991 was nearly seven and one-half million (7,350,023), whereas the District of Columbia's population was just over one-half million (598,000).

Let's take the size of each city's population into account in understanding these raw murder counts by calculating the rate of murder per 100,000 people. For New York this would be (2154/7,350,023) $\times$ 100,000 = 29.3 murders per 100,000. The murder rate for the District of Columbia would be 482/598,000 = 80.6 murders per 100,000. Whoa! It appears that, at least so far as murder is concerned, Washington, DC, is a far more dangerous place than New York. Now where would you rather go for a visit?

If we were interested in specific subgroups of the population, we could calculate separate rates for males and females or separate rates for different ages. To do this, we would have to make both the numerator and denominator that we use in our rate calculations specific to these demographic characteristics. To calculate sex-specific rates, for example, the numerator would have to consist of frequency counts for males only. The corresponding denominator would be the number of males in the population, rather than the entire population. Table 2.4 presents sex-specific average annual rates and counts of violent and theft victimizations from the National Crime Victimization Survey (NCVS) data for the years 1987–1991. Also included in the table are the average annual male and female population counts used as the denominators in these rate calculations. As illustrated in the table, to compute the rate of violent victimization per 1000 females, we had to divide the number of violent victimizations experienced by females by the total number of females in the population and then multiply this by 1000.[4] These rates indicate that, on average, 25 out of every 1000 women and 40 out of every 1000 men become the victims of violence, including rapes, robberies, and assaults. Rates of theft are higher than rates of violent victimization for both sex groups, indicating that 64 thefts per 1000 women and 72 thefts per 1000 men occur in the United States each year.

A *ratio* is a number that expresses the relationship between two numbers and indicates their relative size. The ratio of $x$ to $y$ is determined by dividing $x$ by $y$. For example, in our example, the homicide rate for Washington, DC, was 80.6 per

**TABLE 2.4. Average Annual Number of Violent and Theft Victimizations for Males and Females and Average Annual Rate of Victimization per 1000 Males and Females, NCVS Data for 1987–1991**

|  | Average Annual Number | | Average Annual Rate | |
|---|---|---|---|---|
| Type of Crime | Male | Female | Male | Female |
| Crimes of violence | 3,926,415 | 2,600,607 | 40.5 | 24.8 |
| Personal larceny | 6,943,990 | 6,712,738 | 71.6 | 64.2 |

Male victimization rates

$$Rate\ of\ violence: \frac{3,926,415}{96,878,403} = .041 \times 1000 = 40.5$$

$$Rate\ of\ theft: \frac{6,943,990}{96,878,403} = .072 \times 1000 = 71.6$$

Female victimization rates

$$Rate\ of\ violence: \frac{2,600,607}{104,548,368} = .024 \times 1000 = 24.8$$

$$Rate\ of\ theft: \frac{6,712,738}{104,548,368} = .064 \times 1000 = 64.2$$

Average male population: 96,878,403. Average female population: 104,548,368.
*Source:* Bachman, R. (1994) Violence Against Women: A National Crime Victimization Survey Report. U.S. Department of Justice, Bureau of Justice Statistics, Washington, D.C.

100,000, whereas that for New York City was 29.3 per 100,000. The ratio of murders in Washington to New York is 80.6/29.3 = 2.75. This means that for every one homicide that occurs in New York, there are nearly three in the District of Columbia. We can state this differently by saying that there were almost three times more homicides in the District than in New York for that year. In Table 2.3, the ratio of murders committed in the South to murders committed in the West is 10,517/5202 = 2.02. For each murder that occurs in the West, two were committed in the South.

## Proportions and Percents

Two other common techniques used to present information about variables are *proportions* and *percentages*. These measures are really special kinds of ratios obtained by dividing the number of observations from a subset of your sample by the total number in your sample. In other words, a proportion is obtained by dividing the number of counts for a given event (*f*) by the total number of events (*N*). More specifically, proportions are obtained by using the following simple formula:

$$Proportion = \frac{Number\ in\ Subset\ of\ Sample}{Total\ Number\ in\ Sample} = \frac{f}{N}$$

Another name for a proportion is a **relative frequency** because it expresses the number of cases in a given subset (*f*) relative to the total number of cases (*N*). In this text we use the terms proportion and relative frequency interchangeably.

Percentages are obtained simply by multiplying the proportion by 100. This standardizes everything to a base of 100, which is generally easier to interpret than a proportion:

$$\text{Percent} = \frac{f}{N} \times 100 = \text{Proportion} \times 100$$

Let's go through an example. Using data from the NCVS from 1987 to 1990, Table 2.5 presents the number of weapon-specific stranger-perpetrated robberies and the calculations used to compute proportions and percentages from these numbers. From this table, we can immediately ascertain that most robberies (68 percent) involved the use of some type of weapon as only 32 percent of robbery offenders were unarmed. We can also identify that in all robberies guns were used 21 percent of the time, followed by knives and other sharp objects (19 percent of the time).

Another application of ratios in criminological research is the computation of percentage change scores, a common practice when criminal justice agencies are interested in tracking the levels of crime from one year to the next. Because a percentage increase of zero has inherent meaning (i.e., there was no change), ratios computed from percent change scores also have inherent meaning. Table 2.6 displays the number of arrests for various offenses in 1982 and 1992 and the percent change in these numbers between the two time periods.

Here is how percent change scores are derived. Let's look at murder in Table 2.6. What you want to know is the percent change in murder arrests from 1982 to 1992. What you first need to do is to determine whether the raw number of murder arrests decreased or increased over 1982–1992. To find this, subtract the number of arrests in 1982 from the number of arrests in 1992: 22,510 − 21,810 = 700 murder arrests. You now know that there were 700 more murder arrests in 1992 than in 1982. What you want to know next is what percent of 1982 murders this increase of 700 represents. To calculate this, simply divide 700 by the number of murders in 1982 (700/21,810) = .032. This figure represents the ratio of increases in murder arrests

TABLE 2.5. **Stranger-Perpetrated Robberies by Type of Weapon Used, NCVS Data, 1987–1990**

| Weapon Type | Number ($f$) | Proportion ($f/N$) | Percent ($f/N$) × 100 |
|---|---|---|---|
| Armed | | | |
| Handgun | 743,900 | .21 | 21% |
| Other gun | 53,900 | .02 | 2% |
| Knives | 657,000 | .19 | 19% |
| Other weapons | 361,200 | .10 | 10% |
| Weapon not known | 560,000 | .16 | 16% |
| Total armed | 2,376,000 | .68 | 68% |
| Not armed | 1,138,700 | .32 | 32% |
| Total robberies: | $N = 3,514,600$ | | |

*Source:* Bureau of Justice Statistics, 1994, p. 10.

**TABLE 2.6. Number of Arrests in 1982 and in 1992 by Offense Type and Percent Change, UCR Data**

| Offense | 1982 Number of Arrests | 1992 Number of Arrests | Percent Change |
|---|---|---|---|
| Murder | 21,810 | 22,510 | 3.2 |
| Robbery | 157,630 | 173,310 | 9.9 |
| Drug abuse violations | 676,000 | 1,066,400 | 57.0 |
| Driving under the influence | 1,778,400 | 1,624,500 | − 8.6 |

*Source:* FBI, 1983, Table 23, p. 167, and 1993, Table 29, p. 217.

from 1982 to 1992 to the total number of murder arrests in 1982. To convert this ratio to a percent, simply multiply this proportion by 100: .032 × 100 = 3.2 percent. Thus, the percent increase in murder arrests from 1982 to 1992 was 3.2 percent.

Using the percent change scores shown in Table 2.6, we can then compute ratios between the two time periods to determine the magnitude of change in the number of arrests by offense type. Again, remember that ratios are computed by dividing the quantity of one group by the quantity of another. For example, we can compute the ratio between the increase in drug abuse violations relative to the increase in robberies:

$$\frac{\text{Percent Increase in Drug Arrests}}{\text{Percent Increase in Robbery Arrests}} = \frac{57}{9.9} = 5.7$$

This ratio of 5.7 shows that the percent increase in arrests for drug abuse violations from 1982 to 1992 was almost six times greater than the percent increase in robbery arrests.

## 2.5 UNITS OF ANALYSIS

The final issue we discuss in this chapter is often referred to as the *units of analysis*. The units of analysis are the particular objects we have gathered our data about and to which we apply our statistical methods. It refers to what constitutes an observation that comprises our data set. For example, are our observations or data points comprised of persons? prisons? court cases? arrests? states?

As implied, in criminological research we employ many different units of analysis. Sometimes we use questionnaires or interviews to obtain data from individuals. The NCVS, for example, interviews individuals in households from around the United States and asks them about their experiences with criminal victimization. The National Survey of Youth, conducted by Delbert Elliott and his colleagues (1985), consists of interviews with a representative sample of U.S. high school students. In both cases, the units of analysis are the individuals or persons, because the data are obtained from individual respondents.

In other instances, the units of analysis consist of a group or collectivity. Often, this data originally was collected from individuals and then combined or aggregated to form a collectivity. For example, someone interested in the effects of neighborhood characteristics on crime rates might first identify particular neighborhoods in an urban area and take a sample of the residents in each neighborhood, asking the residents such questions as whether they have been the victim of a burglary and how many hours per day no one is home. They may then combine or pool the data from the individuals living in each neighborhood, calculating the number or rate of burglaries and the average number of empty "house hours" for each neighborhood. The data no longer reflect the characteristics of individuals, but rather they are the characteristics of neighborhoods. A neighborhood may have a burglary rate of 25 per 1000 homes and each house may be empty of people an average of 6.5 hours per day. In this case, because the data have been combined or aggregated, the units of analysis are the neighborhoods, not the persons.

As another example of aggregated data, the FBI collects information about the number of crimes reported by individuals to local police departments. The FBI then aggregates this information, identifying what state the report came from and, in some cases, what city and/or county, and whether the report came from an urban, suburban, or rural area of a state. Depending on what data you use, the units of analysis may be the city, county, or state. Sometimes the units of analysis are something called the "city group," which refers to the size of the city.

As an example of data at the city level of analysis, Table 2.7 presents violent and property crime rates for cities by city size. Each of these rates was calculated by using information from local law enforcement agencies in cities of a given size and then aggregating this information to reflect a "group" rate. Even though the information is based on local-level data, the units of analysis in this case are actually the "city groups," not individual cities.

We see from Table 2.7 that both violent and property crime rates are lower for groups made up of smaller cities than for groups made up of larger cities. Notice that this statement is specific to the units of analysis, the group, not to individual cities. If we examined a table with individual agency- or individual city-level data, only then could we make a statement regarding the distribution of crime specifically by city.

**TABLE 2.7.   Violent Crime and Property Crime Rate by City Size Group, UCR Data, 1992**

|  | Violent Crime Rate | Property Crime Rate |
|---|---|---|
| Group I (cities with populations 250,000 and over) | 535.2 | 1046.7 |
| Group II (cities with populations 100,000–249,999) | 431.2 | 1224.7 |
| Group III (cities with populations 50,000–99,999) | 309.6 | 1095.6 |
| Group IV (cities with populations 25,000–49,999) | 253.3 | 1006.6 |
| Group V (cities with populations 10,000–24,999) | 193.2 | 956.5 |

*Source:* FBI, 1993, Table 31, p. 219.

# 2.6 SUMMARY

We hope that you now have a better understanding of the differences that exist between the many types of variables and many levels of measurement used in criminological research. It is essential that you understand these concepts so that you can study their statistical applications.

We have classified the two most general measurement levels of variables as qualitative or categorical and quantitative or continuous. Henceforth, we will most often refer to this distinction as qualitative variables and quantitative variables. Be forewarned, however, that we may, at times, interchange them with the terms "categorical" and "continuous." Qualitative variables tell us "what kind" or "what category" a variable's value denotes, and the values of quantitative variables give us numerical information regarding "how much" or the "quantity" a value contains.

Within these two categories, we have also specified the conditions under which a variable can be defined as measured at the nominal, ordinal, interval, or ratio level. These levels are progressive and can be thought of as a sort of quantitative hierarchy. Values of nominal-level variables tell us the categories or qualities of each case only. Values of ordinal-level variables not only represent categories, but also can be rank-ordered. In addition to an inherent rank order, the distance between categories of an interval-level variable have a known and constant value, but an arbitrary zero point. Finally, not only are there equal distances between any pair of adjacent values on a ratio-level scale, but also there exists a true-zero point.

We next discussed the difference between independent and dependent variables. Independent variables are the variables in our research thought to affect some outcome variable, referred to as the dependent variable.

The remainder of the chapter examined the differences between simple counts of a phenomenon, rates, proportions, and percentages. The final section provided a discussion of the units of analysis used in research.

## Key Terms

alphanumeric data
categorical variable
constant
continuous variable
count
dependent variable
distribution
empirical distribution
frequency count
frequency distribution
independent variable
interval-level variable
level of measurement
nominal-level variable

numeric data
ordinal-level variable
outcome variable
percentage
proportion
qualitative variable
quantitative variable
rate
ratio
ratio-level variable
relative frequency
units of analysis
variable

## Problems

1. For each of the following variables, define the level of measurement as either qualitative or quantitative, and also as one of the four more distinct levels: nominal, ordinal, interval or ratio.

   a. A convicted felon's age in years

   **b.** A driver's score on the breathalizer exam

   **c.** The fine for a parking ticket

   **d.** The specific offense code of a felony

   **e.** A defendant's sex

   **f.** Fines given to industrial companies convicted of violating the Clean Air Act

   **g.** A juvenile offender's grade in school

**2.** What distinguishes an ordinal-level variable from an interval-level variable? What does the ratio level of measurement add?

**3.** In a study examining the effects of arrest on convicted drunk drivers' future drunk driving behavior, which is the independent variable and which is the dependent variable?

**4.** If we are interested in determining the extent to which males and females are more or less afraid to walk outside alone at night, which variable would we designate as our independent and which would be our dependent?

**5.** To compute a rate of violent crime victimizations against 14- to 18-year-olds, what would we use as the numerator and what would we use as the denominator?

**6.** What are the advantages of rates over frequency counts? Give an example.

**7.** In the table that follows, compute the proportion and percent of the household crime victimizations reported to the police according to the monetary loss value.

| | $f$ | Proportion | Percent |
|---|---|---|---|
| Less than $10 | 16 | | |
| $10–$49 | 39 | | |
| $50–$99 | 48 | | |
| $100–$249 | 86 | | |
| $250–$999 | 102 | | |
| $1000 or more | 251 | | |
| | $N = 542$ | | |

**8.** Jeffrey Benoit and Wallace Kennedy (1992) performed a study of 100 adolescent males incarcerated in a secure residential training school in Florida, examining the relationship between prior sexual and physical abuse in their childhoods and the type of offense they were convicted of. What are the units of analysis for this study? What are the independent and dependent variables?

**9.** To test the existence of a relationship between unemployment and crime, we use data from 50 U.S. states. What are the units of analysis? What would you select as independent variable and dependent variable?

**10.** Suppose we are interested in the amount of time police departments took to respond to reports of crime. We track response times for several police departments within large metropolitan areas to see if there are any differences based on the location of the jurisdiction. In this study, what are the units of analysis?

## Solutions to Problems

**1. a.** Interval- or ratio-level measurement. Remember, in the social sciences, it is really splitting hairs to designate a variable as either interval or ratio. We therefore accept both answers. It is also a quantitative variable.

   **b.** Interval/ratio. It is a quantitative variable.

   **c.** Interval/ratio. It is a quantitative variable.

**d.** Nominal, unless the offenses are arranged in order of severity, in which case you could reasonably argue that it was ordinal. Qualitative.

**e.** Nominal. Qualitative.

**f.** Interval/ratio. Quantitative.

**g.** Ordinal if the grade was a letter grade (e.g., A, B, C) because in this instance we would only have order (an A is a better grade than a B, etc.), but it would be classified as an Interval- or ratio-level variable if it were in the form of a GPA. Both would be quantitative variables.

2. The values of ordinal-level variables are not only categorical in nature, but the categories also are related. So the values of ordinal-level variables have the added distinction of meaning and order. That is, there is some inherent and logical order to the categories that represent the values of an ordinal-level variable. In addition to enabling us to rank-order values, interval-level variables allow us to quantify the exact numeric relationship between values. To be classified as an interval-level variable, the categories of the variable must have an equal and known quantity. The zero point on an interval scale, however, is arbitrary.

   Ratio-level variables have all of the qualities of interval-level variables, but in addition, the calibrations that allow us to measure the numerical difference between values are based on a natural or true-zero point. Although many variables we use in criminological research do have a true-zero point (e.g., prior felonies, sentence length received, a person's age, income), this level of measurement is perhaps more pertinent to the physical sciences. Therefore, we will not split hairs in trying to distinguish between interval and ordinal levels of measurement.

3. In this study, you would be trying to predict future drunk driving behavior and you believe that previous arrests would have some impact on this behavior. Arrest is therefore the independent variable and future drunk driving behavior is the dependent variable.

4. In this case, you are trying to predict levels of fear. You believe that a respondent's sex has some impact on an individual's perception of this fear. Therefore, respondent's sex would be used as the independent variable used to predict levels of fear, the dependent variable.

5. To compute age-specific rates of anything, you must utilize both age-specific numerators and denominators. In this case, you would use the number of violent victimizations committed against 14 to 18-year-olds as the numerator and the total number of 14- to 18-year-olds in the population as the denominator. In addition, you would usually multiply this ratio by some base number such as 1000 or 100,000 to ascertain a rate of victimization per 1000 or 100,000 14- to 18-year-olds.

6. The most elementary way of presenting information is to use counts, or frequencies, of the phenomenon you are interested in; this is usually referred to as the ***frequency count.*** These simple counts would be fine if we were not interested in making comparisons across counts. In most cases, however, we are interested in such comparisons. To make comparisons more accurately, it is important to control for the size of the populations you are comparing. To do this, you need to calculate rates of some occurrence. Rates are derived by dividing the observed number of an occurrence or phenomenon by the total number that could have been observed within the population of interest. Examples that illuminate the importance of rates over counts are comparisons across different demographic categories, such as race, age, geographical location. For example, when you examine the number of violent victimizations occurring for blacks and whites in the United States, it may appear from the simple counts that whites are more likely to become the victims of violence than blacks. When the population is controlled, however, the reverse is found. Therefore, the original conclusion you would reach when using

counts as the comparison is actually false. The counts indicate that there are more victimizations against whites, but one because there are more whites in the population.
When this number of victimizations is standardized and based on the total number of
all potential white victims, the rate of victimization is actually lower than for African
Americans.

7.

| | $f$ | Proportion | Percent |
|---|---|---|---|
| Less than $10 | 16 | .029 | 2.9 |
| $10–$49 | 39 | .072 | 7.2 |
| $50–$99 | 48 | .089 | 8.9 |
| $100–$249 | 86 | .159 | 15.9 |
| $250–$999 | 102 | .188 | 18.8 |
| $1000 or more | 251 | .463 | 46.3 |
| | $N = 542$ | 1.0 | 100% |

8. The units of analysis are juvenile male offenders. The researchers thought sexual and physical abuse in childhood would be related to the type of offense committed by juvenile offenders. The presence of sexual or physical abuse in childhood histories would therefore be
the independent variable and type of offense committed would be the dependent variable.
9. The units of analysis would be the 50 states of the United States. We would select unemployment rates for the 50 states as the independent variable and select the types of
crime rates (e.g., violent, property) within the states as the dependent variable. This scenario would presume that levels of unemployment in one state affect levels of crime in
that state.
10. This is a bit tricky. We would ultimately have aggregate data on police response times
for several police departments. Even though the data originally came from individual
incidents of crime, we are using the data only to make comparisons across jurisdictions.
Jurisdictions are therefore the units of analysis.

## *Endnotes*

1. Data obtained from the *United States Sentencing Commission Annual Report, 1992,* Washington, DC, United States Sentencing Commission.
2. There is a proliferation of literature on this subject and the relationship between defendant's
sex and sentencing has been found to be much more complex than this simplistic representation. For example, some have found that when important legal variables (e.g., prior record)
and extralegal variables (e.g., marital status, number of dependent children) are controlled, the
effect of defendant's sex on sentencing outcomes is actually negligible. Results of even the
most current research, however, does not establish equivocal results. For a more detailed discussion of this issue, see Steffensmier et al., 1993, and Daly, 1994.
3. Data from the *Uniform Crime Reports, 1992,* Washington, DC, Federal Bureau of Investigation, U.S. Department of Justice, Table 4, pp. 60–67.
4. The NCVS interviews only individuals 12 years of age or older. Therefore, the population
bases used to calculate rates from NCVS data must also be only for individuals 12 or older.

# CHAPTER 3

# Interpreting Data Distributions

## Graphical Techniques

*Modern data graphics can do much more than simply substitute for small statistical tables. At their best, graphics are instruments for reasoning about quantitative information. Often the most effective way to describe, explore, and summarize a set of numbers—even a large set—is to look at pictures of those numbers. Furthermore, of all methods for analyzing and communicating statistical information, well-designed data graphics are usually the simplest and at the same time the most powerful.*

—EDWARD TUFTE

## 3.1 INTRODUCTION

The importance of understanding the distribution and general characteristics of your data set cannot be overemphasized. One theme that we highlight in this chapter and throughout the text is that you should always know your data—its shape, form, and so on—before proceeding to any more sophisticated statistical analysis. This chapter illustrates a set of graphical techniques to help you better understand and summarize your data distributions. We examine some very effective techniques used for analyzing and describing the characteristics of your data through graphical displays. At a glance, a graphical display of the distribution of a given variable can tell you many important things about your data, such as where the most scores seem to fall and the existence of extreme scores (called outliers) or other unexpected variations that numerical summaries often hide.

Even the simplest charts can prove extremely useful. Take, for example, the trials of the alleged notorious gangster John Gotti. Mr. Gotti, who was believed to be the head of a powerful Mafia crime family, was convicted of several racketeering charges. However, he was also acquitted of many charges at the same trial. One of the aides used by Gotti's defense counsel in his 1987 racketeering trial was a chart illustrating the criminal backgrounds of the prosecution's witnesses. Figure 3.1 presents an excerpt from *The New York Times* that describes the case.

The chart used by Gotti's defense lawyer is displayed in Figure 3.2. This chart lists 69 crimes, including murder, drug possession, and even pistol-whipping a

# GOTTI IS ACQUITTED BY A FEDERAL JURY IN CONSPIRACY CASE

---

## NEW CHARGES ARE LIKELY

---

### Verdict is the First Setback in Recent Government Drive Against Mafia Leaders

---

**By LEONARD BUDER**

John Gotti was acquitted of Federal racketeering and conspiracy charges yesterday in the Government's first major setback in its recent assault on organized crime.

Mr. Gotti, who the Government says is the leader of the nation's most powerful Mafia family, and six co-defendants were found not guilty of charges they took part in a criminal enterprise. They were accused of carrying out illegal gambling and loan-sharking operations, armed hijackings and at least two murders over an 18-year period.

Despite yesterday's verdict, Federal investigators said the 46-year-old Mr. Gotti might face indictment on new charges as head of the Gambino crime family. "I can't comment but I won't deny it," said Thomas L. Sheer, head of the Federal Bureau of Investigation in New York, when asked if the F.B.I. was building up another case against Mr. Gotti.

#### 'We'll Be Starting Again'

"They'll be ready to frame us again in two weeks," Mr. Gotti told a reporter before leaving the Brooklyn courthouse in a gray Cadillac that was waiting for him. "In three weeks we'll be starting again, just watch."

Until yesterday, Federal prosecutors in the Southern and Eastern Districts of New York had recorded a string of successes in major organized-crime cases.

Within the last six months, the heads of the city's four other Mafia families have been convicted after trials in Manhattan and Brooklyn. They, like Mr. Gotti and his co-defendants, had been charged under the Federal Racketeer Influenced and Corrupt Organizations Act, or RICO.

#### Key Witnesses Were Criminals

"Obviously they perceived there was something wrong with the evidence," said Andrew J. Maloney, the United States Attorney in Brooklyn, referring to the jury.

Many of the Government's key witnesses were criminals who testified for the prosecution under grants of immunity or in return for payments and other benefits.

The last piece of evidence requested by the jury for re-examination was a chart introduced by the defense that showed the criminal backgrounds of seven prosecution witnesses. It listed 69 crimes, including murder, drug possession and sales and kidnapping.

Mr. Gotti's lawyer, Bruce Cutler, said the jury showed "courage" because "it's not easy to say no to a Federal prosecutor." He said the jury had not been impressed with the testimony of "paid Government informants who lie, who use drugs, who kill people."

The verdict, which came on the seventh day of jury deliberations after a trial that lasted almost seven months, surprised many in the packed courtroom. Friends of the defendants cheered and applauded; the Government prosecutors, Diane F. Giacalone and John Gleeson, looked glum.

Mr. Gotti, who has been dubbed "Dapper Don" because of his expensive attire and impeccable grooming, and his co-defendants hugged and kissed each other and their lawyers.

Then they stood and applauded as the 12 members of the jury — whose identities had been kept secret to prevent possible tampering — left the room escorted by Federal marshals....

The New York Times

John Gotti

FIGURE 3.1. (The New York Times, *March 14, 1987,* p. 1. *Reprinted by permission from Edward R. Tufte, Envisioning Information, Cheshire, CN: Graphics Press.*)

priest. The chart indicates each crime committed by each witness for the prosecution with an X. It is not hard to detect patterns from this chart. Those who testified against Mr. Gotti were not exactly choir boys! How credible could they have been as witnesses? Rather than simply talking to the jury about the lengthy and serious criminal history of those who testified against his client and letting his words make his case, Gotti's lawyer used a picture, a very simple picture. This graphical display was, however, an excellent and persuasive tool, and it obviously worked for the defense. One lesson to derive from the Gotti case is that the presentation of data does not have to have a lot of fancy numbers and calculations; sometimes a very simple

| Crime | Cardinale | Lofaro | Maloney | Polisi | Senatore | Foronjy | Curro |
|---|---|---|---|---|---|---|---|
| Murder | X | X | | | | | |
| Attempted murder | | X | X | | | | |
| Heroin possession and sale | X | X | | X | | | X |
| Cocaine possession and sale | X | | X | X | | | |
| Marijuana possession and sale | | | | | | | X |
| Gambling business | | X | | X | | X | |
| Armed robberies | X | | X | X | X | | X |
| Loansharking | | X | | X | | | |
| Kidnapping | | | X | X | | | |
| Extortion | | | X | X | | | |
| Assault | X | | X | X | | | X |
| Possession of dangerous weapons | X | X | X | X | X | | X |
| Perjury | | X | | | | X | |
| Counterfeiting | | | | | X | X | |
| Bank robbery | | | X | X | | | |
| Armed hijacking | | | | X | X | | |
| Stolen financial documents | | | X | X | X | | |
| Tax evasion | | | | X | | X | |
| Burglaries | X | X | | X | X | | |
| Bribery | | X | | X | | | |
| Theft: auto, money, other | | | X | X | X | X | X |
| Bail jumping and escape | | | X | X | | | |
| Insurance frauds | | | | | X | X | |
| Forgeries | | | | X | X | | |
| Pistol-whipping a priest | X | | | | | | |
| Sexual assault on minor | | | | | | | X |
| Reckless endangerment | | | | | | | X |

FIGURE 3.2. (United States v. Gotti et al., *1987. Chart supplied by counsel, Bruce Cutler and Susan G. Kellman. Reprinted by permission from Edward R. Tufte, Envisioning Information, Cheshire, CN: Graphics Press.*)

graphical description of the data is very effective in communicating what you want to communicate.

In addition to being presentational props, graphical displays of data are also important analytical tools. As suggested, in criminological research, before more advanced statistical analyses are performed, the following simple questions must be asked. What do my data look like? What does this question mean? How much variation do I have for each variable, are the scores mostly alike, or are they in general very different from one another? Like most things in life, the best course of action is to proceed slowly and cautiously. To use an automobile metaphor, get to know your data in the parking lot before heading out onto the information highway.

In the preceding chapter, we described two different types of variables (qualitative, or categorical, and quantitative, or continuous) and how the type of variable we have in part determines the appropriate analytical technique we use. Similarly, the type of variable you have also determines which type of graphical technique is most appropriate to display your data. Because qualitative variables are best described in table form, this chapter only briefly describes two types of graphical displays used for qualitative variables: pie charts and bar charts. The second part of the chapter focuses on various techniques for graphing quantitative variables, including histograms, frequency polygons, cumulative frequency polygons, relative frequency polygons, and time-series plots.

## 3.2 ORGANIZING QUALITATIVE DATA

Remember from our earlier discussion that whereas quantitative or continuous variables tell us "how much" of something each case has, qualitative or categorical variables tell us "what kind" or "what category" a case belongs in. One way of organizing crime data in the United States is to analyze how rates of criminal victimization vary by certain demographic characteristics, such as regional location or the sex and race of the offender.

Table 3.1 displays 1991 homicide and property crime rates for selected states and for the four regions of the country. Each state listed in the table is followed by its corresponding homicide and property crime rates. Although the rates displayed in this table are themselves quantitative in nature, we are interested here in the qualitative variable State. We can aggregate this information further by calculating regional rates of crime. Table 3.2 displays the regional homicide and property crime rates that were calculated from the numbers displayed in Table 3.1.

Think of it in this way. Similar to tallying up how many Republicans and Democrats may be in your class, think of this as tallying up how many incidents of homicide and property crime occurred in each of the four regions of the country during 1991. Each rate of homicide or property crime therefore represents "what region" the homicide or property crime case "took place" or "belongs in." The next section describes how the information from Table 3.2 can be graphically illustrated by using *pie charts*.

## 3.3 PIE CHARTS AND BAR GRAPHS

Looking at Table 3.2, it does not take long to determine by examining the rates alone that the South has the highest rate of homicides whereas the South and West have higher rates of property crime than the other regions of the country. For most purposes, this table would be all that is necessary to convey these differential rates of crime by region to an audience. However, in some instances, graphical display such as a *pie chart* can make this type of information easier to convey.

Figures 3.3 and 3.4 display pie charts for homicide and property crime rates by region, respectively. The size of the "slice" of the pie is proportional to the number,

## TABLE 3.1. Homicide and Property Crime Rates per 100,000 Population by Selected State and Region of the Country, UCR Data, 1991

| Region | State | Homicide | Property |
|---|---|---|---|
| 1 | Connecticut | 5.70 | 4824.40 |
| 1 | Maine | 1.20 | 3635.60 |
| 1 | Massachusetts | 4.20 | 4586.20 |
| 1 | New Hampshire | 3.60 | 3328.50 |
| 1 | New Jersey | 5.20 | 4796.50 |
| 1 | New York | 14.20 | 5080.70 |
| 1 | Pennsylvania | 6.30 | 3108.60 |
| 1 | Rhode Island | 3.70 | 4577.40 |
| 1 | Vermont | 2.10 | 3838.40 |
| 2 | Illinois | 11.30 | 5092.90 |
| 2 | Indiana | 7.50 | 4312.50 |
| 2 | Iowa | 2.00 | 3830.70 |
| 2 | Kansas | 6.10 | 5034.70 |
| 2 | Michigan | 10.80 | 5335.00 |
| 2 | Minnesota | 3.00 | 4180.20 |
| 2 | Missouri | 10.50 | 4652.60 |
| 2 | Nebraska | 3.30 | 4019.50 |
| 2 | North Dakota | 1.10 | 2728.50 |
| 2 | Ohio | 7.20 | 4471.20 |
| 2 | South Dakota | 1.70 | 2897.00 |
| 2 | Wisconsin | 4.80 | 4188.90 |
| 3 | Alabama | 11.50 | 4521.40 |
| 3 | Arkansas | 11.10 | 4581.70 |
| 3 | Delaware | 5.40 | 5155.10 |
| 3 | DC | 80.60 | 8314.70 |
| 3 | Florida | 9.40 | 7362.90 |
| 3 | Georgia | 12.80 | 5755.20 |
| 3 | Kentucky | 6.80 | 2920.30 |
| 3 | Louisiana | 16.90 | 5473.50 |
| 3 | Maryland | 11.70 | 5253.10 |
| 3 | Mississippi | 12.80 | 3831.70 |
| 3 | North Carolina | 11.40 | 5230.30 |
| 3 | Oklahoma | 7.20 | 5085.00 |
| 3 | South Carolina | 11.30 | 5206.70 |
| 3 | Tennessee | 11.00 | 4640.70 |
| 3 | Texas | 15.30 | 6979.00 |
| 3 | Virginia | 9.30 | 4234.20 |
| 3 | West Virginia | 6.20 | 2472.40 |
| 4 | Alaska | 7.40 | 5087.70 |
| 4 | Arizona | 7.80 | 6734.90 |
| 4 | California | 12.70 | 5682.70 |
| 4 | Colorado | 5.90 | 5541.80 |

1, North East; 2, North Central; 3, South; 4, West.
*Source:* FBI, 1992.

**TABLE 3.2. Homicide and Property Crime Rates per 100,000 Population by Region, UCR Data, 1991**

|  | North East | North Central | South | West |
|---|---|---|---|---|
| Homicide | 5.1 | 5.7 | 14.7 | 6.1 |
| Property Crime | 4197.3 | 4228.6 | 5118.7 | 5237.3 |

*Source:* FBI, 1992.

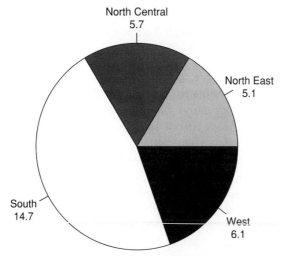

FIGURE 3.3. Homicide rates per 100,000 population by region, 1991.
(*Source: FBI, 1992.*)

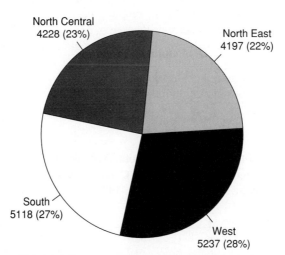

FIGURE 3.4. Property crime rates per 100,000 population by region, UCR data, 1991.
(*Source: FBI, 1992.*)

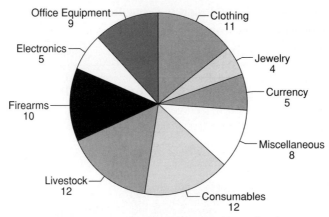

FIGURE 3.5. Percentage of property recovered by police from NCVS victims, 1991.
(*Source: FBI, 1992.*)

or proportion of events for that region. The bigger the slice, therefore, the more crimes. From these figures, we can see at a glance that the South has the highest homicide rate compared to the other regions of the country. It is not so easy, however, to ascertain from a glance the region where the majority of property crimes occur. Therefore, it is helpful to display the percentages (percent of total pie that region comprises) as well as the actual numbers you are trying to convey on your graphical display, as we have done in Figure 3.4.

Technically, a pie chart is constructed by apportioning the 360 degrees of a circle (a pie) in relation to the percentage in each category, in this case a region. These proportions are calculated by adding up the entire number of incidents of property crime (or the rates in this case) and then dividing each region's rate by this total. For example, the South has a property crime rate of 5118 per 100,000, which, when divided by the total rate obtained from adding each region's property crime rate together (18,780), represents approximately 27 percent of all incidents of property crime that were reported to police during 1991.

There are some important guidelines to follow when constructing a pie chart. First, you should utilize this graphical technique *only* when you want to summarize

TABLE 3.3. Percent of Total Arrests for
Violent Crime, Property Crime, and Total
Crime Index Rate by Sex, 1991

|  | Male (%) | Female (%) |
|---|---|---|
| Violent crime | 88.7 | 11.3 |
| Property crime | 74.7 | 25.3 |
| Total crime index | 78.1 | 21.9 |

*Source:* FBI, 1992.

a qualitative variable that consists of five or fewer categories. A variable with too many categories may present a confusing picture, thereby undermining the goal of a graphical display in the first place. For example, Figure 3.5 presents the percentages for each type of stolen property that was recovered by police. So many types of property are displayed in this pie, however, that someone would have a difficult time making sense out of this figure. Second, it is also a good idea, as illustrated in Figure 3.4, to display the category percentages in addition to the actual rates; it is usually easier for audiences to compare percentages across each category rather than to compare rates.

## *Bar Graphs*

An alternative way graphically to present qualitative variables is with a *bar graph.* Based on data taken from Table 3.3, Figure 3.6 presents a bar graph that displays the percent of total arrests made in 1990 for males and females for violent, property, and total crime index. The question is, "What proportion of those arrested for violent crime are male and what proportion are female?" From the bar graph presented in Figure 3.6, an observer can easily determine that even though there is a larger percentage of men arrested for all forms of crime than women, women have higher percentages of arrest for property crime than they do for violent crime.

FIGURE 3.6. Percent of total arrests by type of crime, UCR data, 1991.
(*Source: FBI, 1992.*)

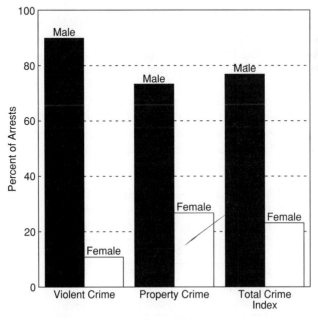

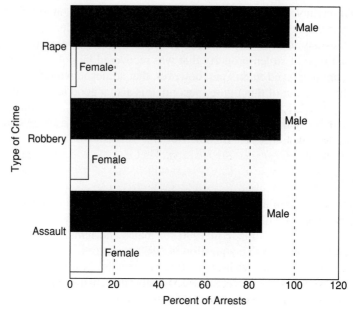

FIGURE 3.7. Percent of offenders perceived to be male and female,
NCVS data, 1991.
(*Source: Bureau of Justice Statistics, 1992.*)

Typically, the percent or frequencies you want to display are labeled along the
vertical axis (ordinate) of the bar graph, and categories of the qualitative variable
are labeled along the horizontal axis (abscissa). Rectangles (bars) are then constructed over each category, with the height of each rectangle equal to the frequency
or percent. Bar graphs can also be displayed horizontally.

If you select a horizontal mode of presentation, the horizontal and vertical axes
should be reversed as shown in Figure 3.7 (see Table 3.4 for original data). The bar
graph presented here uses data from the National Crime Victimization Survey
(NCVS; Bureau of Justice Statistics, 1990) showing the proportion of violent crime
victims who perceived their assailants to be either male or female. Consistent with
arrest data obtained for this same year from the FBI and displayed in Figure 3.6, it

**TABLE 3.4. Percent of Single Offenders
Perceived by the Victim to be Either
Male or Female, NCVS Data, 1990**

|         | Male (%) | Female (%) |
|---------|----------|------------|
| Rape    | 98.0     | 2.0        |
| Robbery | 92.5     | 7.5        |
| Assault | 85.2     | 14.3       |

*Source:* Bureau of Justice Statistics, 1992.

appears that victims of violent crime also reported their assailants to be male far more often than they reported them to be female.

## *3.4 GRAPHING QUANTITATIVE DATA*

To begin our discussion of organizing and graphing quantitative data, we have listed in Table 3.5 in ascending order the violent crime rate per 100,000 population for each of the fifty states plus the District of Columbia. Technically, this table is called an *ungrouped frequency distribution.* That is, each state's violent crime rate is listed along with the frequency $(f)$ with which each score occurs in the data. In this distribution, no two states have the same violent crime rate; therefore, each state's rate occurs only once and represents a frequency $(f)$ of 1. Because there are so many values (50), the data would be better displayed in a grouped frequency format.

The first step necessary in order to construct a *grouped frequency distribution* from ungrouped data is to decide on the number of *class intervals* necessary to group your data. This decision is a matter of judgment (as much art as science), but it is a very crucial decision. If you choose too many intervals, the table will be no more informative than an ungrouped frequency distribution. If too few intervals are used, important features of the data may be hidden. In addition, the intervals must not overlap and every value in your distribution must fall within one, and only one, class interval.

Let's go through an exercise of placing the data presented in Table 3.5 into a grouped frequency distribution. The first step, which we have already done for you, is to put all of your data into ascending order. This is done simply by reordering your data from the lowest to the highest value. Note from Table 3.5 that the violent crime rate for Washington, DC, is the highest (2453 per 100,000) and is more than double that of the next highest (Florida with 1184.3 violent crimes per 100,000 population). Because the District of Columbia often has extremely high rates of crime and is not officially given statehood status, most analysts usually drop it from state-level analyses. For this reason, the next examples will be based on the 50 states, excluding Washington, DC.

After our data are placed in ascending order, we must calculate the range of our scores and then decide on the number of intervals necessary to describe the distribution—the rule of thumb is usually between 10 to 20 intervals. The range of a set of scores is defined as the difference between the largest and the smallest values. For these state-level violent crime rates, the highest value is Florida with a rate of 1184.3 per 100,000 and the lowest value is North Dakota with a rate of 65.4. This gives us a range of $(1184.3 - 65.4) = 1118.9$.

We must now divide this range into a sufficient number of intervals that will give us an accurate and detailed picture of our data. Again, the rule of thumb is that there should usually be between 10 and 20 intervals. Keeping within these limits, let's say that we decide this distribution would best be described by using 10 intervals. (It is your decision as to how many intervals to use; if you try it and don't like the way it portrays your data, select a different number of intervals.) The next step

**TABLE 3.5. Rank-Order Listing of the Violent Crime Rate by State, UCR Data, 1991**

| Rank | State | Violent Crime Rate | Frequency | Percent |
|------|-------|--------------------|-----------|---------|
| 1 | North Dakota | 65.40 | 1 | 1.96 |
| 2 | Vermont | 116.80 | 1 | 1.96 |
| 3 | New Hampshire | 119.30 | 1 | 1.96 |
| 4 | Maine | 132.10 | 1 | 1.96 |
| 5 | Montana | 139.90 | 1 | 1.96 |
| 6 | South Dakota | 182.20 | 1 | 1.96 |
| 7 | West Virginia | 191.00 | 1 | 1.96 |
| 8 | Hawaii | 241.80 | 1 | 1.96 |
| 9 | Utah | 268.80 | 1 | 1.96 |
| 10 | Wisconsin | 277.00 | 1 | 1.96 |
| 11 | Idaho | 290.30 | 1 | 1.96 |
| 12 | Iowa | 303.30 | 1 | 1.96 |
| 13 | Wyoming | 310.20 | 1 | 1.96 |
| 14 | Minnesota | 316.00 | 1 | 1.96 |
| 15 | Nebraska | 334.60 | 1 | 1.96 |
| 16 | Virginia | 373.20 | 1 | 1.96 |
| 17 | Mississippi | 389.10 | 1 | 1.96 |
| 18 | Kentucky | 438.00 | 1 | 1.96 |
| 19 | Pennsylvania | 450.00 | 1 | 1.96 |
| 20 | Rhode Island | 462.00 | 1 | 1.96 |
| 21 | Kansas | 499.60 | 1 | 1.96 |
| 22 | Indiana | 505.30 | 1 | 1.96 |
| 23 | Oregon | 506.30 | 1 | 1.96 |
| 24 | Washington | 522.60 | 1 | 1.96 |
| 25 | Connecticut | 539.70 | 1 | 1.96 |
| 26 | Colorado | 559.30 | 1 | 1.96 |
| 27 | Ohio | 561.80 | 1 | 1.96 |
| 28 | Oklahoma | 583.70 | 1 | 1.96 |
| 29 | Arkansas | 593.30 | 1 | 1.96 |
| 30 | Alaska | 613.90 | 1 | 1.96 |
| 31 | New Jersey | 634.80 | 1 | 1.96 |
| 32 | North Carolina | 658.40 | 1 | 1.96 |
| 33 | Arizona | 670.70 | 1 | 1.96 |
| 34 | Nevada | 677.00 | 1 | 1.96 |
| 35 | Delaware | 714.30 | 1 | 1.96 |
| 36 | Tennessee | 725.90 | 1 | 1.96 |
| 37 | Massachusetts | 736.10 | 1 | 1.96 |
| 38 | Georgia | 738.20 | 1 | 1.96 |
| 39 | Missouri | 763.00 | 1 | 1.96 |
| 40 | Michigan | 803.10 | 1 | 1.96 |
| 41 | New Mexico | 834.80 | 1 | 1.96 |
| 42 | Texas | 840.10 | 1 | 1.96 |
| 43 | Alabama | 844.20 | 1 | 1.96 |
| 44 | Louisiana | 951.00 | 1 | 1.96 |
| 45 | Maryland | 956.20 | 1 | 1.96 |
| 46 | South Carolina | 972.50 | 1 | 1.96 |
| 47 | Illinois | 1039.20 | 1 | 1.96 |
| 48 | California | 1089.90 | 1 | 1.96 |
| 49 | New York | 1163.90 | 1 | 1.96 |
| 50 | Florida | 1184.30 | 1 | 1.96 |
| 51 | DC | 2453.30 | 1 | 1.96 |

*Source:* FBI, 1992.

is to determine the width of our intervals. We do this by dividing the range of our data by the number of intervals we have selected. You can round this number to an even and convenient *interval width*. In our example, we have a range of 1118.9 and we decided on 10 intervals. To determine the interval width, we divide the range by the number of intervals. Our range of 1118.9 divided by 10 is equal to 111.89, so we round this number down to an even interval width of 110.

Now that we have determined our interval width, we can construct our class intervals and begin to group our data. When selecting the first interval, we must make sure that it includes the smallest value in our distribution. As a rule, most analysts select the lower limit of the first interval to be either zero or an integral multiple of the interval width. It is also important to make sure that no observation can fall on a point of division between two class intervals. To help avoid this, it usually is a good idea to take the limits of your interval an extra decimal place than that in the data. For example, the data in Table 3.5 extends to one decimal place (the last digit is always a zero), so our interval limits should extend to two decimal places. This means that the size of our interval width will really be 109.99, not 110.

Let's use zero as the lower limit of our first interval (for North Dakota, with a violent crime rate of 65.4) and construct intervals with a width of 109.99 thereafter. Table 3.6 displays the resulting grouped frequency distribution. Because we rounded the class interval width down to 110, we had to add an additional interval to include our two highest scores for New York and Florida. We therefore ended up with 11 rather than 10 class intervals. The first interval has a lower value of 0.00 and an upper value of 109.99; these values are called the *stated class limits*. There is a lower stated class limit and an upper stated class limit. The lower stated class limit for the first interval is zero, and the upper stated class limit is 109.99. The stated class limits for the second interval are 110.00 and 219.99, and for the eleventh interval they are 1100.00 and 1209.99.

**TABLE 3.6. Grouped Frequency Distribution of Violent Crime Rates for 50 States, UCR Data, 1991**

| Interval | Class Interval | Frequency | Porportion | Percent |
|---|---|---|---|---|
| 1 | 0.00–109.99 | 1 | .02 | 2 |
| 2 | 110.00–219.99 | 6 | .12 | 12 |
| 3 | 220.00–329.99 | 7 | .14 | 14 |
| 4 | 330.00–439.99 | 4 | .08 | 8 |
| 5 | 440.00–549.99 | 7 | .14 | 14 |
| 6 | 550.00–659.99 | 7 | .14 | 14 |
| 7 | 660.00–769.99 | 7 | .14 | 14 |
| 8 | 770.00–879.99 | 4 | .08 | 8 |
| 9 | 880.00–989.99 | 3 | .06 | 6 |
| 10 | 990.00–1099.99 | 2 | .04 | 4 |
| 11 | 1100.00–1209.99 | 2 | .04 | 4 |
| Totals | | $N = 50$ | 1.0 | 100% |

*Source:* FBI, 1992.

After your intervals are created, you can easily tally up the number of violent crime rates that fall within each of the intervals. This number is called a *frequency* and is usually denoted with a lowercase italic *f*. Notice that only one state, North Dakota, with a violent crime rate of 65.40, falls into the first interval. The state with the next highest violent crime rate is Vermont with a rate of 116.80, which is greater than 109.99, so it falls out of the first interval and into the second. Notice that six states have a violent crime rate 110.0 or over and 219.99 or under (Vermont, New Hampshire, Maine, Montana, South Dakota, and West Virginia), so these six states fall into the second interval. The number of states that fall into each interval are included in the column labeled "frequency." The sum of your interval frequencies should equal your total sample size *(N)* as shown in Table 3.6. In addition to the frequency, proportion and percentage columns also are displayed in the table. Remember from Chapter 2 that the proportions are the frequencies *(f)* divided by the total number of cases in your sample *(N)*. As discussed in that chapter, another way to think of the proportion is as a *relative frequency,* because it reflects the frequency of a given value relative to the total number of cases *(f/N)*. Again, just to remind you, percentages can easily be obtained by multiplying these proportions or relative frequencies by 100.

## Refinements to a Grouped Frequency Distribution

For general purposes, the grouped frequency distribution shown in Table 3.6 will suffice. However, in several instances, which we will get to later, other information is needed. The first example is more conceptual in nature and revolves around the issue of continuity. Certain cases demand that we conceptualize our class intervals as a continuous series of contiguous categories, not as a series of discrete class intervals. In reality, this is the "real" nature of a quantitative variable. For example, even though a survey respondent may state that she or he is 21 years of age, in reality, age is not so discrete. If we wanted to get technical, age could be broken down into a number of ways to reflect the fact that it really is continuous. Is the respondent actually 19 years, 4 months, 6 hours, and 5 minutes old?

To reflect this actual continuity in a grouped frequency distribution, statisticians often use something called the *real class limits* of the class intervals. To find the real class limits of your class intervals, you simply do the following. Starting at

---

STEPS FOR CONSTRUCTING A GROUPED FREQUENCY DISTRIBUTION

1. Arrange original data points in ascending order.
2. Determine number of intervals by using the range of your data as an indicator—usually between 10 and 20 intervals.
3. Determine the width of your intervals.
4. Construct class intervals; intervals must not overlap, and every value in the distribution must fall within one, and only one, class interval.
5. Complete the frequency *(f)* column by tallying the number of cases that fall within each interval.
6. Complete grouped frequency distribution by computing the proportion and percentage columns.

the first interval, subtract the upper stated class limit of the first interval from the lower stated class limit of the second interval. Then divide this number by 2. Finally, add this last number to the upper stated class limit of every interval and subtract it from the lower stated class limit of every interval.

For example, suppose we had a grouped frequency distribution of age with stated class intervals as follows: 13–15, 16–18, and 19–21. To find the real class limits, start at the first interval (13–15) and subtract the upper stated class limit of this interval (15) from the lower stated class limit of the second interval (16). This will equal $16 - 15$, or 1. Then divide this number by 2: 1/2, or .5. Finally, add this number to the upper stated class limit of every interval and subtract it from the lower stated class limit of every interval. This will produce the following stated and real class limits:

| Stated Class Limits | Real Class Limits |
|:---:|:---:|
| 13–15 | 12.5–15.5 |
| 16–18 | 15.5–18.5 |
| 19–21 | 18.5–21.5 |

Notice that the real interval limits converge. That is, the class limits of one interval run imperceptibly into the limits of the next interval. This illustrates the continuous nature of the variable, in spite of the fact that we have expressed it in terms of intervals or categories. Where, you may be thinking, do you place a value of 15.5? Well, remember that if you extended your decimal or digit one place past the decimal point in your original data points, no values should fall there.

Other useful pieces of information that can be added to a grouped frequency distribution are the *midpoints* of the class intervals. Midpoints are exactly that: the middle point of the class interval. Midpoints are obtained by taking the sum of the upper and lower limits and dividing it by 2. It makes no difference whether you use the real or stated class limits to find the midpoint, the result will be the same. For example, the midpoint for the first interval from the age data we just used would be obtained like this: $(12.5 + 15.5)/2 = (28/2) = 14$. Notice that we would have obtained the same results had we used the stated class limits $(13 + 15)/2 = 28/2 = 14$. Midpoints can be calculated for any and all intervals in a grouped frequency distribution.

Table 3.7 displays stated and real limits along with the midpoints of the intervals for the data originally displayed in Table 3.6. The first interval has a lower stated class limit of 0.00 and an upper stated class limit of 109.99. To find the midpoint of this interval, add the two limits together and divide by 2: $(0 + 109.99)/2 = 109.99/2 = 54.995$. To find the midpoint of the second interval (110.00 − 219.99), simply add these class limits together and also divide by 2: $(110.0 + 219.99)/2 = 329.99/2 = 164.995$. Now you can calculate the midpoints for the rest of the intervals.

Cumulative frequencies, cumulative relative frequencies, and cumulative percentages are the final three pieces of information we discuss about frequency distributions. Again, the term cumulative is very descriptive. *Cumulative frequency* columns within a frequency distribution table quantify the extent to which frequencies or cases within the distribution accumulate. *Cumulative relative frequency,* or *cumulative proportion,* columns within a frequency distribution table quantify the extent to which relative frequencies or proportions within the distribution accumulate. *Cumulative percent* columns show the same accumulation with

**TABLE 3.7. Grouped Frequency Distribution of Violent Crime Rates for 50 States, Including Real Limits and Midpoints, UCR Data, 1991**

| Interval | Class Interval | Real Limits | Midpoint | $f$ | Percent |
|---|---|---|---|---|---|
| 1 | 0.00–109.99 | −.005–109.995 | 54.995 | 1 | 2 |
| 2 | 110.00–219.99 | 109.995–219.995 | 164.995 | 6 | 12 |
| 3 | 220.00–329.99 | 219.995–329.995 | 274.995 | 7 | 14 |
| 4 | 330.00–439.99 | 329.995–439.995 | 384.995 | 4 | 8 |
| 5 | 440.00–549.99 | 439.995–549.995 | 494.995 | 7 | 14 |
| 6 | 550.00–659.99 | 549.995–659.995 | 604.995 | 7 | 14 |
| 7 | 660.00–769.99 | 659.995–769.995 | 714.995 | 7 | 14 |
| 8 | 770.00–879.99 | 769.995–879.995 | 824.995 | 4 | 8 |
| 9 | 880.00–989.99 | 879.995–989.995 | 934.995 | 3 | 6 |
| 10 | 990.00–1099.99 | 989.995–1099.995 | 1044.995 | 2 | 4 |
| 11 | 1100.99–1209.99 | 1099.995–1209.995 | 1154.995 | 2 | 4 |
| Totals | | | | $N = 50$ | 100% |

*Source:* FBI, 1992.

percentages. Cumulative proportion and cumulative percent columns are primarily used to communicate how many cases or what percentage or proportion of the total distribution falls above or below a given class interval.

The cumulative frequency column simply is a summation of the frequency of the class intervals either from lowest to highest or highest to lowest. For example, the cumulative frequency for the first interval would be equal to the frequency $(f)$ of that interval because no other cases fall below it. The cumulative frequency for the second interval would be all cases in the first interval plus all cases in the second interval, and so on. This additive procedure is continued until the final interval is tallied. The cumulative frequency listed in the final interval of the distribution should be equal to the total number of cases in the sample, or $N$. For example: In Table 3.8 the frequency for the first interval is one because there is only one case in that interval. Because this is the first interval, the cumulative frequency is also one. When these six cases in the second interval are added to the one case in the first interval, the cumulative frequency through the second interval is seven. When the seven cases in the third interval are added to the frequencies in the first two intervals, the cumulative frequency is 14. The 14 is the sum of the frequencies in the first $(f = 1)$, second $(f = 6)$, and third $(f = 7)$ intervals. To complete the cumulative frequency distribution, simply add the frequencies in each subsequent interval to the existing cumulative frequency. Notice that when the two cases in the last interval are added, the cumulative frequency becomes 50, which is the total number of observations.

Now, just repeat the same process using relative frequencies or proportions to obtain the cumulative relative frequencies. Remember, the relative frequency is the same thing as the proportion. It is found by dividing the frequency in the interval by the total number of cases $(f/N)$. The cumulative relative frequency for the first interval would be equal to the relative frequency (proportion) of that interval. The cumulative relative frequency for the second interval would be found by adding the relative

**TABLE 3.8. Grouped Frequency Distribution of Violent Crime Rates for 50 States, Including Cumulative Frequencies, Cumulative Relative Frequencies (Proportions), and Cumulative Percents, UCR Data, 1991**

| Interval | Class Interval | Frequency | Cumulative Frequency | Proportion | Cumulative Proportion | Percent | Cumulative Percent |
|---|---|---|---|---|---|---|---|
| 1 | 0.00–109.99 | 1 | 1 | .02 | .02 | 2 | 2 |
| 2 | 110.00–219.99 | 6 | 7 | .12 | .14 | 12 | 14 |
| 3 | 220.00–329.99 | 7 | 14 | .14 | .28 | 14 | 28 |
| 4 | 330.00–439.99 | 4 | 18 | .08 | .36 | 8 | 36 |
| 5 | 440.00–549.99 | 7 | 25 | .14 | .50 | 14 | 50 |
| 6 | 550.00–659.99 | 7 | 32 | .14 | .64 | 14 | 64 |
| 7 | 660.00–769.99 | 7 | 39 | .14 | .78 | 14 | 78 |
| 8 | 770.00–879.99 | 4 | 43 | .08 | .86 | 8 | 86 |
| 9 | 880.00–989.99 | 3 | 46 | .06 | .92 | 6 | 92 |
| 10 | 990.00–1099.99 | 2 | 48 | .04 | .96 | 4 | 96 |
| 11 | 1100.00–1209.00 | 2 | 50 | .04 | 1.00 | 4 | 100 |
| Totals | | 50 | | | 1.00 | | 100% |

frequency of that interval to the first. The cumulative relative frequency for the third interval would be found by adding the relative frequency of the third interval to the sum of the first two intervals. Continue with this for each interval. Because we are dealing with relative frequencies or proportions, the cumulative relative frequency of the last interval should be 1.0. For example: In Table 3.8 the proportion of cases in the first interval is .02 (1/50 = .02). Because this is the first interval, the cumulative proportion is also .02. There are six cases in the second interval, so the proportion of cases is .12 (6/50 = .12). When this proportion (.12) is added to the proportion in the first interval (.02), the cumulative proportion through the second interval is .14. When the proportion in the third interval (.14) is added to the proportion in the first two intervals, the cumulative proportion is .28. The .28 is the sum of the proportions in the first ($p = .02$), second ($p = .12$), and third ($p = .14$) intervals. To complete the cumulative proportion distribution, simply add the proportions in each subsequent interval to the existing cumulative proportion. Notice that when the proportion in the last interval is added, the cumulative proportion is 1.0.

The cumulative percentage column is calculated in the same additive manner, but by summing the percentages instead of the frequencies or proportions. The cumulative percent for the first interval will be equal to the percent of that interval. The cumulative percent for the second interval would be found by adding the percent found for that interval to the first. The cumulative percent for the third interval would be found by adding the percent in the third interval to the sum of the first two intervals. Continue with this for each interval. Because we are dealing with percentages, the cumulative percent for the last interval should be 100%. For example: In Table 3.8, the first interval contains 2 percent of the cases (1/50 = .02 × 100 = 2%). Because this is the first interval, the cumulative percent is also 2 percent. There are six cases in the second interval, so the second interval contains 12 percent of the cases (6/50 = .12 × 100 = 12%). When the percentage in the second interval is added to the percentage in the first interval (2%), the cumulative percent through the second interval is 14 percent. This tells us that 14 percent of the total number of cases are in the first two intervals. When the percentage in the third interval (14%) is added to the percentage in the first two intervals, the cumulative percent is 28 percent, which is the sum of the percents in the first (2%), second (12%), and third (14%) intervals. The cumulative percent tells us that 28 percent of the total number of cases are found in the first three intervals. To complete the cumulative percent distribution, simply add the percentages in each subsequent interval to the existing cumulative percent. Notice that when the percentage of cases in the last interval is added, the cumulative percent equals 100 percent.

## 3.5 HISTOGRAMS

*Histograms* are perhaps the most typical way of displaying graphically the distributions of quantitative variables. As with bar graphs, histograms can be created by using either the horizontal or vertical axes for the class intervals. However, we create histograms in this chapter with the more conventional horizontal axis (abscissa) for the class intervals and display the frequency, relative frequency (proportion), or percentage along the vertical (ordinate) axis.

In creating a histogram from the data in Table 3.6, we simply place rectangles over each class interval, with the height of each rectangle equal to the frequency of a given class interval. For example, in the first class interval, only one state has a violent crime rate that falls within these limits (North Dakota), so we make the height of our first rectangle equal to 1. The height of each rectangle, then, reflects the frequency of each interval along the vertical axis. What results is a histogram such as that displayed in Figure 3.8A. Note that the histogram looks very much like the bar graph used for qualitative data. However, because histograms are used with quantitative data, the bars are placed side by side, with no space in between them. This is done to reflect the continuous nature of quantitative data as opposed to the categorical nature of qualitative data. In addition, instead of marking the variable categories under each bar, the numerical limits (stated or real) of each interval are displayed along the horizontal axis. We should note here that, rather than the frequency, we could have placed the relative frequency (proportion) or percent on the vertical axis. The height of each bar would then reflect each interval's relative frequency or percent. We graph the relative frequencies for you in Figure 3.8B.

By examining Figures 3.8A and 3.8B, we can not only determine specifics about our distribution but also get an overall picture of the shape of our distribution. For example, we can see that the majority of states have violent crime rates that fall between 440 and 769 per 100,000 population, but we also can see that there are a few very low rates of violent crime and even fewer very high rates. Knowing what your distribution looks like is a very important first step in any data analysis.

Typically, social data from a very large sample tend to take the form of a bell-shaped curve, similar to that superimposed on our original histogram and displayed in Figure 3.9. When a distribution has this shape, it is often called a *normal distribution*. Although the distribution illustrated is not completely normal, it approximates one enough to give you the idea. More important, if a distribution's left or lower half resembles the right or upper half, it is called a *symmetrical distribution*. Both halves are equal—the left or lower half is a mirror image of the right or upper half (see Figure 3.10).

More often than not, however, we are not so fortunate and the distributions we must work with are not symmetrical but are *skewed distributions*. Because there are two sides to any distribution, there are two ways in which our data can be skewed. If the right tail of the distribution extends out farther than the left tail, the distribution is said to be *positively skewed* (Figure 3.11). Here, most of the data are in the lower left tail, and a few cases are straggling off at the high end, pulling the distribution out to the right. This distribution is referred to as positively skewed because the long tail of the distribution trails off on the positive side of a number line. You may remember that a number line is a line with zero in the middle. To the right of zero are the positive numbers extending to infinity; to the left of zero are the negative numbers extending to infinity:

$$\longleftrightarrow$$
$$-\infty \ldots -3 \quad -2 \quad -1 \quad 0 \quad 1 \quad 2 \quad 3 \ldots \infty$$

A distribution is said to be *negatively skewed* if the left tail extends out farther than the right tail (Figure 3.12). In this case, most of the data points are at the upper

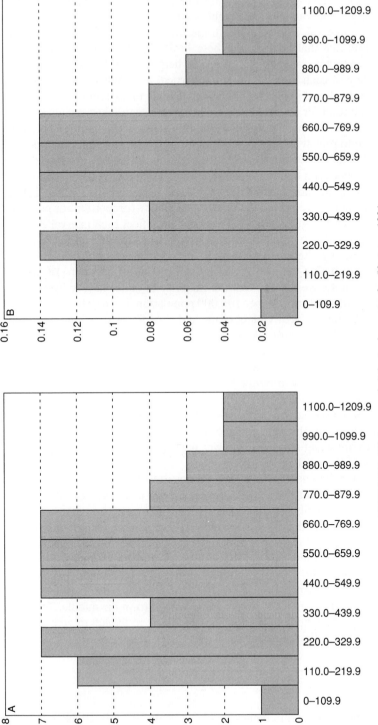

FIGURE 3.8. Histogram of violent crime rates for 50 states, 1991. (*Source: FBI, 1992.*)

FIGURE 3.9. Histogram of violent crime rates for 50 states, 1991. (*Source: FBI, 1992.*)

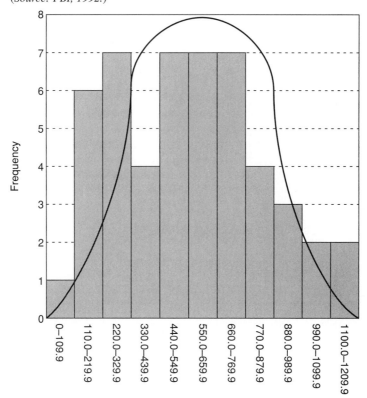

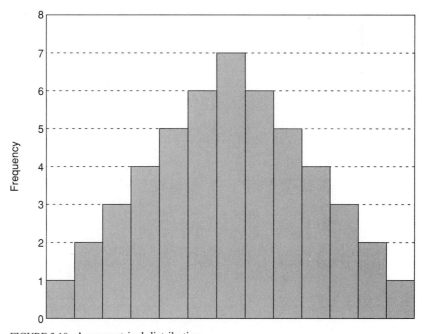

FIGURE 3.10. A symmetrical distribution.

FIGURE 3.11. A positively skewed distribution.

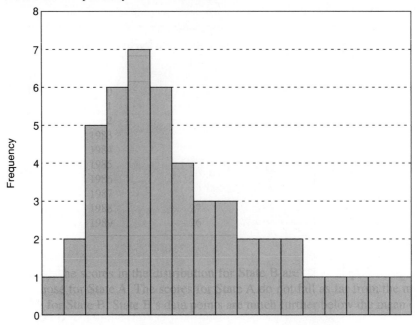

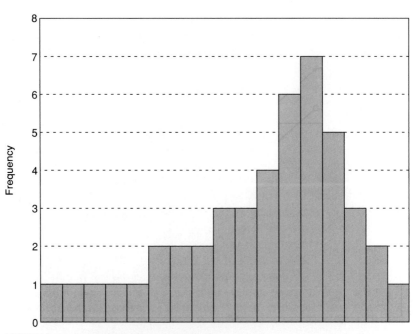

FIGURE 3.12. A negatively skewed distribution.

right hand side of your distribution with a few data points straggling off at the low end—pulling the tail of the distribution out to the left. This distribution is referred to as negatively skewed because the long tail of the distribution trails off on the negative side of a number line.

# 3.6 FREQUENCY POLYGONS

An alternative way graphically to present the frequency distribution of a quantitative variable is with a *frequency polygon.* A polygon is a figure consisting of straight lines joined end to end. Instead of rectangular bars representing the frequencies within intervals, then, dots connected by line segments are used to create a frequency polygon. The real limits of the class intervals are displayed along the horizontal axis, and the vertical axis displays the frequencies. The frequency associated with each interval is then indicated by placing a dot over the midpoint of each class interval. The height of the dot is equal to the interval's frequency. These points are then connected with line segments.

To illustrate a frequency polygon, let's use violent crime rates within metropolitan statistical areas (MSAs) from Uniform Crime Reports (UCR) data (Table 3.9). We have placed these original data into a grouped frequency distribution in Table 3.10, however. As a learning exercise, you could create your own grouped distribution before moving on. We also report the interval percents and cumulative percents in Table 3.10.

The frequency polygon created from the data in Table 3.10 is presented in Figure 3.13. For the sake of display simplicity, we have rounded up the interval labels along the horizontal axis. From this graph, it is easy to discern the shape of the distribution. Violent crime rates within metropolitan areas have an obvious positive skewness. The vast majority of MSAs have rates of violent crime under 1050, a minority of areas fall above this, and even fewer lie in the upper tail with very high rates of violent crime.

Notice that one class interval has a frequency of zero, two intervals have very high frequencies, and the last three intervals contain only one MSA each (Los Angeles, New York, and Miami). These illustrate other irregularities that data distributions may display. In addition to positive skewness, this distribution also contains abnormalities that are called *gaps, multiple peaks,* and *outliers.* To emphasize these abnormalities, Figure 3.14 presents this same frequency distribution in histogram form. There you can clearly see the multiple peaks in the distribution, the gaps where no frequencies are found, and outliers for unusually high or unusually low scores. In this case we have unusually high scores, or positive, outliers. Three MSAs have very high crime rates compared with the others (Los Angeles, New York, and Miami).

In addition to being shown in a frequency polygon, cumulative frequencies can also be graphically displayed in what is called, you guessed it, a *cumulative frequency polygon.* The cumulative frequency polygon is constructed in the same manner as the frequency polygon. However, instead of having frequencies plotted at each interval, cumulative frequencies are plotted. The vertical axis is therefore

**TABLE 3.9. MSA Rank-Order Listing of Violent Crime Rate per 100,000 Population, UCR Data, 1991**

| Rank | MSA | State | Rate of Violent Crime | Rank | MSA | State | Rate of Violent Crime |
|---|---|---|---|---|---|---|---|
| 1 | Bismark | ND | 73.20 | 50 | Cleveland | OH | 669.30 |
| 2 | Nashua | NH | 73.40 | 51 | Reno | NV | 673.70 |
| 3 | Billings | MT | 81.90 | 52 | Tucson | AZ | 688.80 |
| 4 | Eau Claire | WI | 109.10 | 53 | Trenton | NJ | 689.10 |
| 5 | Bangor | ME | 118.00 | 54 | Corpus Christi | TX | 697.20 |
| 6 | Altoona | PA | 137.70 | 55 | Lexington | KY | 711.30 |
| 7 | Provo | UT | 140.00 | 56 | Anchorage | AK | 711.50 |
| 8 | Rochester | MN | 140.90 | 57 | San Antonio | TX | 712.20 |
| 9 | Danbury | CT | 161.00 | 58 | Jackson | MS | 715.60 |
| 10 | Manchester | NH | 189.90 | 59 | Columbus | OH | 720.80 |
| 11 | Green Bay | WI | 225.80 | 60 | Oklahoma City | OK | 723.90 |
| 12 | Cheyenne | WY | 237.20 | 61 | Bridgeport | CT | 726.10 |
| 13 | Honolulu | HI | 240.30 | 62 | Denver | CO | 730.10 |
| 14 | Olympia | WA | 276.10 | 63 | Indianapolis | IN | 732.90 |
| 15 | Portland | ME | 276.10 | 64 | Phoenix | AZ | 771.40 |
| 16 | Boulder | CO | 276.70 | 65 | Las Vegas | NV | 788.10 |
| 17 | Hagerstown | MD | 291.00 | 66 | Portland | OR | 798.30 |
| 18 | Vancouver | WA | 296.60 | 67 | Tulsa | OK | 829.80 |
| 19 | Eugene | OR | 298.40 | 68 | Boston | MA | 832.30 |
| 20 | Springfield | MO | 300.60 | 69 | Buffalo | NY | 850.00 |
| 21 | Boise | ID | 300.80 | 70 | Montgomery | AL | 853.80 |
| 22 | Charlottesville | VA | 304.10 | 71 | Atlantic City | NJ | 879.20 |
| 23 | Sioux Falls | SD | 319.70 | 72 | Daytona Beach | FL | 911.90 |
| 24 | Bellingham | WA | 320.30 | 73 | Battle Creek | MI | 917.30 |
| 25 | Syracuse | NY | 321.30 | 74 | New Bedford | MA | 949.40 |
| 26 | Madison | WI | 340.10 | 75 | Tuscaloosa | AL | 965.30 |
| 27 | Medford | OR | 349.50 | 76 | San Diego | CA | 966.80 |
| 28 | Fort Wayne | IN | 371.10 | 77 | Fayetteville | NC | 967.20 |
| 29 | Decatur | AL | 371.80 | 78 | Charleston | SC | 972.50 |
| 30 | Charleston | WV | 372.20 | 79 | San Francisco | CA | 983.70 |
| 31 | Salt Lake City | UT | 373.70 | 80 | Atlanta | GA | 987.90 |
| 32 | Erie | PA | 374.20 | 81 | El Paso | TX | 991.70 |
| 33 | Albany | NY | 410.60 | 82 | Detroit | MI | 1001.20 |
| 34 | Pittsburgh | PA | 429.10 | 83 | Nashville | TN | 1014.50 |
| 35 | Lynchburg | VA | 429.90 | 84 | Fresno | CA | 1021.30 |
| 36 | Lawrence | KS | 443.10 | 85 | Newark | NJ | 1028.50 |
| 37 | Minneapolis-St. Paul | MN | 470.00 | 86 | Houston | TX | 1076.60 |
| 38 | Rapid City | SD | 494.20 | 87 | Flint | MI | 1092.80 |
| 39 | Austin | TX | 506.90 | 88 | Birmingham | AL | 1127.70 |
| 40 | Casper | WY | 508.90 | 89 | Gainesville | FL | 1152.00 |
| 41 | Providence | RI | 509.10 | 90 | Baltimore | MD | 1255.00 |
| 42 | Athens | GA | 515.80 | 91 | Baton Rouge | LA | 1286.00 |
| 43 | Lincoln | NB | 519.40 | 92 | Jackson | MI | 1296.00 |
| 44 | Amarillo | TX | 519.50 | 93 | Dallas | TX | 1333.60 |
| 45 | Omaha | NB | 546.90 | 94 | New Orleans | LA | 1407.70 |
| 46 | Seattle | WA | 596.40 | 95 | Little Rock | AR | 1408.90 |
| 47 | Grand Rapids | MI | 645.80 | 96 | Los Angeles | CA | 1795.90 |
| 48 | Hartford | CT | 648.40 | 97 | New York | NY | 2044.20 |
| 49 | Panama City | FL | 669.10 | 98 | Miami | FL | 2194.90 |

*Source:* FBI, 1992.

TABLE 3.10. Grouped Frequency Distribution of MSA Violent Crime Data, UCR Data, 1991

| Interval | Real Limits of Class Interval | Midpoint | Frequency | Cumulative Frequency | Percent | Cumulative Percent |
|---|---|---|---|---|---|---|
| 1 | −0.005–209.995 | 104.995 | 10 | 10 | 10 | 10 |
| 2 | 209.995–419.995 | 314.995 | 23 | 33 | 23 | 33 |
| 3 | 419.995–629.995 | 524.995 | 13 | 46 | 13 | 46 |
| 4 | 629.995–839.995 | 734.995 | 22 | 68 | 22 | 68 |
| 5 | 839.995–1049.995 | 944.995 | 17 | 85 | 17 | 85 |
| 6 | 1049.995–1259.995 | 1154.995 | 5 | 90 | 5 | 90 |
| 7 | 1259.995–1469.995 | 1364.995 | 5 | 95 | 5 | 95 |
| 8 | 1469.995–1679.995 | 1574.995 | 0 | 95 | 0 | 95 |
| 9 | 1679.995–1889.995 | 1784.995 | 1 | 96 | 1 | 96 |
| 10 | 1889.995–2099.995 | 1994.995 | 1 | 97 | 1 | 97 |
| 11 | 2099.995–2309.995 | 2204.995 | 1 | 98 | 1 | 98 |
| Totals | | | $N = 98$ | | 98% | |

Note: Percent total does not add to 100 because of rounding.

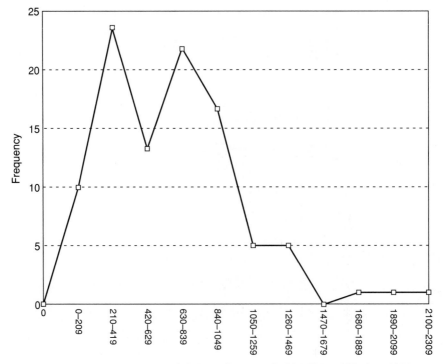

FIGURE 3.13.  Frequency polygon of violent crime rates in 98 MSAs, UCR data, 1991.
(*Source: FBI, 1992.*)

labeled Cumulative Frequency, and the height of the point is equal to the cumulative frequency of each interval. The horizontal axis is labeled with the upper limits of each class interval, and the dots are placed above this point. In addition, only the starting point of the plot is based at zero.

The cumulative frequencies of the MSA violent crime rates in Table 3.10 are displayed in a cumulative frequency polygon in Figure 3.15. The information in this graph conveys the number of metropolitan areas that have violent crime rates below or equal to a given rate. For example, we can see that 95 of the 98 metro areas had rates that fell below the seventh interval of 1469 (again, we have rounded up the points on the horizontal axis for display purposes) and that only three areas are represented in the final four intervals. This tells us that there are only a few cases at the very high end of the distribution. The cumulative frequency polygon, then, also illustrates the shape of a distribution, but in a somewhat different manner. Notice that because the graph displays cumulative frequencies, the line will always be rising or flat, because in calculating cumulative frequencies you are always adding frequencies, even if the frequency is zero. The cumulative frequency line, therefore, will never drop below its previous level. If it does, retrace your steps because something is wrong.

In addition to using frequencies, the vertical or left-hand axis could have shown the category cumulative proportions or cumulative percentages. Like a cumulative

FIGURE 3.14.  Histogram of violent crime rates in 98 MSAs, UCR data, 1991. (*Source: FBI, 1992.*)

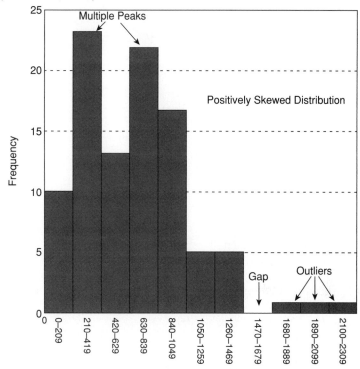

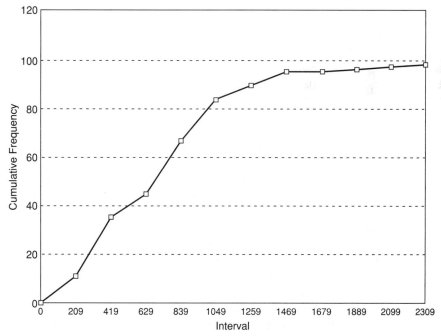

FIGURE 3.15.  Cumulative frequency polygon of MSA violent crime rates, UCR data, 1991.
(*Source: FBI, 1992.*)

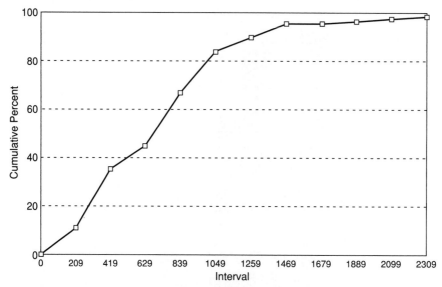

FIGURE 3.16. Cumulative percent polygon of MSA violent crime rates, UCR data, 1991. (*Source: FBI, 1992.*)

frequency polygon a *cumulative percent polygon* or *cumulative proportion polygon* will never drop below its previous level; it will always be rising or flat. In Figure 3.16 we have recreated Figure 3.15 using cumulative percents. The advantage of this graph over the cumulative frequency polygon is that percentages can be very easily discerned and interpreted. For example, you can easily see that almost one-half (46 percent) of the jurisdictions have violent crime rates under 700 per 100,000 and that 85 percent have rates under 1050 per 100,000.

## 3.7 TIME PLOTS

One question that often arises in criminological research is the extent to which there has been a change in the rates of criminality or victimization over time. *Time plots* are used to show a variable's change over time, such as how crime rates have evolved over the years or how they fluctuate from month to month during a given year. Table 3.11 presents rape and robbery rates known to police in the United States from 1972 to 1991 based on UCR data. Although we can determine how the rates of these crimes have changed over time from this table, a graphical display in the form of a time plot allows us to ascertain more easily the kind and extent of change that has taken place.

As with the frequency polygons we created in the preceding section, to create a time plot, we place a point above the unit of analysis being used, in this case year, to designate the rate or frequency of a given variable during that time. Line seg-

**TABLE 3.11. Robbery and Rape
Rates, UCR Data, 1972–1991**

| Year | Rape | Robbery |
|------|------|---------|
| 1972 | 22.5 | 180.7 |
| 1973 | 24.5 | 183.1 |
| 1974 | 26.2 | 209.3 |
| 1975 | 26.3 | 220.8 |
| 1976 | 26.6 | 199.3 |
| 1977 | 29.4 | 190.7 |
| 1978 | 31.0 | 195.8 |
| 1979 | 34.7 | 218.4 |
| 1980 | 36.8 | 251.1 |
| 1981 | 36.0 | 258.7 |
| 1982 | 34.0 | 238.9 |
| 1983 | 33.7 | 216.5 |
| 1984 | 35.7 | 205.4 |
| 1985 | 37.1 | 208.5 |
| 1986 | 37.9 | 225.1 |
| 1987 | 37.4 | 212.7 |
| 1988 | 37.6 | 220.9 |
| 1989 | 38.1 | 233.0 |
| 1990 | 41.2 | 257.0 |
| 1991 | 42.3 | 272.7 |

*Source:* FBI, 1992.

ments are then drawn to connect these points. Figure 3.17 presents a time plot of rape and robbery rates from 1972 to 1991 from the data in Table 3.11. From this graph, we can see that, although both types of crime have generally increased during this period, robbery rates in the United States have fluctuated much more than rates of rape. Rates of robbery peaked during the mid-1970s after the lows experienced in 1972, at which point they began to decrease. During the early 1980s, robbery rates increased again and similarly decreased during the mid- to late 1980s. Since 1987, however, rates of robbery have been steadily increasing.

Another invaluable source of data that is available to monitor changes in rates of crime and other issues regarding victimization over time is the National Crime Victimization Survey (NCVS). As the NCVS collects information of criminal victimizations that were both reported and not reported to the police, one question we can answer using these data is the extent to which victims of crime have over time become more or less reluctant to report their victimizations to police. Figure 3.18 presents a time plot of the proportion of rape and robbery victims who reported their crime to police from 1973 through 1990.

Note that trends within this time plot, particularly those for rape, are not as easy to see as trends in Figure 3.17. The year-to-year fluctuations are more rapid and sporadic. For variables such as these, some researchers prefer a technique called

FIGURE 3.17. Time plot of rape and robbery rates, UCR data, 1972–1991.
(*Source: FBI, 1992.*)

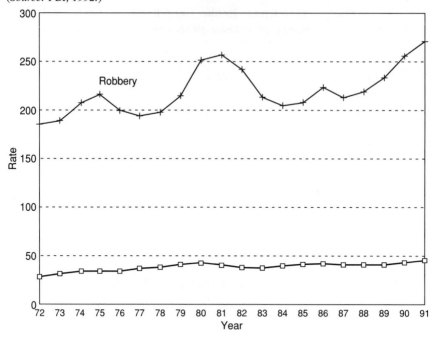

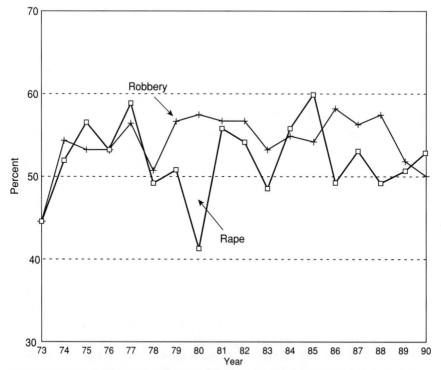

FIGURE 3.18. Proportion of NCVS rape and robbery victims who reported their victimization to police, 1973–1990.
(*Source: Bureau of Justice Statistics, 1973–1990.*)

*smoothing,* which removes the more severe irregularities in the data, thereby making trends in the plot easier to discern. Several statistical manipulations can be used to smooth data. However, we show you only one of the most popular techniques, called a "moving average span of 3."

In general, smoothing a set of raw data creates a new data point for each case called the *smoothed score.* Table 3.12 presents the raw and smoothed data points from the proportion of rape victims who reported their victimization to police during the 1973 to 1990 period. In all smoothing techniques, the first and last case in your data remain the same; they are not transformed. So in this table, the smoothed proportion of victim reports in 1973 and 1990 are the same as those points in the raw data. Smoothing the remainder of data points is done by computing the average proportion of interest by adding this point to the data points before and after it and then dividing this sum by 3.

We start at the second year in the time series because the first data point does not get smoothed. We take the score for the second year and add to this the score for the first and third year. We then divide these three scores by 3. This becomes our new score for the second year (it is actually the average of the scores for the first, second, and third year in the time series). This yields your smoothed data point, and because we smoothed it by averaging 3 years, it is called a "moving average span of 3." Then, we move on to the third year and sum the scores for the

**TABLE 3.12. Raw and Smoothed Proportion of Rape Victims Who Reported Their Victimizations to the Police, NCVS Data, 1973–1990**

| Year | Raw Proportion | Smoothing Technique | Smooth Proportion |
|------|------|------|------|
| 1973 | 44 | Endpoints remain | 44 |
| 1974 | 56 | (44 + 56 + 53)/3 | 51 |
| 1975 | 53 | (56 + 53 + 58)/3 | 56 |
| 1976 | 58 | (53 + 58 + 49)/3 | 53 |
| 1977 | 49 | (58 + 49 + 51)/3 | 53 |
| 1978 | 51 | (49 + 51 + 42)/3 | 47 |
| 1979 | 42 | (51 + 42 + 55)/3 | 49 |
| 1980 | 55 | (42 + 55 + 53)/3 | 50 |
| 1981 | 53 | (55 + 53 + 48)/3 | 52 |
| 1982 | 48 | (53 + 48 + 56)/3 | 52 |
| 1983 | 56 | (48 + 56 + 60)/3 | 54 |
| 1984 | 60 | (56 + 60 + 49)/3 | 55 |
| 1985 | 49 | (60 + 49 + 53)/3 | 54 |
| 1986 | 53 | (49 + 53 + 51)/3 | 51 |
| 1987 | 49 | (53 + 49 + 51)/3 | 51 |
| 1988 | 51 | (49 + 51 + 54)/3 | 51 |
| 1989 | 54 | (51 + 54 + 54)/3 | 53 |
| 1990 | 54 | Endpoints remain | 54 |

*Source:* Data compiled from *Criminal Victimization in the U.S., 1973–1990,* Bureau of Justice Statistics.

third year along with the second (the one before it) and the fourth (the one after it). We divide this sum by 3. This becomes the smoothed score for the third year. We continue to do this until we reach the last year in the time series. This last data point does not get smoothed. For example, by smoothing the proportion of rapes reported to the police for 1974, we simply add the proportions from 1973, 1974, and 1975 and divide this sum by 3. This is illustrated for you step-by-step in Table 3.12.

Figure 3.19 presents a time plot of both the raw and smoothed proportions of rape victims who reported their victimization to the police. With the smooth line, it is much easier to determine what was happening during the period covered than using the raw data points. The smoothing process did not drastically change gradual year-to-year fluctuations, but it did make trends easier to discern between years in which extreme fluctuations occurred. In general, we can see that, although victims of rape did not report their victimizations as much to police in the late 1970s, the 1980s have witnessed a general increasing trend in the proportion of rape victims willing to report their victimization to the police.

FIGURE 3.19. Raw (squares) and smooth (crosses) percentages of rape victims who reported their victimization to police, NCVS data, 1973–1990. (*Source: Bureau of Justice Statistics, 1973–1990.*)

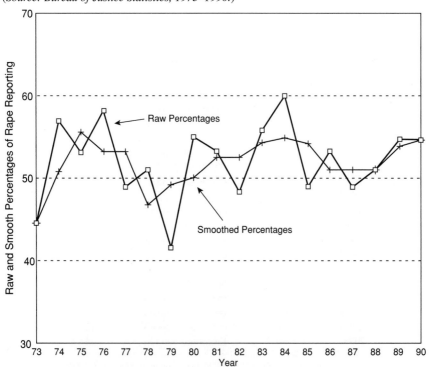

# 3.8 SUMMARY

In this chapter we introduced you to the most popular ways in which to display both qualitative and quantitative variables graphically. We discussed two techniques for displaying qualitative data: pie charts and bar graphs. At a glance, these tell us "how much" of something a qualitative category has, such as how many crimes per 100,000 population the South has in this country versus the Northeast. Because it is often necessary to group the distributions of quantitative variables into a more manageable number of categories instead of using each original data point, we began the second section of this chapter by illustrating the appropriate way in which to construct a grouped frequency distribution.

We outlined four ways in which to graph quantitative distributions: histograms, frequency polygons, cumulative frequency polygons, and time plots. With these graphical techniques, we can easily determine what our distribution looks like. For example, if our distribution resembles a bell, with both halves being equal, we know that we have a symmetrical distribution. On the other hand, if the upper tail of our distribution extends out farther than the lower left tail, our distribution is said to be positively skewed. If the lower or left tail extends out farther than the upper right tail, it is said to be negatively skewed.

Unlike histograms and frequency polygons, which are used to graph a quantitative variable at one point in time, time plots graph a quantitative variable over a given set of time segments, such as days, weeks, months, or years. In this case, the unit of analysis is the type of time segment you are using. With time plots, we can easily determine the extent of change that has taken place in a variable over time. We also introduced the technique of smoothing, which enables us better to discern trends in time-series data that fluctuate erratically.

## Key Terms

bar graph
class intervals
cumulative frequency
cumulative frequency polygon
cumulative percent
cumulative percent polygon
cumulative proportion
cumulative proportion polygon
cumulative relative frequency
frequency
frequency polygon
gaps
grouped frequency distribution
histogram
interval width
midpoint

multiple peaks
negative skew
normal distribution
outliers
pie chart
positive skew
real class limits
relative frequency
skewed distribution
smoothed score
smoothing
stated class limits
symmetrical distribution
time plot
ungrouped frequency distribution

## Problems

1. If your data consist of motor vehicle theft rates for every state in the United States, what is your unit of analysis?
2. If your data consist of purse snatching rates for every month of 1990, what is your unit of analysis?

3. The following list presents the rate of violent crime victimizations (NCVS data; Bureau of Justice Statistics, 1992) in 1991 by marital status of the victim. Assuming that the variable of interest here is marital status, what type of variable is this? What type(s) of graphical display(s) would be appropriate? What would they tell us about this variable?

| Never married: | 62.6 | Widowed: | 6.2 |
| Married: | 14.8 | Divorced/separated: | 44.5 |

4. The following list presents motor vehicle theft rates for each state in the United States in 1991 (VCR data; FBI, 1992). Construct a grouped frequency distribution from these motor vehicle rates.

| Alabama | 363 | Louisiana | 573 | Ohio | 500 |
| Alaska | 533 | Maine | 163 | Oklahoma | 556 |
| Arizona | 861 | Maryland | 730 | Oregon | 474 |
| Arkansas | 341 | Massachusetts | 918 | Pennsylvania | 481 |
| California | 1038 | Michigan | 679 | Rhode Island | 794 |
| Colorado | 426 | Minnesota | 363 | South Carolina | 387 |
| Connecticut | 795 | Mississippi | 286 | South Dakota | 114 |
| Delaware | 375 | Missouri | 558 | Tennessee | 613 |
| Florida | 783 | Montana | 206 | Texas | 944 |
| Georgia | 611 | Nebraska | 212 | Utah | 241 |
| Hawaii | 336 | Nevada | 652 | Vermont | 144 |
| Idaho | 178 | New Hampshire | 220 | Virginia | 338 |
| Illinois | 655 | New Jersey | 925 | Washington | 444 |
| Indiana | 464 | New Mexico | 346 | West Virginia | 174 |
| Iowa | 170 | New York | 1003 | Wisconsin | 436 |
| Kansas | 351 | North Carolina | 299 | Wyoming | 154 |
| Kentucky | 214 | North Dakota | 126 | | |

5. Construct a histogram from the grouped frequency distribution you just created.
6. What does this distribution of motor vehicle thefts look like? How would you classify this distributional shape (symmetrical, positively skewed, negatively skewed)?
7. The following table presents rates of personal crimes of violence and personal theft per 1000 persons aged 25 to 34 from 1973 to 1990 (NCVS data). Create a time plot for each of these data points. What does this tell us about rates of violence and theft during this time?

| | Crimes of Violence | Crimes of Theft | | Crimes of Violence | Crimes of Theft |
|---|---|---|---|---|---|
| 1973 | 34 | 99 | 1982 | 46 | 98 |
| 1974 | 38 | 106 | 1983 | 41 | 88 |
| 1975 | 39 | 109 | 1984 | 38 | 84 |
| 1976 | 40 | 113 | 1985 | 37 | 83 |
| 1977 | 42 | 115 | 1986 | 34 | 76 |
| 1978 | 40 | 117 | 1987 | 34 | 81 |
| 1979 | 44 | 108 | 1988 | 35 | 82 |
| 1980 | 40 | 99 | 1989 | 35 | 84 |
| 1981 | 44 | 101 | 1990 | 36 | 77 |

*Source:* Bureau of Justice Statistics, 1992.

8. What is the unit of analysis in the table in Question 7?

9. Smooth the original data points for rates of personal theft for those age 25 to 34 in the preceding table using a moving average span of 3. Plot both original and smooth data points. What does this tell us?

## Solutions to Problems

1. The 50 states of the United States are the units of analysis.
2. Months of the year are the units of analysis.
3. Marital status is a nominal-level variable; the categories imply no order. For variables of this nature, bar charts and pie charts would be appropriate types of graphical presentation. Both would generally tell us that those individuals who had never been married had higher victimization rates than any other marital status categories.
4. The first step in constructing a grouped frequency distribution is to place all of the rates into ascending order. This is done simply by re-ordering your data from the lowest to the highest value. Then, you must calculate the range of your data and then decide on the number of intervals necessary to describe the distribution—the rule of thumb is usually between 10 and 20 intervals. The range of a set of scores is defined as the difference between the largest and the smallest values. In this distribution, motor vehicle theft rates range from 114 to 1038, so the range is $1038 - 114 = 924$. As the data range is almost 1000, an appropriate number of intervals to select would be 10, ranging from 100 through 1100. After the intervals are created, you can now easily tally up the number of violent crime rates that fall within each of the intervals. This number is called frequency and is usually denoted with a small $f$. The sum of your interval frequencies should equal your total sample size $(N)$, which is 50. In addition to the frequency, you should include a percentage column displayed in the table as shown:

**Grouped Frequency Distribution for Motor Vehicle Theft Rates for Each State, UCR Data, 1991**

| Interval | Class Interval | $f$ | Percent |
|---|---|---|---|
| 1 | 101–200 | 8 | 16 |
| 2 | 201–300 | 7 | 14 |
| 3 | 301–400 | 9 | 18 |
| 4 | 401–500 | 6 | 12 |
| 5 | 501–600 | 5 | 10 |
| 6 | 601–700 | 5 | 10 |
| 7 | 701–800 | 4 | 8 |
| 8 | 801–900 | 1 | 2 |
| 9 | 901–1000 | 3 | 6 |
| 10 | 1001–1100 | 2 | 4 |
| | | $N = 50$ | 100% |

*Source:* FBI, 1992.

5. A histogram constructed from the above grouped frequency distribution of motor vehicle theft rates would look like the one in Figure 3A.1.
6. The histogram of state-level motor vehicle theft rates reveals a positively skewed distribution. Most of the state rates cluster around the lower end of the distribution, with a few states dragging the high end of the distribution out.

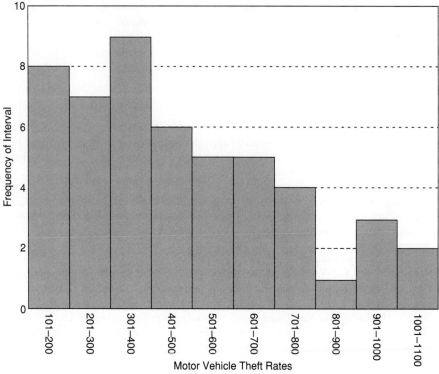

FIGURE 3A.1. Histogram of state-level motor vehicle theft rates, 1991.
(*Source: FBI, 1992.*)

7. Both theft and violent rates of victimization for 1973 to 1990 are plotted in Figure 3A.2. The plots indicate that rates of theft victimization against 25- to 34-year-olds increased during the early 1970s and then began to decline steadily. Rates of violence during this time have remained relatively stable.
8. The units of analysis in this table are years.
9. The original theft rates and smoothed rates are as follows:

| | Original Rates of Theft | Smoothed Rates | | Original Rates of Theft | Smoothed Rates |
|---|---|---|---|---|---|
| 1973 | 99 | 99 | 1982 | 98 | 95.7 |
| 1974 | 106 | 104.7 | 1983 | 88 | 90 |
| 1975 | 109 | 109.3 | 1984 | 84 | 85 |
| 1976 | 113 | 112.3 | 1985 | 83 | 81 |
| 1977 | 115 | 115 | 1986 | 76 | 80 |
| 1978 | 117 | 113.3 | 1987 | 81 | 79.7 |
| 1979 | 108 | 108 | 1988 | 82 | 82.3 |
| 1980 | 99 | 102.7 | 1989 | 84 | 81 |
| 1981 | 101 | 99.3 | 1990 | 77 | 77 |

*Source:* Bureau of Justice Statistics, 1992, rounded data.

FIGURE 3A.2. Time plot for rates of theft and violent victimizations per One Thousand 25- to 34-year-olds.
(*Source: Bureau of Justice Statistics, 1992.*)

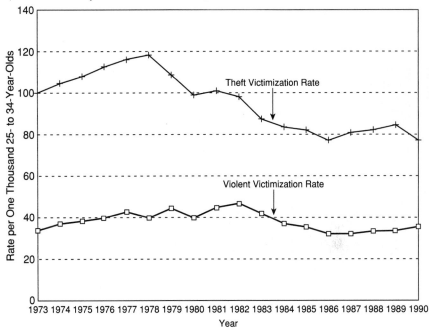

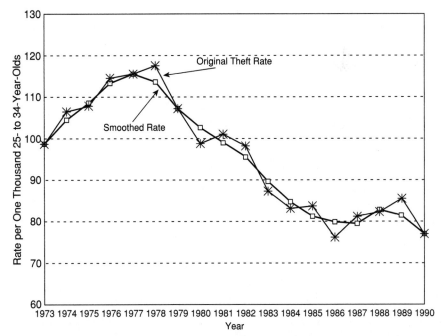

FIGURE 3A.3. Time plot for rates of theft, original rates, and smoothed rates using a running average span of 3.

A time plot of both original rates and smoothed rates is presented in Figure 3A.3. Because there are no severe rate aberrations within the original data points, there is not much difference between the time plot for original and smoothed rates. The smoothed trend line, however, does reveal a somewhat smoother transition than the original data points.

# CHAPTER 4

# *Measures of Central Tendency*

*The Normal is the good smile in a child's eyes—all right. It is also the dead stare in a million adults. It both sustains and kills—like a God. It is the Ordinary made beautiful; it is also the Average made lethal.*

—PETER SHAFFER

## 4.1 INTRODUCTION

In the preceding chapters we have discussed some ways of presenting our data in the form of charts, diagrams, and distributions. There are times, however, when we want to summarize our data in a more succinct or compact form. We may not want to nor be able to summarize very easily the important features of our data with graphical displays. For example, suppose that a police department gave a paper-and-pencil performance evaluation test to each of its new recruits after their first year of service. In addition to each person's score on the test, we probably would like to know how well the group of new officers did overall. That is, we would like to know what the "typical" or "average" score on the test was. We can use this information in other ways. For instance, we might also eventually want to know whether the "average" for this set of rookies was better or worse than for those in the past. Or, we might want to know how a particular individual officer performed relative to the rest of the group, whether his or her score was better or worse than the "typical" score.

The descriptive statistics that inform us about the most common, or "typical," score, or the score around which other scores tend to cluster, are called *measures of central tendency*. They are called measures of "central tendency" because they describe the center point on a distribution of scores. The use of the plural here should immediately let you know that there is more than one measure of central tendency. We will examine three of the most frequently used measures: the mode, the median, and the mean. Each of these measures is calculated in a different manner, each describes the "typical" score differently, and each has its own advantages and disadvantages. Because the mode, median, and mean are based on different understandings of what the notion of "average" or "typical" is, they will, under some circumstances, give us very different results. We will examine the circumstances when one measure of central tendency may be more appropriate to use than another.

## 4.2 THE MODE

### *Ungrouped Data*

The *mode* is the most easily calculated measure of central tendency. In fact, it requires no real mathematical calculation to determine what the mode is, just a reasonably discerning eye. In a distribution of scores, either categorical or continuous, the mode is that score or scores that occurs most frequently. It is in the sense that it is the most frequent score that the mode is used as a measure of central tendency.

Table 4.1 reports scores for 20 rookies on a hypothetical police officer performance evaluation test. The most frequent score on this test is 75, as six of twenty officers received it. We can conceive of the mode as a measure of central tendency in two ways. One is to look at the frequency distribution of the scores where the mode appears as the highest point on the curve. In our example you can see that the top of the curve corresponds to the score of 75 (Figure 4.1). Another way to think of the mode is that it is the most likely or most probable score if we were to pick one by chance. If we randomly selected any of the twenty scores it would most likely be a 75 because the chance of picking a 75 (6/20, or .30) is higher than for any other score.

Sometimes there is more than one frequently occurring score in a distribution. Suppose that our 20 scores looked like the following: 40, 50, 60, 65, 65, 65, 65, 65, 70, 70, 75, 75, 80, 80, 80, 80, 80, 85, 90, 95. In this distribution there are two frequent scores, 65 and 80, because each occurs five times. This distribution, therefore, does not have one mode, it has two, and is called a *bimodal distribution.* A bimodal distribution has two high points on a frequency distribution (see Figure 4.2). As you can see, in our example the chance of randomly selecting a score of 65 (5/20, or .25) is the same as the chance of selecting a score of 80 (5/20), both of which are

---

The **mode** is the most frequent score or scores in a distribution of scores.

---

**TABLE 4.1. Twenty Scores on a Hypothetical Police Performance Evaluation Test**

| Person | Score | Person | Score |
|--------|-------|--------|-------|
| 1 | 40 | 11 | 75 |
| 2 | 50 | 12 | 75 |
| 3 | 55 | 13 | 75 |
| 4 | 59 | 14 | 78 |
| 5 | 62 | 15 | 79 |
| 6 | 69 | 16 | 80 |
| 7 | 70 | 17 | 80 |
| 8 | 75 | 18 | 80 |
| 9 | 75 | 19 | 90 |
| 10 | 75 | 20 | 95 |

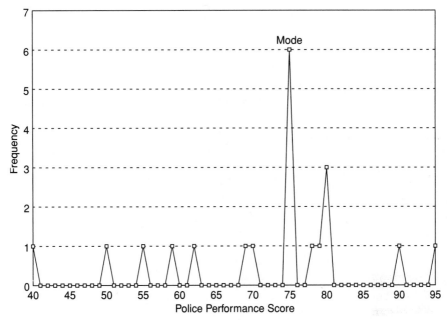

FIGURE 4.1. Scores on a hypothetical police performance test.

higher than the chance of selecting any other score. In bimodal distributions the two scores do not have to have the same frequency, just greater frequencies than other values. Had there been only four scores of 80 rather than five we would still describe the distribution as possessing two modes (bimodal) rather than one (*unimodal*).

FIGURE 4.2. Scores on a hypothetical police performance test.

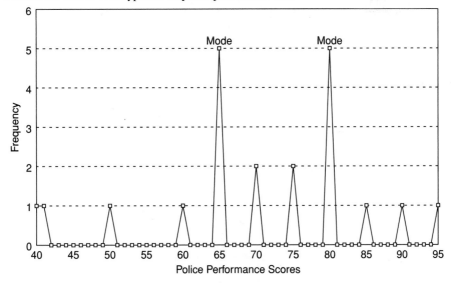

Sometimes our data may happen to have three scores that occur more frequently than others. In this case we would say that there are three modes (a *trimodal* distribution). As an informal rule of thumb, when there are more than three scores that appear most frequently, it is probably better not to use the mode as the measure of central tendency. In that case, you may accurately say that the data have no real mode because there are several frequently appearing scores and calculate an alternative measure of central tendency.

There is one other thing you should remember about the mode. Although the mode may be used as the measure of central tendency for both continuous and categorical data, it is the *only* measure of central tendency that can be employed with nominal-level categorical data. Table 4.2 shows the number of index crimes (except arson) committed in the United States in 1992. The variable, index crime, is a categorical, nominal-level variable, because the crimes represent differences in quality or type. Murder differs from armed robbery, which differs from burglary, but we cannot say that one offense has more of the thing called "crime" than another. What we can say, however, is that one kind of crime is different from another type and was committed more frequently. If we want some indication of the most "typical" or likely crime, then, we must use the mode. For the data in Table 4.2, the mode is represented by the crime category Larceny/theft because this crime was committed more often than any other of the index offenses in 1992 (7,915,199 thefts). Approximately 55% of the index offenses were larceny/theft; the probability, therefore, that a randomly selected index crime in 1992 was a larceny/theft is .55 (7,915,199/14,438,191). Both the frequency and the probability of this crime are higher than for any other of the seven index offenses in 1992.

## Grouped Data

If our data are in the form of a grouped frequency distribution rather than a distribution of raw scores, we may still describe their central tendency with the mode or

**TABLE 4.2. Number of Index Crimes Committed in the United States, 1992**

| Index Offense | Frequency |
|---|---|
| Murder | 23,760 |
| Rape | 109,062 |
| Armed robbery | 672,478 |
| Aggravated assault | 1,126,974 |
| Burglary | 2,279,884 |
| Larceny/theft | 7,915,199 |
| Motor vehicle theft | 1,610,834 |
| Total | 14,438,191 |

*Source:* U.S. Department of Justice, Federal Bureau of Investigation, *Crime in the United States, 1992.* Washington, DC: USGPO, 1993.

**TABLE 4.3. Rate of Violent Crime
(per 100,000) for 50 U.S. States, 1992**

| Rate of Violent Crime | Frequency |
|:---:|:---:|
| 49–199 | 6 |
| 200–350 | 9 |
| 351–501 | 5 |
| 502–652 | 11 |
| 653–803 | 9 |
| 804–954 | 4 |
| 955–1105 | 3 |
| 1106–1256 | 3 |
| | $N = 50$ |

modes. In this case the mode is calculated as the midpoint of the interval that contains the most cases. Table 4.3 shows the rate of violent crime (per 100,000) in 1992 for the 50 U.S. states. Rather than providing the exact raw score, however, the data are grouped into eight rank-ordered categories. Six states, for example, had a rate of violent crime in 1992 between 49 and 199 per 100,000. Nine states had a rate of violent crime between 200 and 350 per 100,000, and so on. One way to get an idea of the typical rate of violent crime for these 50 states would be to determine the mode. In this case, the mode would not be a score but an interval or category, so we would talk about the "modal category." The category with the greatest frequency is the interval 502–652 (11 states). Because there are more states in this interval than in any other, we might want to call this our modal category.

To describe our data more accurately, however, we should probably say that the distribution of violent crime rates in Table 4.3 is trimodal, because it looks as if there are three modes. One mode is the interval 506–652 because 11 states fall in this range; another mode is the interval 200–350 with 9 states; a third is the interval 653–803, which also contains 9 states. These three intervals are by far the most frequently occurring intervals, and the two latter intervals contain only two fewer states than the one with the greatest number. You can see this from the histogram for the distribution in Figure 4.3, where you can see three "peaks" corresponding to the three modes. That is why we might want to describe this data set as having three modes.

## Advantages and Disadvantages of the Mode

As a measure of central tendency, the mode has a few advantages over the other measures. First of all, it is very easy to ascertain because it involves no real arithmetic calculation. Second, there is no assumption regarding the level of measurement. The mode can be used as a measure of central tendency for nominal-, ordinal-, interval-, and ratio-level data. An example of the use of the mode for nominal-level data was Table 4.2, which showed the number of index crimes committed in the United States in 1992. In this data set, crime type (type of index

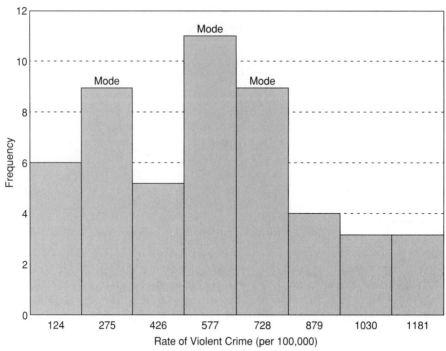

FIGURE 4.3. Rates of violent crime for 50 states.

offense) is a nominal-level categorical variable. The mode for this data was Larceny/theft because this crime type had the greatest number of crimes.

The most substantial disadvantage of the mode is that it fails to take into account all of the data. Because the mode also concerns the value or category with the highest frequency, it ignores all other values and categories. By only considering part of the data distribution, the mode could, under some circumstances, give a misleading impression of the central tendency. Consider a criminal justice experiment involving domestic violence in which police officers arrest husbands for assaulting their wives instead of merely separating the parties or counseling them. A domestic violence experiment very similar to what follows has been recently conducted in several U.S. cities (Sherman, 1992).

Let's say that 20 men were arrested as a result of their violent behavior and then followed up for 2 years to see whether they were arrested for assaulting their partner again. At the end of the 2-year follow-up period here are the number of times that each of the 20 arrested men had again assaulted their partner: 0, 0, 0, 0, 0, 0, 0, 0, 1, 2, 3, 4, 4, 4, 5, 5, 5, 6, 6, 6. The mode for this distribution of arrests is zero as 8 of the 20 men had no arrests during the follow-up period. The score of zero occurs at least twice as frequently as any other score. The value of zero for the mode, however, fails to reveal the fact that there is a clustering of scores at the other end of the distribution. That is, although 8 men had zero arrests, 3 men had 4 arrests during the follow-up period, 3 had 5 arrests, and 3 more had 6 arrests. The central tendency of the data may, therefore, be more toward the center of the distribution of assaults than at zero. Because the mode does not take into account all of the data but only the most frequently occurring score or category, we fail to notice this.

## 4.3 THE MEDIAN

### Ungrouped Data

If our variable is measured at the ordinal level or higher, we can use another measure of central tendency, the *median.* The median is defined as that score which divides the distribution of scores exactly into half. That is, it is the middle value in a distribution of scores such that one half of the scores are higher and one half are lower.

The median is often referred to as a "positional measure" of central tendency because we are looking for the score that lies at a particular position within a distribution (i.e., the score that is in the middle position).

The following box explains the two easy steps to compute the median with ungrouped data.

The two sets of rank-ordered scores below show the position of the medians:

| | |
|---|---|
| −13 | 2 |
| −10 | 5 |
| − 5 Median | 8 ⎤ Median lies in between |
| 4 | 10 ⎦ these two scores |
| 7 | 15 |
| | 22 |

In the first set of scores we can easily locate the position of the median with our formula. Because $N = 5$, the median is in the $(5 + 1)/2$, or third, position. The value of the median is −5. Notice that this is the score that divides the distribution in half because two scores are greater than it is (4 and 7) and two scores are less (−13 and −10). In the second set there are an even number of scores ($N = 6$). The median in this case is located at the $(6 + 1)/2 = 3.5$th position, or in between the third and fourth positions. Therefore, the median lies in between the two middle scores of 8 and 10. To find the midpoint between these two scores, we simply take their average $(8 + 10)/2 = 9$. The median is 9, then, because there are three lower scores (2, 5, and 8) and three higher scores (10, 15, and 22). In both sets, the median divides the distribution of scores into two exact halves.

As another example, we will demonstrate how to determine the median with the data provided in Table 4.4, which contains the homicide rates for 10 randomly selected American cities. In column 1 of Table 4.4 we have the homicide rates for nine cities, and in column 2 we have added a tenth city, Washington, DC. Notice that we have already completed the first step in the calculation of the median by

---

The **median** is the score that divides the distribution of scores into two exact halves. It is, then, that score that is less than one half of the scores and greater than the other half of the scores.

---

**Step 1.** Rank-order the scores from lowest to highest or highest to lowest.

**Step 2.** Then, find the position of the median with the following formula: $(N + 1)/2$. For example, with five scores the median is that score at the $(5 + 1)/2$, or 3rd, position in the rank order of scores. If there are an odd number of scores in the distribution (if $N$ is an odd number), the median is at the $(N + 1)/2$ position. If there are an even number of scores ($N$ is an even number), the median is the midpoint of the two middle positions of the distribution. In this case, the midpoint is found with the same formula $(N + 1)/2$, and the value of the median is calculated as the average or mean of the scores at the two adjacent positions. For example, with eight scores the median is at the $(8 + 1)/2$, or 4.5th, position. The position of the median, then, is in between the 4th and 5th positions in the rank order of scores. To determine the value of the median, find the scores at the 4th and 5th positions and calculate the average by adding the two scores and dividing by 2. Remember that the formula $(N + 1)/2$ is a formula not to calculate the value of the median, but to find the position of the median. Once you have found the position of the median by the formula, you must go to the rank-ordered distribution of scores to find the value.

---

rank-ordering the homicide rates for each of the cities. Remember that, because you are looking for the score that is lower than one half of the scores and higher than the other half, you must first rank-order your scores in order to determine the median. In other words, the median is not the middle score of any distribution of scores, but the middle score in a *rank-ordered distribution.*

In Table 4.4 we have ranked scores from low to high. We could have put the city with the highest homicide first and ranked the others from high to low. It does not make a difference for the median how they are ranked, but again *the scores must be placed rank-ordered first.* Once we have rank-ordered the scores, all we have to do is find the score that corresponds to the middle of the distribution of rank-ordered scores.

In the first column of Table 4.4 we have the homicide rates for our nine American cities ranked from lowest to highest. Because we have an odd number of

**TABLE 4.4. Homicide Rate (per 100,000) for Random Sample of American Cities, 1991**

| City | Homicide Rate | Homicide Rate |
|------|---------------|---------------|
| Pittsburgh, PA | 9.7 | 9.7 |
| Austin, TX | 10.3 | 10.3 |
| Anchorage, AK | 10.7 | 10.7 |
| Tulsa, OK | 11.3 | 11.3 |
| Raleigh, NC | 11.8 | 11.8 |
| Phoenix, AZ | 12.9 | 12.9 |
| Albuquerque, NM | 13.0 | 13.0 |
| Fresno, CA | 14.4 | 14.4 |
| Cincinnati, OH | 14.7 | 14.7 |
| Washington, DC | – | 80.1 |
| | $N = 9$ | $N = 10$ |

scores (9), the median is located at the 5th position ([9 + 1]/2 = 5). *Please remember that this does not mean that the median is 5; it means that we have to find the median that is located in the fifth position.* Counting down four positions from the top or counting up four positions from the bottom, we find that the fifth position is occupied by the score of 11.8 homicides per 100,000 for the city of Raleigh, North Carolina. The median homicide rate for this distribution of 9 cities is, then, 11.8 per 100,000.

In the second column we have added one more city so we have an even number of cities (10). In this case, the median is located at the (10 + 1)/2, or 5.5th, position, or the midpoint between the fifth and sixth positions. To determine the median in this distribution, we need to find first the scores at the fifth and sixth positions and then take the average of the two. To do this, we can go down four and five positions from the top to find the fifth and sixth score, or we can go up four and five positions from the bottom—our location will be the same. Whichever way we do this, we find that the fifth and sixth scores are 11.8 and 12.9, which corresponds to the homicide rates of Raleigh, North Carolina, and Phoenix, Arizona. The median lies in the middle, or midpoint, between these two scores. We can calculate this midpoint as the average of the two scores by adding them together and dividing by 2 ([11.8 + 12.9]/2 = 12.35). The median homicide rate for this group of 10 cities is, then, 12.35 per 100,000.

Another way to describe the median is to say that because it divides the distribution of scores into exact halves, the median is the score that lies at the 50th percentile in a cumulative percent distribution because the 50th percentile is the middle position of a percentile distribution. To see this, let's assume that we have a set of 100 hypothetical scores ranging from 0 to 14. In the following list we show four pieces of information, (1) the actual score (column 1), (2) the frequency for that particular score (column 2), (3) the percent of the total for that score (column 3), and (4) the cumulative frequency for that score (column 4):

| Score | Frequency | Percent | Cumulative Percent |
|---|---|---|---|
| 0 | 20 | 20 | 20 |
| 1 | 13 | 13 | 33 |
| 2 | 11 | 11 | 44 |
| 3 | 9 | 9 | 53 |
| 4 | 15 | 15 | 68 |
| 5 | 5 | 5 | 73 |
| 6 | 7 | 7 | 80 |
| 7 | 4 | 4 | 84 |
| 8 | 4 | 4 | 88 |
| 9 | 3 | 3 | 91 |
| 10 | 2 | 2 | 93 |
| 11 | 2 | 2 | 95 |
| 12 | 3 | 3 | 98 |
| 13 | 1 | 1 | 99 |
| 14 | 1 | 1 | 100 |

1. With an odd number of scores, the median is the score that lies exactly in the middle of a distribution of rank-ordered scores.
2. With an even number of scores, the median is the average of the two middle scores in a distribution of rank-ordered scores.

From this distribution of scores, we can see that 20 percent of the 100 respondents obtained a score of 0, 13 percent obtained a score of 1, and 1% obtained a score of 14. To determine the median, we rank-order the 100 scores, and then locate the $(100 + 1)/2$, or 50.5th, position. The median, then, would be the average of the scores in the 50th and 51st positions. If we were to do this, the first 20 positions would be taken up by the score of 0 (20 persons had a score of 0), the next 13 positions would be taken up by the score of 1. With scores of 0 and 1, then, we would be up to the 33rd score. The next 11 positions would be taken up by the 11 scores of 2, which would bring us to the 44th position. In order to get to the 50th position, then, we would have to count 6 more positions. Because the next 9 scores are scores of 3, the 50th score and the 51st scores would both be 3s. After we average these two scores, we would obtain a median of 3.

If instead of going through this process we simply looked at the last column, the cumulative percent distribution, we would discover that scores of 2 will go up to the 44th percentile and that the score corresponding to the 50th percentile is 3. The median, then, is that score at the 50th percentile.

## Median with Grouped Data

The median also is a useful measure of central tendency when we do not have individual scores but grouped data. Table 4.5 reports the homicide rates for 100 U.S. cities in group intervals. Notice that with these grouped data we have lost some information from the previous example in which we had the exact homicide rate of each city. Although we know that there are 14 cities with homicide rates somewhere in between 11.0 and 16.4 per 100,000, we do not know their exact rate. As a result, we do not know how the various homicide rates are distributed within the interval. We do not know, for instance, if they cluster around the rate of 11.0 or 16.4 or if they are evenly distributed within the interval.

**TABLE 4.5. Homicide Rates per 100,000 for 100 American Cities**

| Homicide Rate Interval | True Limits | Frequency ($f$) | Cumulative Frequency ($cf$) |
|---|---|---|---|
| 0–5.4 | −.05–5.45 | 37 | 37 |
| 5.5–10.9 | 5.45–10.95 | 36 | 73 |
| 11.0–16.4 | 10.95–16.45 | 14 | 87 |
| 16.5–21.9 | 16.45–21.95 | 9 | 96 |
| 22.0–27.4 | 21.95–27.45 | 3 | 99 |
| 27.5–32.9 | 27.45–32.95 | 0 | 99 |
| 33.0–38.4 | 32.95–38.45 | 1 | 100 |

In order to calculate the median as the midpoint of the interval, therefore, we must make some simplifying assumptions about how the cases are distributed or positioned within each interval. Our assumption will be that all cases are located at equal distances throughout the interval. Because we are forced to make this assumption, which may or may not be true, the value of the median we will obtain from grouped data will generally be different from the one we would obtain had the data not been grouped (the raw data). If there are a large number of cases, the error we introduce from making this assumption will be small—and well worth the time saved.

The steps involved in calculating the median with grouped data are comparable to those with ungrouped data. We first must rank the scores in order. In the case of grouped data, we rank *the intervals* from high to low. In Table 4.5, the interval with the lowest magnitude is the interval 0–5.4 homicides per 100,000; the next lowest is 5.5–10.9 per 100,000 and so on up to the interval with the highest magnitude, 33.0–38.4 homicides per 100,000. Once we have rank-ordered the intervals, we can determine the median for grouped data with the following formula:

$$mdn = L + \frac{([N + 1]/2) - cf}{f} \, i \tag{4.1}$$

where

$Mdn$ = the median
$L$ = the lower true limit of the interval that contains the median
$cf$ = the cumulative frequency corresponding to the interval just below the interval that contains the median
$f$ = the frequency in the interval that contains the median
$i$ = the width of the interval

For the grouped data in Table 4.5 we can estimate the median as:

$$\text{Median} = 5.45 + \left(\frac{101/2 - 37}{36}\right) 5.5$$

$$= 5.45 + \left(\frac{50.5 - 37}{36}\right) 5.5$$

$$= 5.45 + 2.06$$

$$= 7.51$$

## Advantages and Disadvantages of the Median

Notice that in finding the median we do not use all of the data. With the median we are interested in identifying the score that corresponds to a particular position (the 50th percentile). In finding the median, therefore, it does not matter if there are extreme (very high or very low) scores. That is, it would not affect the median if the lowest score were 0, −200, or 1000, or if the highest scores were 1, 25 or a million as long as these were the lowest and highest scores in the distribution. In other words, the median would stay the same no matter how skewed the data are as long as the position of the median did not change.

For example, the following two data distributions have the same median of 10 because in both distributions it is the score that occupies the middle position. In both instances there are three scores lower and three scores higher than the median:

| | |
|---|---|
| −100,000 | 4 |
| −25,000 | 5 |
| −8,973 | 8 |
| 10 = Median | 10 = Median |
| 275,000 | 15 |
| 800,127 | 20 |
| 989,581 | 28 |

No matter how extreme the scores are, then, the median is that score in the middle of the rank-ordered distribution. This should convince you that the value of the median is not greatly disturbed whenever there are either extremely high or extremely low scores in a distribution. One of the most important advantages of the median, then, is that it is insensitive to extreme scores, and is, therefore, the preferred measure of central tendency when we have skewed data.

Finally, the median also is a very useful measure of central tendency because it is used in graphical displays of data and some advanced statistical procedures. In Chapter 6 we examine the median in connection with something called a stem-and-leaf display and a box-and-whisker plot. In these two graphical representations of our data the median is the measure of central tendency that we use. In addition, on occasion we use the median as our indicator of central tendency in hypothesis tests with one or more samples of data. As an example, we test a hypothesis that the median score on some variable between two samples are equal to one another.

The only real disadvantage of the median is that many of the most frequently used statistics in criminology and criminal justice are based on the mean and its property of least squares (we discuss this property of the mean in a later section of this chapter). This is not a very substantial disadvantage, however, because as we will see shortly, the median has a unique statistical property of its own. In addition, the median is used as the measure of central tendency in a class of statistics commonly referred to as "nonparametric statistics." We discuss these statistics in Chapter 16.

## 4.4 THE MEAN

### Ungrouped Data

Perhaps the most common measure of central tendency is the *mean*. You probably are already very familiar with what the mean is because you know what such things as the "class average" for a particular test is or what your "grade point average" is. When you calculate the former, you simply add each persons' test grade and divide by the total number of people in the class. To calculate your GPA, you add up the scores for each letter grade you received (a 4.0 for an "A," 3.0 for a "B," 2.0 for a "C," and so on) and divide by the number of scores or classes. The "average" calculated in this manner reflects another meaning of the term "the most typical score" and is the measure of central tendency called the mean.

The **mean** is defined as the arithmetic average of a defined group of scores.

Simply, the mean is the arithmetic average of a group of scores and is calculated by summing all scores and dividing by the number of cases involved.

The formula for the mean is defined as:

$$\bar{x} = \frac{x_1 + x_2 + x_3 + \cdots + x_N}{N} \tag{4.2}$$

where

$\bar{x}$ = the symbol for the mean (read "*x* bar")
$x$ = a raw score in a distribution of raw scores
$N$ = the total number of scores

To calculate the mean with ungrouped data, perform the two simple steps outlined in the box below.

This formula for the mean can be written more formally as:

$$\bar{x} = \frac{\displaystyle\sum_{i=1}^{N} x}{N} \tag{4.3}$$

The Greek letter $\Sigma$ (sigma) in Equation 4.3 is an instruction for you to conduct the operation of summing a series of numbers. Specifically, this equation tells us to sum all the scores from $i$ (where the subscript $i = 1$ tells us to start with the first observation) to $N$ (where the superscript $N$ tells us to end with the last, or $N$th, observation). After these numbers are added, divide this sum by $N$ (the total number of observations). If you are not familiar with the summation notion (what $\Sigma$ tells you to do), look at the review of mathematics provided in Appendix A at the back of the book.

We can apply the formula for the mean to the data reported in Table 4.1. First we add all 20 scores: $40 + 50 + 55 + \cdots + 95 = 1437$. Then we divide by 20: $1437/20 = 71.85$. The mean or arithmetic average for this set of 20 scores is, then, 71.85 (remember that the median was 75).

The question now is how to interpret the mean. It is relatively easy to interpret both the mode (it is the most frequently occurring score) and the median (it is the score at the 50th percentile or the middle score in a distribution of scores), but what about the mean? To say that it is the arithmetic average is not very helpful because that does not tell us in what sense it is the "average" score.

One useful way to interpret the mean is to think of it as a kind of balancing score. That is, the mean is the score in a distribution of scores that is the balancing point between all scores that are lower and higher than the mean. For example, suppose that we have the following 10 scores: 8, 13, 14, 16, 18, 20, 22, 25, 26, 28.

**Step 1.** Add up each of the raw scores ($x_1 + x_2 + \cdots + x_n$).
**Step 2.** Divide this sum by the total number of scores ($N$).

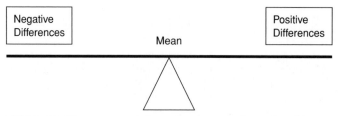

FIGURE 4.4. The mean as a balance between negative and positive differences.

The mean for these scores is 19 (190/10). In Table 4.6 we subtract the mean from each of the scores $(x - \bar{x})$ and obtain a difference score $d$. Notice that the sum of the negative difference scores $(-11 + -6 + -5 + -3 + -1 = -26)$ is equal in absolute value to the sum of the positive difference scores $(1 + 3 + 6 + 7 + 9 = 26)$. The sum of the positive differences between each score and the mean is always equal to the sum of the negative differences. It is in this sense that the mean is the "balancing score" in a distribution. It is the one value that, when each score is subtracted from it and these scores are summed, will be zero because the sum of the positive numbers will be exactly equal to the sum of the negative numbers (see Figure 4.4). In Table 4.6, the +26 is equal to the −26. If we add the negative differences to the positive differences we will have a sum of zero. The *sum of the differences* (also called the sum of the deviations) of each score from the mean is always zero $(\Sigma d = 0)$. In mathematical terms this means that:

$$\Sigma (x - \bar{x}) = 0$$

We will use this valuable property of the mean in Chapter 5 and in some more complex statistical analyses later in the book.

As another example, let's calculate the mean homicide rate for our nine cities in Table 4.4. First, we add up the scores $9.7 + 10.3 + 10.7 + 11.3 + \cdots + 14.7 =$

TABLE 4.6.  **Differences ($d$) of a Set of Scores from the Mean of the Score**

| $x$ | $x - \bar{x}$ | $d$ |
|---|---|---|
| 8 | 8 − 19 | −11 |
| 13 | 13 − 19 | −6 |
| 14 | 14 − 19 | −5 |
| 16 | 16 − 19 | −3 |
| 18 | 18 − 19 | −1 |
| 20 | 20 − 19 | 1 |
| 22 | 22 − 19 | 3 |
| 25 | 25 − 19 | 6 |
| 26 | 26 − 19 | 7 |
| 28 | 28 − 19 | 9 |
| | | $\Sigma d = 0$ |

108.8. Then we divide this sum by the total number of cities 108.8/ 9 = 12.09. This is the mean. For these nine cities, then, the average or mean homicide rate is 12.09 per 100,000.

Notice that with a small number of scores it is relatively easy to calculate the mean with the formula in Equations 4.2 and 4.3. If, however, we have a large number of scores, it may not be so easy. In many cases we can make our calculations easier and take a short-cut in calculating the mean by multiplying a score by its frequency, then summing the obtained values and dividing by the total number of scores. The formula for the mean in this case is defined as:

$$\bar{x} = \frac{\Sigma fx}{N} \tag{4.4}$$

where

$\bar{x}$ = the mean
$x$ = the raw score in the distribution
$f$ = the frequency of that score
$fx$ = a score multiplied by its frequency
$\Sigma fx$ = the sum of the scores multiplied by their frequency
$N$ = the total number of scores

The steps involved in calculating the mean using frequency counts are found in the box on page 96.

This method is illustrated in Table 4.7, which uses exactly the same data as in Table 4.1. Check to verify that the sum of the scores is the same in both tables ($\Sigma x = \Sigma fx = 1437$), as is the number of observations ($N = \Sigma f = 20$). To determine

**TABLE 4.7. Twenty Scores on a Hypothetical Police Officer Performance Evaluation Test**

| Score ($x$) | $f$ | $fx$ |
|:-----------:|:---:|:----:|
| 40 | 1 | 40 |
| 50 | 1 | 50 |
| 55 | 1 | 55 |
| 59 | 1 | 59 |
| 62 | 1 | 62 |
| 69 | 1 | 69 |
| 70 | 1 | 70 |
| 75 | 6 | 450 |
| 78 | 1 | 78 |
| 79 | 1 | 79 |
| 80 | 3 | 240 |
| 90 | 1 | 90 |
| 95 | 1 | 95 |
| | 20 | $fx = 1437$ |

Data correspond to those on Table 4.1.

> **Step 1.** Multiply the number of times a score occurs, or the frequency of a score, $f$, by the value of the score, $fx$. If a score has a frequency of 1, obtain the product the same way, $1x = x$. If a score has a zero frequency, either omit that score or obtain the product as before. In this case, you would multiply the frequency by zero ($0x$) and your product would be zero.
> **Step 2.** Do this for each combination of frequencies and scores, and add them up, $\Sigma fx$.
> **Step 3.** Divide by the total number of scores (the total frequency), the total number of scores equal to $\Sigma f$.

the mean, we simply sum the different products formed when we multiply each score by its frequency and divide by the total number of scores. In this case, the value of the mean is $1437/20 = 71.85$, the same value we obtained from Table 4.1.

Please remember that, when you are calculating the mean from a frequency distribution such as that in Table 4.6, the denominator you use is the total number of observations $N$ (or $\Sigma f$), not the number of different scores. For example, in Table 4.7 we have 20 observations, but only 13 different scores. You may be tempted simply to sum down the first column of scores and divide by the number of different scores ($[40 + 50 + 55 + \cdots + 95]/13$). This will give you the correct mean only if each score has a frequency of 1. In Table 4.7, and in most other frequency distributions, however, some scores will have a frequency greater than one ($f > 1$) and we will have to reflect this in both our sum of scores (the numerator of the mean) by multiplying each score by its frequency and our sum of observations (the denominator of the mean). Thus, the correct mean for Table 4.7 would be arrived at by summing $40 + 50 + \cdots + 450 + \cdots + 240 + \cdots + 95 = 1437$, and then dividing by 20.

Notice one very important feature about the mean. Unlike the case of the median where we are looking for a score that corresponds to a certain position (the 50th percentile) and thereby virtually ignoring other scores, in calculating the mean we use each and every score because in calculating the mean we add *each* score, omitting no score in our addition. Because we employ every score in calculating the mean, we do not have first to rank-order the data as we did when calculating the median. The sum of the scores will always be the same if you add them from low to high, high to low, or any other order or in no particular order. As we will see in a moment, however, because we use every score in calculating the mean, its value is sensitive to the presence of very high or very low scores (skewed data). For this reason the mean may at some times provide a distorted view of the central tendency of our data.

## Grouped Data

The procedures involved in calculating the mean from grouped data are essentially the same as for ungrouped data. Keep in mind, however, that with grouped data we do not have each individual score, only the interval that a case falls into. We must therefore make a simplifying assumption about the distribution of scores within each interval that *every case within an interval is located exactly at the midpoint of the interval.* Because all cases within an interval are treated as having the same value, the value of the midpoint of the interval, we can easily calculate the mean by multiplying the number of cases in the interval by the midpoint, sum across each interval, and then divide by the total number of observations or scores. The formula for calculating the mean from grouped data is a special case of Equation 4.4:

$$\bar{x} = \frac{\sum_{i}^{k} f_i m_i}{N} = \frac{\sum_{i}^{k} f_i m_i}{\Sigma f_i} \tag{4.5}$$

where

$f_i$ = the number of cases in the $i$th interval, with $\Sigma f_i N$
$m_i$ = the midpoint of $i$th interval
$k$ = the number of intervals

In the special case of grouped data we multiply the frequency of each interval by the midpoint of the interval, sum across all intervals, and divide by $N$. As with nongrouped data in the form of a frequency distribution, when calculating the mean from grouped data make sure that you multiply the midpoint of each interval by its respective frequency as your numerator for the mean, and make sure that you sum up the frequencies ($\Sigma f$) to arrive at $N$ (the total number of observations) as your denominator. In other words, the numerator for the mean with grouped data is the sum of the product of each interval midpoint times the frequency of the interval ($\Sigma fm$); the denominator is $N$, the total number of *observations,* not the number of intervals.

Table 4.8 shows an example of how to calculate the mean with grouped data. The data in Table 4.8 are hypothetical data of the self-reported number of delinquent acts committed by 789 youths. The data are grouped into 11 intervals. To obtain the mean we must first locate the midpoint of the interval. Then we multiply the frequency of each interval by each midpoint, then we sum the obtained products and divide by $N$. For this example, the sum of the midpoint of each interval multiplied by its frequency is obtained as $0 + 375 + 880 + \cdots + 1872)$ and is

**TABLE 4.8. Self-Reported Number of Delinquent Acts Committed by 789 Youths**

| Stated Interval | True Interval | Midpoint ($mi$) | Frequency ($fi$) | $fimi$ |
|---|---|---|---|---|
| 0 | 0 | 0 | 50 | 0 |
| 1–5 | .5–5.5 | 3 | 125 | 375 |
| 6–10 | 5.5–10.5 | 8 | 110 | 880 |
| 11–15 | 10.5–15.5 | 13 | 75 | 975 |
| 16–20 | 15.5–20.5 | 18 | 80 | 1440 |
| 21–25 | 20.5–25.5 | 23 | 78 | 1794 |
| 26–30 | 25.5–30.5 | 28 | 72 | 2016 |
| 31–35 | 30.5–35.5 | 33 | 65 | 2145 |
| 36–40 | 35.5–40.5 | 38 | 50 | 1900 |
| 41–45 | 40.5–45.5 | 43 | 45 | 1935 |
| 46–50 | 45.5–50.5 | 48 | 39 | 1872 |
| | | | $\Sigma = 789$ | 15,332 |

$x = 15,332/789 = 19.43$.

**TABLE 4.9.  Calculating the Mean for the State Violent Crime Rate Data in Table 4.3**

| Rate of Violent Crime | Midpoint (*m*) | Frequency (*f*) | *fm* |
|---|---|---|---|
| 49–199 | 124 | 6 | 744 |
| 200–350 | 275 | 9 | 2475 |
| 351–501 | 426 | 5 | 2130 |
| 502–652 | 577 | 11 | 6347 |
| 653–803 | 728 | 9 | 6552 |
| 804–954 | 879 | 4 | 3516 |
| 955–1105 | 1030 | 3 | 3090 |
| 1106–1256 | 1181 | 3 | 3543 |
| | | $\Sigma = 50$ | $\Sigma = 28397$ |

$fm = 28{,}397$; $\bar{x} = 28{,}397/50 = 567.94$.

found in the last column of Table 4.8. To determine the mean, then, we divide this sum by the total number of observations ($\Sigma f = 789$). The mean is equal to 15,332/789 = 19.43. In the example from Table 4.8, the youths committed an average of 19.43 delinquent acts.

As another example of how to calculate the mean with grouped data, let's return to the state-level violent crime rate data from Table 4.3. In this table, the rates of violent crime per 100,000 are divided into equally sized intervals. To determine the mean violent crime rate for the 50 states, then, we need to do the following:

1. Determine the midpoint of each interval (*m*).
2. Multiply the midpoint of each interval by the frequency of the interval (*fm*).
3. Add these products for each of the intervals ($\Sigma fm$).
4. Divide by the total number of observations (*N*).

We show the necessary calculations for you in Table 4.9. You can see from there that the mean is 567.94. For the 50 states, then, the average rate of violent crime is 567.94 per 100,000.

## Advantages and Disadvantages of the Mean

The mean offers an important advantage over the median. Unlike the median, the mean uses all of the available data, which, as long as there are no very extreme scores, is a considerable advantage. Because the mean uses all scores, it will generally be a more consistent measure of central tendency than the median. That is, if we take many samples from the same population and calculate both the mean and median with each sample, the medians will differ from one another more than the means. Because we usually draw only one sample from a population, we want a measure of central tendency that is stable. In most cases, this is the mean.

Another advantage of the mean is that it has desirable mathematical properties. We have already seen that one property of the mean is that the sum of the difference between each score and the mean is zero. We will use this property of the mean in more complex statistics.

**TABLE 4.10.  Average Prison Sentence for Nine Offenses Tried in the Four Federal Districts of California**

| District | $n$ | $\bar{x}$ |
|----------|-----|-----------|
| Northern | 243 | 59.8 |
| Eastern | 559 | 62.6 |
| Central | 1166 | 74.2 |
| Southern | 1380 | 44.8 |
| | $N=3348$ | |

A final valuable property of the mean that the median does not have is that we can, in appropriate circumstances, estimate a *weighted mean*. The weighted mean gives us an arithmetic average from several different data sets that takes into account or is weighted by the number of observations in each data set. An example can be found in Table 4.10. The state of California is divided into four different federal court circuits for the purpose of trying and sentencing federal crimes, the Northern District, the Eastern District, the Central District, and the Southern District. Table 4.10 reports the average prison length (in months) for nine offenses within each of the four federal districts in California for the year 1992. We can see that the average prison length in the Northern District was 59.8 months, 62.6 months in the Eastern District, 74.2 months in the Central District, and 44.8 months in the Southern District. Let's say that we wanted to calculate the mean prison time given to defendants in California as a whole, that is, we wanted a mean sentence length for all 3348 federal offenders convicted for these crimes in California. We might be tempted to simply calculate a California mean by adding the means for the four separate districts in California and then divide by the number of districts (4): ([59.8 + 62.6 + 74.2 + 44.8]/4 = 60.35 months). Had the individual district means been based on the same number of cases, we would be able to do this. But notice that there are about five times as many cases in the Central and Southern District as in the Northern District of California and that there are nearly twice the cases in the latter two as in the Eastern District of California. If we were to calculate a mean as we did above, we would be ignoring the fact that different numbers of cases came from different judicial districts where the sentence lengths were very different.

In order to estimate the mean from data sets with different numbers of observations, we must first weight each mean by its respective number of cases, sum this product, and then divide by the total number of cases. The weighted mean has the formula:

$$\bar{x} = \frac{\sum_{i=1}^{k} n_i \bar{x}_i}{N} \tag{4.6}$$

where

$\bar{x}$ = the overall mean

$n_i$ = the number of observations in the $i$th data set or group

$\bar{x}_i$ = the mean of the *i*th data set or group

$N$ = the total number of observations

In our example from Table 4.10, there are four data sets or groups, each corresponding to a federal judicial district in California. To calculate the mean, we should multiply each of the four group means by its respective sample size, or *n*, add these products up for each group, and then divide the sum by the total number of observations in all the groups, or *N*. Here are the necessary calculations:

$$\text{Weighted } \bar{x} = \frac{n_1(\bar{x}_1) + n_2(\bar{x}_2) + n_3(\bar{x}_3) + n_4(\bar{x}_4)}{N}$$

$$\bar{x} = \frac{243(59.8) + 559(62.6) + 1166(74.2) + 1380(44.8)}{3348}$$

$$= \frac{14,531.4 + 34,993.4 + 86,517.2 + 61,824}{3348}$$

$$= \frac{197,866}{3348}$$

$$= 59.10$$

The average prison sentence given to federal offenders tried in California was 59.1 months, or almost 5 years. In this example, our weighted mean is very similar to our unweighted mean, but this is not the case in general. In the event that you wish to calculate a grand mean from the means of subgroups with different numbers of cases, you should always calculate a weighted mean. More in general, the group means $(X_i)$ can be weighted by the weight $w_i$, so that the equation for the weighted mean becomes:

$$\bar{x} = \frac{\Sigma w_i \bar{x}_i}{\Sigma w_i} \tag{4.7}$$

Conventionally, the weights are constructed so that they sum to a known quantity, such as the total number of observations or unity. In the latter case, for example, we would have constructed the weights to reflect the proportion of each group to the total number of cases. In this case the proportional weights would have to sum to 1.0: for example, $w_1 = 243/3348.07$; $w_2 = 559/3348.17$; $w_3 = 1166/3348 = .35$; $w_4 = 1380/3348 = .41$; and $\Sigma w_i = 1.0$. In using proportional weights we would have obtained the same result for our weighted mean:

$$\bar{x} = \frac{.07(59.8) + .17(62.6) + .35(74.2) + .41(44.8)}{1}$$

$$= \frac{4.19 + 10.64 + 25.97 + 18.37}{1}$$

$$= 59.17$$

The most important disadvantage of the mean, however, is a by-product of its advantage—in taking every score into account the mean may be distorted by very extreme scores. When we add each score to calculate our mean, we may at times be adding either very large values or very small values. In either case, the effect is to provide a somewhat distorted picture of the central tendency of our data. As an example, let's return to the city homicide data in Table 4.4.

We have reproduced this table with one change in Table 4.11, the addition of a third column where we replace Washington, DC, with the city of Honolulu, Hawaii, which had a homicide rate of 3.4 per 100,000 in 1991. Notice that for these three groups of cities the median homicide rate is very comparable (11.80, 12.35, 11.55). The addition of Washington, DC, with its very high homicide rate did not disturb the median that much, nor did the addition of Honolulu with its very low homicide rate. However, notice what happens to the value of the mean when extreme observations are included. The addition of Washington, DC, with its homicide rate of 80.1 per 100,000, increases the mean by about 50% from 12.09 to 18.89.

For the 10 cities in column 2, if we use the median as the measure of central tendency, we conclude that the typical homicide rate is 12.35 per 100,000. If we use the mean as the measure of central tendency to describe the same set of data, we conclude that the typical homicide rate is 18.89 per 100,000. Why such different estimates for central tendency?

By including Washington, DC, in our data we naturally include its very high homicide rate into our calculation of the mean. Its rate of 80.1 is added to other homicide rates that are much lower, such as 10.3 and 13.0. In effect, then, in calculating the mean in this case we are adding a very large number to a set of much less larger numbers. As a result of the influence of this large score, the average or mean score increases. The median does not change so drastically because the addition of Washington, DC, only moves the position of the median in the distribution of scores. The District of Columbia's homicide rate of 80.1 is not directly calculated into the median, which hence is less affected than the mean is.

**TABLE 4.11. Homicide Rate (per 100,000) for Random Sample of American Cities, 1991**

| City | Homicide Rate | Homicide Rate | Homicide Rate |
|---|---|---|---|
| Honolulu, HI | — | — | 3.4 |
| Pittsburgh, PA | 9.7 | 9.7 | 9.7 |
| Austin, TX | 10.3 | 10.3 | 10.3 |
| Anchorage, AK | 10.7 | 10.7 | 10.7 |
| Tulsa, OK | 11.3 | 11.3 | 11.3 |
| Raleigh, NC | 11.8 | 11.8 | 11.8 |
| Phoenix, AZ | 12.9 | 12.9 | 12.9 |
| Albuquerque, NM | 13.0 | 13.0 | 13.0 |
| Fresno, CA | 14.4 | 14.4 | 14.4 |
| Cincinnati, OH | 14.7 | 14.7 | 14.7 |
| Washington, DC | — | 80.1 | — |
| $N =$ | 9 | 10 | 10 |
| Median = | 11.80 | 12.35 | 11.55 |
| Mean = | 12.09 | 18.89 | 11.22 |

Adding a large score, then, inflates the mean relative to the median as a measure of central tendency of the data. In other words, the mean gets larger than the median and becomes "pulled out" away from the median. Because we are adding a large positive number to the mean, the direction of the "pull" is to the right, or toward positive scores. How much greater the mean becomes relative to the median is a function of how extreme the extreme score is. In the case of Washington, DC, because its homicide rate is more than five times greater than the next highest homicide rate, its effect is pretty substantial. As you can see for yourself, to say that the average or most typical homicide rate for these 10 cities is about 19 per 100,000 is somewhat of a distortion. We now know that the only reason why the mean is so high for the second column of cities ($\bar{x} = 18.89$) is because it includes one extremely high score. It would appear, then, that a more appropriate measure of central tendency would be the median.

Notice what happens when Washington, DC, is replaced with Honolulu, Hawaii. Honolulu has a much smaller than normal homicide rate, only 3.4 per 100,000. When we calculate the mean with Honolulu rather than Washington, DC, in the data, it is 11.22. In this scenario, when an extremely low score is added to the other scores, the value of the mean is less than the value of the median. How much less it becomes is a function of how much lower the extremely low score is relative to the other scores. The homicide rate for Honolulu is about one-half of the next lowest homicide rate. It has a less extreme score difference than Washington, DC, so its effect on the mean is less dramatic. In general, the effect of adding an extremely low score to the mean is to deflate the value of the mean relative to the median. An extremely low score will pull the mean away from the median to the left of the median. In the absence of extreme scores, the value of the mean and median is roughly comparable, as seen in the first column of Table 4.11, which does not include either Washington, DC, or Honolulu.

In sum, because the mean takes every score into account, we can see that it is very sensitive to high and low values in our distribution. That is, the mean can change dramatically whenever our data sets have very high or very low values, that is, whenever it is *skewed*. A major disadvantage of the mean, therefore, is that it may not be the most appropriate measure of central tendency whenever we have skewed data because it will give us a misleading measure of the central tendency of our data.

## 4.5 STATISTICAL PROPERTIES OF THE MEDIAN AND MEAN

The median and mean each have a unique statistical property that helps make clear why they are referred to as measures of central tendency. What are the statistical properties of the median?

In a given distribution of scores, the median is the value of $m$ that minimizes the expression $1/n \sum |x - m|$. That is, if we take the absolute value of each score from the median and then divide by the total number of scores, that number will be at a minimum. By minimum we mean that it will be the lowest number you could possibly obtain. (You may remember from your math classes that the absolute value of a number is the value of that number without its sign. For example, the absolute value of $-3$ [expressed as $|-3|$]) is 3.) In other words, if we use any value for $m$ other than the median, we will get a larger value. The median, therefore, is the least absolute deviations (LAD) estimator of central tendency. An example may help you see this.

Suppose we have seven scores, 2, 2, 5, 6, 7, 12, and 15. The median for this distribution is 6 (three scores are lower and three are higher). Let's now subtract the median from each score and take the absolute value of these differences.

$$|2 - 6| = |-4| = 4$$
$$|2 - 6| = |-4| = 4$$
$$|5 - 6| = |-1| = 1$$
$$|6 - 6| = |0| = 0$$
$$|7 - 6| = |1| = 1$$
$$|12 - 6| = |6| = 6$$
$$|15 - 6| = |9| = 9$$

If we sum these absolute values, we get $4 + 4 + 1 + 0 + 1 + 6 + 9 = 25$. If we then divide by the number of scores, we get $25/7 = 3.57$. By subtracting the median from each score rather than any other number, the value of 3.57 is at a minimum; it is the LAD. If we subtract any other value from each score, the average absolute deviation will be greater than 3.57. Don't take our word, try it! Substitute the value of 7 instead of the median of 6. You will find that the average absolute deviation is 3.71. The median is a measure of central tendency, then, because it is the value that minimizes the absolute value of the difference with each score.

The mean has a related, though somewhat different, statistical property. The mean minimizes not the absolute value of the difference, but the square of the difference or deviation. That is, the mean is the value of $m$ that minimizes the expression $1/n \Sigma (x - m)^2$. In this expression, we subtract a given value $m$ from each score, square this difference, and then divide this squared difference by the total number of scores. This final value will be at a minimum whenever $m$ is the mean of the scores. The mean, therefore, is the least-square measure of central tendency.

As an example of this property, let's return to our seven scores above. If we calculate the mean for this data set, we discover that it is 49/7, or 7. Let's now subtract the mean from each score and square this difference:

$$2 - 7 = -5 \quad (-5)^2 = 25$$
$$2 - 7 = -5 \quad (-5)^2 = 25$$
$$5 - 7 = -2 \quad (-2)^2 = 4$$
$$6 - 7 = -1 \quad (-1)^2 = 1$$
$$7 - 7 = 0 \quad (0)^2 = 0$$
$$12 - 7 = 5 \quad (5)^2 = 25$$
$$15 - 7 = 8 \quad (8)^2 = 64$$

If we sum these squared differences (also called squared deviations), we get $25 + 25 + 4 + 1 + 0 + 25 + 64 = 144$, and if we then divide by the total number of scores, we get $144/7 = 20.57$. By subtracting the mean from each score and taking the average squared difference, the value of 20.57 is at a minimum. It is the least-squared difference. Again, try substituting any other value but the mean and see what you get. For example, instead of the mean (7), subtract the median (6) from each score. Here is what you would get:

$$2 - 6 = -4 \qquad (-4)^2 = 16$$
$$2 - 6 = -4 \qquad (-4)^2 = 16$$
$$5 - 6 = -1 \qquad (-1)^2 = 1$$
$$6 - 6 = 0 \qquad (0)^2 = 0$$
$$7 - 6 = 1 \qquad (1)^2 = 1$$
$$12 - 6 = 6 \qquad (6)^2 = 36$$
$$15 - 6 = 9 \qquad (9)^2 = 81$$

If we now sum these numbers, we get $16 + 16 + 1 + 0 + 1 + 36 + 81 = 151$. This sum of 151 is greater than the sum of 144 we obtained when we subtracted the mean from each score. If we divide 151 by the number of scores, the average squared difference is $151/7 = 21.57$, which is greater than 20.57. The mean, then, is a measure of central tendency because it is the value that minimizes the squared difference between itself and each score. It is a least-squares estimator of central tendency.

## 4.6 SELECTING THE APPROPRIATE MEASURE OF CENTRAL TENDENCY

In this chapter we discuss three somewhat different measures of central tendency: the mode, the median, and the mean. You may be wondering which measure you should use in reporting your data. Which measure of central tendency is appropriate depends upon two things: (1) the level of measurement of your data, and (2) the distributional form or skewness of your data.

The mode can be used as a measure of central tendency with data at the nominal level or higher because we only need to know which score or category has the highest frequency. For instance, we could use the mode to describe the central tendency of a distribution of offending data. We could report that of the following offenses, burglary, armed robbery, simple assault, auto theft, larceny, and drug possession, the most frequent offense in a given jurisdiction was larceny. Or we could report that the most frequently given sentence in a judicial jurisdiction for embezzlement is probation, with the next most frequent a fine and the least frequent a prison sentence. The mode is appropriate because we can speak of the most frequent offense or sentence. In fact, the mode can be used in any instance because we can always speak of the most frequent category or score. It would make little sense, however, to compute the median because we cannot rank-order the offenses. We cannot find the median with nominal-level data because we cannot rank-order the categories—burglary is not "more crime" than armed robbery or larceny. You should keep in mind, then, that the mode is *the only* measure of central tendency when you have nominal-level data.

The median, therefore, requires that we have data at the ordinal level or higher. In order to locate the median, we must first be able to rank-order our scores or intervals, we must therefore be able to determine that one score or category has

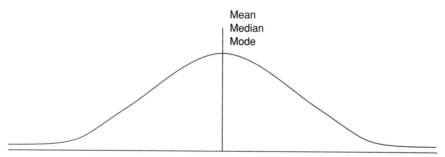

FIGURE 4.5. Symmetrical distribution.

"more" or "less" of a given characteristic than another category. For example, if we had persons' actual incomes (say, in dollars earned) or the income category into which they fell, we would be able to determine the median of the data. The mean demands even more rigid properties of our variables; it requires data at the interval or ratio level. The frequency distribution may be grouped, as in Table 4.7, but the particular variable being examined (such as the number of offenses committed or one's income in dollars) must be measured at the interval or ratio level.

If our data are at the interval or ratio level, then, we may appropriately use all three measures of central tendency. Which should we use? The easiest answer to this question would be to report the value of all three measures. If we wish to use only one measure of central tendency, which of the three we select depends on the shape of the distribution of our data. If our data are measured at the interval or ratio level and are perfectly symmetrical (and unimodal), the mode, median, and mean will all be the same. Looking at Figure 4.5 you can see that the top or apex of the curve is the score that appears most frequently (the mode); it is the score that lies in the exact middle of the distribution (the median); and it is the arithmetic average of all scores (the mean).

FIGURE 4.6. Positively skewed distribution.

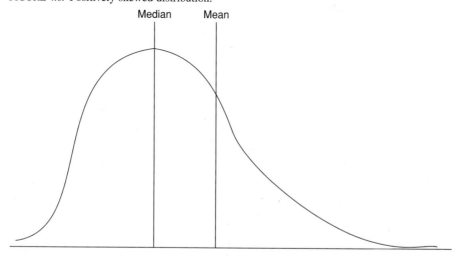

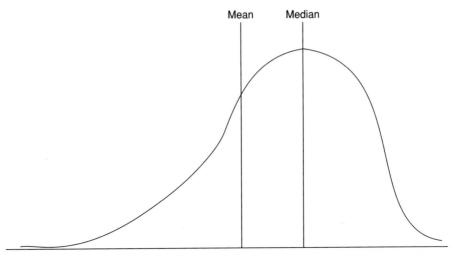

FIGURE 4.7. Negatively skewed distribution.

If the distribution of the data is not symmetrical, that is, if it is skewed, the mode, median, and mean will not coincide and the extent of the skewness will determine the selection of the appropriate measure of central tendency. In Figure 4.6 the distribution of the data is skewed to the right (there is a long "tail" at the right of the distribution) where there are a few extremely high scores. In this case the mean is greater than the median. In Figure 4.7 the distribution of the data is skewed to the left (there is a long "tail" at the left of the distribution) where there are extremely low scores. In this case the mean is less than the median. You now know that the mean may at times be very different from the median because it takes into account all of the scores in the distribution, even the extreme ones, and so it is "pulled" toward those extreme scores. Skewed data appears frequently in criminological research (such as in number of prior arrests, number of offenses committed, length of sentence received), and in such instances it is usually better to report the median as the measure of central tendency or report both the mean and median.

## 4.7 SUMMARY

In this chapter we summarized the typical score or value of our data, that is, the score around which the others cluster. We discovered that the measures that describe the typical score in our distribution of scores or data set are called *measures of central tendency*. There are three main measures of central tendency, the *mode, the median,* and the *mean.*

The *mode* is the score or interval with the highest frequency. It is possible to have one mode in our data (a *unimodal distribution*), two modes (a *bimodal distribution*), or more. As a measure of central tendency the mode is the easiest to obtain (it requires no real calculation, only the identification of the most frequent score), and it is appropriate for all levels of data. Unfortunately, in many instances the mode is not very informative.

The *median* is the score that occupies the middle position in a rank-ordered distribution of scores. A characteristic feature of the median, then, is that one half of the scores are higher and the other half is lower than the median. Because we must rank-order the scores (or intervals with grouped data) to locate the median, it requires data at the ordinal level or higher. Because the median does not take into account all of the data, but only identifies the position of the middle of our distribution, it is insensitive to very high or very low scores. It is, then, a very good measure of central tendency with skewed data.

The *mean* is the arithmetic average of all of our scores. Because to calculate it, we use mathematical operations such as addition and division, we must have data at the interval or ratio level. The mean has the normally desirable property of employing all of the data, and is therefore a generally stable and consistent measure of central tendency. It also has the property that the sum of the differences or deviations from the mean is zero. Unfortunately, because it does use all of the data, it is affected by the presence of extreme scores. It may not, therefore, be the most desirable measure of central tendency with skewed data.

## Key Terms

bimodal distribution

mean

measures of central tendency

median

mode

skewed distribution

sum of the differences

trimodal distribution

unimodal distribution

weighted mean

## Problems

1. David Nurco and his colleagues (1988) have investigated the relationship between drug addiction and criminal activity. The hypothetical data that follows represent the number of crimes committed during a 2-year period by 20-heroin addicts. Calculate the mean and the median for these 20 persons. Which measure of central tendency do you think best summarizes the central tendency of these data? Why?

| Person Number | Number of Crimes Committed | Person Number | Number of Crimes Committed |
|---|---|---|---|
| 1 | 4 | 11 | 4 |
| 2 | 16 | 12 | 11 |
| 3 | 10 | 13 | 10 |
| 4 | 7 | 14 | 88 |
| 5 | 3 | 15 | 9 |
| 6 | 112 | 16 | 12 |
| 7 | 5 | 17 | 8 |
| 8 | 10 | 18 | 5 |
| 9 | 6 | 19 | 7 |
| 10 | 2 | 20 | 10 |

2. In a study of "911 calls" made to a large midwestern police department, Gilsinan (1989: 335) reported the following distribution of caller requests:

| Request | Frequency |
|---|---|
| Information | 65 |
| Police assistance due to a crime | 29 |
| Police assistance for other reasons | 82 |
| Police assistance for a traffic problem | 19 |
| Police assistance because of an alarm sounding | 9 |

What is the measure of central tendency most appropriate for these data? Why? What does this measure of central tendency tell you about the "most typical" reason for a 911 call?

3. The following hypothetical data show the distribution of the percent of total police officers that do narcotics investigation work in 100 American cities. Identify the mode, median, and mean.

| Percent of Force Involved in Narcotics Investigation | Frequency |
|---|---|
| 0–9 | 5 |
| 10–19 | 13 |
| 20–29 | 26 |
| 30–39 | 38 |
| 40–49 | 14 |
| 50–59 | 2 |
| 60–69 | 2 |
| 70–79 | 0 |
| 80–89 | 0 |
| 90–99 | 0 |

4. In a study of Baltimore neighborhoods in the period 1970–1980, Taylor and Covington (1988) found a relationship between neighborhood change (whether "good" or "bad") and violent crime. The following are some hypothetical data on the rates of violent crime (per 100,000) for three types of neighborhoods, those "becoming worse," those "becoming better," and "relatively stable" neighborhoods. Calculate a weighted mean for these 50 neighborhoods.

| Type of Neighborhood | Number of Neighborhoods | Mean Rate of Violent Crime |
|---|---|---|
| Becoming worse | 28 | 612 |
| Stable | 10 | 342 |
| Becoming better | 12 | 489 |

5. The following data represent the number of persons executed in the United States from 1977 to 1983:

| Year | Number of Executions |
|---|---|
| 1977 | 1 |
| 1978 | 0 |
| 1979 | 2 |
| 1980 | 0 |
| 1981 | 1 |
| 1982 | 2 |
| 1983 | 5 |

What was the mean and median number of executions over this period? What happens to the median and mean when we add the year 1984 where there were 21 executions? Which measure of central tendency would you use to describe the 1977–1984 distribution?

6. Let's say you had the following data on the mean sentence length (in months) for four groups of juvenile offenders of differing sample size, property offenders, drug offenders, violent offenders, and status offenders.

| Type of Offender | Mean Sentence Length | Sample Size |
|---|---|---|
| Property | 18 | 670 |
| Drug | 12 | 450 |
| Violent | 38 | 120 |
| Status | 4 | 1575 |

Calculate the weighted mean for these data.

**7.** One seemingly inconsistent finding in criminological research is that women have a greater subjective fear of crime than men, even though their objective risk of being the victim of a crime is lower. In one study, Kelly and DeKeseredy (1994) tried to explain this fact by suggesting that women are often the psychological or physical victim of a crime within their own homes by someone who is an intimate. The following hypothetical data represent the responses of a sample of 200 women who were asked to report to an interviewer the number of times that they had been hit by a spouse, partner, or intimate in the previous 2 years. With these data, calculate the mean, median, and mode.

| Number of Times Hit | Frequency |
|---|---|
| 0–2 | 36 |
| 3–5 | 87 |
| 6–8 | 45 |
| 9–11 | 23 |
| 12–14 | 9 |

**8.** Research reported in Raine (1993) has suggested that there is a link between hypoglycemia (low blood sugar levels) and violent and aggressive behavior. He notes that the brain requires at least 80 mg of glucose per minute to function normally and that with reduced levels aggression may occur. In a random sample of 20 violent offenders currently incarcerated in a state penitentiary, the prison doctor finds the following levels of milligrams of glucose per minute. Calculate the mean and median for these data. Do these two indicators of central tendency give you very different or comparable understandings of the "most typical" level of glucose? Why do you think this is?

| Person | Level of Glucose per Minute | Person | Level of Glucose per Minute |
|---|---|---|---|
| 1 | 65 | 11 | 65 |
| 2 | 68 | 12 | 72 |
| 3 | 69 | 13 | 66 |
| 4 | 62 | 14 | 75 |
| 5 | 69 | 15 | 68 |
| 6 | 70 | 16 | 71 |
| 7 | 73 | 17 | 67 |
| 8 | 74 | 18 | 72 |
| 9 | 71 | 19 | 70 |
| 10 | 67 | 20 | 72 |

## Solutions to Problems

**1.** $\bar{x} = \dfrac{339}{20} = 16.95$

The median is the average of the 10th and 11th scores in the rank-ordered frequency distribution:

$$mdn = \frac{8 + 9}{2} = 8.5$$

The median is the preferred measure of central tendency for these data. The value of the mean is inflated by the existence of two extremely large scores (88, 112).

**2.** The most appropriate measure of central tendency for this data set is the mode because the data are measured at the nominal level. The modal, or "most typical," reason for requesting the police is for "Other Reasons."

**3.** The mode is the interval 30% to 39% because this interval has the highest frequency (38). The median is:

$$mdn = 29.5 + \left( \dfrac{\dfrac{100 + 1}{2} - 44}{38} \right)(10) = 31.2$$

The mean is:

$$\bar{x} = \dfrac{4.5(5) + 14.5(13) + 24.5(26) + 34.5(38) + 44.5(14) + 54.5(2) + 64.5(2)}{100}$$

$$= 30.2$$

**4.** Weighted mean:

$$\bar{x} = \dfrac{28(612) + 10(342) + 12(489)}{28 + 10 + 12} = \dfrac{26,424}{50} = 528.48$$

**5.** Mean number of executions:

$$\bar{x} = \dfrac{11}{7} = 1.57 \text{ executions}$$

The median number of executions is 1. When executions for the year 1984 (21) are added to the data, the mean becomes:

$$\bar{x} = \dfrac{32}{8} = 4 \text{ executions}$$

The median becomes 1.5 executions. The median is the more appropriate measure of central tendency for the 1977–1984 data distribution because it is less affected by the inclusion of the 1984 data than the mean.

**6.** The weighted mean for the data can be determined by:

$$\bar{x} = \dfrac{18(670) + 12(450) + 38(120) + 4(1575)}{670 + 450 + 120 + 1575} = \dfrac{28,320}{2815} = 10.06 \ months$$

**7.** The mean is:

$$\bar{x} = \dfrac{1(36) + 4(87) + 7(45) + 10(23) + 13(9)}{200} = \dfrac{1046}{200} = 5.23 \ times$$

The median is:

$$mdn = 2.5 + \left( \dfrac{\dfrac{201}{2} - 36}{87} \right)(3) = 4.72 \ times$$

The mode is equal to the interval 3–5 times because it contains the highest frequency (87).

**8.** The mean is equal to:

$$\bar{x} = \dfrac{1386}{20} = 69.3 \ mg \ of \ glucose \ per \ minute$$

The median is equal to 69.5. The mean and the median are very comparable. This suggests that there are no or few extreme scores in the data, that the data are not skewed.

# CHAPTER 5

# Measures of Dispersion

*Resemblances are the shadows of differences. Different people see different similarities and similar differences.*

—Vladimir Nabokov

## 5.1 INTRODUCTION

In the preceding chapter we learned how to summarize a very important property of a data distribution by calculating a measure of central tendency, which tells us what the most typical score is in a distribution, or the score around which the other scores cluster. However important a measure of central tendency is to an understanding of our data, it is not in itself all the information we would like to know about a data distribution. If we want to know the distribution more accurately, in addition to the score around which the other scores cluster, we also would want to know how different they are from one another or how tightly the scores cluster about that central tendency. That is, in addition to an estimate of the most typical score, it also is important for us to know how widely the scores are scattered about this measure of central tendency. We need, then, a measure of how different or how variable the scores are. A measure that reflects the distribution of scores about its central point is often referred to as a *measure of dispersion* because it measures how different or how "dispersed" the scores in a distribution are.

As a simple idea of what measures of dispersion actually measure, take a look at the two groups of scores in Table 5.1. These hypothetical scores represent the percentage of convicted felons who get sentenced to prison (rather than fined or given probation) in two states over a 10-year period. The mean proportion of defendants sentenced to prison is approximately the same for the two states (25.8% for State A and 25.9% for State B). In spite of the fact that over the 10-year period the mean percentage of inmates sentenced to prison was roughly the same for both states, the two distributions are not at all alike in a different sense. In State A, for example, the percentages for the different years cluster very closely around the overall mean, whereas in State B the scores are more widely scattered about the same approximate mean.

The difference between the two distributions can be seen in Figure 5.1. Notice that, even though their means are very comparable (shown in Figure 5.1 by the

---

**Measures of dispersion** reflect how different or variable the scores in a distribution are.

---

**TABLE 5.1.  Percent of Felony Defendants
Sentenced to Prison from Two States**

| Year | State A | State B |
|------|---------|---------|
| 1980 | 28 | 15 |
| 1981 | 22 | 17 |
| 1982 | 26 | 20 |
| 1983 | 25 | 22 |
| 1984 | 27 | 26 |
| 1985 | 26 | 28 |
| 1986 | 24 | 29 |
| 1987 | 28 | 34 |
| 1988 | 27 | 35 |
| 1989 | 26 | 33 |

straight line), the scores in the distribution for State B are more disperse and variable than those for State A. The scores for State A do not fall as far from the mean as do those for State B. State B's data points are much further below the mean during the early part of the time series and much further above it in the later years. The corresponding scores for State A are much closer to the mean throughout the time series. Another way to express this is to say that the scores for State A are more homogeneous than those for State B.

FIGURE 5.1. Percent of felony defendants sentenced to prison.

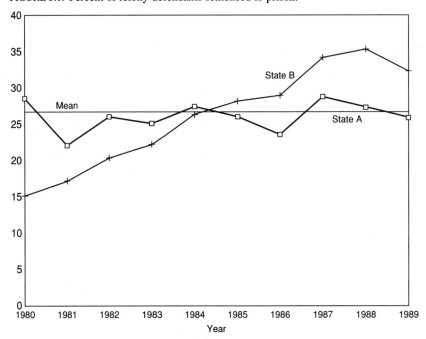

With a measure of dispersion we hope to communicate the amount of variation within a distribution of scores. The numerical value of this measure of dispersion should be greater for State B than for State A, telling us that the scores in the former are more spread out than those in the latter. In addition to a measure of central tendency, then, a measure of dispersion will help us understand what the data look like. Just as there is more than one measure of central tendency, depending on what kind of data you have, there is more than one measure of dispersion.

## 5.2 THE INDEX OF QUALITATIVE VARIATION

As the term implies, the *index of qualitative variation (IQV)* is a measure of dispersion to employ whenever you have qualitative or nominal-level data. It is the measure of dispersion that corresponds to the mode as a measure of central tendency. Because nominal-level data (such as type of crime committed or type of sentence received) provide information about the qualities or attributes of things, and not numerical attributes, we can only estimate how evenly or unevenly the data are distributed into our particular nominal-level categories. The IQV provides a numerical estimate of how evenly or unevenly the cases are distributed across a given number of categories. More specifically, the IQV measures the percentage of maximum variation or heterogeneity in the data. The formula for the IQV is:

$$IQV = \frac{\text{Observed Heterogeneity}}{\text{Maximum Heterogeneity}} \times 100 \qquad (5.1)$$

where

observed heterogeneity is the sum of the product of all *observed* category totals
maximum heterogeneity is the sum of the product of all *expected* category totals

The IQV requires us to find two quantities, the *observed heterogeneity* and the *maximum heterogeneity*. The observed heterogeneity we can calculate from the observed frequencies. To determine what the maximum heterogeneity is, however, we must calculate the *expected frequencies* under the assumption of maximum heterogeneity.

We illustrate the use of the IQV with data from a study of Florida homicide cases (Bowers, 1984). Table 5.2 shows the distribution of homicides by both the race of the offender and the race of the victim for two types of homicides, felony-type homicides (murders that involve the commission of another felony in addition to the murder, such as rape or armed robbery), and nonfelony-type homicides. The distinction is an important one because felony-type murders are punishable by death under existing Florida law. One thing we might want to know about these data is whether the amount of racial heterogeneity is comparable across the two types of homicide. That is, is there more racial variation in felony or nonfelony-type homicides?

Felony-type murders include 617 cases distributed across four race of offender and victim categories. The observed frequencies can be seen from the category frequencies shown in Table 5.2. We determine the expected frequencies by assuming that the data have the maximum amount of heterogeneity. The maximum amount of heterogeneity would exist in the data if the 617 cases were equally

**TABLE 5.2. Number of Felony and Nonfelony-Type Homicides by Race of Offender and Victim for Florida, 1972–1977**

| Racial Combination | Felony-Type Murders | Nonfelony-Type Murders |
|---|---|---|
| Black kills white | 143 | 97 |
| White kills white | 303 | 1465 |
| Black kills black | 160 | 1762 |
| White kills black | 11 | 69 |
| Total | 617 | 3393 |

| Expected frequencies under the assumption of maximum heterogeneity | | |
|---|---|---|
| Black kills white | 154.25 | 848.25 |
| White kills white | 154.25 | 848.25 |
| Black kills black | 154.25 | 848.25 |
| White kills black | 154.25 | 848.25 |
| Total | 617 | 3393 |

*Source:* Bowers (1984).

distributed among the four categories of homicides. In the case of maximum heterogeneity for the felony-type homicides, then, there would be 154.25 (617/4) cases in each of the four categories. For nonfelony-type homicides, the maximum amount of heterogeneity would exist if there were 3393/4, or 848.25, homicides in each racial category. In general, we can find the expected category frequency under the condition of maximum heterogeneity by dividing the total number of observations by the number of categories. We have included the expected frequencies under the assumption of maximum heterogeneity in the lower half of Table 5.2. Once we have found the observed frequencies and expected frequencies under maximum heterogeneity, we can then estimate both the observed and maximum heterogeneity by multiplying each pair of category frequencies (only once) and summing.

The formula for finding the total observed heterogeneity is:

$$\sum_{i=1}^{k-1} \sum_{j=i+1}^{k} (f_i f_j) \tag{5.2}$$

where

$k$ = the number of categories
$f_i$ = the frequency of category $i$
$f_j$ = the frequency of category $j$

If there are four categories as in our example, the formula becomes:

$$\sum_{i=1}^{3} \sum_{j=i+1}^{4} (f_i f_j) = f_1 f_2 + f_1 f_3 + f_1 f_4 + f_2 f_3 + f_2 f_4 + f_3 f_4 \tag{5.3}$$

Please note that we want to multiply each pair of category frequencies only once. That is, once we have calculated $f_1 f_3$ we do not have to calculate and include $f_3 f_1$

because the two are equivalent. Thus, in the formula we used two subscripts, $i$ and $j$, and require that $i$ be less than $j$.

We also can use this formula to estimate the maximum possible heterogeneity. In this case we simply find the maximum expected frequency for each category ($N/k$, where $N$ = the total number of cases and $k$ = the total number of categories) and apply the formula. In this case, however, the category frequencies are not the observed frequencies but the expected frequencies given maximum heterogeneity. We can also find the maximum amount of heterogeneity by the following formula:

$$\text{Maximum Heterogeneity} = \frac{k(k-1)}{2} \left(\frac{N}{k}\right)^2 \tag{5.4}$$

where
  $k$ = the number of categories
  $N$ = the total number of cases

We carry out the necessary calculations to estimate both the observed and maximum amount of heterogeneity for each felony-type homicide in Table 5.2:

$$\begin{aligned}
\text{Observed Heterogeneity} &= (143)(303) + (143)(160) + (143)(11) \\
&\quad + (303)(160) + (303)(11) + (160)(11) \\
&= 43{,}329 + 22{,}880 + 1573 + 48{,}480 + 3333 + 1760 \\
&= 121{,}355
\end{aligned}$$

$$\begin{aligned}
\text{Maximum Heterogeneity} &= (154.25)(154.25) + (154.25)(154.25) \\
&\quad + (154.25)(154.25) + (154.25)(154.25) \\
&\quad + (154.25)(154.25) + (154.25)(154.25) \\
&= 23{,}793 + 23{,}793 + 23{,}793 + 23{,}793 \\
&\quad + 23{,}793 + 23{,}793 \\
&= 142{,}758
\end{aligned}$$

Instead of multiplying expected frequencies, we could have determined the maximum heterogeneity for felony-type murders from equation 5.4:

$$\begin{aligned}
\text{Maximum Heterogeneity} &= \left(\frac{4(4-1)}{2}\right)\left(\frac{617}{4}\right)^2 \\
&= 6(23{,}793) \\
&= 142{,}758
\end{aligned}$$

As you can see, both procedures produce the same results. With these quantities, we can now determine the IQV as:

$$\begin{aligned}
\text{IQV} &= \frac{121{,}355}{142{,}758} \times 100 \\
&= 85.01
\end{aligned}$$

For felony-type murders, we would interpret the IQV by saying that the maximum heterogeneity for these data is approximately 85 percent. Because it measures the percent of possible variation, the IQV will always be a value between 0 percent and 100 percent. A higher IQV value suggests that there is a higher percent of variation given the number of categories in the data.

By way of comparison, we can now compute the IQV for the nonfelony-type murders:

$$IQV = \frac{\begin{array}{c}(97)(1465) + (97)(1762) + (97)(69) \\ + (1465)(1762) + (1465)(69) + (1762)(69)\end{array}}{\begin{array}{c}(848.25)(848.25) + (848.25)(848.25) + (848.25)(848.25) \\ + (848.25)(848.25) + (848.25)(848.25) + (848.25)(848.25)\end{array}} \times 100$$

$$= \frac{\begin{array}{c}(142,105) + (170,914) + (6,693) \\ + (2,581,330) + (101,085) + (121,578)\end{array}}{\begin{array}{c}(719,528) + (719,528) + (719,528) \\ + (719,528) + (719,528) + (719,528)\end{array}} \times 100$$

$$= \frac{3,123,705}{4,317,168} \times 100$$

$$= 72.35$$

For nonfelony-type murders, there is 72 percent of the maximum amount of possible variation. The IQV for nonfelony-type murders (72 percent) is less than that found for felony-type murders (85 percent). There is less racial heterogeneity in the nonfelony murders, then, than for felony-type murders because there is 72 percent of the total possible amount of variation in the former and 85 percent of the maximum for the latter. In comparing two or more IQV values, it must be remembered that the amount of possible variation depends on the number of *categories* in a variable, not the number of cases or observations. A variable with more categories has more possible variation; hence two IQV values should be compared only when the variables have the same number of categories. The IQV is useful, then, when we want to compare the amount of variation in one variable with two different samples or data sets (such as males/females, neighborhoods, types of homicides).

In addition to using raw category frequencies, the IQV can also be calculated with percentages. When using percentages, the category percents are used in the calculation of observed and maximum heterogeneity, and the value of $N$ is 100 percent. For example, in the following table we substitute percentages for the frequencies for felony-type murders and calculate the value of the IQV. The maximum possible heterogeneity (100 percent/4 = 25 percent) is in parentheses:

| Racial Combination | Felony-Type Murders |
|---|---|
| Black kills white | 23% (25%) |
| White kills white | 49% (25%) |
| Black kills black | 26% (25%) |
| White kills black | 2% (25%) |
| Total | 100% (100%) |

$$\text{Maximum Possible Heterogeneity} = (4[4 - 1])/2 \ (100/4)^2$$

$$= 6 \ (625)$$

$$= 3750$$

Observed Heterogeneity = (23)(49) + (23)(26) + (23)(2) + (49)(26)
$$+ (49)(2) + (26)(2)$$
$$= 1127 + 598 + 46 + 1274 + 98 + 52$$
$$= 3195$$

IQV = 3195/3750 × 100

IQV = 85.2 percent

As you can see, the results are the same whether you use category frequencies or percents. The calculations are usually less cumbersome with percents than with frequencies.

Another measure of dispersion with nominal-level data that is somewhat different from the IQV is called the *variation ratio (VR)*. The IQV measures the degree to which the cases are distributed evenly across all categories, whereas the variation ratio measures the extent to which the cases are not concentrated in the modal category. If a high proportion of the cases fall into one category (the mode), then the data are not very dispersed. High VR values therefore indicate greater dispersion or variability in the data. The VR is defined by the formula:

$$\text{Variation Ratio} = 1 - \frac{f_{modal}}{N} \tag{5.5}$$

where

$f_{modal}$ = the number of cases (frequency) in the modal category
$N$ = the total number of cases

The VR for the two types of murder we examined can be easily calculated as:

$$VR_1 = 1 - \frac{303}{617}$$
$$= .51$$
$$VR_2 = 1 - \frac{1762}{3393}$$
$$= .48$$

The VR indicates that the variability in the two types of homicide is roughly comparable, with slightly less variation for nonfelony murders.

## 5.3 THE RANGE

When we have continuous-level data, we can move beyond merely describing how the data are evenly or unevenly distributed into categories. One measure of dispersion with continuous data is the range. The *range* is the easiest measure of dispersion to compute. The range is simply calculated as the difference between the highest and lowest score in a distribution. For example, for the data in Table 5.1 the range is 6 for State A (28 percent to 22 percent) and 20 for State B (35 percent to

15 percent). When the data are rank ordered, the range is expressed as the difference between the midpoints of the two extreme intervals or categories.

Sometimes the range is expressed not as the difference between the two scores, but by the two extreme scores themselves (the range for State A in Table 5.1 would be 28 and 22). Either way, the range is very simple and quick to calculate. Unfortunately, this simplicity may come at a high price because the range may in some instances provide a very distorted picture of the variability in our data.

Suppose, for example, that we have two hypothetical data distributions that represent the number of prison escapes for 20 correctional institutions in each of two states during the past 5 years (Table 5.3). The distribution of the number of escapes in the two states looks reasonably similar, but the ranges are very different. The highest score for State A is 33 (institution 4), whereas the lowest is 0 (institution 14). The range, therefore, is $33 - 0 = 33$. The range of escapes in State B, however, is only 9 $(9 - 0)$. In spite of the fact that the two distributions look very similar, the range in State A is almost four times what it is in State B. Had we used the range as our measure of dispersion, we would be led to conclude that the distribution of escapes in one state is substantially greater than that in the other. Although technically correct, looking at the data, we can see that this clearly is not the case. The reason why the range of escapes is so large in State A is because it happens to include one institution (institution 4) that had an unusually high number of escapes (33).

Because the range is calculated as the difference between the two extreme scores, it is very sensitive to unusually high or low values. Although the range may provide a reasonable measure of dispersion in the absence of extreme values, when such atypical scores are present it can at times provide a misleading estimate of the amount of variability in the data. Because the range can be grossly distorted by just one score, it tends to be a very unstable indicator of dispersion. In view of this limitation, variations of the range have been devised.

One of these variations on the range is called the *interquartile range (IQR)*. A "quartile" refers to the division of a percent distribution into four equal parts. The first quartile, $Q_1$, contains the first 25 percent of the cases in a distribution. The second quartile, $Q_2$, contains the 25 percent of the cases from the first quartile to the

**TABLE 5.3. Hypothetical Data on the Number of Escapes from 20 Correctional Institutions in Two States**

| Institution | State A | State B | Institution | State A | State B |
|---|---|---|---|---|---|
| 1 | 3 | 3 | 11 | 4 | 5 |
| 2 | 2 | 4 | 12 | 5 | 2 |
| 3 | 4 | 1 | 13 | 2 | 3 |
| 4 | 33 | 2 | 14 | 0 | 5 |
| 5 | 2 | 3 | 15 | 7 | 8 |
| 6 | 5 | 6 | 16 | 1 | 0 |
| 7 | 6 | 5 | 17 | 7 | 6 |
| 8 | 4 | 3 | 18 | 6 | 8 |
| 9 | 1 | 4 | 19 | 9 | 9 |
| 10 | 3 | 4 | 20 | 3 | 1 |

50th percentile or the median. The third quartile, $Q_3$, contains the 25 percent of the cases from the median to the 75th percentile. The fourth quartile, $Q_4$, contains the 25 percent of the cases from the 75th to the 100th percentile. The specific terms for the divisions of a percent distribution are as follows:

| Percentile | Decile | Quartile |
|---|---|---|
| 100th | 10th | 4th |
| 90th | 9th | |
| 80th | 8th | |
| 75th | | 3rd |
| 70th | 7th | |
| 60th | 6th | |
| 50th | 5th | 2nd (Median) |
| 40th | 4th | |
| 30th | 3rd | |
| 25th | | 1st |
| 20th | 2nd | |
| 10th | 1st | |

Instead of taking the difference between the highest and lowest scores (which the range does), the interquartile range takes the difference between the score at the 25th percentile (referred to as the first quartile, $Q_1$) and the 75th percentile (referred to as the third quartile, $Q_3$). The interquartile range, then, is defined by the following formula:

$$\text{Interquartile Range} = Q_3 - Q_1 \tag{5.6}$$

where

$Q_3$ = the score at the 75th percentile
$Q_1$ = the score at the 25th percentile

As you can see, the interquartile range is not based on the scores at the two extreme ends of the distribution, but instead measures the variation in the data of the middle 50% of the distribution (the variation between the 75th and 25th percentiles).

To determine the interquartile range, we rank-order the scores by frequency of occurrence. Once this is done, we calculate a cumulative frequency distribution to determine what the scores at the 75th and 25th percentiles are. Once we know the scores at these two percentiles, we can easily determine the interquartile range.

In Table 5.4, we have constructed a frequency distribution for the data in Table 5.3, and have calculated both a percent and a cumulative percent distribution. From this we can determine what the value of the interquartile range would be for each of the two states:

State A Interquartile Range = $6 - 2 = 4$

State B Interquartile Range = $5 - 2 = 3$

The score at the 75th percentile for State A is 6, because a score of 6 corresponds to the 70th to 80th percentile. The score at the 25th percentile is 2, because a score of 2 corresponds to the 15th to 30th percentile. The interquartile range for State A is, therefore, $6 - 2 = 4$. The corresponding value of the interquartile range for

**TABLE 5.4. Frequency Distribution and Cumulative Percent Distribution for the Data in Table 5.3**

| Number of Escapes | State A | Percent | Cumulative Percent | State B | Percent | Cumulative Percent |
|---|---|---|---|---|---|---|
| 0 | 1 | 5 | 5 | 1 | 5 | 5 |
| 1 | 2 | 10 | 15 | 2 | 10 | 15 |
| 2 | 3 | 15 | 30 | 2 | 10 | 25 |
| 3 | 3 | 15 | 45 | 4 | 20 | 45 |
| 4 | 3 | 15 | 60 | 3 | 15 | 60 |
| 5 | 2 | 10 | 70 | 3 | 15 | 75 |
| 6 | 2 | 10 | 80 | 2 | 10 | 85 |
| 7 | 2 | 10 | 90 | 0 | 0 | 85 |
| 8 | 0 | 0 | 90 | 2 | 10 | 95 |
| 9 | 1 | 5 | 95 | 1 | 5 | 100 |
| 33 | 1 | 5 | 100 | 0 | 0 | 100 |
|  | $N = 20$ |  |  | $N = 20$ |  |  |

State B is 3. We can now see that the interquartile range suggests that the dispersion in escapes is very comparable for the two states. The range, you remember, indicated that the variability in the first state (a range of 33) was substantially greater than that in the second (a range of 9). In this case, the interquartile range, because it is not affected by scores at the extremes of the distribution, gives us a more accurate picture of the variability in our data than the range.

There is a way to calculate the interquartile range without constructing a cumulative percent distribution. This alternative procedure involves determining something called the "truncated median position." The truncated median position simply is the position of the median with the decimal place (if there is one) dropped off or truncated. Once this truncated median position is determined, the location or position of the first and third quartiles ($Q_1$ and $Q_3$, respectively) can then be determined with the following formula:

Quartile Position (QP) = (Truncated Median Position + 1)/2

The quartile position (QP) tells us how many scores we need to go down to find the first quartile in a distribution of scores ranked in ascending order and how many scores we need to go up to find the third quartile. Let's illustrate with an example.

Let's continue to use the hypothetical escape data in Table 5.3. In order to find the IQR with this alternative method, first rank-order the scores from low to high:

*State A.* 0, 1, 1, 2, 2, 2, 3, 3, 3, 4, 4, 4, 5, 5, 6, 6, 7, 7, 9, 33

*State B.* 0, 1, 2, 2, 2, 3, 3, 3, 3, 4, 4, 4, 5, 5, 5, 6, 6, 8, 8, 9

Second, find the position of the median. Remember that with an even number of scores the median is the average of the two middle positions. In our example, the position of the median is at the midpoint of the 10th and 11th position, that is, at position 10.5 in our distribution of 20 scores (using the formula we learned in Chapter 4, the median is located at ([N + 1]/2 or [10 + 1]/2 = 10.5). The truncated median position simply is the median position with the decimal place dropped off or truncated, so the truncated median position in this example is 10 rather than 10.5. With the truncated median position, we can now find the position of our two quartiles:

QP = (Truncated Median Position + 1)/2

QP = (10 + 1)/2

QP = 5.5

The quartile position is 5.5. This tells us that the first quartile ($Q_1$) can be found by going 5.5 scores down from the top (the lowest score) of the distribution. The 5.5 position is the midpoint of the 5th and 6th position. For State A these two positions are occupied by the score of 2, so the first quartile for this state is 2. For State B, the 5th position is occupied by the score of 2 and the 6th position is occupied by the score of 3, so the first quartile for this state is 2.5 ([2 + 3]/2). To find the third quartile ($Q_3$) for the two states we simply go 5.5 scores up from the bottom of the distribution (the highest score). Again, the 5.5 position is the midpoint of the 5th and 6th position. For State A both the 5th and 6th positions from the bottom are occupied by the score of 6, so the third quartile for this state is 6. For State B the 5th position up from the bottom is occupied by the score of 6 and the 6th position is occupied by the score of 5, so the third quartile for this state is 5.5 ([6 + 5]/2). We now have the information we need to calculate the IQR for the two states:

IQR = $Q_3 - Q_1$

State A IQR = 6 − 2 = 4

State B IQR = 5.5 − 2.5 = 3

The IQR for State A is 4, and it is 3 for State B. These are exactly the same values we obtained when we used a cumulative frequency distribution to find the values of the first and third quartiles. Of the two methods, the cumulative percent procedure may be easier to use when there are a large number of scores, which must be rank-ordered first. With a smaller number of scores, the IQR may more easily be determined by the truncated median position method.

## 5.4 THE MEAN DEVIATION

Recall the properties of the mean discussed in Chapter 4. The mean, you remember, is the arithmetic average of a set of scores and is defined as the sum of the scores divided by the total number of scores. The mean, therefore, uses all of the data. In addition, in describing the mean we noted that it can be thought of as the balancing score in a set of scores. We noted this balancing property of the mean when we found that by subtracting each score from the mean ($x - \bar{x}$) the value of all of the minus scores are equal to the value of all of the positive scores. When the negative and positive differences are added, then the sum is zero. In other words, the sum of the differences or the sum of the deviations about the mean is equal to zero. Maybe we can use the fact that the mean is the balancing score in a distribution of scores to create a useful measure of dispersion.

If we want our measure of dispersion to tell us how variable or different the scores are from one another, a good way to express how different they are is to use their deviations about the mean. The mean is a measure of central tendency or typicality, so in using the difference of each score from the most "typical" score, we can have some idea of how different the scores are. Perhaps we could take the average or mean of these difference or deviation scores, that is, an average of difference scores. Then, our measure of dispersion would be a reflection of the average distance of each score from the mean. The higher this number, the more different scores are from the mean, the more variability in the data. The lower this number, the less different scores are from the mean, the less variability in the data.

However, we cannot simply take the average of these differences or deviations from the mean, because, as you remember, the sum of the deviations from the mean is zero ($\Sigma[x - \bar{x}] = 0$). We need, therefore, to somehow get rid of the negative signs. There are two ways to get rid of these signs; one is to ignore them, the other is to square the number. Squaring a negative number gets rid of the negative sign because a negative number times a negative number is equal to a positive number ($-3^2 = +9$). First, we consider ignoring the signs of the numbers. Then we will look at two other measures of dispersion that square the deviation scores.

**TABLE 5.5. Calculation of the Mean Deviation for the Number of Escapes from 20 Correctional Institutions in State A of Table 5.3**

| Number of Escapes | $(x - \bar{x})$ | | $\lvert(x - \bar{x})\rvert$ |
|---|---|---|---|
| 3 | $(3 - 5.35)$ = | $-2.35$ | 2.35 |
| 2 | $(2 - 5.35)$ = | $-3.35$ | 3.35 |
| 4 | $(4 - 5.35)$ = | $-1.35$ | 1.35 |
| 33 | $(33 - 5.35)$ = | $27.65$ | 27.65 |
| 2 | $(2 - 5.35)$ = | $-3.35$ | 3.35 |
| 5 | $(5 - 5.35)$ = | $-.35$ | .35 |
| 6 | $(6 - 5.35)$ = | $.65$ | .65 |
| 4 | $(4 - 5.35)$ = | $-1.35$ | 1.35 |
| 1 | $(1 - 5.35)$ = | $-4.35$ | 4.35 |
| 3 | $(3 - 5.35)$ = | $-2.35$ | 2.35 |
| 4 | $(4 - 5.35)$ = | $-1.35$ | 1.35 |
| 5 | $(5 - 5.35)$ = | $-.35$ | .35 |
| 2 | $(2 - 5.35)$ = | $-3.35$ | 3.35 |
| 0 | $(0 - 5.35)$ = | $-5.35$ | 5.35 |
| 7 | $(7 - 5.35)$ = | $1.65$ | 1.65 |
| 1 | $(1 - 5.35)$ = | $-4.35$ | 4.35 |
| 7 | $(7 - 5.35)$ = | $1.65$ | 1.65 |
| 6 | $(6 - 5.35)$ = | $.65$ | .65 |
| 9 | $(9 - 5.35)$ = | $3.65$ | 3.65 |
| 3 | $(3 - 5.35)$ = | $-2.35$ | 2.35 |
| $\Sigma = 107$ | | 0 | 71.80 |

**Step 1.** Subtract the mean from each score.
**Step 2.** Take the absolute value of each difference.
**Step 3.** Sum up all of the absolute differences.
**Step 4.** Divide this sum by the total number of scores.

As we noted in the previous chapter, whenever we consider a number without regard for its sign we are using the *absolute value* of that number. The absolute value of a number is usually shown in bars, like $|-3|$. For example, $|-3| = 3 = |+3|$. In words, the absolute value of $+3$ or $-3$ is 3. We can use the absolute value of numbers when creating a measure of dispersion by subtracting the mean from each score, ignoring the sign (that is, taking the absolute value of that number), summing these values, and then dividing by the total number of scores. We are, then, simply taking the mean of the absolute value of the deviation or difference scores. This is the idea behind the *mean deviation* and is expressed by the following formula:

$$\text{Mean Deviation} = \frac{\Sigma\,|x_i - \bar{x}|}{N} \tag{5.7}$$

where

$x_i$ = the score for the *i*th case
$\bar{x}$ = the mean
$N$ = the total number of scores

The mean deviation, then, is the average or mean of the absolute value of the difference between each score and the mean of those scores.

The mean deviation can be calculated from a few very simple steps, as shown in the box above. We use data from Table 5.3 to illustrate the calculation of the mean deviation. The necessary calculations are shown in Table 5.5 for State A and Table 5.6 for State B.

In Table 5.5 we first determine the mean for State A, which is 5.35 (107/20). Then in the second column, we subtract the mean from each score and retain the sign. The sum of these deviations from the mean $(x - \bar{x})$ will be zero, and you should use this fact to check your arithmetic. We then take the absolute value of these deviations in the third column, sum them, and divide by the total number of observations (20 in this case). The mean deviation in this example is 71.8/20, or 3.59. In other words, the average difference from the mean number of escapes for these 20 institutions is 3.59. The calculation of the mean deviation for State B is shown in Table 5.6. For this set of 20 institutions we find a mean deviation of 1.92. The variation in escapes from correctional institutions is greater in State A than State B; however, the difference in the dispersion between the two states is much less when we use the mean deviation than the range.

## 5.5 THE VARIANCE AND STANDARD DEVIATION

In the previous section we saw that we could calculate a measure of dispersion by ignoring (taking the absolute value of) the sign of the difference between each score and the mean, and then taking the mean of these difference or deviation scores. The

**TABLE 5.6. Calculation of the Mean Deviation for the Number of Escapes from 20 Correctional Institutions in State B of Table 5.3**

| Number of Escapes | $(x - \bar{x})$ | $\lvert (x - \bar{x}) \rvert$ |
|:---:|:---:|:---:|
| 3 | $(3 - 4.10) = -1.10$ | 1.10 |
| 4 | $(4 - 4.10) = \ -.10$ | .10 |
| 1 | $(1 - 4.10) = -3.10$ | 3.10 |
| 2 | $(2 - 4.10) = -2.10$ | 2.10 |
| 3 | $(3 - 4.10) = -1.10$ | 1.10 |
| 6 | $(6 - 4.10) = \ \ 1.90$ | 1.90 |
| 5 | $(5 - 4.10) = \ \ .90$ | .90 |
| 3 | $(3 - 4.10) = -1.10$ | 1.10 |
| 4 | $(4 - 4.10) = \ -.10$ | .10 |
| 4 | $(4 - 4.10) = \ -.10$ | .10 |
| 5 | $(5 - 4.10) = \ \ .90$ | .90 |
| 2 | $(2 - 4.10) = -2.10$ | 2.10 |
| 3 | $(3 - 4.10) = -1.10$ | 1.10 |
| 5 | $(5 - 4.10) = \ \ .90$ | .90 |
| 8 | $(8 - 4.10) = \ \ 3.90$ | 3.90 |
| 0 | $(0 - 4.10) = -4.10$ | 4.10 |
| 6 | $(6 - 4.10) = \ \ 1.90$ | 1.90 |
| 8 | $(8 - 4.10) = \ \ 3.90$ | 3.90 |
| 9 | $(9 - 4.10) = \ \ 4.90$ | 4.90 |
| 1 | $(1 - 4.10) = -3.10$ | 3.10 |
| $\Sigma = 82$ | 0 | 38.40 |

*variance* and *standard deviation,* too, use differences or deviations about the mean on which to build a measure of dispersion. In the latter two cases, however, the minus signs are dealt with by squaring this difference.

We begin by examining the formula for the variance ($s^2$):

$$\text{Variance} = s^2 = \frac{\Sigma(x - \bar{x})^2}{N} \tag{5.8}$$

where

$x$ = each $x$ score
$\bar{x}$ = the mean
$N$ = the total number of scores

The steps involved in the calculation of the variance are shown in the box below.

---

**Step 1.** Subtract the mean from each score.
**Step 2.** Square this difference.
**Step 3.** Sum these squared differences for each score.
**Step 4.** Divide by the total number of scores.

---

Notice how close the variance is to the mean deviation. Just as we did for the mean deviation, in calculating the variance, we subtract the mean from each score. Instead of taking the absolute value, however, in calculating the variance we square this deviation (thus getting rid of the minus signs). Then we sum over all scores and divide by the total number of scores (*N*). The variance, then, is the mean of the squared deviations about the mean. The mean deviation was the mean of the absolute deviations about the mean. We illustrate the calculation of the variance with the escape data in Table 5.3. The deviation of each score from the mean is shown in Tables 5.5 and 5.6. The calculations for the variance for State A and State B are reported in Tables 5.7 and 5.8, respectively. We can see from these calculations that, consistent with our findings for the mean deviation, the dispersion within State A is greater than that for State B. The variance for State A is 45.32, and for State B it is only 5.69.

There is one possible problem with the variance as a measure of dispersion. Notice that in calculating the variance we square the deviations from the mean for each score. In doing this, we are actually changing the unit of measurement of our variable, making the variance more difficult to interpret. For example, because the mean number of escapes for the 20 institutions in State A was 5.35, the first institution in that state had about two fewer escapes than the average (3 − 5.35), the

**TABLE 5.7. Calculation of the Mean Deviation for the Number of Escapes from 20 Correctional Institutions in State A of Table 5.3**

| Number of Escapes | $(x - \bar{x})$ | $(x - \bar{x})^2$ |
|---|---|---|
| 3 | $(3 - 5.35) = -2.35$ | 5.52 |
| 2 | $(2 - 5.35) = -3.35$ | 11.22 |
| 4 | $(4 - 5.35) = -1.35$ | 1.82 |
| 33 | $(33 - 5.35) = 27.65$ | 764.52 |
| 2 | $(2 - 5.35) = -3.35$ | 11.22 |
| 5 | $(5 - 5.35) = -.35$ | .12 |
| 6 | $(6 - 5.35) = .65$ | .42 |
| 4 | $(4 - 5.35) = -1.35$ | 1.82 |
| 1 | $(1 - 5.35) = -4.35$ | 18.92 |
| 3 | $(3 - 5.35) = -2.35$ | 5.52 |
| 4 | $(4 - 5.35) = -1.35$ | 1.82 |
| 5 | $(5 - 5.35) = -.35$ | .12 |
| 2 | $(2 - 5.35) = -3.35$ | 11.22 |
| 0 | $(0 - 5.35) = -5.35$ | 28.62 |
| 7 | $(7 - 5.35) = 1.65$ | 2.72 |
| 1 | $(1 - 5.35) = -4.35$ | 18.92 |
| 7 | $(7 - 5.35) = 1.65$ | 2.72 |
| 6 | $(6 - 5.35) = .65$ | .42 |
| 9 | $(9 - 5.35) = 3.65$ | 13.32 |
| 3 | $(3 - 5.35) = -2.35$ | 5.52 |
| $\Sigma = 107$ | 0 | 906.50 |

$s^2 = 906.5/20 = 45.32.$

**TABLE 5.8. Calculation of the Mean Deviation for the Number of Escapes from 20 Correctional Institutions in State B of Table 5.3**

| Number of Escapes | $(x - \bar{x})$ | $(x - \bar{x})^2$ |
|---|---|---|
| 3 | $(3 - 4.10) = -1.10$ | 1.21 |
| 4 | $(4 - 4.10) = -.10$ | .01 |
| 1 | $(1 - 4.10) = -3.10$ | 9.61 |
| 2 | $(2 - 4.10) = -2.10$ | 4.41 |
| 3 | $(3 - 4.10) = -1.10$ | 1.21 |
| 6 | $(6 - 4.10) = 1.90$ | 3.61 |
| 5 | $(5 - 4.10) = .90$ | .81 |
| 3 | $(3 - 4.10) = -1.10$ | 1.21 |
| 4 | $(4 - 4.10) = -.10$ | .01 |
| 4 | $(4 - 4.10) = -.10$ | .01 |
| 5 | $(5 - 4.10) = .90$ | .81 |
| 2 | $(2 - 4.10) = -2.10$ | 4.41 |
| 3 | $(3 - 4.10) = -1.10$ | 1.21 |
| 5 | $(5 - 4.10) = .90$ | .81 |
| 8 | $(8 - 4.10) = 3.90$ | 15.21 |
| 0 | $(0 - 4.10) = 4.10$ | 16.81 |
| 6 | $(6 - 4.10) = 1.90$ | 3.61 |
| 8 | $(8 - 4.10) = 3.90$ | 15.21 |
| 9 | $(9 - 4.10) = 4.90$ | 24.01 |
| 1 | $(1 - 4.10) = -3.10$ | 9.61 |
| $\Sigma = 82$ | 0 | 113.803 |

$s^2 = 113.803/20 = 5.69.$

seventh institution had about one more escape than the average $(6 - 5.35)$. The mean deviation for these 20 escapes was 3.59, so the average difference was about three and one-half escapes more or less than the average. The mean deviation is expressed, then, in terms of something we clearly understand, the original unit of measurement, which in this case is the number of escapes. When we calculate the variance, however, we do not use the absolute value of the difference between a score and the mean. Instead we use the square of the difference. What exactly is the number of escapes squared? The variance, then, is interpreted in something that is not so easily understood, the unit of measurement squared.

**Step 1.** Calculate the mean.
**Step 2.** Subtract the mean from each score.
**Step 3.** Square the difference.
**Step 4.** Sum the deviations for all scores.
**Step 5.** Divide by the number of scores—this is the variance.
**Step 6.** Take the square root of that value—this is the standard deviation.

All is not lost however. Having first squared the deviations from the mean to get rid of the minus signs, we can convert our computed differences from the mean back into their original unit of measurement by taking the square root of the deviations. If we do this, we have calculated the measure of dispersion called the standard deviation. The standard deviation $(s)$ is the square root of the variance $(s^2)$ and is expressed by the following formula:

$$\text{Standard Deviation} = (s) = \sqrt{s^2} = \sqrt{\frac{\Sigma(x - \bar{x})^2}{N}} \tag{5.9}$$

where

$x$ = each score
$\bar{x}$ = the mean
$N$ = the total number of scores

To calculate the standard deviation, there are six steps that must be followed in *exact order,* as listed in the box on page 126. For State A, the standard deviation is equal to 6.73 ($\sqrt{45.32}$); for State B, it is 2.38 ($\sqrt{5.69}$).

We would like to note at this point that this formula is for the standard deviation of the sample. If you wanted to use the sample standard deviation $s$ as an estimate of the population standard deviation, then the denominator would be $N - 1$, not $N$. That is why some statistics texts initially define $s$ with $N - 1$ in the denominator. The reason why $N - 1$ is in the denominator when $s$ is used to estimate $\sigma$ (the population standard deviation) is because $s$ is a biased estimator of the *population standard deviation* $\sigma$. Subtracting 1 from the sample size corrects for this bias. We prefer to define the sample standard deviation with $N$ in the denominator, because it is the definition of a sample standard deviation. In the chapters on inferential statistics, however, we comment that $s$ is a biased estimator of $\sigma$ and make the appropriate correction. We symbolize the sample standard deviation by $s$, the population standard deviation by $\sigma$, and the sample estimate of the population standard deviation by $\hat{\sigma}$. We illustrate the calculation of the variance and standard deviation for both ungrouped and grouped data.

## Calculation of Variance and Standard Deviation from Ungrouped Data

Table 5.9 lists the number of executions that occurred in the United States from 1930 to 1990 for the 50 states and the District of Columbia (first column). We use these data to calculate a variance and standard deviation. In step 1 we calculate the mean number of executions (the mean is 3969/51, or 77.8, which we have rounded up to 78, second column). In step 2 we subtract the mean from each score (third column). In step 3 we square that difference (fourth column). In step 4 we sum those squared differences (bottom of the fourth column). For the time being, ignore the fifth column of Table 5.9. Now that we have the sum of the squared differences, we can complete step 5, which is to divide the sum of the squared deviations by the total number of observations. This quantity is 483,389/51 = 9478 and is the variance. In the sixth and final step we take the square root of the variance to get the standard deviation ($\sqrt{9478}$ = 97). The variance and standard deviation for this data, then, are 9478 and 97, respectively.

**TABLE 5.9. Number of Persons Executed for 50 States and the District of Columbia, 1930–1990**

| State | Number of Persons Executed | $(x - \bar{x})$ | $(x - \bar{x})^2$ | $(x^2)$ |
|---|---|---|---|---|
| Georgia | 380 | $(380 - 78)$ | 91,204 | 144,400 |
| Texas | 334 | $(334 - 78)$ | 65,536 | 111,556 |
| New York | 329 | $(329 - 78)$ | 63,001 | 108,241 |
| California | 292 | $(292 - 78)$ | 45,796 | 85,264 |
| North Carolina | 266 | $(266 - 78)$ | 35,344 | 70,756 |
| Florida | 195 | $(195 - 78)$ | 13,689 | 38,025 |
| Ohio | 172 | $(172 - 78)$ | 8836 | 29,584 |
| South Carolina | 165 | $(165 - 78)$ | 7569 | 27,225 |
| Mississippi | 158 | $(158 - 78)$ | 6400 | 24,964 |
| Pennsylvania | 152 | $(152 - 78)$ | 5476 | 23,104 |
| Louisiana | 152 | $(152 - 78)$ | 5476 | 23,104 |
| Alabama | 143 | $(143 - 78)$ | 4225 | 20,449 |
| Arkansas | 120 | $(120 - 78)$ | 1764 | 14,400 |
| Kentucky | 103 | $(103 - 78)$ | 625 | 10,609 |
| Virginia | 103 | $(103 - 78)$ | 625 | 10,609 |
| Tennessee | 93 | $(93 - 78)$ | 225 | 8649 |
| Illinois | 91 | $(91 - 78)$ | 169 | 8281 |
| New Jersey | 74 | $(74 - 78)$ | 16 | 5476 |
| Maryland | 68 | $(68 - 78)$ | 100 | 4624 |
| Missouri | 67 | $(67 - 78)$ | 121 | 4489 |
| Oklahoma | 61 | $(61 - 78)$ | 289 | 3721 |
| Washington | 47 | $(47 - 78)$ | 961 | 2209 |
| Colorado | 47 | $(47 - 78)$ | 961 | 2209 |
| Indiana | 43 | $(43 - 78)$ | 1225 | 1849 |
| West Virginia | 40 | $(40 - 78)$ | 1444 | 1600 |
| District of Columbia | 40 | $(40 - 78)$ | 1444 | 1600 |
| Arizona | 38 | $(38 - 78)$ | 1600 | 1444 |
| Nevada | 34 | $(34 - 78)$ | 1936 | 1156 |
| Massachusetts | 27 | $(27 - 78)$ | 2601 | 729 |
| Connecticut | 21 | $(21 - 78)$ | 3249 | 441 |
| Oregon | 19 | $(19 - 78)$ | 3481 | 361 |
| Iowa | 18 | $(18 - 78)$ | 3600 | 324 |
| Utah | 16 | $(16 - 78)$ | 3844 | 256 |
| Kansas | 15 | $(15 - 78)$ | 3969 | 225 |
| Delaware | 12 | $(12 - 78)$ | 4356 | 144 |
| New Mexico | 8 | $(8 - 78)$ | 4900 | 64 |
| Wyoming | 7 | $(7 - 78)$ | 5041 | 49 |
| Montana | 6 | $(6 - 78)$ | 5184 | 36 |
| Vermont | 4 | $(4 - 78)$ | 5476 | 16 |
| Nebraska | 4 | $(4 - 78)$ | 5476 | 16 |
| Idaho | 3 | $(3 - 78)$ | 5625 | 9 |
| South Dakota | 1 | $(1 - 78)$ | 5929 | 1 |
| New Hampshire | 1 | $(1 - 78)$ | 5929 | 1 |
| Wisconsin | 0 | $(0 - 78)$ | 6084 | 0 |
| Rhode Island | 0 | $(0 - 78)$ | 6084 | 0 |
| North Dakota | 0 | $(0 - 78)$ | 6084 | 0 |
| Minnesota | 0 | $(0 - 78)$ | 6084 | 0 |
| Michigan | 0 | $(0 - 78)$ | 6084 | 0 |
| Maine | 0 | $(0 - 78)$ | 6084 | 0 |
| Hawaii | 0 | $(0 - 78)$ | 6084 | 0 |
| Alaska | 0 | $(0 - 78)$ | 6084 | 0 |
| | $\Sigma = 3969$ | $\Sigma = 0$ | $\Sigma = 483,389$ | $\Sigma = 792,269$ |

You have probably by now figured out that the variance and standard deviation can be quite cumbersome to calculate by hand because you have to subtract each and every score from the mean, square it, and sum across all scores. Moreover, the calculations can become even more tedious when there are large numbers or decimals involved (we avoided the latter in the example by rounding the mean to 78). Now imagine how difficult it would be if there were a large number of scores, or if there were many numbers with decimals! To avoid the tedious and error-prone calculations involved in determining the squared deviations from the mean, alternative computational formulas for determining the variance and standard deviation can be used.

The following are computational formulas for the variance and standard deviation:

$$\text{Variance} = S^2 = \frac{\Sigma x^2 - \frac{(\Sigma x)^2}{N}}{N} \tag{5.10}$$

$$\text{Standard Deviation} = S = \sqrt{\frac{\Sigma x^2 - \frac{(\Sigma x)^2}{N}}{N}}$$

where

$\Sigma x^2$ = the sum of each squared $x$ score
$(\Sigma x)^2$ = the sum of the $x$ scores squared
$N$ = the total number of scores

The computational formulas require that we obtain three quantities. The first of these quantities ($\Sigma x^2$) is the sum of the squared scores. To get this, we first square each $x$ score and then add up these squared values ($x_1^2 + x_2^2 + \cdots + x_n^2$). The second quantity ($\Sigma x^2$) is the sum of the $x$ scores squared. To obtain this value, we first sum all of the scores and then square this sum ($[x_1 + x_2 \cdots + x_n]^2$). The third quantity is the total number of scores ($N$). The computational formulas may not seem as intuitive as the definitional formulas, but they are far simpler to use. Rather than taking the square of the deviations from the means, all we have to do is to take the square of the raw scores and the sum of the raw scores squared.

We now use these formulas to calculate the variance and standard deviation of the data in Table 5.9. The last column of that table provides the square of each score. The steps in the computational formulas are shown in the box below.

---

**Step 1.** Square each score and sum the squares.
**Step 2.** Add all the scores together, square this value, and divide by the total number of scores.
**Step 3.** Subtract the value in step 2 from the value in step 1.
**Step 4.** Divide by the total number of scores. This is the variance.
**Step 5.** Take the square root. This is the standard deviation.

---

For the data in Table 5.9, we have the following calculations:

$$\text{Variance} = \frac{792{,}269 - \dfrac{(3969)^2}{51}}{51}$$

$$= \frac{792{,}269 - 308{,}882}{51}$$

$$= \frac{483{,}387}{51}$$

$$= 9478$$

$$\text{Standard Deviation} = \sqrt{\text{Variance}}$$

$$= \sqrt{9478}$$

$$= 97$$

Note that the estimated values of the variance and standard deviation found with the computational formulas are comparable to those found with the longer and more cumbersome mean-square or definitional formulas.

## Calculation of Variance and Standard Deviation from Grouped Data

You will remember that when we calculate the mean from grouped data, we treat each case as if it were at the midpoint of the interval it is in. Then, to obtain the mean we multiply the number of cases in the interval ($f$, or the frequency) by the midpoint, sum each of these products, and divide by the total number of cases ($N$). We follow this procedure in calculating the variance and standard deviation from grouped data, using the following definitional formula:

$$\text{Variance} = \frac{\displaystyle\sum_{i=1}^{k} f_i(m_i - \bar{x})^2}{N}$$

$$\text{Standard Deviation} = \sqrt{\frac{\displaystyle\sum_{i=1}^{k} f_i(m_i - \bar{x})^2}{N}} \qquad (5.11)$$

where
$f$ = the frequency of the $i$th interval
$m_i$ = the midpoint of the $i$th interval
$N$ = the total number of cases

Let us first describe this formula in words. To calculate the variance with this formula, we must first determine the midpoint of each interval ($m_i$). This midpoint then becomes the score for all of the cases that are within the interval; that is, all

> **Step 1.** Calculate the mean (in this case the mean rate of violent crime is 1567 per 100,000 population).
> **Step 2.** Determine the midpoint of each interval.
> **Step 3.** Subtract the mean from the midpoint of each interval.
> **Step 4.** Square this value.
> **Step 5.** Multiply this by the frequency of the interval.
> **Step 6.** Sum these values across all intervals.
> **Step 7.** Divide by the total number of cases (*N*), *not* the number of intervals. This value is the variance.
> **Step 8.** Take the square root of this number. This value is the standard deviation.

scores within that given interval are treated as if they were at the midpoint. Once we have the midpoint for an interval, we subtract the mean from this midpoint ($m_i - \bar{x}$). This is the same as subtracting the mean from a given score because the midpoint is taken as the score for each observation in that interval. Then, square this difference ($[m_i - \bar{x}^2]$). Multiply this number by the frequency of the interval because we have to subtract the mean from the midpoint of every case in the interval, or *f* number of times. Then, divide by the total number of cases (not the number of intervals). The result of this operation is the variance. To calculate the standard deviation, we then take the square root of this variance.

To illustrate these formulas, we use the grouped data in Table 5.10 and calculate the variance and standard deviation. The table reports the violent crime rate (per 100,000 population) for 60 U.S. cities with a population over 250,000. The steps involved in the calculations are listed in the box on this page.

For the data in Table 5.10, we obtain the following results:

$$f(m_i - \bar{x})^2 = 43,984,651$$

$$\frac{f(m_i - \bar{x})^2}{N} = \frac{43,984,651}{60}$$

Variance = 733,077

Standard Deviation = $\sqrt{\text{Variance}} = \sqrt{733,077} = 856$

The variance for these data is 733,077 and the standard deviation is 856.

Before we discuss in more detail the interpretation of the variance and standard deviation, we should also examine the corresponding computational formulas for the variance and standard deviation with grouped data. As with ungrouped data, these computational formulas will make your calculations less cumbersome. The computational formulas for grouped data are derivatives of those for ungrouped data. To refresh your memory, the ungrouped data formulas were:

$$\text{Variance} = \frac{\Sigma x^2 - \frac{(\Sigma x)^2}{N}}{N}$$

**TABLE 5.10. Violent Crime Rate (per 100,000 population) for U.S. Cities over 250,000—Calculating the Variance and Standard Deviation**

| Violent Crime Rate | $f$ | Midpoint ($m$) | $(m - \bar{x})$ | $(m - \bar{x})^2$ | $f(m - \bar{x})^2$ |
|---|---|---|---|---|---|
| 0–500 | 1 | 250 | 250–1567 | 1,734,489.00 | 1,734,489.00 |
| 501–1000 | 15 | 750.5 | 750.5–1567 | 6,666,672.25 | 10,000,083.00 |
| 1001–1500 | 20 | 1250.5 | 1250.5–1567 | 100,172.25 | 2,003,445.00 |
| 1501–2000 | 9 | 1750.5 | 1750.5–1567 | 33,672.25 | 303,050.25 |
| 2001–2500 | 8 | 2250.5 | 2250.5–1567 | 467,172.25 | 3,737,378.00 |
| 2501–3000 | 3 | 2750.5 | 2750.5–1567 | 1,400,672.25 | 4,202,016.75 |
| 3001–3500 | 1 | 3250.5 | 3250.5–1567 | 2,834,172.25 | 2,834,172.25 |
| 3501–4000 | 1 | 3750.5 | 3750.5–1567 | 4,767,672.25 | 4,767,672.25 |
| 4001–4500 | 2 | 4250.5 | 4250.5–1567 | 7,201,172.25 | 14,402,344.50 |
| | | | | | $\Sigma = 43,984,651$ |

$$\text{Standard Deviation} = \sqrt{\frac{\Sigma x^2 - \frac{(\Sigma x)^2}{N}}{N}}$$

We use a similar formula for the standard deviation and variance when our data happen to be in groups or intervals. For grouped data, however, the scores within each interval are all treated as if they were at the midpoint of the interval. Thus, all cases within a given interval have the same value of $x$ — the midpoint ($m$) of the interval ($x - m$). Moreover, we can take advantage of the fact that, if we have $n$ scores within a given interval, we can quickly sum them by multiplying the frequency in the interval by the midpoint of the interval ($fm$). Hence, the scores are the midpoints of the intervals, and the sum of the scores is the sum of the midpoint ($m$) of each interval times the frequency ($f$) of the interval ($mf$). We can now rewrite the equation as follows:

$$\text{Variance} = \frac{\Sigma f(m^2) - \frac{(\Sigma fm)^2}{N}}{N}$$

$$\text{Standard Deviation} = \sqrt{\frac{\Sigma f(m^2) - \frac{(\Sigma fm)^2}{N}}{N}} \qquad (5.12)$$

We now use the computational formulas to calculate the variance and standard deviation for the grouped data in Table 5.10. The necessary calculations are shown in Table 5.11. First, we calculate the sum of the $x$ scores, which with grouped data is the sum of each midpoint times the frequency of the interval ($\Sigma x = \Sigma mf = 94,029.5$). Then, as the midpoint is taken as the score for its respective interval, we determine the sum of the $x^2$'s by squaring the value of each midpoint, multiplying

**TABLE 5.11. Use of Computational Formula in Calculating Variance and Standard Deviation from Grouped Data in Table 5.10**

| Midpoint (m) | Frequency (f) | mf | m² | fm² |
|---|---|---|---|---|
| 250.0 | 1 | 250.0 | 62,500.00 | 62,500 |
| 750.5 | 15 | 11,257.5 | 563,250.25 | 8,448,754 |
| 1250.5 | 20 | 25,010.0 | 1,563,750.25 | 31,275,005 |
| 1750.5 | 9 | 15,754.5 | 3,064,250.25 | 27,578,252 |
| 2250.5 | 8 | 18,004.0 | 5,064,750.25 | 40,518,002 |
| 2750.5 | 3 | 8251.5 | 7,565,250.25 | 22,695,751 |
| 3250.5 | 1 | 3250.5 | 10,565,750.25 | 10,565,750 |
| 3750.5 | 1 | 3750.5 | 14,066,250.25 | 14,066,250 |
| 4250.5 | 2 | 8501.0 | 18,066,750.25 | 36,133,500 |
| | $\Sigma = 60$ | 94,029.5 | | $\Sigma = 191,343,764$ |

by the frequency of the interval, and summing ($\Sigma fm^2$). Finally, we can "plug" these numbers into our formulas:

$$\text{Variance} = \frac{191{,}343{,}764 - \dfrac{(94{,}029.5)^2}{60}}{60}$$

$$= \frac{43{,}984{,}649.5}{60}$$

$$= 733{,}077$$

$$\text{Standard Deviation} = \sqrt{\text{Variance}} = \sqrt{733{,}077} = 856$$

We can now see that the values of the variance (733,077) and standard deviation (856) that we have obtained from our computational formulas are identical to what we found with the definitional or mean-square formula.

## Interpretation of the Variance and Standard Deviation

The variance and standard deviation are measures of variability or dispersion in our data, such that the larger these two values are, the less homogeneous our data are (i.e., they do not cluster very tightly around the mean). So, we know that the greater the variance and standard deviation, the greater the variability of our scores around the mean. This statement is not all that helpful, however, because the magnitude of the variance and standard deviation is a function of a variable's unit of measurement. If two variables are measured in the same unit, we can directly compare the size of their respective variances and standard deviations. For example, if the standard deviation for the distribution of homicide rates from 1900 to 1990 is larger for Texas than for Minnesota, we would know that homicide rates varied over the years more in Texas than in Minnesota. If two variables are measured in different units, however, we cannot directly compare their standard deviations. The same income distribution measured in pennies, for example, will have a much higher variance and standard deviation than one measured in dollars (the former will be 100 times higher). If two variables are measured in different units, therefore, we may not easily be able to determine which distribution is more dispersed.

In order to compare the standard deviations of variables that have different units of measurement, you could calculate the *coefficient of variation*. The coefficient of variation is defined as the ratio of the standard deviation of a variable to its mean ($s/\bar{x}$). In this manner, the standard deviation is "standardized" by dividing it by its mean. The larger this ratio, the more disperse the data. For example, assume that we have the distributions of two variables: age in years and age in months. The standard deviation for the first age distribution is 9.3 years with a mean of 30. The standard deviation for the second distribution is 72 months with a mean of 276. The coefficient of variation for the first distribution is 9.3/30 = .31. The coefficient of variation for the second distribution is 72/276 = .26. Comparing the magnitude of these two coefficients, we can see that there is more variation in the first distribution than in the second. You can use the coefficient of variation to compare standard deviations of different variables, such as age with income or with number of arrests.

But what else does the variance and standard deviation tell us? What can we tell, for example, if we know that a distribution of scores has a mean of 10 and a standard deviation of 3 (and therefore a variance of 9)? Other than in terms of more or less variability, how do we make sense of these two measures of dispersion?

Unfortunately, there is not much more we can say about the variance. We have already noted that the variance is difficult to interpret because squaring the standard deviation of each score from the mean changes the metric or the level of measurement of our variable. The concept of the variance is valuable for statisticians, but it is of less interest to us. Because the standard deviation, by taking the square root of the variance, retains our original level of measurement and because of its relationship to *normal distributions,* we can have a more definitive and clear understanding of it.

We discuss the normal distribution in more detail in subsequent chapters of this book (especially in Chapter 8, which is devoted to the normal distribution and standard normal, or *z,* scores). For now, however, we think of the normal distribution as a symmetrical, unimodal distribution. That is, if we drew a horizontal line down the middle curve, each half of the curve would be the perfect mirror image of the other. This means that the greatest proportion of the cases falls in the middle of the distribution (the mean, median, and mode are the same) with fewer cases lying at either of the two ends, or "tails," of the distribution. This normal distribution looks somewhat like a bell and is often called the bell-shaped distribution or the bell-shaped curve (Figure 5.2). One thing to remember is that a normal distribution refers to the properties of the distribution, not its content, so that we could have a normal distribution of persons' height, weight, IQ scores, income. Figure 5.2 shows a special kind of normal distribution called the standard normal distribution. This standard normal distribution has all the properties of any other normal distribution (bell-shaped, unimodal, etc.), and it has a population mean of zero and a standard deviation of 1. We talk more about the standard normal distribution in Chapter 8.

When using the standard normal distribution to think about the standard deviation, the area under the curve includes 100 percent of the cases in a distribution. Think of it, then, as a type of frequency distribution in which all of the cases lie under the curve. An important property of the normal distribution is that, no matter what the particular value of its mean or standard deviation, there is a constant or fixed proportion of cases between the mean and a point that is a given standard deviation away from the mean. Figure 5.3 shows the area under the normal curve in terms of the proportion of cases that fall within a given standard deviation unit away from the mean.

We can see that, if we move one standard deviation to the right of the mean (that is, the mean + 1 standard deviation unit), we will find approximately 34

FIGURE 5.2. Illustration of a normal distribution.

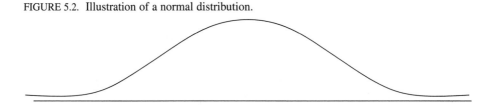

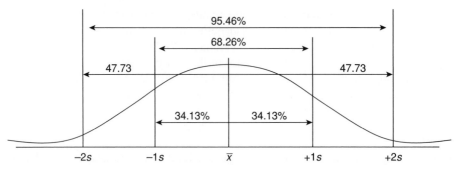

FIGURE 5.3. Areas under the normal curve.

percent, or .34 of our total number of cases. If we move one standard deviation to the left of the mean (the mean $-$ 1 standard deviation unit), we will find another .34 of our cases. Therefore, approximately .68, or 68 percent, of the total number of observations in a normal distribution lie within $\pm$ 1 standard deviations of the mean. If we move two standard deviations to the right of the mean, we will find approximately 47 percent of our cases, and another 47 percent two standard deviations to the left of the mean. Thus, slightly more than 95 percent of our cases can be found within $\pm$ 2 standard deviations. You can now see that almost all of our cases will lie within three standard deviations of the mean (99 percent).

If we know, then, that a score is two standard deviations above the mean of its distribution and that the scores can be assumed to be normally distributed, we know that it is an extremely rare score because it is greater than 95 percent of all the scores. For example, we know that in a given distribution of IQ scores that are presumed to be normally distributed with a mean of 100 and a standard deviation of 10, an IQ of 60 is fairly rare, because it lies four standard deviations away from the mean. In examining the normal curve and the distribution of cases in Figure 5.3, we know that very few persons will have IQ scores that low. One thing we can learn, therefore, from the standard deviation and our knowledge of the normal distribution, is the probability of a given score occurring. We will learn more about deviations from the mean and standard deviation units in subsequent chapters when we discuss hypothesis testing.

## 5.6 SUMMARY

In this chapter we have learned about measures of dispersion. Measures of dispersion tell us how variable or different our scores are from one another. Just as the correct measure of central tendency depends on the level of measurement of our variables, so does the correct measure of dispersion. When our data are at the nominal level our question about dispersion concerns how qualitatively different our data are. In this case the appropriate measure of dispersion is the *index of qualitative variation (IQV)* or the *variation ratio (VR)*. When our data are at the ordinal level or higher we can estimate the *range* or *interquartile range*. Finally, when our data are at the interval or ratio level, where the calculation of a mean is meaningful, we can employ mean-based measures of dispersion such as the *mean deviation,* the *variance,* and the *standard deviation.*

# Key Terms

| | |
|---|---|
| absolute value | normal distribution |
| interquartile range (IQR) | range |
| index of qualitative variation (IQV) | standard deviation |
| mean deviation | variance |
| measures of dispersion | variation ratio (VR) |

# Problems

**1.** As part of the National Survey of Youth, a nationwide study of juvenile delinquency and drug use, Delbert Elliott (1985) and his colleagues asked his adolescent respondents to describe how their classmates saw them. The following data represent their responses:

| | Males ($f$) | Females ($f$) |
|---|---|---|
| Athlete | 158 | 62 |
| Activities member | 34 | 46 |
| Social type | 162 | 197 |
| Good student | 205 | 223 |
| Average student | 284 | 223 |
| Total | 843 | 751 |

Using either raw frequencies or percentages, calculate the IQV for the male and female distribution. For which gender is there greater variability in how they feel they are perceived by peers?

**2.** The following data represent the number of offenders sentenced to death from 1968 to 1990.

| Year | $f$ | Year | $f$ |
|---|---|---|---|
| 1968 | 138 | 1980 | 198 |
| 1969 | 143 | 1981 | 245 |
| 1970 | 133 | 1982 | 264 |
| 1971 | 113 | 1983 | 259 |
| 1972 | 83 | 1984 | 280 |
| 1973 | 42 | 1985 | 273 |
| 1974 | 167 | 1986 | 297 |
| 1975 | 322 | 1987 | 299 |
| 1976 | 249 | 1988 | 296 |
| 1977 | 159 | 1989 | 251 |
| 1978 | 209 | 1990 | 244 |
| 1979 | 172 | | |

   **a.** Find the range.
   **b.** Find the interquartile range.
   **c.** Find the variance and standard deviation.

**3.** Calculate the range, the standard deviation, and the variance for the two columns of city homicide rate data in Table 4.4 (p. 88).

**4.** In the following data, youths arrested for a property offense, violent offense, drug offense, or a status offense were asked what type of crime their previous offense was. As you can see, of the 125 youths whose current offense was a property offense, 75 of them committed a property offense the last time, 10 committed a violent offense, 20 a drug crime, and 20 a status offense. Calculate the IQV and VR for each type of current offense. Which type of offense has the most variation? the least variation?

| Last Offense | Current Offense | | | |
|---|---|---|---|---|
| | Property | Violent | Drug | Status |
| Property | 75 | 50 | 40 | 120 |
| Violent | 10 | 30 | 30 | 20 |
| Drug | 20 | 10 | 110 | 115 |
| Status | 20 | 20 | 50 | 320 |
| Total | 125 | 110 | 230 | 575 |

5. A group of 205 high school males were asked to report the number of times in the past year that they had stolen something that was worth at least $25 in value. Their responses are shown in the following intervals. For these data, determine the standard deviation and variance.

| Number of Thefts | Frequency |
|---|---|
| 0–4 | 76 |
| 5–9 | 52 |
| 10–14 | 38 |
| 15–19 | 21 |
| 20–24 | 10 |
| 25–29 | 8 |
| Total | 205 |

6. The following data show the 1991 arrest rate for rape (per 100,000 persons) for a sample of 18 states. For these data, determine:

| State | 1991 Arrest Rate for Rape (per 100,000) |
|---|---|
| Arizona | 42.4 |
| Arkansas | 44.6 |
| Colorado | 47.0 |
| Georgia | 42.3 |
| Illinois | 40.0 |
| Kentucky | 35.4 |
| Louisiana | 40.9 |
| Maryland | 45.9 |
| Missouri | 34.0 |
| New York | 28.2 |
| North Carolina | 34.6 |
| North Dakota | 18.3 |
| Oregon | 53.4 |
| Pennsylvania | 28.7 |
| South Carolina | 58.9 |
| Texas | 53.4 |
| Utah | 45.6 |
| Wyoming | 25.9 |

a. The range
b. The interquartile range
c. The standard deviation
d. The variance

## Solutions to Problems

1. The value of the IQV for the males is:

$$\text{Males IQV} = \frac{267{,}802}{284{,}259.6} \times 100 = 94.21$$

The value of the IQV for the females is:

$$\text{Females IQV} = \frac{209{,}887}{225{,}600.4} \times 100 = 93.03$$

The two groups display approximately the same amount of variability.

2. a. The range is $322 - 42 = 280$ executions.
   b. The interquartile range is:

   $$\text{IQR} = 268.5 - 151 = 117.5$$

   c. We use the computational formula (formula 5.10) to determine the variance and standard variation:

   $$\text{Variance} = \frac{1{,}147{,}422 - \dfrac{23{,}386{,}896}{23}}{23}$$

   $$= \frac{1{,}147{,}422 - 1{,}016{,}821.56}{23}$$

   $$= \frac{130{,}600.44}{23}$$

   $$= 5678.28$$

   $$\text{Standard Deviation} = \sqrt{5678.28} = 75.35$$

3. The range is equal to $14.7 - 9.7 = 5$ for the first column of cities, and $80.1 - 9.7 = 70.4$ for the second column.

   The standard deviation and variance for the first column of cities are equal to:

   $$\text{Variance} = \frac{1340.46 - \dfrac{11{,}837.44}{9}}{9}$$

   $$= \frac{1340.46 - 1315.27}{9}$$

   $$= \frac{25.19}{9}$$

   $$= 2.80$$

   $$\text{Standard Deviation} = \sqrt{2.80} = 1.67$$

The standard deviation and variance for the second column of cities are equal to:

$$\text{Variance} = \cfrac{7756.47 - \cfrac{35{,}683.21}{10}}{10}$$

$$= \frac{7756.47 - 3568.32}{10}$$

$$= 4188.15/10$$

$$= 418.82$$

$$\text{Standard Deviation} = \sqrt{418.82} = 20.46$$

4. The IQV for property offenders is:

$$\text{IQV} = \frac{4550}{5859.36} \times 100 = 77.65$$

For violent offenders:

$$\text{IQV} = \frac{4100}{4537.5} \times 100 = 90.36$$

For drug offenders:

$$\text{IQV} = \frac{17{,}900}{19{,}837.5} \times 100 = 90.23$$

For status offenders:

$$\text{IQV} = \frac{100{,}100}{123{,}984.37} \times 100 = 80.73$$

The greatest variability is found for violent and drug offenders followed by status and property offenders. The variation ratios for each offense are as follows:

$$\text{Variation Ratio}_{property} = 1 - \frac{75}{125} = .40$$

$$\text{Variation Ratio}_{violent} = 1 - \frac{50}{110} = .54$$

$$\text{Variation Ratio}_{drug} = 1 - \frac{110}{230} = .52$$

$$\text{Variation Ratio}_{status} = 1 - \frac{320}{575} = .44$$

According to the variation ratio, violent and drug offenders evidence the greatest variation. A smaller proportion of their cases fall at the mode than for property and drug offenders.

**5.** The standard deviation and variance are:

$$\text{Variance} = \frac{25{,}065 - \dfrac{(1765)^2}{205}}{205}$$

$$= \frac{25{,}065 - 15{,}196.22}{205}$$

$$= 48.14$$

$$\text{Standard Deviation} = \sqrt{48.14} = 6.94$$

**6. a.** The range is:

$58.9 - 18.3 = 40.6$

**b.** The interquartile range is:

$\text{IQR} = 45.9 - 34.0 = 11.9$

**c.** The standard deviation is:

$$\text{Standard Deviation} = \sqrt{\frac{30{,}647.47 - \dfrac{(719.5)^2}{18}}{18}}$$

$$= \sqrt{\frac{30{,}647.47 - 28{,}760.01}{18}}$$

$$= \sqrt{\frac{1887.46}{18}}$$

$$= \sqrt{104.86}$$

$$= 10.24$$

**d.** Knowing what the standard deviation is, we can easily determine the variance:

$\text{Variance} = (\text{standard deviation})^2 = (10.24)^2 = 104.86$

# CHAPTER 6

# Exploratory Data Analysis

*Exploratory data analysis is a state of mind, a way of thinking about data analysis—and also a way of doing it . . . the exploratory approach to data analysis seeks to maximize what is learned from the data, and this requires adherence to two principles: skepticism and openness. One should be skeptical of measures which summarize data since they can sometimes conceal or even misrepresent what may be the most informative aspects of the data, and one should be open to unanticipated patterns in the data since they can be the most revealing outcomes of the analysis.*

—HARTWIG AND DEARING

## 6.1 INTRODUCTION

In the preceding three chapters, we have examined the more traditional techniques used to determine what data distributions look like. In this chapter, we are also concerned with exploring the shape of our distributions, but we will go about the task somewhat differently. We are going to use a class of techniques originally developed by the statistician John W. Tukey (1977) that are subsumed under the name *exploratory data analysis* (EDA). The name is fitting because this is what Tukey intended when he developed this type of analysis. The techniques of EDA allow us to "explore" the distribution of the variables in our data set; they facilitate our understanding of what our distributions look like, what abnormalities might be present (e.g., outliers), and what secrets they might hold.

Although EDA techniques have been around since the 1970s, they have only recently begun to be routinely used by researchers, primarily because most statistical software packages did not have the capability of performing them. Today, however, we can perform many EDA techniques with several popular statistical software packages, including SPSS. These new computer applications have increased the use of EDA in contemporary research.

In this chapter, we focus on two of the most widely used EDA techniques: *stem-and-leaf displays* and *boxplots*. It is difficult to categorize these techniques in any conventional way because they are both graphical and numerical. They offer visual displays of the data and, in addition, provide the analyst with numerical information about the distribution's center, spread, and outliers. The novelty of EDA, however, is that all of this information is available at a glance. EDA is a great way to get up close and personal with your data!

## 6.2 STEM-AND-LEAF DISPLAYS

Although the name "stem-and-leaf display" sounds more botanical than statistical, the statistical reasoning behind it becomes apparent when we begin to construct one. This technique utilizes every data point in a variable distribution to draw a picture. From this picture, we can easily determine many things about our distribution, including:

1. The range of values in our variable distribution
2. Where the majority of our data points lie (the center)
3. The shape of our distribution (symmetrical or skewed)
4. The existence of gaps or outliers in our distribution.

To illustrate the construction of a stem-and-leaf display, let's utilize data from Tables 6.1 and 6.2. Table 6.1 displays two kinds of adjudication data for felony arrests from 34 urban counties in the United States, the percent of all felony cases in each county that were disposed of within the first year, and the percent of the disposed cases in each county that resulted in a conviction. Using this same data set, Table 6.2 displays the percent of all convictions for each county that resulted in either felony or misdemeanor charges.

The first step necessary to begin constructing a stem-and-leaf display is to rank-order the distribution in ascending order. As you can see, this has already been done in each of the tables. With data sorted in this way, it is easy to ascertain the range of the distribution, and this makes the subsequent steps of stem-and-leaf construction much easier.

Because we already have our data ordered in Table 6.1, we can move on to the next step in constructing our stems and our leaves. The stems of a display generally list the first digit of a value, and the leaves generally list each value's subsequent digits. This jargon is probably very confusing right now. It would be best to begin by showing you what a complete stem-and-leaf display actually looks like and then go over the steps.

Figure 6.1 presents a complete stem-and-leaf display of the variable found in the second column of numbers in Table 6.1: percent of felony arrests that resulted in a conviction within 1 year (labeled as Percent Convicted in Table 6.1). The first column of numbers in Figure 6.1 ($f$) simply represents the frequency of cases in each row. The second column of numbers represent the stems, and the remaining columns after that represent each of the leaves.

Remember that the first step was to place this distribution in ascending order. The next step in constructing a display is to decide which digits from the data points will represent the stems and which will represent the leaves. In this example, this was a very easy decision to make because there were only two digits in each data point. We simply used the first digit in each case to represent the stem and the remaining digit to represent each leaf. So, for example, for the case of Suffolk, MA, where 32 percent of adjudicated cases resulted in a conviction, the 3 was our stem and the 2 our leaf. Next, simply split each data point in the distribution into a stem portion and a leaf portion and then fill out your display giving each value in the variable distribution a place in the display.

144   CHAPTER 6

**TABLE 6.1. Percent of Felony Arrests Adjudicated and Percent Resulting in a Conviction, 34 Counties, 1990**

| Rank | County | State | Percent Adjudicated in 1 Year | County | State | Percent Convicted |
|---|---|---|---|---|---|---|
| 1 | St. Louis | MO | 56.00 | Suffolk | MA | 32.00 |
| 2 | Tarrant | TX | 69.00 | Erie | NY | 37.00 |
| 3 | Essex | MA | 73.00 | Dade | FL | 39.00 |
| 4 | Philadelphia | PA | 73.00 | Cook | IL | 48.00 |
| 5 | Suffolk | MA | 76.00 | Philadelphia | PA | 51.00 |
| 6 | Shelby | TN | 77.00 | Dallas | TX | 54.00 |
| 7 | Bronx | NY | 81.00 | Tarrant | TX | 55.00 |
| 8 | Washington | DC | 83.00 | Washington | DC | 56.00 |
| 9 | Fulton | GA | 85.00 | Essex | MA | 59.00 |
| 10 | Cook | IL | 87.00 | New York | NY | 60.00 |
| 11 | Kings | NY | 87.00 | Broward | FL | 61.00 |
| 12 | New York | NY | 87.00 | Wayne | MI | 62.00 |
| 13 | Queens | NY | 88.00 | Kings | NY | 63.00 |
| 14 | Orange | CA | 90.00 | Queens | NY | 64.00 |
| 15 | Allegheny | PA | 90.00 | St. Louis | MO | 65.00 |
| 16 | Erie | NY | 91.00 | Bronx | NY | 66.00 |
| 17 | Los Angeles | CA | 93.00 | Duval | FL | 68.00 |
| 18 | Sacramento | CA | 94.00 | Fairfax | VA | 69.00 |
| 19 | San Bernardino | CA | 94.00 | Harris | TX | 70.00 |
| 20 | Hills | FL | 94.00 | Hamilton | OH | 72.00 |
| 21 | Wayne | MI | 94.00 | Los Angeles | CA | 73.00 |
| 22 | Dade | FL | 95.00 | Sacramento | CA | 73.00 |
| 23 | King | WA | 95.00 | Salt Lake City | UT | 76.00 |
| 24 | Santa Clara | CA | 96.00 | Palm Beach | FL | 77.00 |
| 25 | Broward | FL | 96.00 | San Bernardino | CA | 78.00 |
| 26 | Harris | TX | 96.00 | King | WA | 79.00 |
| 27 | Fairfax | VA | 96.00 | Shelby | TN | 82.00 |
| 28 | Maricopa | AZ | 97.00 | Fulton | GA | 82.00 |
| 29 | San Diego | CA | 97.00 | Hills | FL | 82.00 |
| 30 | Duval | FL | 97.00 | Orange | CA | 83.00 |
| 31 | Hamilton | OH | 97.00 | San Diego | CA | 83.00 |
| 32 | Dallas | TX | 97.00 | Maricopa | AZ | 85.00 |
| 33 | Salt Lake City | UT | 97.00 | Allegheny | PA | 86.00 |
| 34 | Palm Beach | FL | 100.00 | Santa Clara | CA | 86.00 |

*Source:* Adapted from P. Z. Smith (1993), *Felony Defendants in Large Urban Counties, 1990* (Publication #NCJ-141872), Bureau of Justice Statistics, U.S. Department of Justice, Washington, DC: U.S. Government Printing Office, Appendix table E.

The bottom of Figure 6.1 displays a legend that gives readers the information necessary to interpret the display. The legend tells readers that the stem width in the display is equal to 10. This indicates that a value of 1 would be equal to 10, a value of 3 would be equal to 30, a value of 4 would be equal to 40, and so on. The legend also indicates that each leaf value represents one case. Therefore, a value

**TABLE 6.2. Percent of Felony Arrest Convictions That Resulted in a Felony Charge and Percent That Resulted in a Misdemeanor Charge, 34 Counties, 1990**

| Rank | County | State | Percent Felony | County | State | Percent Misdemeanor |
|---|---|---|---|---|---|---|
| 1 | Erie | NY | 21.00 | Tarrant | TX | .00 |
| 2 | Washington | DC | 21.00 | Broward | FL | .00 |
| 3 | Kings | NY | 26.00 | Essex | MA | 1.00 |
| 4 | Suffolk | MA | 28.00 | Wayne | MI | 1.00 |
| 5 | New York | NY | 28.00 | Cook | IL | 3.00 |
| 6 | Bronx | NY | 28.00 | Philadelphia | PA | 3.00 |
| 7 | Fairfax | VA | 31.00 | King | WA | 3.00 |
| 8 | Dade | FL | 35.00 | Suffolk | MA | 4.00 |
| 9 | Queens | NY | 37.00 | Harris | TX | 4.00 |
| 10 | Palm Beach | FL | 41.00 | Los Angeles | CA | 4.00 |
| 11 | Cook | IL | 45.00 | San Diego | CA | 4.00 |
| 12 | Hamilton | OH | 45.00 | St. Louis | MO | 5.00 |
| 13 | Philadelphia | PA | 47.00 | Fulton | GA | 5.00 |
| 14 | Shelby | TN | 47.00 | Hills | FL | 5.00 |
| 15 | Dallas | TX | 48.00 | Dallas | TX | 6.00 |
| 16 | Salt Lake City | UT | 48.00 | San Bernardino | CA | 8.00 |
| 17 | Duval | FL | 51.00 | Dade | FL | 11.00 |
| 18 | Tarrant | TX | 55.00 | Sacramento | CA | 11.00 |
| 19 | Essex | MA | 58.00 | Orange | CA | 11.00 |
| 20 | Allegheny | PA | 58.00 | Maricopa | AZ | 15.00 |
| 21 | St. Louis | MO | 60.00 | Erie | NY | 16.00 |
| 22 | Broward | FL | 61.00 | Santa Clara | CA | 16.00 |
| 23 | Wayne | MI | 61.00 | Duval | FL | 17.00 |
| 24 | Sacramento | CA | 62.00 | Queens | NY | 26.00 |
| 25 | Harris | TX | 65.00 | Hamilton | OH | 27.00 |
| 26 | Los Angeles | CA | 69.00 | Salt Lake City | UT | 28.00 |
| 27 | Maricopa | AZ | 69.00 | Allegheny | PA | 28.00 |
| 28 | San Bernardino | CA | 70.00 | New York | NY | 32.00 |
| 29 | Santa Clara | CA | 70.00 | Washington | DC | 35.00 |
| 30 | Orange | CA | 72.00 | Shelby | TN | 35.00 |
| 31 | King | WA | 76.00 | Palm Beach | FL | 36.00 |
| 32 | Fulton | GA | 76.00 | Kings | NY | 38.00 |
| 33 | Hills | FL | 77.00 | Fairfax | VA | 38.00 |
| 34 | San Diego | CA | 79.00 | Bronx | NY | 39.00 |

*Source:* Adapted from P. Z. Smith (1993), *Felony Defendants in Large Urban Counties, 1990* (Publication #NCJ-141872), Bureau of Justice Statistics, U.S. Department of Justice, Washington, DC: U.S. Government Printing Office, Appendix table E.

of 4 in the stem and 4 on the leaf would indicate that there is a single value of 44 in the distribution (in this case, it is 44 percent). In addition to giving the total number of cases represented in the display, it is also a good idea to add an example of how to interpret the stem-and-leaf digits (e.g., 4|8 represents 48 percent). Knowing all of this information allows readers accurately to interpret a stem-and-leaf display.

| f | Stem | Leaves |
|---|------|--------|
| 3 | 3 | 279 |
| 1 | 4 | 8 |
| 5 | 5 | 14569 |
| 9 | 6 | 012345689 |
| 8 | 7 | 02336789 |
| 8 | 8 | 22233566 |

Stem unit = 10%
1 leaf represents 1 case
4 | 8 represents 48%
$N = 34$

FIGURE 6.1. Stem-and-leaf display of county data indicating percent of felony arrests resulting in conviction.

Now that we have completed one, what does the stem-and-leaf display in Figure 6.1 tell us? Well, we see that the first case in the distribution has a stem of 3 and a leaf of 2; this represents the county with the lowest conviction rate of 32 percent (Suffolk, MA). The highest value on the display has a stem of 8 and a leaf of 6 and represents a county with an 86 percent conviction rate (Santa Clara, CA). Thus, the stem-and-leaf display tells us that our county conviction rate data ranges from 32 percent to 86 percent.

We can also see that the majority of the values fall in the higher range, from about 60 percent to 80 percent. Now transpose the image in Figure 6.1 right side up in your mind. What do you see now? If you cannot visualize this, look at Figure 6.2, which does the transposing for you. From this figure, you can actually see the shape of the distribution this way, can't you? If you placed a bell-shaped curve over the display, what would you see? What does this distribution look like? It has a

FIGURE 6.2. Transposed stem-and-leaf display of Figure 6.1.

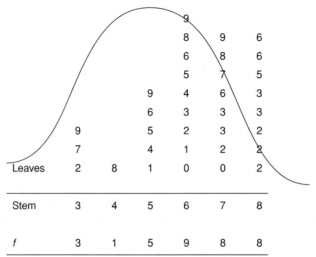

slight negative skew because the bulk of the cases fall at the high end and only a few cases trail off at the low end of the distribution.

Another piece of information you can easily obtain from a stem-and-leaf display is the median. Remember that the median simply is the score that divides your distribution into two equal halves. Remember from Chapter 4 that the position of the median in a rank-ordered distribution of scores is $(N + 1)/2$. The median is relatively easy to find with our data already sorted here. In this example, we have a sample size of 34 counties. The 50th percentile or median position would therefore lie at the 17.5th position ([34 + 1]/2 = 17.5). Again, remember that when the median position falls between two points like this, we simply take the average of the values in both positions. Because the data are already ordered, all we have to do to find the median is to count up to the 17th and 18th positions beginning with our first leaf, and take the average of these two scores. Because these positions are 68 percent and 69 percent, respectively, our median value would be 68.5 percent ([68 + 69]/2). How do we interpret this? Well, we can say that 50 percent of the counties in this sample have conviction rates lower than 68.5 percent within the first year of arrest and that 50 percent of the counties have conviction rates higher than 68.5 percent.

Are you beginning to see the beauty of stem-and-leaf displays? So much information is communicated from just a glance. We have the luxury of a visual display without losing the specific numerical points of our data. With this one simple display, we can find the range of our variable distribution, where the data points are concentrated, what the shape of our distribution is, and whether there are any gaps or outliers in our distribution.

Now that you are feeling a little confidence, let's construct a stem-and-leaf display from a somewhat more difficult variable distribution. Table 6.3 displays the average annual salaries for a sample of criminal justice and correctional facility personnel in the United States in rank order from lowest to highest. Because we have more than two digits for each data point, we have to decide which numbers will represent the stems and which will represent the leaves. When we are working with large numbers such as these, it is best to round up the digits so that each leaf represents only one case. This makes the display much easier to interpret. For the sake of example, let's make the stems the first digit in each case, the leaves the second digit, and drop the remaining numbers. In this way, we would know that someone made $16,000 but we wouldn't know that exact hundred amount. The stem unit would therefore be equal to $10,000, and the leaves would be equal to $1000.

Figure 6.3 displays the stem-and-leaf display we would obtain if we constructed the data from Table 6.3. We lost some specificity to our salary distribution, but, again, this was a judgment call. We opted for ease of presentation and interpretation over specificity in this case. Even though we do not know exactly how much over $14,000 our lowest income point falls, we do know from this display that our salary distribution from this sample of criminal justice personnel ranges from $14,000 to $59,000. We also know that the distribution is positively skewed with most of the cases falling at the low end of the income scale and only a few cases falling above $40,000.

```
 f    Stem   Leaves
 8     1     46688999
 7     2     2234488
 4     3     1346
 3     4     036
 1     5     9

Stem unit = $10,000
1 leaf represents 1 case
3 | 1 represents $31,000
N = 23
```

FIGURE 6.3. Stem-and-leaf display of the average annual salaries from a sample of criminal justice and correctional facilities personnel in the United States.

Notice that this display looks a little scrunched together. As with any graph, when constructing a stem-and-leaf display, we have the option of spreading it out or condensing it. When we have a variable distribution with many values but a small range, it is sometimes necessary to extend it out to determine the distribution's shape. One way of doing this is to place multiple leaf lines on each stem. We

**TABLE 6.3. Average Annual Salaries for a Sample of Criminal Justice and Correction Facilities Personnel in the United States**

| Rank | Job | Average Annual Salary |
|---|---|---|
| 1 | State correctional officer (entry level) | $14,985.00 |
| 2 | State correctional officer (maximum) | 16,427.00 |
| 3 | Local jail officer (entry level) | 16,939.00 |
| 4 | State trooper (entry level) | 18,170.00 |
| 5 | City police officer (entry level) | 18,913.00 |
| 6 | State probation officer (entry level) | 19,402.00 |
| 7 | Deputy U.S. Marshal | 19,585.00 |
| 8 | State parole officer (entry level) | 19,986.00 |
| 9 | Federal probation officer (entry level) | 22,458.00 |
| 10 | Federal correctional officer | 22,857.00 |
| 11 | U.S. border patrol agent | 23,058.00 |
| 12 | City police officer (maximum) | 24,243.00 |
| 13 | U.S. immigration inspector | 24,719.00 |
| 14 | State trooper (maximum) | 28,033.00 |
| 15 | State chief probation officer | 28,600.00 |
| 16 | State chief parole officer | 31,233.00 |
| 17 | City police chief | 33,158.00 |
| 18 | U.S. immigration agent | 34,259.00 |
| 19 | Federal drug agent | 36,973.00 |
| 20 | FBI agent | 40,321.00 |
| 21 | State parole board member | 43,429.00 |
| 22 | State parole board chairman | 46,100.00 |
| 23 | State director of corrections | 59,947.00 |

*Source:* Adapted from Bureau of Justice Statistics, U.S. Department of Justice, (1988), *Report to the Nation on Crime and Justice,* (Publication Number NCJ-105506), Washington, DC: U.S. Government Printing Office, p. 126.

DOUBLE STEM-AND-LEAF DISPLAYS

Have two stems for each stem digit and label as follows:

1*   leaf digits of 0–4 are displayed here

1•   leaf digits of 5–9 are displayed here

can actually stretch out a display as long as we want by splitting the stems into equal parts. For example, if we had many data points that only fell within a range of 20 to 30, we could divide the data into five equal stems with the first stem listing all those data points that were either 20 or 21, the second stem listing all those data points that were either 22 or 23, the third stem listing all those data points that were either 24 or 25, and so on.

One of the most common methods used to increase the spread of a display is to split the stems into two equal parts. In this way, the leaf digits 0, 1, 2, 3, and 4 are placed on the first stem line (indicated by a * after the stem) and the leaf digits 5, 6, 7, 8, and 9 placed on the second stem line (indicated by a • after the stem).

The salary data from Table 6.3 are reconstructed with multiple stems and presented in Figure 6.4. We still have truncated the salaries, leaving only the first two digits of each average annual income; $28,033 has been truncated to $28,000, $22,857 to simply $22,000, and so forth. By adding double stems to the display, the shape of the distribution is a little easier to visualize. For example, it reveals the gap that exists between the majority of salaries that fall between $10,000 and $20,000 and the extreme high salary of $59,000. What else can we determine from this display? As with the general income distribution in this country, we see that the income distribution among this sample of criminal justice employees also is positively skewed. Most criminal justice personnel have annual incomes in the low to middle ranges of the distribution, a few trail off in the middle to high ranges, and only a very small proportion make the highest incomes.

FIGURE 6.4. A double stem-and-leaf display of the average annual salaries from a sample of criminal justice and correctional facilities personnel in the United States.

| f | Stem | Leaves |
|---|---|---|
| 1 | 1 * | 4 |
| 7 | 1 • | 6688999 |
| 5 | 2 * | 22344 |
| 2 | 2 • | 88 |
| 3 | 3 * | 134 |
| 1 | 3 • | 6 |
| 2 | 4 * | 03 |
| 1 | 4 • | 6 |
| 0 | 5 * | |
| 1 | 5 • | 9 |

Stem unit = $10,000
1 leaf represents 1 case
4 | 0 represents $40,000
N = 23

STEM-AND-LEAF DISPLAYS

**Step 1.** Rank-order your variable distribution in ascending order from lowest to highest values.

**Step 2.** Decide which digits you will use as your stems and which you will use as your leaves. If each case contains more than two digits, will you truncate or round them?

**Step 3.** Decide whether multiple stems are necessary to properly display your distribution.

**Step 4.** List your selection of stems, and place each leaf value on to its respective stem.

**Step 5.** Finish the display with a legend containing interpretation information: stem width, leaf width, sample size, and sample interpretation.

Where does the median fall in this distribution? Because there are 23 cases, the median would be in the 12th position ([23 + 1]/2 = 12) of our rank-ordered scores. The score that occupies the 12th position is $24,000. This indicates that 50 percent of those working in the criminal justice field earn less than $24,000 and 50 percent earn more than $24,000. Remember that this data set was obtained for the years 1985–1987; the figures would undoubtedly be higher if we were to obtain a sample today.

## 6.3 BOX-AND-WHISKER PLOTS

Boxplots, originally coined by Tukey (1977) as box-and-whisker plots, are another technique in the EDA family that is used to convey information about the distribution of a variable. Although you can generally ascertain the same information from boxplots as you can from stem-and-leaf displays, boxplots are more graphically and less numerically oriented. Instead of focusing on the individual data points, boxplots provide a more general picture of the overall shape and variability of a distribution. At a glance, you can ascertain what the distribution looks like, how spread out it is, where its approximate center lies, and how far out on the ends of the distribution any trailing data points lie.

Essentially, constructing a boxplot involves calculating particular statistical values from your data and then forming the boxplot based on these values. The statistics that a boxplot is primarily based on are the values of the median, the quartiles, and the interquartile range (IQR). We have already covered these statistics in preceding chapters; what we do with a box plot is to combine them into a picture. Let's illustrate these steps through an example by using the felony charge data from Table 6.2 (labeled Percent Felony in Table 6.2). Specifically, we will construct a boxplot from the first column of data presented in Table 6.2, which lists in ascending order those convictions from felony arrests that resulted in a felony charge by each county.

If the values of this variable were not already rank-ordered, the first step in constructing a boxplot would be to place the values in ascending order. Because all other points necessary to construct a boxplot can be obtained by knowing the median and first ($Q_1$ = 25th percentile) and third ($Q_3$ = 75th percentile) quartiles, the next step is to find these values from the rank-ordered scores. Because we have an even number of scores in this data distribution (34), the median can be found at the midpoint of the 17th (34/2) and 18th (36/2) positions. The score at the 17th position is 51 percent, and the score at the 18th position is 55 percent. The median, then, is (51 + 55)/2 = 53 percent.

We can easily find the first and third quartiles ($Q_1$ and $Q_3$), respectively, by first finding the Truncated Median Position (TMP). The TMP, you will remember from Chapter 5, is the position of the median truncated at the decimal point. For example, the position of the median in this instance is the midpoint between the 17th and 18th positions. In other words, the median is at the 17.5th position in our distribution of scores. When we drop off the decimal place, the truncated median position is 17. We have truncated or eliminated the decimal place so that we have an integer or whole number. We can now find the position of the first and third quartile with the simple formula:

$$\text{Quartile Position} = \frac{(\text{Truncated Median Position} + 1)}{2}$$

$$= \frac{(17 + 1)}{2}$$

$$= 9$$

Using the results of this formula, we see that the first quartile can be found nine scores from the lowest score in the distribution (counting the lowest score as one), and the third quartile can be found nine scores from the highest score in the distribution (counting the highest score as one). The ninth score from the lowest score is 37 percent (Queens, NY), and the ninth score from the highest is 69 percent (Los Angeles, CA). The first quartile, then, is 37, and the third quartile is 69.

Knowing the values of the quartiles and the median, we can determine all of the other values we need for our boxplot. We must now calculate the IQR. Remember from Chapter 5 that this simply is the difference between the first and third quartiles (IQR = $Q_3 - Q_1$). For our data, then, the IQR is 69 percent − 37 percent = 32 percent. With this piece of information we can construct the box part of our boxplot. Although a boxplot can be constructed either vertically or horizontally, computer programs usually display them with the axis running along the vertical axis; we will follow this guideline for the examples that follow.

The first element to be entered into our boxplot design is the vertical axis. Construct a vertical axis along the side of the paper that will accommodate all of the data points for your variable. In our example the variable of interest is the felony charge variable in Table 6.2. Next, along this vertical axis, we construct the first part of our boxplot by simply drawing a box the length of the IQR that runs from our first quartile to the third quartile. In our example, the box would extend from 69 percent to 37 percent of the vertical axis, the length of the interquartile range. Across this box, we place a line indicating where the median falls within the distribution. In our example, this line is drawn at 53, because the median was 53 percent. We now have the dimensions for our box and can draw all four sides and a line through the box showing where the median is. The box for the as-yet-unfinished boxplot from the felony charge data of Table 6.2 is shown for you in Figure 6.5.

The next step is to add what Tukey called the "whiskers" to the box. These whiskers are actually lines that extend out from both the top and bottom of the box. These lines denote how far the data extend up and down to a calculated value called a *fence*. We must determine four fences when constructing a boxplot. We can calculate the fences from the following formulas:

Low Inner Fence $= Q_1 - 1.5$ (IQR)

Lower Outer Fence $= Q_1 - 3.0$ (IQR)

High Inner Fence $= Q_3 + 1.5$ (IQR)

Higher Outer Fence $= Q_3 + 3.0$ (IQR)

The inner fences are, then, placed at a distance one and one-half times the IQR above (high inner) and below (low inner) the edges of the box. The outer fences are placed at a distance three times the IQR above (higher outer) and below (lower outer) the edges of the box. Let's state this a different way. There are two inner fences in a boxplot, one coming out of the bottom of the box (the low inner fence) and one coming out of the top of the box (the high inner fence). These two inner fences extend a distance from the box equal to 1.5 times the value of the IQR (1.5[IQR]). There are two outer fences, one coming out of the bottom of the box (the lower outer fence), and one coming out of the top of the box (the higher outer fence). These two outer fences extend a distance from the box equal to three times

FIGURE 6.5.  Skeleton boxplot for felony charge data.

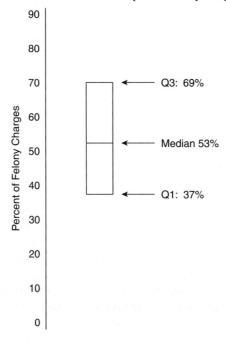

the value of the IQR (3[IQR]). Notice, however, that the values for the two bottom fences (low and lower) are found by subtracting 1.5(IQR) or 3.0(IQR) from $Q_1$ because these fences are found *below* the box and are therefore below or less than the median. The values for the two upper fences (high and higher) are found by adding 1.5(IQR) or 3.0(IQR) to $Q_3$ because these fences are found *above* the box and are therefore above or greater than the median.

Let's return to our example. For our felony conviction data we would obtain the following fence values:

Low Inner Fence $= [37 - 1.5(32)] = 37 - 48 = -11$

Lower Outer Fence $= [37 - 3.0(32)] = 37 - 96 = -59$

High Inner Fence $= [69 + 1.5(32)] = 69 + 48 = 117$

Higher Outer Fence $= [69 + 3.0(32)] = 69 + 96 = 165$

Again, notice that the values for the low and lower fences are obtained by subtracting the distance of each fence from the median, whereas the values for the high and higher fences are obtained by adding the distance of each fence from the median.

With these values, we can finish the boxplot by adding the whiskers. We use the values of our fences to determine the exact length of each whisker. There are two whiskers, a top one extending up from the top of the box, and a bottom one extending down from the bottom of the box. Before we can draw the whiskers from the box, however, we must find one more set of numbers. These are what are called the *adjacent values* in our distribution.

The adjacent values in a boxplot are the highest and lowest scores in our data distribution that do not fall outside either of the inner fences (either the low inner or the high inner). There are, then, two adjacent values. The *low adjacent value* is the lowest value in our distribution that does not fall outside of the low inner fence. In our example the value of this low inner fence was $-11$. The *high adjacent value* is the highest value in our distribution that does not fall outside of the high inner fence. In our example the value of this high inner fence was 117. Examining our felony conviction data, we see that none of our values fall outside of these fences. There were no scores higher than 117 or lower than $-11$. Our adjacent values, then, are the actual scores in the distribution that are closest to these. Our lower adjacent value would be the lowest value in the distribution, 21 percent. The high adjacent value would be the highest value in the distribution, 79 percent. These adjacent values denote how far out the whisker lines extend from the box. The upper whisker extends from the box up to the value of 79 percent on the vertical axis. Draw a line from the middle of the box up to that point, make another small line the width of the box perpendicular to that. There is one of your whiskers. The bottom whisker extends from the box down to the value of 21 percent on the same vertical axis. Draw a line from the middle of the box down to 21 percent, and make another small perpendicular line the width of the box. There is the other whisker (Figure 6.6).

Let's return to the almost completed box-and-whisker plot in Figure 6.6. In addition to the whiskers, it is also possible and very useful in describing your data to denote *outliers* in your boxplots. Outliers, you may remember, are unusually high or unusually low scores in our distribution. They do strange things to our statistical

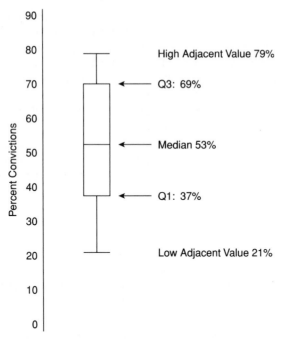

FIGURE 6.6. Complete boxplot for felony conviction data.

analyses at times (you already know what an outlier can do to the value of the mean), so we want to know where they are and how extreme they are. Box-and-whisker plots are a very good way to identify the presence and magnitude of such outliers.

There are usually two types of outliers displayed in a box-and-whisker plot. These are called *mild outliers* and *extreme outliers.* As their respective terms imply, extreme outliers are even more unusual scores than mild outliers. Mild outliers are labeled with the symbol O and are those values in the distribution that fall outside either of the calculated inner fences but do not fall outside the calculated outer fences. Extreme outliers are labeled with the symbol • and are those values in the distribution that fall outside of both the inner and outer fences. Because no values in the felony conviction data of Figure 6.6 fall outside of either the inner or outer fences, we do not have any outliers to label for this boxplot. But, be warned, they do exist.

Now that we have created the masterpiece displayed in Figure 6.6, what can it tell us about the distribution of our variable, percent of felony convictions? Think about it. What information is this boxplot made up of? We know from looking at the display that the median in our distribution falls around 53 percent. We also know that the box represents the IQR range marked off by the first and third quartiles. Thus, we know where the middle 50 percent of our cases lie and how spread out they are around the median. In addition, we have lines extending from the box that indicate where and to what extent the values of the data fall beyond 1.5 interquartile ranges below the first and above the third quartiles. If the median fell exactly in the middle of the box and each whisker line was the same length, what would this tell us? It would tell us that our distribution is almost perfectly symmetrical, wouldn't it? Remember that this box represents only the middle 50 percent of the cases. Therefore, we can ascertain symmetry information at two levels: in the middle of the distribution and at the tails. The location of the median line in the box tells us about the shape of the middle of the distribution, and the length of the whiskers tells us about the distribution of the top and bottom 25 percent of our data.

If the median line is closer to the lower quartile than to the upper one (that is, if the median line is lower than half-way down the box), there would be a greater concentration of scores on the lower side of the median. This would indicate a positive skew, or a long right tail of the distribution. Conversely, if the median line is closer to the third quartile in the box (that is, if the median line is higher than half-way up the box), this would indicate that there is a greater concentration of scores on the higher side of the median. This would indicate a negative skew, or a long left tail of the distribution.

Skewness can also be detected from the length of the whisker lines. Suppose that the whisker on the bottom end of the box is longer than the whisker at the top end. What would this mean? This would indicate a negative skew. Why? Think of the bottom whisker as representing the left tail of the distribution. This would indicate a higher concentration of cases falling on the lower end of the distribution. A long left tail, therefore, means a negative skew. Suppose that the whisker on the top end of the box is longer than the whisker at the bottom. What would this mean? If the whisker at the top end of the box is longer than the lower whisker, this would indicate a higher concentration of cases falling on the upper end of the distribution, hence, a positive skew.

Figure 6.7 shows a sample of a horizontal box-and-whisker plot with a curve above the box to show the approximate shape of the distribution. It does not matter if the graph is vertical or horizontal. You can still get a good idea of the shape of the distribution with the box-and-whisker plot.

Transposing the image in your head and placing the box horizontally may help you see the shape of the distribution better. This way you can impose a bell-shaped curve over the box to help you visualize what the distribution looks like. Of course, another fantastic tool that helps understanding is repetition, so let's go over another example. An outline of the steps used for boxplot construction is highlighted for you in the box on page 156.

Table 6.4 provides a rank-order listing of the number of individuals who were sentenced to death in 1991 in the 36 states that authorized capital punishment at that time. We can tell just by glancing at the table that a few states sentenced many more people to death than the majority of states. In fact, the number of defendants sentenced to death ranges from a low of 0 (New Hampshire) to a high of 340 (Texas). Let's construct a boxplot of this distribution.

The first step in constructing a box-and-whisker plot is to order the data. Because the data are already ordered for you, we can begin to calculate the values we need as follows:

Median Position $= (n + 1)/2$

$$= (36 + 1)/2 = 18.5$$

$$= \text{Midpoint of 18th and 19th position (position 18.5)}$$

Median Value $= (37 + 45)/2 = 41$

---

### BOXPLOTS

**Step 1.** Rank your data in ascending order.

**Step 2.** Find the following values:

Median (Median position $= [n + 1]/2$)

$Q_1$ and $Q_3$ (Quartile depth $= [tmp + 1]/2$)

IQR $= Q_3 - Q_1$

**Step 3.** Draw scale along vertical axis to accommodate all data values.

**Step 4.** Draw box indicating the width of IQR from first to third quartile with a line drawn through the box indicating the median.

**Step 5.** Find fences:

Low inner fence        $= Q_1 - 1.5$ (IQR)

Lower outer fence     $= Q_1 - 3.0$ (IQR)

High inner fence       $= Q_3 + 1.5$ (IQR)

Higher outer fence    $= Q_3 + 3.0$ (IQR)

**Step 6.** Find adjacent values—those values that are closest to the inner fences but do not fall outside of them.

**Step 7.** Draw whisker lines to each adjacent value.

**Step 8.** Find mild outliers—those values that fall outside of inner fences but *not* outside of outer fences—and mark with the symbol.

**Step 9.** Find extreme outliers—those values that fall outside of the outer fences.

---

Quartile Position $= [(tmp + 1)/2] = [(18 + 1)/2] = 9.5$

$\qquad\qquad\qquad$ = Midpoint of 9th and 10th position from top and bottom of distribution

$$Q_1 = (7 + 9)/2 = 8$$

$$Q_3 = (101 + 97)/2 = 99$$

$$\text{IQR} = (99 - 8) = 91$$

Low Inner Fence $= [8 - 1.5(91)] = -128.5$

Lower Outer Fence $= [8 - 3.0(91)] = -265$

High Inner Fence $= [99 + 1.5(91)] = 235.5$

Higher Outer Fence $= [99 + 3.0(91)] = 372$

Low Adjacent Value $= 0$

High Adjacent Value $= 137$

Mild Outliers $= 301$ (California), $311$ (Florida), $340$ (Texas)

Extreme Outliers $=$ No values fall outside of outer fences

**TABLE 6.4. Number of Prisoners Sentenced to Death by State, 1991**

| Rank | State* | Number Sentenced to Death | Rank | State* | Number Sentenced to Death |
|------|--------|---------------------------|------|--------|---------------------------|
| 1 | New Hampshire | .00 | 19 | South Carolina | 45.00 |
| 2 | South Dakota | .00 | 20 | Virginia | 47.00 |
| 3 | New Mexico | 1.00 | 21 | Indiana | 49.00 |
| 4 | Wyoming | 1.00 | 22 | Mississippi | 51.00 |
| 5 | Colorado | 3.00 | 23 | Nevada | 60.00 |
| 6 | Connecticut | 4.00 | 24 | North Carolina | 74.00 |
| 7 | New Jersey | 4.00 | 25 | Missouri | 77.00 |
| 8 | Montana | 6.00 | 26 | Tennessee | 97.00 |
| 9 | Delaware | 7.00 | 27 | Arizona | 97.00 |
| 10 | Oregon | 9.00 | 28 | Georgia | 101.00 |
| 11 | Nebraska | 12.00 | 29 | Ohio | 111.00 |
| 12 | Utah | 12.00 | 30 | Alabama | 119.00 |
| 13 | Washington | 12.00 | 31 | Oklahoma | 125.00 |
| 14 | Maryland | 16.00 | 32 | Illinois | 132.00 |
| 15 | Idaho | 21.00 | 33 | Pennsylvania | 137.00 |
| 16 | Kentucky | 30.00 | 34 | California | 301.00 |
| 17 | Arkansas | 34.00 | 35 | Florida | 311.00 |
| 18 | Louisiana | 37.00 | 36 | Texas | 340.00 |

*States not listed and the District of Columbia did not authorize the death penalty as of 12/31/90.
*Source:* Adapted from L. A. Greenfeld (1992), *Capital Punishment, 1991* (Publication #136946), Bureau of Justice Statistics, U.S. Department of Justice, Washington, DC: U.S. Government Printing Office, Table 4.

To obtain a finished boxplot display like that presented in Figure 6.8, we must first construct the vertical axis to accommodate all of our values. Because we have such a large range in this distribution (340), we have labeled the axis at every 50th point beginning with 0. The next step is to draw the box the length of the IQR using the vertical axis as your reference from the first to the third quartiles (8 to 99) and then place a horizontal line across the box where the median falls (41).

Adding the whiskers to the box is our next task. Our low adjacent value—the lowest value in our distribution that is closest to but not outside of the low inner fence—is 0; this is where the end of our low whisker line is marked off. Our high adjacent value—which is the highest value in our distribution that is closest to but

FIGURE 6.7. A horizontal box-and-whisker plot with a curve.

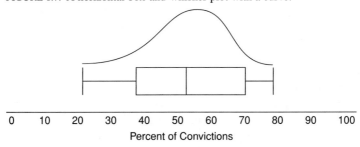

Percent of Convictions

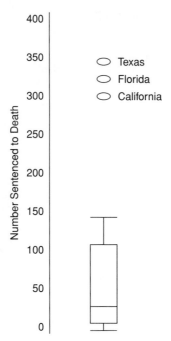

FIGURE 6.8. Number of people sentenced to death for 36 states that authorize the death penalty, 1991.

not outside of the high inner fence—is 137; this is where the end of our high whisker line is marked off. Draw the vertical lines connecting the whiskers to the box.

The final step we must take is to locate any outliers that exist in the distribution. We have three high values left in our distribution that are not represented in the boxplot: 301, 311, and 340. These values fall outside of the high inner fence but do not fall outside of the higher outer fence; they would therefore be mild outliers and are labeled with the symbol on the boxplot as shown in Figure 6.8.

What can we say about the number of people sentenced to death in the United States in 1991 based on the boxplot presented in Figure 6.8? We can say that the majority of states have sentenced less than 100 people to death; 50 percent of the states in 1991 sentenced less than 41 people to death, and 50 percent sentenced more than 41 people to die. The distribution of death sentences by state is positively skewed, indicating that only a few states have sentenced many people to die and are pulling the distribution upward. In fact, there are three states that are classified as outliers in this distribution and fall more than 1.5 IQRs above the third quartile. California, Florida, and Texas each sentenced over 300 people to death in 1991 (301, 311, and 340, respectively).

We hope that you have become a convert of EDA by now and agree that these techniques are very effective methods for examining the shape of your distributions. Researchers often forget this crucial step in the process of statistical analysis and sometimes rush ahead to inferential statistics unaware that they may be working with distributions that are extremely skewed or have other abnormalities such as outliers. If, in the initial phase of your research, you use the EDA techniques we have just gone over, you will avoid many of these mistakes. You can then move more confidently on to multivariate methods of statistical analysis. But hold on! There is even more we can do with these EDA techniques. Not only do they illuminate the univariate distributions of your data set, but also they are very useful for comparing the distributions of the same variable among different samples or distributions among subsets of the same sample. Now that we have mastered the construction of boxplots, the next section demonstrates how to use them to draw comparisons among distributions.

## 6.4 COMPARING DIFFERENT DISTRIBUTIONS WITH BOXPLOTS

As with the regional comparisons we made in Chapter 3, this section relies on state and regional crime data from the United States to explore the regional variability of crime with EDA techniques. Table 6.5 displays a rank-order listing of violent crime rates per 100,000 population by state within each of the four regions of the country. Because the purpose of this section is to enhance our understanding of interpreting these displays, not to construct them, Table 6.6 presents the summary statistics for these regional distributions necessary to construct boxplots for each region. This would be a good opportunity, however, to construct boxplots on your own from the raw data presented in Table 6.5.

The question to be addressed here is, How does the variability of violent crime rates among regions compare to the variability of the distribution of the United States as a whole? Figure 6.9 presents a boxplot that would be obtained from the entire distribution of violent crime rates by each state. Because the gap between the extreme outlier of the District of Columbia and the rest of the state rates was so large, it was deemed necessary to place a break along the vertical axis. The gap indicates that the data values are not eliminated, just condensed.

What does Figure 6.8 tell us about the distribution of state-level violent crime rates? In general, we see that, although most of the distribution is relatively symmetrical, a few states are outliers: both Florida and New York fall over 1.5 IQRs from the third quartile, and the District of Columbia is an extreme outlier falling over 3 IQRs from the third quartile. We can see that the median is approximately 525 crimes per 100,000 population. This indicates that about 50 percent of the states had violent crime rates lower than 525 per 100,000 population and that 50 percent of states experienced rates higher than 500. Notice that the median line is just about in the center of the box. This tells us that the middle 50 percent of the distribution is approximately symmetrical, roughly spanning between the rates of 300 to 735 violent crimes per 100,000.

Does this general distribution of violent crime rates also reflect what is happening in each of the four regions of the country? Do the boxplots for these four regions look like the one for the United States as a whole? Figure 6.10 presents a multiple boxplot display of the four regional distributions of violent crime. As you can tell, this type of display is an excellent way to compare the variability of

**TABLE 6.5. Violent Crime Rates per 100,000 Population by Region, Rank-Ordered by State, 1990**

| Northeast | | Midwest | |
|---|---|---|---|
| Vermont | 127.00 | North Dakota | 74.00 |
| New Hampshire | 132.00 | South Dakota | 163.00 |
| Maine | 143.00 | Wisconsin | 265.00 |
| Pennsylvania | 431.00 | Iowa | 300.00 |
| Rhode Island | 432.00 | Minnesota | 306.00 |
| Connecticut | 554.00 | Nebraska | 330.00 |
| New Jersey | 648.00 | Kansas | 448.00 |
| Massachusetts | 736.00 | Indiana | 474.00 |
| New York | 1181.00 | Ohio | 506.00 |
| South | | Missouri | 715.00 |
| West Virginia | 169.00 | Michigan | 790.00 |
| Mississippi | 340.00 | Illinois | 967.00 |
| Virginia | 351.00 | West | |
| Kentucky | 390.00 | Montana | 159.00 |
| Arkansas | 532.00 | Idaho | 276.00 |
| Oklahoma | 547.00 | Hawaii | 281.00 |
| North Carolina | 624.00 | Utah | 284.00 |
| Delaware | 655.00 | Wyoming | 301.00 |
| Tennessee | 670.00 | Washington | 502.00 |
| Alabama | 709.00 | Oregon | 507.00 |
| Georgia | 756.00 | Alaska | 525.00 |
| Texas | 761.00 | Colorado | 526.00 |
| Louisiana | 898.00 | Nevada | 601.00 |
| Maryland | 919.00 | Arizona | 652.00 |
| South Carolina | 977.00 | New Mexico | 780.00 |
| Florida | 1244.00 | California | 1045.00 |
| District of Columbia | 2458.00 | | |

*Source:* Adapted from Bureau of the Census, *Statistical Abstract of the United States, 1992* (112 ed.), Washington, DC: U.S. Government Printing Office, p. 181.

different distributions. You can not only determine how violent crime is distributed within each region, but also how this variability compares to that of other regions of the country. What can you tell about the variability, center, shape (symmetry), or abnormalities of regional rates of violence from Figure 6.10? Let's begin with variability. We can tell that the Northeast has the largest variability of any region because the length of the box, the IQR, is the longest. For the northeastern states the middle 50 percent of the data range from 100 to approximately 600 (an IQR of 500), whereas in the other three regions the IQR is about 300.

What about the median rate of violent crime in each region? It appears that the South has the highest median rate of violent crime, followed by the West, Northeast, and Midwest, respectively. The median violent crime rate in southern states is 670 per 100,000, which is higher than any other region. The highest rates of violence are found in the southern and northeastern regions as the whisker lines for the

**TABLE 6.6. Summary Statistics for Violent Crime
Rates from Table 6.5, by Region**

Northeast

| | | |
|---|---|---|
| $N$ = 9 | Low inner fence = | −614.5 |
| $Mdn$ = 432 | Lower outer fence = | −1,372 |
| $Q_1$ = 143 | High inner fence = | 1,405.5 |
| $Q_3$ = 648 | Higher outer fence = | 2,163 |
| IQR = 505 | Low adjacent value = | 127 |
| | High adjacent value = | 1,181 |

Midwest

| | | |
|---|---|---|
| $N$ = 12 | Low inner fence = | −209.5 |
| $Mdn$ = 389 | Lower outer fence = | −701.5 |
| $Q_1$ = 282.5 | High inner fence = | 1,102.5 |
| $Q_3$ = 610.5 | Higher outer fence = | 1,594.5 |
| IQR = 328 | Low adjacent value = | 74 |
| | High adjacent value = | 967 |

South

| | | |
|---|---|---|
| $N$ = 17 | Low inner fence = | −17 |
| $Mdn$ = 670 | Lower outer fence = | −566 |
| $Q_1$ = 532 | High inner fence = | 1,447 |
| $Q_3$ = 898 | Higher outer fence = | 1,996 |
| IQR = 366 | Low adjacent value = | 169 |
| | High adjacent value = | 1,244 |

West

| | | |
|---|---|---|
| $N$ = 13 | Low inner fence = | −191.5 |
| $Mdn$ = 507 | Lower outer fence = | −667 |
| $Q_1$ = 284 | High inner fence = | 1,076.5 |
| $Q_3$ = 601 | Higher outer fence = | 1,552 |
| IQR = 317 | Low adjacent value = | 159 |
| | High adjacent value = | 1,045 |

South extend up the highest followed by those for the Northeast. The only outlier present in any regional distribution falls in the South; the District of Columbia falls more than 3 IQRs from the third quartile in the South and thus represents an extreme outlier. This is not surprising considering that the rate of violent crime in the District of Columbia is nearly 2500 per 100,000, compared to the median rate in the South of only 670. When we get into inferential statistics that investigate relationships among variables, it will become clear to you just how important information about the distribution of our variables is. An outlier such as this one can severely compromise the integrity of the results you obtain from a statistical analysis investigating how one variable affects another.

Finally, what conclusions can we draw about the shape or symmetry of these four regional violent crime distributions? In general, we can conclude that all of the regional distributions of violent crime rates have a slight positive skew, although the evidence we use to draw this conclusion is different for different regions. For states in the Northeast and West, the evidence of a positive skew takes the form of

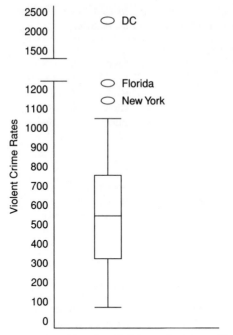

FIGURE 6.9.  Boxplot of violent crime rates, 50 states.

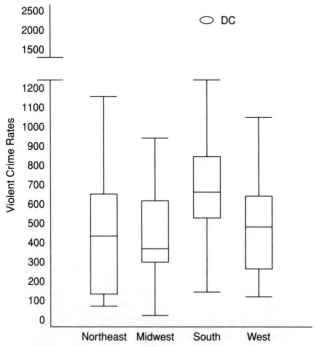

FIGURE 6.10.  Boxplot for violent crime rates by region.

a very long upper whisker and a very short lower one. This suggests that there are a larger number of scores at the upper levels of violent crime than at the lower levels. For both regions, the median is not far off-center, though slightly above it, suggesting that the middle half of the distribution shows some slight negative skew. For states in both the Midwest and South, our evidence of a positive skew does not come in the form of an elongated upper whisker, for the length of the upper and lower whiskers is about the same for these two regions. Instead, we would conclude that there is a slight positive skew because the median line falls closer to the bottom of the box than the middle.

## 6.5 SUMMARY

We have examined two techniques from a genre of statistics called *exploratory data analysis (EDA)* originally developed by the statistician John Tukey (1977). The goal behind the development of EDA was to help analysts obtain a better understanding about the distributional properties of the variables in their data sets. From the simple displays we have covered in this chapter, we can tell at a glance many important things about the distribution of the variables in our data set: the central location of the distributions (central tendency), the extent of variability (dispersion), the shape of the distribution (symmetrical or skewed), and any abnormalities that exist within the distributions, such as outliers. Many of us would like to think that our data are free from skewness or abnormalities, but most distributions we work with tend to be far from normal. This is particularly true with many criminological variables. With the techniques of EDA, we cannot help but be aware of the peculiarities in our data. They literally jump off the page at us.

### Key Terms

| | |
|---|---|
| **adjacent values** | **fences** |
| **boxplot (box-and-whisker plot)** | **outliers** |
| **exploratory data analysis (EDA)** | **stem-and-leaf display** |

### Problems

1. Why did John Tukey develop EDA techniques?
2. List the steps necessary to construct a stem-and-leaf display from a data distribution.
3. In a study of the social background and sentencing practices of a sample of Georgia judges, Myers (1988) found that older judges imposed more punitive sentences than younger judges. With the data that follow, which represents the ages of a hypothetical sample of 20 judges, construct a stem-and-leaf display. What is the range of ages and the median age? What would you conclude about the shape of this distribution?

Judges' Age

| | | |
|---|---|---|
| 58 | 70 | 58 |
| 63 | 65 | 50 |
| 65 | 61 | 46 |
| 57 | 59 | 61 |
| 49 | 62 | 67 |
| 51 | 71 | 70 |
| 60 | 66 | |

**4.** What are the differences between a stem-and-leaf display and a boxplot?

**5.** From the employment data in the following table, construct a box-and-whisker plot. What is the median number of employed police? Are there any outliers in this data set? What would you conclude about the overall shape of the distribution?

Police Protection Personnel Employed Full-Time by State and Region; Rank-Ordered by State, 1988

| Northeast | | | Midwest | |
|---|---|---|---|---|
| Vermont | 1224.00 | | North Dakota | 1303.00 |
| New Hampshire | 2756.00 | | South Dakota | 1497.00 |
| Maine | 2777.00 | | Nebraska | 3619.00 |
| Rhode Island | 2803.00 | | Iowa | 5713.00 |
| Connecticut | 9355.00 | | Kansas | 6520.00 |
| Massachusetts | 17,881.00 | | Minnesota | 8564.00 |
| Pennsylvania | 28,653.00 | | Indiana | 12,306.00 |
| New Jersey | 30,476.00 | | Wisconsin | 12,896.00 |
| New York | 66,261.00 | | Missouri | 13,665.00 |
| **South** | | | Michigan | 23,463.00 |
| Delaware | 1769.00 | | Ohio | 24,947.00 |
| West Virginia | 3184.00 | | Illinois | 38,541.00 |
| District of Columbia | 4594.00 | | **West** | |
| Arkansas | 4782.00 | | Alaska | 1562.00 |
| Mississippi | 5497.00 | | Wyoming | 1633.00 |
| Kentucky | 7326.00 | | Montana | 1811.00 |
| South Carolina | 8335.00 | | Idaho | 2434.00 |
| Oklahoma | 8632.00 | | Hawaii | 2959.00 |
| Alabama | 9556.00 | | Utah | 3596.00 |
| Tennessee | 11,435.00 | | Nevada | 4101.00 |
| Louisiana | 12,090.00 | | New Mexico | 4438.00 |
| Maryland | 14,041.00 | | Oregon | 6174.00 |
| Virginia | 14,136.00 | | Colorado | 8941.00 |
| North Carolina | 15,728.00 | | Washington | 10,081.00 |
| Georgia | 16,532.00 | | Arizona | 10,232.00 |
| Florida | 38,583.00 | | California | 79,868.00 |
| Texas | 42,384.00 | | | |

*Source:* Adapted from Bureau of the Census, *Statistical Abstract of the United States, 1992* (112 ed.), Washington, DC: U.S. Government Printing Office, p. 191.

**6.** The following data represent the number of prior self-reported offenses from a sample of 30 adult property offenders incarcerated in a state penitentiary. Construct a double stem-and-leaf display from these data. What is the median number of offenses?

| | | | | |
|---|---|---|---|---|
| 18 | 27 | 24 | 12 | 22 |
| 17 | 18 | 14 | 24 | 17 |
| 29 | 23 | 10 | 26 | 14 |
| 11 | 18 | 21 | 29 | 13 |
| 25 | 10 | 20 | 19 | 28 |
| 13 | 18 | 15 | 17 | 21 |

**7.** In their extensive review of the literature on IQ and delinquency, Hirschi and Hindelang (1977) found that low IQ was very consistently related to the commission of delinquent acts. The following hypothetical data are the IQ scores from a sample of 40 youths who appeared in a local juvenile court. Construct a box-and-whisker plot for the data. What is the mean IQ score? Is the distribution skewed?

| | | | |
|---|---|---|---|
| 95 | 92 | 104 | 68 |
| 80 | 103 | 78 | 102 |
| 88 | 67 | 66 | 92 |
| 67 | 60 | 52 | 74 |
| 89 | 74 | 63 | 81 |
| 93 | 87 | 95 | 75 |
| 104 | 101 | 105 | 62 |
| 100 | 78 | 92 | 69 |
| 99 | 93 | 90 | 75 |
| 84 | 69 | 87 | 77 |

## Solutions to Problems

**1.** John Tukey developed the techniques of EDA to allow researchers to explore the distribution of the variables in their data sets. They permit us visually to see and comprehend what our distributions look like, what abnormalities might be present (e.g., outliers), and what secrets they might hold.

**2.** There are five steps involved in the construction of a stem-and-leaf display:

**Step 1.** Rank-order your variable distribution in ascending order from lowest to highest values.

**Step 2.** Decide which digits you will use as your stems and which you will use as your leaves. If each case contains more than two digits, will you truncate or round them?

**Step 3.** Decide whether multiple stems are necessary to properly display your distribution.

**Step 4.** List your selection of stems and place each leaf value on to its respective stem.

**Step 5.** Finish the display with a legend containing interpretation information: stem width, leaf width, sample size, and sample interpretation.

**3.** The first thing to do is to rank-order the 20 judges' age from low to high. Then, let the stem represent units of 10 and the leaves represent units of 1. We will let one leaf represent each case as follows:

| f | Stem | Leaves |
|---|---|---|
| 2 | 4 | 69 |
| 6 | 5 | 017889 |
| 9 | 6 | 011235567 |
| 3 | 7 | 001 |

Stem unit = 10 years
1 leaf represents 1 case
5 | 1 represents 51 years old
$N = 20$

The range in age is:

$71 - 46 = 25$ years

The median score is:

$$\frac{61 + 61}{2} = \frac{122}{2} = 61$$

The shape of the distribution is approximately symmetrical. There is no negative or positive skew.

4. A stem-and-leaf display shows every data point of the distribution. From it you can comprehend the general shape and skewness of the distribution. With a little counting, you can easily determine the median. A box-and-whisker plot does not display all the data points. It is more visual, whereas the stem-and-leaf display is more numerical. From the box of the box-and-whisker plot you can determine the shape of the middle 50 percent of a distribution of scores. From the length of the whiskers and the location of the median in the box, you can get some sense of the skewness of the distribution.

5. To construct a box-and-whisker plot from this data set, first rank-order all scores from low to high. The median is equal to 8564 persons.
The first quartile is:

$$Q_1 = \frac{3184 + 3596}{2} = 3390$$

The third quartile is:

$$Q_3 = \frac{14,041 + 14,136}{2} = 14,088.5$$

The IQR, then, is:

$$IQR = 14,088.5 - 3390 = 10,698.5$$

The fences are:

Low Inner Fence = $3390 - [(1.5)\ 10,698.5] = -12,657.75$

Lower Outer Fence = $3390 - [(3.0)\ 10,698.5] = -28,705.50$

High Inner Fence = $14,088.5 + [(1.5)\ 10,698.5] = 30,136.25$

Higher Outer Fence = $14,088.5 + [(3.0)\ 10,698.5] = 46,184$

The adjacent values are:

Low Adjacent Value = 1224

High Adjacent Value = 28,653

We can also determine that we have four mild outliers (New Jersey, Illinois, Florida, and Texas) and two extreme outliers (New York and California). Now we have all the information we need to construct our box-and-whisker plot. We show this at the top of page 167.

6. Before constructing a double stem-and-leaf display, you should rank-order the data from low to high. The double stem-and-leaf display should look something like this:

| f | Stem | Leaves |
|---|------|--------|
| 8 | 1* | 00123344 |
| 9 | 1• | 577788889 |
| 7 | 2* | 0112344 |
| 6 | 2• | 567899 |

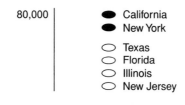

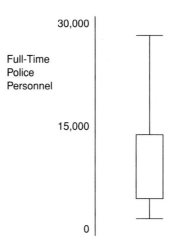

Stem unit = 10 offenses

1 leaf represents 1 case

1 | 7 represents 17 offenses

$N = 30$

The median is 18 offenses.

7. Rank the data from low to high. The median IQ score is 85.5.

The first quartile is the average of the 10th and 11th scores from the lowest score:

$$Q_1 = (69 + 74)/2 = 143/2 = 71.5$$

The third quartile is the average of the 10th and 11th scores from the highest score:

$$Q_3 = (95 + 93)/2 = 188/2 = 94$$

The interquartile range is equal to:

$$IQR = 94 - 71.5 = 22.5$$

The fences and adjacent values are:

Low Inner Fence = $71.5 - [(1.5)22] = 38.5$

Lower Outer Fence = $71.5 - [(3.0)22] = 5.5$

High Inner Fence = $93.5 + [(1.5)22] = 126.5$

Higher Outer Fence = $93.5 + [(3.0)22] = 159.5$

Low Adjacent Value = 52

High Adjacent Value = 105

There are no outliers. The completed box-and-whisker plot is shown as follows.

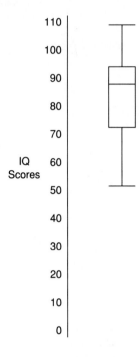

Because the bottom whisker is slightly longer than the upper whisker and the median line in the box is above the half-way point, we would conclude that there is a small negative skewness to the distribution of these IQ scores.

# CHAPTER 7

# Introduction to Probability Theory

*Probable impossibilities are to be preferred to improbable possibilities.*
—ARISTOTLE

## 7.1 INTRODUCTION

Although we might not be able to provide a precise mathematical definition of what it is, most of us have some understanding of what is meant by the concept of *probability*. Our intuitive knowledge of probability is captured by other words that we may substitute for it, such as the odds, likelihood, or the chance of something happening. For example, most of us have probably wondered what the odds are that we will win the state lottery if we purchased a lottery ticket. We have also probably asked ourself about the chance of getting into a class before it closes or have asked a professor how likely it is that we can still get an A (or a C!) out of her course.

People also make frequent probability judgments in the criminal justice world. Jurors in criminal cases, for example, are asked to determine how probable it is that an accused defendant actually committed an offense (and are told that the probability must be very high—"beyond a reasonable doubt"—before they can convict). Before setting or denying bail, judges make estimates of the probability that a defendant will appear later in court for trial. Members of parole boards make rough estimates of the likelihood of inmates recidivating before releasing them on parole or continuing to confine them in a penal institution. Finally, criminal justice researchers also are frequently concerned with the notion of probability. They wish to know how likely it is that their sample data and their findings accurately capture or reflect the larger population that they are interested in generalizing to.

Notions of probability are implied in each of these uses, although in a slightly different sense. What is common to all of them, however, is that probability estimates are used to enhance and inform decision making. The concept of probability forms the foundation for much research and statistical work. To understand the concept of probability more precisely and how it applies to problems of criminal justice policy and research, we need to acquaint you with the mathematical notion of probability. This chapter introduces you to some of the basic concepts and rules of probability.

## 7.2 PROBABILITY CONCEPTS

When we flip a coin, we know that there are two and only two possible outcomes to the flip. We get either a head or a tail. In the language of probability, the act of flipping a coin is called a *trial* or an *experiment*. The outcome of obtaining either a head or a tail on our one flip is called an *event*. The total number of possible outcomes or events from a trial is often referred to as a *sample space*. The trial of flipping a coin, therefore, has a sample space of two, because a single flip can have two possible outcomes, either a head or a tail. It is conventional to refer to the appearance of an event as a *success* and to the nonappearance of an event as a *failure*. We use these terms in this chapter.

In the classical notion of probability, the probability of an event, event *A*, referred to by the term P(*A*), is defined as the number of observations of *A* divided by the total number of possible observations or events (the sample space):

$$P(A) = \frac{\text{Number of Observations Favoring Event A}}{\text{Total Number of Possible Observations}} \qquad (7.1)$$

For example, in our coin flip, there are two possible observations (a sample space of two), one observation of a head and one observation of a tail. The probability of a head appearing, then, is 1/2, or .50.

As a second example, let us suppose we have a deck of fair cards. Because there are 52 cards in the deck, the total number of outcomes (the sample space) is 52. There are 52 total possible outcomes because there are 52 different cards. With this deck, what is the probability of drawing a club in a single pick? Because there are 52 total possible observations and there are 13 clubs in the deck, the probability of drawing a club from a single trial is 13/52, or .25. In this sense of the term, then, the probability of an event refers to the proportion of successes relative to the total number of possible outcomes or events.

To say that the probability of a head on a coin flip is .50 does not mean that, if we flip a coin twice (two trials), we will always get a head on one trial and a tail on the other. Although the probability of getting a head on a coin flip is .50 (as is the probability of a tail), the notion of probability implies that "over the long run" or with a very large number of coin flips, we would expect the proportion of heads (and tails) to be .50. Even if we were to flip a coin 10 times, we would not usually expect to get exactly five heads and five tails. We may instead get seven heads, three heads, or no heads. If, however, we were to continue to flip our coin, say for 100 trials, the proportion of heads would approximate .50, and after 1000 trials it would even be closer to .50. Probability in this sense of the term, then, indicates the proportion of times that we would expect an event to occur if the trial were repeated a large number of times.

## 7.3 THE RULES OF PROBABILITY

Remember that a sample space refers to the total possible number of outcomes. With a sample space of *N*, we can have no fewer than zero and no more than *N* successes. The first rule of probability, therefore, is that for any event *A*, the probability of *A* occurring [P(*A*)] must be greater than or equal to zero and less than or equal to 1. This rule expressed in equation form is:

$$0 \leq P(A) \leq 1 \tag{7.2}$$

We will call this the *bounding rule* because it indicates that any probability is bounded by zero and 1. Events with probabilities close to zero are very unlikely to occur, whereas events with probabilities close to 1 are very likely to occur.

P(*A*) is referred to as the probability of an event occurring. The probability of an event not occurring, what we will call the probability of "not A," also has a special term. It is called the *complement of an event.* The complement of an event is the probability of any event in the sampling space other than *A* occurring and is mathematically defined as 1 − P(*A*). For example, if the probability of selecting a heart from a deck of cards is .25 (13/52), the probability of not drawing a heart, that is, the probability of drawing anything but a heart, is (1 − .25), or .75. Because one or the other event must occur, you should notice that the sum of the probability of an event and its complement must be 1:

P(*A*) + P(not *A*) = 1

Notice one other thing about the probability of an event and its complement: they cannot both occur at the same time. We cannot have both the occurrence of event *A* and the occurrence of event not *A*. In other words, we cannot in a single draw select both a heart from a deck of cards and any other card besides a heart. The probability of event *A* occurring and the probability of event not *A* occurring at the same time, then, is zero. If two events, like an event and its complement, cannot both occur at the same time, they are said to be *mutually exclusive.* The probability of two events occurring at the same time is referred to as the *joint probability* of the events, and the joint probability of two mutually exclusive events is zero.

With our knowledge of mutually exclusive events, we can now discuss a second rule of probability, the *addition rule.* A limited case of the addition rule of probability can be stated as follows: If events *A* and *B* are mutually exclusive, the probability of observing *either* event *A* or event *B*, written as P(*A* or *B*), is equal to the probability of *A* [P(*A*)] plus the probability of *B* [P(*B*)]:

$$P(A \text{ or } B) = P(A) + P(B) \tag{7.3}$$

Please note that Equation 7.3 is only true if the two events are mutually exclusive. For example, the drawing of both a heart and a spade in a single draw from a deck of cards are mutually exclusive events. If we wanted to know the probability of drawing either a heart or a spade, we can use our addition rule:

P(♥ or ♠) = P(♥) + P(♠) = 13/52 + 13/52 = 26/52 = .50

The addition rule tells us that the appearance of either of two events is the sum of their separate probabilities. You can think of the addition rule as the "or" rule. It is

---

**The bounding rule:** The probability of any event occurring must be between zero and 1.

---

**The addition rule:** The probability of either of two mutually exclusive events occurring is equal to the probability of one event plus the probability of the other:

$$P(A \text{ or } B) = P(A) + P(B)$$

---

applicable whenever we are interested in the probability of either one event *or* another occurring, but not both simultaneously.

We will now extend this addition rule to cover more than two mutually exclusive events. If events $A, B, C, \ldots, K$ are *all mutually exclusive,* then the probability of any one of them occurring is equal to the sum of their respective separate probabilities. That is:

$$P(A \text{ or } B \text{ or } C \ldots \text{ or } K) = P(A) + P(B) + P(C) + \ldots + P(K) \tag{7.4}$$

The probability of drawing a heart, spade, or club in a single draw from a deck of cards would be:

$$P(\heartsuit \text{ or } \spadesuit \text{ or } \clubsuit) = P(\heartsuit) + P(\spadesuit) + P(\clubsuit)$$

$$= 13/52 + 13/52 + 13/52$$

$$= 39/52$$

$$= .75$$

Let's use an example more applicable to criminology. The data in Table 7.1 refer to defendants charged with violating U.S. drug laws who were tried in U.S. District Courts in 1991. Let's use this data set to examine further the addition rule of

**TABLE 7.1. Defendants Charged with Drug Law Violations and Tried in U.S. District Courts, 1991**

| Disposition | Number of Defendants |
|---|---|
| Not convicted | |
| Case dismissed | 2444 |
| Acquitted by court | 39 |
| Acquitted by trial | 398 |
| Convicted | |
| Guilty plea | 13,554 |
| Convicted by court | 93 |
| Convicted by jury | 2699 |
| Total | 19,227 |

*Source:* Kathleen Maguire and Ann L. Pastore, eds., Sourcebook of Criminal Justice Statistics, 1993. U.S. Department of Justice, Bureau of Criminal Statistics. Washington, DC: USGPO, 1994.

probability. The probability of selecting a defendant who was acquitted either by the court ($A$) or by trial ($B$) is:

$$P(A) + P(B) = 39/19,227 + 398/19,227$$

$$= .0020 + .0207$$

$$= .0227$$

The probability of selecting any convicted defendant, that is, one convicted either by guilty plea ($A$), by the court ($B$), or by jury ($C$) is:

$$P(A) + P(B) + P(C) = 13,554/19,227 + 93/19,227 + 2699/19,227$$

$$= .7049 + .0048 + .1404$$

$$= .8501$$

If the probability of selecting a convicted defendant is .85, from our knowledge of complements and mutually exclusive probabilities, we can determine that the probability of selecting a defendant who was not convicted is $1 - .85 = .15$.

So far, we limited our discussion to mutually exclusive events. We can now discuss a more general form of the addition rule that includes nonmutually exclusive events. If $A$ and $B$ are any events that are not necessarily mutually exclusive, then the probability of $A$ or $B$ is equal to the probability of $A$ [P($A$)] plus the probability of $B$ [P($B$)] minus the probability of *both* $A$ and $B$ occurring [P($A$ and $B$)]:

$$P(A \text{ or } B) = P(A) + P(B) - P(A \text{ and } B) \tag{7.5}$$

We have mentioned the notion of the probability of both events $A$ and $B$ occurring simultaneously, or the *joint probability* of an event. The joint probability of two events is written P($A$ and $B$) because we are now interested in both $A$ *and* B happening at the same time. In Equation 7.5 the joint probability of $A$ and $B$ must be subtracted because it has been considered twice, once in the calculation of P($A$) and once in the calculation of P($B$). An example may help us understand this more general addition rule.

Suppose we wanted to know the probability of selecting either a diamond or a king from a deck of cards. We show the 52 possible cards in a deck (our sample space) and underline those cards that would constitute a success:

```
♥ ♥ ♥ ♥ ♥ ♥ ♥ ♥   ♥ ♥ ♥ ♥
2 3 4 5 6 7 8 9  10 J  Q K A
♦ ♦ ♦ ♦ ♦ ♦ ♦ ♦   ♦ ♦ ♦ ♦
2 3 4 5 6 7 8 9  10 J  Q K A
♣ ♣ ♣ ♣ ♣ ♣ ♣ ♣   ♣ ♣ ♣ ♣
2 3 4 5 6 7 8 9  10 J  Q K A
♠ ♠ ♠ ♠ ♠ ♠ ♠ ♠   ♠ ♠ ♠ ♠
2 3 4 5 6 7 8 9  10 J  Q  K A
```

When selecting a card from a deck, we find a success when we select either a diamond or a king. We can do this by drawing any of the 13 diamonds (13/52) or by drawing any of the four kings (4/52). So the probability of drawing either a diamond or king might seem to be equal to the sum of these two probabilities: 13/52 + 4/52 = 17/52 (.327). Notice, however, that we have counted one card, the king of diamonds, twice (it is underlined twice). The king of diamonds is counted once as a diamond and again as a king. The king of diamonds is the joint occurrence of two events. Event one is the occurrence of a diamond, and event two is the occurrence of a king. These two events are not mutually exclusive, however, because they both can occur at the same time (in the king of diamonds). The probability of obtaining both a diamond and a king, therefore, is not zero. It is equal to 1/52, or .019, which corresponds to the king of diamonds out of 52 cards.

Therefore, because we have counted the king of diamonds twice, we must then subtract the probability of selecting it when calculating the probability of selecting either a diamond or a king. We must do this, remember, because we use the addition rule whenever we want to know the probability of either one event or another, but not both simultaneously. The probability of selecting either a diamond or a king, therefore, is equal to the probability of selecting a diamond plus the probability of selecting a king minus the probability of selecting the king of diamonds:[1]

$$P(\diamond \text{ or } K) = P(\diamond) + P(K) - P(K\diamond)$$

$$= 13/52 + 4/52 - 1/52$$

$$= .25 + .08 - .02$$

$$= .31$$

The concept of mutually exclusive and nonmutually exclusive events and their associated addition rules are shown with Venn diagrams in Figures 7.1 and 7.2. In Figure 7.1 the two events, A and B, are mutually exclusive because they do not intersect. As you can see, the probability of both A and B occurring is zero. In this case, the probability of either event A or event B occurring is the sum of each separate probability.

In Figure 7.2, however, the two events are not mutually exclusive. In this case the probability of A and B occurring at the same time (their joint probability) is greater than zero. This joint probability is illustrated as the small space where the two circles intersect (denoted by A and B). You can now see that, if we want to know the probability of either A or B occurring with nonmutually exclusive events,

FIGURE 7.1. Mutually exclusive events: P(A and B) = 0; P(A or B) = P(A) + P(B).

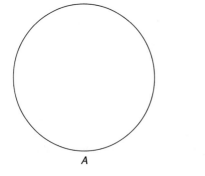
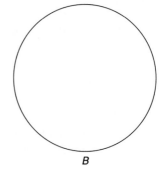

A                    B

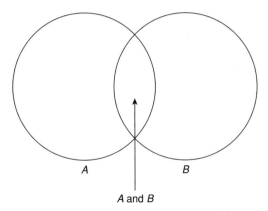

FIGURE 7.2. Nonmutually exclusive events: $P(A \text{ and } B) > 0$; $P(A \text{ or } B) = P(A) + P(B) - P(A \text{ and } B)$.

we have to adjust our addition rule. If we sum the probabilities of both events $A$ and $B$, we count the area noted by their joint occurrence ($A$ and $B$) twice. We count it once when we consider the probability of event $A$, and we count this common area again when we consider the probability of event $B$. We must, therefore, subtract this from the sum of the two probabilities. Hence, our addition rule for nonmutually exclusive events includes the final term, $- P(A \text{ and } B)$.

Let's use the data in Table 7.2 to illustrate further the general application of the addition rule of probability. Table 7.2 reports the number of crimes known to the police in 1990 for three states, Illinois, Michigan, and Texas. The number in each state is further divided into whether the crime was committed in a central city, a suburban area, or a rural area. Let's begin by calculating the probability that any crime will have been committed in the state of Texas:

P(Texas) = 16,986,510/37,712,409

= .45

and the probability of selecting a crime committed in a rural area of any of the three states:

P(Rural) = [978,687 + 1,167,831 + 1,766,780]/37,712,409

= 3,913,298/37,712,409

= .104

and finally, the probability of selecting a crime that is committed either in Texas or in a rural area:

P(T or R) = P(T) + P(R) − P(T and R)

= 16,986,510/37,712,409 + 3,913,298/37,712,409 −
1,766,780/37,712,409

= .450 + .104 − .047

= .507

**TABLE 7.2.  Number of Offenses Known to Police in Illinois, Michigan, and Texas by Extent of Urbanization, 1990**

| State | Number of Offenses |
|---|---|
| Illinois | 11,430,602 |
| Central city | 9,413,349 |
| Suburban | 1,038,566 |
| Rural | 978,687 |
| Michigan | 9,295,297 |
| Central city | 7,449,768 |
| Suburban | 677,698 |
| Rural | 1,167,831 |
| Texas | 16,986,510 |
| Central city | 13,864,735 |
| Suburban | 1,354,995 |
| Rural | 1,766,780 |
| Total | 37,712,409 |

*Source:* Crime in the United States, 1990. Federal Bureau of Investigation Uniform Crime Reports, U.S. Department of Justice, Washington, DC: USGPO, 1991.

The last term, P(*T* and *R*), is the probability of a crime occurring both in Texas and in a rural area simultaneously. It is a joint probability because it is the probability of two events occurring at the same time. It is possible for a crime to be committed both in a rural area and in Texas, so the events are not mutually exclusive and their joint probability is not zero. We therefore have to subtract it from our other two probabilities because we counted it twice: we added it into the number of crimes for Texas and we added it into the number of rural crimes.

The third rule of probability builds on the idea of nonmutually exclusive events and joint probabilities; it is the *multiplication rule*. The multiplication rule is concerned with the probability of two or more events occurring simultaneously (event *A and* event *B*) or the joint probability of two or more events. We first state the multiplication rule with reference to only two events and then provide a general multiplication rule that is applicable for all joint probability instances. After this, we illustrate a special case of the multiplication rule.

If *A* and *B* are any two events, the probability of both *A* and *B* occurring, written as P(*A* and *B*), is the product of the probability of one event occurring (*A*) times the probability of the other event occurring (*B*) given that the first event has already occurred $P(B \mid A)$:

$$P(A \text{ and } B) = P(A) \times P(B \mid A) = P(B) \times P(A \mid B) \tag{7.6}$$

We have two new terms in Equation 7.6 that we need to discuss and understand. The terms $P(B \mid A)$ and $P(A \mid B)$ are referred to as *conditional probabilities*. The con-

ditional probability P(B|A) (read as "the probability of B given A") is the proba-
bility of B occurring conditional on the fact that A has occurred. It is the probability of B occurring in the sample space defined by A. The conditional probability of
an event is a recognition that the probability of one event (B) may be dependent on
whether or not another event (A) has first occurred. This is probably very confusing
to you right now, so let's give an example.

From Table 7.2, we learned that the probability that a crime being committed
in a rural area is .104. We calculated this by dividing the number of rural crimes by
the total sample space − the total number of crimes (3,913,298/37,712,409). The
probability that a crime was committed in Illinois is .303. This is determined by dividing the number of crimes committed in Illinois by the total sample space
(11,430,602/37,712,409). Now let's say that we are interested in the probability that
a crime was committed both in a rural area [P(A)] *and* in Illinois [P(B)]. This probability concerns the joint probability or simultaneous occurrence of two events.

To determine this probability, we use the multiplication rule. First, we determine
the probability of a crime being committed in a rural area, P(A). We already know
this is .104. Next, based on Equation 7.6, we need to know the probability of a crime
being committed in Illinois given the fact that it is a rural crime P(B|A). This prob-
ability is a conditional probability. To determine this, we ask ourselves how many
rural crimes there were in all three states. The answer to this question is 3,913,298
(978,687 + 1,167,831 + 1,766,780). This is our sample space for the conditional
probability. Now, we want to know, given the fact that a crime is rural (i.e., given the
fact that it is one of the 3,913,298 rural crimes committed), what is the probability
that it was committed in Illinois. This probability is the probability that a crime was
committed in Illinois given the fact that it was rural. Because there were 3,913,298
rural crimes, of which 978,687 occurred in Illinois, the conditional probability is
978,687/3,913,298, or .25. Notice that in the conditional probability the sample
space is not the total number of cases, but the total number of event A cases, because
that is what event B is conditioned on. What we are actually saying is, "assume that
A has already occurred, and then determine the probability of B occurring."

We now have the two probabilities we need to determine the joint probability
of a crime being both rural, P(A), and occurring in Illinois, P(B):

P(A and B) = P(A) P(B|A)

= (.104) × (.250)

= .026

For those of you who are still a little confused, another example may help. Still
using the data in Table 7.2, let's determine the probability of a crime being committed both in Texas P(A) and within a central city P(B). You already know that this
joint probability is written as:

P(A and B) = P(A) P(B|A)

P(A), or the probability of a crime being committed in Texas is equal to .45
(16,986,510/37,712,409). The probability of a crime being committed in a cen-
tral city given the fact that it was committed in Texas, P(B|A), is determined by

determining first how many crimes were committed in Texas (16,986,510) and then how many of those were committed in a central city (13,864,735). The probability of a crime being committed in a central city given the fact that it occurred in Texas, then, is .816 (13,864,735/16,986,510). The probability that a crime was committed in Texas and in a central city can then be calculated as:

$$P(A \text{ and } B) = P(A) \, P(B \mid A)$$

$$= (.45) \, (.816)$$

$$= .367$$

Equation 7.5 is the general multiplication rule of probability. Before we discuss a special instance of the multiplication rule, we need to examine one additional concept based on the notion of conditional probability. This is the concept of *statistical independence*. An event $A$ is said to be statistically independent of another event $B$ if the probability of $A$ is equal to the probability of $A$ given $B$. That is, an event is statistically independent of another if its probability is not affected by the occurrence of the other event. In probability terms, $A$ and $B$ are statistically independent if:

$$P(A \mid B) = P(A) \text{ and } P(B \mid A) = P(B) \qquad (7.7)$$

In words, this means that the conditional probability of $A$ given $B$ is equal to the probability of $A$, and the conditional probability of $B$ given $A$ is equal to the probability of $B$.

If two events are statistically independent, knowing that event $B$ has occurred will not help us predict whether event $A$ will occur, and knowing that event $A$ has occurred will not help us predict whether event $B$ will occur. For instance, in a deck of cards the face value of a card (2, 3, 4, . . ., king, ace, etc.) is statistically independent of the suit of a card (♥, ♦, ♣, ♠). The conditional probability of selecting an ace given a club—the probability of selecting the ace given that a card is a club: $P(A \mid ♣) = 1/13$—is the same as the unconditional probability of selecting an ace from the entire deck—$P(A) = 4/52 = 1/13$. Knowing that a card is a club, therefore, will not help us predict what face value it has because suit and face value are statistically independent. By definition, this is true because each suit has the same number of aces, kings, queens, and so on. Similarly, knowing what face value a card is will not help us predict what suit it is.

When two events are not statistically independent, they are said to be dependent. How can we determine when events are dependent? Well, we can use probability Equation 7.7 to help us define when an event is dependent. When event $A$ is not statistically independent of event $B$, the probability of $A$ is not equal to the probability of $A$ given $B$: $P(A) \neq P(A \mid B)$. When an event is dependent, the conditional probability of $A$ given $B$ is less than or greater than the probability of $A$. In

---

**The general multiplication rule:** The probability of two events occurring simultaneously is equal to the probability of one event times the conditional probability of the other:

$$P(A \text{ and } B) = P(A) \, P(B \mid A)$$

> **Statistical independence:** Event *A* is statistically independent of event *B* when the probability of *A* is equal to the probability of *A* given *B:* $P(A) = P(A \mid B)$. When two events are statistically independent, knowledge of one event does not help us predict the occurrence of the other.

the case of dependent events, then, knowledge about the occurrence of one event does help us predict the occurrence of the other. This probably all sounds very confusing, so it might be time for a few examples.

Let's take as our first example a fictitious deck of cards. In this fictitious deck of 52 cards there are four suits (spades, clubs, diamonds, and hearts) but only four face values (ace, king, queen, and jack). Moreover, all 13 of the spades are aces, all 13 of the clubs are kings, all of the diamonds are queens and all of the hearts are jacks. Unlike a regular deck of cards, then, each suit does not have one of each different face value. Let's let event *A* be the selection of a spade and event *B* be the selection of a jack. With a random draw from a shuffled deck, we can determine that the probability of event *A* (selecting a spade) is .25 (13/52). Is the probability of event *A* (selecting a spade) equal to the probability of selecting event *A* (selecting a spade) given event *B* (that the card is a jack)? The answer is no. Given that a card is a jack, the probability that it is a spade is equal to zero because in this fictitious deck all jacks are hearts. The condition of a statistically independent event described in Equation 7.7 is therefore not met:

$P(A) = P(A \mid B)$ for statistically independent events

$P(A) = .25$

$P(A \mid B) = 0$

$P(A) \neq P(A \mid B)$: events *A* and *B* are not statistically independent

The events of drawing a spade and drawing a jack are not, therefore, independent events. The probability of drawing a spade depends on the card's face value, because if the card is a jack, the probability that it is a spade is equal to zero and the probability that it is a heart is equal to 1. Knowing that a card is a jack, then, will help us predict its suit, and knowing its suit will help us predict its face value. The two events are dependent.

Let's return to the data in Table 7.2 for another example. We already know from this data set that the probability that a crime was committed in a rural area is .104. Let's set the probability of a rural crime as event *A* and let the state the crime was committed in be event *B*. Is the probability that a crime was rural independent of the state in which it occurred? The answer is no. The probability that a crime was rural is not equal to the probability that the crime was rural given that it was committed in a given state. Although the probability of a rural crime is .104 (3,913,298/ 37,712,404), the probability of a rural crime given that the crime occurred in Illinois is .086. The probability of a rural crime given that it occurred in Michigan is .126 (1,167,831/9,295,297), and it is .10 for Texas (1,766,780/16,986,510). The conditional probabilities are not equal to the unconditional probability. The probability of a rural crime and the state are not, therefore, independent events. Because conditional probabilities are not equal to the unconditional probabilities when events are statistically dependent, we have to use the former in our general case of the multiplication rule (Equation 7.6). When events are independent, however, there is a special case of the multiplication rule.

When events $A$ and $B$ are statistically independent [$P(A | B) = P(A)$], the multiplication rule takes a simplified form:

$$P(A \text{ and } B) = P(A) \times P(B) \tag{7.8}$$

The probability of two independent events occurring simultaneously (the joint probability) is equal to the product of their separate probabilities.[2] With our previous example, because suit and face value are statistically independent, the probability of selecting a diamond and a queen is equal to the probability of selecting a diamond (13/52) times the probability of selecting a queen (4/52):

$$(13/52) \times (4/52) = 52/2704 = .019$$

What happens when two events are not statistically independent? We already know that two things will happen. One is that the probability of an event will not be equal to the conditional probability of that event. We also know that, when two events are dependent, knowledge that one event has occurred will help us predict the occurrence of another event. We can further speculate that the more dependent the two events are, the more help one event will be in predicting the other. This predictive ability is very important in criminological research and is the cornerstone of most inferential statistics. Let's look at some more real data to help us understand further the concept of statistical independence.

Figures 7.3 and 7.4 provide some data from a study one of the authors conducted. Questionnaires were administered to more than 2000 students in nine high schools concerning issues related to juvenile delinquency. Figure 7.3 shows the number of male and female students and whether they reported drinking liquor when they were under age in the year before completing the questionnaire. Let's take event $A$ as the probability of drinking, and let event $B$ be the probability of being male. Of 2546 students, 1806 of them admitted drinking liquor in the previous year. Therefore, the probability that we will select a high school student who drank liquor in the past year is .71 [$P(A) = 1806/2546$]. Now, does knowing the person's gender help us predict whether someone reported drinking in the past year? Does the condition of being male, for example, increase the probability that someone will drink? Is drinking statistically independent of gender?

FIGURE 7.3. Number of high school students who reported drinking alcohol in past year, by gender.

| Gender | | No | Yes | Totals |
|---|---|---|---|---|
| | Male | 377 | 901 | 1278 |
| | Female | 363 | 905 | 1268 |
| Totals | | 740 | 1806 | 2546 |

Remember that two events are statistically independent if $P(A|B) = P(A)$. We know that $P(A) = .71$. What is $P(A|B)$? There were a total of 1278 male students, of whom 901 admitted to drinking in the past year. The conditional probability of being a drinker given that the person is a male, then, is 901/1278, or .71. The unconditional probability of selecting a student who drank (.71) is the same as the conditional probability of selecting a drinking student given the fact that the student is a male (.71). By our definition, because the probability of event $A$ (drinking) is equal to the conditional probability of $A$ given $B$ (drinking given male), the two events are statistically independent.

Because the two events are statistically independent, we can apply our simplified multiplication rule in determining the probability that someone will both have drunk liquor in the past and be male. The probability of selecting someone who has reported drinking and is male is equal to the product of their separate probabilities:

$$P(\text{Drinking and Male}) = P(D) \times P(M) = 1806/2546 \times 1278/2546$$

$$= .71 \times .50$$

$$= .355$$

Figure 7.4 reports data from the same study. In this figure we have the joint occurrence of drinking in the past year (event $A$) and the grades that the student received in their most recent report card (event $B$). The probability of selecting a student who reported drinking in the past year is the same as before, .71 (1805/2542). We now ask whether drinking is statistically independent of grades. Is $P(A) = P(A|B)$? The probability of drinking in the past year is .60 for those whose grades are As and Bs (377/632), .73 for those who get Bs and Cs (919/1259), .77 for those who get Cs and Ds, and .94 for those who get Ds and Fs. The probability that a student drank in the past year [$P(A)$] is not equal to the conditional probability of drinking given what grades they get [$P(A|B)$]. We noted that, when two events ($A$ and $B$) are statistically independent, the probability of $A$ does not vary with $B$. This is decidedly *not* the case with drinking and grades. The probability that a student drank liquor in the past year (event $A$) changes dramatically with event $B$—the worse the student's grades were, the higher the probability that they

FIGURE 7.4. Number of high school students who reported drinking alcohol in past year, by grades received.

| | | No | Yes | Totals |
|---|---|---|---|---|
| | A's & B's | 255 | 377 | 632 |
| | B's & C's | 340 | 919 | 1259 |
| Grades | | | | |
| | C's & D's | 138 | 451 | 589 |
| | D's & F's | 4 | 58 | 62 |
| Totals | | 737 | 1805 | 2542 |

had drunk liquor in the past year. If we know that someone gets Ds and Fs in school, we know that he or she has a higher probability of also having been a drinker in the past than one with better grades. In other words, knowing grades helps us predict past drinking. These two events, drinking and grades, are not statistically independent.

We will now use the more general multiplication rule in Equation 7.6 to determine the probability that we will select someone from Figure 7.4 who has both reported drinking in the past year (event A) and has grades of Cs and Ds (event B):

$$P(A \text{ and } B) = P(A) \, P(B \,|\, A)$$

$$= (1805/2542) \, (451/1805)$$

$$= (.71) \, (.25)$$

$$= .18$$

and the probability of selecting someone who both reported not drinking (event A) and who has grades of As and Bs (event B):

$$P(A \text{ and } B) = P(A) \, P(B \,|\, A)$$

$$= (737/2542) \, (255/737)$$

$$= (.29) \, (.34)$$

$$= .10$$

The multiplication rule can easily be extended to cover three or more events. If events A, B, C, . . ., K are all statistically independent of one another, the probability of A, B, C, . . ., and K occurring simultaneously is the product of their separate probabilities:

$$P(A \text{ and } B \text{ and } C \ldots K) = P(A) \, P(B) \, P(C) \ldots P(K) \tag{7.9}$$

If events A, B, C, . . . , K are not statistically independent, the probability of A, B, C, . . . , and K occurring simultaneously can be determined by the formula:

$$P(A \text{ and } B \text{ and } C \ldots \text{ and } K) = P(A) \, P(B \,|\, A) \, P(C \,|\, A \text{ and } B) \ldots$$
$$P(K \,|\, A \text{ and } B \text{ and } C \ldots) \tag{7.10}$$

The term $P(C \,|\, A \text{ and } B)$ is the conditional probability of event C occurring given the fact that both events A and B have also occurred.

To examine the probability of three events that are not statistically independent we use the data in Figure 7.5, from the same study of high school students and delinquency. Figure 7.5 shows the joint distribution of three events or variables; whether the student reported drinking liquor (event A), the grades the student received (event B), and the proportion of the student's friends under age who drink liquor (event C). What is the probability of selecting a student who (1) drank liquor in the past year, *and* (2) gets Cs and Ds in their class work, *and* (3) has many friends who also drink liquor? We can use the formula for conditional probabilities in Equation 7.10:

$$P(A \text{ and } B \text{ and } C) = P(A) \, P(B \,|\, A) \, P(C \,|\, A \text{ and } B)$$

> **The multiplication rule with independent events:** The probability of two independent events occurring simultaneously is equal to the probability of one event times the probability of the other:
>
> $P(A \text{ and } B) = P(A) \, P(B)$

Let's first determine the probability of A, the probability of selecting a student who reported drinking in the past year. This probability is calculated as 722 + 1068 (the number of students who reported drinking) divided by 1368 + 1150 (the total number of students in the table). Hence, $P(A) = 1790/2518 = .71$. Now, let's calculate the probability of B given A (the probability of selecting a student who gets Cs and Ds given that they reported drinking). Because we want to know the number of students who got Cs and Ds given the fact that they reported drinking, let's first determine how many students reported that they drank liquor in the past year. This number is the sum of 722 + 1068, which is 1790. Now, let's determine of these who reported drinking, how many received C and D grades. This number is the sum of 169 + 280, which is 449. The probability of selecting a student who gets C and D grades given the fact that they drink $[P(B \,|\, A)]$, then, is 449/1790, or .25. Last, let's calculate the probability of C given A and B. This conditional probability is the

FIGURE 7.5. Number of high school students who reported having friends who drank alcohol in the past year, by grades received.

No or Only a Few Friends Drank Liquor in Past Year

|        |         | No | Yes | Totals |
|--------|---------|-----|-----|--------|
|        | A's & B's | 236 | 182 | 418 |
| Grades | B's & C's | 287 | 361 | 648 |
|        | C's & D's | 120 | 169 | 289 |
|        | D's & F's | 3   | 10  | 13  |
| Totals |         | 646 | 722 | 1368 |

Most or All Friends Drank Liquor in Past Year

|        |         | No | Yes | Totals |
|--------|---------|-----|-----|--------|
|        | A's & B's | 17 | 192 | 209 |
| Grades | B's & C's | 46 | 549 | 595 |
|        | C's & D's | 18 | 280 | 298 |
|        | D's & F's | 1  | 47  | 48  |
| Totals |         | 82 | 1068 | 1150 |

---

**Rules of Probabilities**

**Rule 1.** The Bounding Rule

$0 \leq P(A) \leq 1$

The probability of an event, $P(A)$, must always be greater than or equal to zero and less than or equal to 1.

**Rule 2.** The Addition Rule

For mutually exclusive events:

$P(A \text{ or } B) = P(A) + P(B)$

For mutually exclusive events, the probability of either event $A$ occurring or event $B$ occurring is equal to the sum of their separate probabilities.

For nonmutually exclusive events:

$P(A \text{ or } B) = P(A) + P(B) - P(A \text{ and } B)$

For two events that are not mutually exclusive, the probability of either event $A$ or event $B$ occurring is equal to the sum of their separate probabilities minus the probability of their joint occurrence.

**Rule 3.** The Multiplication Rule

For statistically independent events:

$P(A \text{ and } B) = P(A) \times P(B)$

If two events are statistically independent, the probability of both event $A$ and event $B$ occurring simultaneously is equal to the product of their separate probabilities.

For statistically dependent events:

$P(A \text{ and } B) = P(A) \times P(B \mid A)$

If any two events are not statistically independent, the probability of both event $A$ and event $B$ occurring simultaneously is equal to the product of the probability of one event and the conditional probability of the second.

---

probability of selecting someone with many or most drinking friends (event $C$) given the fact that they get Cs and Ds (event $B$) and that they reported drinking (event $A$). The denominator of our probability is the number of students who both get Cs and Ds and reported drinking. From Figure 7.5, we can see that this number is the sum of $169 + 280$, which is 449. We now want to know how many of these students also have many friends who drink, which is 280. The probability, then, of selecting someone with many friends who drink, given the fact that they get Cs and Ds and reported drinking themselves is $280/449 = .62$. We now have all the information we need to solve our problem:

$$P(A \text{ and } B \text{ and } C) = P(A) \, P(B \mid A) \, P(C \mid A \text{ and } B)$$

$$= (.71)\,(.25)\,(.62)$$

$$= .11$$

The three rules of probabilities are summarized for you in the box.

# 7.4 THE RULES OF COUNTING

In addition to the above rules of probabilities, we need to add one more complexity. This complexity concerns counting rules. What exactly do we mean by counting rules, and what part do they play in our discussion of probabilities? You will notice that the rules of probabilities discussed in the previous sections are really all about counting. To calculate the probability of an event, remember that we needed to count the number of occurrences, or "successes," of event *A* and divide by the total possible number of occurrences (the sample space). For example, to determine the probability of selecting a male from Figure 7.3, we counted the number of males (1278) and divided by the total number of students (2546). In some instances the counts are provided for us, are relatively easy to list, or few in number, as in Figure 7.3. At other times, however, the number of outcomes of an event are not so easily derived and may be so large that they cannot easily be listed. In these instances, we need to determine our own counts of events. There are a few simple rules to follow when counting events for probability analysis.

The first rule is the most fundamental counting rule of all, and we will refer to it as the basic counting rule. It concerns the total number of possible sequences or occurrences for a given event and a specified number of trials.

## Rule 1: The Basic Counting Rule

If there is an event with *K* possible mutually exclusive outcomes on any given trial and *N* number of trials, the total number of possible occurrences can be determined as $K^N$. For example, let's say we plan to flip three coins, a quarter, a dime, and a penny. The event of a coin flip has two outcomes, either heads or tails ($K = 2$), so with three flips ($N = 3$) the total number of possible occurrences is $2^3$, or 8. The eight possible outcomes from flipping the coins three times are shown in the following list (H = heads, T = tails):

| Trial | Outcome |
|-------|---------|
| 1 | H H H |
| 2 | H H T |
| 3 | H T H |
| 4 | H T T |
| 5 | T T T |
| 6 | T T H |
| 7 | T H T |
| 8 | T H H |

From this listing of all possible sequences, you can see that the probability of obtaining three heads in three coin flips is 1/8, or .125. The probability of getting two and only two tails is 3/8, or .375, and the probability of getting at least one tail is 7/8, or .875.

This counting formula applies when the *N* trials each have the same number of outcomes (*K*). A more general counting rule can now be stated: If there are $T_1$ distinct outcomes that can occur on the first trial and $T_2$ distinct outcomes that can occur on

> **The general counting rule:** If there are *N* events that occur in a definite order and there are *K* different outcomes for each event, the total number of possible outcomes is equal to:
>
> $$K_1 \times K_2 \times K_3 \times \cdots \times K_N$$

the second trial and $T_N$ outcomes that can occur on the *N*th trial, then the total number of different outcomes can be determined by $T_1 \times T_2 \times \cdots \times T_N$. For example, imagine that a judicial administrator has four courtrooms to use ($C_1$, $C_2$, $C_3$, and $C_4$) and three times a day to schedule jury questioning, or *voir dire* (8:00 A.M., 11:00 A.M., and 3:00 P.M.). From our general counting rule there would be 4(3), or 12, outcomes of distinct courtrooms and time. You can perhaps see the different listing of all events more clearly from Figure 7.6. The tree has two limbs, one for each of the two events. The number of branches corresponds to the number of distinct possibilities. With four courtrooms and three times, we have twelve branches. The first branch of the tree corresponds to an 8:00 A.M. time in the first courtroom. The second branch corresponds to an 11:00 A.M. time in the first courtroom and so on. Now you can see that the total number of events can always be determined by multiplying the number of outcomes for the first event by the number of outcomes for the second event for each of the different events.

FIGURE 7.6. Tree diagram for courtroom and court time example.

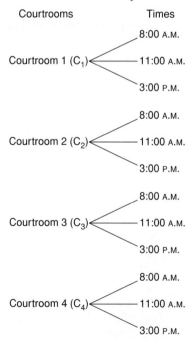

In the coin toss example, we treated each ordering of events as unique. That is, the sequence HHT was treated as different from the sequence THH, and both were treated as different from HTH, even though all three sequences contain two heads and one tail. They are different in this case because the outcomes appear in a different order. In the first sequence, two successive heads are followed by a tail; in the second, two heads follow a tail; and in the third, the tail comes in between two heads. Thus, although all three sequences contain the same number of heads (2), they are different because of the *ordering* of the heads and tails.

Sometimes the ordering of events matters. Up to this point we have been concerned with the ordering of events. For example, using our multiplication rule we could calculate the probability of getting two heads and one tail on three successive coin flips as the probability of getting a head, followed by another head, followed by a tail. This probability is $.5 \times .5 \times .5 = .125$. We can verify this by looking at the sequences in the list of possible outcomes. We see there that the sequence head, head, tails (HHT) occurs only once out of eight total possible sequences. The probability is 1/8, or .125. The probability of .125, then, is the probability of getting a head, a head, and a tail *in that exact order.*

In many instances, however, we are not concerned about the ordering of events. That is, we want to know the probability of getting two heads and one tail *in any order* from flipping a coin three times. In simple cases we can determine this by examining all of the total possible sequences of outcomes, such as that displayed in the list. We can see, for example, that there are three possible ways we can obtain exactly two heads and one tail in any order from flipping a coin three times (Trials 2, 3, and 8). This probability, then, is 3/8, or .375.

At other times it is rather tedious to list all possible sequences of events and then find the number of sequences that define a success like we just did. It would be more helpful if we could use other counting rules. This brings us to our second rule of counting.

## Rule 2: The Permutation Rule

An important probability rule concerns the number of different ways that objects may be arranged in order. For instance, let's say we have four distinct cards [♥, ♦, ♣, ♠], ignoring the face value for the moment. How many different ways can these four cards be arranged? Any one of the four cards could be selected to fill the first position, making four possibilities for position one (let's say a heart occupies the first position). Given the heart in the first position there are only three suits left for the second position. Similarly, with a diamond in the first position, there are only three suits left for the second position. With a club in the first position, there are only three left for the second position, and with a spade in the first position, there are three suits left for the second. The total number of different ways in which the first two positions could be filled, then, is 4(3), or 12. They are: ♥ ♦, ♥ ♣, ♥ ♠, ♦ ♣, ♦ ♠, ♦ ♥, ♣ ♥, ♣ ♥, ♣ ♦, ♠ ♥, ♠ ♦, ♠ ♣. What about the third position? With the first two positions taken, two cards remain, so that there are (4)(3)(2), or 24 ways, to fill positions one to three. Finally, with three positions filled there is only one card left to fill the remaining position. In sum, there are (4)(3)(2)(1), or 24, different ways in which the four cards can be displayed:

| | |
|---|---|
| 1. ♥♠♦♣ | 13. ♦♣♠♥ |
| 2. ♥♠♣♦ | 14. ♦♣♥♠ |
| 3. ♥♦♠♣ | 15. ♦♥♠♣ |
| 4. ♥♦♣♠ | 16. ♦♥♣♠ |
| 5. ♥♣♠♦ | 17. ♦♠♥♣ |
| 6. ♥♣♦♠ | 18. ♦♠♣♥ |
| 7. ♠♥♦♣ | 19. ♣♠♥♦ |
| 8. ♠♥♣♦ | 20. ♣♠♦♥ |
| 9. ♠♦♥♣ | 21. ♣♥♠♦ |
| 10. ♠♦♣♥ | 22. ♣♥♦♠ |
| 11. ♠♣♥♦ | 23. ♣♦♠♥ |
| 12. ♠♣♦♥ | 24. ♣♦♥♠ |

Notice what we have done. We have taken four cards (♥ ♦ ♣ ♠) and determined the number of different ways in which they can be ordered among themselves. In other words, we determined the number of ways in which four objects can be ordered from a collection of four objects. Each different ordering of the four cards is treated as a different outcome. Even though they all contain the same four cards, the events are different because the cards occur in a different *order* in each outcome.

Each one of the 24 outcomes is called a *permutation* of the four cards. A permutation of $r$ objects from a group of $N$ objects is any *ordered* arrangement of the $r$ objects from the $N$ objects. In the card example, we are determining the number of arrangements of four objects (the four cards) from a group of four objects. In counting the permutation of objects, then, the ordering of events matters. The second rule of counting concerns how to derive the number of these permutations, and we will call it the permutation rule. The total number of permutations of $N$ objects among themselves is ($N!$ (the symbol $N!$ is called "$N$ factorial"),[3] where ! is $N \times (N - 1) \times (N - 2) \times (N - 3) \times \cdots \times 1$. For example:

$$4! = (4)(3)(2)(1) = 24$$

$$3! = (3)(2)(1) = 6$$

$$10! = (10)(9)(8)(7)(6)(5)(4)(3)(2)(1) = 3,628,800$$

Imagine that you are asked to put together a police lineup with five suspects. In how many different ways can the lineup be ordered? With five persons (events) objects, there are 5!, or 120 different possible lineup orderings, or 120 different permutations of the five persons. Again, each distinct lineup of persons is counted as a different outcome, even though the same five persons are in the lineup because in permutations the ordering of objects matters.

---

**Permutation rule:** $N$ different objects can be arranged in order $N!$ different ways, where

$$N! = 1 \times 2 \times 3 \times \ldots \times (N - 1) \times N$$

In these examples we have determined the number of permutations of $N$ objects among themselves. Sometimes we may want to order a smaller subset of objects from a collection of $N$ objects. In this case we need to define a more general permutation rule. Recall the definition of a permutation. A permutation of $r$ objects from a collection of $N$ objects is any *ordered* arrangement of the $r$ from the $N$ objects. In the lineup case, $r = N$. This is not always the case. For example, suppose that we wanted to determine the total number of ways in which we can arrange any two of the four cards (♥ ♦ ♣ ♠). In this case we want the number of permutations of two objects from four objects, where $r = 2$ and $N = 4$. The general formula for determining the total number of possible permutations of $r$ objects from a group of $N$ objects is:

$$\frac{N!}{(N - r)!}$$

where $r < N$                                              (7.11)

In our card example, the number of permutations of any two cards from the collection of four cards is:

$$\frac{4!}{(4 - 2)!} = \frac{4!}{2!}$$

$$= \frac{(4)(3)(2)(1)}{(2)(1)}$$

$$= \frac{24}{2} = 12$$

We show each of these 12 outcomes in the list that follows for you to examine. Notice that because these are permutations, the ordering of events matters so that a heart followed by a spade (the first permutation) is different from a spade followed by a heart (the fourth permutation).

1. ♥ ♠        7. ♦ ♣
2. ♥ ♦        8. ♦ ♥
3. ♥ ♣        9. ♦ ♠
4. ♠ ♥      10. ♣ ♠
5. ♠ ♦      11. ♣ ♥
6. ♠ ♣      12. ♣ ♦

## Rule 3: The Combination Rule

In counting the number of permutations, we have learned that the order of events matters. Whenever the order in which events occur is of no concern, the grouping of events is called a *combination*. In a combination, therefore, the sequence of ♥ ♥ ♦ is not treated as different from the sequence ♥ ♦ ♥ or ♦ ♥ ♥ because all three contain two hearts and one diamond. In contrast to a permutation, then, a combination of $r$ objects from a group of $N$ objects is any *unordered* arrangement of the $r$ objects from the $N$ objects. That is, a combination of $r$ objects is any subset of objects from a collection of $N$ objects. The rule for calculating the total number of combinations of $r$ objects from $N$ objects is:

$$\frac{N!}{r!(N-r)!} = \binom{N}{r} \tag{7.12}$$

where the symbol $\binom{N}{r}$ is not a fraction denoting $N$ divided by $r$, but refers to the number of combinations of $N$ objects taken $r$ at a time.

Let's return to our card example for a moment. In how many ways can we arrange two suits from four suits without regard for the order in which they appear? In other words, how many combinations of two cards are there from the four? Using Equation 7.12, we can calculate this to be $4!/(2!2!) = 24/4 = 6$ ways. The six ways are: ♥ ♣ ♥ ♠ ♥ ♦ ♠ ♦ ♠ ♣ ♦ ♣. Although there were twelve permutations of two cards from four, there are only six combinations, because order does not matter in combinations. For each of the six combinations of cards, we know from our permutation rule that there are 2!, or two, permutations: ♥♣ ♣♥ ♥♠ ♠♥ ♥♦ ♦♥ ♠♦ ♦♠ ♠♣ ♣♠ ♦♣ ♣♦. This implies that there are $r!$ as many permutations of $r$ objects from $N$ as there are combinations.

In the special case where there are only two kinds of events (say, flipping a coin and calling heads a "success" and tails a "failure"), the formula in Equation 7.12 is referred to as the *binomial coefficient*.

Before going on, take some time to review the three counting rules listed in the box.

We can now use both our addition/multiplication rules and counting rules to answer some complex probability questions. These questions will serve as the in-

---

**The basic counting rule:** If there are $N$ distinct events that occur in a specific order and there are $k_1$ outcomes for the first event, $k_2$ outcomes for the second event . . . and $k_n$ outcomes for the $n$th event the total number of possible outcomes is equal to

$$k_1 \times k_2 \times \cdots \times K_n$$

**The permutation rule:** A permutation of $r$ objects from a collection of $N$ objects is any ordered arrangement of the $r$ objects from the $N$ objects. The number of permutations of $r$ objects from $N$ objects is determined by:

$$\frac{N!}{(N-r)!}$$

**The combination rule:** A combination of $r$ objects from a collection of $N$ objects is any *unordered arrangement* of the $r$ objects from the $N$ objects. The number of combinations of $r$ objects from $N$ objects is determined by:

$$\frac{N!}{r!(N-r)!}$$

troduction to a very important part of the scientific process, hypothesis testing. For example, what is the probability of getting exactly two heads out of five flips of a coin? First of all, let's calculate the probability of getting two heads and three tails *in a given order.* Let's take the order (H,H,T,T,T). We know from our multiplication rule that the probability of obtaining the sequence H,H,T,T,T from five flips of a coin is (.5)(.5)(.5)(.5)(.5), or (.5)$^5$. This is not the answer to our probability question, however, because there are other ways to get exactly two heads from the five flips of a coin than just the sequence we considered. How can we calculate the number of ways in which we can get two heads out of five flips of a coin regardless of the order? Using our counting rules, we use the following calculations:

$$\binom{N}{r} = \frac{N!}{r!(N-r)!} \text{ with } N = 5 \text{ and } r = 2$$

$$\binom{5}{2} = \frac{5!}{2!(5-2)!}$$

$$= \frac{5!}{(2!)(3!)}$$

$$= \frac{5 \times 4 \times 3 \times 2 \times 1}{(2 \times 1)(3 \times 2 \times 1)}$$

$$= \frac{120}{(2)(6)}$$

$$= \frac{120}{12}$$

$$= 10$$

There are 10 ways, then, in which we can arrange exactly two heads from five flips of a coin:

(H,H,T,T,T) (H,T,H,T,T) (H,T,T,H,T) (H,T,T,T,H) (T,H,T,T,H) (T,H,H,T,H)
(T,T,H,H,T) (T,T,H,T,H) (T,T,T,H,H) (T,H,T,H,T)

We can now use our addition rule to determine the probability of getting two heads on five coin flips as the sum of the probability of getting two heads in any of these 10 possible orders. In sum, then, the probability of getting two heads on five flips (without regard to their order) can be found in two steps, as shown in the box. Let's take as our first sequence two heads followed by three tails (H,H,T,T,T). The probability of this sequence is (.5)(.5)(.5)(.5)(.5), or (.5)$^5$ = .031.

---

**Step 1.** Determine the probability of getting two heads and three tails on five flips in any order.

**Step 2.** Determine the total number of ways of arranging two heads and three tails from five flips of a coin.

---

We next determine the total number of combinations of two heads and three tails using Equation 7.12:

$$\frac{5!}{2!(3!)} = \frac{120}{(2)(6)} = \frac{120}{12} = 10$$

From the probability of observing an event in any order and the number of times the event can be ordered, we can determine the probability of getting exactly two heads in five flips of a coin as 10 (.031) = .31.

In this and a large number of other probability problems it is easy to determine the solution by first calculating the probability of getting any arrangement of events (Step 1) and multiplying this by the number of possible orderings (Step 2). In this way, we are using both our addition and multiplication rules and our counting rules of probability. In the next section, we apply these rules to the process and logic of hypothesis testing.

## 7.5 TESTING HYPOTHESES WITH THE BINOMIAL DISTRIBUTION

In a great number of instances in criminological and criminal justice research we are interested in events that have only two outcomes. For example, whether a defendant appears for trial, whether one who appears for trial tested positively or negatively for drug use, or whether someone released from prison is rearrested or reincarcerated. An event or process that can have only two outcomes is called a *Bernoulli process.* We can label the two outcomes of a Bernoulli process as either a success or a failure. In this section, the probability of obtaining a success will be denoted by $p$ and the probability of a failure by $q$. The sum of $p$ and $q$ is of course 1, so that the probability of $q$ is $1 - p$. If there are $N$ Bernoulli trials, the number of successes can only take on a whole value from zero to $N$ (that is, we can have no less than zero or no more than $N$ successes). We can, then, determine the probability of observing any number of $r$ successes from $N$ trials. Just as we have frequency distributions of raw data, then, we can also have *probability distributions* that tell us the probability of getting a certain number of successes and failures from a given number of trials. The probability distribution based on a Bernoulli process is referred to as the *binomial distribution.*

We examine in some detail the intricacies of the binomial distribution. Our purpose is to explore the logic of hypothesis testing in research. During the course of this book we use a number of such probability distributions, such as the normal, or $z$, distribution, Student's $t$, chi-square, and $F$ distributions. The binomial distribution is simply one type of probability distribution used whenever there are only two outcomes.

## 7.6 BERNOULLI PROCESS EVENTS

Before we begin, let's examine how the binomial distribution is obtained. In a Bernoulli process with $N$ trials we have two and only two possible outcomes, whose probabilities are $p$ and $q$. For simplicity we restrict our example to the case of a coin of a coin toss. Here we have only two outcomes, a head and a tail. The trial of flipping a coin, then, fits our description of a Bernoulli process. In the first example, we define the outcome of a head as a success ($p$) and that of a tail as a failure ($q$). With $N$ trials we can now easily calculate the probability of obtaining any number of $r$ heads and $(N - r)$ tails. Using the multiplication rule, the probability of obtaining three heads and two tails in succession (H,H,H,T,T) in five flips is: $(p,p,p,q,q)$ or $p^3q^2$. Because there is a constant probability of success in statistically independent trials, the probability of obtaining any other ordering of $r$ heads and $N - r$ tails is $p^rq^{N-r}$. Of course, this is true not only of coin flips but also of any event that fits the definition of a Bernoulli process. More in general, the probability of any given sequence of $N$ independent Bernoulli trials is:

$$p^rq^{N-r}$$

Returning to our coin example, the probability of obtaining three heads and two tails in succession in five flips (H,H,H,T,T) was found to be $p^3q^2$. But remember, this is the probability of getting three heads exactly in the order shown. To calculate the probability of obtaining exactly three heads and two tails *in any order,* we only need to know the number of different ways we can order the three heads and two tails. We have a simple formula from the previous section to determine this. Equation 7.12 stated that the number of possible ways in which we can order $r$ distinct objects from $N$ objects was defined as:

$$\binom{N}{r} = \frac{N!}{r!(N - r)!}$$

If we are interested in calculating the probability of getting exactly $r$ successes and $N - r$ failures in $N$ trials, regardless of the order of successes and failures, we can use the following formula:

$$P(r) = \binom{N}{r}(p^rq^{N-r}) \tag{7.13}$$

where

    $P(r)$ = the probability of getting exactly $r$ successes

    $\binom{N}{r}$ = the number of different ways of getting $r$ successes, originally defined in Equation 7.12

    $p^rq^{N-r}$ = the probability of getting any sequence

For example, the probability of getting exactly three heads in 10 coin flips is:

$$P(3) = \binom{10}{3}(.5)^3 (.5)^7$$

$$= \left(\frac{10!}{3!(7!)}\right)(.5)^3(.5)^7$$

$$= 120(.5)^{10}$$

$$= 120(.0009766)$$

$$= .117$$

We now calculate a complete probability distribution for this example and determine the probability of getting 0, 1, 2, 3, . . ., 10 heads in 10 coin flips. Remember, in this case $p = .5$, $q = .5$, and $N = 10$. The results are shown in Table 7.3.

You can see that whenever $r = 0$ the binomial $\binom{N}{r}$ is undefined (it refers to the number of combinations of $N$ things taken zero at a time). You will notice, however, that there can be only one combination when $r = 0$ (no heads). In this case, the probability of 10 successive tails is $(.5)^{10}$.

In Table 7.3, we list the probabilities for each possible outcome when a coin is flipped 10 times and we record the number of heads and tails. We can get anywhere from zero heads (with a probability of .001) to 10 heads (with a probability of .001). This and any other compilation of probabilities with each possible outcome of a given number of trials is referred to as a *probability distribution*. The probability distribution just discussed has the special property of being perfectly symmetrical. This is the case with Bernoulli events where $p = q = .5$. Notice that you can also calculate a cumulative probability distribution (*cp*). Unlike the case of a raw frequency distribution where the cumulative frequency always sum to the total

**TABLE 7.3. Probability Distribution for 10 Coin Flips**

| Number of Heads | Probabilities | C(p) |
|---|---|---|
| 0 | $\binom{10}{0}\left(\frac{1}{2}\right)^0\left(\frac{1}{2}\right)^{10} = .001$ | .001 |
| 1 | $\binom{10}{1}\left(\frac{1}{2}\right)^1\left(\frac{1}{2}\right)^9 = .010$ | .011 |
| 2 | $\binom{10}{2}\left(\frac{1}{2}\right)^2\left(\frac{1}{2}\right)^8 = .044$ | .055 |
| 3 | $\binom{10}{3}\left(\frac{1}{2}\right)^3\left(\frac{1}{2}\right)^7 = .117$ | .172 |
| 4 | $\binom{10}{4}\left(\frac{1}{2}\right)^4\left(\frac{1}{2}\right)^6 = .205$ | .377 |
| 5 | $\binom{10}{5}\left(\frac{1}{2}\right)^5\left(\frac{1}{2}\right)^5 = .246$ | .623 |
| 6 | $\binom{10}{6}\left(\frac{1}{2}\right)^6\left(\frac{1}{2}\right)^4 = .205$ | .828 |
| 7 | $\binom{10}{7}\left(\frac{1}{2}\right)^7\left(\frac{1}{2}\right)^3 = .117$ | .945 |
| 8 | $\binom{10}{8}\left(\frac{1}{2}\right)^8\left(\frac{1}{2}\right)^2 = .044$ | .989 |
| 9 | $\binom{10}{9}\left(\frac{1}{2}\right)^9\left(\frac{1}{2}\right)^1 = .010$ | .999 |
| 10 | $\binom{10}{10}\left(\frac{1}{2}\right)^{10}\left(\frac{1}{2}\right)^0 = .001$ | 1.000 |

number of cases (*N*), in the cumulative probability distribution the sum of the cumulative probabilities will be 1. From the cumulative probability distribution you can determine that the probability of getting at least four heads is equal to .001 + .010 + .044 + .117 + .205 + .246 + .205 = .828.

In thinking about this and other probability distributions, you should keep in mind our notion of probability that stresses the chance or the likelihood that an event will occur "in the long run," that is, in a very large or infinite number of trials. The probability distribution shown in Table 7.3 is a *theoretical* distribution, based on the mathematics of probability theory. It indicates the probability of each outcome if the experiment of flipping a coin 10 times were repeated an infinite number of times, *not* what we would expect in any single or small number of trials.

In Table 7.4 we report the results of repeating the coin flip experiment only 20 times. That is, we flipped a coin 10 times and recorded the number of heads and then repeated this for 20 trials. Table 7.4 is a *frequency* distribution, not a theoretical probability distribution. It shows the number of times we actually obtained zero heads (0), 1 head (2), 2 heads (1), and so on out of 10 flips, and the corresponding probabilities. The probabilities we obtained from doing the experiment 20 times is very different from the theoretical probability distribution in Table 7.3. If we were to do this experiment 100 times, the actual distribution of the number of heads for our trials would most likely still not equal what would be expected from Table 7.3, but it would be closer than this experiment in which we only performed 20 trials. If we were to conduct the experiment 10,000 times, it would come closer and would be even closer if we conducted the experiment 1,000,000 times. The general rule is that the greater the number of trials, the more our empirical distribution would resemble the theoretical binomial probability distribution. The important point to remember is that like the binomial distribution, probability distributions do not actually appear in the real world. These distributions are based on probability theory and tell us what *should* happen in an infinite number of trials.

We have thus far been discussing a very simple distribution, the binomial distribution. The probability distribution is only one of several kinds of probability dis-

**TABLE 7.4. Frequency Distribution of 20 Flips of 10 Coins**

| Number of Heads | Frequency | Probability |
|---|---|---|
| 0 | 0 | .00 |
| 1 | 2 | .10 |
| 2 | 3 | .15 |
| 3 | 3 | .15 |
| 4 | 2 | .10 |
| 5 | 4 | .20 |
| 6 | 3 | .15 |
| 7 | 2 | .10 |
| 8 | 1 | .05 |
| 9 | 0 | .00 |
| 10 | 0 | .00 |

tributions you will eventually become acquainted with in this book. The computations for the probabilities in these other distributions are very complex and are far beyond this text. We have delineated the computations of the binomial distribution because it is very important that you understand how probability distributions are formed and their role in inferential statistics and research.

## 7.7 THE LOGIC OF HYPOTHESIS TESTS

A great deal of empirical research in criminology and criminal justice involves the testing of hypotheses. In this section we discuss the logic of hypothesis testing with a very simple example that is an extension of what we already know about the binomial distribution.

Let's suppose that we have a friend who makes the following proposal to us: "Each time we go out for entertainment, for example, to dinner, to the movies, or to an athletic event, I will flip a coin. If the coin comes up heads, I will treat you, and if it comes up tails, you will treat me." This strikes us as an eminently fair proposal and we agree. At the end of the first month, however, we discover that out of 10 coin flips we have lost all 10 times. We begin to suspect (i.e., we make a hypothesis) that we are being cheated, but do not want to accuse our friend of being a swindler without reasonably solid evidence. We want to think that our friend is not cheating us. Perhaps the coin is actually a fair one, and it's just that we have been temporarily unlucky. We also, however, don't want to make the mistake of believing the coin is fair when, in fact, it's not. This creates somewhat of a dilemma because we face two risks. If we accuse our friend of being a cheater and he really is not, we run the risk of ruining our friendship. If, however, we fail to accuse our "friend" of cheating and stopping the coin flips, we run the risk of always paying his way and being a "chump." How do we handle these two risks, which are unequal in importance to us?

This case involves the test of a simple hypothesis. We test this cheating hypothesis exactly as we would test a scientific hypothesis. There are a number of specific steps involved in the testing of a hypothesis, as shown in the box.

There are a number of new terms here. In the course of our discussion of the hypothesis test, we provide a definition of each of them. Do not get too involved in the definitions, however; what we would like you to understand at the moment are the logic and process of hypothesis testing. We discuss the process of hypothesis testing in much more detail in subsequent chapters. Right now, however, let's apply these steps to our specific example of the maybe-cheating friend.

---

**Step 1.** Making assumptions and formally stating hypotheses.
**Step 2.** Obtaining the probability distribution of our statistic.
**Step 3.** Selecting a level of significance and a critical value.
**Step 4.** Calculating the test statistic.
**Step 5.** Making a decision about the hypothesis.

---

## *Step 1: Making Assumptions*

Before we can obtain a probability distribution, we have to make certain assumptions about the population of events we wish to generalize to and the sampling procedure used in the trials. In our coin example, we make the assumption that the 10 flips conducted by our friend comprise a random sample of all possible coin flips with the same coin. That is, we are willing to accept that the flipping process is fair.[4] Another assumption that we will make is that the coin itself is fair—that it is not a coin with two tails or is badly unbalanced so that it always lands on the tails after a fair flip.

If we accept the validity of the first assumption, we will suspend our acceptance of the second assumption. The hypothesis that we actually examine is traditionally known as the *null hypothesis* and is symbolized as $H_0$. It is called the null hypothesis because it usually is stated in such a way as to suggest that there is nothing going on in the data—the coin is not unfair, our friend is not cheating us, two groups are not different from each other, there is no relationship between two variables. The alternative to the null hypothesis is often called the *research,* or *alternative, hypothesis* (symbolized as $H_1$) and states that there is something going on in the data—the coin is not fair, our friend is cheating us, two groups are different from each other, there is a relationship between two variables. Sometimes the alternative hypothesis is stated as a nondirectional alternative to the null hypothesis, such as the coin is unfair, or group 1 is different from group 2. However, it also may be stated in a more specific way, such as the coin is biased against heads, or group 1 has more or less of some attribute than group 2. When the research hypothesis is stated more specifically, it is referred to as a *directional alternative hypothesis.*

Whether the alternative hypothesis is stated as a directional or nondirectional alternative, however, *the hypothesis test is always made of the null hypothesis.* Therefore, it is the validity or truthfulness of the null hypothesis we wish to examine. Essentially, what we do in a hypothesis test is make an assumption that the null hypothesis is true. We then examine our observed information (the sample data) to see how reasonable or likely the null hypothesis is *given* the evidence provided by the sample data. Think of a hypothesis test as analogous to a trial in criminal court.[5] In a hypothesis test a researcher assumes that the null hypothesis is true. In a criminal proceeding, the jury gives the defendant a presumption of innocence. In a hypothesis test the researcher collects information or data from the sample. In a criminal proceeding the jury listens to evidence presented by the prosecution and defense about the defendant's guilt and innocence from physical evidence, witnesses, and other sources. In a hypothesis test if the sample information convinces the researcher that given the evidence from the sample, the initial assumption made in the null hypothesis is unreasonable (unlikely), then the null hypothesis will be rejected, and the original assumption is retained. If, however, the sample evidence indicates that the assumption in the null hypothesis is very likely, the assumption is not rejected. Similarly, in a criminal proceeding if the evidence convinces the jury that its initial presumption of innocence is unlikely given the evidence collected and heard, that presumption is rejected and the defendant is convicted. If, however, the evidence is not strong enough to convince the jury that the presumption of innocence should be rejected, it is retained, and the defendant is acquitted.

We should add here that the appropriateness of the analogy between a hypothesis test and a criminal proceeding continues after the verdict of the jury is made. In rendering a decision, a jury can make two kinds of correct decisions or two kinds of incorrect decisions. If a jury acquits a truly innocent person or convicts a truly guilty person, it has made a correct decision. If, however, a jury acquits a defendant who is really guilty, it has made an error. If a jury convicts a defendant who is really innocent, it has made a different kind of error. Similarly, a researcher can make two correct decisions and two kinds of errors. If a researcher fails to reject a null hypothesis that is really true, or rejects a null hypothesis that is really false, she has made a correct decision. If, however, she fails to reject a false null hypothesis, she has made a mistake. If she rejects a null hypothesis that is really true, she also has made a mistake. In both the null hypothesis and the criminal proceeding, therefore, decisions have to be made, and the decision maker rarely knows for certain that the decision is correct. To help people avoid making mistakes, both processes are bound by strict rules that minimize making incorrect decisions. In a criminal proceeding the rule of law or due process protections comprise one set of rules; in hypothesis testing the canons of science (the rules you are now learning) provide guidance for the researcher.

Keeping this in mind, let's return to our example. In the case at hand, our null hypothesis is that the coin is fair, and our research hypothesis is the directional alternative that the coin is biased against landing on heads.[6] The two hypotheses, then, are as follows:

$H_0$: The coin is fair.

$H_1$: The coin is biased against heads.

The goal of a hypothesis test is to reject or accept the null hypothesis rather than the research hypothesis. This seems like a very strange way to go about the business of doing research, but there is a reason for this. In doing criminological research we are frequently driven by a theory or an informed hunch about what we will find. This theory or hunch specifies a number of consequences that should occur if the theory is true. That is, because there is no direct way to examine our theory, we do it indirectly by stating something like the following: "If my theory is true, then $X$ should occur." If $X$ has not occurred when it should have, then I may conclude that the theory must not be true. If, however, $X$ has occurred, can we automatically conclude that the theory is true? Not necessarily. Suppose there exists an alternative theory that also predicts that $X$ should occur. Our research cannot tell us whether the first or second (or both) theories are true. Because alternative theories frequently compete with our own, we will rarely be able to prove definitively that ours is true. What we can do, however, is to try and disprove our theory by stating and testing null hypotheses. If we continue to reject null hypotheses (and thus fail to disprove our theory), we will gain more credibility for our theory (expressed in the alternative hypothesis). What we do, then, is to try and prove our theory wrong. To the extent that we fail to prove it wrong, we add to the notion that it may be true.

Because hypothesis testing actually involves decision making about the truthfulness of our null hypothesis, we should now explicitly recognize that the decision we eventually make may be correct or wrong. As suggested in the opening paragraphs to this section, in testing the assumption that the coin is fair (our null hypothesis), we run the risk of making one of two possible errors. One error occurs if we decide that the coin is not fair and we accuse our friend of cheating us when in fact he is not actually cheating (we just happened to be unlucky). In this case the null hypothesis is really true, but we decided to reject it. In statistics, this type of decision making error is called a ***Type I error.*** A second possible error occurs if we decide that the coin is fair and that our friend is not cheating us when in reality the coin is not fair. In this case the null hypothesis is really false, but we decided to accept it. This type of error is called a ***Type II error.*** In a Type I error, then, we reject a null hypothesis that is really true; in a Type II error we fail to reject a null hypothesis that is really false.

Another way to think of Type I and Type II errors is to consider the case of a jury's decision to convict a given criminal defendant. Take the assumption of innocence in a criminal proceeding as the null hypothesis. The jury has to make a decision either to fail to reject this null hypothesis and acquit the person or to reject it and find the accused guilty. Let's say it has found a given defendant innocent of a particular charge (it fails to reject the null hypothesis). If, however, the defendant is really guilty, then the decision of the jury is incorrect. It should have rejected the null hypothesis. The decision to fail to reject a false null hypothesis is an example of a Type II error. Now let's presume that it has found the defendant guilty (it has rejected the null hypothesis). If the defendant is really guilty, the decision to reject the null hypothesis is the correct one. If, however, the defendant was really innocent, then the decision of the jury is incorrect. The decision to reject a null hypothesis that is really true is an example of a Type I error. What the legal system does is to minimize the risk of a Type I error because we want to avoid at all possible costs to declare a defendant guilty when he is really innocent. Science does much the same thing when it makes very demanding decision rules before you can reject the null hypothesis. The two types of errors and the two kinds of correct decisions are shown for you in Figure 7.7.

We would naturally like to avoid both types of error if we could, because each comes at some cost. In our coin example, if we make a Type I error and reject the null hypothesis that the coin is fair when in fact it is not, we run the cost of ruining a good relationship by accusing our friend of cheating. If we make a Type II error and mistakenly fail to reject a false null hypothesis, we run the cost of losing further bets with our "friend" and of having to incur the cost of additional social outings.

FIGURE 7.7. Decision making in hypothesis tests.

| | | Decision | |
| --- | --- | --- | --- |
| | | Accept the Null Hypothesis | Reject the Null Hypothesis |
| Reality | Null Hypothesis Is True | Correct Decision | Type I Error |
| | Null Hypothesis Is False | Type II Error | Correct Decision |

Although we would like to avoid both kinds of errors, there is a trade-off between preventing the occurrence of each. As we will see, if we make it more difficult to make a Type I error by being "absolutely sure" that the coin is not fair before rejecting the null hypothesis, we increase the risk of making a Type II error. Similarly, if we make it easier to reject the null hypothesis by interpreting even the flimsiest data as evidence of cheating, we increase the risk of making a Type I error. What we must do is make a decision as to which error is more costly for us; would we rather keep our friend even if there is a slight risk that we are being cheated, or would we rather not be swindled out of money and risk losing a good friend? We will return to this question in the third step. For now we will assume that our friendship is more valuable than losing a little money.

## Step 2. Obtaining a Sampling or Probability Distribution

In assuming that the coin is fair as we did in our null hypothesis, we are actually assuming that there is a known and constant probability of events. In our coin example, a fair coin has a .5 probability of landing on tails (or heads) on each and every one of the 10 flips. As you can perhaps see now, another advantage of testing the null hypothesis is that we can calculate an exact probability distribution.[7] In the example at hand, we want to know the probability of getting $r$ heads in 10 flips of a fair coin (where $0 \leq r \leq 10$). We now know that this is a Bernoulli problem that makes use of the binomial distribution. This exact probability distribution can be easily calculated. In fact, we have already calculated the probability distribution for this specific example in Table 7.3. In other examples throughout this book we do not calculate the exact probability distribution but rely on the labors of others who have already calculated them for us for several other types of statistics, such as the chi-square distribution, the $t$ distribution, and the normal distribution. For all of these distributions, however, the logic of hypothesis testing that we are now examining holds. We calculate a "test statistic" from our data that will have a known *sampling distribution.* (We discuss sampling distribution in more detail in later chapters.) For now, just think of a sampling distribution as a theoretical distribution of the results of an infinite number of trials, experiments, or studies. These sampling distributions take on particular forms or shapes such as the normal or binomial probability distribution, and we base our decision about the null hypothesis on these probabilities. Before doing this, however, we must select the level of risk we are willing to take in making a Type I error.

## Step 3: Selecting a Level of Significance and Critical Region

In Step 1, we discussed a Type I error. This error occurs whenever we reject a true null hypothesis that is correct. In our coin example, we make a Type I error if we reject the assumption that the coin is fair when in fact it is fair. When conducting a hypothesis test, we must specify in advance how often we are willing to make such a Type I error. This risk of making a Type I error is set by selecting what is called a *significance level,* which is usually referred to by the Greek letter alpha ($\alpha$). For example, we can set a significance level at $\alpha = .05$, which indicates that we are willing to be wrong 5% of the time in rejecting the null hypothesis. In other words, out of 100 experiments or trials, we are willing to reject the null hypothesis when in fact it is correct five times (5% of the trials). In this case, therefore, our level of significance is said to be .05. Remember, the level of significance is the risk we accept of making a Type I error.

At first, it may seem strange to talk about how willing we are to make a Type I error. You may think that, because we have the actual number of coin flips (10) and the number of "successes" (zero), we can determine with 100% accuracy whether or not the coin is fair. For example, because we got no heads out of 10 coin flips, the coin must be unfair and our friend is cheating us. Not so. Remember that the probability distribution reported in Table 7.3 is a theoretical distribution. If we were to conduct 100 trials of 10 coin flips, we would not get exactly the distribution predicted from Table 7.3. We may get a combination of five heads and five tails 20, 30, or 40 percent of the time, or we may not even get one head or one tail three, four, or more times.[8] The point is, even if the coin is perfectly fair, we may actually get 10 coin flips with no heads by chance alone. For example, our friend may have gotten tails 10 times out of 10 simply because we just happened to be unlucky. The question, of course, is where we draw the line between assuming that the coin is really fair and assuming that the coin is really unfair? Where do we draw the line and reject the null hypothesis? This line is established by our level of significance ($\alpha$).

In selecting a significance level, we need to weigh the relative costs of making a Type I and Type II error, because the more we protect ourselves from making a Type I error, the more likely it is that we will make a Type II error. In our coin toss example, we may figure that, although we generally value our friend's companionship more than we do our money, we are also poor students that cannot pay for our friend's company continuously. We may decide that we want to be fairly sure that we are not just being unlucky before we accuse him of being a cheat, but we don't have to be *very* sure. We therefore establish a significance level of .05. An alpha of .05 means that we are willing to make a Type I error 5 percent of the time, or five times out of 100. Had we been more interested in saving money than friends, we might have set a lower significance level, say .10 or .20. Had we been more interested in saving our friendship than in not being cheated, we might have set a higher significance level, say .01. Notice, however, that had we made a very strict decision rule and determined that we would reject the null hypothesis only if we got 10 tails, we would still run a risk of making a Type I error, because, even with a fair coin we would expect to get all 10 tails one time out of 1000 simply by chance alone. For now, we will use the value of $\alpha = .05$ for this example.

Before moving on, we need to address one final point. Our research hypothesis was that the coin our friend flipped was biased against landing on heads because then our friend was required to treat us. The cheating, then, was suspected to occur only in one direction. When the alternative hypothesis is stated with a specific direction, the hypothesis test is conventionally called a *directional hypothesis,* or a *one-tailed significance test.* It is called a one-tailed test because the unusual event we are interested in occurs at only one tail of the distribution. We can see this more clearly in Figure 7.8 where we have represented the probability distribution of Table 7.4 in graphic form. Because we are interested in knowing how likely it is that a fair coin would come up with so few heads, we are concerned only with the left end or left tail of the probability distribution. This tail reports the probability of getting 0, 1, 2, . . ., heads out of 10 flips. Notice that with a one-tailed test using

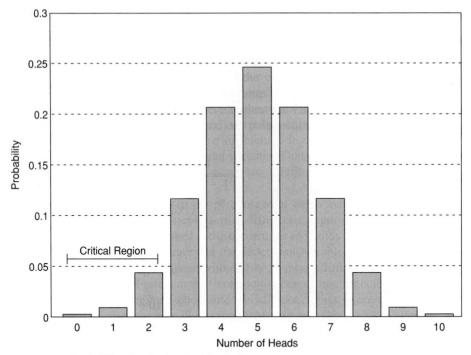

FIGURE 7.8. Probability distribution for 10 coin flips.

$\alpha = .05$, we can place all of the alpha level in the left tail. Every outcome that falls beyond the .05 probability level is said to lie in the *critical region* because any outcome within this region of our probability distribution leads us to reject the null hypothesis. In other words, the critical region is the area in our sampling distribution that, if our sample statistic falls into it, leads us to reject the null hypothesis. For this reason, the critical region is also called the region of rejection. In a one-tailed hypothesis test the critical region lies in only one tail or end of the probability distribution; in a two-tailed test the critical region lies in both tails of the distribution.

Had we not specified a direction in our alternative hypothesis and simply stated that the coin was biased but not in which direction, we would have to divide our critical region into two equal halves, one at each end of the probability distribution. When we fail to specify a direction for our hypothesis test, we have a *nondirectional hypothesis,* or a *two-tailed significance test.* Notice that the advantage of employing a one-tailed significance test is that the critical region is larger. Thus, we will be more likely to reject the null hypothesis. This reduces the risk of a Type II error.

Back to our hypothesis test concerning the coin toss! We have selected an alpha level of .05 using a one-tailed test. Examining Table 7.4 and Figure 7.8, we can see that the critical region for this test consists of the outcomes zero heads, 1 head, and 2 heads. Whenever we get two or fewer heads from 10 flips, we will conclude that the null hypothesis of a fair coin is untenable and we will reject it. The outcome of three heads does not lie within the critical region because the probability of obtaining three heads (.117) is greater than .05.[9] The next step is to perform our hypothesis test by calculating our test statistic.

## Step 4: Calculating the Test Statistic

A test statistic is a statistic that we calculate from our data and that we use to test our hypothesis. There are many test statistics; which one is selected is determined primarily by the research question and the type of data (nominal, interval, etc.) you are using. Every test statistic has a sampling distribution that is described by probability theory. What we do in a hypothesis test is to compare the value of the test statistic we obtain from our test with this probability distribution and determine how likely it is that we have obtained our test statistic by chance. Our decision to reject or fail to reject the null hypothesis is based on this probability. If we determine that it is very unlikely that we would get a test statistic of a given magnitude, we can reject the null hypothesis. In rejecting the null hypothesis we reject the assumption that it is true. If, on the other hand, we determine that the value of our test statistic is not so unlikely, we must fail to reject the null hypothesis. What makes a statistic unlikely? This judgment is based on our selected alpha level or level of significance. This may all be very confusing to you right now, but it will make more sense once we have completed our example.

In our coin toss example, the test statistic we calculate is relatively simple. It is the number of successes ($r$) in a given number of trials ($N$). In our case we have zero heads out of 10 flips. We already know that this test statistic has a sampling distribution that is binomial. We are now ready to test our null hypothesis and make a decision about its truth.

## Step 5: Making a Decision about the Hypothesis

Thus far, we have calculated our sampling distribution (Table 7.4), selected an alpha level ($\alpha = .05$), determined a critical region (0, 1, 2 heads), and computed the test statistic (zero heads). If our test statistic falls within the critical region, we will reject the null hypothesis with a known probability of a Type I error. If it does not fall within the critical region, we must fail to reject the null hypothesis and take the chance of making a Type II error. In our case, the test statistic of zero heads falls within our critical region. We therefore reject the null hypothesis that the coin is fair.

Before we accuse our friend of cheating us, however, we should keep in mind that there is a 1 in 20 chance (5 times out of 100) that we will get fewer than two heads in 10 flips, even if the coin is an honest one. In other words, we have not definitively "proven" that our friend is a cheat—just that our outcome of 0 heads in 10 flips is not a very likely outcome if the coin is indeed fair. Either we are very unlucky or the coin is not honest. Based on the scientific game of hypothesis testing we have just conducted, we have decided that the coin is not honest.

## 7.8 SUMMARY

In this chapter we have considered a very difficult concept—the idea of probability. Though an intuitive concept, the definition of probability in statistics involves both the notion of the likelihood or chance of a single event (the probability of drawing an ace from a deck of cards) relative to all possible events and the likelihood of an event over an infinitely large number of trials.

Probability theory is guided by a number of rules; the *bounding rule,* the *addition rule,* and the *multiplication rule.* In addition, we also learned in this chapter about counting rules. The first rule was that for any event with $K$ possible mutually exclusive outcomes and $N$ number of trials, the total number of possible unique sequences is $K^N$. Other rules concern the arrangements of events in a sequence. Rule 2 stated that $N$ objects can be arranged in $N!$ ($N$ factorial) ways. When there are $N$ different events that occur in a particular order, we have a *permutation* of those events. Whenever we do not care about the ordering in which the events occur, the grouping of events is referred to as a *combination.* Two other counting rules concern the arrangement of a subset of objects from a larger set. Rule 3 stated that the number of ways of arranging r unique objects from a larger set of $N$ unique objects is $N!/(N-r)!$. If we want to know the number of ways of arranging $r$ objects from $N$ distinct objects without regard for their order, we must use the formula

$$N!/[r!\ (N-r)!],\ \text{or}\ \binom{N}{r}.$$

Finally, we used all of our rules of probability and counting to calculate a probability distribution. More specifically, we calculated a binomial probability distribution. We examined the binomial distribution to illustrate more in general the logic of testing hypotheses in scientific research. In doing research we actually test the *null hypothesis,* which usually makes a statement that goes against our theory or hunch. The *alternative,* or *research, hypothesis* is usually derived from our theory or experience. We usually proceed with our research as if the null hypothesis was true. The object of scientific research, then, is to disprove the null hypothesis rather than to prove the research hypothesis. In testing hypotheses we learned that a five-step process should be followed in explicit order. In Step 1 we make assumptions about our data and formally state our null and alternative hypotheses. In Step 2 we obtain a sampling distribution. In Step 3 we select a significance level and critical region. In Step 4 we calculate our test statistic. In Step 5 we make a decision about our null hypothesis.

## Key Terms

addition rule
alpha level
alternative hypothesis
basic counting rule
Bernoulli process
Bernoulli process events
binomial coefficient
binomial distribution
bounding rule
combination
complement of an event
conditional probability
critical region
critical value
directional alternative hypothesis
event
experiment
failure
joint probability

level of significance
multiplication rule
mutually exclusive events
nondirectional alternative hypothesis
null hypothesis
one-tailed significance test
permutation
probability
probability distribution
research hypothesis
sample space
sampling distribution
significance level
statistical independence
success
trial
two-tailed significance test
Type I error
Type II error

## Problems

1. The following table lists the number of prisoners under state and federal jurisdiction on December 31, 1989. Using this table, answer the following questions:
   a. What is the probability that a randomly selected prisoner would be incarcerated in the South? In New York, California, or Texas?
   b. What is the probability that a randomly selected prisoner is under federal jurisdiction?
   c. What is the probability that a randomly selected prisoner would be incarcerated either in the Northeast or in the West?
   d. What is the probability that a randomly selected prisoner is from Michigan? Given that a prisoner is incarcerated in the Midwest, what is the probability that he or she is from Michigan? Why are these two probabilities different? Given that a prisoner is incarcerated in the Midwest, what is the probability that he or she is from Illinois, Ohio, or Indiana?
   e. Given that a prisoner is from the Northeast, what is the probability that he or she is from New York? From either New Jersey or Pennsylvania?
   f. What is the probability that a prisoner is from both Maine and Louisiana?

| Jurisdictiton | Number of Prisoners | Jurisdiction | Number of Prisoners |
|---|---|---|---|
| U.S. total | 680,907 | Federal institutions total | 47,168 |
| NORTHEAST | 109,399 | MIDWEST | 136,046 |
| Connecticut | 6309 | Illinois | 24,712 |
| Maine | 1432 | Indiana | 12,220 |
| Massachusetts | 7268 | Iowa | 3584 |
| New Hampshire | 1166 | Kansas | 5616 |
| New Jersey | 19,439 | Michigan | 31,639 |
| New York | 51,232 | Missouri | 13,921 |
| Pennsylvania | 20,458 | Nebraska | 2278 |
| Rhode Island | 1469 | North Dakota | 404 |
| Vermont | 626 | Ohio | 30,538 |
| SOUTH | 252,799 | South Dakota | 1256 |
| Alabama | 13,575 | Wisconsin | 6775 |
| Arkansas | 6546 | WEST | 135,525 |
| Delaware | 2284 | Alaska | 1908 |
| District of Columbia | 6650 | Arizona | 12,726 |
| Florida | 39,996 | California | 84,338 |
| Georgia | 19,619 | Colorado | 6908 |
| Kentucky | 8289 | Hawaii | 1757 |
| Louisiana | 17,257 | Idaho | 1850 |
| Maryland | 15,378 | Montana | 1328 |
| Mississippi | 7,700 | Nevada | 5112 |
| North Carolina | 16,628 | New Mexico | 3120 |
| Oklahoma | 11,608 | Oregon | 6156 |
| South Carolina | 14,808 | Utah | 2368 |
| Tennessee | 10,630 | Washington | 6928 |
| Texas | 44,022 | Wyoming | 1026 |
| Virginia | 16,273 | | |
| West Virginia | 1536 | | |

2. In drawing a single card from a deck of cards, what is the probability of selecting:
   a. An ace?
   b. The king of spades?
   c. Either a heart or a seven?
   d. A king, a two, or a club?
   e. An odd-numbered diamond?
   f. A heart and a spade?
3. In six flips of a fair coin, what is the probability of getting?
   a. No heads?
   b. Exactly one head or one tail?
   c. Exactly three tails?
   d. Four or fewer heads?
4. Complete the full probability distribution for an experiment involving four flips of a coin. What is the most likely outcome? Why? What is the least likely outcome? Let's say you test the null hypothesis that the coin is fair (i.e., that the probability of a head is .5). If you flip the coin four times and obtain four tails, would you reject this null hypothesis with a .05 level of significance?
5. The following data show the number of youths appearing in juvenile courts across the United States in 1991, by the race and the offense they were charged with. With this table answer the following questions:
   a. What is the probability that a randomly selected youth is black? Is white?
   b. What is the probability that a randomly selected youth is in court for a person-related crime? A public order offense?
   c. What is the probability that a youth is both black and a property offender?
   d. What is the probability that a youth is both white and a drug offender?
   e. What is the probability that a youth is both a drug and a property offender?
   f. What is the probability that a youth is both white and black?
   g. What is the probability that a youth is both white and a property offender?
   h. What is the probability that a youth committed an offense against a person?
   i. What is the probability that a youth is both black and committed an offense against a person?
   j. What is the probability that a youth is both white and committed an offense against a person?

| Offense | White Youths | Black Youths | Total |
|---|---|---|---|
| Person | 144,500 | 108,500 | 253,000 |
| Property | 550,000 | 214,200 | 764,200 |
| Drugs | 29,800 | 28,600 | 58,400 |
| Public order | 146,300 | 71,400 | 217,700 |
| Total | 870,600 | 422,700 | 1,293,300 |

6. In a 1988 article, Gary Kleck reported that citizens' use of firearms against violent criminals and burglars was about as frequent as an arrest and often a more severe and swift punishment. Answer the following questions with the following hypothetical data from a survey of 2000 gun owners.

| Used Against | Severe Injury | Minor Injury | No Injury | Total |
|---|---|---|---|---|
| Violent criminal | 425 | 115 | 20 | 560 |
| Burglar | 415 | 140 | 10 | 450 |
| Family member | 625 | 200 | 50 | 675 |
| Total | 1465 | 455 | 80 | 2000 |

What is the probability that:

**a.** The use of a firearm produced some kind of injury?
**b.** A firearm was used against a violent criminal or burglar?
**c.** A firearm was used against a burglar and involved severe injury?
**d.** A firearm was used against a family member?
**e.** A firearm was used against a family member and involved severe injury?

## Solutions to Problems

**1. a.** $P_{South} = \dfrac{292,769}{680,907} = .37$

Because these are mutually exclusive events,

$P(NY \text{ or } CA \text{ or } TX) = P(NY) + P(CA) + P(TX)$

$$= \frac{51,232}{680,907} + \frac{84,338}{680,907} + \frac{44,022}{680,907} = .07 + .12 + .06 = .25$$

**b.** $P_{Federal} = \dfrac{47,168}{680,907} = .07$

**c.** Because these are mutually exclusive events,

$P(\text{Northeast or West}) = P(\text{Northeast}) + P(\text{West})$

$$= P_{Northeast \text{ or } West} = \frac{109,399}{680,907} + \frac{135,525}{680,907} = .16 + .20 = .36$$

**d.** $P_{Michigan} = \dfrac{31,639}{680,907} = .05$

Given the 136,046 prisoners in the Midwest, what is the probability that the prisoner is from Michigan?

$$P_{(Michigan \mid Midwest)} = \frac{31,639}{136,046} = .23$$

These two probabilities are different because the second probability is a conditional probability so the denominator is the total number of prisoners incarcerated in the Midwest. Michigan prisoners make up 5 percent of the total prisoner population, but 23 percent of the prisoners are in the Midwest.

Because these are mutually exclusive events,

$P(\text{Illinois, Ohio or Indiana} \mid \text{Midwest}) = P(\text{Illinois}) + P(\text{Ohio}) + P(\text{Indiana})$

$$P_{(Illinois\ Ohio\ or\ Indiana \mid Midwest)} = \frac{24,712}{136,046} + \frac{30,538}{136,046} + \frac{12,220}{136,046}$$

$$= .18 + .22 + .09 = .49$$

**e.** $P(\text{New York} \mid \text{Northeast}) = \dfrac{51,232}{109,399} = .47$

$$P(\text{New Jersey or Pennsylvania} \mid \text{Northeast}) = \frac{19,439}{109,399} + \frac{20,458}{109,399} = .18 + .19 = .37$$

**f.** P(Maine and Louisiana) = 0 because these are mutually exclusive events. A prisoner cannot at the same time be incarcerated both in Maine and Louisiana.

**2. a.** Because there are four aces in a deck of 52 cards,

$$P(Ace) = \frac{4}{52} = .08$$

**b.** $P(\text{King of Spades}) = \dfrac{1}{52} = .02.$

**c.** These are not mutually exclusive events because a heart can also be a seven (the seven of hearts). Therefore,

P(Heart or Seven) = P(Heart) + P(Seven) − P(Seven of Hearts)

$$= \frac{13}{52} + \frac{4}{52} - \frac{1}{52} = \frac{16}{52} = .31$$

**d.** Therefore,

P(King or Two or Clubs) = P(King) + P(Two) + P(Clubs) − P(King of Clubs) − P(Two of Clubs)

$$= \left(\frac{4}{52} + \frac{4}{52} + \frac{13}{52} - \frac{1}{52} - \frac{1}{52}\right) = \frac{19}{52} = .37$$

**e.** The odd diamonds are the three, five, seven, and nine of diamonds.

$$P = \left(\frac{1}{52} + \frac{1}{52} + \frac{1}{52} + \frac{1}{52}\right) = \frac{4}{52} = .077$$

**f.** These are mutually exclusive events because one card cannot be both a heart and a spade. Therefore P(Heart and Spade) = 0.

**3. a.** The probability of getting no heads is the probability of getting six tails in six flips of a coin.

P(T T T T T T) = (.5)(.5)(.5)(.5)(.5)(.5) = $(.5)^6$ = .0156

**b.** Using our addition rule, the probability of getting one head in six flips of a coin or one tail in six flips of a coin is:

.0936 + .0936 = .1872

**c.** The probability of getting three tails and three heads in any order is:

20(.0156) = .312

**d.** The probability of four or fewer heads is:

.234 + .312 + .234 + .094 + .0156 = .89

**4.** The full probability distribution of four flips of a coin is as follows:

P(T T T T) = $(.5)^4$ = .0625

$$P(H\,T\,T\,T) = \frac{4!}{1!\,3!} = 4(.0625) = .25$$

$$P(H\,H\,T\,T) = \frac{4!}{2!\,2!} = 6(.0625) = .375$$

$$P(H\,H\,H\,T) = \frac{4!}{3!\,1!} = 4(.0625) = .25$$

$$P(H\,H\,H\,H) = (.5)^4 = .0625$$

The most likely outcome of four flips of a coin is two heads and two tails [P(HHTT) = .375]. The least likely outcomes are no heads and no tails. No, you would not reject the null hypothesis that the coin is fair. With a fair coin, where the probability of a head is .5, the probability that you would get four tails from four flips is .0625. This is greater than the .05 level of significance you chose.

**5. a.** $P(\text{Black}) = \dfrac{422,700}{1,293,300} = .327$

$P(\text{White}) = \dfrac{870,600}{1,293,300} = .673$

**b.** $P(\text{Person Crime}) = \dfrac{253,000}{1,293,300} = .196$

$P(\text{Public Order Offense}) = \dfrac{217,700}{1,293,300} = .168$

**c.** P(Black and Property Crime) = P(Black)P(Property Crime | Black)

$$= \left(\frac{422,700}{1,293,300}\right)\left(\frac{214,200}{422,700}\right) = (.327)(.507) = .166$$

**d.** $P(\text{White and Drug Crime}) = \left(\dfrac{870,600}{1,293,300}\right)\left(\dfrac{29,800}{870,600}\right) = (.673)(.034) = .023.$

**e.** P(Drug Crime and Property Crime) = 0.

**f.** P(White and Black) = 0.

**g.** $P(\text{White and Property Crime}) = \left(\dfrac{870,600}{1,293,300}\right)\left(\dfrac{550,000}{870,600}\right) = (.673)(.632) = .425.$

**h.** $P(\text{Person Crime}) = \dfrac{253,000}{1,293,300} = .196.$

**i.** $P(\text{Black and Person Crime}) = \left(\dfrac{422,700}{1,293,300}\right)\left(\dfrac{108,500}{422,700}\right) = (.327)(.257) = .084.$

**j.** $P(\text{White and Person Crime}) = \left(\dfrac{870,600}{1,293,300}\right)\left(\dfrac{144,500}{870,600}\right) = (.673)(.166) = .112.$

**6. a.** $P(\text{Severe Injury}) + P(\text{Minor Injury}) = \left(\dfrac{1465}{2000}\right) + \left(\dfrac{455}{2000}\right) = (.73) + (.23) = .96.$

**b.** $P(\text{Violent Criminal}) + P(\text{Burglar}) = \left(\dfrac{560}{2000}\right) + \left(\dfrac{565}{2000}\right) = (.28) + (.28) = .56.$

**c.** $P(\text{Burglar and Severe Injury}) = \left(\dfrac{565}{2000}\right)\left(\dfrac{415}{565}\right) = (.282)(.734) = .207.$

**d.** $P(\text{Family Member}) = \left(\dfrac{875}{2000}\right) = .44$

**e.** $P(\text{Family Member and Severe Injury}) = \left(\dfrac{875}{2000}\right)\left(\dfrac{625}{875}\right) = (.437)(.714) = .312.$

## Endnotes

1. You can perhaps see this more clearly if you reason as follows: The probability of selecting either a diamond or a king is equal to the probability of selecting a diamond (13/52) plus the probability of selecting any one of the other three kings that are not the king of diamonds (K♥, K♣, K♠; [3/52]): (13/52) + (3/52) = 16/52 = .31.

2. You will probably now recognize that we calculated a joint probability when we used the general form of the addition rule (Equation 7.5). In our example, we needed to calculate the probability of selecting a king of diamonds from a deck of cards, which is the joint probability of selecting both a king and a diamond. This is the same as the conditional probability of selecting a king given a diamond. We found this probability to be 1/52 from looking at the display from a full deck of cards. We can obtain the same result now with our use of the simplified multiplication rule in Equation 7.8. Because the suit of a card and its face value are statistically independent, the probability of drawing a king and a diamond is equal to:

$$P(K \text{ and } \blacklozenge) = P(K) \times P(\blacklozenge)$$

$$= (4/52)(13/52)$$

$$= 52/2704$$

$$= 1/52$$

3. By convention, $0! = 1$.

4. By this we simply mean that the observed outcome of all tails was not the result of biased sampling. In this case, biased sampling would occur if the flipper did not actually flip the coin so that it tumbled repeatedly in the air but instead tossed the coin flatly with the tails side up, always ensuring that it would "land" on tails.

5. We would like to thank Professor Daniel A. Powers in the Department of Sociology at the University of Texas-Austin for calling this analogy to our attention.

6. We say that the coin is biased against heads because our original bet was that, if the coin landed on heads, our friend will treat us. Because we have no reason to believe that our friend would deliberately rig the game so as to prejudice his own chances, we predict that the coin is biased so that it is more likely to land on tails than heads.

7. If we were to assume that the coin was unfair, before we could calculate a probability distribution we would have to be precise in describing how "unfair" it was. That is, we would have to state that the probability of getting a heads was not .5 but was .4 or .3 or .2 or .1, or some other probability less than .5. It is not often that we are able to state with any degree of precision this alternative probability, so we simply assume that the coin is fair, that the probability of a heads is equal to the probability of a tails ($p = .5$).

8. Based on the theoretical probabilities listed on p. 194, out of 100 trials we should get a combination of five heads and five tails approximately 25 times (.246 × 100), and no heads or tails less than one time (.001 × 100).

9. Had we not predicted the direction of our alternative hypothesis, we would have divided our selected alpha level ($\alpha = .05$) into two equal halves (.025) at each end of the probability distribution. In this case the critical region would include the two sets of outcomes; 0, . . . 1 heads and 9, . . . 10 heads. In both of these instances the probability is less than .025. When we predicted the direction as the coin being biased against heads, the critical region included 0, 1, or 2 heads. As you can see, if we can predict the direction of our alternative hypothesis we are more likely to reject the null hypothesis *as long as we predict the correct direction.*

# CHAPTER 8

# The Normal Distribution

*The normal is what you find but rarely. The normal is an ideal. It is a picture that one fabricates of the average characteristics of men, and to find them all in a single man is hardly to be expected.*
—WILLIAM SOMERSET MAUGHAM

## 8.1 INTRODUCTION

In previous chapters we have discussed two major types of distributions, a frequency distribution and a probability distribution. A frequency distribution displays an array of scores or values that are found in our data and the associated frequency count for each value. The frequency distributions we have seen thus far are *empirical probability distributions* in that the data on which they are based are observed in the real world. A probability distribution, however, displays an array of values and the associated *theoretical* probabilities of each value. These probabilities reflect the chance or likelihood of a particular value occurring in our data "in the long run" or in an infinite number of frequency distributions. The probability distribution of 10 coin flips discussed in the preceding chapter is an example.

At the end of the preceding chapter, we discussed one type of probability distribution, the binomial distribution. The binomial distribution is a probability distribution of events with only two outcomes. It is, therefore, a distribution of discrete events. In this chapter we examine in detail another kind of probability distribution that has much wider applicability in criminological and social science research, the *normal distribution,* or, more accurately, the normal probability density function. The normal distribution, like the binomial, is a *theoretical probability distribution* that is defined by its mathematical equation. Unlike the binomial, however, the normal is a continuous distribution. The rather hefty mathematical formula for the normal probability density function is:

$$Z = 1 \backslash \sigma \sqrt{2\pi} \, e^{-\frac{1}{2} \left( \frac{Y - \mu}{\sigma} \right)^2} \tag{8.1}$$

where $Z$ is the height of the normal curve for any given value of $Y$ and $\pi$ and $e$ are constants (approximately equal to 3.14 and 2.72, respectively).

There are two parameters in the normal density function, the population mean ($\mu$) and standard deviation ($\sigma$). These two values determine the location and shape of the distribution. As we discuss later, this should tell you that there is more than

**211**

one normal distribution. Although you have seen the typical bell-shaped curve form of the normal distribution many times, this is only one of its forms or shapes. It is not necessary to know this equation (thank goodness!), but it is important for us to become familiar with the basic properties of the normal distribution. We then examine some statistical theorems that provide the basis for the normal distribution's wide applicability.

## 8.2 CHARACTERISTICS OF THE NORMAL DISTRIBUTION

The general form of the normal distribution is shown in Figure 8.1. As you can see, the normal distribution has a shape that should be familiar to you. The smooth symmetrical shape of the normal curve gives it the appearance of a bell, and it is frequently known as the "bell-shaped" curve. Many empirical distributions take the shape of the normal distribution. For example, height and weight are approximately normally distributed in the population. Most persons are about of average, or "normal," height (between 5 and 6 feet) with fewer people being shorter than 5 or taller than 6 feet. IQ is also approximately normally distributed; most persons have an IQ score near the average of 100. As you move away from this average score, there are increasingly fewer persons with IQ scores at either the high end (IQ > 100) or low end (IQ < 100) of the distribution. Other traits or characteristics in the real world have a similar distribution, so it is not surprising that the normal distribution is a very helpful tool for statisticians and researchers.

The reference to the normal distribution as a bell-shaped curve is generally descriptive, but it may be misleading at times. Some curves may depart from the typical bell-shaped appearance shown in Figure 8.1 but are nonetheless normal in terms of their mathematical properties. The equation for the normal curve (Equation 8.1) indicates that the normal curve is defined in part by its mean ($\mu$) and standard deviation ($\sigma$). This suggests that there is not one normal distribution, but a *family* of nor-

FIGURE 8.1.  A normal distribution.

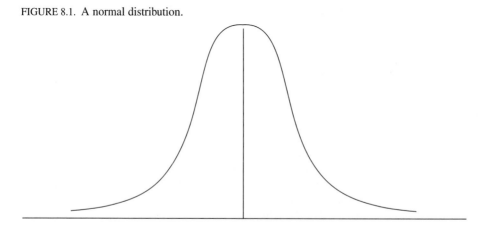

mal distributions or curves, one for each combination of a given mean and standard deviation. This means that normal distributions may differ in terms of their means, standard deviations or both, and that, of course, their specific shape will vary accordingly. Figures 8.2 through 8.4 show normal curves with varying characteristics. Figure 8.2 shows two normal curves that differ with respect to their means but have the same standard deviation. In Figure 8.3 the three curves all have the same mean but different standard deviations. In 8.4 the two curves have different means and standard deviations. In spite of their very different shapes, all of the curves shown in Figures 8.2–8.4 are normal curves and have a normal distribution.

Whatever the exact shape of a normal curve, it has a number of distinctive features, which are true no matter what specific shape the curve has. One clear feature of any normal distribution is that it is a perfectly symmetrical curve. This means that if you were to draw a line through the middle of a normal distribution at the highest point of the curve and fold it at this center point you would have two perfectly equal halves. A second feature of the normal curve is that it is unimodal.

FIGURE 8.2. Normal distributions with equal standard deviations and different means.

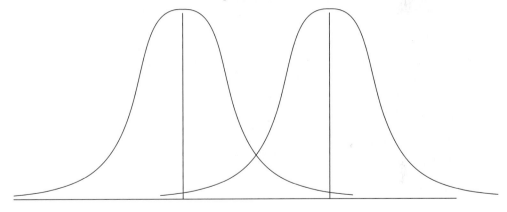

FIGURE 8.3. Normal distributions with equal means and different standard deviations.

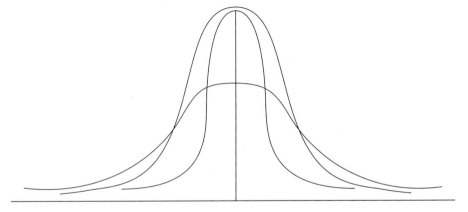

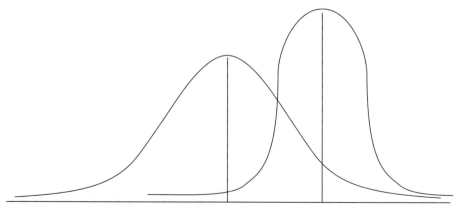

FIGURE 8.4. Normal distributions with different means and standard deviations.

There is only one distinguishing high point of the curve where the mean, median, and mode all coincide. From its rounded peak at the center of the distribution, the curve gradually tails off infinitely (yes, infinitely, because it is a theoretical distribution) in both directions where it comes close to but never actually touches the *x* axis. A final characteristic of the normal curve is that, no matter what its particular shape (i.e., regardless of its specific mean or standard deviation), there will be a constant area (or a constant proportion of cases) under the curve between its mean and any given distance away from that mean measured in terms of standard deviation units. This final property is so important that we spend some additional time understanding it and its implications.

## *8.3 THE AREA UNDER THE NORMAL CURVE*

Let's begin our discussion of the normal curve by reiterating the point made in the introduction to this chapter that the normal distribution is a *theoretical probability distribution.* As a theoretical distribution, the normal distribution does not appear in the real world with our empirical frequency distributions. For the purposes of this discussion, let's assume that we are able to measure the height (in inches) of each person in the world who has ever lived and from this we created a very large (but not infinite) frequency distribution. Let's say that we then graphed this large frequency distribution. With the several billion observations of height we would have an approximation to the theoretical normal distribution. This hypothetical graph of the frequency distribution of the height of every person in the world is illustrated in Figure 8.5.

One observation we can make from this distribution, which of course holds for the theoretical normal distribution, is that all cases or observations can be found under the curve. That is, the area that lies between the line of the curve on its surface and the *x* (horizontal) axis is equal to 100 percent of all the cases. The proportion of cases, then, that lies under the normal curve is 1.0 (that is, 100 percent). The line down the center of the curve from its highest point is the mean. The mean divides

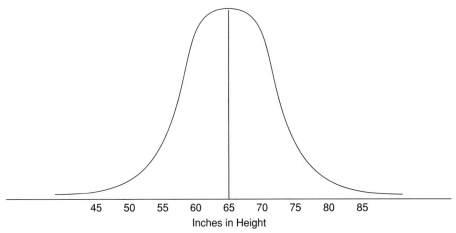

FIGURE 8.5. Normal distribution of height.

the normal curve into two equal parts. In empirical distributions (samples), the mean is denoted with the term $\bar{x}$ and the standard deviation as $s$. In theoretical probability distributions, the mean is denoted with the Greek letter $\mu$ (mu) and the standard deviation by the Greek letter $\sigma$ (sigma).

Knowing this, we can now repeat the statement at the end of the preceding section regarding the normal curve: no matter what its shape, there will be a constant area (a constant proportion of cases) between the mean and any given distance from the mean measured in standard deviation units. Based on mathematical theory, we can determine these exact proportions. For example, we know that in every normal distribution, .3413 (34.13 percent) of the cases will fall in the area between the mean and one standard deviation unit ($\mu \pm 1\sigma$). In other words, if we drew a line through a normal curve that is one standard deviation away from its mean, the proportion of the distribution in the normal curve that would lie between the mean and this line would always be .3413 (see Figure 8.6). There will be .4772, or 47.72 percent, of the cases in the area between the mean and two standard deviation units, and .4987, or 49.87 percent, of the cases will lie in the area between the mean and three standard deviation units.

We can now combine this information with our knowledge that the normal distribution is perfectly symmetrical. Because the normal distribution is symmetrical, 34.13 percent of the cases will lie within one standard deviation to the right of the mean (greater than the mean) and exactly 34.13 percent of the cases will lie within one standard deviation to the left of the mean (less than the mean). Adding these two values, we can note that 68.26 percent of the cases in a normal distribution will lie within ±1 standard deviation unit of the mean. Similarly, 95.44 percent of the cases in a normal distribution will lie within ±2 standard deviation units of the mean, and almost all of the cases (99.74 percent) will lie within ±3 standard deviation units (see Figure 8.6).

You should remember that we introduced these principles in Chapter 5 (Measures of Dispersion) when we discussed an interpretation of the standard deviation.

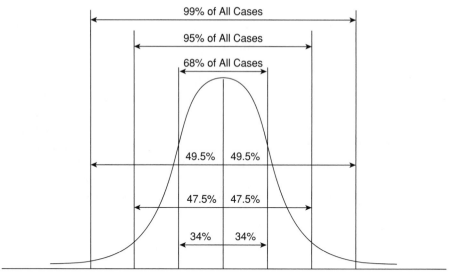

FIGURE 8.6. Area under the normal curve in standard deviation units.

With what we know about the normal curve, we now should have a better under-standing of the standard deviation as a measure of dispersion. Because a number of empirical frequency distributions in the real world approximate the properties of the normal distribution, the relationship between standard deviations and areas un-der the curve becomes very meaningful. For example, if we have a given distribu-tion that we believe is approximately normal, we may assume that 95 percent of the cases will lie within ±2 standard deviation units of the mean of the distribution.

A knowledge of both normal distributions and standard deviations is very help-ful, then, in understanding what constitutes an extreme score. If we have a given score (say, a sample mean), we can now determine how many standard deviation units away from the population mean it is. Or we can determine such things as the score that is so extreme that 95 percent or 99 percent of all other scores are higher (or lower) than it is. You may remember from the preceding chapter that this is the kind of information we want to have when we conduct hypothesis tests.

Because normal distributions have the very desirable property that a fixed pro-portion of its cases falls in an interval between the mean and a given standard de-viation unit, all we need to know is the form or shape of any given normal distri-bution. Unfortunately, the shape of each normal distribution differs depending on its mean and standard deviation (see Equation 8.1), so we have to determine the ex-act form of the curve with each new distribution. Another way to do this, however, is to transform our original data scores into other scores where we know the mean, standard deviation, and hence the precise form of its normal distribution. If we did this, we could use this standard normal distribution in all our empirical problems. That way, we would have only one normal distribution to worry about. This is the idea behind the *standard score* and the *standard normal distribution,* which we ex-amine in the next section.

## *8.4 THE STANDARD NORMAL DISTRIBUTION AND STANDARD SCORES*

In creating standard scores from raw scores (scores from our original data), we simply convert or transform our raw score into a hypothetical score that comes from a known normal distribution. This known distribution has a mean of zero and a standard deviation of 1. This does not affect the properties of our original distribution but simply standardizes the original level of measurement. In doing this, we then have only one normal distribution to worry about. And because this distribution has already been determined by mathematical theory (we know its mean, (0), and standard deviation, 1), it is a very handy statistical tool to use in our research.

The specific type of normal distribution we are referring to with a mean of zero and standard deviation of 1 is called the *standard form* of the normal distribution or the *standard normal distribution.* The standard score that we calculate to refer to the standard normal distribution is called a *z score* and is calculated as follows:

$$z = \frac{x - \bar{x}}{s} \tag{8.2}$$

where
$x$ = the given raw score
$\bar{x}$ = the mean of the empirical distribution
$s$ = the standard deviation of the empirical distribution

If, for example, we have an empirical distribution that is normally distributed, we can calculate $z$ scores from our original data points. With a mean of 25 and a standard deviation of 5, we can transform the raw score of 32 into a $z$ score as follows:

$$z = \frac{32 - 25}{5} = 1.4$$

The $z$ score of 1.4 tells us that a raw score of 32 is 1.4 standard deviation units *above* the mean of the standard normal distribution. If we calculate the $z$ score for a raw score of 18 we will see that it is:

$$z = \frac{18 - 25}{5} = -1.4$$

This $z$ score of $-1.4$ tells us that a raw score of 18 is 1.4 standard deviation units *below* the mean of the standard normal distribution. Thus, the sign of the transformed $z$ score will indicate whether the raw score is less than or equal to the mean of the standard normal distribution, and the magnitude of the $z$ score will tell us how many standard deviation units away from the mean the score is.

At this point, you may be wondering, "To get a $z$ score distribution with a mean of zero and a standard deviation of 1, why do we subtract the mean from our raw score and then divide by the standard deviation of our scores?" There is a good reason for this, which we explain next.

Figure 8.7 shows two normal distributions. The one on the right is the distribution from our raw scores for the example where the mean was 25 and the standard deviation was 5. The distribution on the left is the standard normal distribution of $z$ scores with a mean ($\mu$) of zero and a standard deviation ($\sigma$) of 1. The calculation of a $z$ score requires that the mean be subtracted from each score. In subtracting the mean from each score, we are moving or shifting each of the raw $x$ scores a constant value. This constant value is a distance on the $x$ axis equal to the mean. In our example we are moving each score by a constant of 25. In subtracting 25 from each score, we are moving them 25 units to the left where the scores are now centered on a mean of zero. The mean of the old raw scores is 25, and the mean of the new scores (the $z$ scores) is now zero.

When we divide the difference of each score from the mean ($x - \bar{x}$) by the standard deviation of the raw scores, we are changing the shape of the distribution. If the standard deviation of the raw scores is greater than 1, we are narrowing the original distribution. If the standard deviation of the raw scores is less than 1, the $z$ transformation broadens the original distribution. The result is that not only are the scores shifted so that they are centered over a mean of zero, but also the curve now takes the appearance of the one on the left. The original distribution on the right is now exactly superimposed on the distribution of the left.

Notice that all we have done is to alter the measurement scale of the underlying variable so that a change in five units in the raw distribution (one standard deviation) is the same as a 1 unit change in the $z$ distribution (one standard deviation). Therefore, a raw score of 32 from a distribution whose mean is 25 and standard deviation is 5 is seven units from that mean and corresponds to 1.4 standard deviation units in $z$ score terms (5 units is one standard deviation, and 2 units equal .4 of a standard deviation unit; $7/5 = 1.4$).

Let's now examine how we can determine the proportion of cases that fall within a given interval on the standard normal distribution. We continue with our example of a normal distribution of raw data with a mean of 25 and a standard deviation of 5. As seen, a raw score of 32 corresponds to a $z$ score of 1.4, thus indicating that it is 1.4 standard deviation units to the right of the mean in the standard

FIGURE 8.7. The standard normal distribution and a normal distribution with a mean of 25.

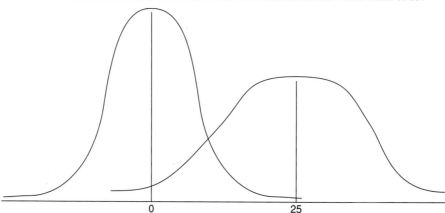

0                                    25

normal distribution. In essence, what we are saying is that a raw score of 32 corresponds to a score of 1.4 on the $z$ scale.

Let's say that we are interested in knowing the proportion of cases that fall in between the mean and a $z$ score of 1.4. To determine this, we must go to what is called a $z$ table that shows the exact area under the standard normal curve. Table B.2 in Appendix B is such a table. The values of $z$ can be found by going down the left-hand margin for the first two digits of the $z$ score and across the top of the table for the third digit. The numbers within the body of the table are the proportion of the cases (the proportion of the area of the curve) between the mean and the location on the curve corresponding to a particular $z$ score. For example, with a $z$ score of 1.40 we go down the left margin of the table to the value of 1.4 and then to the first column for the value .00. This location corresponds to our $z$ score of 1.40. The number in the table associated with that $z$ score is .4192. What this means is that the proportion of the curve lying between the mean and a $z$ score of 1.40 is .4192. In other words, approximately 42 percent of the area of the standard normal curve lies between the mean and a $z$ score of 1.40. Because the normal curve is symmetrical, we can deduce that approximately 42 percent of the area of the curve lies between the mean and a $z$ score of $-1.40$. In this case, we are moving 1.4 standard deviations to the left of the mean. Therefore, we can furthermore conclude that approximately 84 percent (exactly $.4192 \times 2$, or .8384 [83.84 percent]) of the area of the curve lies between $-1.40$ and $+1.40$ standard deviation units from the mean.

What is the area under the curve for a $z$ score of 1.37? We find this in the same way by going down the column to the $z$ score value of 1.37. From this we find the area between 1.37 and the mean is .4147. We can also deduce that the area between the mean and a $z$ score of $-1.37$ also is .4147. Thus, the total area under the curve for $z$ scores of $\pm 1.37$ is equal to .8294 ($.4147 \times 2$), or 82.94 percent.

Not only can we determine the area of the curve between the mean and a given $z$ score, we can also use the standard normal table to find the area between any pair of $z$ scores or between any pair of raw scores. For example, suppose that we have a normal distribution of data with a mean of 75 and standard deviation of 9. Suppose furthermore that we wanted to know the proportion of cases that fall between the raw scores of 60 and 89. To determine this, we first obtain the corresponding $z$ scores for our two raw scores:

$$z = \frac{60 - 75}{9} = \frac{-15}{9} = -1.67$$

$$z = \frac{89 - 75}{9} = \frac{14}{9} = 1.56$$

We now need to know the proportion of cases that fall between a $z$ score of $-1.67$ and 1.56. The first thing we do is go to our standard normal $z$ table, where we find the area under the curve between the mean and the first $z$ score of $-1.67$ (.4525) and then find the area under the curve between the mean and the second $z$ score of 1.56 (.4406). The proportion of cases between a $z$ of $-1.67$ and 1.56, then, simply, is the sum of these two areas:

Proportion of cases between the mean and −1.67     .4525
Proportion of cases between the mean and 1.56      .4406
Proportion of cases between −1.67 and 1.56         .8931

Thus, approximately 90 percent of the cases lie between the raw scores of 60 and 89. We can follow this procedure whenever we wish to know the area of the curve (the proportion of cases) between any two points.

We can also use the standard normal table and $z$ scores to answer probability questions. For example, suppose that we wanted to know what $z$ scores are so far out on the right end of the tail that 95 percent of the area of the curve lies to their left. That is, what $z$ scores are so extreme that they lie in the upper 5 percent of the tail of the standard normal curve? This area is shown as the cross-hatched area in Figure 8.8. To answer this question, we need to keep in mind that the normal curve is symmetrical. Exactly one-half of the cases fall to the left of the mean, and exactly one half of the cases fall to the right of the mean. We know, then, that the area under the curve from the infinite end of the left tail to the mean is .50. Therefore, we need to find the score to the right of the mean that corresponds to .45 of the remaining area under the curve. We need to go into the body of the normal curve table and find the $z$ score that corresponds to the area .45. We can see that a $z$ score of 1.64 corresponds to .4495 of the area to the right of the mean. When we add this to the .50 of the area that lies on the left side of the mean, we will find that .9495 (.50 + .4495) of the area under the normal curve lies to the left of a $z$ score of 1.64.

Proportion of the curve to the left of the mean                   .5000
Proportion of the curve from the mean to a $z$ score of 1.64      .4495
Total area to the left of a $z$ score of 1.64                     .9495

The shaded area in Figure 8.8, then, corresponds to all $z$ scores of 1.64 and higher.

We know that, because 100 percent of all cases lie under the normal curve, the probability of a case falling somewhere under that curve is 1.0. Because only .0505 (1 − .9495) of the curve lies in the cross-hatched area of Figure 8.8, we know that the probability of a score being in that cross-hatched area is approximately .05. In other words, approximately 5 percent of the cases have a $z$ score of 1.64 or

FIGURE 8.8. Area of the normal curve to a $z$ score of 1.64.

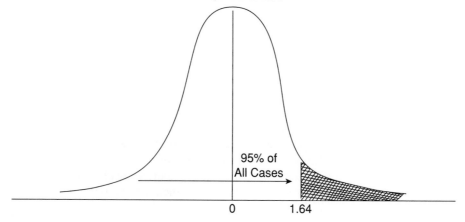

95% of
All Cases

0          1.64

higher. If we wanted to know what a $z$ score of 1.64 corresponds to in raw score terms with our earlier example data (where $\bar{x} = 25$ and $s = 5$), we can find that value with our $z$ score formula by substituting the $z$ score of 1.64 and solving for $x$ as shown:

$$z = \frac{x - \bar{x}}{sd}$$

$$1.64 = \frac{x - 25}{5}$$

$$(1.64)\,(5) = x - 25$$

$$8.2 = x - 25$$

$$8.2 + 25 = x$$

$$33.2 = x$$

To verify this result, simply substitute the raw score into the $z$ score formula and solve for $z$:

$$z = \frac{33.2 - 25}{5} = \frac{8.2}{5} = 1.64$$

Thus, raw scores of 33.2 and higher in our original distribution are higher than 95 percent of all of the scores in that given empirical distribution. In probability language, the probability of getting a raw score of above 33.2 is only .05, or 5 percent.

As a final illustration, let's determine the probability of getting a raw score of 14 or lower from our example empirical distribution. As shown in the following, a raw score of 14 corresponds to a $z$ score of $-2.20$:

$$z = \frac{14 - 25}{5} = \frac{-11}{5} = -2.20$$

Because the $z$ score is negative, we are interested in the left tail of the standard normal distribution (see Figure 8.9). Our question, then, is how much of the area of the curve lies in the cross-hatched area. Let's solve this by first finding the area under

FIGURE 8.9. Area under the curve for a $z$ score of $-2.20$ or less.

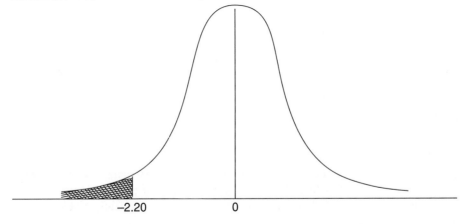

the curve that is in the non–cross-hatched area. We know that the total proportion under the curve is 1.0, so we can subtract the non–cross-hatched area from this in order to find the area that is shaded.

To begin with, we know that the area to the right of the mean out to the infinite end of the right tail is equal to .50 of the cases. To find the area under the curve from the mean to a $z$ score of $-2.20$ (the non–cross-hatched area under the curve to the left of the mean), we simply go to our standard normal table in Appendix B, go down 2.2 on the left margin and .00 at the top of the table. A normal distribution is symmetrical, so we can drop the negative sign. The area of the curve between the mean and a $z$ of $-2.20$ is the same as that between the mean and a $z$ of 2.20. Looking at Table B2, we see that the area of the curve from the mean to a $z$ score of 2.20 is .4861. Thus, the total area of the curve that is not in the cross-hatched interval (the area to the right of a $z$ score of $-2.20$) is:

| | |
|---|---|
| Proportion of the curve to the right of the mean | .5000 |
| Proportion of the curve from the mean to a $z$ score of $-2.20$ | .4861 |
| Total area to the right of a $z$ score of $-2.20$ | .9861 |

The proportion of the unshaded area of the curve is .9861, or roughly 98.6 percent. Therefore, the proportion under the curve that falls within the cross-hatched area is $1 - .9861 = .0139$. If we have a $z$ score of $-2.20$ or lower, then, we know that it lies in the cross-hatched area where only .0139 of the area of the curve is found; that is, fewer than 1.5 percent of the cases have a raw score of 14 or lower.

If this discussion sounds a bit abstract, let's examine the idea of standard scores in relation to some criminological data. The data below represent the raw scores on a verbal IQ test and the number of self-reported delinquent acts for a sample of 15 youths:

| Person | Verbal IQ | Delinquent Acts |
|:---:|:---:|:---:|
| 1 | 85 | 7 |
| 2 | 104 | 0 |
| 3 | 110 | 1 |
| 4 | 78 | 16 |
| 5 | 100 | 2 |
| 6 | 107 | 3 |
| 7 | 101 | 1 |
| 8 | 76 | 13 |
| 9 | 89 | 8 |
| 10 | 112 | 4 |
| 11 | 101 | 2 |
| 12 | 99 | 1 |
| 13 | 89 | 8 |
| 14 | 100 | 4 |
| 15 | 82 | 9 |

Looking at the two sets of scores does not tell you very much because they are measured on what are called different metrics or scales of measurement. The verbal IQ test is measured with a scale that ranges from approximately 30 to 150. The measure of self-reported delinquent acts is measured on a different scale, one with a minimum value of zero. If we were to try and compare the two groups of scores, then, we would be in the position of comparing the proverbial "apples and oranges." One way to get a better understanding about these scores and what they mean is to convert them to $z$ scores. If we convert these raw scores into $z$ or standard scores, they will be measured on the same scale or metric. We can then make some comparisons more easily.

We can convert our raw scores into $z$ scores by first calculating the mean and standard deviation for each set of scores. The mean for the sample of verbal IQ scores is 95.53, and the standard deviation is 11.15. The mean for the self-reported delinquency scores is 5.26 with a standard deviation of 4.61. After you have worked out the $z$ score transformations, check them with the following results:

| Person | Verbal IQ | Self-Reported Delinquency |
|:------:|:---------:|:-------------------------:|
| 1 | −.95 | .38 |
| 2 | .76 | −1.14 |
| 3 | 1.26 | −.92 |
| 4 | −1.57 | 2.33 |
| 5 | .40 | −.71 |
| 6 | .01 | −.49 |
| 7 | .49 | −.92 |
| 8 | −1.75 | 1.68 |
| 9 | −.59 | .59 |
| 10 | 1.48 | −.27 |
| 11 | .49 | −.71 |
| 12 | .31 | −.92 |
| 13 | −.59 | .59 |
| 14 | .40 | −.27 |
| 15 | −1.21 | .81 |

With the two sets of scores now transformed as $z$ scores, so that they are measured on the same underlying scale, we can see a pattern to the data that we may have overlooked in the raw scores. Notice that there are a few verbal IQ $z$ scores that are very low. For example, person number 4 has a verbal IQ $z$ score of −1.57. This means that his or her score on the verbal IQ test was one and one-half standard deviations *below* the mean. Person number 8 has a verbal IQ $z$ score of −1.75, that is, his or her score on the verbal IQ test was one and three quarters—almost two standard deviations—below the mean. Notice also that the self-reported delinquency $z$ scores for these two youths are 2.33 and 1.68, telling us that they are over two and one and one-half standard deviations *above* the mean delinquency score, respectively. This would seem to indicate that youths with low verbal IQ scores tend to have higher levels of delinquency than those with higher verbal IQ scores. This pattern would be difficult to see with the raw scores but becomes quite clear with the $z$ scores. As you can see, then, the $z$ score allows us to convert any variable, no matter how it is measured, into a score with a common mean (zero) and standard deviation (1).

## 8.5 THE NORMAL DISTRIBUTION AND THE CENTRAL LIMIT THEOREM

A good understanding of the properties of the normal distribution is very important for statistical work. At some point in your reading of this chapter, though, you may have wondered just why the normal distribution is so important. You may have thought that, although some variables certainly are normally distributed in the population, most are certainly not. For example, population characteristics such as the number of crimes committed or convictions experienced by persons are not likely to be normally distributed. The same holds for such things as neighborhood crime rates or the number of parole violations. If few variables are normally distributed in the population, the utility of the normal distribution must be rather restricted. Not so!

The normal distribution has wide applicability that makes it invaluable for us as aspiring researchers. The generality of the normal distribution is based on one of the most important and remarkable theorems of statistics, the *central limit theorem.* This theorem is what enables us to employ the standard normal distribution in so much of our statistical work. Before we discuss this theorem and its implications, however, we need to discuss some preliminary issues.

Recall that in conducting our research we almost always draw a sample from a large population rather than study the entire population. We draw a sample from our population and collect data on characteristics of the sample, with the intention of making an *inference* about the corresponding, but unknown, characteristic in the population. The puzzle that the subject of inferential statistics attempts to solve is that, although we know a great deal about the characteristics of our sample (we know its mean, standard deviation, skew of the distribution, etc.), we know virtually nothing about the characteristics of the population. (If we knew about the characteristics of the population, why would we even bother to select a sample?) This is a big problem because it is the population that we really want to know about. Through inferential statistics we can estimate the characteristics of populations from our knowledge of the sample. The connection between sample information and population characteristics is made through a *sampling distribution.*

As an example, let's assume that we are interested in the variable of height. We collect data on the height of those selected into our sample so that we can make inferences about the height of those in the larger population. Let's also assume for the moment that the distribution of height in the population is normal. We draw a random sample of 100 persons, so our sample size is 100. Both our sample and the larger population from which it was drawn have a mean value. For our sample the mean height is symbolized by the term "$x$ bar" ($\bar{x}$); this is our sample *statistic.* The corresponding population value is called the *parameter,* and the population mean is symbolized by the Greek letter mu ($\mu$). Not all of the values in our sample are equal to the mean value, however—some scores are lower or higher than the mean. That is, although there is a mean height for our sample, not all 100 persons in our sample are that exact height. Some are taller, some are shorter, and some may actually be equal to the mean. We have, then, variation about our sample mean, which we measure with the sample standard deviation ($s$). Similarly, in our population there is variation about the population mean height, which is measured in terms of the population standard deviation ($\sigma$). Keep in mind that, although the population is normally distributed (we have assumed this), our sample of heights may not be. The distribution of height from our sample may be very skewed.

Now, instead of taking just one random sample of size 100 from our population, let's imagine taking an infinite number of random samples of size 100 one at a time. Remember, the number of samples is infinite but the sample size is finite and equal to $N$ (i.e., 100 in this case). For each one of these samples we can determine the mean ($\bar{x}$). That is, we draw a sample size of 100 and then calculate the mean of that sample. We draw a second random sample of size 100 and determine the mean of that sample. We continue drawing a random sample from a population for an infinite number of samples, each of size 100, and calculate the mean of the sample. If we do this for each sample drawn, we will have an infinite number of sample means. Because not all these infinite number of sample means are alike (that is, the value of the mean will vary from sample to sample because a different 100 people are in each sample), there is a corresponding distribution of means and a corresponding standard deviation of this distribution of means. The fact that we are referring to an *infinite* number of means should alert you to the fact that we are speaking about a theoretical distribution, not a distribution based on empirical information. The distribution of these infinite number of means from sample size $N$ is called a sampling distribution of means or just a *sampling distribution.* Keep in mind that in this sampling distribution, we have an infinite distribution of theoretical sample means ($\bar{x}$), not raw scores or "cases."

Although the value of the mean varies from sample to sample, data points cluster about the true population mean ($\mu$). The standard deviation of this distribution of sample means is $\sigma/\sqrt{N}$. Based on this formula, you can see that the larger the size of the random sample we select from this normal population ($N$), the smaller the standard deviation of the sampling distribution will be. In other words, as our sample size increases, the narrower the clustering of the sample means ($\bar{x}$) about the true population mean ($\mu$) becomes. Stated in yet another way, the means display less variation from sample to sample with a large $N$. Therefore, we have more faith in our sample mean as an estimate of the population mean if we have a large sample size. The mean of the sample is seen as an estimate of the mean of the population, so we can draw two conclusions: (1) there is a certain amount of error in using a sample mean to estimate a population mean because the means vary from sample to sample, and (2) the amount of this error decreases as the size of the sample ($N$) increases. Because it reflects the amount of error due to sampling variation, the standard deviation of the sampling distribution ($\sigma/\sqrt{N}$) is generally referred to as the *standard error* or the standard error of the mean ($\sigma_{\bar{x}}$).

Figure 8.10 shows the relationship between the standard error of a sampling distribution and sample size. Notice that (1) the distribution of the sample means is narrower than the population and (2) the larger the sample size ($N$), the narrower that distribution is. As you can see, with a larger sample size, it is likely that the mean of any randomly drawn sample of size $N$ will be closer to the population mean ($\mu$). In other words, the larger the sample size, the less error there is in using a sample statistic ($\bar{x}$) to estimate a population parameter ($\mu$). The general rule here is that larger samples are always better than smaller ones.

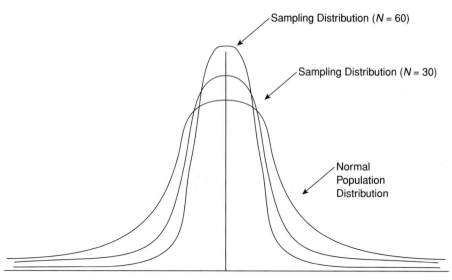

FIGURE 8.10. Population and sampling distributions.

In addition to having a known mean and standard deviation ($\mu$ and $\sigma/\sqrt{N}$, respectively), according to an important statistical theorem, the distribution of this infinite number of sample means drawn from a normal population will also be normal. We will state this theorem explicitly in the first box at the bottom of this page. In other words, the theoretical sampling distribution of the means of an infinite number of random samples drawn from a normal population will have a normal distribution.

Before we introduce an even more useful and important statistical theorem, the central limit theorem, you need to remember that we have referred to three distinct distributions, only two of which are normal. First, we have a distribution of raw scores from the single random sample that we actually draw and investigate. These scores are the heights of the individual persons in our random sample. The scores within our sample differ, so there is a distribution of sample scores with a mean $\bar{x}$ and standard deviation ($s$). Our distribution of sample values *is not* presumed to be normal. The characteristic of interest (mean height) is referred to as a sample statistic.

---

If an infinite number of random samples of size $N$ are drawn from a normal population, with a mean equal to $\mu$ and standard deviation equal to $\sigma$, the sampling distribution of the sample means ($\bar{x}$) will itself be normally distributed with mean equal to $\mu$ and standard deviation equal to $\sigma/\sqrt{N}$.

---

If we have a characteristic that is normally distributed in the population, take an infinite number of random samples of size $N$ from that population, and calculate a mean for each sample, the sampling distribution of these means will be normally distributed. In other words, if the population is normally distributed, the sampling distribution will be normally distributed.

A *sample* is a distribution of scores of size $N$ drawn from some population. The scores in our sample are empirically observed in the world.

A *population* is the much larger distribution of scores or cases from which we draw our sample. The scores in the population are empirical (they exist in the world) but are not known.

A *sampling distribution* is a distribution of means from an infinite number of samples drawn from our population. A sampling distribution is a theoretical probability distribution. It is nonempirical (we do not observe it in the real world), but we can know its features (shape, central tendency) from the laws of probability.

The second distribution is the distribution of our population characteristic (height). The scores in this distribution vary and are presumed to be normally distributed with mean $\mu$ and standard deviation $\sigma$. The characteristic of interest in this distribution (mean height) is called the population parameter.

The third distribution is the distribution of sample means of an infinite number of random samples drawn from our normally distributed population. Based on the theorem just discussed this distribution also is assumed to be normally distributed, with a mean equal to the population parameter ($\mu$) and standard deviation equal to $\sigma/\sqrt{N}$. The three distributions and their associated characteristics are summarized in Table 8.1.

You should keep in mind that these are three distinct distributions. The first is a distribution of sample scores (empirical), the second is a distribution of population values (empirical but not known). What connects these two is the third distribution (theoretical), which is a distribution of sample means. That is, we can make inferences from our sample mean to the population mean by considering it as one sample mean from a theoretical distribution of all possible sample means (the sampling distribution). With our sampling distribution we can determine the probability of obtaining our sample statistic. Because the sampling distribution of means is normal and the population is assumed to be normal, we can make use of the standard normal distribution to determine this probability.

These ideas can be illustrated from the inference flow diagram in the box at the top of page 228. We collect data from a random sample and use the theoretical sampling distribution to make inferences from these sample data to the population parameter.

You may be thinking to yourself right now, "What about the vast majority of cases in which we cannot reasonably make the assumption that the population characteristic is normally distributed? Does this mean that the normal distribution is inapplicable?" No. We can employ the normal distribution even if our population is not normally distributed. This is because of the remarkable nature of the central limit theorem. The central limit theorem is stated in the second box on page 228.

**TABLE 8.1. Characteristics of Three Types of Statistical Distributions**

| | Mean | Standard Deviation | Distribution |
|---|---|---|---|
| Sample | $\bar{x}$ | $s$ | Empirical, known |
| Population | $\mu$ | $\sigma$ | Empirical, unknown |
| Sampling distribution | $\mu$ | $\sigma/\sqrt{N}$ | Theoretical |

> Sample→Sampling Distribution→Population

> If an infinite number of random samples of size $N$ are drawn from *any population* with mean $\mu$ and standard deviation $\sigma$, then as the sample size ($N$) becomes larger, the sampling distribution of sample means will approach normality, with mean $\mu$ and standard deviation $\sigma/\sqrt{N}$, even if the population distribution is not normally distributed.

The importance of this theorem is that it does not depend on normality in the population. No matter what the shape of the distribution in the population, the theoretical probability distribution of sample means approximates a normal distribution as the sample size becomes large. Not only will the sampling distribution be normal, it will have a mean equal to the population mean $\mu$ and a standard deviation equal to $\sigma/\sqrt{N}$. This is quite an important theorem because it suggests that, even if our population distribution is quite skewed (like the number of arrests in the population), we can still assume that our sampling distribution of means will be normal as the size of the sample becomes large. Because it is the sampling distribution that links our sample estimate to the population parameter, we can employ the normal probability distribution in instances where our population is not normal.

The important and practical question to ask now is, "How large is large enough so we can relax the normality assumption and use the central limit theorem?" A good rule of thumb (and only a rule of thumb) is that the assumption of normality can almost always be relaxed when the sample size is 100 or more ($N \geq 100$). If there is some empirical evidence to suggest that the population is not terribly skewed, then it is recommended that the sample size be at least 50 ($N \geq 50$). With sample sizes under 50, the normality assumption should generally not be relaxed, unless there is fairly strong empirical evidence indicating that the population is normally distributed. In the case of small samples, you must use statistics that are not based on the central limit theorem and on the normal distribution. Many of these so-called distribution-free or nonparametric statistics are covered in Chapter 16. Before departing this chapter, however, you should convince yourself that the claim of the central limit theorem is a valid one. Let's look at an example.

> **THREE CHARACTERISTICS OF THE SAMPLING DISTRIBUTION BASED ON THE CENTRAL LIMIT THEOREM**
>
> Whenever the sample size is large:
> 1. We can assume that the mean of the sampling distribution is equal to the population mean, $\mu$.
> 2. We can assume that the standard deviation of the sampling distribution is equal to $\sigma/\sqrt{N}$.
> 3. We can assume that the sampling distribution is normally distributed even if the population from which the sample was drawn is not.

Let's assume that we have five cards (an ace, a two, a three, a four, and a five). To make things simple, these five cards are all of the same suit. You know that the five cards have an equal probability of being drawn in a random selection, so that $p = 1/5 = .20$ for each card. The probability distribution for the selection of a single card is shown for you in Figure 8.11. As you can see, this distribution is not normal at all. In a normal distribution the most likely events are in the center of the distribution with less likely events occurring as you move toward each tail.

Now let's take a sample of two ($N = 2$) by randomly selecting two cards from the five. We then take the mean of this sample; that is, first, we select one card and record its face value (the ace will be equal to 1), replace the card, select a second one, and record its face value. Then, we sum the values of these two cards and divide by 2. This is our mean value. With these five cards, the sums of our sample of two cards ranges in value from a low of 2 (both cards are aces) to a high of 10 (both cards are fives). What we want to do now is to determine the probability distribution of the means for an infinite number of samples of size two from this population of five cards.

To do this, let's first use our counting rules of probability. With five distinct outcomes on the first random card selection (ace, two, three, four, five) and the same five distinct outcomes on the selection there are (5)(5), or 25, possible different outcomes. This is our sample space. Because the sum of our two cards can range from

FIGURE 8.11. Probability distribution of five cards.

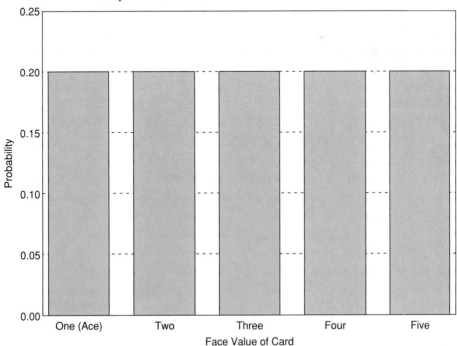

2 to 10 (and the means, therefore, can range from 1 to 5 as $N = 2$), we need to determine the number of ways in which two cards can total to these different sums.

There is only one way to obtain a sum of 2 (and a mean of 1). This occurs only if both cards are aces. Similarly, there is only one way to obtain a sum of 10 (and a mean of 5), when both cards are fives. There are two ways to obtain a sum of 3 (and a mean of 1.5). This occurs when the first card is an ace and the second is a two or if the first card is a two and the second is an ace. Similarly, there are two ways to obtain a sum of 9 (and a mean of 4.5), when the first card is a four and the second a five or when the first is a five and the second card is a four. A sum of 4 (and a mean of two) can occur any of three ways, a two on both cards, an ace on the first and three on the second, and a three on the first and an ace on the second. Table 8.2 lists the total possible sums, the corresponding mean values, the number of ways to obtain each sum, and the probability of each mean. You can see from this table that the probability of obtaining a mean of 1 or 5 is 1/25, or .04. The probability of obtaining a mean of 2 or 4 is 3/25, or .12. The most likely sum is 6, and the most likely mean is 3, with a probability of 5/25, or .20.

In Figure 8.12 we graph the probability distribution of these sample means. Notice that even with a sample size of only 2, the sampling distribution of means is starting to take on the appearance of a normal distribution. The most probable mean occurs in the middle of the distribution of means with more extreme mean values (both high and low) less likely. We admit that this does not look exactly like a "normal" normal distribution, but remember, in this example we only have a sample size of 2.

Let's now increase our sample size to 3 and determine the probability distribution of sample means. With three cards, the range of possible sums is from 3 (three aces are drawn) to 15 (three fives are drawn). The range of means, therefore, is from 1 to 5. We have calculated the probability distribution for you with $N = 3$ (Table 8.3). The sampling distribution is plotted in Figure 8.13. Compare Figure 8.11 with Figure 8.13. Figure 8.11 is the probability distribution for our five cards. It is rectangular in shape with equal probabilities for each card. Figure 8.13 shows the dis-

**TABLE 8.2. Sums, Means, and Probability of Means for Random Samples of Size Two from Five Cards**

| Sum | Mean | Number of Ways of Obtaining Sum | | Probability of Mean | |
|---|---|---|---|---|---|
| 2 | 1 | 1 | (Ace, Ace) | 1/25 | (.04) |
| 3 | 1.5 | 2 | (Ace, 2) (2, Ace) | 2/25 | (.08) |
| 4 | 2 | 3 | (2, 2) (Ace, 3) (3, Ace) | 3/25 | (.12) |
| 5 | 2.5 | 4 | (Ace, 4) (4, Ace) (2, 3) (3, 2) | 4/25 | (.16) |
| 6 | 3 | 5 | (3, 3) (2, 4) (4, 2) (Ace, 5) (5, Ace) | 5/25 | (.20) |
| 7 | 3.5 | 4 | (3, 4) (4, 3) (5, 2) (2, 5) | 4/25 | (.16) |
| 8 | 4 | 3 | (4, 4) (5, 3) (3, 5) | 3/25 | (.12) |
| 9 | 4.5 | 2 | (4, 5) (5, 4) | 2/25 | (.08) |
| 10 | 5 | 1 | (5, 5) | 1/25 | (.04) |
| Total | | 25 | | 25/25 | 1.00 |

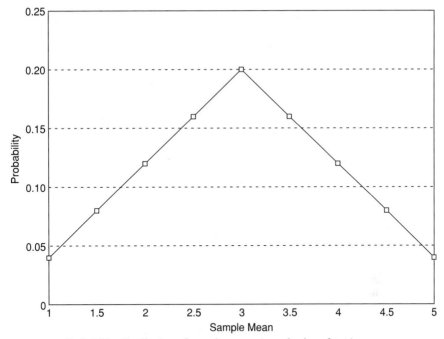

FIGURE 8.12. Probability distribution of sample means (sample size of two).

tribution of sample means when the sample size is 3. The distribution of sample means with $N = 3$ is beginning to take on the shape of the normal distribution, even though the population from which the sample was drawn was decidedly non-normal (Figure 8.11).

**TABLE 8.3. Sums, Means, and Probability of Means for Random Samples of Size Three from Five Cards**

| Sum | Mean | Probability of Mean |
|-----|------|---------------------|
| 3   | 1.00 | .01 |
| 4   | 1.33 | .02 |
| 5   | 1.67 | .05 |
| 6   | 2.00 | .08 |
| 7   | 2.33 | .12 |
| 8   | 2.67 | .14 |
| 9   | 3.00 | .15 |
| 10  | 3.33 | .14 |
| 11  | 3.67 | .12 |
| 12  | 4.00 | .08 |
| 13  | 4.33 | .05 |
| 14  | 4.67 | .02 |
| 15  | 5.00 | .01 |

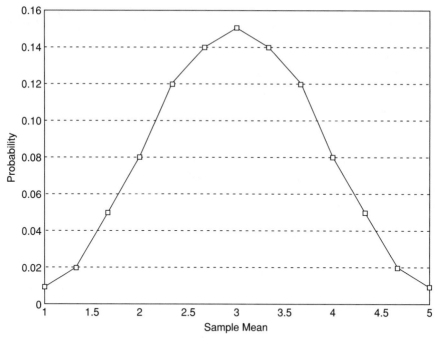

FIGURE 8.13. Probability distribution of sample means (sample size of 3).

We hope this exercise has convinced you that the assumptions the central limit theorem allows us to make are indeed valid. Our ability to use the inferential statistics that we examine in the next few chapters is inextricably linked to these assumptions.

## 8.6 SUMMARY

In this chapter we examined one important kind of theoretical probability distribution, the normal distribution. There is not one normal distribution; there is instead a family of normal curves that are defined by their specific mean and standard deviation. Whatever the particular normal distribution in question, all have the useful property that there is a constant area under the normal curve between the mean and given points, measured in standard deviation units, away from the mean. This is a very useful probability distribution for research purposes because many empirical frequency distributions approximate (or can be considered to approximate) a normal distribution.

Although there are many normal distributions, the most important one for our purposes here is the standard normal distribution. This is a normal distribution with a mean of zero and standard deviation equal to 1. We can use the standard normal distribution by converting our raw scores into $z$ scores. With the standard normal probability distribution and an empirical distribution that is assumed to be normally distributed, we can begin to test specific research hypotheses.

The normal distribution comes in handy because, even if we cannot assume that our population is normally distributed, we can assume that the distribution of sample means, the sampling distribution, will approximate a normal distribution as our sample size increases. The sampling distribution is a theoretical probability distribution of an infinite number of sample means with sample size *N*. The central limit theorem allows us to make three assumptions about sampling distributions when the sample size is large: (1) that the mean of the sampling distribution is equal to the population mean, $\mu$; (2) that the standard deviation of the sampling distribution is equal to $\sigma \backslash \sqrt{N}$; and (3) that the sampling distribution is normally distributed, even if the population from which the sample was drawn is not.

## Key Terms

**central limit theorem**
**empirical probability distribution**
**normal distribution**
**parameter**
**sampling distribution**
**standard error**

**standard normal distribution**
**standard score (z score)**
**statistic**
**theoretical probability distribution**
**z score (standard score)**

## Problems

1. Assume that you have a normal distribution of IQ scores with a mean of 100 and a standard deviation of 10:
   **a.** What is the *z* score for a raw score of 115?
   **b.** What is the *z* score for a raw score of 83?
   **c.** What is the *z* score for a raw score of 70?
   **d.** What proportion of the cases have an IQ score above 115?
   **e.** What proportion of the cases have an IQ score between 90 and 110?
2. A state department of corrections has a policy whereby it accepts as correctional officers only those who score in the top 5 percent of a qualifying exam. The mean of this test is 80 and the standard deviation is 10.
   **a.** Would a person with a raw score of 95 be accepted?
   **b.** Would a person with a raw score of 110 be accepted?
   **c.** What is the minimum score you would have to have on the test to be accepted?
3. Given a normal distribution of raw scores with a mean of 60 and a standard deviation of 8, what proportion of cases fall:
   **a.** In between a raw score of 55 and 71?
   **b.** In between a raw score of 50 and 80?
   **c.** In between a raw score of 48 and 57?
   **d.** What raw score is better than at least 90 percent of the others?
4. Draw a picture and indicate what the area under the standard normal curve is between:
   **a.** The mean and a *z* score of .20?
   **b.** The mean and a *z* score of −2.34?
   **c.** A *z* score of −1.23 and a *z* score of .67?
5. Given a normal distribution of raw data with a mean of 28 and a standard deviation of 4:
   **a.** What proportion of the cases lies between the mean and a raw score of 30?
   **b.** What proportion of the cases lies between the raw scores of 25 and 36?
   **c.** What raw score is larger than 95 percent of all the other raw scores?
   **d.** What raw score is less than 99 percent of all the other raw scores?
6. Draw a picture indicating what proportion (area) of the normal curve lies:
   **a.** To the right of a *z* score of 1.65.
   **b.** To the left of a *z* score of −1.65.
   **c.** Either to the left of a *z* score of −1.65 or to the right of a *z* score of 2.33.

7. A jail has an inmate population with a mean number of prior arrests of 6 and a standard deviation of 2.
   a. Would a new inmate with nine prior arrests have an unusually higher number, where unusual is in the top 5 percent?
   b. Would a new inmate with 11 prior arrests have an unusually higher number, where unusual is in the top 5 percent?
   c. Would an inmate with two prior arrests have an unusually lower number, where unusual is in the bottom 5 percent?
8. What is the central limit theorem? What does it allow us to assume about sampling distributions given the fact that we have a large enough sample?
9. What are the three types of distributions we have examined in this chapter, and how are they related in regard to making inferences to a population?

## Solutions to Problems

1. a. $z = 1.5$.
   b. $z = -1.7$.
   c. $z = -3.0$.
   d. .0548, or slightly more than 5 percent, of the cases have an IQ score above 115.
   e. .6832.
2. a. A raw score of 95 is better than .9332, or 93 percent of the scores. It is not in the top 5 percent of scores. Therefore this candidate would not be accepted.
   b. A raw score of 110 corresponds to a $z$ score of 3.0:

   $$z = \frac{110 - 80}{10} = \frac{30}{10} = 3.0$$

   This score is better than 99 percent of the scores. It is in the top 5 percent. This candidate would be accepted.
   c. You must have a raw score of at least 96.5 on the test to be accepted as a correctional officer.
3. a. The area of the curve between the two points is .2357 + .4147 = .6504.
   b. The area in between the two scores is .3944 + .4938 = .8882.
   c. The area of the curve between the two scores is .4332 − .1433 = .2899.
   d. The raw score that is better than at least 90 percent of the other scores is 70.32.
4. The area under the standard normal ($z$) curve between:
   a. The mean and a $z$ score of .20 is equal to .0793.
   b. The mean and a $z$ score of −2.34 is .4904.
   c. A $z$ score of −1.23 and a $z$ score of .67 is .3907 + .2486 = .6393.
5. a. The area of the curve is .1915.
   b. The area of the curve between the two $z$ scores is .2734 + .4772 = .7506.
   c. Raw scores that are 34.6 or higher are in the top 5 percent of all scores.
   d. Scores that are 18.68 or lower are less than 99 percent of all the other raw scores.
6. a. The area to the right of a $z$ score of 1.65 is equal to .0495.
   b. The area to the left of a $z$ score of −1.65 is equal to .0495.
   c. The area either to the left of a $z$ score of −1.65 or to the right of a $z$ score of 1.65 is equal to .099.
7. a. To see how unusual nine prior arrests are in this population, let's transform the raw score into a $z$ score:

   $$z = \frac{9 - 6}{2} = \frac{3}{2} = 1.5$$

The area to the right of this score comprises approximately 7 percent of the area of the normal curve. Those who have nine prior arrests, then, are in the top 7 percent of this population. Because they are not in the top 5 percent, we would not consider them unusual.

**b.** A raw score of eleven prior arrests corresponds to a $z$ score of:

$$z = \frac{11 - 6}{2} = \frac{5}{2} = 2.50$$

A $z$ score of 2.50 is way at the right or upper end of the distribution. $z$ scores of 2.50 or above are higher than approximately 99 percent of all the other scores. This person does have an unusually large number of prior arrests because he or she is in the top 5 percent.

**c.** A raw score of two prior arrests corresponds to a $z$ score of:

$$z = \frac{2 - 6}{2} = \frac{-4}{2} = -2.0.$$

A $z$ score of $-2.0$ or less is lower than almost 98 percent of all the other scores. The person with only two prior arrests, then, does have an unusually low number for this population because he or she is in the bottom 5 percent.

**8.** The central limit theorem is a statistical proposition that holds that, if an infinite number of random samples of size $N$ are drawn from *any* population with mean $\mu$ and standard deviation $\sigma$, then as the sample size becomes large, the sampling distribution of sample means will become normal with mean $\mu$ and standard deviation equal to $\sigma/\sqrt{N}$. The central limit theorem allows us to make three assumptions about sampling distributions when the sample size is large: We can assume that (1) the mean of the sampling distribution is equal to the population mean, $\mu$, (2) the standard deviation of the sampling distribution is equal to $\sigma/\sqrt{N}$, and (3) the sampling distribution is normally distributed, even if the population from which the sample was drawn is not.

**9.** The first distribution is a distribution of sample scores. This distribution is empirical in that it comes from our observed data. There is no assumption that the distribution of sample scores is normal. The second distribution is a distribution of population values. This distribution also is empirical, in that it exists, although we usually do not know much about its characteristics. What connects these two distributions is the third distribution, which is a distribution of sample means. This distribution is theoretical and based on probability theory. It is the theoretical distribution of an infinite number of sample statistics of sample size $N$. The sampling distribution is what connects our known sample mean to our unknown population mean. We can make inferences from our sample mean to the population mean by considering it as one sample mean from a theoretical distribution of all possible sample means. With our sampling distribution we can determine the probability of obtaining our sample statistic. Because the sampling distribution of means is normal and the population is assumed to be normal, we can make use of the standard normal distribution to determine this probability.

## CHAPTER 9

# Point Estimation and Confidence Intervals

*There is only one thing certain, namely, that we can have nothing certain;
therefore it is not certain that we can have nothing certain.*

—SAMUEL BUTLER

### 9.1 INTRODUCTION

We are about to take our first step into the world of inferential statistics. Remember that the objective of inferential statistics is to make inferences about a population characteristic based on information obtained from a sample. In this chapter, we examine different ways in which to estimate a population parameter based on a sample statistic. Estimation is an interest common to many criminologists. How many children become the victims of abuse and neglect annually in this country? Does the average citizen believe that incarceration should or should not include access to education or job training? How often do teenagers use alcohol or other drugs? The answers to each of these questions begin with estimation.

In this chapter we want to evaluate how accurate our sample statistic (mean or proportion) is as an estimate of the true population value. The sample mean is referred to as our *point estimate* of the population mean. Because this estimate is subject to some measurement error, we want to surround it with a margin of error. This margin of error consists of a range of values or an interval into which we believe, with some established degree of confidence, the population value falls. That is, instead of estimating just one value for our population characteristic (our point estimate), we estimate a range of values or an interval within which we believe or are confident that the population value falls. This interval is called a *confidence interval*. Think of a confidence interval as an estimated interval that we are reasonably confident contains the true population value over the long run. The advantage of creating a confidence interval is that, by stipulating a range of values instead of a point estimate, the population parameter is more likely to be included.

Each of you has undoubtedly heard these intervals being referred to without even realizing that it was a statistical confidence interval. For example, every time the media covers the results of a new opinion poll, they will often caveat the story with a phrase such as, "A Gallup poll released today indicates that 79 percent (plus

**236**

or minus 2 percent) of Americans believe that crime is the most important problem for the current administration to address." The 79 percent is the point estimate of the population value. In this case the 79 percent is an estimate of the percent of Americans who believe that crime is the most important problem. The "plus or minus 2 percent" is the interval the researchers drew around the point estimate of 79 percent. With this confidence interval these pollsters are saying that they are reasonably confident that the true population percent may be as low as 77 percent or as high as 81 percent.

Let's describe the concept of a confidence interval in a different way. As with sampling distributions, think of a confidence interval in "long-run" terms. For example, let's say we took repeated samples of the same size from the same population. For each sample we calculated the proportion who believed crime to be the most important problem in America today and built a 95% confidence interval (c.i.) around that sample proportion. A 95% confidence interval indicates that approximately 95 percent of these estimated intervals would contain the true population proportion and approximately 5 percent would not.

Figure 9.1 illustrates the concept of a 95% confidence interval. It shows a hypothetical example in which 20 samples ($n = 100$) are drawn from the same population. From each sample, the mean number of times individuals from each sample ran a stop sign per month was calculated and 95% confidence intervals were drawn around each mean. The horizontal lines across the figure represent these 95 percent confidence intervals, and the vertical line running down the middle of the figure represents the true population mean of stop sign violations. From Figure 9.1, you can see that 95 percent (19) of these confidence intervals actually contain the true population mean, whereas 5 percent (1) do not. Even though each of these confidence intervals varies from sample to sample, 95 percent of them nevertheless contain the true population parameter. This is the goal of *inferential statistics.*

You should also notice that the true population parameter does not change, but the estimated interval does vary from sample to sample. What we are 95 percent confident about, then, is the procedure, not the particular confidence interval we estimate with our sample data. That is, we should interpret our confidence interval as saying that over the long run, 95 percent of the confidence intervals we would estimate would include the true population parameter.

Of course, in the real world, we never take repeated samples from the population and we never really know whether our confidence intervals contain the "true" population parameter. But if we have drawn our sample using probability sampling techniques (e.g., a simple random sample), we can use both probability theory and what we know about areas under the normal curve to estimate a population parameter from only one sample. Moreover, probability theory allows us to make numerical statements about the accuracy of our estimates.

We begin the chapter by examining the properties that any good estimate should have. We then examine confidence interval estimation procedures for sample means based on large samples ($n > 100$). We utilize the $z$ distribution to do this. In the second section of the chapter we introduce the $t$ distribution, which is used for estimating means from small samples ($n < 100$). In the final section of the chapter we examine estimation procedures used for proportions and percentages.

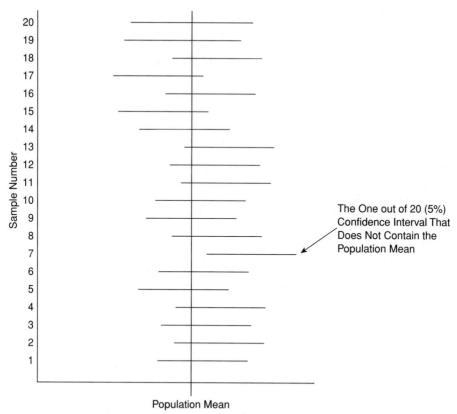

The One out of 20 (5%) Confidence Interval That Does Not Contain the Population Mean

Population Mean

FIGURE 9.1. A hypothetical example of 95% confidence intervals computed from 20 different samples of the same size drawn from the same population.

## 9.2 PROPERTIES OF GOOD ESTIMATES

The first parameter we are going to estimate is a population mean $\mu$. We are going to use the sample mean as our point estimate of the population mean. Why use the sample mean? Why not the sample median or the average of the mean and the median values as our point estimator? We choose the sample mean as our estimator because it is an unbiased estimate of the population mean. Any given estimate of a population parameter is unbiased if the mean of its sampling distribution is equal to the parameter being estimated. In the preceding chapter we learned that the mean of the sampling distribution of means ($\mu_{\bar{x}}$) is the population mean ($\mu$). Of course, this does not mean that any given sample mean ($\bar{x}$) will equal the population mean. Think of bias in the long run. With an infinite number of samples of size $n$, the mean of the samples will be equal to the population value.

We also know from the two theorems we presented in Chapter 8 that if the sample size is large enough, the distribution of the sample means will be approximately normal. We can, then, determine the probability that our sample statistic lies within a given number of standard deviation units from the population mean. We

---

PROPERTIES OF THE SAMPLING DISTRIBUTION OF THE MEAN

1. The mean of this sampling distribution of $\bar{x}$ is $\mu$.
2. The standard deviation of the sampling distribution of $\bar{x}$ is

$$\sigma_{\bar{x}} = \frac{\sigma}{\sqrt{n}}$$

where $\sigma$ is the standard deviation of the original population and $n$ is the sample size. $\sigma_{\bar{x}}$ is used to denote the standard deviation of the sampling distribution. This entire term is called the *standard error of the mean.*
3. Because of the central limit theorem, when $n$ is large (safely, when $n \geq 100$), the sampling distribution of $\bar{x}$ is normally distributed regardless of the distribution of the population from which the sample was drawn.
4. As the sample size increases, the standard deviation of the sampling distribution (the standard error of the mean) decreases.

---

know, for example, that there is a 68 percent chance that our sample mean is within one standard deviation unit of the population mean and a 95 percent chance that it is within $\pm 2$ standard deviation units. It is important, therefore, that our estimate be unbiased. The sample mean and proportion are unbiased estimates of their respective population values. In addition to bias, a second important property of an estimate is that it be efficient.

The efficiency of an estimate refers to the degree to which the sampling distribution is clustered about the true population value. In this case, an efficient estimate is one where the sampling distribution of means is clustered close to the population mean. The greater the clustering, the greater the efficiency of the estimate. Recall from Chapter 8 that sampling distributions are simply theoretical distributions that we would obtain if we were to draw many random samples of the same size from the same population and calculate the statistic of interest. In this case we are talking about the mean. As with any theoretical distribution such as the normal distribution, there are theoretical properties behind the sampling distribution of the mean. These properties are displayed in the box at the top of this page.

You will remember from the preceding chapter that the standard deviation of the sampling distribution of means is equal to $\sigma/\sqrt{n}$. The standard deviation of the sampling distribution, therefore, is in proportion to $n$, that is, the sample size. As the sample size increases, the standard deviation of the sampling distribution decreases (see Figure 8.10). This means that the sample means themselves differ less from one another and cluster more tightly about the population mean. The practical implication of this is that our sample estimate becomes more efficient when the sample size increases. We repeat this important lesson throughout this and other chapters.

## 9.3 ESTIMATING A POPULATION MEAN FROM LARGE SAMPLES

We know now that a sample mean is an unbiased estimate of the population mean and that the efficiency of the sample mean as an estimate is heightened by increasing the sample size. We are now ready to get down to the business of constructing confidence intervals. Relying on the properties of the sampling distribution of the mean and on what we know about the normal distribution and probability theory, we can utilize the following formula to construct a confidence interval around a sample mean ($\bar{x}$):

$$\bar{x} \pm z_\alpha (\sigma_{\bar{x}}) = \bar{x} \pm z_\alpha \left( \frac{\sigma}{\sqrt{n}} \right) \tag{9.1}$$

where

$\bar{x}$ = the mean of our sample

$z_\alpha$ = the $z$ score corresponding to the level of alpha we are using to construct our interval

$\sigma_{\bar{x}}$ = the standard deviation of the sampling distribution (i.e., the standard error)

The confidence interval, then, is determined by going out in both a positive and negative direction from the point estimate (the mean in Equation 9.1) a specified multiple of standard errors ($\sigma/\sqrt{n}$). How many standard errors we go out from the point estimate is a function of the confidence level we select.

The first order of business, therefore, is the size of our confidence interval or the strength of our confidence. What size should our confidence interval be, or, expressed differently, how confident should we be in creating our interval? Typically, criminologists choose an alpha level of .05 and construct 95% confidence intervals, although the choice is yours. The alpha we select will determine our *confidence level*. If $\alpha$ = .05, we have a 95% confidence level; if $\alpha$ = .01, we have a 99% confidence level. A 95% confidence level means that over the long run, we are willing to be wrong only 5 percent of the time. Being wrong in this case means not having the population mean within the boundaries established by the confidence interval. We see later that the size of the confidence interval is a function of how confident you want to be and how large your sample is.

Let's begin with a 95% confidence interval. No matter what confidence interval we select, we must determine the corresponding $z$ score for that level of confidence. The $z$ score corresponding to an alpha of .05 is 1.96. Why is it 1.96? With a 95% confidence interval we are concerned with 5 percent of the tail of the standard normal distribution. However, because we do not know whether our sample statistic ($\bar{x}$) is less than or greater than the true population value ($\mu$), we are really concerned about *both* tails of the distribution. Hence, we divide our 5 percent into two equal halves (2.5 percent) and place them at each tail of the distribution. The proportion of the normal curve corresponding to 2.5 percent is .025. The $z$ score that corresponds to .4750 of the normal curve (.50 − .025) is 1.96 (from Table B.2 in Appendix B). To find this $z$ score, simply go into the body of the table until you see the proportion .4750. The $z$ score for this proportion is 1.96. Because we are interested in both tails of the distribution, our $z$ score is ±1.96. In Table 9.1 we provide a list of some common confidence intervals and their corresponding $z$ score.

You know from the preceding chapter that the term ($\sigma_{\bar{x}}$) in Equation 9.1 is the standard deviation of the sampling distribution or the standard error. When the standard deviation of the population is known, we can easily determine the stan-

**TABLE 9.1. Common Confidence Intervals and Their $z$ Scores**

| Confidence Level | Alpha | | Proportion from the mean | $z$ score |
|---|---|---|---|---|
| | $\alpha$ | $\alpha/2$ | | |
| 90% | .10 | .050 | .4500 | 1.65 |
| 95% | .05 | .025 | .4750 | 1.96 |
| 99% | .01 | .005 | .4950 | 2.58 |
| 99.9% | .001 | .0005 | .4995 | 3.27 |

dard error of the sampling distribution by dividing the population standard deviation by the square root of the sample size ($\sigma/\sqrt{n}$). When we know the population standard deviation, then, the standard error of the sampling distribution can be directly determined, and we can create our confidence intervals from Equation 9.1.

As an example, let's imagine that we have selected a random sample of 200 residents from a youth training school. We want to estimate the mean IQ score for the population of incarcerated youths. We find that the mean IQ for our group of training school youths was 97. Remember that this sample mean, $\bar{x}$, is the point estimate of our population mean ($\mu$). Based on years of work with IQ testing we know that the general population mean is 100 and the standard deviation is 15. We can set the population standard deviation at 15, then, and using Equation 9.1 we can create a 95% confidence interval for our point estimate of 97:

$$95\% \text{ c.i.} = \bar{x} \pm z_\alpha \left( \frac{\sigma_x}{\sqrt{n}} \right)$$

$$= 97 \pm 1.96 \left( \frac{15}{\sqrt{200}} \right)$$

$$= 97 \pm 1.96(1.06)$$

$$= 97 \pm 2.08$$

$$95\% \text{ c.i.} = 94.92 - 99.08$$

This confidence interval indicates that our estimate of the mean IQ score for the population of youth training school residents is between 94.92 and 99.08.

The end points of our estimated confidence interval (94.92 and 99.08) are referred to as our *confidence limits*. This indicates that we are 95 percent confident that our interval contains the population mean of the training school youths. Another way to express this confidence interval would be:

$$94.92 \leq \mu \leq 99.08$$

We are 95 percent confident that the population mean is greater than or equal to 94.92 and less than or equal to 99.08.

However, we rarely know the standard deviation of our population. If we knew it, we would probably also be in a good position to know the mean, so our point estimate and confidence interval construction would be unnecessary. Most of the time, then, we do not know our population standard deviation and the standard error of the sampling distribution must be estimated. If the sample size is large enough we can use our sample standard deviation ($s$) to estimate the population standard deviation ($\sigma$), and then use the $z$ distribution to obtain the critical value needed for our confidence interval. The sample estimate of the standard deviation of the sampling distribution is $s/\sqrt{n}$. However, because $s$ is a slightly biased estimator of $\sigma$, we need to adjust Equation 9.1 to take this bias into account. The adjustment is in the denominator of the standard error where $n - 1$ replaces $n$. The sample estimate for the standard deviation of the sampling distribution is now $\dfrac{s}{\sqrt{n - 1}}$, and the formula for our confidence interval is:

$$\bar{x} \pm z_\alpha \left( \frac{s}{\sqrt{n - 1}} \right) \tag{9.2}$$

You can probably see from this that, as $n$ becomes larger, the substitution of $n - 1$ for $n$ in the denominator of the standard error makes less of a difference because, as $n$ increases, the sample standard deviation becomes a less biased estimate for the population standard deviation. Why? Before we continue, let's review what we know about the error in sampling distributions.

Recall from the box on p. 239 that $\sigma/\sqrt{n}$ is an estimate of the standard deviation of the sampling distribution of means and is referred to as the standard error. Standard errors, like standard deviations, describe the variability a distribution has. A large standard error for the mean indicates that the mean varies a great deal from sample to sample, whereas, a small standard error indicates that there is little variation from sample to sample.

It should be apparent to you by now that, as the size of the standard error decreases, the level of confidence we have in sample estimates typically increases. You should also notice that, the larger the sample size ($n$), the smaller the standard deviation of the sampling distribution. Less sample-to-sample variation indicates that we can be more confident that our sample statistic actually reflects the population parameter we are trying to estimate. Stated another way, if the standard error of the sampling distribution of means is small, then all samples drawn from a given population will have fairly similar means. The means from these samples will cluster tightly about the true population mean ($\mu$). In this case, any given sample mean will be a good estimate of the population mean. We then have a small (narrow) confidence interval.

However, if the standard error is large, then the means obtained from these same-size samples tends to be very different. Some may be close to the true population mean, and some may be far away. In this case we are less confident that any one sample mean is a good estimate of the true population mean, and the confidence interval will be large (wide).

Let's go through the calculation procedures for constructing a 95% confidence interval around a mean using a hypothetical example where the population standard deviation is not known. Suppose that we conducted interviews with individuals drawn from a random sample ($n = 140$) in a large metropolitan area. We assured these individuals that their answers would be confidential, of course, and we asked them about their law-breaking behavior. Among the questions was the number of times per month they exceeded the speed limit. One of the objectives of the study was to estimate (make an inference about) the average number of times per month residents in all metropolitan areas across the country exceeded the speed limit. The sample statistics we obtained were as follows:

$\bar{x} = 12.4$ times
$s = 3.2$
$n = 140$

The sample mean above tells us that, on average, the individuals from our sample exceed the speed limit about 12.4 times a month. To remind you, this sample statistic ($\bar{x}$) is referred to as our *point estimate* of the true population parameter ($\mu$). What does our sample mean tell us about the mean of the entire population of metropolitan residents? This is the question we are really trying to answer. We want to make our point estimate of 12.4 more reliable and at the same time, give ourselves the ability to make a probability statement about the confidence we have in our estimate. To do this, we use Equation 9.2 to construct a 95% confidence interval around the sample mean estimate of 12.4:

$$95\% \text{ c.i.} = 12.4 \pm 1.96 \left( \frac{3.2}{\sqrt{140 - 1}} \right)$$

$$= 12.4 \pm 1.96 \left( \frac{3.2}{11.79} \right)$$

$$= 12.4 \pm 1.96 \, (.27)$$

$$= 12.4 \pm .53$$

$$12.4 - .53 = 11.87$$

$$12.4 + .53 = 12.93$$

$$95\% \text{ c.i.} = 11.87 \text{ to } 12.93$$

So, what does this interval tell us? It tells us that based on our sample data, we can be 95 percent confident that the mean number of self-admitted speeding violations among all residents of metropolitan areas lies between 11.87 and 12.93 times per month. That is, theoretically speaking, if we had taken a large number of random samples from this same population and calculated 95% confidence intervals around the means obtained from each sample, approximately 95 percent of these intervals would include the true population mean ($\mu$) and 5 percent would not.

Let's say for the sake of argument that we only wanted a 90% confidence interval about our sample mean, rather than a 95% confidence interval for our point estimate of 12.4. From Table 9.1 we see that the $z$ score corresponding to an alpha level of .10 or a 90% confidence interval is 1.65. As before, using Equation 9.2 we construct our confidence interval as follows:

$$90\% \text{ c.i.} = 12.4 \pm 1.65 \left( \frac{3.2}{\sqrt{140 - 1}} \right)$$

$$= 12.4 \pm 1.65(.27)$$

$$= 12.4 \pm .44$$

$$90\% \text{ c.i.} = 11.96 \text{ to } 12.84$$

This interval indicates that we are 90 percent confident that the true population mean speeding violation score falls between 11.96 to 12.84. Notice that the interval for a 90% confidence interval is narrower than for a 95% confidence interval. You can see, then, that we are less confident (90 percent vs. 95 percent confident) that our true population mean falls into this interval. By lowering our level of confidence, we gained some precision in our estimate. We could reduce the width of our confidence interval even more, but we would have to pay the price in levels of confidence.

Because repetition is the key to acquiring skill, let's go through another example from the literature. Miller et al. (1990) investigated the relationship between alcohol and spousal violence using a sample of male parolees ($n = 82$). One of the first objectives of this study was to assess the extent of alcohol problems in the parolees' lives. To do this, parolees were asked 20 questions relating to alcohol dependence (e.g., "Do friends or family members tell you that you drink too much?" "Have you wanted to stop drinking but couldn't?"). Based on these questions, these investigators constructed an index measured at the interval/ratio level to quantify the extent of drinking problems in each parolee's life. For the sample, the mean number of alcohol problems obtained from this index was $\bar{x} = 5.09$ with a sample standard deviation equal to 5.11. Let's construct a 95% confidence interval around this estimate:

$$95\% \text{ c.i.} = 5.09 \pm 1.96 \left( \frac{5.11}{\sqrt{82 - 1}} \right)$$

$$= 5.09 \pm 1.96 \left( \frac{5.11}{9.00} \right)$$

$$= 5.09 \pm 1.96 \,(.57)$$

$$= 5.09 \pm 1.12$$

$$5.09 - 1.12 = 3.97$$

$$5.09 + 1.12 = 6.21$$

$$95\% \text{ c.i.} = 3.97 \text{ to } 6.21$$

The 95% confidence interval indicates that we can be 95 percent confident, based on our sample statistics, that the average number of drinking problems present in the lives of offenders on parole lies between 3.97 and 6.21.

Let's now take the same data, and, instead of constructing a 95% confidence interval, let's increase the confidence we have in our interval estimate by calculating a 99% interval. The only change that is necessary in the formula is the value of $z$. Because we have increased the level of confidence we wish to have about our point estimate ($\bar{x}$), the value of $z$ increases from 1.96 to 2.58 (Table 9.1). Using Equation 9.2:

$$99\% \text{ c.i.} = 5.09 \pm 2.58 \left( \frac{5.11}{\sqrt{82 - 1}} \right)$$

$$= 5.09 \pm 2.58 \left( \frac{5.11}{9.00} \right)$$

$$= 5.09 \pm 2.58 \, (.57)$$

$$= 5.09 \pm 1.47$$

$$5.09 - 1.47 = 3.62$$

$$5.09 + 1.47 = 6.56$$

$$99\% \text{ c.i.} = 3.62 \text{ to } 6.56$$

Based on our sample statistics, then, we are 99 percent confident that the average number of drinking problems among spouse abuse offenders on parole is between 3.62 and 6.56.

Notice that this 99% confidence interval (3.62 to 6.56) is wider than that from the same data with only a 95% confidence interval (3.97 to 6.21). Because we want to be more confident that our interval contains the population mean, this increased confidence comes at the price of a wider confidence interval. By now, this should make intuitive sense to you. It suggests that, if we want to be more confident that the true population mean falls into our estimated interval, we have to make the interval wider (other things being equal). To reiterate, greater confidence comes at a price, and the price we pay is the width of the confidence interval.

Think for a minute about this question: If we wanted to be more confident without increasing the size of the interval, what can we do? If you thought that by increasing our sample size we could achieve more confidence without widening our intervals you would be right!

Let's take the same example and calculate a 99% confidence interval for our point estimate of 5.09, but let's assume that we have a much larger sample now (150 rather than 82). What would our 99% confidence interval be when we almost double our sample size?

$$99\% \text{ c.i.} = 5.09 \pm 2.58 \left( \frac{5.11}{\sqrt{150 - 1}} \right)$$

$$= 5.09 \pm 2.58 \left( \frac{5.11}{12.21} \right)$$

$$= 5.09 \pm 2.58(.418)$$

$$= 5.09 \pm 1.08$$

$5.09 - 1.08 = 4.01$

$5.09 + 1.08 = 6.17$

99% c.i. = 4.01 to 6.17

The 99% confidence interval when $n = 150$ is 4.01 to 6.17. As you can see, our confidence interval in this case is actually narrower than the 95% confidence interval obtained with a sample size of only 82. Although we increased our confidence level, we did not increase the width of our confidence interval because our sample size was larger. In other words, our confidence interval did not increase, even though our confidence level did because we increased the size of our sample. By increasing our sample size, we reduced the estimated standard deviation of the sampling distribution. When our sample size was 82, the estimated standard deviation of the sampling distribution was .570. With a sample size of 150, that was reduced to .419. The confidence interval is smaller with a larger sample size because, when the standard deviation of the sampling distribution is lower, the sample value is a more accurate estimate of the true population mean. The lessons to be learned from this are as follows:

- The larger the sample size, the smaller the standard deviation of the sampling distribution of means (the standard error).
- The smaller the standard error, the more accurate our sample mean is as an estimate of the population mean.
- To increase the confidence that our interval contains the population mean, we can increase the confidence level (and widen the confidence interval) or increase the sample size.

After this discussion of different confidence levels, you may be asking yourself now when we want to use a 99% confidence interval compared to a 95% interval or a 90% interval? What guides us in our decision to select a level of confidence? Unfortunately, there are no hard-and-fast rules for this. The decision you make is in part a judgment call that depends on the nature of your research. Just remember that there usually is a trade-off between confidence and precision. Generally speaking, at a fixed sample size you will get a smaller interval and therefore more precision with lower levels of confidence. The lower your confidence, however, the less sure you are that your interval contains the true population mean. If you want to attain greater confidence that your interval actually contains the population mean, increase your confidence level. The trade-off you make in doing this is a larger confidence interval (unless you increase sample size). Because the 95% confidence interval is most typical in the criminology and criminal justice literature, we construct intervals at this level throughout the remainder of the chapter.

## *9.4 ESTIMATING CONFIDENCE INTERVALS WITH SMALL SAMPLES*

In constructing confidence intervals with Equation 9.2, we used the sample standard deviation to estimate the population standard deviation. When our sample size is large (in the preceding chapter we noted, when the sample size is at least 100, the assumption of a normal population can almost always be relaxed and can generally be relaxed whenever $n > 50$), $s$ is a fairly good estimate of $\sigma$. This is not true, however, when our sample size is small. With small sample sizes, the sample standard deviation shows substantial variation from sample to sample. For small samples, therefore, the standard deviation of the sampling distribution (standard error) is greater than for large samples. The practical implication of this is that the $z$ distribution cannot be used for constructing confidence intervals when the sample size is small.

There are many times in criminological research, however, when we must rely on small samples. In such instances, therefore, the assumptions we make about the normal distribution do not apply. Why? Well, recall that the properties described in the preceding chapter about the central limit theorem applied only to large-size samples. Therefore, if our sample is small, we must use statistics that violate this large-sample assumption. When our research dictates that we have no choice and must use a small sample, the Student's $t$ distribution is typically used to make inferences from the sample mean, $\bar{x}$, to the population mean, $\mu$.

The theoretical sampling distribution called Student's $t$ was calculated by W. E. Gosset and published in 1908. Gosset was a statistician for the Guinness brewing company. Although Guinness did not usually allow its employees to publish their own work, Gosset was permitted to under the *nom de plume* of "Student." Hence, his distribution has been called the *Student's t distribution.*

The $t$ distribution is flatter and has a greater spread than the $z$ distribution, which indicates that there is more sample-to-sample variation in the former. The two sampling distributions are shown in Figure 9.2. The smaller the sample size, the flatter the $t$ distribution is compared to the normal distribution. Just as with the standard normal distribution of $z$, the $t$ distribution also has several known properties, which are listed in the following box.

As noted in the box, there are actually several different $t$ distributions depending on the degrees of freedom present in the sample. The degrees of freedom are equal to the sample size minus 1 $(n - 1)$. As the sample size (and df) becomes larger, the $t$ distribution more closely approximates the standard normal distribution ($z$ distribution). When $n > 100$, the two distributions are virtually identical, but the $t$ distribution will always be flatter than the $z$. The values of $t$ associated with these degrees of freedom and different levels of alpha ($\alpha$) are displayed in Table B.3 in Appendix B.

---

### Properties of the Sampling Distribution of $t$

1. The $t$ distribution is bell shaped and symmetrical and centers around $t = 0$.
2. The $t$ distribution exhibits more variability than the $z$ distribution. It is flatter and has wider tails than the $z$ distribution.
3. There are many different $t$ distributions based on the sample size. More specifically, the distribution of $t$ we use for our statistical test is based on a parameter called the *degrees of freedom (df)*. The degrees of freedom are calculated as the sample size minus 1 $(n - 1)$.
4. With samples of size 100 or more the $t$ distribution becomes virtually identical to the $z$ distribution.

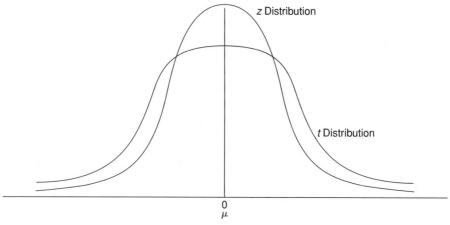

FIGURE 9.2. The *z* distribution and the *t* distribution.

As an example, let's say we had a sample size of $n = 10$ and wanted to make an inference to the population mean $\mu$ at the 95 percent level. With this, we would go into the *t* table using a $t_\alpha = .05$ for a two-tailed test and 9 degrees of freedom $(n - 1:10 - 1 = 9)$. In doing this, we would obtain a critical value of $t = 2.262$. Remember that by definition, confidence intervals are two-sided tests because we do not know whether our sample statistic is greater than or less than the true population value.

In Table B.3 of Appendix B, notice that, when the sample size is greater than 100, the critical values of *t* are about the same as those for *z*. This reflects the fourth property listed that states that, as the sample size approximates 100, the *t* distribution begins to look more and more like the *z* distribution. This should make intuitive sense to you based on our discussion in the preceding chapter. Remember that with large samples (over 100) the assumption of a normal population can almost always be relaxed. The sampling distribution of the mean can now be assumed to be approximately normal, which would allow us to utilize the *z* distribution to make inferences.

The formula for calculating a confidence interval around a mean using the *t* distribution follows. It looks almost exactly like that used when calculating confidence intervals using the *z* distribution, doesn't it?

$$\bar{x} \pm t_\alpha(\sigma_{\bar{x}}) = \bar{x} \pm t_\alpha\left(\frac{s_x}{\sqrt{n-1}}\right) \tag{9.3}$$

Let's go through a hypothetical example of making inferences about $\mu$ with a small sample using the *t* distribution. Research has shown that men convicted of rape usually have committed the crime of rape once if not several times before they were eventually caught and incarcerated (Abel et al., 1987). Suppose that you are a criminologist interested in the number of rapes committed by rapists before they are arrested. One way to examine this issue would be to calculate the average number of self-reported rapes incarcerated rapists committed before they were caught. To do this, you conduct interviews with a sample of 15 convicted rapists who were incarcerated in a state prison. You find that the mean number of rapes these men committed before being convicted on the count they are currently serving time for is 5.3. You calculate the standard deviation of this distribution to be 3.4. Because you want to infer this sample information to the population of all incarcerated rapists, you decide to calculate a 95 percent confidence interval around the $\bar{x}$.

The first step in this procedure is to calculate the degrees of freedom you have and find the critical value of $t$. With a sample size of 15, our degrees of freedom are equal to 14 ($n - 1$). Going down the appropriate column and across the appropriate row in the $t$ table (Appendix B, Table B.3) you find the critical value needed is 2.145. As before, the selection of the confidence level (and corresponding critical value) is up to you. Once you have selected your confidence level, you can construct your confidence interval with Equation 9.3 as shown:

$$95\% \text{ c.i.} = 5.3 \pm 2.145 \left( \frac{3.4}{\sqrt{15 - 1}} \right)$$

$$= 5.3 \pm 2.145 \left( \frac{3.4}{3.74} \right)$$

$$= 5.3 \pm 2.145 \, (.91)$$

$$= 5.3 \pm 1.95$$

$$5.3 - 1.95 = 3.35$$

$$5.3 + 1.95 = 7.25$$

$$95\% \text{ c.i.} = 3.35 \text{ to } 7.25$$

This interval tells us that using our sample data, we can be 95 percent confident that the mean number of self-admitted rapes committed by incarcerated rapists lies somewhere between 3.35 and 7.25 offenses. If we had taken a large number of random same-size samples from this same population of incarcerated rapists and calculated 95 percent confidence intervals around the mean obtained from each sample, approximately 95 percent of these intervals would include the true population mean $\mu$ and 5 percent would not.

Notice the difference between the critical value in this confidence interval for small samples and that for the same 95% confidence interval we calculated earlier for large samples. If we had a larger sample in this case, we could have used a $z$ value of 1.96 instead of the larger $t$ value of 2.145 that was necessary here. To reiterate the reasoning behind this, remember that because the $t$ distribution is flatter than the $z$ distribution, we have to go farther out in the tail to find our critical region. Again, the smaller the sample size, the flatter the $t$ distribution is and the farther we will have to move out in the tail. At the same alpha level, with very small sample sizes the critical value of $t$ will be much larger than the large sample $z$.

For the $t$ distribution, the normal relationships between confidence levels, sample sizes, and confidence intervals are still applicable. At a fixed sample size, decreasing the confidence level will narrow the confidence interval, whereas increasing the confidence level will widen the confidence interval. The confidence interval can be narrowed (even when increasing the confidence level) by increasing the sample size. For example, let's take the same data on self-reported rape offenses and first increase the confidence level and then the sample size.

A 99% confidence interval around our point estimate of 5.3 would be:

$$99\% \text{ c.i.} = 5.3 \pm 2.977 \left( \frac{3.4}{\sqrt{15 - 1}} \right)$$

$$= 5.3 \pm 2.977\,(.91)$$

$$= 5.3 \pm 2.71$$

$$5.3 - 2.71 = 2.59$$

$$5.3 + 2.71 = 8.01$$

$$99\% \text{ c.i} = 2.59 \text{ to } 8.01$$

This indicates that we are 99 percent confident that the population mean of self-reported rapes is between 2.59 and 8.01. Notice that, because we increased our confidence level from 95 percent to 99 percent, we have increased the width of our interval. Let's now estimate the 99% confidence level and assume that we had a sample size of 30 rather than 15. The confidence interval in this case would be:

$$99\% \text{ c.i.} = 5.3 \pm 2.977 \left( \frac{3.4}{\sqrt{30 - 1}} \right)$$

$$= 5.3 \pm 2.977\,(.63)$$

$$= 5.3 \pm 1.88$$

$$5.3 - 1.88 = 3.42$$

$$5.3 + 1.88 = 7.18$$

$$99\% \text{ c.i.} = 3.42 \text{ to } 7.18$$

As shown, with a 99% confidence level and $n = 30$, our confidence interval is 3.42 to 7.18. This interval is smaller than the interval at the same confidence level for an $n$ of 15. The reason the interval is smaller is because the estimated standard deviation of the sampling distribution ($s/[\sqrt{n - 1}]$) gets smaller when the sample size is increased. In the example with $n = 15$, the standard error was .91. When we increased our sample size to 30, the standard error was reduced to .63. By increasing our sample size, we have decreased the standard deviation of the sampling distribution and we have increased the precision of our estimate.

## 9.5 ESTIMATING CONFIDENCE INTERVALS FOR PROPORTIONS AND PERCENTS

Compared to the confidence intervals around means we have just examined, you are perhaps more familiar with confidence intervals constructed around proportions. The media bombards us with examples of these all the time. As said, results of opinion polls are usually quickly followed by a phrase that says something like "plus or minus 2 percent." This is one way of presenting a confidence interval to the public that is understandable. The confidence intervals we discuss in this section are for large samples only. The calculation of a confidence interval around a proportion is done by using the following formula:

Confidence Interval $= \hat{p} + z_\alpha(\sigma_p)$

where $\hat{p}$ = sample proportion

$$\sigma_p = \sqrt{\frac{p(1 - p)}{n}} \tag{9.4}$$

where $p$ = population proportion

This formula is very similar to the confidence interval formula for sample means. With a large sample, sample proportions have sampling distributions that are approximately normal with a mean $(\mu_p)$ equal to the true population proportion $(p)$ and a standard deviation $(\sigma_p)$ equal to $\sqrt{p(1 - p)/n}$. The latter term is referred to as the *standard error of the proportion.* In the confidence interval formula for proportions, we simply replace the sample mean $(\bar{x})$ with the sample proportion $(\hat{p})$ and the standard error of the mean $(\sigma/\sqrt{n})$ by the standard error of the proportion $\sqrt{p(1 - p)/n}$.

In Equation 9.4, the value of $\hat{p}$ in the confidence interval is the sample proportion. It is the sample point estimate $(\hat{p})$ of the unknown population parameter $(p)$. The term $z_\alpha$ is the value of $z$ we obtain from the standard normal table, as in confidence interval problems for the mean. As before, the precise value of $z$ depends on the particular confidence level we select. Notice that the standard error of the proportion $(\sigma_p = \sqrt{p(1 - p)/n})$ is based on the *population proportion* $(p),$ a quantity we do not know and are in fact trying to estimate with our sample statistic $(\hat{p})$. Because $p$ is not known, it must be estimated, and the standard error of the proportion must be estimated. The symbol for the estimate of the standard error of the proportion is $\sigma_{\hat{p}}$. How do we estimate this quantity? There are two solutions to this estimation problem. One is more conservative than the other.

One solution would be simply to use the sample proportion $(\hat{p})$ to estimate the population proportion $(p)$. In most instances this will be a reasonable solution because the sample size must be large to use the normal approximation (the $z$ table) for our confidence interval, and the sample proportion will provide a good estimate of the population proportion in the case of large samples. Therefore, the first possible solution would be to substitute $\hat{p}$ for $p$ in Equation 9.4 and to proceed with the construction of the confidence interval. In this approach, the estimated standard error of the proportion is:

$$\hat{\sigma}_p = \sqrt{\frac{\hat{p}(1 - \hat{p})}{n}}$$

where $\hat{p}$ is simply the sample proportion. However, because we know that $\hat{p}$ is a biased estimate of $p$, we may want to be more conservative in estimating the confidence interval.

The second, more conservative solution, would be always to use the proportion .5 as the value of $p$ (and, of course, .5 would always be the value of $1 - p$) in the estimate for the standard error of the proportion: $\sigma_{\hat{p}} = \sqrt{(.5)\,(.5)/n}$. In this solution the term $p(1 - p)$ would always be $(.5)(.5) = .25$, which is the maximum value this term can have. For any other value of $p$, the expression produces a smaller value. In using .5 as our estimate of the population proportion, then, we are ensuring that our confidence interval will be at its maximum width, thereby making it the most conservative interval we could obtain. We illustrate both solutions to the problem of estimating $p$.

Let's first go through an example using data provided from a study by Greenwood and Turner (1993). These researchers investigated the extent to which recidivism rates differed between convicted delinquents (males over 15 years of age convicted of a class 1 or 2 felony) who were assigned to a small experimental program and those who were assigned to a traditional training school. The experimental program, Paint Creek Youth Center, was designed to provide the youths with a comprehensive and highly structured array of intervention services and activities. Recidivism in this study was operationalized by computing the percent of youths who had been arrested for any crime within 12 months of their release from the programs.

Approximately .61 of the youths assigned to the traditional program ($n = 75$) were arrested in the 12-month period following their release, and .51 of the youths assigned to the new experimental program were rearrested ($n = 73$). Using a confidence limit of 95 percent, we already know that the critical value of $z$ is 1.96. The calculation of a 95 percent confidence interval around the recidivism proportions for both programs based on Equation 9.4 is:

$$95\% \text{ c.i. for the Traditional Treatment} = .61 \pm 1.96 \sqrt{\frac{.61(1 - .61)}{75}}$$

$$= .61 \pm 1.96 \sqrt{\frac{.24}{75}}$$

$$= .61 \pm 1.96 \sqrt{.003}$$

$$= .61 \pm 1.96(.055)$$

$$= .61 \pm .108$$

$$.61 - .108 = .50$$

$$.61 + .107 = .72$$

$$95\% \text{ c.i.} = .50 \text{ to } .72$$

$$95\% \text{ c.i. for the Experimental Treatment} = .51 \pm 1.96 \sqrt{\frac{.51(1 - .51)}{73}}$$

$$= .51 \pm 1.96 \sqrt{\frac{.25}{73}}$$

$$= .51 \pm 1.96 \sqrt{.003}$$

$$= .51 \pm 1.96(.055)$$

$$= .51 \pm .108$$

$$.51 - .108 = .40$$

$$.51 + .108 = .62$$

$$95\% \text{ c.i.} = .40 \text{ to } .62$$

What do these confidence intervals tell us? The first interval, which was calculated for youths who received the traditional treatment, tells us that, based on our sample proportion $\hat{p}$, we can be 95 percent confident that the true proportion of youths who are rearrested within 12 months of release from a traditional treatment program lies somewhere between .50 and .72. We could, of course, express this confidence interval in percentages by reporting that between 50 percent and 72 percent of those released from a traditional program are rearrested within 12 months.

Similarly, based on the sample statistic for the youths who received the experimental treatment program, we can be 95 percent confident that the true proportion of recidivism among the population of youth who receive a similar treatment program lies between .40 and .62. Expressed in percents, we can say that we are 95% confident that between 40 percent and 62 percent of delinquents released from programs similar to the experimental treatment are rearrested within 12 months.

Now let's estimate comparable 95% confidence intervals for the two programs, this time using .5 as our estimate of the population proportion ($p$) rather than the sample proportion:

$$95\% \text{ c.i. for the Traditional Treatment} = 61 \pm 1.96 \sqrt{\frac{.50(1 - .50)}{75}}$$

$$= .61 \pm 1.96 \sqrt{\frac{.25}{75}}$$

$$= .61 \pm 1.96 \sqrt{.0033}$$

$$= .61 \pm 1.96(.0577)$$

$$= .61 \pm .113$$

$$.61 - .113 = .497$$

$$.61 + .113 = .723$$

$$95\% \text{ c.i.} = .497 \text{ to } .723$$

$$95\% \text{ c.i. for the Experimental Treatment} = .51 \pm 1.96 \sqrt{\frac{.50(1 - .50)}{73}}$$

$$= .51 \pm 1.96 \sqrt{\frac{.25}{73}}$$

$$= .51 \pm 1.96 \sqrt{.0034}$$

$$= .51 \pm 1.96(.0585)$$

$$= .51 \pm .115$$

$$.51 - .115 = .395$$

$$.51 + .115 = .625$$

$$95\% \text{ c.i.} = .395 \text{ to } .625$$

As you can see, the confidence intervals with the more conservative .5 estimate of the population proportion are about the same size as those we obtained when we used the sample proportion as our estimate of $p$. This is because the sample proportions were not far from .5 (.61 and .49 for the traditional program and .51 and .49 for the experimental program). In general, the two methods yield approximately the same results whenever the sample proportion is between .3 and .7. When sample proportions approach 0 or 1, the different methods for estimating the standard error tends to yield different results. The method of estimation you select, of course, is your choice. Again, there are no hard-and-fast rules for selection. We would, however, recommend using the most conservative estimation procedure of .5 for $p$, particularly if your sample proportions fall below .3 or above .7.

## 9.6 SUMMARY

In this chapter we examined the procedures used to estimate population parameters using confidence intervals. To estimate confidence intervals around a $\bar{x}$ obtained from a large sample, we used estimation procedures based on the $z$ distribution. We also looked at the formula based on the $t$ distribution used to construct confidence intervals around means obtained from small samples. We concluded the chapter with estimation procedures used to construct confidence intervals around proportions.

Each of the above types of intervals could have been constructed using any level of confidence (e.g., 75 percent, 88 percent, 95 percent). However, we focused almost exclusively on confidence levels of 95 percent as this is the typical level used in criminological research. We discussed the trade-offs made when adopting particular levels of confidence: higher levels of confidence (e.g., 99 percent compared to 95 percent) produce wider intervals, so, although you gain confidence in your estimation, you also lose precision. In this chapter we also emphasized the importance of sample sizes. Smaller samples always inflate the standard error of the sampling distribution, thereby increasing the width of the confidence interval. Thus, larger samples are more desirable than smaller ones.

# Key Terms

confidence interval
confidence level
degrees of freedom (df)
inferential statistics
point estimate
population parameter

population proportion
sample statistic
standard error of the proportion
student's *t* distribution
*z* distribution

# Problems

1. What is the purpose of confidence intervals?
2. Describe the differences between the *z* distribution and the *t* distribution? When is it appropriate to use the *z* distribution for estimation procedures?
3. A hypothetical study concerned with estimating the amount of marijuana use per year among a teenage population obtained a sample of 110 high school students. With the following sample statistics, construct a 95% confidence interval around the mean number of times this sample used marijuana in a given 1-year period:

$\bar{x} = 4.5$ times per year

$s = 3.2$

$n = 110$

What does the interval you constructed tell us about marijuana use in the population? Interpret these results.
4. Using the same mean and standard deviations as in Question 2, change the sample size to 55 and construct a confidence interval around the mean using the appropriate procedures. How does the interval change? Provide an interpretation for your interval.
5. What does the standard deviation of the sampling distribution of the mean tell us? What will affect the size of the standard error?
6. In a 1993 article, Terrie Moffitt identified a group of young offenders called "life course persistent" offenders, who commit both frequent and serious offenses throughout their life. Let's say you have a sample of 20 young males who have been in juvenile institutions at least twice. The mean age of their first arrest was 11 and the standard deviation is 1.7. Build a 99% confidence interval around this point estimate.
7. A mayor of a large city wants to know how long it takes the police to respond to a call for service. In a random sample of 15 citizens who called the police for service, the mayor's research director found that the average response time was 560 seconds with a standard deviation of 45 seconds. Construct a 95% confidence interval around your point estimate. What would the research director say to the mayor?
8. A hypothetical study investigating the attitudes American citizens have toward incarcerated felons being allowed to work in jail revealed that, of the 66 people interviewed, 87 percent (.87) approved of prisoners being allowed to work if a percentage of their wages went toward paying for their incarceration and other taxes. Construct a 95% confidence interval around this percentage. What can you infer from this?
9. Using the same information from Question 8, construct a 99% confidence interval around the percentage. How does this change the interval and why?

## Solutions to Problems

1. The purpose of confidence intervals is to give us a range of values for our estimated population parameter rather than a single value or a point estimate. The estimated confidence interval gives us a range of values within which we believe, with varying degrees of confidence, that the true population value falls. The advantage of providing a range of values for our estimate is that we will be more likely to include the population parameter.

2. At small sample sizes, the $t$ distribution is flatter than a $z$ distribution and has fatter tails on both ends of the distribution. When the sample size is 100 or more, the two distributions are virtually identical. We can use the $z$ distribution rather than the $t$ distribution when our sample size is 100 or more.

3. Our 95% confidence interval is:

$$4.5 \pm 1.96 \left( \frac{3.2}{\sqrt{110 - 1}} \right)$$

$$= 4.5 \pm 1.96 \left( \frac{3.2}{10.44} \right)$$

$$= 4.5 \pm 1.96(.31)$$

$$= 4.5 \pm .61$$

$$3.89 \leq \mu \leq 5.11$$

We are 95 percent confident that the mean level of marijuana use in our population of teenagers is between 3.89 and 5.11 times a year.

4. $$4.5 \pm 1.96 \left( \frac{3.2}{\sqrt{55 - 1}} \right)$$

$$= 4.5 \pm 1.96 \left( \frac{3.2}{7.35} \right)$$

$$= 4.5 \pm 1.96(.43)$$

$$= 4.5 \pm .84$$

$$3.66 \leq \mu \leq 5.34$$

Our confidence interval is much wider when our sample size is 55 than when it was 110 because with a smaller sample size, our sampling error becomes larger.

5. The standard deviation of the sampling distribution is the standard deviation of an infinite number of sample estimates (means [$\bar{x}$] or proportions [$p$]) each drawn from a sample with sample size of $n$. The sample size affects the value of the standard error. At a fixed confidence level, increasing the sample size will reduce the size of the standard error (and, consequently, the width of the confidence interval).

6. Because we have a small sample ($n = 20$), we have to use the $t$ distribution to build our 99% confidence interval around the sample mean:

$$99\% \text{ c.i.} = 11 \pm 2.861 \left( \frac{1.7}{\sqrt{20 - 1}} \right)$$

$$= 11 \pm 2.861 \left( \frac{1.7}{4.36} \right)$$

$$= 11 \pm 2.861(.39)$$

$$= 11 \pm 1.11$$

$$9.89 \le \mu \le 12.11$$

**7.** $95\% \text{ c.i.} = 560 \pm 2.145 \left( \dfrac{45}{\sqrt{15 - 1}} \right)$

$$= 560 \pm 2.145 \left( \frac{45}{3.74} \right)$$

$$= 560 \pm 2.145 (12.03)$$

$$= 560 \pm 25.80$$

$$534.2 \le \mu \le 585.8$$

You can say that you are 95 percent confident that the true police response time is between 534 seconds (almost 9 minutes) and 586 seconds (almost 10 minutes).

**8.** We will treat the 87 percent as a proportion (.87), and then express the confidence interval as a percent. First, the conservative solution:

$$95\% \text{ c.i.} = .87 \pm 1.96 \sqrt{\frac{(.5)(.5)}{66}}$$

$$= .87 \pm 1.96 \sqrt{\frac{.25}{66}}$$

$$= .87 \pm 1.96(.06)$$

$$= .87 \pm .12$$

$$.75 \le p \le .99$$

$$75\% \le p \le 99\%$$

If you used the sample proportion in your estimate of the standard error of the proportion, you would have:

$$95\% \text{ c.i.} = .87 \pm 1.96 \sqrt{\frac{(.87)(.13)}{66}}$$

$$= .87 \pm 1.96 \sqrt{\frac{.11}{66}}$$

$$= .87 \pm 1.96(.04)$$

$$= .87 \pm .08$$

$$.79 \le p \le .95$$

$$79\% \le p \le 95\%$$

In this case, you would state that there is a 95 percent chance that the true population percent in favor of inmates working to compensate the state is between 79 percent and 95 percent.

9. We show the results only for the more conservative solution:

$$99\% \text{ c.i.} = .87 \pm 2.58 \sqrt{\frac{(.5)(.5)}{66}}$$

$$= .87 \pm 2.58 \sqrt{\frac{.25}{66}}$$

$$= .87 \pm 2.58(.06)$$

$$\text{c.i.} = .87 \pm .15$$

$$.72 \le p \le 1.0 \ (1.02)$$

$$72\% \le p \le 100\% \ (102\%)$$

Although the upper confidence limit is 1.02 (102%), because no proportion is greater than 1.0 and no percent higher than 100%, we have truncated these values at the upper possible limit. When we increase the confidence interval from a 95% to a 99% confidence interval, the width of the confidence interval increased.

# CHAPTER 10

# *From Estimation to Statistical Tests:*

*Hypothesis Testing
for One Population Mean
and Proportion*

*That is a question which has puzzled many an expert, and why? Because
there was no reliable test. Now we have the Sherlock Holmes test, and
there will no longer be any difficulty.*

—SHERLOCK HOLMES TO WATSON

## *10.1 INTRODUCTION*

In the preceding chapter, we focused exclusively on techniques of point and confidence interval estimation. We examined how we could utilize confidence intervals based on information from samples to place boundaries on our estimates of population parameters. We were primarily interested in finding out what the value of the population mean (proportion) is. In this chapter, we focus on a somewhat different type of question. We make an assumption about what the value of the population parameter is, and the question we ask is whether this assumption is realistic given the particular sample statistic we observe from our data. Our question in this chapter is, "Is it likely that the unknown population mean (proportion) is equal to what we have presumed it to be, given what we know about our sample mean (proportion)?"

We want to know whether we can continue to assume that our population parameter is equal to a hypothesized value in the face of the evidence we have from our sample. We presume something about our population characteristic (that the population mean or proportion is equal to some given value), and we have some real information from our sample (that the sample mean or sample proportion is actually equal to some value). What we want to know is whether our assumption about the value of the population parameter is reasonable, given the sample value. Either it is—and we conclude that our presumption about the population parameter is true—or it is not, and we conclude that our presumption about the population parameter is not true, and we reject it.

Essentially in this chapter we compare information we have from our sample with what we presume to be true about our population. We then use probability theory to provide a decision rule to determine the truth or falseness of our presumption. The decision we make, however, is not without some risk of error. Recall from Chapter 7 the coin flip problem with our friend that, no matter what we decide, there is always a chance that we have made the wrong decision. What probability theory permits us to do is to estimate the probability of making the wrong decision.

Suppose, for example, that you have been hired by the warden of a correctional institution to evaluate a literacy program in the prison. After reviewing records at the state department of corrections you know that the reading level for the entire population of incarcerated inmates in the state is 7.5 years with a standard deviation of 2.2. You take a random sample of 90 "graduates" of the literacy program and find that their mean reading level is 9.3 years. You want to know whether the mean reading level for the sample of literacy program graduates is equal to the general population mean, that is, whether the population mean of literacy program graduates is equal to 7.5 years. The question you must ask yourself is, "Is it reasonable to assume that the population mean for program graduates is 7.5 years, given that my sample mean is 9.3 years?"

If, instead of a sample of 90 graduates, you had information about every graduate that had ever completed the program (the population of program graduates), you would be better able to answer your question. In this case, you could simply compute the average reading level for your population of program graduates and see if it is equal to 7.5 years. Either it would be or it would not be. You would have no doubt, and there would be no risk of error about your conclusion.

With sample information, however, you cannot be so sure. Even if your sample mean is very different from the presumed value of the population mean, you cannot automatically conclude that your assumption about the value of that population mean was wrong. The difference between your sample mean and the presumed population mean might be due simply to sampling variation, the fact that the means of repeated samples from the same population are invariably different from the true population value. Herein lies the applicability of probability theory and sampling distributions. With the information provided by your sample and the presumed value of the population mean, you can determine the probability that the population has that mean value given the value of the sample mean. We do this through the formal procedures of conducting a hypothesis test.

The remainder of this chapter examines the ways to test a hypothesis about a single population mean using both large and small samples, and a population proportion using a large sample. We also examine the differences between hypothesis testing using nondirectional (one-tailed) versus directional (two-tailed) tests. Before we begin this new section, let's refresh our memory from Chapter 7 about the steps involved in any hypothesis test by looking at the box on top of page 261.

---

**Step 1.** Formally state your null ($H_0$) and research ($H_1$) hypotheses.

**Step 2.** Select an appropriate test statistic and the sampling distribution of that test statistic.

**Step 3.** Select a level of significance (alpha), and determine the critical value and rejection region of the test statistic based on the selected level of alpha.

**Step 4.** Conduct the test: Calculate the obtained value of the test statistic and compare it to the critical value.

**Step 5.** Make a decision about your null hypothesis and interpret this decision in a meaningful way based on the research question.

---

In the following sections, we apply these steps to the problems of testing a hypothesis first about a sample mean and then a sample proportion.

## 10.2 TESTING A HYPOTHESIS ABOUT A SINGLE POPULATION MEAN: THE z TEST

Let's begin our discussion of hypothesis testing using the example about reading levels for the sample of prison literacy program graduates and the general population of inmates. We can summarize what we know about the two groups as follows:

|  | Population | Sample |
|---|---|---|
| Mean reading level | $\mu = 7.5$ | $\bar{x} = 9.3$ |
| Standard deviation | $\sigma = 2.2$ | $n = 90$ |

What we know for sure, then, is that the mean reading level of our sample of 90 literacy program graduates ($\bar{x} = 9.3$) is different from the mean for the entire population of incarcerated inmates ($\mu = 7.5$). We will initially assume that the population of literacy program graduates has the same mean reading level as the rest of the inmates, that is, 7.5 years. We need to ask how reasonable an assumption this is, given the fact that our sample value (9.3 years) is different. What sense do we make of the difference between the presumed population mean of 7.5 years and our observed sample mean of 9.3 years? Because we have a *sample* of literacy program graduates, we can account for this apparent difference in one of two ways.

One explanation for the difference between our sample mean of 9.3 and the population mean of 7.5 years is that the population mean is not really 7.5 years. This means that our assumption about the value of the population mean is incorrect and that the true population mean for the literacy program graduates is different from 7.5. The implication of this is that literacy program graduates come from a different population with a different mean than nonprogram inmates. By this we mean that our sample did not come from the population of all other incarcerated offenders but from another population, the population of literacy program graduates, which has a different mean.

Figures 10.1 and 10.2 illustrates this explanation by showing the distribution of reading levels for the two populations. In Figure 10.1 the curve on the left is the population of incarcerated offenders with a mean reading level of 7.5 years ($\mu = 7.5$). The one on the right is a different population with a higher population

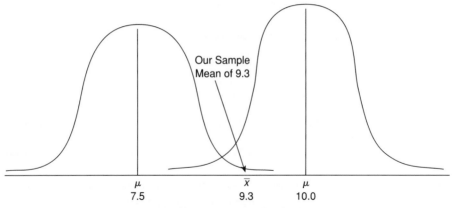

FIGURE 10.1. Two populations with different mean reading levels.

mean ($\mu = 10$). One explanation for the difference between our sample mean (9.3) and what we have assumed as the true population mean (7.5) is that our sample was actually drawn from a different population. Perhaps our sample was drawn from the population on the right, where the population mean is 10 rather than 7.5. If this is true, our assumption that the population mean reading level for literacy program graduates is 7.5 years is not correct.

A second explanation for the difference between the presumed population mean (7.5 years) and the observed sample mean (9.3 years) is based on sampling variation. Figure 10.2 illustrates this state of affairs. In this explanation the true population mean for both program graduates and nongraduates is 7.5 years. There is only one population with a mean reading level of 7.5 years. If this is true, our assumption that the population mean is 7.5 years is correct. Well, you may wonder, "if the true population mean is 7.5, why is our sample mean different from this?" The second explanation is that the only reason the sample mean (9.3 years) is different from the presumed population mean (7.5) is because of the fact that not every sample selected from a population will have a mean equal to that population mean. The means of many samples drawn from the same population will not be equal to the mean of that population. There will be variation in the proximity of the many sample means to the true sample mean. In other words, simple sampling variation can account for the difference between a sample mean and the mean of the population from which that sample was drawn.

Remember our discussion of the distribution of sample means in Chapter 8 where we said that, if we take a very large or infinite number of samples of size $n$ from a population whose mean is $\mu$, the individual sample means would differ from one another but the mean of the infinite number of sample means would be $\mu$. Well, maybe what happened here is that we have selected one of those samples from the population in which the sample mean is quite different from the population mean. In this case, the sample we have was drawn from a population with a mean reading level of 7.5 years, but the sample is different from that (9.3 years). Our sample mean happens to be different from the population mean simply because of sampling variation. That is, sample means differ from the true population mean because dif-

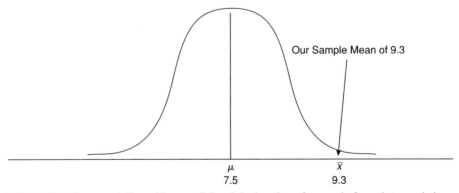

FIGURE 10.2. One population with mean 7.5 and the location of a sample from that population with a higher mean.

ferent cases are selected in each sample. There is a standard deviation to the distribution of sample means, also called the *standard error of the mean*. A glance back at Figure 9.1 illustrates this fact. In that figure, confidence intervals were drawn around sample means taken from 20 different samples, all of which were different. In sum, it may be possible for a sample mean to be very different from a population mean and still have been drawn from the same population the population mean was calculated for.

As you can perhaps imagine, the implications of the two explanations are quite different. In the first explanation, the implication is that there are two different populations with two different population means. In this scenario, our sample mean differs from the presumed population mean because the sample was drawn from an entirely different population. If this explanation is correct, we would conclude that the observed difference between the sample and population means is "statistically significant." In other words, it is a difference due to a difference in population means, not to chance factors, such as sampling variation. In drawing this conclusion, we would be saying that our initial assumption that the population mean is equal to 7.5 years was incorrect.

If the second explanation is correct, however, the observed difference between our sample and population mean is more likely attributable to the fact that we happened to pick a sample whose mean reading level was different from the population mean. In this case, the observed difference is not "statistically significant," that is, due to a real difference between the two groups; it is just due to chance, that is, *sampling variation*. In drawing this conclusion, we have not rejected our initial assumption that the population mean is 7.5 years.

We have, then, two possible and equally compelling explanations for the difference between our sample mean and population mean—two explanations with very different implications. Which explanation is correct? Unfortunately, because we have sample data, not information from a population, we cannot know for certain which explanation is correct. Remember that we did not know what the population mean was; rather, we presumed that it was a given value and wondered how safe an assumption that was (given what we observed our sample mean to be).

What we can do, however, is to set up a decision-making rule that will help us decide whether one of the explanations is very likely. This decision rule will also tell us how likely "very likely" is. The basis of this decision rule is the subject matter of *hypothesis testing.*

In making a hypothesis test about our two explanations, we begin by assuming that the second explanation is correct, that is, that the sample actually was drawn from the population in question. We are assuming that the population mean is a particular value (in our example, that was a reading level in the population of 7.5 years). We have suggested to you that this assumption implies that the literacy program graduates come from the same population as do nonprogram inmates. In essence, the two groups come from the same population. We want to be very conservative in our decision making and not jump to any conclusion that the two groups are different. We proceed, then, by initially assuming that they are not different and see whether that assumption can be maintained given the sample information.

The assumption that there is one population with a mean of 7.5 years constitutes our *null hypothesis.* The word *"null"* implies that the entity considered is "of no consequence or value." We stated that the null hypothesis is the hypothesis of no difference. Our hypothesis that the population mean is 7.5 years is a null hypothesis because we are assuming that there is no "real" difference between the observed sample mean of 9.3 years and the population mean of 7.5 years. The difference is "null" or "of no consequence" because it is due simply to sampling variation, not to any "real" difference between the sample and the population. The starting point of the process of hypothesis testing, then, is an assumption of no differences—a null hypothesis. In a hypothesis test, we determine whether this assumption is reasonable given the evidence we have from our sample data.

In Chapter 7 we made an analogy between the null hypothesis and the presumption of innocence in criminal proceedings. Just as a defendant is presumed to be innocent, a null hypothesis is presumed to be true. Similarly, just as the state must present considerable evidence ("beyond a reasonable doubt") to overcome this presumption of innocence and convince the jury to convict the defendant, the research scientist must present considerable evidence to overcome the presumption that the null hypothesis is not true. If there is enough evidence to suggest that the null hypothesis is probably not true, the scientist rejects it. Let's remind you, however, that both the jury and the scientist can make an error in rejecting their initial presumptions. The jury may convict an innocent person, and a researcher may reject a null hypothesis that happens to be true. The legal procedures of the criminal trial and the methodological and statistical rigor of science are there to keep this risk of error small.

In our research example, the null hypothesis is the hypothesis that the true population mean is equal to 7.5 years. It specifically refers to the fact that the sample mean and the population mean are not really different. So our assumption or null hypothesis is: $H_0$: *The population mean is equal to 7.5 years. The sample mean is not different from the population mean.* Since the null hypothesis is symbolized by a capital *H* with a subscript of zero (the zero symbolizes the null condition or no difference), two ways to state this hypothesis are:

$H_0$: $\mu$ = 7.5 years

$H_0$: $\bar{x} - \mu = 0$

After making that assumption, we ask whether this assumption or hypothesis is true and what is the probability of getting the particular sample mean ($\bar{x}$) that we observe in our data. In other words, we want to know how likely it is that we would observe the value of our sample mean if the population mean is what we have assumed it to be. In our specific example, we determine the probability of selecting a sample with a mean reading level of 9.3 years from a population whose mean is 7.5. If the null hypothesis is true, we can determine the probability of observing the given value of our sample mean. Moreover, we can state in advance that, if this probability is very small (say 5 chances out of 100, which translates to an alpha level of .05, or 1 chance out of 100, $\alpha$ = .01), we will conclude that the assumption behind the null hypothesis must be false. In other words, if it is very unlikely that we would have observed the sample mean if the population mean was what we have presumed it to be under the null hypothesis, we will reject that hypothesis.

This is exactly the procedure we used in Chapter 7 with our "friend" who flipped a coin to determine who paid for our social events. We determined there that, if the probability of getting 8 out of 10 heads was very unlikely given a fair coin, we would reject the assumption that the coin was fair. We remind you repeatedly that because we are asking questions about a sample, there is no way of knowing for sure whether the decision we make is the correct one. What we do know when we reject the null hypothesis is that the outcome or sample mean we have observed is so unlikely that "chances are" that it came from a different population. The risk or chance that we are wrong is determined by the alpha level we set in our hypothesis test.

Although we have previously suggested that .05 and .01 are commonly chosen alpha levels, this is just conventional practice. There are at times compelling reasons why you may want to use a larger (.10) or much smaller alpha level (.001). Recall that in choosing a particular alpha level, we are selecting the risk we are willing to take of making a Type I error, that is, of rejecting a null hypothesis that is actually true. In rejecting a null hypothesis that is true, we are saying that the sample mean is significantly different from the population mean when in fact it is not.

Sometimes the cost of a Type I error may be very great and we may want to be very sure before we reject the null hypothesis. Suppose, for instance, that we know of a treatment program that successfully reduces a person's level of violence. This treatment, however, is expensive and we want to determine if a slightly cheaper treatment is just as effective. In this case, because we have a treatment program with proven success we do not want to abandon it in favor of another program that is only marginally less expensive. In addition, reducing violence is more important than saving a little money, so we want to be very careful not to reject our null hypothesis of no difference between the two treatments if it is really true. Given these interests, we might want to set our alpha at a lower level than usual, say .001 instead of .05. If we do this, the probability that we will reject a null hypothesis that is really true will be only 1 out of 1000, rather than 5 out of 100. Selecting a lower alpha level will make it more difficult for us to reject the proven treatment program.

Consider a different research situation. As a police chief you have instituted a policy of foot patrols in a high crime area in an attempt to reduce crime. These foot patrols do not create any real added expense, and after a few months it appears that residents in the affected neighborhoods report that they feel safer. After a year of trying foot patrols you request that some research be done on whether or not crime in these areas is significantly lower than before. Because there have been many favorable by-products of these foot patrols and no increase in cost, you are more willing to risk a Type I error. In this situation you might want to have a more generous level of alpha, such as .10. Just remember that the decision as to what level of significance or alpha to use is one the researcher must make after very careful thought about the respective costs of making a Type I and Type II error. Unfortunately, there is no way you can minimize the cost of both errors simultaneously. As you reduce the risk of one type of error, you increase the risk of making the other.

There are a few remaining questions before we begin the nitty-gritty work of hypothesis testing with one sample mean. One concerns how we determine the likelihood of observing a particular sample mean ($\bar{x}$) given a population with mean μ. How do we know whether a sample mean of 9.3 from a population with a mean of 7.5 is likely to occur or not? We can determine this likelihood or probability based on what we know about the theoretical sampling distribution of means, the central limit theorem, and the standard normal distribution (the $z$ distribution). From the central limit theorem, we know that, with a large enough sample ($n \geq 50$), the sampling distribution of an infinite number of sample means from a population with mean μ and standard deviation σ will be normally distributed and have a mean of μ and a standard deviation of $\sigma_{\bar{x}}$ ($\sigma_{\bar{x}} = \sigma_x / \sqrt{n}$). We also know that, if the sampling distribution of means is normally distributed with a known mean and standard deviation, we can convert our sample mean into a standard normal score called a $z$ score. With our given sample mean expressed as a $z$ score, we can then use our knowledge of the standard normal distribution and determine the probability of observing a mean of this value given the known population mean. If this probability is very small, we will reject the null hypothesis.

The only piece of information we lack now is how to translate our sample mean ($\bar{x}$) into a $z$ score. We transformed a raw score into a $z$ score in Chapter 8 with the following formula:

$$z = \frac{x - \bar{x}}{s} \qquad (10.1)$$

where $x$ = our raw score

$\bar{x}$ = the mean for the sample

$s$ = the sample standard deviation.

To transform our sample mean into a $z$ score, all we need to do is to modify slightly Equation 10.1:

$$z = \frac{\bar{x} - \mu_{\bar{x}}}{\sigma / \sqrt{n}} \qquad (10.2)$$

In this equation our raw score is replaced by the sample mean, the sample mean in formula 10.1 is replaced by the mean of the sampling distribution (which is $\mu$, the population mean), and the standard deviation of the sample is replaced by the standard deviation of the sampling distribution of means (the standard error of the mean). We are now ready to conduct our hypothesis test with our hypothetical data about mean reading levels.

To refresh your memory, we have a sample of 90 graduates from a prison literacy program where the sample mean was 9.3 years and a population of incarcerated inmates whose mean reading level was 7.5 years. We want to know if our sample came from a population whose mean is 7.5. We begin our hypothesis test by stating the null and research or alternative hypotheses:

$H_0$: The two means are equal ($\bar{x} = \mu$). We could also state this null hypothesis by giving the value of the population parameter ($\mu = 7.5$). Our hypothesis test is whether the sample, whose mean we have observed, comes from this population.

$H_1$: The two means are not equal ($\bar{x} \neq \mu$; in our example, $\mu \neq 7.5$).

Notice that the alternative, or research, hypothesis simply states that the two means are not equal. You may remember from a previous chapter that this is called a *nondirectional alternative hypothesis* because it does not state that the mean of the population from which the sample was drawn is greater than or less than the population mean referred to in the null hypothesis. It simply assumes that they are different. We have more to say about directional and nondirectional tests later in this chapter.

The next step in hypothesis testing is to select an appropriate test statistic and obtain the sampling distribution for that statistic. Because the population standard deviation is known ($\sigma = 2.2$), we can use the $z$ score formula in Equation 10.2. Accordingly, we use the standard normal distribution ($z$ distribution) as our sampling distribution. By calculating the test statistic $z$ with Equation 10.2, what we are actually doing is to obtain a measurement of the distance in "standard error units" between the sample statistic ($\bar{x}$) and the hypothesized population parameter ($\mu$). If, for example, we obtained a $z$ score of 1.5, this would indicate that our sample mean was 1.5 standard errors above $\mu$. An obtained $z$ score of $-2.3$ would indicate that our sample mean was 2.3 standard errors below $\mu$, and so on.

The next step in formal hypothesis testing is to select a level of significance, termed our alpha level ($\alpha$), and identify the critical region. Remember that the alpha level we set determines our risk of making a Type I error, that is, of rejecting a null hypothesis that is really true. Also remember that the selection of an alpha level is a judgment call. However, the usual alpha levels in criminology and most other social sciences are .05 and .01. Based on our selected level of alpha, we must then find the *critical value* of our test statistic, which we refer to as $z_{crit}$. This critical value determines the rejection region for our test.

For the sake of illustration, let's opt for an alpha level of .05 ($\alpha = .05$). Because we are testing a nondirectional hypothesis, we have to divide our selected alpha level into two equal halves and place one half in each tail of the distribution (hence it is referred to as a two-tailed test). With an alpha level of .05, we are interested in identifying that $z$ score that corresponds to $.05/2 = .025$ of the area at each tail of the normal curve. This .025 of the area at each tail of the normal distribution defines our *critical region*. The remaining area of the curve up to the mean is equal to $.50 - .025 = .4750$, so we need to find the $z$ score that corresponds to .4750 of the curve. We find this from the $z$ table in Table B.2 in Appendix B. Going into the body of the table until we find .4750, we can determine that the corresponding $z$ score is 1.96. Because the normal curve is symmetrical, we do the same thing for the other tail of the distribution where the corresponding $z$ score is $-1.96$. The critical value of $z$ for a two-tailed test with an alpha level of .05, then, is $\pm 1.96$ ($z_{\text{crit}} = \pm 1.96$). This means that, in order to reject the null hypothesis at the .05 level based on our sample data, the value of $z$ we obtain from our test ($z_{\text{obt}}$) must either fall 1.96 standard errors or more above or below the population mean ($\mu$). Stated another way, our decision rule is to fail to reject the null hypothesis if $-1.96 < z_{\text{obt}} < 1.96$ and to reject the null hypothesis if $z_{\text{obt}} \leq -z_{\text{crit}}$ or if $z_{\text{obt}} \geq +z_{\text{crit}}$. For future reference, we have provided the most often used critical values of $z$ in Table 10.1.

Now that we have our critical value of $z$, we can define the *critical region* in the sampling distribution. The critical region defines the area of the sampling distribution that contains all unlikely sample outcomes. We use the word "region" because the critical value of our test statistic defines the class of all obtained values that would lead us to reject the null hypothesis. For example, if we defined our critical value of $z$ as $\pm 1.96$, one critical region would consist of all obtained $z$ scores under $-1.96$. The second critical region would consist of all obtained $z$ scores greater than $+1.96$. The critical value of $z$ at $\pm 1.96$ and the corresponding regions of rejection are illustrated for you in Figure 10.3. Because we selected a .05 alpha level and conduct a two-tailed hypothesis test, the critical region is equal to .025 $(.05/2)$ of the area of the normal curve at each tail. You can see from this figure that, if we obtained a $z$ score of 2.3 from our statistical test, we would be able to reject the null hypothesis because our obtained value would fall inside the rejection region on the right tail of the $z$ distribution. Similarly, if the value of $z$ we obtained from our test was $-2.3$, we would also be able to reject the null hypothesis because this value would fall inside the rejection region on the left side of the distribution.

**TABLE 10.1. Alpha Levels and Critical Values of $z$ for One- and Two-Tailed Hypothesis Tests**

| Type of Hypothesis Test | Alpha Level | Critical Area in Each Tail | Critical $z$ |
|---|---|---|---|
| Two-tailed | .10 | .05 | 1.65 |
| One-tailed | .10 | .10 | 1.29 |
| Two-tailed | .05 | .025 | 1.96 |
| One-tailed | .05 | .05 | 1.65 |
| Two-tailed | .01 | .005 | 2.58 |
| One-tailed | .01 | .01 | 2.33 |
| Two-tailed | .001 | .0005 | 3.27 |
| One-tailed | .001 | .001 | 3.08 |

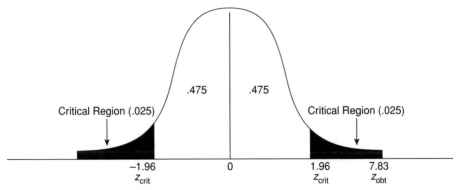

FIGURE 10.3. Critical $z$ and critical region for two-tailed test and alpha = .05.

If you are getting a little lost, remain calm and just continue through the entire example. We know that the small pieces of the picture are often illuminated by observing the picture in its entirety. So let's move on with the remaining steps. Using the data we obtained from our sample, the fourth step is to calculate the obtained test statistic, in this case $z_{obt}$. We have the sample size ($n$ = 90), sample mean ($\bar{x}$ = 9.3), and known population standard deviation ($\sigma$ = 2.2), so we can simply plug them into Equation 10.2. The value of $\mu$ that is used in our calculations is always the value of $\mu$ we are testing in the null hypothesis; in this case it is 7.5. The calculation of the $z_{obt}$ statistic is:

$$z_{obt} = \frac{\bar{x} - \mu}{\sigma/\sqrt{n}}$$

$$= \frac{9.3 - 7.5}{2.2/\sqrt{90}}$$

$$= \frac{1.8}{2.2/9.49}$$

$$= \frac{1.8}{.23}$$

$$= 7.83$$

The obtained value of $z$, then, is 7.83. Using this value, the final step of our hypothesis testing enterprise involves making a decision about the validity of the null hypothesis based on the results of our statistical test. We do this by comparing our critical value of $z$ ($z_{crit}$ = 1.96) with the value we obtain from our statistical test ($z_{obt}$ = 7.83). We see that the obtained $z$ value of 7.83 is higher than 1.96. In fact, it falls well into the critical region, almost 8 standard error units above the hypothesized $\mu$. This outcome is highly unlikely if the null hypothesis is true. Because $z_{obt} > 1.96$, we will reject the null hypothesis that the population mean is equal to 7.5. We will conclude instead that the sample of literacy program graduates comes from a population where the mean reading level is not equal to 7.5 years. In fact, based on our sample statistic, we can also infer that our sample comes from a population where the mean reading level is greater than 7.5 years.

In our hypothetical example, the population standard deviation was known and using the $z$ score formula was straightforward. Unfortunately, the population standard deviation rarely is known. If it is not known, and if our sample size is large ($n \geq 50$), we can use the sample standard deviation ($s$) to estimate the population standard deviation. As mentioned in the preceding chapter, however, the sample standard deviation is a biased estimate of the population standard deviation. As before, we correct for this bias by using the term $n - 1$ rather than $n$ in the denominator of the standard error. Whenever $\sigma$ is not known and the sample size is large, then, the estimate for the standard deviation of the sampling distribution becomes $s/\sqrt{n - 1}$. The formula for the $z$ test when the population standard deviation is not known and our sample size is large enough, then, becomes:

$$z_{obt} = \frac{\bar{x} - \mu}{s/\sqrt{n - 1}} \tag{10.3}$$

All of the other procedures remain the same: we use the standard normal table as before to find a critical value of $z$ and a critical region at a selected alpha level.

Let's do another example. Suppose we were interested in the mean sentence length given to convicted armed robbers in a given state after the passage of a new firearms law. This new legislation provides for an automatic 3-year additional prison term for those convicted offenders sentenced for a felony in which a gun was used during the commission of a crime. We know that the mean sentence length given to convicted armed robbers in the 3 years before the new legislation was passed was 52.5 months. This is our population mean. We take a random sample of 110 armed robbers who were convicted under the new law and sentenced to prison. The mean sentence length given to these 110 offenders was 54 months, with a standard deviation of 6. We want to know if this sample mean is significantly different from the known population mean, and will conduct a hypothesis test to determine this. Let's state each step along the way.

The first step is to state our null and research hypothesis. Our null hypothesis in this example is that the mean sentence length for our sample of armed robbers sentenced under the new law is the same as the population of previously sentenced armed robbers. Formally, the null hypothesis is that our sample is drawn from a population with a mean of 52.5 months:

$H_0$: $\mu = 52.5$

For our research hypothesis we will state the nondirectional alternative that the population from which our sample was drawn has a mean that is not equal to 52.5. We are not stating direction in this research hypothesis because we do not know for sure whether the mean sentence length under the new law will be more than or less than the previous mean sentence. We are hesitant to predict direction because other things are working to affect the mean sentence length of armed robbers in addition to the new legislation. For example, the state may be experiencing tremendous prison overcrowding and judges might respond to this by decreasing the average prison sentence they impose in all cases. In addition, judges might not like the fact that the state legislators are "meddling" in their sentencing domain. They might respond to the automatic 3-year addition to a sentence length by taking off 3 years to what they normally would impose. Because of these countervailing effects, the only alternative hypothesis we feel comfortable in asserting is that the mean sentence length for newly convicted armed robbers is not 52.5.

$H_1$: $\mu \neq 52.5$

Step number two requires that we select our test statistic and the sampling distribution of that statistic. In this example, our test statistic is the $z$ test and the sampling distribution is the standard normal ($z$) distribution. The population standard deviation ($\sigma$) is not known, so we will use Equation 10.3:

$$z = \frac{\bar{x} - \mu}{s/\sqrt{n - 1}}$$

Our third step in hypothesis testing is to select a level of significance (alpha level) and determine the critical value and critical region of our test statistic. We select a .01 alpha level for this example. As we have stated a nondirectional research hypothesis, we place one-half of our selected alpha level (.01/2 = .005) in each tail of the $z$ distribution. This area comprises our critical region, and it is marked for you in Figure 10.4. As you can see from Table 10.1, the $z$ score corresponding to this alpha level using a nondirectional (two-tailed) test is 2.58. This is the critical value of our $z$ ($z_{\text{crit}}$), and the critical region is any $z$ score less than or equal to $-2.58$ or greater than or equal to $+2.58$. Any obtained $z$ score that falls into the critical region will lead us to reject the null hypothesis. Thus, our decision rule is to fail to reject the null hypothesis if $-2.58 < z_{\text{obt}} < 2.58$ and to reject the null hypothesis if either $z_{\text{obt}} \leq -2.58$ or $z_{\text{obt}} \geq +2.58$.

FIGURE 10.4. Critical $z$ and critical region for two-tailed test and alpha = .01.

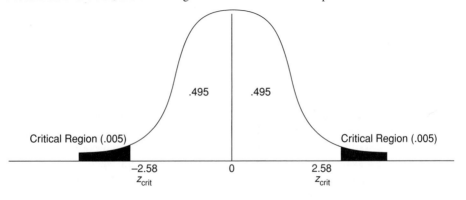

Now that we have our critical value of $z$ ($z_{crit} = \pm 2.58$) we need to compute our test statistic ($z_{obt}$). Using Equation 10.3, we can transform our sample mean into a $z$ score as follows:

$$z_{obt} = \frac{\bar{x} - \mu}{s/\sqrt{n-1}}$$

$$= \frac{54 - 52.5}{6/\sqrt{110 - 1}}$$

$$= \frac{1.5}{6/10.44}$$

$$= \frac{1.5}{.57}$$

$$= 2.63$$

With our sample data, we have an obtained $z$ score of 2.63. Using this obtained value of $z$, our fifth and final step is to make a decision about our null hypothesis. Because our obtained $z$ score of 2.63 is greater than our critical $z$ score of 2.58 ($z_{obt} > z_{crit}$), we will reject the null hypothesis and conclude that the sample does not come from a population where the mean sentence length is 52.5 months. We can therefore conclude that our sample was probably drawn from a population where the mean number of months sentenced is not equal to 52.5 and, in fact, appears to be greater than that. Remember, it is not only necessary to make a decision about your null hypothesis, but also it is equally important to interpret this decision based on the data and research issues you are working with.

## 10.3 DIRECTIONAL AND NONDIRECTIONAL HYPOTHESIS TESTS

The choice between a *directional* or *nondirectional hypothesis test* depends on the researcher's beliefs about the population from which the sample was drawn. Directional research hypotheses are referred to as "one-tailed" statistical tests, and nondirectional research hypotheses are called "two-tailed" statistical tests. In our one sample mean problem above, the null hypothesis stated that the sample came from a population with a known mean ($\mu$). In general, the research hypothesis always states our beliefs about what we think to be the "truth." This truth has three possibilities: (1) the sample was drawn from a population with a different mean, (2) the sample was drawn from a population with a higher mean, and (3) the sample was drawn from a population with a lower mean. Notice that the last two of these possibilities are subsets of the first. The first possibility simply states a difference, the latter two state a more specific direction of difference.

The first possibility is a nondirectional hypothesis. As seen, nondirectional hypotheses are tested by a two-tailed hypothesis test. The second two possibilities are variations on a directional research hypothesis. Directional hypotheses are tested with one-tailed hypothesis tests. The researcher will state one of these three possibilities in his or her research hypothesis.

In the preceding examples, the research hypothesis was always stated as a nondirectional alternative. In both cases, although we did not think that our sample came from the null hypothesis population, we did not know whether the population from which the sample was drawn had a mean higher or lower than that stated in the null hypothesis. For example, maybe the population of convicted armed robbers from which we drew our sample above had a mean sentence length higher than 52.5, or maybe it had a mean sentence lower than that. These two possibilities are shown in Figure 10.5. You can perhaps see from this figure why we are interested in both tails of a sampling distribution when we have a nondirectional research hypothesis.

Unlike this scenario, directional research hypotheses state a more precise relationship between the sample and null hypothesis means. When we use directional hypotheses, we believe not only that the sample and population means are different but also that we can define the exact direction of that difference. For example, in the previous problem, if we were more firm in our belief that the effect of the firearm law was to increase the prison terms of those convicted of a felony involving a weapon, we could have stated our alternative hypothesis more specifically as $H_1$: $\mu > 52.5$. This is a directional hypothesis because we are specifically stating what type of difference the population mean has from our sample mean. In this case, we are saying that our sample was drawn from a population whose mean is greater than the population mean expressed in the null hypothesis. This is illustrated for you in Figure 10.6, which shows two curves. The curve on the left is the curve for the population defined by the null hypothesis with a mean of 52.5. The curve to the right is the population defined by the directional alternative hypothesis ($H_1$: $\mu > 52.5$). In this population the mean is hypothesized to be greater than that for the population of the null hypothesis. Had our directional research hypothesis stated that the sample mean came from a population whose mean was less than 52.5 ($H_1$: $\mu < 52.5$), our two curves would look like those in Figure 10.7. Thus, when stating a directional alternative or research hypothesis, we are stating a direction that we believe the population from which our sample was drawn lies, either above (Figure 10.6) or below (Figure 10.7) the mean specified by the null hypothesis.

FIGURE 10.5. Three populations of convicted armed robbers with different mean sentence lengths.

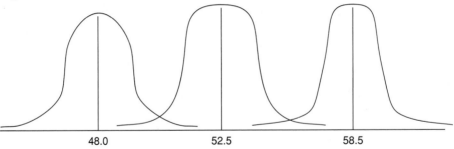

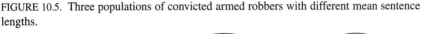

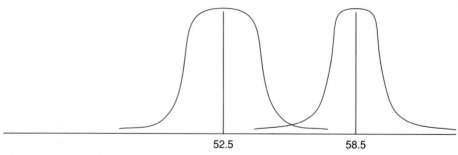

FIGURE 10.6. Two populations of convicted armed robbers, one with mean = 52.5 and one with mean = 58.5.

You may be wondering what possible difference it makes if we make our research hypothesis nondirectional or directional. If you can, it is to your advantage as a researcher to specify a specific direction for your research hypothesis. This does not mean that in the absence of prior knowledge you should always make a directional research hypothesis, just that if you can, it is to your advantage to do so. Like most answers, however, this one is not very satisfactory because it only leads to another question. "Why is testing a directional rather than a nondirectional hypothesis to my advantage?" Well, let's think about this for a minute.

When we state a nondirectional research hypothesis, we hypothesize that our sample was drawn from a population with a mean that is different from that specified in the null hypothesis. We do not know, then, whether our real population mean is larger or smaller than that found in the null hypothesis. These two possibilities, and the null hypothesis, are illustrated in Figure 10.5. As you can see, in the nondirectional case we are interested in both tails of the distribution for the null hypothesis. That is why we divide our alpha level into two equal halves and place one half in the right tail and one half of the left tail of the distribution. Notice that, when we divide our alpha level in half, we are cutting the area of the critical region in the tail of the sampling distribution in half. Instead of .05 of the area of the curve in one tail, we have .025 (.05/2) of the area in both tails. Because we are interested in a smaller area of the curve, the effect of this is to push the critical region further out

FIGURE 10.7. Two populations of convicted armed robbers, one with mean = 48.0 and one with mean = 52.5.

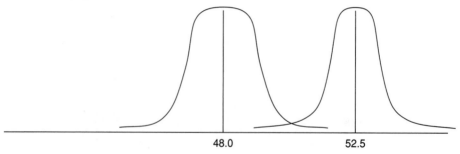

into the tail of the distribution. As you can see, it is not that our critical region is smaller in the two-tailed (nondirectional) research hypothesis; our critical area (alpha level) is still .05 of the curve. The important point is that this total area is now divided into two equal halves.

When we state a directional research hypothesis, however, we make the much more specific statement that we believe that the true population mean is higher (or lower) than that specified in the null hypothesis. Examples of a directional research hypothesis are shown in Figures 10.6 and 10.7. In these directional hypotheses we are only interested in one tail. Figure 10.6 illustrates the case when we hypothesize that the sample comes from a population with a higher mean than that specified in the null hypothesis. Because we suspect a higher population mean, our attention is directed at the right tail. Figure 10.7 illustrates the case when we hypothesize that the sample comes from a population with a lower mean than that stated in the null hypothesis. Because we hypothesize a lower population mean, we are interested in the left tail of the distribution. Both instances are, therefore, examples of one-tailed hypothesis tests. Unlike the case with the nondirectional hypothesis, we do not have to divide our alpha level in two parts. In the one-tailed case all of our alpha level is in one tail of the distribution.

The practical implication of this is that, when using a two-tailed hypothesis test, we are pushed out further into the tail of the distribution, and as a result, in order to reject the null hypothesis, our obtained $z$ will have to be greater compared to a directional (one-tailed) alternative hypothesis at the same alpha level. Figures 10.8 and 10.9 illustrate this point.

In Figure 10.8 we show the critical region for a two-tailed hypothesis test with an alpha of .05. Each critical region is equal to .025 of the area under the normal curve, and the critical value of $z$ is $\pm 1.96$. Thus, to reject the null hypothesis, we would need to obtain a $z$ score under $-1.96$ or above $+1.96$. This two-tailed hypothesis test would correspond to the situation of Figure 10.5. In Figure 10.9 we have a one-tailed hypothesis test at the same alpha level ($\alpha = .05$). In this test all .05 of our critical region is in one tail of the sampling distribution. You can see that the critical region in the right tail of Figure 10.9 is much larger than that in Figure 10.8; in fact, it is twice as large. Because we do not have to go so far out into the

FIGURE 10.8. Critical $z$ and critical region for two-tailed test and alpha = .05.

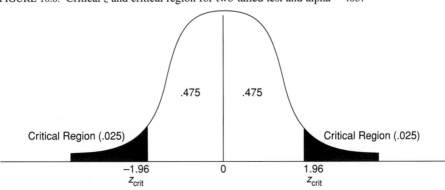

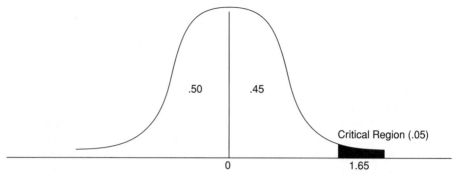

FIGURE 10.9. Critical $z$ and critical region for one-tailed test and alpha = .05.

right tail, our critical value of $z$ is only 1.65 in comparison to the 1.96 $z$ value for the nondirectional two-tailed test in Figure 10.8.

As you can see, then, at any given level of alpha, we will need a smaller $z_{obt}$ to reject the null hypothesis in the one-tailed (directional) hypothesis test. Now you can see that it is to your advantage to specify a directional alternative hypothesis *if you can.*

The critical $z$ values reported in Table 10.1 clearly reveal that at each level of alpha, you will need a smaller value of $z_{obt}$ to reject the null hypothesis using a one-tailed versus a two-tailed test. Remember, though, that, no matter which type of test you are conducting, directional or nondirectional, the steps necessary to conduct a hypothesis test remain the same. Let's go through an example.

Some criminologists and psychologists have long contended that there are important and stable personality differences between criminal offenders and the nonoffending "normal" population. One of these supposed personality differences is psychopathology—the degree to which persons feel antisocial or lack any regard for the feelings of others. A frequently used psychological test that has been assumed to measure the trait of psychopathology is the Socialization (SO) scale of the California Psychological Inventory (Megargee 1972). The SO scale measures such things as one's ability to form close social relationships, the extent to which they are concerned with the rights and feelings of others, and a tendency for deliberately planned rather than impulsive behavior. As a measure of healthy socialization, then, we would expect that adult criminal offenders would score lower on the SO Scale than nonoffenders. Megargee (1972) has reported a mean SO scale score of 35.99 for a large group of working-class male adults. We will take this as our population value. Let's suppose that we collected a sample of 177 prison inmates in California with a mean SO scale score of 27.76 and a standard deviation of 6.03. We want to know if our sample of California prison inmates came from the population with a mean of 35.99. Because we expect the mean for the prisoners to be less than for the nonincarcerated population, we can state a directional research hypothesis. We now explicitly go through our formal hypothesis test.

**Step 1.** Our null hypothesis is $H_0$: $\mu = 35.99$. Our research hypothesis is: $H_1$: $\mu < 35.99$. We are specifically stating that the true population mean is less than

35.99, so we are stating a directional research hypothesis and will conduct a one-tailed test.

**Step 2.** Our test statistic will be the $z$ statistic (where the population standard deviation is not known), and our sampling distribution will be the standard normal distribution.

**Step 3.** We will select .01 as our alpha level. The critical value of $z$ for $\alpha = .01$ with a one-tailed test in this direction is $-2.33$ ($z_{crit} = -2.33$). The critical value of $z$ is negative because in our research hypothesis we have predicted that the true population mean is less than the mean expressed in the null hypothesis. We are, therefore, interested in the left tail of the sampling distribution. The critical region will consist of all $z_{obt}$ scores less than or equal to $-2.33$. Our decision rule, therefore, is to reject $H_0$ if $z_{obt} \le -2.33$.

**Step 4.** The value of $z_{obt}$ is:

$$z_{obt} = \frac{27.76 - 35.99}{6.03/\sqrt{177 - 1}}$$

$$= \frac{-8.23}{6.03/13.27}$$

$$= \frac{-8.23}{.45}$$

$$= -18.29$$

**Step 5.** As $z_{obt} < z_{crit}$ we would reject the null hypothesis. This is illustrated for you in Figure 10.10. We would therefore conclude that the population of incarcerated offenders has a mean SO scale score that is less than 35.99. Based on this test, then, we can also conclude that incarcerated offenders demonstrate greater psychopathology than nonoffenders.

Because hypothesis testing involves probabilities and not certainties, let us remind you yet another time that there is some known risk of error in rejecting the null hypothesis. Our alpha level of .01 serves notice that there is 1 chance in 100, or a 1 percent chance, that we could have observed a sample mean of

FIGURE 10.10. Critical $z$ and critical region for one-tailed test and alpha $= .01$.

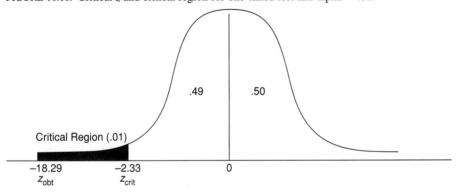

27.76 even if the true population mean was 35.99. Because the probability of that occurring is very small, however, we have opted to reject the null hypothesis. Nevertheless, there is no way of knowing for sure whether we are correct. Keep in mind that the risk of rejecting a true null hypothesis is always present and is equal to alpha.


## 10.4 HYPOTHESIS TESTING FOR POPULATION MEANS USING SMALL SAMPLES

In the previous section we have discussed hypothesis testing about one sample mean when either the population standard deviation ($\sigma$) was known or our sample size was large enough that we could use the sample standard deviation ($s$) as our estimate and proceed with the $z$ score as our test statistic. When we have small samples ($n \leq 50$), however, the sample standard deviation is a more biased estimate of $\sigma$ and we cannot take advantage of the central limit theorem and employ the standard normal distribution as our sampling distribution. As with the differences we observed between calculating confidence intervals when we have large and small samples, the techniques we use when testing a hypothesis about a population mean also are a little different when we are utilizing a small sample. With small samples, the appropriate test statistic is the $t$ test we used in Chapter 9 with confidence intervals. Our sampling distribution, then, is the Student's $t$ distribution.

As stated in Chapter 9, the $t$ distribution is different from the $z$ distribution. The $t$ distribution is flatter than the $z$ distribution, and it is much flatter when the sample size is small. This means that the critical value of $t$ at a given alpha level will be greater than the comparable critical value of $z$ and can be much greater when $n$ is small. As an example, you know that the critical value of $z$ for a one-tailed test at $\alpha = .05$ is 1.65. Let's take the same alpha level and find the critical value of $t$ with an $n$ of 10. To find the critical value of $t,$ go to the table of $t$ values in Table B.3 of Appendix B. You may remember that to find the critical $t$ value, you first locate the appropriate alpha level and type of test (one- or two-tailed) at the top of the table. After that you must determine the correct degrees of freedom (df), where df is equal to $n - 1$. With a sample size of 10, therefore, we have nine degrees of freedom. Keep in mind that unlike the $z$ table, the numbers in the body of the $t$ table correspond to values of critical $t,$ not to areas under the curve. We can see from the table that the critical value of $t$ for a one-tailed test and an alpha of .05 with nine degrees of freedom is 1.833. This is greater than the critical value of $z$ at the same alpha level (1.65).

As an exercise, stay in the same column of $t$ and move down the page. Notice what happens when the size of the sample increases. The size of critical $t$ decreases. At a sample size of 121 (120 degrees of freedom) the critical value of $t$ (1.658) is almost the same as the critical value of $z$ (1.65). Therefore, you can see that, as the sample size increases, the more the $t$ distribution approximates the shape of the $z$ distribution. When our sample size has reached about 100, the two distributions are virtually identical.

We now go through an example of conducting a hypothesis test about a mean obtained from a small sample. The formula for the *t* test used to conduct a hypothesis test about a population mean using small samples is identical to the formula used for the *z* test when the population standard deviation was unknown:

$$t = \frac{\bar{x} - \mu}{\hat{\sigma}_{\bar{x}}}$$

(10.4)

where $\sigma_{\bar{x}} = s/\sqrt{n-1}$

The steps involved in conducting a hypothesis test with *t* are the same as in the previous section with the *z* test. We first state the null and research hypotheses. We determine our test statistic and sampling distribution. We select an alpha level, and based on this, we determine the critical value of our test statistic ($t_{crit}$) and the critical region of our sampling distribution. We calculate our test statistic ($t_{obt}$) and compare it to the critical value. Finally, we make a decision about our null hypothesis and interpret this decision in a way that is meaningful to the research question at hand. The main difference between hypothesis testing using the *t* test and the *z* test lies in these statistics' respective sampling distributions and, consequently, the critical values and rejection regions for a given level of alpha.

Using data from the *Sourcebook of Criminal Justice Statistics,* let's go through an example. In 1992, the *Sourcebook* reported that the average area per inmate in all state confinement facilities was 56 square feet. For the sake of example, let's assume that we obtain a sample of 14 correctional facilities from one state and calculate the mean square footage of space per inmate to be $\bar{x} = 55.8$ with a standard deviation of .6.

With these data we want to test the null hypothesis that the population mean square footage of space per inmate for our state is equal to 56. Our research hypothesis states that $\mu$ is not equal to 56 feet, so our alternative hypothesis is nondirectional. Formally, both hypotheses would be stated like this:

$H_0$: $\mu = 56$

$H_1$: $\mu \neq 56$

We decide to adopt an alpha level of .01. The next step is to find the critical value of *t* and to map out our rejection region. We know that we are conducting a nondirectional test using $\alpha = .01$, but we also need to calculate how many degrees of freedom we have in our sample. Remember that this is equal to $n - 1$ (14 − 1), which gives us 13 degrees of freedom. From Table B.3 of Appendix B we find that for a two-tailed test with an alpha of .01 and 13 degrees of freedom, our critical value of *t* is 3.012. Recall that when doing a nondirectional test we are interested in both tails of our sampling distribution. In a nondirectional test, then, the critical value corresponds to both positive and negative values. Our critical value of *t*, therefore, is $t_{crit} = \pm 3.012$. Our decision rule will be to reject the null hypothesis if $t_{obt}$ is less than or equal to −3.012 or greater than or equal to +3.012. Stated differently, we must fail to reject the null hypothesis if $-3.012 < t_{obt} < 3.012$. We are now ready to compute our test statistic:

$H_0$: $\mu = 56$

$H_1$: $\mu \neq 56$

$\alpha = .01$

$df = 14 - 1 = 13$

$z_{crit} = \pm 3.012$

$$t_{obt} = \frac{55.8 - 56}{.6/\sqrt{14 - 1}}$$

$$= \frac{55.8 - 56}{.6/3.61}$$

$$= \frac{-.2}{.17}$$

$$= -1.18$$

The value of $t$ we obtained from our statistical test was $-.118$. Figure 10.11 shows the obtained value of $t$ relative to critical regions on the sampling distribution. Because our obtained test statistic does not fall into either of the two critical regions, we must fail to reject the null hypothesis that inmates in this state's correctional facilities receive an average of 56 square feet of space per inmate.

Let's go through another example. The *Sourcebook of Criminal Justice Statistics* (1991) also reports that the mean entry-level salary for police officers in all metropolitan areas is $23,474 annually. Let's say that, even though we believe that this figure accurately reflects entry-level salaries of police officers in cities, we do not believe that this population mean represents entrance salaries of police officers in rural communities. In fact, we believe that police officers in rural communities probably receive much lower salaries than those working in urban and suburban jurisdictions. To test this, we first formalize our null and research hypotheses as:

$H_0$: $\mu = \$23,474$

$H_1$: $\mu < \$23,474$

FIGURE 10.11.  Critical $t$ and critical region for two-tailed test and alpha $= .01$.

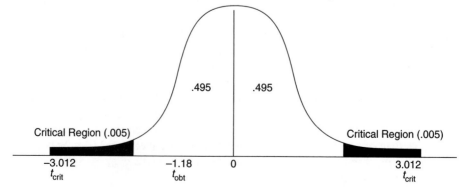

Our null hypothesis is that the population mean is equal to $23,474; our research hypothesis suggests that the sample was actually drawn from a different population with a lower mean salary. Next, we collect information on entrance-level salaries from a random sample of nine rural communities ($n = 9$). From this sample of rural police departments, we find that the mean entrance level salary is $19,889 with a standard deviation of $446. We decide that an alpha level of .05 is sufficient to test our hypothesis. Given this information, along with our sample statistics, we next define our critical value of $t$ and calculate the test statistic as:

$H_0$: $\mu = \$23,474$

$H_1$: $\mu < \$23,474$

$\alpha = .05$

$df = 9 - 1 = 8$

$t_{\text{crit}} = -1.86$

$$t_{\text{obt}} = \frac{19,889 - 23,474}{446/\sqrt{9 - 1}}$$

$$= \frac{19,889 - 23,474}{446/2.83}$$

$$= \frac{-3585}{157.6}$$

$$= -22.75$$

Our critical value of $t$ is $-1.86$ because in our research hypothesis we have specifically hypothesized that the sample comes from a population with a lower mean than that expressed in the null hypothesis. We are, therefore, only interested in the left tail of the $t$ distribution and in negative values of $t_{\text{obt}}$. If $t_{\text{obt}}$ is positive, we would fail to reject the null hypothesis even if it is greater than the absolute value of $t_{\text{crit}}$ because it is in the wrong direction. In Figure 10.12 we illustrate the critical value of $t$ and the rejection region relative to the value of $t$ we obtained in our test.

The obtained $t$ statistic ($-22.75$) is much larger than the critical value of $t$ ($-1.86$) needed to reject the null hypothesis. This is shown for you in Figure 10.12. We can therefore reject the null hypothesis and conclude that the mean entry-level salary for rural police officers is, indeed, under $23,474.

So far, we have talked about hypothesis tests for population means only. We have conducted hypothesis tests for a population mean $\mu$ using data from both large samples ($z$ test) and small samples ($t$ test). Before we move on to hypothesis tests for proportions, let us just summarize the types of tests that we can use when conducting hypothesis tests about a single population mean ($\mu$). The following box displays the three combinations of hypothesis tests that can be conducted when making an inference about $\mu$.

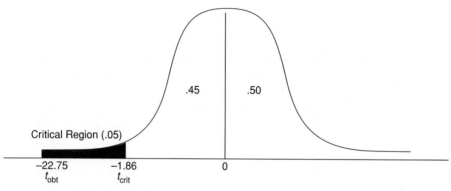

FIGURE 10.12. Critical *t* and critical region for one-tailed test and alpha = .05.

---

**Formal Statements of the Null and Research Hypotheses for Both Nondirectional (Two-Tailed) and Directional (One-Tailed) Tests with a Population Mean of 5**

Nondirectional hypotheses for a population mean:

$H_0$: $\mu = 5$

$H_1$: $\mu \neq 5$

Directional hypotheses for a larger population mean:

$H_0$: $\mu = 5$

$H_1$: $\mu > 5$

Directional hypotheses for a smaller population mean:

$H_0$: $\mu = 5$

$H_1$: $\mu < 5$

---

## 10.5 HYPOTHESIS TESTING FOR POPULATION PROPORTIONS AND PERCENTS USING LARGE SAMPLES

Very frequently we find that our data will not be measured at the interval or ratio level, and we will not be able to calculate a mean. These data include such things as the percentage of the American public who support the death penalty or own firearms, the proportion of arrested defendants who test positively for drugs, and the proportion of arrested defendants who plead guilty in exchange for a lesser charge. Even though we have percent and proportion data, we still may be interested in the kind of problem we have been examining thus far in the chapter, testing the difference between a sample statistic and a population parameter. What we want to know now is whether any observed difference between a sample proportion and population parameter is "significantly different" or whether this difference is due simply to chance or due to sampling variation.

The general procedures used to conduct hypothesis tests about a single population proportion are almost identical to those used for a population mean, so we will not reiterate them here. We use $\hat{p}$ to denote the proportion obtained from our sample data and $p$ to denote the population proportion. In this chapter, we focus exclusively on tests used for proportions obtained from large samples. With large samples, we can use our familiar $z$ test. The general rule regarding sample size in tests of proportions is that the normal approximation (standard normal or $z$ distribution) can be used when both $n$ $(\hat{p}) \geq 5$ and $n$ $(\hat{p} - 1) \geq 5$. For example, if $\hat{p} = .5$, we would need a sample size of at least 10 to conduct a $z$ test, because $10(.5) \geq 5$. If $\hat{p} = .10$, we would need a sample size of at least 50 $(50[.10] \geq 5)$. Small sample tests of hypotheses for proportions are discussed in Chapter 16.

To perform a hypothesis test about a population proportion using large samples, we again use the $z$ test as our test statistic and the $z$ distribution as our sampling distribution. If you are wondering why we are able to use the $z$ or standard normal distribution with proportion data that clearly are not normally distributed, recall the central limit theorem from Chapter 8. That theorem stated that, no matter what the shape of the population distribution, the sampling distribution of repeated random samples of size $n$ is normally distributed as $n$ becomes large. Recall that we also used the $z$ distribution when we estimated population proportions by calculating confidence intervals around sample proportions. The formula used to conduct a $z$ test for proportions is comparable to the formula for hypothesis tests with a mean:

$$z = \frac{\hat{p} - p}{\sigma_{\hat{p}}} \tag{10.5}$$

where

$$\sigma_{\hat{p}} = \sqrt{\frac{p(q)}{n}}$$

$\hat{p}$ = the sample proportion

$p$ = the population proportion

$q = 1 - p$ or 1 minus the population proportion

The numerator of this formula simply is the difference between the sample and population proportion. This represents the distance between the sample statistic and the hypothesized population parameter. The denominator $(\sigma_{\hat{p}} = \sqrt{pq/n})$ is an estimate of the standard deviation of the sampling distribution. This standard deviation is also called the *standard error of the proportion,* and the form of this formula should be very familiar to you by now.

Let's go through the procedures of conducting a hypothesis test for a population proportion. In September of 1990, the Gallup Polling Organization included in one of its polls this question, "Do you think there should or should not be a law that would ban the possession of handguns except by the police and other authorized persons?" The proportion of the total population who believed there *should* be such a law was 41 percent. Let's say that we believe that attitudes regarding a law like this varies significantly by gender, between males and females. In fact, let's say that we think females would be much more likely on average to believe that such a law should exist. To test our hypothesis, we collect a random sample of 107 females and ask them the same question. As all good researchers do, we formally state our hypothesis (a directional or one-tailed hypothesis) as shown before conducting the statistical test:

$H_0$: $p = .41$

$H_1$: $p > .41$

We next specify the level of alpha at .05 and determine the critical region. The critical value of $z$ with $\alpha = .05$ using a directional hypothesis is equal to 1.65 (Table 10.1). The critical value is positive in this case because we believe the proportion of females who believe in such a law will be greater than the null hypothesis proportion. We will reject the null hypothesis, then, if $z_{obt} \geq 1.65$.

The results of our sample indicate that 51 of the 107 females from our sample believed that there should be a law banning the possession of handguns except by the police and other authorized persons. Remember, to obtain the proportion, we simply divide the frequency of interest, in this case those in favor of the law, by the total number in the sample ($f/n = 51/107$), which gives us a sample proportion of $\hat{p} = .48$. With this information, we calculate the obtained test statistic of $z$:

$$z_{obt} = \frac{.48 - .41}{\sqrt{\dfrac{.41(.59)}{107}}}$$

$$= \frac{.07}{\sqrt{\dfrac{.24}{107}}}$$

$$= \frac{.07}{\sqrt{.002}}$$

$$= \frac{.07}{.047}$$

$$= 1.49$$

The value of $z$ we obtain from our statistical test indicates, just as all $z$ scores do, that if the null hypothesis were true, the sample proportion $\hat{p} = .48$ falls only about 1.49 standard errors above the hypothesized population proportion $p$ of .41. This does not fall within our rejection region. The obtained value of $z$ relative to the critical value of $z$ is displayed for you in Figure 10.13. Because $z_{obt} < z_{crit}$, we must fail to reject the null hypothesis and conclude that the true proportion of females favoring such a ban on handguns is not significantly different from .41. We can state this in terms of percentages by simply multiplying the proportions by 100. We

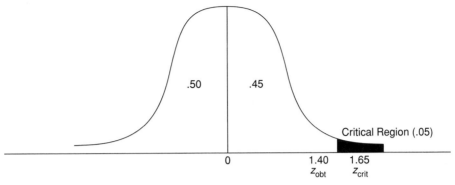

FIGURE 10.13. Critical $z$ and critical region for one-tailed test and alpha = .05.

could then conclude that, based on our hypothesis test, the proportion of females favoring a ban on handguns probably does fall somewhere around 41 percent.

Let's do another example, this time using percents. Imagine that you have passed your statistics course with flying colors, got your degree, and are now the research specialist for a municipal jail. During the course of your duties, you notice that in a random drug test of 100 new pretrial detainees, 36 percent tested positive for some form of cocaine. You begin to wonder whether perhaps the population of pretrial detainees contains a higher than normal percentage of cocaine users. You do a little background research and discover that, according to the National Institute on Drug Abuse, approximately 19 percent of young adults (age 18–25) have used cocaine at some time in their life (Akers 1992:50). You decide to test the hypothesis that the percent of cocaine use among pretrial detainees is significantly higher than 19 percent.

You have the following information:

| Population: | Sample: |
|---|---|
| $p$ = 19 percent | $\hat{p}$ = 36 percent |
| $n$ = 100 | |

With your well-honed statistical skills you identify this as a call for a hypothesis test of a one sample proportion and go through each step in order.

**Step 1.** You state the null and research hypothesis:

$H_0$: $p$ = 19 percent     $H_1$: $p > 19$ percent

As you suspect that the sample of pretrial detainees comes from a population where the percent of cocaine use is greater than 19 percent, you state a directional research hypothesis.

**Step 2.** Because you have a large sample ($n$ = 100), you select the $z$ test for proportions as your statistical test and the $z$ distribution as your sampling distribution.

**Step 3.** You select an alpha level of .01. With a one-tailed test, the critical level of $z$ at this level of alpha is 2.33. Your decision is to reject the null hypothesis if $z_{obt} > 2.33$.

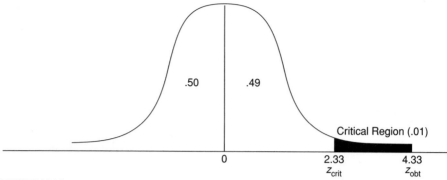

FIGURE 10.14.

**Step 4.** You calculate the obtained value of your test statistic, $z_{obt}$:

$$z_{obt} = \frac{\hat{p} - p}{\sqrt{pq/n}} = \frac{36 - 19}{\sqrt{(19)(81)/100}} = \frac{17}{\sqrt{1539/100}}$$

$$= \frac{17}{3.92} \qquad = 4.34$$

**Step 5.** The location of the obtained value of $z$ relative to the critical value and the critical region are illustrated in Figure 10.14. As $z_{obt} > 2.33$, you would reject the null hypothesis, knowing that there is a 1 in 100 chance that you are making the wrong decision (Type I error). From this hypothesis test, you can conclude that in the population of pretrial detainees the percentage who have ever used cocaine is greater than 19 percent.

## 10.6 SUMMARY

In this chapter, we have examined the procedures used to make inferences about two population parameters: inferences from a sample mean ($\bar{x}$) about a population mean ($\mu$), and inferences from a sample proportion ($\hat{p}$) to a population proportion ($p$). We used a $z$ test when making inferences about both sample means and sample proportions when we had large samples. When working with small samples, we demonstrated the steps necessary for hypothesis testing involving a mean using a $t$ test.

Each of these hypothesis tests involved a series of decisions. The first one is whether to state a directional or nondirectional research hypothesis. If there are sound reasons to state your research hypothesis as a directional one, you should do so. Another decision to make concerns which test statistic and which corresponding sampling distribution to use. The third decision pertains to which level of significance (the alpha level) to use in conducting your hypothesis test, one of the most important decisions you will make in hypothesis testing because the alpha level determines the risk you accept of rejecting a null hypothesis that is really true (i.e., making a Type I error). Finally, the last and easiest decision you have to make is whether to fail to reject or reject your null hypothesis. This is the easiest decision because, if you have properly conducted the hypothesis test and followed the order of the steps, this last decision will have essentially been made for you. Once you have chosen your alpha level and found the critical value and critical region, all you need to do is to determine if the obtained value of your test statistic falls in the critical region. If it does, you reject the null hypothesis, if it does not you fail to reject the null hypothesis. What else could be easier?

## Key Terms

critical region

critical value

directional hypothesis test

hypothesis testing

nondirectional hypothesis test

null hypothesis

one-tailed test

sampling distribution of the mean

sampling variation

standard error of the mean

standard error of the proportion

two-tailed test

## Problems

1. When is it appropriate to use a $t$ test for hypothesis testing instead of a $z$ test?
2. We are interested in the average dollar amount lost by victims of burglary. The National Insurance Association has reported that the mean dollar amount lost by victims of burglary is $2,333. Assume that this is the population mean. We believe that the true population mean loss is different from this. Formally state the null and research hypotheses we would test to investigate this question. What if we believed the dollar amount to be higher?
3. The Internal Revenue Service claimed that the mean number of times the average U.S. citizen has cheated on taxes in the last 10 years was 4.6 times. Assume that this is your population value. We believe the actual population mean ($\mu$) of the number of times individuals cheat on their taxes is higher than this. We collect a random sample of 64 tax-paying citizens and find the following sample statistics: $\bar{x} = 6.3$, $s = 1.9$. Perform all of the procedures necessary for conducting a hypothesis test based on our assumption. Set your alpha level at .01. What do you conclude?
4. A major research study concluded that the mean number of times that adolescents had engaged in vandalism during the previous 12 months was 3.5 times. We believe the true population mean to be less than this. After collecting our own sample of 59 adolescents, we find that the mean number of times they have vandalized property during a 1-year period was $\bar{x} = 2.9$ with a standard deviation equal to .7. Perform all of the procedures necessary for conducting a hypothesis test based on our assumption. What do you conclude? Set your alpha level at .05.
5. Over a 20-year period, the average sentence given to defendants convicted of aggravated assault in the United States was 25.9 months. Assume this to be your population mean. You think that it might be different in your home state and conduct a little study to examine this question. You take a random sample of 75 jurisdictions in your home state and find that the mean aggravated assault sentence is 27.3 months, with a standard deviation of 6.5. Test the null hypothesis that the mean sentence is 25.9 months against the alternative hypothesis that it is different from that. Set your alpha level at .01.
6. A study conducted by Research Institute of America has concluded that the average number of hours inmates at state correctional facilities spend in their cells during a day is 15. We believe the population mean number of hours to be different from this. We contacted a sample

of 15 state correctional facilities and inquired about the mean number of hours inmates housed in their facilities spent in their cells and came up with the following sample data:

| Facility Number | Spend in Cells |
|:---:|:---:|
| 1 | 16.3 |
| 2 | 21.1 |
| 3 | 14.9 |
| 4 | 13.5 |
| 5 | 22.2 |
| 6 | 15.3 |
| 7 | 18.1 |
| 8 | 19.0 |
| 9 | 14.2 |
| 10 | 9.3 |
| 11 | 10.1 |
| 12 | 21.1 |
| 13 | 22.3 |
| 14 | 15.4 |
| 15 | 13.2 |

Calculate the mean number of hours inmates spend in their cells from the sample data. Test the null hypothesis that the mean number of hours inmates spend in their cells is 15 against the null hypothesis that it is different from that. Set your alpha level at .05. Hint: you will also have to calculate the standard deviation. Remember, practice makes perfect! What do you conclude?

7. You are on the police force in a small town. During an election year, a candidate for mayor claims that fewer police are needed because the average police officer makes only four arrests per year. You think the population mean is much higher than that, so you conduct a small research project. You ask 12 other officers how many arrests they made in the past year. The average for this sample of 12 is 6.3 with a standard deviation of 1.5. With your sample evidence, test the null hypothesis that the population mean is four arrests against the alternative that it is greater than four. Set your alpha level at .01.

8. The American Bar Association reports that the mean length of time for a hearing in juvenile court is 25 minutes. Assume that this is your population mean. As a lawyer who practices in the juvenile court, you think that the average hearing is much shorter than this. You take a sample of 20 other lawyers who do juvenile work and ask them how long their last case in juvenile court was. The mean hearing length for this sample of 20 was 23 minutes, with a standard deviation of 6. Test the null hypothesis that the population mean is 25 minutes against the alternative that it is less than 25. Set your alpha level at .05.

9. A spokesperson for the National Rifle Association states that 45 percent of the households in the United States contain at least one firearm. Assume that this is your population value. You take a random sample of 200 homes and find that about 23 percent of them contained a firearm. Test the null hypothesis that the population proportion is 45 percent against the alternative that it is less than that. Set your alpha level at .01.

10. A friend of yours claims that 20 percent of the people in your neighborhood have been the victim of a crime. Take this as your population value. You take a random sample of 60 homes and find that about 31 percent of the homes reported some kind of crime. Test the null hypothesis that the population proportion is 20 percent against the alternative that it is different from 20 percent. Set your alpha level at .05.

**11.** A public opinion study concluded that the proportion of Americans agreeing with the statement "Prisons should be for punishment, not rehabilitation" was .31. You believe the true population proportion who agree with this statement is actually higher than this. After collecting your own sample of 110 individuals and asking them the same question, you find that .46 agree with the statement. Test the null hypothesis that the population proportion is .31 against the alternative that it is more than this. Set your alpha level at .05.

## Solutions to Problems

**1.** The $z$ test and $z$ distribution may be used for making one sample hypothesis tests involving a population mean under two conditions: (1) if the population standard deviation ($\sigma$) is known, or (2) if the sample size is large enough ($n \geq 50$ or more), so that the sample standard deviation ($s$) can be used as an unbiased estimate of the population standard deviation. If either of these two conditions is not met, hypothesis tests about one population mean must be conducted with the $t$ test and $t$ distribution.

**2.** In our first hypothesis test, the null and alternative hypotheses would be:

$H_0$: $\mu = \$2,333$

$H_1$: $\mu \neq \$2,333$

If we believed the dollar amount lost by burglary victims to be *higher* than \$2,333, our null hypothesis would be the same, but we would assume the following about the alternative hypothesis: $H_1$: $\mu > \$2,333$

**3.** The null and alternative hypotheses are:

$H_0$: $\mu = 4.6$

$H_1$: $\mu > 4.6$

Although we do not know the population standard deviation, our sample size is greater than 50 ($n = 64$), so we can use the $z$ test and the $z$ distribution. Our decision rule is to reject the null hypothesis if our obtained value of $z$ is 2.33 or greater (reject $H_0$ if $z_{obt} \geq 2.33$). The value of $z_{obt}$ is:

$$z_{obt} = \frac{6.3 - 4.6}{1.9/\sqrt{64 - 1}} = 7.08$$

Because 7.08 is higher than the critical value of 2.33 and falls in the critical region, we will reject the null hypothesis that the population mean is equal to 4.6 times.

**4.** The null and alternative hypotheses are:

$H_0$: $\mu = 3.5$

$H_1$: $\mu < 3.5$

Although we do not know the population standard deviation, our sample size is greater than 50 ($n = 59$), so we can use the $z$ test and the $z$ distribution. Our decision rule is to reject the null hypothesis if our obtained value of $z$ is 1.65 or less. The value of $z_{obt}$ is:

$$z_{obt} = \frac{2.9 - 3.5}{.7/\sqrt{59 - 1}} = -6.67$$

Because this is lower than the critical value of 1.65 and falls in the critical region, we will reject the null hypothesis that the population mean is equal to 3.5 acts of vandalism.

**5.** The null and alternative hypotheses are:

$H_0$: $\mu = 25.9$

$H_1$: $\mu \neq 25.9$

Although we do not know the population standard deviation, our sample size is greater than 50 ($n = 75$), so we can use the $z$ test and the $z$ distribution. Our decision rule is to reject the null hypothesis if our obtained value of $z \geq 2.58$ or if $z_{obt} \leq -2.58$. The value of $z_{obt}$ is:

$$z_{obt} = \frac{27.3 - 25.9}{6.5/\sqrt{75 - 1}} = 1.87$$

Because this value is not higher than the critical value of 2.58 and does not fall in the critical region, we fail to reject the null hypothesis that the population mean is equal to 25.9 months.

**6.** The null and alternative hypotheses are:

$H_0$: $\mu = 15$

$H_1$: $\mu \neq 15$

Because we do not know the population standard deviation and our sample size is substantially less than 50 ($n = 15$), we must use the $t$ test and the $t$ distribution. Our decision rule is to reject the null hypothesis if our obtained value of $t \geq 2.145$ or if $t_{obt} \leq -2.145$. The value of $t_{obt}$ is:

$$t_{obt} = \frac{16.4 - 15}{4/\sqrt{15 - 1}} = 1.31$$

Because this value is not higher than the critical value of 2.145 and does not fall in the critical region, we fail to reject the null hypothesis that the population mean is equal to 15 hours.

**7.** The null and alternative hypotheses are:

$H_0$: $\mu = 4$

$H_1$: $\mu > 4$

Because we do not know the population standard deviation and our sample size is substantially less than 50 ($n = 12$), we must use the $t$ test and the $t$ distribution. Our decision rule is to reject the null hypothesis if our obtained value of $t \geq 2.718$. The value of $t_{obt}$ is:

$$t_{obt} = \frac{6.3 - 4}{1.5/\sqrt{12 - 1}} = 5.11$$

Because this is greater than the critical value of 2.718 and falls in the critical region, we decide to reject the null hypothesis that the population mean is equal to four arrests.

**8.** The null and alternative hypotheses are:

$H_0$: $\mu = 25$

$H_1$: $\mu < 25$

Because we do not know the population standard deviation and our sample size is substantially less than 50 ($n = 20$), we must use the $t$ test and the $t$ distribution. Our decision rule is to reject the null hypothesis if our obtained value of $t \leq -1.729$. The value of $t_{obt}$ is:

$$t_{\text{obt}} = \frac{23 - 25}{6/\sqrt{20 - 1}} = -1.45$$

Because this value is not lower than the critical value of $-1.729$ and does not fall in the critical region, we fail to reject the null hypothesis that the population mean is equal to 25 minutes.

9. The null and alternative hypotheses are:

$H_0$: $p = .45$

$H_1$: $p < .45$

Because this is a problem involving a population proportion with a large sample size ($n = 200$), we can use the $z$ test and the $z$ distribution. Our decision rule is to reject the null hypothesis if our obtained value of $z$ is $-2.33$ or less. The value of $z_{\text{obt}}$ is:

$$z_{\text{obt}} = \frac{.23 - .45}{\sqrt{\dfrac{(.45)(.55)}{200}}} = -6.29$$

Because this is less than the critical value of $-2.33$ and falls in the critical region, we will reject the null hypothesis that the population proportion is equal to .45, or 45 percent.

10. The null and alternative hypotheses are:

$H_0$: $p = .20$

$H_1$: $p \neq .20$

Because this is a problem involving a population proportion with a large sample size ($n = 60$; $60 \times .2 > 5$), we can use the $z$ test and the $z$ distribution. Our decision rule is to reject the null hypothesis if our obtained value of $z \geq 1.96$ or if $z_{\text{obt}} \leq -1.96$. The value of $z_{\text{obt}}$ is:

$$z_{\text{obt}} = \frac{.31 - .20}{\sqrt{\dfrac{(.20)(.80)}{60}}} = 2.20$$

Because this is greater than the critical value of 1.96 and falls in the critical region, we decide to reject the null hypothesis that the population proportion is equal to .20, or 20 percent, of the homes.

11. The null and alternative hypotheses are:

$H_0$: $p = .31$

$H_1$: $p > .31$

Because this is a problem involving a population proportion with a large sample size ($n = 110$), we can use the $z$ test and the $z$ distribution. Our decision rule is to reject the null hypothesis if our obtained value of $z$ is 1.65 or greater. The value of $z_{\text{obt}}$ is:

$$z_{\text{obt}} = \frac{.46 - .31}{\sqrt{\dfrac{(.31)(.69)}{110}}} = 3.41$$

Because this is greater than the critical value of 1.65 and falls in the critical region, we will reject the null hypothesis that the population proportion is equal to .31, or 31 percent.

# CHAPTER 11

# Data Analysis with Two Categorical Variables:

## The Chi-Square Test and Measures of Association

*There can be little liking where there is no likeness.*

—AESOP

## 11.1 INTRODUCTION

In this chapter, our data take the form of categories, either unordered or ordered. An example of an unordered category would be the variable gender. The variable gender has two categories, male and female, that cannot be ordered, as neither category has more "gender" than the other. Another example of an unordered category would be a person's race or ethnicity. People can be classified into categories as "African Americans," "Asians," "Hispanics/Latinos," or "whites," but they cannot be ordered, because one racial/ethnic group does have more race or ethnicity than another. Variables that consist of unordered categories are nominal-level variables because the values differ in quality only, not in quantity.

An example of an ordered category would be self-reported delinquency when measured as the following: "zero delinquent acts committed," "1–5 delinquent acts committed," "more than 5 delinquent acts committed." Unlike gender, these categories can be ordered because someone placed in the third category (let's call it category C) has committed more delinquent acts than someone placed in the second category (let's call it category B), who in turn has committed more delinquent acts than someone placed in the first category (let's call that category A). Not only is category A different from categories B and C, and category B different from category C, but also we can say that $A < B < C$. That is, the category values can be numerically ordered in terms of having "more than" or "less than" the variable in question. Variables that consist of ordered categories are ordinal-level variables.

The kind of research problem that concerns us in this chapter involves the joint distribution of two categorical variables. We want to know if the distribution of one variable is related to or depends on the distribution of another. By examining the joint distribution of two variables, we can determine whether there is a relationship between them or not. If there is no relationship between the two distributions, we say that the variables are independent of one another. In this instance, knowing the category that someone is in for one variable will not help us understand the category that person is in for the other. If, however, the two distributions are related, then we can predict which category the person is in for the second variable based on our knowledge of the first variable. In this instance, the two variables are said to be dependent. That is why this type of problem is referred to as a problem of independence.

In examining this problem, we learn about the chi-square statistic ($\chi^2$) and the chi-square distribution. The chi-square statistic (the chi is pronounced "ki," as in *kite*) is symbolized by the Greek letter chi ($\chi$). The chi-square distribution is the theoretical sampling distribution of the chi-square statistic. When we want to know whether two categorical variables are independent or are related to one another, we use a statistical test called the chi-square test of independence. Many criminological and criminal justice variables are categorical, so chi-square tests of independence are very common.

The chi-square test tells us whether two variables are significantly related to one another. However, it tells us nothing about how strongly they are related. We therefore conclude the chapter with a discussion of different statistics that measure the strength of the association between two categorical variables. Before we discuss the chi-square test, however, we need to digress a little and discuss the joint distribution of two categorical variables in the form of percent, or contingency, tables.

## 11.2 READING AND UNDERSTANDING CONTINGENCY TABLES

One of the most frequent ways of presenting the relationship between two categorical variables is by showing their joint frequency in a contingency table, sometimes referred to as a cross-tabulation table. Recall that frequency distribution tables (Chapter 3) display the distribution of a single variable. Contingency tables display the *joint distribution* of two variables. By joint distribution, we mean how two variables are distributed when considered simultaneously or jointly.

As an example, the top of Table 11.1 shows the distribution of two categorical variables, the decision of South Carolina prosecutors to charge a homicide as a capital or noncapital murder, and the race of the victim in a murder. As you can see, there are a total of 302 cases. In 188 of these cases a noncapital offense was charged, and in the other 114 cases a capital offense was charged by the prosecutor. In 215 of the latter cases a white victim was killed, and in the other 87 cases an African American victim was killed. Now, what about the joint distribution of these two variables? In other words, for how many of the white victim murders was there a capital charge? a noncapital charge? Likewise, how many of the African American victim murders resulted in capital and noncapital charges?

The bottom of Table 11.1 shows the joint distribution of the two categorical-level variables. This joint distribution takes the form of a *contingency table*. A contingency table is usually defined by the number of rows and columns that it has. The bottom table of Table 11.1 is a 2 × 2 contingency table because it has two columns

**TABLE 11.1.  Contingency Table of White South Carolina Prosecutors' Charging Decision (Noncapital, Capital), by Race of Homicide Victim, 1982**

| | Frequency | | |
|---|---|---|---|
| Prosecutors' charging decision | | | |
|    Noncapital charge | 188 | | |
|    Capital charge | 114 | | |
|    Total | 302 | | |
| Race of victim | | | |
|    White victim | 215 | | |
|    Nonwhite victim | 87 | | |
|    Total | 302 | | |

| Prosecutors' Charging Decision | White | Nonwhite | |
|---|---|---|---|
| Noncapital | 118 | 70 | 188 |
| Capital | 97 | 17 | 114 |
| Total | 215 | 87 | 302 |

(white victims and nonwhite victims) and two rows (noncapital and capital charging decisions). The product of the number of rows (R) and columns (C) within a contingency table is equal to the total number of *cells* in the table (R × C = Number of Cells). There are four cells in Table 11.1 (2 × 2 = 4). Each cell corresponds to the joint distribution of the categories of both variables (white victim and capital charge; nonwhite victim and capital charge; white victim and noncapital charge; nonwhite victim and noncapital charge). These cells are labeled A through D in Table 11.2.

Table 11.2 also labels other important pieces of information found in a contingency table. $R_1$ and $R_2$ indicate the *row marginals*. They correspond to the total number of cases or frequencies found in each of the row categories. $C_1$ and $C_2$, the *column marginals,* correspond to the total number of cases found in each of the column categories. The sum of the row marginals $(R_1 + R_2)$ should equal the sum of the column marginals $(C_1 + C_2)$, and both of these should equal the total sample size in the table $(R_1 + R_2 = C_1 + C_2 = n)$. For example, in Table 11.1, the two row marginals are 188 and 114, and the two column marginals are 215 and 87. The sum of the row marginals = the sum of the column marginals = the total number of cases, that is, here 302.

It might be helpful at this stage to stop here and examine where the numbers in Table 11.1 came from. First of all, the total number of cases $(n)$ is 302 because there were 302 homicide cases charged by South Carolina prosecutors during the period studied. The distribution of the row marginals $(R_1$ and $R_2)$ is the frequency distribution of a single variable, Prosecutors' Charging Decision. From Table 11.1 we see that of the 302 homicides, the local prosecutors charged a noncapital offense in 188 cases $(R_1)$ and a capital offense in 114 cases $(R_2)$. Notice that $R_1 + R_2 = n$ (188 + 114 = 302). The distribution of the column marginals also is the frequency distribution of a single variable, Race of Victim. From Table 11.1 we see that of the

### TABLE 11.2. Labeling a 2 × 2 Contingency Table

| Number of Rows | Number of Columns | | Row Marginals | Total Sample Size |
|---|---|---|---|---|
| | 1 | 2 | | |
| 1 | A* | B* | $R_1$ | |
| 2 | C* | D* | $R_2$ | |
| Column Marginals | $C_1$ | $C_2$ | | $n$ |

*Cell frequencies.

302 homicides, 215 ($C_1$) involved white victims and 87 ($C_2$) involved nonwhite victims. Note that $C_1 + C_2 = n$ (215 + 87 = 302).

Now, let's look at the joint distribution of the two variables within each cell. Remember that by joint distribution, we mean how the two variables are distributed when we consider them simultaneously. How many of the 215 white victim cases also involved a noncapital charge? From Table 11.1 we can see that 118 of the 215 white victim cases involved a noncapital charge. You can see that we would have obtained the same result had we asked for the number of noncapital cases that had white victims. Of the 188 noncapital cases, 118 involved a white victim. Either way, considering the two variables together there were 118 white victim/noncapital charge cases. From our notation in Table 11.2, there are 118 cases in cell A of Table 11.1.

Let's fill in the rest of the table. We can see from Table 11.1 that of the 188 noncapital cases, 70 involved a nonwhite victim. The frequency in cell B, then, is 70. Of the 114 capital cases 97 were committed against a white (Cell C) and 17 were committed against a nonwhite (Cell D). In summary, when the race of the victim is cross-classified with the South Carolina prosecutors' charging decision, we have the following: 118 noncapital charges with white victims, 70 noncapital charges with nonwhite victims, 97 capital charges with white victims, and 17 capital charges with nonwhite victims. This is the information that is displayed in Table 11.1.

Because we are interested in testing hypotheses, now we would like to know whether the decision of the prosecutors to charge a capital offense, making a defendant eligible for the death penalty, is influenced or affected by the race of the victim in the homicide. In this case, Race of Victim would be our independent variable and Prosecutors' Charging Decision would be our dependent variable. Our null hypothesis would state that there is no relationship between these two variables; that they are independent of one another. More specifically, that the prosecutors' charging decision is in a sense "color blind," that these decisions are not affected by the race of the victim.

Based on previous research that examines the relationship between race and the imposition of capital punishment in America, our alternative hypothesis is the directional one that states that the prosecutors are more likely to make a capital charge against those defendants who slay white rather than nonwhite victims. More specifically, the alterative hypothesis states that for white South Carolina prosecutors, the killing of a white will be seen as a more severe crime than the slaying of a nonwhite, and therefore more likely to deserve a capital rather than a noncapital charge. These hypotheses are formally stated as:

$H_0$: There is no relationship between the race of the homicide victim and the decision of the prosecutors to charge a homicide as a capital crime: $\chi^2 = 0$.

$H_1$: The prosecutors are more likely to charge a homicide defendant with a capital offense if he or she kills a white than if he or she kills a nonwhite: $\chi^2 > 0$.

Before we discuss the specifics of hypothesis testing using the chi-square statistic, let's first discuss how we can read and understand contingency tables like Table 11.1.

Because our research hypothesis is that the race of the victim affects the prosecutors' charging decision, what we really want to know from Table 11.1 is the extent to which white victim homicides result more often in a capital charge than do nonwhite victim homicides. It would not be a good idea, however, simply to compare the frequencies of white and nonwhite homicides that resulted in a capital charge (Cell C with Cell D) because there are many more white victims than black victims. To take into account these differences in number, we must compare the *percentage* of white and nonwhite victim homicides that resulted in a capital charge.

In general, it is better to use percentages rather than raw frequencies when making comparisons across the categories of a contingency table. The comparison of frequencies may lead to erroneous conclusions if the marginal frequencies are very different from one another. Take, for example, Table 11.3. Here we have data showing the relationship between whether or not a youth likes school and the number of delinquent acts he or she has committed. If we examine the raw frequency data, we see that a greater number of the youths who reported either liking school (52) or feeling indifferent toward school (162) committed two or more delinquent acts compared to those who disliked school (only 35). If we based our conclusions on these raw frequencies, then, it would appear that having a favorable attitude toward school was related to committing more acts of delinquency.

**TABLE 11.3. Relationship between Attitude toward School and Delinquency, Raw Frequencies**

| Number of Delinquent Acts | "Do you like school?" | | | |
| --- | --- | --- | --- | --- |
| | Like | Neither Like nor Dislike | Dislike | |
| 0 | 395 | 314 | 24 | 733 |
| 1 | 133 | 172 | 13 | 318 |
| 2+ | 52 | 162 | 35 | 249 |
| Total | 580 | 648 | 72 | 1300 |

Adapted from Travis Hirschi (1969), Table 33, p. 121. Reprinted by permission of the author.

However, notice that there are far more youths who reported liking school (580) or being indifferent to school (648) than disliking school (72). Because there are far more cases in these former two categories, compared to the dislike category, it is more likely that there will be greater frequencies for these two groups in every cell. In other words, the marginal frequencies are very different across these categories, and this may explain the relationship we noted.

Table 11.4 describes the very same data, this time using percentages in the cells in addition to the frequencies. In calculating percentages, we are taking into account different marginal frequencies because the percentages in each column must all sum to 100 percent. When we examine these percentage differences, we see that 9 percent of those youths who liked school committed two or more delinquent acts, 25 percent of those who were neutral about school committed more than one delinquent offense, and nearly one-half (49 percent) of those who disliked school committed more than one delinquent act. There are far fewer youths who dislike school, but they are about twice as likely to commit two or more delinquent acts than those who are neutral about school and over five times more likely than those who like school. It would appear, then, that the table using raw frequencies alone led us to the wrong conclusion. It turns out that frequent delinquent behavior is more likely for those who dislike school.

A good rule to follow in constructing contingency tables, then, is to report both frequencies and percentages. Given this guide, you may now be asking, "How do you calculate percentages using two variable distributions? In which direction should percentages be calculated?" In Table 11.4, we calculated the percentages so that they summed to 100 percent down the columns. That is, we calculated our percentages using the column marginals. But why do it that way? We could have, for example, calculated the percentages so that they summed to 100 percent across the rows using the row marginals as our denominators. The general rule is to calculate

**TABLE 11.4. Relationship between Attitude toward School and Delinquency, Percentages Based on Column Marginals**

| | *"Do you like school?"* | | | |
|---|---|---|---|---|
| Number of Delinquent Acts | Like | Neither Like nor Dislike | Dislike | |
| 0 | 395 (68.1%) | 314 (48.5%) | 24 (33.3%) | 733 |
| 1 | 133 (22.9%) | 172 (26.5%) | 13 (18.1%) | 318 |
| 2+ | 52 (9%) | 162 (25%) | 35 (48.6%) | 249 |
| Total | 580 (100%) | 648 (100%) | 72 (100%) | 1300 |

Adapted from Travis Hirschi (1969), Table 33, p. 121. Reprinted by permission of University of California Press.

percentages using the marginals of the independent variable as the denominator. Let's look at an example.

In Table 11.3, the research hypothesis was that a student's attitude toward school influenced whether or not they committed delinquent acts. It was assumed that having a positive attitude toward school was one of the things that kept youths from breaking rules. In other words, good feelings about school "controlled" deviant impulses. In this scenario, attitudes toward school would be seen as the independent variable and self-reported delinquency as the dependent variable. Given this, what we want to know is whether differences in the independent variable correspond to differences in the dependent variable. That is, we want to know if those who differ in their attitudes toward school also differ in the extent to which they engage in delinquent activity.

To do this, we must look at the percentage of cases that fall within the same category of the dependent variable across different categories of the independent variable. In Table 11.4, we looked at the percentage of youths reporting two or more delinquent acts (the same category of the dependent variable) for those who liked, those who were neutral, and those who disliked school (different categories of the independent variable). For example, to obtain the percentage for cell A, we took the frequency of those who liked school and who did not engage in any delinquent acts (395) divided by all those who liked school (580) to come up with 68.1 percent. To get the percentage for the cell to the right of that, we took the frequency of those who neither liked nor disliked school and who did not engage in any delinquent acts (314) divided by all those who neither liked nor disliked school (648) to obtain 48.5 percent, and so on. What we found was that, as one's attitude toward school became more negative, the percentage of delinquent acts increased substantially. This would lead us to conclude that attitude toward school is related to the commission of delinquent acts.

A general rule to follow when calculating percentages in contingency tables is that, if you can distinguish between the independent and dependent variable, percentages should be calculated using the marginal totals of the independent variable as the denominator for each cell. Comparisons should then be made between percentages found in *different* categories of the independent variable *at the same category level* of the dependent variable. In general, the independent variable is used as the column variable. However, this convention is not always followed in the research literature. For this reason, the independent variable may be found as either the column and row variable in this chapter.

Let's go back to our data in Table 11.1 that presented prosecutors' charging decisions by the race of the victim in homicide cases. In this table, our independent variable (the column variable) is the victim's race, and our dependent variable is the prosecutors' charging decision. We calculate our percentages on the race of the victim because we want to know whether a greater percentage of white victim homicides result in a capital charge than the percentage for nonwhite victims (Table 11.5). When percentages are calculated in this way, we see that 45 percent (97/215) of those defendants who killed a white victim were charged with a capital offense, whereas only 20 percent (17/87) of those defendants who killed a nonwhite victim were charged with a capital offense. This percentage comparison indicates that

**TABLE 11.5.  Race of the Victim and Prosecutors' Charging Decision (data from Table 11.1) with Percentages Based on Column Marginals**

| Prosecutors' Charging Decision | White | Nonwhite | |
|---|---|---|---|
| Noncapital | 118 | 70 | 188 |
| | (55%) | (80%) | |
| Capital | 97 | 17 | 114 |
| | (45%) | (20%) | — |
| Total | 215 | 87 | 302 |
| | (100%) | (100%) | |

homicide defendants who killed white victims were more than twice as likely as defendants who killed nonwhites to be charged with a capital homicide.

A comparison of the percentages, then, would suggest that prosecutors do seem to be influenced by the race of the victim in their decision to charge a homicide as a capital offense. Although these percent differences can be very informative, they do not take us very far in hypothesis testing because we have no reliable decision rule by which to reject or fail to reject a null hypothesis. For example, how large should the percentage difference be before we can claim that our null hypothesis is false? Five percentage points, 10 percentage points? Any decision based on percentage differences would be arbitrary. In addition, the use of percentage comparisons may get unwieldy as the number of categories in our independent variable increases.

There is a more definitive and consistent way to conduct a hypothesis test with these type of data that is based on a known probability distribution. It is called the *chi-square test of independence.* In the next section, we describe this commonly used statistical test of significance.

## 11.3 UNDERSTANDING AND CALCULATING THE CHI-SQUARE STATISTIC

Before examining the calculations of the chi-square statistic, let's try to understand exactly what this statistical test does. To illustrate the logic of the chi-square test, we will continue to use the data presented in Table 11.1. Again, this table shows the joint distribution of two variables: the decision of white South Carolina prosecutors to charge a crime as a capital offense and the race of the victim. Our plan is to test the null hypothesis that the two variables are independent against the alternative that they are not independent. As we have done in previous hypothesis tests, we explicitly state the null and alternative hypotheses:

$H_0$: Race of victim and the prosecutor's charging decision are independent events.

$H_1$: Race of victim and the prosecutor's charging decision are not independent events.

When conducting a hypothesis test and calculating the chi-square statistic, we must first ask ourselves the following question, "If these two variables are not related to one another and the null hypothesis is true, what would the table showing their joint distribution look like?" We first calculate the value of the cell frequencies we would *expect* to obtain if the null hypothesis were true. This table is called the *table of expected frequencies*. After we have calculated the expected frequency table, we will then have two tables. One table is based on the frequencies we would expect to have if there was no association between the two variables. The second table is the table we actually observe with our data (in our example this is Table 11.1). The latter is referred to as the *table of observed frequencies*. We show you how to determine the expected frequencies in a moment, but before we get to that, let's continue.

The next question we ask ourselves is whether the *expected frequencies* table looks like the table of *observed frequencies?* That is, do the cell frequencies in the expected table equal the cell frequencies in the observed table, and if they differ, how much do they differ? If they are not significantly different from one another, based on an exact probability of error (our alpha level), we will fail to reject the null hypothesis and conclude that the variables are not related to one another. If, however, the two tables are so different that we cannot presume that this difference is due to chance alone or sampling variation, we will instead reject the null hypothesis and conclude that the two variables are related.

The actual arithmetic procedure involved in this is fairly simple. The formula for the chi-square statistic is as follows:

$$\chi^2 = \sum_{i=1}^{k} \frac{(f_{o_i} - f_{e_i})^2}{f_{e_i}} \tag{11.1}$$

where
  $f_o$ = the observed cell frequency
  $f_e$ = the expected cell frequency
  $k$ = the number of cells in the table

To calculate the chi-square statistic for independence, we simply subtract each cell's expected cell frequency from the observed cell frequency, square that difference, and divide by the expected cell frequency. We perform the last step to standardize the value of chi-square so that the greatest difference does not always come from the cell with the largest frequency. We do this for each cell in our table. The sum of these values is equal to the value of chi-square.

Well, this is easy enough, you may be thinking, but how do we obtain the expected cell frequencies? Because we have to "fill in" the expected cell frequencies under the assumption of independence, let's start our calculations by looking at Table 11.6, which includes only the row and column marginals and the total sample size for the prosecutor data from Table 11.1.

**TABLE 11.6. Race of the Victim and Prosecutors' Charging Decision (data from Table 11.1) with Percentages Based on Column Marginals**

| Prosecutors' Charging Decision | White | Nonwhite | |
|---|---|---|---|
| Noncapital | Cell A | Cell B | 188 |
| Capital | Cell C | Cell D | 114 |
| Total | 215 (100%) | 87 (100%) | 302 |

To calculate the expected frequency of cell A, we must first calculate the probability of a case falling into cell A. From this probability, we can obtain the expected frequency of cell A by simply multiplying this probability by the total sample size. How do we obtain the probability that a case will fall into cell A? Well, in reality, the frequency of cell A involves the joint probability of two nonmutually exclusive events. For example, in cell A, event A is the event that the prosecutor charges a noncapital offense, and event B is the event that the victim is white. Recall from our chapter on probability that the probability of two independent events occurring simultaneously is defined as:

$$P(A \text{ and } B) = P(A) \times P(B)$$

Therefore, the probability that a homicide is both a noncapital homicide and involves a white victim is the product of the two separate probabilities. The probability that a homicide is a noncapital homicide is 188/302, or .622. The probability that a homicide involves a white victim is 215/302, or .712. The joint probability that a homicide is both a noncapital and a white victim homicide, then, is (.622)(.712), or .443.

To determine the expected frequency of noncapital/white victim homicides, we simply multiply this probability by the total number of cases: (.443)(302) = 134. Therefore, if the prosecutors' charging decision is unrelated or independent of the race of the victim, we would expect to have 134 noncapital/white victim cases. We place the frequency of 134 in cell A of our expected frequency table displayed in Table 11.7.

**TABLE 11.7. Race of the Victim and Prosecutors' Charging Decision (data from Table 11.1) with Percentages Based on Column Marginals**

| Prosecutors' Charging Decision | White | Nonwhite | |
|---|---|---|---|
| Noncapital | 134 | | 188 |
| Capital | | | 114 |
| Total | 215 | 87 | 302 |

What about cell B, the expected frequency of noncapital/nonwhite murders? We can determine the expected frequency of this cell in the same way. First, let's calculate the joint probability of a noncapital/nonwhite homicide. The probability that a homicide involves a noncapital charge is 188/302, or .622. The probability that a homicide was of a nonwhite victim is 87/302, or .288. The joint probability that a homicide is both noncapital and nonwhite, therefore, is: (.622)(.288) = .179. Given the assumption of independence, then, the expected frequency for cell B is (.179)(302) = 54. This indicates that, if the two variables are unrelated, we would expect to find 54 noncapital/nonwhite homicides. We will put that expected frequency in cell B of Table 11.8.

Following the same procedure we fill in the other two cells of table. For cell C, the expected frequency of capital/white homicides is:

$$P(\text{Capital and White Homicide}) = P(\text{Capital})\ P(\text{White})$$
$$= (114/302)(215/302)$$
$$= (.377)(.712)$$
$$= .268$$

Expected Frequency = (.268)(302) = 81

For cell D, the expected frequency of capital/nonwhite homicides is:

$$P(\text{Capital and Nonwhite Homicide}) = P(\text{Capital})\ P(\text{Nonwhite})$$
$$= (114/302)(87/302)$$
$$= (.377)(.288)$$
$$= .109$$

Expected Frequency = (.109)(302) = 33

Table 11.9 shows the full table of expected cell frequencies. In brackets we also report the observed cell frequencies taken from Table 11.1. Notice that for both sets of frequencies, the cell frequencies sum to the row and column marginals. Now that we have the expected cell frequencies, we can calculate the value of the chi-square statistic and conduct our hypothesis test.

**TABLE 11.8.  Race of the Victim and Prosecutors' Charging Decision (data from Table 11.1) with Percentages Based on Column Marginals**

| Prosecutors' Charging Decision | White | Nonwhite | |
|---|---|---|---|
| Noncapital | 134 | 54 | 188 |
| Capital | ___ | ___ | 114 |
| Total | 215 | 87 | 302 |

**TABLE 11.9. Table of Expected and Observed (in brackets) Cell Frequencies (data from Table 11.1)**

| Prosecutors' Charging Decision | White | Nonwhite | |
|---|---|---|---|
| Noncapital | [118] | [70] | 188 |
| | 134 | 54 | |
| Capital | [97] | [17] | 114 |
| | 81 | 33 | |
| Total | 215 | 87 | 302 |

Let's return to the formula for the chi-square statistic found in Equation 11.1:

$$\chi^2 = \sum_{i=1}^{k} \frac{(f_{o_i} - f_{e_i})^2}{f_{e_i}}$$

In words, this formula gives us four steps to obtain the value of our chi-square, as shown in the box at the bottom of this page.

Table 11.10 provides the necessary calculations for chi-square using the observed and expected frequencies found in Table 11.9. You will notice that the absolute value of the difference between the expected frequency and observed frequency is the same for each cell. This is always the case in a $2 \times 2$ table, but it will not be true for larger tables. When we square the difference between the observed and expected frequencies, we get rid of the negative signs. Note that the denominator always is the expected cell frequency ($f_e$) rather than the observed cell frequency.

We also want you to notice that the obtained value of chi-square will be zero when the expected cell frequencies are exactly the same as the observed cell frequencies. The magnitude of chi-square will increase whenever the difference between the expected and observed cell frequencies becomes larger. Because we square the difference, it does not matter if it is negative or positive—large differences will produce a large chi-square value. Because of this, the critical value of chi-square always is found in the right-hand tail of the chi-square distribution.

In this example, our obtained value of chi-square is 17.57. To make our decision about the validity of the null hypothesis, we need to determine whether the value of our obtained chi-square is above the critical chi-square value at a given significance level. To locate the critical chi-square value, we go to a chi-square table (see Table B.4 of Appendix B). Before we can find the correct critical value of

---

**Step 1.** Subtract the value of the expected frequency from the observed frequency ($f_o - f_e$).
**Step 2.** Square this difference ($f_o - f_e$)$^2$.
**Step 3.** Divide this by the expected frequency ($f_o - f_e$)$^2/f_e$.
**Step 4.** Do this for each cell, and sum the values for all cells.

**TABLE 11.10. Calculating the Chi-Square Statistic
for the Data Reported in Table 11.9**

| Cell | $f_o$ | $f_e$ | $f_o-f_e$ | $(f_o-f_e)^2$ | $(f_o-f_e)^2/f_e$ |
|------|------|------|------|------|------|
| A | 118 | 134 | − 16 | 256 | 1.91 |
| B | 70 | 54 | 16 | 256 | 4.74 |
| C | 97 | 81 | 16 | 256 | 3.16 |
| D | 17 | 33 | − 16 | 256 | 7.76 |
| Total | 302 | 302 | | | 17.57 |

chi-square at a selected alpha level, however, we first need to determine the appropriate degrees of freedom.

In the case of contingency tables, the degrees of freedom are determined not by the size of the sample, but by the number of cells in the table. In the general case, the degrees of freedom in a contingency table are determined as follows:

$$df = (R − 1)(C − 1)$$

The degrees of freedom is equal to the number of rows $(R)$ minus 1 times the number of columns $(C)$ minus 1. In the $2 \times 2$ case of Table 11.1, we have only 1 degree of freedom, so we get: $(2 − 1)(2 − 1) = 1$. These degrees of freedom indicate the number of cell frequencies that are free to vary within a given distribution of row and cell marginals. Let us explain this concept.

Take, for example, a $2 \times 2$ table such as that displayed in Table 11.6. In this table all of the cells are empty. Using this table, we could think of a number of cell frequencies that would sum to the given row and column marginals. In Table 11.7, however, we have fixed one of the cell frequencies at 134. Once we have done this, all of the other cell frequencies are determined because they must sum to the given marginal frequencies. For example, if cell A is 134, then cell B has to be 54 because the row total must be 188. By the same reasoning, cell C must be 81 because the column frequency must be 215. In other words, once one cell frequency is fixed in a $2 \times 2$ table, the remaining cells can only take on one value. Thus, there is only one cell frequency that is free to vary and, hence, one degree of freedom.

Let's get back to the example at hand. To test the extent to which there is a significant relationship between prosecutors' decisions and the race of the homicide victim, let's adopt an alpha level of .05. Using this alpha level and our degrees of freedom, we can find the critical value of chi-square from Table B.4 in Appendix B. Going across the table until we find our desired level of significance (.05) and using 1 degree of freedom, we see that the critical value of chi-square necessary to reject the null hypothesis is 3.841. Our decision rule, then, is to reject the null hypothesis if the obtained chi-square is greater than or equal to 3.841.

The chi-square value we obtained from our statistical test was 17.57. This value is greater than our critical value, so we can reject the null hypothesis that there is no relationship between a homicide victim's race and the prosecutors' charging decision. Using the cell percentages to interpret this relationship, it appears that offenders who kill whites are more likely to be charged by prosecutors with a capital offense than those who kill nonwhites.

## 11.4 A COMPUTATIONAL FORMULA
## FOR EXPECTED CELL FREQUENCIES

By calculating the expected frequencies as we did in our example, we have shown how they are based on the multiplication rule of probabilities. We hope that this example has helped you understand the rationale behind the chi-square statistic. However, the use of the multiplication rule in obtaining expected frequencies is somewhat complicated and tedious, particularly when we have larger tables. An easier way to obtain the expected cell frequencies is through the following formula:

$$\text{Expected Cell Frequency of cell } f_{ij} = \frac{RM_iCM_j}{n} \tag{11.2}$$

where
$RM$ = the row marginal for row $i$
$CM$ = the column marginal for column $j$

In words, to calculate the expected frequency for any cell, simply multiply the row marginal for that cell by its column marginal and divide this product by the total sample size. Applying this simple formula, we can recalculate the expected frequencies in Table 11.10:

Cell A   (188)(215)/302 = 134

Cell B   (188)(87)/302  =  54

Cell C   (114)(215)/302 =  81

Cell D   (114)(87)/302  =  33

You will notice that these are exactly equal to the expected frequencies we obtained when we used the conditional probability method of calculation. The row/column marginal method, however, is a bit easier to use, so we use it throughout the rest of the chapter.

## 11.5 A COMPUTATIONAL FORMULA FOR
## THE GENERAL CHI-SQUARE CASE

In this section, we go through another example of the chi-square test. However, this time we use an easier-to-calculate computational formula. In this example, we also discover that the chi-square significance test is not the end of our research job.

Let's use a data set obtained by one of the authors to examine delinquency within a large sample of high school students. Table 11.11 shows the joint distribution between two variables from this survey, the grades received by a student in their sophomore year in high school and self-reported involvement in theft during the junior year. Social control theory (Hirschi, 1969) would lead us to predict that there would be a significant inverse (negative) relationship between school performance and delinquency. That is, we would predict that students with higher grades would tend to have lower rates of delinquency. Is this true for the data in Table 11.11?

**TABLE 11.11. Self-Reported Acts of Petty Theft by Grades Received in Last Year of School (Observed Frequencies)**

| Grades in School | Self-Reported Acts of Theft | | | |
|---|---|---|---|---|
| | 0 | 1–5 | 6+ | |
| As | 418 | 166 | 56 | 640 |
| Bs | 762 | 345 | 155 | 1262 |
| Cs | 307 | 157 | 123 | 587 |
| Ds and Fs | 23 | 19 | 20 | 62 |
| Total | 1510 | 687 | 354 | 2551 |

Let's conduct a hypothesis test to explore this question. Our null hypothesis is that there is no relationship between the two variables. The alternative hypothesis is that there is a relationship:

$H_0$: There is no relationship between school grades and self-reported involvement in theft: $\chi^2 = 0$.

$H_1$: There is a relationship between school grades and self-reported involvement in theft: $\chi^2 > 0$.

We conduct our hypothesis test using the chi-square statistic and chi-square distribution. Remember that the chi-square test does not tell us the direction of the relationship because the obtained value of chi-square always is equal to or greater than zero. We examine the exact nature of the relationship later if we find that a significant relationship exists.

The next step is to select our alpha level and obtain the corresponding critical chi-square value. We have a $4 \times 3$ table, which means that we have $(4 - 1)(3 - 1) = 6$ degrees of freedom. Let's select an alpha level of .001 for this test. We now go to our chi-square table and find the critical chi-square value with 6 degrees of freedom and an alpha level of .001. Going down the column of degrees of freedom until we find 6, then over the row of alpha values until we find .001, we see that our critical chi-square value is 22.457. Our decision rule will be to reject the null hypothesis if $\chi^2_{obt} \geq 22.457$.

Next we calculate what the expected cell frequencies would be under the assumption of the null hypothesis. Using our row/column marginal formula (Equation 11.2) we calculate the following expected frequencies:

Cell A   $(640 \times 1510)/2551 = 379$

Cell B   $(640 \times 687)/2551 = 172$

Cell C   $(640 \times 354)/2551 = 89$

Cell D   $(1262 \times 1510)/2551 = 747$

Cell E   $(1262 \times 687)/2551 = 340$

Cell F   $(1262 \times 354)/2551 = 175$

Cell G     (587 × 1510)/2551 = 347
Cell H     (587 × 687)/2551 = 158
Cell I     (587 × 354)/2551 = 81
Cell J     (62 × 1510)/2551 = 37
Cell K     (62 × 687)/2551 = 17
Cell L     (62 × 354)/2551 = 9

These expected cell frequencies are placed in their correct cells in Table 11.12. Now, let's go through the steps of calculating the chi-square statistic:

Step 1. Subtract the value of the expected frequency from observed frequency $(f_o - f_e)$.
Step 2. Square this difference $(f_o - f_e)^2$.
Step 3. Divide this by the expected frequency $(f_o - f_e)^2/f_e$.
Step 4. Do this for each cell, and sum the values for all cells.

Table 11.13 shows all the calculations to obtain our chi-square value using this original formula. You see that we have a chi-square of 64.48. There is an easier-to-use computation formula for the chi-square statistic that reduces the number of arithmetic operations that you have to perform:

$$\chi^2 = \sum \frac{f_o^2}{f_e} - n \tag{11.3}$$

In this formula, the observed frequency of each cell is first squared and then divided by the expected cell frequency. We do this for each cell and then add these results across each of the cells. From this total sum, we subtract the sample size. This value represents the obtained chi-square. Table 11.14 displays the calculations for the high school delinquency data (Tables 11.11 and 11.12). Not surprisingly, the obtained value of chi-square of 64.50, which, within rounding error, is the same as the chi-square we found using the more complicated definitional formula.

The final step in our hypothesis test is to make a decision about the validity of our null hypothesis. Because the obtained chi-square value (64.48 or 64.50) is greater than our critical value (22.457), we can reject the null hypothesis. This decision only

**TABLE 11.12. Self-Reported Acts of Petty Theft by Grades Received in Last Year of School (Expected Frequencies)**

| Grades in School | Self-Reported Acts of Theft | | | |
|---|---|---|---|---|
| | 0 | 1–5 | 6+ | |
| As | 379 | 172 | 89 | 640 |
| Bs | 747 | 340 | 175 | 1262 |
| Cs | 347 | 158 | 81 | 586 |
| Ds and Fs | 37 | 17 | 9 | 63 |
| Total | 1510 | 687 | 354 | 2551 |

**TABLE 11.13.  Calculating the Chi-Square Statistic for the Data from Tables 11.8 and 11.12\***

| Cell | $f_o$ | $f_e$ | $f_o - f_e$ | $(f_o - f_e)^2$ | $(f_o - f_e)^2/f_e$ |
|------|------|------|------|------|------|
| A | 418 | 379 | 39 | 1521 | 4.01 |
| B | 166 | 172 | −6 | 36 | .21 |
| C | 56 | 89 | −33 | 1089 | 12.24 |
| D | 762 | 747 | 15 | 225 | .30 |
| E | 345 | 340 | 5 | 25 | .07 |
| F | 155 | 175 | −20 | 400 | 2.29 |
| G | 307 | 347 | −40 | 1600 | 4.61 |
| H | 157 | 158 | −1 | 1 | .01 |
| I | 123 | 81 | 42 | 1764 | 21.77 |
| J | 23 | 37 | −14 | 196 | 5.3 |
| K | 19 | 17 | 2 | 4 | .23 |
| L | 20 | 9 | 11 | 121 | 13.44 |

\*Degrees of freedom: $(4-1)(3-1) = 6$; $\chi^2 = 64.48$; critical $\chi^2$ with $\alpha = .001 = 22.457$.

indicates, however, that school grades and self-reported theft are significantly related to one another. In other words, that they are not independent events.

We should now refine this interpretation by calculating appropriate percentages from the frequencies in the table. Because social control theory would lead us to define school grades as the independent variable, we would like to know whether poor grades are related to higher rates of delinquency. We should therefore calculate our percentages based on the independent variable marginals, which in this case are the row marginals. To obtain the percentage value in cell A, then, we divide the frequency in cell A (418) by the row marginal of 640 to obtain 65.3 percent. All cell percentages and observed frequencies (in parentheses) are displayed in Table 11.15.

**TABLE 11.14.  Calculating Chi-Square Using the Computational Formula for Delinquency Data in Tables 11.11 and 11.12**

| Cell | $f_o$ | $f_o^2$ | $f_o^2/f_e$ | | |
|------|------|------|------|------|------|
| A | 418 | 174,724 | 174,724/379 | = | 461.01 |
| B | 166 | 27,556 | 27,556/172 | = | 160.21 |
| C | 56 | 3,136 | 3136/89 | = | 35.24 |
| D | 762 | 580,644 | 580,644/747 | = | 777.30 |
| E | 345 | 119,025 | 119,025/340 | = | 350.07 |
| F | 155 | 24,025 | 24,025/175 | = | 137.29 |
| G | 307 | 94,249 | 94,249/347 | = | 271.61 |
| H | 157 | 24,649 | 24,649/158 | = | 156.01 |
| I | 123 | 15,129 | 15,129/81 | = | 186.78 |
| J | 23 | 529 | 529/37 | = | 14.30 |
| K | 19 | 361 | 361/17 | = | 21.24 |
| L | 20 | 400 | 400/9 | = | 44.44 |
| | | | **Total** | **=** | **2615.50** |

$$\chi^2 = \sum \frac{f_o^2}{f_e} - n$$

$$\chi^2 = 2615.50 - 2551 = 64.50$$

**TABLE 11.15.  Percentages for Self-Reported Acts of Petty Theft by Grades Received in Last Year of School**

| Grades in School | Self-Reported Acts of Theft | | | |
| | 0 | 1–5 | 6+ | |
|---|---|---|---|---|
| As | 418 (65.3%) | 166 (25.9%) | 56 (8.8%) | 640 (100%) |
| Bs | 762 (60.4%) | 345 (27.3%) | 155 (12.3%) | 1262 (100%) |
| Cs | 307 (52.3%) | 157 (26.7%) | 123 (21.0%) | 587 (100%) |
| Ds and Fs | 23 (37.1%) | 19 (30.6%) | 20 (32.3%) | 62 (100%) |
| Total | 1510 | 687 | 354 | 2551 |

Looking at Table 11.15, we can see that less than 10 percent (8.8 percent) of those youths who received mostly As reported committing six or more acts of delinquency. This increased to 12.3 percent for those getting mostly Bs, 21 percent for those with mostly C grades, and 32.3 percent for those who said that they received mostly Ds and Fs. Consistent with social control theory, then, there does appear to be a significant relationship between an adolescent's grades in school and self-reported delinquency. Results from our sample of high school students indicate that students who did poorly in school were more likely to report committing acts of delinquency than students who did well.

## 11.6 LIMITATIONS OF THE CHI-SQUARE TEST FOR INDEPENDENCE

Here's an interesting question. Suppose that the researcher in the high school example could only obtain a sample of 255 high school students rather than 2551? What would happen to the chi-square statistical test in this case? Table 11.16 shows the cross-tabulation of grades in school and self-reported acts of theft for 255 hypothetical students. The percentages indicate that the relationship between grades and delinquency is essentially the same as in our previous tables. Approximately 8 percent of those students getting As report committing six or more thefts. This increases to approximately 13 percent of those getting Bs, 20 percent for those getting Cs, and 33 percent for those getting Ds and Fs.

When we calculate our chi-square statistic, however, we find that it is only 6.06. These calculations are also shown in Table 11.16. This compares with a chi-square of 64.48 (or 64.50) that was obtained using the larger sample. With the same six degrees of freedom, the chi-square statistic for the small sample table is not significant at the .001 level ($\chi^2_{crit} = 22.457$), contrary to our earlier finding. In fact, this obtained value is not even significant at the .01 or .05 level. With a sample size of 255 rather than 2551, we must fail to reject the null hypothesis and conclude that there is no association between grades in school and self-reported theft. Why are we led to such different conclusions from the chi-square test when the percentages indicate that the two variables are related to one another to about the same degree?

**TABLE 11.16. Hypothetical Data for Self-Reported Acts of Petty Theft by Grades Received in Last Year of School**

| Grades in School | Self-Reported Acts of Theft | | | |
|---|---|---|---|---|
| | 0 | 1–5 | 6+ | |
| As | 42 [38] (65.6%) | 17 [17] (26.6%) | 5 [9] (7.8%) | 64 (100%) |
| Bs | 76 [75] (60.3%) | 34 [34] (27.0%) | 16 [17] (12.7%) | 126 (100%) |
| Cs | 31 [35] (52.5%) | 16 [16] (27.1%) | 12 [8] (20.3%) | 59 (100%) |
| Ds and Fs | 2 [3] (33.3%) | 2 [2] (33.8%) | 2 [1] (33.3%) | 6 (100%) |
| Total | 151 | 69 | 35 | 255 |

| Cell | $f_o$ | $f_o^2$ | $f_o^2/f_e$ |
|---|---|---|---|
| A | 42 | 1764 | $1764/38 = 46.42$ |
| B | 17 | 289 | $289/17 = 17.0$ |
| C | 5 | 25 | $25/9 = 2.78$ |
| D | 76 | 5776 | $5776/75 = 77.01$ |
| E | 34 | 1156 | $1156/34 = 34.0$ |
| F | 16 | 256 | $256/17 = 15.06$ |
| G | 31 | 961 | $961/35 = 27.46$ |
| H | 16 | 256 | $256/16 = 16.0$ |
| I | 12 | 144 | $144/8 = 18.0$ |
| J | 2 | 4 | $4/3 = 1.33$ |
| K | 2 | 4 | $4/2 = 2.0$ |
| L | 2 | 4 | $4/1 = 4.0$ |
| | | | Total    261.06 |

$$x^2 = \sum \frac{f_o^2}{f_e} - n$$
$$= 261.06 - 255$$
$$= 6.06$$

You may remember from other chapters that with very large samples, we were likely to reflect the null hypothesis even when we observed only small differences between two variables (or groups). This is because the probability of observing an extreme result decreases as sample size increases when the null hypothesis is true. With any statistical test, we are more likely to reject the null hypothesis with large samples than we are with small samples. In general, the value of chi-square increases at the same rate as the sample size. That is, if the sample is increased by a factor of four, the obtained chi-square value will also tend to be four times higher.

The important lesson to be drawn from this is the size of the obtained test statistic tells us very little about the strength of the relationship between two variables. From earlier chapters, you should be aware that the strength of the association between two variables is a separate issue from statistical significance. For this reason, what we need, in addition to our chi-square test of significance, is a *measure of association*. This *measure of association* tells us about the *strength* of the relationship between two variables. There are several measures of association, which we discuss next.

## 11.7 MEASURES OF ASSOCIATION FOR CATEGORICAL VARIABLES: THE CASE OF NOMINAL-LEVEL VARIABLES AND 2 × 2 TABLES

The measures of association we discuss in this section describe the *strength*, or *magnitude*, of the relationship between two categorical variables. One important property that a good measure of association should have is that it should be easy to interpret. The easiest measures to interpret are those which take on the value of zero when there is no relationship between the two variables and a maximum value of 1 ($\pm 1$) when there is a perfect association between the two, no matter what size the contingency table is. Measures that can be interpreted in this way allow comparisons across different contingency tables.

A second property that an ideal measure of association should have is a *proportionate reduction in error* (*PRE*) interpretation. For categorical variables, a PRE measure would compare the amount of prediction error we would make without knowing the independent variable to the amount of prediction error we would make when knowing the independent variable. In other words, a PRE measure of association tells us how much better we can predict a dependent variable with the information we have about the independent variable than without it.

If knowledge about an independent variable tells us nothing about a dependent variable, then our predictions will not improve. In this instance, we would have no association between the two variables and the value of the PRE measure of association would be zero. If, however, knowledge about an independent variable allowed us to predict the distribution of the categories of the dependent variable without error, we would have a perfect association between the two variables and the value of the PRE measure would be $\pm 1$. The PRE values that fall between these two extremes of zero and 1 indicate how much better we are at predicting the dependent variable with our knowledge of the independent variable. The amount by which we can reduce our prediction error, then, serves as our interpretation of the association between the two variables.

To help you understand PRE measures and how they reflect improvement in prediction, carefully examine Table 11.17. Here we display several panels that show the joint association between two variables ($V_1$ and $V_2$) for 900 persons. Does knowing a person's position on $V_2$ help us predict their position on $V_1$? In panel *A*, the cases are evenly distributed throughout each cell in the table. The same proportion of respondents fall in each cell. In this case, knowing the category a person falls into on $V_2$ will not help us predict that person's category of $V_1$ at all. For example, if we knew that a person fell into the first category of $V_2$, what would we predict his or her $V_1$ category to be? Because it is equally likely that he or she will be in the first (100/300), second (100/300), or third (100/300) category of $V_1$, we will get absolutely no help in our predictions from knowledge of $V_2$. In this case our PRE measure of association between the two variables will be 0.00. The variables are unrelated to one another.

In panel *B*, however, knowing the distribution of cases within $V_2$ allows us to predict the distribution of $V_1$ with perfect accuracy. For example, if we know that someone falls into the first category of $V_2$, we know that he or she always will fall

**TABLE 11.17. Interpretation of PRE Measures Using a Second-Independent Variable ($V_2$) to Help Predict a First-Dependent Variable ($V_1$)**

| A | $V_1$ | | | | |
|---|---|---|---|---|---|
| $V_2$ | 3 | 2 | 1 | | |
| 1 | 100 | 100 | 100 | 300 | |
| 2 | 100 | 100 | 100 | 300 | |
| 3 | 100 | 100 | 100 | 300 | |
| Total | 300 | 300 | 300 | 900 | PRE = 0.00 |

| B | $V_1$ | | | | |
|---|---|---|---|---|---|
| $V_2$ | 3 | 2 | 1 | | |
| 1 | | | 300 | 300 | |
| 2 | | 300 | | 300 | |
| 3 | 300 | | | 300 | |
| Total | 300 | 300 | 300 | 900 | PRE = +1.00 |

| C | $V_1$ | | | | |
|---|---|---|---|---|---|
| $V_2$ | 3 | 2 | 1 | | |
| 1 | 300 | | | 300 | |
| 2 | | 300 | | 300 | |
| 3 | | | 300 | 300 | |
| Total | 300 | 300 | 300 | 900 | PRE = −1.00 |

| D | $V_1$ | | | | |
|---|---|---|---|---|---|
| $V_2$ | 3 | 2 | 1 | | |
| 1 | 15 | 60 | 225 | 300 | |
| 2 | 100 | 180 | 20 | 300 | |
| 3 | 185 | 60 | 50 | 300 | |
| Total | 300 | 300 | 300 | 900 | 0.00 > PRE < 1.00 |

into the first category of $V_1$. If we know that the person falls into the second category of $V_2$, we know that he or she always will fall into the second category of $V_1$, and so on. In this case, we can predict the distribution of $V_1$ without error if we know the distribution of $V_2$. This type of association also is displayed in panel C. In this case, however, the direction of the relationship is reversed. In both cases, however, the PRE measure is equal to 1.00.

Panel D in Table 11.17 illustrates a final example. In this case, knowing the distribution of $V_2$ will help us predict the distribution of $V_1$, but not with perfect accuracy. Those who fall into the first category of $V_2$ *tend* to fall into the second category of $V_1$, those who fall into the second category of $V_2$ *tend* to fall into the second category of $V_1$, and so on. Most of the cases fall on the diagonal from the bottom left cell to the top right cell. However, we will make some errors in prediction. Not all of those who fall into the first category of $V_2$ also fall into the first category of $V_1$. The point is that, by knowing the distribution of $V_2$, we decrease the amount of prediction errors we would have compared to not knowing the distribution of $V_2$. In this instance, the PRE measure would lie somewhere between 0.00 and $\pm$ 1.00. The more strongly the two variables are related, the closer our PRE measure of association moves away from 0.00 and toward $\pm$ 1.00. The general formula for a PRE measure is as follows:

$$\frac{\text{Prediction Errors without} - \text{Prediction Errors with}}{\text{Independent Variable}} \frac{\text{Independent Variable}}{\text{Prediction Errors without Independent Variable}}$$

Think of the process of estimating the reduction in prediction errors as involving two stages. In the first stage, we predict without knowledge of the independent variable which category a case falls into for the dependent variable. In the second stage we again predict the category a case falls into for this same variable, but this time we base our prediction on our knowledge about the distribution of the independent variable. If the two variables are related, then knowing someone's position on the indpendent variable will help us predict their position on the dependent variable. Hence, we reduce our prediction errors. The stronger the two variables are related, the more we reduce our errors.

As an example, suppose you were asked to predict blindly whether each of 100 persons were either "well-off" (defined as having a yearly income of $50,000 or more) or "not well-off" (having a yearly income under $50,000). If you knew nothing else about these 100 persons, you would likely predict many cases incorrectly. Now, let's assume that you had to do the same thing again, but this time you were given information about each person's level of education. For example, let's say you were told whether or not a person's education level was either "less than college" or "college or more."

Because research indicates that education and income are positively associated, you would probably be better able to predict a person's income. You would more likely predict that someone has a higher income if you knew that they had a college education. You would still make some prediction errors using someone's education to predict income, but the number of errors you make would generally be fewer than without it. The stronger the association between education and income, the fewer errors you would make. This lower rate of errors would be reflected in a nonzero value of the PRE measure. We examine several measures of association in the sections that follow.

## Phi Coefficient

In examining measures of association with categorical variables, let's start out with the most simple case, a 2 × 2 table with nominal-level data. There are several PRE measures of association for the 2 × 2 case with nominal-level data. The first of these is based on the value of the chi-square statistic itself and is called the *phi coefficient* (φ). Although the phi coefficient itself does not have a PRE interpretation, its squared value (φ²) does. The value of φ² is interpreted as the amount of variance in one variable explained by the other. Phi and φ² can be calculated from the following formulas:

$$\phi = \sqrt{\frac{\chi^2}{n}}$$  (11.4)

$$\phi^2 = \frac{\chi^2}{n}$$  (11.5)

The values of phi and phi squared range from zero to 1. Like the correlation coefficient ($r$), larger values of phi indicate a stronger relationship between two variables, and larger values of phi squared indicate more variance explained.

Using our data set from the sample of high school students, Table 11.18 shows the relationship between two dichotomous variables, gender and self-reported theft offenses. In order to calculate the phi and phi-squared coefficients from this data set, we first need to determine the value of the chi-square statistic. We have provided the results of a chi-square test at the bottom of Table 11.18. However, you should practice calculating chi-square values by performing the arithmetic procedures yourself.

**TABLE 11.18. Relationship between Gender and Self-Reported Petty Theft Offenses (expected frequencies in brackets)**

| Gender | Number of Self-Reported Thefts | | |
|---|---|---|---|
| | 0 | 1+ | |
| Male | 625 [754] (49.1%) | 648 [519] (50.9%) | 1273 |
| Female | 891 [762] (69.3%) | 395 [524] (30.7%) | 1286 |
| Total | 1516 (100%) | 1043 (100%) | 2559 |

| Cell | $f_o^2$ | $f_o^2/f_e$ |
|---|---|---|
| A | 390,625 | 390,625/754 = 518.07 |
| B | 419,904 | 419,904/519 = 809.06 |
| C | 793,881 | 793,881/762 = 1041.84 |
| D | 156,025 | 156,025/524 = 297.76 |
| | | Total = 2666.73 |

$\chi^2 = (2666.73 - 2559) = 107.73$

To test the null hypothesis of no relationship between gender and theft violations, let's say we selected an alpha level of .05. With $(2 - 1)(2 - 1) = 1$ degree of freedom, the critical chi-square value is 3.84. As the bottom of Table 11.18 indicates, the obtained chi-square value for this data is 107.73. The obtained value of chi-square far exceeds the critical value necessary to reject the null hypothesis. We can therefore conclude that there is a significant relationship between gender and the number of thefts students engaged in. From our contingency table, we can see that a larger percentage of males than females engaged in acts of theft.

From this test, we know that there is a significant relationship between gender and stealing, but how strong is this relationship? With our chi-square value of 107.73, we can very easily calculate our phi coefficient to be .205 ($\sqrt{107.73/2559}$), and phi squared to be .042. The phi coefficient indicates that the relationship between gender and self-reported theft is moderately low. To reiterate, the PRE measure, phi squared, $(.205)^2 = .042$, indicates the amount of variance explained in theft by knowledge of a student's gender. Thus, only 4 percent of the variance in self-reported theft is explained by gender. Both of these measures indicate, then, that gender and self-reported delinquency are not very strongly related to one another, even though they are significantly related. Unfortunately, phi and phi squared are appropriate *only* for $2 \times 2$ tables.

## Yule's Q

Another measure of association appropriate only for $2 \times 2$ tables is called Yule's $Q$. Unlike the phi coefficient, which is only applicable for nominal-level data, Yule's $Q$ may be used for both nominal- or ordinal-level data. When the cell frequencies of a table are labeled A through D as in Table 11.2, Yule's $Q$ is defined by the following formula:

$$Q = \frac{(AD) - (BC)}{(AD) + (BC)} \tag{11.6}$$

Notice that $Q$ is formed by the cross-product of the pair of cell frequencies diagonal to one another. When there is no association between two variables, the value of $Q$ is zero. Its maximum value is $\pm 1.0$. You should also notice that one of the problems with $Q$ as a measure of association is that it will be $-1.0$ or $+1.0$ whenever one of the cell frequencies is zero, even in the absence of a perfect relationship between the two variables. For this reason, Yule's $Q$ is very sensitive to zero-cell frequencies, and you should carefully inspect a table for zero cells before calculating and reporting $Q$. For the data in Table 11.18 the value of $Q$ is:

$$Q = \frac{(625)(395) - (648)(891)}{(625)(395) + (648)(891)}$$

$$= \frac{246,875 - 577,368}{246,875 + 577,368}$$

$$= -.40$$

The magnitude of $-.40$ for $Q$ tells us that we would make 40 percent fewer errors in predicting acts of theft by knowing a person's gender. The negative sign of the relationship for $Q$ should be interpreted as follows: those who are classified on the first category of the independent variable are more likely to be in the second category of the dependent variable than in the first category. Similarly, those who are classified in the second category of the independent variable are more likely to be in the first category of the dependent variable. In this data set, males (the first category of gender) are more likely to be in the 1+ theft group (the second category of self-reported theft) than in the 0 theft group. Females (the second category of gender) are more likely to be in the 0 theft group (the first category of self-reported theft) than in the 1+ theft group. A positive value of $Q$ would have indicated that those who are classified in the first category of the independent variable are also more likely to be in the first category of the dependent variable than in the second category. Similarly, those who are classified in the second category of the independent variable are more likely to be in the second category of the dependent variable.

## Lambda

Another PRE measure of association for contingency tables using nominal-level data is *Lambda* ($\lambda$). Unlike both Yule's $Q$ and the phi coefficient, Lambda does not require a $2 \times 2$ table. It is, however, generally restricted to nominal-level data. Lambda ranges in magnitude from zero to 1.

Lambda is based on the prediction of the modal category of the dependent variable, that category which has the highest frequency of cases. To calculate lambda, we first make a prediction about the classification of each case on the dependent variable based on the mode for that variable.

In Table 11.18, for example, the self-reported number of thefts is the dependent variable. The mode in this instance is "zero reported thefts" because more cases fall into this category than the "1+ reported thefts" category (1516 v. 1043). If we were to predict which category each of the 2559 persons fell into, without any other information available to us, we would minimize the number of errors we would make by placing them all into the modal category ("no reported thefts"). If we were to make the prediction that all 2559 persons committed 0 acts of theft, we would be correct in 1516 cases because 1516 persons actually fell into this category. We would, however, make $(2559 - 1516) = 1043$ prediction errors, because 1043 persons committed one or more acts of theft.

The next step is to use information about the independent variable to try and reduce this number of prediction errors. To do this, we calculate how many errors we would make by predicting that all cases fall into the modal category of the dependent variable *within* each level of the independent variable. For males, the modal category of the dependent variable is "1+ reported thefts" because this cell has the greatest frequency for males. Based on this, we predict that all 1273 males fall into that category (1+ thefts). Because only 648 males actually fall into this category, we make $(1273 - 648) = 625$ errors. For females, the modal category of the dependent variable is "0 reported thefts." Based on this, we will predict that all 1286 females fall into that category. Because only 891 females actually commit no thefts, we make $(1286 - 891) = 395$ errors.

Combining the number of prediction errors made for both males and females using this method of prediction, we make a total of $(625 + 395) = 1020$ errors. Without using the information from the independent variable we made 1043 errors. When we use the information from the independent variable, then, we make 23 fewer prediction errors. We calculate lambda for this data set with the following formula:

$$\lambda = \frac{\text{Number of Errors Using Mode of } y - \text{Number of Errors Using Mode of } y \text{ within Levels of } x}{\text{Number of Errors Using Mode of } y} \quad (11.7)$$

$$= \frac{1043 - 1020}{1043}$$

$$= .022$$

The value of lambda in this example is only .022. When this value is multiplied by 100, it tells us the proportionate reduction in prediction errors when using the independent variable to predict the dependent variable. In our example, we can reduce our theft prediction errors by 2 percent by basing our predictions on knowledge about a youth's gender. This is not very much! This indicates that gender and self-reported theft are not very strongly related.

Please note that lambda and other PRE measures should be interpreted in terms of the *proportionate* reduction in error, not the percent reduction in prediction errors. Without using gender to predict self-reported theft, we made 1043 errors out of 2559 predictions, for an error rate of approximately 41 percent. When we used gender to help us predict self-reported theft, we reduced this to 1020 errors out of 2559 predictions, an error rate of approximately 40 percent. We actually reduced our errors, then, by only 41 percent $-$ 40 percent $= 1$ percent, but the proportionate reduction in errors is 2 percent. We have reduced our original number of errors by 2 percent because 1 percent of 41 percent is approximately 2 percent. Hence the label "proportionate" reduction in errors.

One other note about lambda: it is generally an asymmetric measure of association. This means that the magnitude of lambda depends on which variable is designated as the independent variable and which the dependent variable. That is, lambda will be different depending on which variable is treated as the independent variable. For example, in Table 11.18, if we had treated self-reported theft as the independent variable and used it to predict gender, our lambda would have been .199. This is greater than the lambda we obtained when we used gender to predict delinquency (.022). It is a good idea, therefore, to state specifically which variable is the independent and which one the dependent variable, particularly when using the lambda coefficient.

Another disadvantage of lambda as a measure of association is that it may have a value of zero even when the two variables being examined are not completely independent. This occurs whenever one of the categories of the dependent variable has a much greater frequency than the others so that, no matter what category of the independent variable we examine, the modal category of the dependent variable is the same. Because of this problem, whenever the marginal frequencies are not approximately equal, a measure of association other than lambda should be used. We discuss yet another measure of association next!

## Goodman and Kruskal's Tau$_{yx}$

In instances when lambda is not appropriate, another useful measure of association with nominal-level data is Goodman and Kruskal's tau$_{yx}$ (given by the Greek letter for tau, $\tau_{yx}$). Like lambda, tau$_{yx}$ may be used on 2 × 2 or larger tables and ranges in magnitude from zero (meaning no association between the two variables) to 1.00 (meaning a perfect association between the two variables). In addition, the prediction logic of tau$_{yx}$ is comparable to that of lambda.

Let's again use the data in Table 11.18 as our example. Suppose that we had to categorize all 2559 students into one of the two categories of the dependent variable (self-reported theft) in such a way that we had to place exactly 1516 persons into the first column and 1043 persons into the second column. In doing this, we are not told the gender of the student. Let's begin by placing 1516 persons into the first column. Because the proportion of people who do not actually belong in this column is equal to .4076 (1043/2559), we can expect to make 1516(.4076) = 618 prediction errors. We then assign 1043 persons to the second column. Because the proportion of people who do not actually belong in this column is equal to .5924 (1516/2559), we can expect to make 1043(.5924) = 618 more prediction errors. Combining these two sources of error, we would make (618 + 618) = 1236 errors in predicting self-reported theft without knowledge of gender.

Now let's suppose we have information about students' gender. As before, we want to know whether knowing a person's gender will help us predict if he or she has committed a theft. Also as before, if the two variables are independent, then knowledge of gender will not help us reduce our errors. How do we calculate the number of errors we will make in the long run when we know a person's gender? If we know that a student belongs in the first row and is therefore a male, we can use this information in our prediction.

For example, we know that exactly 625 of the 1273 males must be placed in the first column of row 1. Because the proportion of males who do not actually belong here is .509 (648/1273), we can expect to make 625(.509) = 318 errors. We must now place 648 males in the second column of the first row. Because the proportion of males who do not actually belong here is .491 (625/1273), we can expect to make another 648(.491) = 318 errors. If we know someone is a male, therefore, we will expect to make 636 (318 + 318) errors in predicting whether or not they committed theft.

The next step is to assign the 1286 female students in the second row. We know that exactly 891 of the 1286 females must be placed in the first column of row 2. Because the proportion of females who do not actually belong here is .307 (395/1286), we can expect to make 891(.307) = 274 prediction errors. We must now place 395 females in the second column of the second row. Because the proportion of females who do not actually belong here is .693 (891/1286), we can expect to make another 395(.693) = 274 errors. If we know someone is a female, therefore, we will expect to make 548 (274 + 274) errors in predicting whether or not they committed theft.

When we add these errors together, we can see that by knowing a student's gender, we can expect to make 636 errors for the males and 548 errors for the women.

Knowing gender, therefore, we will make 1184 (636 + 548) prediction errors. Without knowing gender, you will remember, we would expect to make 1236 prediction errors.

Remembering our general prediction equation for PRE measures, we can estimate our value of $tau_{yx}$ to be:

$$\tau_{yx} = \frac{1236 - 1184}{1236}$$

$$= .042$$

By multiplying this value by 100, we see that we have proportionately reduced our prediction errors by a mere 4 percent. You should note that the value we have obtained here for $tau_{yx}$ is the same as we found for phi squared. For a $2 \times 2$ table $tau_{yx} = \phi^2$. You should also note that as with lambda, Goodman and Kruskal's tau is generally asymmetric. In the $2 \times 2$ case, the value of tau is the same no matter which variable is designated as the independent or dependent variable. In larger tables, however, you generally obtain different results depending on which you treat as the independent and dependent variables. In the case of tables larger than $2 \times 2$, then, $tau_{yx} \neq tau_{xy}$.

The statistical significance of both phi and lambda can be tested with the chi-square test for independence calculated from the frequencies. The null hypothesis we are testing in this case is that the value of phi/lambda in the population is zero. For our student data investigating gender and delinquency, the obtained chi-square value was 107.73, whereas the critical value with 1 degree of freedom was 3.84. Because the obtained value of chi-square is greater than the critical value, we can reject the null hypothesis that phi/lambda equals zero and conclude that gender and self-reported theft are associated in the population. Because the magnitudes of our phi (.21, $\phi^2 = .04$) and lambda (.022) are very small, however, we must also conclude that the relationship is weak.

We can also test for the statistical significance of Yule's $Q$. For this statistic, the significance test is a $z$ test, where:

$$z = \frac{Q}{\sigma_Q} \tag{11.8}$$

where

$\sigma_Q$ = estimated standard error of $Q$

$$= \sqrt{(.25)(1 - Q^2)^2 \left(\frac{1}{A} + \frac{1}{B} + \frac{1}{C} + \frac{1}{D}\right)}$$

For our previous example, the standard error can be calculated as:

$$\sigma_Q = \sqrt{\frac{1}{4}[1 - (-.40)^2]^2 \left(\frac{1}{625} + \frac{1}{648} + \frac{1}{891} + \frac{1}{395}\right)}$$

$$= \sqrt{\frac{1}{4}(1 - .16)^2 (.0068)}$$

$$= \sqrt{\frac{1}{4}(.84)^2\,(.0068)} \qquad = \sqrt{\frac{1}{4}(.7056)\,(.0068)} \qquad = \sqrt{(.1764)\,(.0068)}$$

$$= \sqrt{.0012} \qquad = .035$$

The $z$ test for the null hypothesis that $Q$ is equal to zero is:

$$z = \frac{-.40}{.035} \qquad = -11.43$$

Using an alpha of .01, the critical value of $z$ for a one-tailed test is $-2.33$. Because the obtained value of $z$ is less than the critical value, we would reject the null hypothesis that the value of Yule's $Q$ in the population is zero.

So far we have discussed four measures of association for nominal-level data: lambda and Goodman and Kruskal's $\text{tau}_{yx}$ that can be used with tables of any size, and phi (and $\phi^2$) and Yule's $Q$ that can be used only for 2 × 2 tables. The features of these measures are summarized in the box below. In the next section, we discuss measures of association that can be used with ordinal-level variables.

## 11.8 MEASURES OF ASSOCIATION FOR RANK-ORDERED CATEGORICAL VARIABLES: THE CASE OF ORDINAL-LEVEL VARIABLES

The measures we are going to discuss in this section may be used for tables of any size, but are appropriate only for ordinal-level data. With rank-ordered categories, we can talk not only about the *strength* of a relationship but also about its direction as well. For example, when considering the two variables $V_1$ and $V_2$, if persons are classified as "low"/"low," "medium"/"medium," and "high"/"high," then there is a *positive* association between the two variables. In this instance, higher scores on one variable are associated with higher scores on the other. If, however, those who score "low" on one variable score "high" on the other, then there is a *negative* association between the two variables. In this case, higher scores on one variable are associated with lower scores on the other. We could not make these direction statements using nominal-level variables because the levels were simply named categories with no rank order.

Before we discuss measures of association for ordinal-level categorical variables, however, we first have to understand the concepts of *concordant, discordant,* and *tied pairs.* The concept of "pairs" here refers to pairs of cases. Let's begin by

---

1. Phi (and $\phi^2$) and Yule's $Q$ are valid only for 2 × 2 tables. Yule's $Q$ is generally much larger than phi.
2. Lambda, $\text{tau}_{yx}$, phi, and Yule's $Q$ can be used with nominal-level data.
3. For nominal-level data involving tables larger than 2 × 2, lambda or $\text{tau}_{yx}$ should be used.
4. For 2 × 2 tables $\phi^2 = \text{tau}_{yx}$.

taking five hypothetical persons who fall into different categories of two categorical variables: variable one ($V_1$) and variable two ($V_2$). Both variables contain three levels or categories. The following table shows the categories on both variables each of the five persons fall into. Because the categories or levels are rank ordered, we can assume that the higher the category, the higher the "score" on that variable.

| Person No. | $V_1$ | $V_2$ |
|---|---|---|
| Number 1 | 1 | 2 |
| Number 2 | 2 | 3 |
| Number 3 | 3 | 2 |
| Number 4 | 3 | 3 |
| Number 5 | 3 | 3 |

*Con*cordant pairs are those pairs of cases where the scores on two variables are *con*sistently higher or lower. Let's take as an example the pair of cases formed by person number 1 and number 2. In comparing person 1 with person 2, we see that the second person scores higher than the first person on both variables; 2 versus 1 on $V_1$ and 3 versus 2 on $V_2$. This pair of persons is said to be a *concordant pair* because the value of both variables is greater for one pair (person 2) than for another pair (person 1). Person 4 is concordant with person 1 as well. Pairs can also be concordant if the value of each variable is smaller for one person than for another. For example, person 1 is concordant with person 2 because they are lower on both $V_1$ and $V_2$.

Now look at person number 2 and person number 3. For this pair of cases, person number 3 is higher than person 2 on the first variable but lower than person 2 on the second variable. This pair of persons is said to constitute a *discordant pair*. A pair of cases is discordant if the direction of the difference in scores between two variables in a pair is reversed. Think of *dis*cordant pairs of cases as those where the scores on two variables are *dis*similar. A person is higher than another person on one variable but lower than that person on another variable.

Let's now compare person 4 with person 3. In this instance, the two cases are tied on the first variable because they both fall into the third category. Comparing person 4 with person 2, we see that they are tied on the second variable because they both fall into the third category. Comparing person 5 with person 4, we can see that they are tied on both variables. These last three comparisons involve three pairs of *tied ranks* because they are tied on either the first variable, the second variable, or both variables.

In comparing a pair of cases, then, there are three possible outcomes: concordant, discordant, or tied. In a given table, if most pairs are concordant, we find a positive relationship between the variables because, as the value of one variable increases, so does the value of the second. If most pairs are discordant, we find a negative relationship because, as the value of one variable increases, the value of the second decreases. If there are the same number of concordant as discordant pairs, we find no relationship between the two variables.

The measures of association with ordinal-level data that we discuss in this section are all based on the difference between the number of concordant pairs (symbolized as *CP*) and the number of discordant pairs (symbolized as *DP*). Because we would like to have a measure of association that is based on a proportionate reduction in error interpretation, we need to standardize the difference between *CP* and *DP* so that it falls between −1.00 for a perfect negative relationship, + 1.00 for a perfect positive relationship, with 0.00 indicating no relationship. The PRE measures we will discuss in this section differ primarily in how this standardization is achieved.

## Goodman and Kruskal's Gamma

One of the most popular of these ordinal measures of association is *Goodman and Kruskal's gamma* (symbolized by the Greek letter gamma, $\gamma$). Gamma is a PRE measure that is symmetric, meaning that it doesn't matter which variable is designated as the independent or dependent variable. The values of gamma vary between 0.00 and ± 1.00. Gamma standardizes the difference between the number of concordant and discordant pairs with the formula below:

$$\gamma = \frac{CP - DP}{CP + DP} \tag{11.9}$$

where
$CP$ = the number of concordant pairs
$DP$ = the number of discordant pairs

You can infer from this formula that, when calculating gamma, only the number of concordant and discordant pairs are used. All pairs of tied ranks are ignored. Also notice that, when the number of concordant ranks is greater than the number of discordant ranks, the sign of gamma will be positive, indicating a positive relationship between two variables. When the number of discordant ranks is greater than the number of concordant ranks, the sign of gamma will be negative, indicating a negative relationship.

How do we go about calculating gamma? Let's return to the data reported earlier in this chapter between grades received in school and the self-reported number of committed thefts. We have reproduced this data set in Table 11.19. Our chi-square test told us that these two variables were significantly related to each other ($\chi^2 = 64.48, p < .001$). What we want to know now is the strength of the association between grades and theft. Notice that both of these variables are ordinal. We can rank-order persons in terms of how good or bad their grades are and in terms of the number of thefts they reported.

For this example, we label grades as $V_2$. We also assign an arbitrary number to the four grade levels so that Ds and Fs = 1, Cs = 2, Bs = 3, and As = 4. We label the theft variable as $V_1$. We have assigned an arbitrary number to the three levels of self-reported delinquency so that "0 thefts" = 1, "1–5 thefts" = 2, and "6 + thefts" = 3.

In calculating gamma, we first have to determine the number of concordant and discordant pairs. We have to do this for *each distinct pair* of cases. Unfortunately, this can be an extremely tedious operation. For Table 11.19 where there are

**TABLE 11.19. Cross-Tabulation of Grades in School and Self-Reported Acts of Petty Theft**

| Grades in School ($V_2$) | | Self-Reported Acts of Theft ($V_1$) | | | |
|---|---|---|---|---|---|
| | | 0 | 1–5 | 6+ | |
| | | 1 | 2 | 3 | |
| Ds and Fs | 1 | Cell A<br>23 | Cell B<br>19 | Cell C<br>20 | 62 |
| Cs | 2 | Cell D<br>307 | Cell E<br>157 | Cell F<br>123 | 587 |
| Bs | 3 | Cell G<br>762 | Cell H<br>345 | Cell I<br>155 | 1262 |
| As | 4 | Cell J<br>418 | Cell K<br>166 | Cell L<br>56 | 640 |
| Totals | | 1510 | 687 | 354 | 2551 |

2551 distinct pairs, we would have to make $(n)(n-1)/2$, or 3,252,525 comparisons! That would take us the rest of the semester. Fortunately, there is a fairly easy-to-use procedure for doing this. Instead of trying to explain how this procedure compares each pair of cases, we first take you through the procedure.

To find the number of concordant cells, follow the steps outlined in the box.

---

**Step 1.** Find the cell that corresponds to the pair of cases with the lowest values on both variables. This is cell *A* in Table 11.19 because both cases in this cell have a score of 1 on both variables, the lowest score. Then, ignoring all cell frequencies that are in the same row or column, add the remaining cell frequencies for all cells that *are both* below and to the right of that cell. Finally, multiply this sum by the cell frequency in cell *A*. Your calculations, then, would be: 23(157 + 123 + 345 + 155 + 166 + 56). (Notice that we did not include the frequencies for cells *D, G, J, B*, or *C* because these cells are either in the same column or same row as cell *A*.)

**Step 2.** Staying in the top row of the table, go to the next cell (cell *B*). Again, ignoring all cell frequencies that are in the same row or column, add the remaining cell frequencies below and to the right of this cell, and multiply this by the frequency in cell *B*: 19(123 + 155 + 56).

**Step 3.** Because there are no cases below and to the right of cell *C*, we drop down to the next row. Starting in the first column of that row (cell *D*), ignore all cell frequencies in the same row or column and add the remaining cell frequencies below and to the right of this cell, and multiply this by the frequency in cell *D*: 307(345 + 155 + 166 + 56).

**Step 4.** You should now have the hang of the procedure. Continue to move from the left to the right, multiply each cell frequency by the sum of the frequencies for all cells that lie below it and to the right (ignoring cell frequencies in the same row or column). Do this for each cell.

For the data displayed in Table 11.19, we can summarize our calculations for the number of concordant pairs as follows:

Cell A     23(157 + 123 + 345 + 155 + 166 + 56) = 23,046
Cell B     19(123 + 155 + 56) = 6,346
Cell D     307(345 + 155 + 166 + 56) = 221,654
Cell E     157(155 + 56) = 33,127
Cell G     762(166 + 56) = 169,164
Cell H     345(56) = 19,320

Total      472,657 concordant pairs

Now, before we go through the procedure for calculating the number of discordant pairs, let's figure out why the comparisons involve concordant pairs. Remember that a concordant pair occurs whenever one case is lower (or higher) on both variables than another case. Let's take one case from the original data points from each of the cells A, B, D, E, and F and display their scores on $V_1$ and $V_2$:

|  | $V_1$ | $V_2$ |
|---|---|---|
| Case from Cell A | 1 | 1 |
| Case from Cell B | 2 | 1 |
| Case from Cell D | 1 | 2 |
| Case from Cell E | 2 | 2 |
| Case from Cell F | 3 | 2 |

Let's now compare our cell A case with each one of the others. In comparing a case from Cell A with one from cell B, we can see that they are tied on the second variable. This comparison involves a tied case, then, and we do not count it in calculating gamma. In comparing the same A cell case with one from cell D, we can see that they are tied on the first variable. This comparison also involves a tied case, and we will not count it. Notice that cell B lies in the same row as cell A and cell D lies in the same column. All cases that lie in the same row or column as our comparison case will then be tied with it on one or the other variable (if they are tied on both variables they will be in the same cell). As a result, we do not count these tied cases in calculating the number of concordant (or discordant) pairs for our value of gamma.

In comparing the case from cell A with the one in cell E, however, we see that it is lower on both variables. Because one case is lower than the other on *both* variables, it is a concordant pair. By the same reasoning, all cases in cell A are lower on both variables than all cases in cell E. As a result, in comparing these two cells we have 23(157) = 3611 concordant pairs. In comparing a case from cell A with one from cell F, we can again see that it is lower on both variables. This, too, is a concordant case, and because all cases in cell A will be lower than all cases in cell F, we have 23(123) = 2829 concordant pairs. With these last two comparisons (cell A with cells E and F), we have a total of 23(157 + 123) = 6440 concordant pairs.

Notice that the concordant pairs lie only to the right and below the cell we are examining.

Let's go now through the procedure for calculating the number of discordant pairs from Table 11.19:

1. Find the cell that corresponds to those cases that are "high" on one variable but "low" on another. Let's use cell *J* as persons in that cell are "high" on the grade variable (As) but "low" on the self-reported theft variable (0 thefts). Then, ignoring all cell frequencies that are in the same row or column, add the remaining cell frequencies for all cells that *are both* above and to the right of that cell. Finally, multiply this sum by the cell frequency in cell *J*. Your calculations, then, would be: 418(345 + 155 + 157 + 123 + 19 + 20). Notice that, as before, we did not include the frequencies for cells *G, D, A, K,* or *L* because these cells are either in the same column or same row as cell *J*.

2. Staying in the bottom row of the table, go to the next cell (cell *K*). Again ignoring all cell frequencies that are in the same row or column, add the remaining cell frequencies above and to the right of this cell, and multiply this sum by the frequency in cell *K*: 166(155 + 123 + 20).

3. Because there are no cases above and to the right of cell *L*, we go up to the next row. Starting in the first column (cell *G*), ignore all cell frequencies in the same row or column, add the remaining cell frequencies above and to the right of this cell, and multiply this by the frequency in cell *G*: 762(157 + 123 + 19 + 20).

4. You should now have the hang of the procedure for finding the number of discordant pairs. Continue to move from the left to the right, multiply each cell frequency by the sum of the frequencies for all cells that lie both above it and to the right (ignoring cell frequencies in the same row or column). Do this for each cell.

For this data displayed in Table 11.19, we can summarize our calculations for the number of discordant pairs as follows:

| | |
|---|---|
| Cell *J* | 418(345 + 155 + 157 + 123 + 19 + 20) = 342,342 |
| Cell *K* | 166(155 + 123 + 20) = 49,468 |
| Cell *G* | 762(157 + 123 + 19 + 20) = 243,078 |
| Cell *H* | 345(123 + 20) = 49,335 |
| Cell *B* | 307(19 + 20) = 11,973 |
| Cell *E* | 157(20) = 3,140 |
| Total | 699,336 discordant pairs |

What makes these pairs discordant? Remember that a discordant pair occurs whenever one case is lower than another case on one variable but is higher on the other variable (or higher on one variable and lower on the other). In other words, a *dis*cordant pair is *dis*similar in its ranking on the two variables. To illustrate how this can be found from the table, let's take one case each from cells *J, K, G, H,* and *I* and display their scores on $V_1$ and $V_2$.

|  | $V_1$ | $V_2$ |
|---|---|---|
| Case from Cell *J* | 1 | 4 |
| Case from Cell *K* | 2 | 4 |
| Case from Cell *G* | 1 | 3 |
| Case from Cell *H* | 2 | 3 |
| Case from Cell *I* | 3 | 3 |

Let's now compare our cell *J* case with each one of the others. Comparing a case from cell *J* with one from cell *K,* we can see that they are tied on the second variable. This comparison involves a pair case, then, and we do not count it. Comparing the same *J* cell case with one from cell *G,* we can see that they are tied on the first variable. This comparison also involves a tied pair, and we will not count it in our calculation of gamma. Notice that cell *K* lies in the same row as cell *J* and cell *G* lies in the same column. As we saw in our calculation of the number of concordant pairs, all cases that lie in the same row or column as our comparison case will be tied with it on one or the other variables (if they are tied on both variables, they will be in the same cell). As a result, we do not count these tied cases in calculating the number of discordant pairs.

In comparing the case from cell *J* with the one in cell *H,* however, we see that it is lower on the first variable but higher on the second variable. This is a discordant pair. In fact, we know that all cases in cell *J* are lower on the first variable and higher on the second variable than all cases in cell *H.* As a result, in comparing these two cells we have $418(345) = 144{,}210$ discordant pairs.

Comparing a case from cell *J* with one from cell *I,* we can see that it is lower on one variable and higher on the other variable. This, too, then, is a discordant pair, and because all cases in cell *J* are lower than all cases in cell *I* on one variable and higher than the other, we have an additional $418(155) = 64{,}790$ discordant pairs. Notice that the discordant pairs lie only to the right and above the cell we are examining.

Now that we have the number of concordant and discordant pairs, we can finally calculate our value of gamma. Recall from Equation 11.9 that gamma was obtained as:

$$\gamma = \frac{\text{Number of Concordant Pairs } - \text{ Number of Discordant Pairs}}{\text{Number of Concordant Pairs } + \text{ Number of Discordant Pairs}}$$

For the data in Table 11.19, the value of gamma is:

$$\gamma = \frac{472{,}657 - 699{,}336}{472{,}657 + 699{,}336}$$

$$= \frac{-226{,}679}{1{,}171{,}993}$$

$$= -.193$$

A gamma value of −.193 tells us that there are more "unlike" than "like" pairs. That is, there are more cases high on one variable and low on another than either high or low on both. We can interpret this as saying that those students who get relatively better grades are less likely to report committing theft than those who get relatively low grades. Thus, a negative relationship exists between grades in school and delinquency. As school grades increase, the likelihood of reporting theft decreases. Remember that the ability to speak about the *direction* of a relationship is something that we did not encounter in working with nominal-level data.

The magnitude of gamma tells us that grades and self-reported theft are not very strongly related. Remember that when two variables are not related at all, the value of gamma will be 0.00 and ± 1.00 when perfectly related. Our value of −.19 is not very substantial; it is much closer to zero than it is to ± 1. As a PRE measure, this gamma coefficient informs us that we will proportionately reduce our errors by 19 percent when we use grades to predict theft.

We also can test the statistical significance that the value of gamma in the population is zero. When the sample size is sufficiently large ($n > 50$), the sampling distribution of gamma can be approximated with a normal distribution. The $z$ test for gamma takes the following formula:

$$z = (\gamma) \sqrt{\frac{(CP + DP)}{n(1 - \gamma^2)}} \tag{11.10}$$

where
$CP$ = number of concordant pairs
$DP$ = number of discordant pairs
$\gamma$ = our observed gamma

For our example, with an alpha level of .01 and a one-tailed test, the critical value of $z$ is − 2.33. We calculate the test statistic as:

$$z = (-.193) \sqrt{\frac{(472{,}657 + 699{,}336)}{2551[1 - (-.193)^2]}}$$

$$= (-.193) \sqrt{\frac{1{,}171{,}993}{2457}}$$

$$= (-.193)(21.8)$$

$$= -4.2$$

Because our obtained value of $z$ is less than the critical $z$ score, we can reject the null hypothesis that the value of gamma in the population is zero. We can therefore conclude that there is a significant negative relationship between grades and self-reported theft.

## Kendall's Tau

One of the problems with gamma as a measure of association, however, is that it ignores the number of tied ranks. Whenever there are a large number of tied ranks, then, gamma should probably not be used as the measure of association. Two other PRE measures of association can be used with ordinal-level variables that do take tied ranks into account. They are Kendall's tau (symbolized by the Greek letter $\tau$), and Somers' $d_{yx}$. Kendall's tau takes into account pairs that are tied on either of the two variables (but not those tied on both), and Somers' $d_{yx}$ takes into account pairs tied on the variable that is designated as the dependent variable but not the independent variable.

Because both Kendall's tau and Somers' $d_{yx}$ require that we determine the number of tied rank pairs, let's begin our discussion of these measures by figuring out how to obtain the number of tied pairs. We use the data in Table 11.19 because we are familiar with this table and have already calculated the number of concordant and discordant pairs. In this example, you will remember, we have treated grades as the independent variable and self-reported theft as the dependent variable. To keep distinct the number of pairs tied on the independent variable from those tied on the dependent variable and those tied on both, we will use the following symbols $T_x$, $T_y$, $T_{xy}$, respectively.

Let's begin by finding the number of tied pairs for the independent variable. In Table 11.19, grades, the independent variable, is the row variable. Beginning with the first row, we see that all cases in cell $A$ are tied on the independent variable with everyone in their own row (all have received grades of Ds and Fs). As every case in cell $A$ is tied on the independent variable with every case in both cell $B$ and cell $C$, we have a total of $23(19 + 20) = 897$ tied comparisons. Every case in cell $B$ is the same on the independent variable with every case in the cell to the right (cell $C$: all have received grades of Ds and Fs), adding $19(20) = 380$ more tied comparisons to the total of $T_x$. Because there are no cases to the right of cell $C$, we can drop to the next row.

Starting in the left column in the second row, add the frequencies for each cell to the right and multiply by this cell's frequency. For cell $D$, the number of tied ranks would be $307(157 + 123) = 85,960$. Continue with this simple algorithm in counting to obtain the total number of cases that are tied on the independent variable. We have summarized the calculations for the entire table:

Cell $A$    $23(19 + 20) = 897$
Cell $B$    $19(20) = 380$
Cell $D$    $307(157 + 123) = 85,960$
Cell $E$    $157(123) = 19,311$
Cell $G$    $762(345 + 155) = 381,000$
Cell $H$    $345(155) = 53,475$
Cell $J$    $418(166 + 56) = 92,796$
Cell $K$    $166(56) = 9296$

Total cases tied on independent variable $(T_x) = 643,115$.

The dependent variable is the column variable in Table 11.19. To determine the number of cases tied on the dependent variable, let's again begin with the cell in the top right corner, cell *A*. Cases in cell *A* are tied on the dependent variable with every case that is also in the first column (they all reported "zero thefts"). Because every case in cell *A* is tied on the dependent variable with every case below it, there would be a total of 23(307 + 762 + 418) = 34,201 tied comparisons involving this cell. Staying in the first column, go to the next cell (cell *D*) and multiply this cell frequency by the sum of the frequencies for all cells below it: 307(762 + 418) = 362,260.

Go to the next cell in the column and do the same thing: 762(418) = 318,516. As there are no cases below cell *J*, go to the next column and continue the procedure down the column. These cases are tied on the dependent variable as well because they all reported "1–5 thefts." Continue until you have reached the last cell (cell *L*). The number of cases tied on the dependent variable have been calculated for the entire table with the following results:

| | |
|---|---|
| Cell *A* | 23(307 + 762 + 418) = 34,201 |
| Cell *D* | 307(762 + 418) = 362,260 |
| Cell *G* | 762(418) = 318,516 |
| Cell *B* | 19(157 + 345 + 166) = 12,692 |
| Cell *E* | 157(345 + 166) = 80,227 |
| Cell *F* | 345(166) = 57,270 |
| Cell *C* | 20(123 + 155 + 56) = 6680 |
| Cell *F* | 123(155 + 56) = 25,953 |
| Cell *I* | 155(56) = 8680 |

Total cases tied on dependent variable $(T_y)$ is 906,479.

We now know that there are 472,657 concordant pairs, 699,336 discordant pairs, 643,115 pairs tied on the independent variable (grades), and 906,479 pairs tied on the dependent variable (self-reported theft). With this information, we can calculate both Kendall's tau and Somers' $d_{yx}$.

There are actually two different statistics for Kendall's tau: $tau_b$ and $tau_c$. Both coefficients range in value from 0.00 to ± 1.00 and are equal to 0.00 if the two variables are unrelated. $Tau_b$ is appropriate whenever the number of rows and columns are the same $(R = C)$. $Tau_b$ has a PRE interpretation, but $tau_c$ does not. If the number of rows are equal to the number of columns, then, $tau_b$ is a more satisfactory measure of association. $Tau_b$ is defined by the following formula:

$$\tau_b = \frac{CP - DP}{\sqrt{CP + DP + T_y)\,(CP + DP + T_x)}} \tag{11.11}$$

where
  $CP$ = the number of concordant pairs
  $DP$ = the number of discordant pairs
  $T_y$ = the number of pairs tied on the dependent variable
  $T_x$ = the number of pairs tied on the independent variable

Both tau$_b$ and tau$_c$ measures of association are symmetric, meaning that it does not matter which variable is designated as the dependent or independent variable. In tables in which the number of rows do not equal the number of columns, however, Kendall's tau$_c$ or Somers' $d_{yx}$ should be used. The formula for tau$_c$ is:

$$\tau_c = \frac{2m(CP - DP)}{n^2(m-1)} \tag{11.12}$$

where

$m$ = the smaller of the number of rows or the number of columns

Because the table in Table 11.19 is not square ($R = 4, C = 3$), tau$_c$ is the appropriate tau measure of association. For this data set, our obtained value of tau$_c$ is:

$$\tau_c = \frac{2(3)(CP - DP)}{N^2(3-1)}$$

$$= \frac{(6)(472,657 - 699,336)}{(2551)^2(2)}$$

$$= \frac{-1,360,074}{13,015,202}$$

$$= -.104$$

We can interpret this as indicating that there is a weak negative association between grades and self-reported delinquency.

The statistical significance of both tau$_b$ and tau$_c$ can be easily determined. To test the null hypothesis that the value of tau in the population is zero ($H_0$: $\tau = 0$), we use the $z$ distribution and calculate the value of $z$ using the following formula:

$$z = \frac{\tau}{\hat{\sigma}_\tau} \tag{11.13}$$

where

$\hat{\sigma}_\tau$ = the standard error of tau

$$\hat{\sigma}_\tau = \sqrt{\frac{4(R+1)(C+1)}{9\,nRC}}$$

where

$R$ = the number of rows
$C$ = the number of columns
$n$ = the sample size

For our obtained tau$_c$ value of $-.104$, the value of $z$ is:

$$z = \frac{-.104}{\sqrt{\dfrac{4(4 + 1)(3 + 1)}{9[(2551)(4)(3)]}}}$$

$$= \frac{-.104}{\sqrt{\dfrac{80}{275,508}}}$$

$$= \frac{-.104}{.017}$$

$$= -6.12$$

Using an alpha level of .01 and a one-tailed test to determine the validity of the null hypothesis that tau $= 0$, the critical value of $z$ is $-2.33$. Because our obtained value of $z$ is less than the critical value, we can reject the null hypothesis and conclude that the relationship between grades and self-reported theft in the population is significantly different from zero. Recall, however, that the value of tau$_c$ ($-.104$) indicated that the relationship was very weak.

## Somers' d

Yes, we come now to the final measure of association for ordinal-level categorical variables that we discuss, called Somers' $d_{yx}$. Unlike both gamma and Kendall's tau measures, Somers' $d_{yx}$ is an asymmetric measure of ordinal association. Its value will depend on which variable is designated as the independent and dependent variables. It is important, therefore, that before calculating Somers' $d_{yx}$, you have a sound theoretical reason for treating one variable as the independent and the other as the dependent variable. Unlike gamma, Somers' $d_{yx}$ does take tied ranks into account in its denominator, but unlike Kendall's tau measures, it only includes cases tied on the dependent variable. Cases tied on the independent variable are excluded.
The formula for Somers' $d_{yx}$ is:

$$d = \frac{CP - DP}{CP + DP + T_y} \tag{11.14}$$

where
$\quad CP$ = the number of concordant pairs
$\quad DP$ = the number of discordant pairs
$\quad T_y$ = the number of pairs tied on the dependent variable

This formula should by now be very familiar to you. The numerator is the same as that for gamma and both tau measures. The denominator is the same as that for gamma, except it adds the number of cases tied on the dependent variable (this should tell you that Somers' $d$ will always be lower in magnitude than gamma for the same table). Somers' $d$ varies in magnitude from $-1.00$ to $+1.00$ for variables that are perfectly related, and 0.00 for variables that are unrelated. For our example involving school grades and self-reported theft, we had designated grades as the independent and theft as the dependent variable. Our value of $d$ for this data set would be:

$$d_{yx} = \frac{472{,}657 - 699{,}336}{472{,}657 + 699{,}336 + 906{,}479}$$

$$= \frac{-226{,}679}{2{,}078{,}469}$$

$$= -.109$$

This indicates that there is a weak negative relationship between self-reported theft and grades. More specifically, we can say that we have approximately an 11 percent reduction in PRE when we use grades to predict self-reported theft.

As with our other measures of association, we can test the null hypothesis that our obtained value of Somers' $d$ is zero in the population. The significance test is:

$$z = \frac{d_{yx}}{\hat{\sigma} d_{yx}} \tag{11.15}$$

where

$\hat{\sigma} d_{yx}$ = the standard error of $d_{yx}$

An estimate of the standard error of $d_{yx}$ can be approximated with:

$$\hat{\sigma} d_{yx} = \frac{2}{3R} \sqrt{\frac{(R^2 - 1)(C + 1)}{n(C - 1)}}$$

For our example, we test the null hypothesis that $d_{yx}$ is zero with an alpha of .01 using a one-tailed test. The critical value of $z$ for this test is $-2.33$. We calculate our obtained $z$ statistic as:

$$z_{obt} = \frac{-.109}{\dfrac{2}{(3)(4)} \sqrt{\dfrac{(4^2 - 1)(3 + 1)}{2551(3 - 1)}}}$$

$$= \frac{-.109}{\dfrac{2}{12} \sqrt{\dfrac{(15)(4)}{2551(2)}}}$$

$$= \frac{-.109}{(.166)\sqrt{.012}}$$

$$= -5.96$$

Because our obtained $z$ value ($-5.96$) is less than the critical $z$ ($-2.33$), we can reject the null hypothesis and conclude that there is a significant negative relationship between grades and self-reported theft in the population.

# 11.9 SUMMARY

In this chapter we learned about a significance test to determine whether two categorical variables are statistically independent—the chi-square test of independence. We also learned that, even though the chi-square test may tell us something about whether or not two variables are significantly related to one another within a margin of error (our alpha level), it tells us nothing about the strength of the relationship. To determine how strongly two variables are related to each other, we must calculate *measures of association.*

We have discussed several different measures of association. In fact, you must by now be completely overwhelmed by the different kinds and when they are and are not appropriate. About the only common ground among them is that all of them are appropriate when our data are categorical and that the better measures of association have proportionate reduction in error (PRE) interpretations. Other than these commonalities, however, the different kinds of measures must present a dizzying variety to you. Table 11.20 provides you with a guide to help you select which measure of association is the best under certain circumstances.

**TABLE 11.20. Guide to the Appropriate Measure of Association for Categorical Variables**

| Level of Data | Size of Table | PRE Measure | Symmetric | Statistics |
|---|---|---|---|---|
| Nominal | 2 × 2 | Yes | Yes | Phi squared |
| Nominal-Ordinal | 2 × 2 | Yes | Yes | Yule's $Q$ |
| Nominal | R × C | Yes | No | Lambda |
| Nominal | R × C | Yes | No | Goodman and Kruskal's tau |
| Ordinal | R × C | Yes | Yes | Goodman and Kruskal's gamma |
| Ordinal | R × C (R = C) | Yes | Yes | Kendall's tau$_b$ |
| Ordinal | R × C (R ≠ C) | No | Yes | Kendall's tau$_c$ |
| Ordinal | R × C | Yes | No | Somers' $d$ |

## Key Terms

**asymmetric measure of association**
**cell**
**chi-square test of independence**
**column marginal**
**contingency table**
**expected frequencies**
**Goodman and Kruskal's gamma**
**Goodman and Kruskal's tau (tau$_{yx}$)**
**joint distribution**
**Kendall's tau$_b$**
**Kendall's tau$_c$**
**lambda**

**measure of association**
**observed frequencies**
**phi coefficient**
**phi coefficient squared**
**proportionate reduction in error (PRE)**
**row marginal**
**Somers' $d$**
**symmetric measure of association**
**table of expected frequencies**
**table of observed frequencies**
**tau$_{yx}$ (Goodman and Kruskal's tau)**
**Yule's $Q$**

## Problems

1. The following contingency table describes the joint distribution of two variables, the type of institution a correctional officer works in, and whether or not they report being satisfied with his job.

*Satisfied?*

| Type of Institution | No | Yes | |
|---|---|---|---|
| Medium Security | 15 | 30 | 45 |
| Maximum Security | 100 | 40 | 140 |
| Total | 115 | 70 | 185 |

With these data, answer the following questions:
a. How many total cases are there?
b. What are the two row marginals?
c. What are the two column marginals?
d. How many cases are there in cell *A* of the table? In Cell *D*?
e. How would you describe the size of this contingency table?
f. How many degrees of freedom do you have in this table?
g. Assuming that Type of Institution is the independent variable and Job Satisfaction is the dependent variable, calculate your cell percentages.
h. Are those officers who work in medium security institutions more satisfied with their jobs than those who work in maximum security institutions?

2. In their research on police violence, Bayley and Garofalo (1989) found that some police officers are especially skilled in minimizing conflict and that other police officers can accurately identify those "conflict minimizers." You conduct a similar study on a random sample of 250 officers, 100 of whom have been identified by their peers as "conflict minimizers." You examine whether these "conflict minimizers" resort to force less often in making an arrest than a control group of officers. Here are your results.

*Officer Type*

| Force Used? | Conflict Minimizer | Control | |
|---|---|---|---|
| No | 90 | 98 | 188 |
| Yes | 10 | 52 | 62 |
| Total | 100 | 150 | 250 |

a. Assuming that Officer Type is the independent variable, calculate the cell percentages for the table. Do a lower percentage of the "conflict minimizers" use force than the controls?
b. Using an alpha level of .01, test the null hypothesis that Type of Officer and Use of Force are independent from each other. What do you conclude from this hypothesis test?

c. Calculate the value of Yule's $Q$. What is the strength of the association between Officer Type and Use of Force?

d. Is the value of Yule's $Q$ for this table significantly different from zero with an alpha of .01?

3. You want to conduct some research on the effectiveness of different types of defense counsel in criminal cases. You take a random sample of 80 counsel retained and paid for by the defendant, 125 counsel appointed by the court to serve as defense counsel, and 220 public defenders. You then determine what sentence their last convicted client received. You want to know whether different sentencing outcomes are related to type of counsel. Here's what your data look like.

*Type of Counsel*

| Type of Sentence Received | Retained | Appointed | Public Defender | |
|---|---|---|---|---|
| Jail Only | 18 | 30 | 94 | 142 |
| Fine and Jail | 22 | 37 | 36 | 95 |
| Less than 60 Days of Jail | 24 | 38 | 50 | 112 |
| 60 Days of Jail or More | 16 | 20 | 40 | 76 |
| Total | 80 | 125 | 220 | 425 |

a. Assume that Type of Counsel is the independent variable, and calculate the percentages for the table. Is there a difference by counsel type in the percent who serve 60 days or more in jail?

b. With an alpha level of .05, test the null hypothesis that the two variables are independent. What do you conclude about this hypothesis test?

c. Calculate lambda as a measure of association for your table. What do you conclude about the strength of the association between Type of Counsel and sentencing outcome?

d. Test the null hypothesis that lambda is significantly different from zero with an alpha of .05. What do you conclude?

4. In their recent book, *Crime in the Making*, Robert Sampson and John Laub (1993) found that strong social bonds established later in life serve as effective controls to crime. Let's say you were interested in this notion, and studied the postrelease behavior of random samples of three groups of parolees, those with a stable job, those with intermittent or sporadic employment, and those unable to find a job. In addition to their postrelease employment, you determined how many in each group were arrested within 3 years of their release from prison. Here is what you found:

*Postrelease Employment*

| Number of Postrelease Arrests | Stable Employment | Sporadic Employment | Unemployed | |
|---|---|---|---|---|
| 0 | 30 | 14 | 10 | 54 |
| 1 + | 15 | 16 | 30 | 61 |
| Total | 45 | 30 | 40 | 115 |

**a.** Assume that Postrelease Employment is the independent variable, and calculate the cell percentages. Are those with stable employment less likely to have one or more arrests?

**b.** Using an alpha level of .01, test the null hypothesis that the two variables are related. What do you conclude from this hypothesis test?

**c.** Calculate gamma, Kendall's $tau_c$, and Somers' $d$ as your measure of association. What is the strength of the relationship between postrelease employment and arrest according to these measures? Why do they give us different indications as to the strength of the relationship between employment and arrest? Why would you not want to use Kendall's $tau_b$ as the measure of association for this table?

**d.** Using an alpha of .05, test the null hypothesis that gamma, $tau_c$, and Somers' $d$ are equal to zero against the null hypothesis that each is different from zero. What do you conclude?

**5.** Which measure of association would you use for the following data and table size?

**a.** Nominal-level data and a 2 × 2 table?

**b.** Ordinal-level data and a 2 × 2 table?

**c.** Ordinal-level data $R \times C$ table where $R \neq C$?

**d.** Nominal-level data $R \times C$ table?

**e.** Ordinal-level data $R \times C$ table where $R = C$?

**f.** Ordinal-level data $R \times C$ table where $R \neq C$ and there are a lot of tied ranks.

## Solutions to Problems

**1. a.** There are 185 total cases.

**b.** The two row marginal frequencies are 45 (Medium Security) and 140 (Maximum Security).

**c.** The two column marginal frequencies are 115 (Not Satisfied) and 70 (Satisfied).

**d.** There are 15 cases in Cell $A$, and 40 cases in Cell $D$.

**e.** This is a 2 × 2 contingency table, because there are two columns and two rows.

**f.** With two rows and two columns, the number of degrees of freedom is equal to df = $(2 - 1)(2 - 1) = 1$.

**g.** The cell percentages would look like this:

*Satisfied?*

| Type of Institution | No | Yes | |
|---|---|---|---|
| Medium Security | 33% | 67% | 100% |
| Maximum Security | 71% | 29% | 100% |

**h.** Yes, 67 percent of those officers in medium security institutions are satisfied with their job, whereas only 29 percent of those in maximum security institutions are satisfied with their job.

**2. a.** Assuming that Officer Type is the independent variable, here are the cell percentages:

*Officer Type*

| Force Used? | Conflict Minimizer | Control |
|---|---|---|
| No | 90% | 65% |
| Yes | 10% | 35% |
| | 100% | 100% |

Yes, 35 percent of the control officers used force in making an arrest, compared with only 10 percent of the conflict minimizer officers.

**b.** Our hypotheses are:

$H_0$: Type of Officer is statistically independent of the use of force. In other words, Type of Officer is not related to the use of force. $x^2 = 0$.

$H_1$: Type of Officer is not statistically independent of the use of force. In other words, Type of Officer is related to the use of force. $x^2 > 0$.

Our decision rule is to reject the null hypothesis if our obtained value of chi-square is greater than or equal to 6.635. Our obtained value of chi-square is 20.07. Because our obtained chi-square is greater than the critical value ($20.07 > 6.635$), our decision is to reject the null hypothesis. There is a statistically significant relationship between Type of Officer and Use of Force, conflict minimizers are significantly less likely to use force than control officers.

**c.** The value of Yule's $Q$ is .65. This tells us that there is a moderately strong positive relationship between officer type and use of force.

**d.** $H_0$: $Q = 0$

$H_1$: $Q > 0$

Our decision rule will be to reject the null hypothesis that $Q = 0$ if $z_{obt} \geq 2.33$. The obtained value of $z$ is:

$$z_{obt} = \frac{.65}{\sqrt{(.25)(1 - .65^2)^2 \left(\frac{1}{90} + \frac{1}{98} + \frac{1}{10} + \frac{1}{52}\right)}}$$

$$= \frac{.65}{\sqrt{(.25)(.33)(.01 + .01 + .10 + .02)}}$$

$$= \frac{.65}{\sqrt{(.25)(.33)(.14)}}$$

$$= \frac{.65}{.11}$$

$$= 5.91$$

Because $z_{obt} > z_{crit}$, our decision is to reject the null hypothesis that $Q$ equals zero.

**3. a.**

<table>
<tr><td rowspan="2">Type of Sentence<br>Received</td><td colspan="3" align="center">*Type of Counsel*</td></tr>
<tr><td>Retained</td><td>Appointed</td><td>Public<br>Defender</td></tr>
<tr><td>Jail Only</td><td>23%</td><td>24%</td><td>43%</td></tr>
<tr><td>Fine and Jail</td><td>27%</td><td>30%</td><td>16%</td></tr>
<tr><td>Less than<br>60 Days of Jail</td><td>30%</td><td>30%</td><td>23%</td></tr>
<tr><td>60 Days or More<br>of Jail</td><td>20%</td><td>16%</td><td>18%</td></tr>
<tr><td></td><td>100%</td><td>100%</td><td>100%</td></tr>
</table>

There is only a very slight difference across type of counsel in the percent of convicted defendants who receive a jail sentence of 60 days or more. For example, 20 percent of those with retained counsel received that sentence, compared with 16 percent of those with appointed counsel and 18 percent of those with a public defender. These percent differences are not very large.

**b.** Our hypotheses are:

$H_0$: Type of Counsel is statistically independent of the type of sentence received. In other words, Type of Counsel is not related to type of sentence. $x^2 = 0$.

$H_1$: Type of Counsel is not statistically independent of the type of sentence received. In other words, type of counsel is related to type of sentence. $x^2 > 0$.

Our decision rule is to reject the null hypothesis if our obtained value of chi-square is greater than or equal to 12.592. Because our obtained value of chi-square is 21.85, our decision is to reject the null hypothesis. There is a statistically significant relationship between type of counsel and type of sentence received.

**c.** Type of Counsel clearly is a nominal-level variable, and Type of Sentence Received is most likely nominal. The best measure of association, then, is probably lambda:

$$\lambda = \frac{283 - 269}{283}$$

$$= \frac{14}{283}$$

$$= .05$$

Our lambda value is only .05. This tells us that, by knowing the independent variable, the PRE in predicting the dependent variable is 5 percent. It tells us that Type of Counsel is not very strongly related to type of sentence received.

**d.** $H_0: \lambda = 0$

$H_0: \lambda > 0$

We have already calculated the chi-square for the table of observed and expected frequencies and rejected the null hypothesis. We would conclude, then, that the value of lambda in the population is not zero. We would also conclude that it is not very large, so the relationship between these two variables is not particularly strong.

**4. a.**

Postrelease Employment

| Number of Postrelease Arrests | Stable Employment | Sporadic Employment | Unemployed |
|---|---|---|---|
| 0 | 67% | 47% | 25% |
| 1 + | 33% | 53% | 75% |
|  | 100% | 100% | 100% |

Yes, those with stable employment are less likely to be arrested when released from prison. Seventy-five percent of those without jobs were arrested on release, approximately 50 percent of those only sporadically employed, and only one-third of those with stable employment were arrested.

**b.** Our hypotheses are:

$H_0$: Stability of employment is statistically independent of the number of arrests after release from prison. $x^2 = 0$.

$H_1$: Stability of employment is not statistically independent of the number of arrests. $x^2 > 0$.

Our decision rule is to reject the null hypothesis if our obtained value of chi-square is greater than or equal to 9.210. Our obtained value of chi-square is 15.33, and our decision is to reject the null hypothesis. There is a statistically significant relationship between stability of employment and the number of postprison arrests. Those with more stable employment have fewer postrelease arrests.

**c.** Gamma is equal to:

$$\gamma = \frac{1800 - 520}{1800 + 520}$$

$$= \frac{1280}{2320}$$

$$= .55$$

The gamma value indicates that there is a moderately strong relationship between job stability and the number of arrests. The more unstable the job (from stable to sporadic to unemployed), the more likely it is that there will be at least one postrelease arrest.

The value of Kendall's tau$_c$ is:

$$\tau_c = \frac{[(2)(2)](1800 - 520)}{(115)^2(2 - 1)}$$

$$= \frac{(4)(1280)}{13,225(1)}$$

$$= \frac{5120}{13,225}$$

$$= .39$$

Tau$_c$ indicates a weaker relationship than did gamma. Unfortunately, tau$_c$ does not have a PRE interpretation.

The value of Somers' *d* is:

$$d = \frac{1800 - 520}{1800 + 520 + 2030}$$

$$= \frac{1280}{4350}$$

$$= .29$$

The value of Somers' *d* indicates that there is a 29 percent PRE when using employment stability to predict postrelease arrest.

These measures give us different numerical estimates of the measure of association because gamma does not take tied ranks into account. The gamma value is greater than the other two measures from the same table. Both Kendall's $tau_c$ and Somers' *d* take tied ranks into account and are for that reason lower in magnitude. Kendall's $tau_b$ should not be used for this table. It is appropriate only when the number of rows are equal to the number of columns.

**d.** With a two-tailed alpha of .05, test the null hypotheses that:

$H_0$: $\gamma = 0$

$H_0$: $\tau_c = 0$

$H_0$: $d = 0$

against the alternative hypotheses that

$H_1$: $\gamma \neq 0$

$H_1$: $\tau_c \neq 0$

$H_1$: $d \neq 0$

We have stated all of these alternatives as two-tailed hypothesis tests. All three hypotheses can be tested with the $z$ test, with the $z$ or standard normal distribution as the sampling distribution. With a two-tailed alpha of .05, the critical value of $z$ is 1.96. Our decision rule for each test, therefore, is to reject the null hypothesis if $z_{obt} \leq -1.96$ or if $z_{obt} \geq 1.96$.

The $z$ test for the significance of gamma is:

$$z_{obt} = .55 \sqrt{\frac{1800 + 520}{115(1 - .55^2)}}$$

$$= .55 \sqrt{\frac{2320}{115(.70)}}$$

$$= .55 \sqrt{\frac{2320}{80.5}}$$

$$= 2.95$$

As $z_{obt} > z_{crit}$ we decide to reject the null hypothesis that the population value of gamma is equal to zero.

The $z$ test for the significance of tau$_c$ is:

$$z_{obt} = \frac{.39}{\sqrt{\dfrac{4(2+1)(3+1)}{9(115)(3)(1)}}}$$

$$= \frac{.39}{\sqrt{\dfrac{48}{3105}}}$$

$$= \frac{.39}{.12}$$

$$= 3.25$$

As our obtained value of 3.25 is greater than the critical value of 1.96, we decide to reject the null hypothesis that the population tau$_c$ value is equal to zero.

The $z$ test for the significance of Somers' $d$ is:

$$z_{obt} = \frac{.29}{\dfrac{2}{3(2)}\sqrt{\dfrac{(2^2-1)(3+1)}{115(3-1)}}}$$

$$= \frac{.29}{\dfrac{2}{6}\sqrt{\dfrac{(4-1)(4)}{230}}}$$

$$= \frac{.29}{(.33)(.23)}$$

$$= \frac{.29}{.0759}$$

$$= 3.82$$

As our obtained value of 3.82 is greater than the critical value of 1.96, we decide to reject the null hypothesis that the value of Somers' $d$ in the population is equal to zero.

5. **a.** Phi, Yule's $Q$, lambda, Goodman and Kruskal's tau can all be used.
   **b.** Yule's $Q$; $Q$ is the same as gamma when the table is $2 \times 2$.
   **c.** Gamma, tau$_c$, and Somers' $d$.
   **d.** Lambda, Goodman and Kruskal's tau.
   **e.** Gamma, Kendall's tau$_b$ and Somers' $d$.
   **f.** Kendall's tau$_c$ and Somers' $d$.

# CHAPTER 12

# Hypothesis Tests Involving Two Population Means or Proportions

*Beauty is the first test: There is no permanent place in the world for ugly mathematics.*

—GODFREY HARDY

## 12.1 INTRODUCTION

In Chapter 10, we examined the statistical procedures necessary to conduct a hypothesis test about one population mean ($\mu$) and one proportion ($P$). Very frequently, however, we want to compare the differences that exist between two population means (or proportions) or between the means (or proportions) of two subgroups within a population. In this chapter we focus on the statistical procedures that allow us to test hypotheses about the differences *between* two population means ($\mu_2 - \mu_1$) and two population proportions ($P_2 - P_1$).

We look at two types of mean difference tests: one for independent samples, and one for dependent, or matched, samples. The independent-samples test is designed to measure mean differences between *two* samples or *two* subsets within the same sample, that is, two groups that are assumed to be independent in nature, not related in *any* way. In contrast, the matched-group or dependent-samples test is designed to measure the difference between means obtained for the same sample over time or for two samples that are matched on certain characteristics so as to be as much alike as possible.

In this chapter we also examine a test for the difference between two sample proportions, seen as a special case of a test for mean differences. In this chapter, we may use the terms "sample" and "group" interchangeably. Let's get started.

## 12.2 EXPLAINING THE DIFFERENCE BETWEEN TWO SAMPLE MEANS

In a hypothesis test involving two sample means, we have two variables to consider. One of them is a two-level, or dichotomous, categorical variable, and the other is a continuous variable. The categorical variable generally is thought of as the *inde-*

*pendent variable* and the continuous variable as the *dependent variable*. For example, one of the most persistent findings in criminology is the relationship between gender and the number of delinquent offenses committed. Males consistently report having committed more delinquent acts than females. In a random sample of young males and females, then, the mean for the men is expected to be greater than the mean for the women. In the language of causal analysis, gender is the independent variable that is predicted to "cause" high levels of delinquency, the dependent variable. In this example, gender is the dichotomous independent variable (male/female), and the number of committed delinquent acts is the dependent variable. Let's follow this example through to illustrate the kinds of problems we devote our attention to in this chapter.

If we were to take a random sample of 70 young males and independently select an equal number of young females and then ask each to report the number of times in the past year that they committed each of four delinquent offenses (theft, vandalism, fighting, use of drugs), we would have two means: a mean for the sample of young men ($\bar{x}_m$), and a mean for the sample of young women ($\bar{x}_w$). We also have two population means, one from the population of men ($\mu_m$), and one from the population of women ($\mu_w$). Both the sample and the population also have standard deviations. To keep these different components of samples and populations straight, we show each and their respective notations in Table 12.1.

Let's say that consistent with findings from previous research, the mean for the sample of young men was greater than the mean for the sample of young women ($\bar{x}_m > \bar{x}_w$). As we learned in the preceding chapter, however, we can account for the difference between these two sample means in two different ways.

One explanation is that there really is a difference between the rate at which young men and women offend. What this explanation implies is that males and females come from different offending populations with different population means (Figure 12.1). There are two distributions of the rate of delinquent offending, one for females on the left, and one for males on the right. The population mean for the number of delinquent acts committed is greater for men ($\mu_m = 20$) than it is for women ($\mu_w = 10$; $\mu_m > \mu_w$). Notice that, if this is true, then when we randomly select a sample of men and record their mean and randomly select a sample of women and record their mean, more frequently than not the sample mean for men will be greater than the sample mean for women.

A second explanation for the observed difference in sample means between young men and women is that, even though each sample comes from a different

**TABLE 12.1. Characteristics and Notation for Two-Sample Problems**

|  | Population 1 | Population 2 |
|---|---|---|
| Population mean | $\mu_1$ | $\mu_2$ |
| Population standard deviation | $\sigma_1$ | $\sigma_2$ |
| Sample mean | $\bar{x}_1$ | $\bar{x}_2$ |
| Sample standard deviation | $s_1$ | $s_2$ |
| Sample size | $n_1$ | $n_2$ |

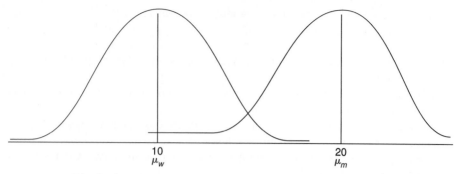

FIGURE 12.1.  Distribution of male and female delinquent offending with different population means.

population, the two population means are equal ($\mu = 17$). This is illustrated in Figure 12.2, which shows two distributions of offending, one for the population of males and one for the population of females. Although they may differ in some respects (e.g., their respective standard deviations may be different), the two population means are the same. In this explanation, when we draw random samples from both populations, the two sample means sometimes differ. In some samples we will select very delinquent males or very delinquent females. Even with equal population means, then, we can expect to find our male and female sample means sometimes to differ from one another simply by chance or sampling variation.

FIGURE 12.2.  Distribution of male and female delinquent offending with equal population means.

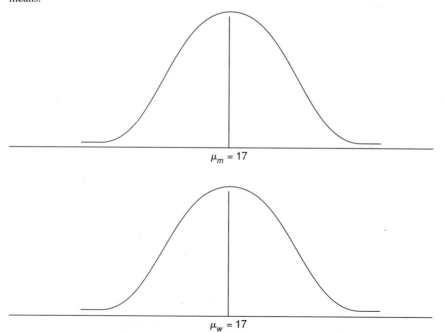

Also as seen in Chapter 10, these two explanations have very different implications. If the first explanation is true, then we would conclude that the mean number of delinquent offenses committed by males is significantly different from the mean number of offenses committed by females. Because the frequency of committing delinquent acts is significantly different between males and females, we would say that there is a "statistically significant" relationship between gender and delinquency. What we are saying here is that the difference between the male and female mean is so large that "chances are" that the samples came from different populations. However, if the second explanation is true, then we would conclude that the observed difference between means is no greater than what we would expect to observe by chance alone, in spite of the fact that the sample means are different.

Because we have sample data, not population data, any difference we observe in our sample means may be due to "real differences" between males and females in how frequently they commit delinquent acts, or just due to chance. We do not and cannot know for sure which explanation is really true. We can, however, determine which explanation is more likely. In deciding which of these two possible explanations is the more likely one, we proceed exactly as we did in Chapter 11.

We begin by assuming that there is no difference between the two population means, that is, that the populations from which each of the two samples were drawn have equal means ($\mu_m = \mu_w$). Using probability theory and a new kind of sampling distribution, we then ask how likely is it that we would have observed the difference between the two sample means if the population means are equal. If it is very unlikely, we will conclude that our presumption of equal population means is not true. This is exactly the procedure we followed in Chapter 10, where our sampling distribution was the sampling distribution of means. In this chapter, we are interested in the *sampling distribution of sample mean differences*. We illustrate the process of hypothesis testing with two sample means in Figure 12.3.

## 12.3 SAMPLING DISTRIBUTION OF MEAN DIFFERENCES

To understand what a sampling distribution of mean differences is, imagine that we take a sample of males and a sample of females from their respective populations, that we compute a mean for each sample, and then calculate the difference between the two means. Imagine that we do this for an infinite number of samples, calculating the mean for each group and the difference between the means. We then plot this frequency distribution of an infinite number of mean differences. This theoretical distribution of all differences between an infinite number of sample means is our sampling distribution of *differences* between sample means. We illustrate what this distribution might look like in Figure 12.4. The following list provides a summary of its characteristics:

1. The mean of the sampling distribution of the difference between two means, $\mu_1 - \mu_2$, is equal to the difference between the population means.

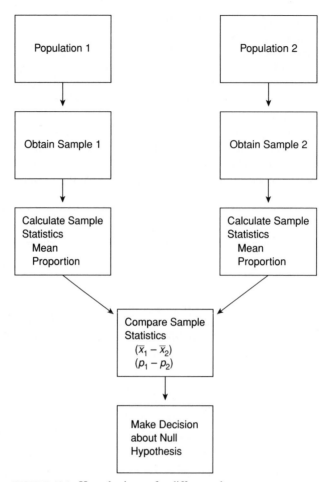

FIGURE 12.3. Hypothesis test for difference between two means or proportions.

2. The standard deviation of the sampling distribution of the difference between two means is called the *standard error of the difference between two means* and reflects how much variation exists from sample to sample. When the population standard deviations are known, the formula for the standard error is:

$$\sigma_{\bar{x}_1 - \bar{x}_2} = \sqrt{\frac{\sigma_1^2}{n_1} + \frac{\sigma_2^2}{n_2}}$$

This sampling distribution of mean differences is analogous to the sampling distribution of the mean that we discussed in Chapter 10. The differences are that the sampling distribution in Figure 12.4 is composed of the *difference* between sample means rather than single means. Second, it is centered around the difference between the *two* population means ($\mu_1 - \mu_2$), not around a *single* population mean ($\mu$).

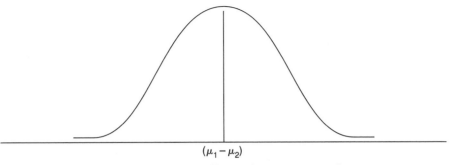

FIGURE 12.4. Sampling distribution of the difference between two sample means.

The mean of this distribution of mean differences is determined by the difference between the two population means. If the two population means are equal ($\mu_m = \mu_w$), as in Figure 12.2, the mean of the sampling distribution of differences will be zero. As stated, even if this is true, not every *sample difference* is expected to be equal to zero. Sometimes the male mean will be greater than the female mean; sometimes the female mean will be greater. What will be true, however, is that with an infinite number of samples, the mean of the distribution of sample differences will be zero.

If the two population means are different, as they are in Figure 12.2 with the population mean for men being greater than that for women ($\mu_m > \mu_w$), then most of the sample mean differences $\bar{x}_m - \bar{x}_w$ will be positive because in most of the samples the male mean will be greater than the female mean. In this case the mean of the sampling distribution of differences will be greater than zero. More specifically, the mean of the sampling distribution will be equal to the difference between the population means ($\mu_m - \mu_w$).

Up to now, we repeatedly have stated that, no matter what the value of the means for the two populations, when repeated random samples are taken, means calculated, and differences taken, not every mean difference will be exactly the same. There will, then, be dispersion about the mean of the sampling distribution of differences. You can see the spread about the mean of the sampling distribution of differences in Figure 12.4. This dispersion is measured by the standard deviation of sample mean differences, or the *standard error of the difference between means* ($\sigma_{(\bar{x}_1 - \bar{x}_2)}$), which is defined as:

$$\sigma_{(\bar{x}_1 - \bar{x}_2)} = \sqrt{\sigma_1^2/n_1 + \sigma_2^2/n_2} \tag{12.1}$$

where
    $\sigma_1$ = the standard deviation of the first population
    $\sigma_2$ = the standard deviation of the second population

As shown in this equation, the standard error of the difference is equal to the sum of the standard deviations of the sampling distributions for the two means.

Not only do we know the mean and standard deviation of the sampling distribution of differences, but we also are in a position to know its shape. This important statistical theorem states that:

> If two independent random samples of size $n_1$ and $n_2$ are drawn from normal populations, then the sampling distribution of the difference between the two sample means $(\bar{x}_1 - \bar{x}_2)$ will be normally distributed.

We can now use the central limit theorem to generalize this to include any population whenever the sample sizes are large. That is, no matter what the shape of the two populations, if independent random samples of size $n_1$ and $n_2$ are drawn, the sampling distribution of the difference between the two sample means will approximate a normal distribution as $n_1$ and $n_2$ become large (both sample sizes over 50). With normal populations or with large enough samples from any population, then, the sampling distribution of differences will approximate normality.

This should sound very familiar to you because it is similar to what we did in Chapter 10. An appropriate statistical test for the difference between two means is either a $z$ test or $t$ test. Therefore, an appropriate sampling distribution would be either the $z$ or $t$ distribution. The $z$ test for two means is appropriate whenever the two population variances ($\sigma_1$ and $\sigma_2$) are known. If these values are unknown, the $t$ test for two means is the appropriate statistical test. Because we seldom know the value of the population variances, the $t$ test is the more frequently applied test. For that reason, we discuss only $t$ tests for the difference between two means.

To refresh your memory, the explicit steps in any hypothesis test are listed in the box at the bottom of the page.

Now, let's go through some examples of different types of hypothesis tests involving two population means.

## 12.4 TESTING A HYPOTHESIS ABOUT THE DIFFERENCE BETWEEN TWO MEANS: INDEPENDENT SAMPLES

In this section, we discuss the case of hypothesis tests for the difference between two *independent random sample* means. In the independent samples case, we have two samples whose elements are randomly and independently selected. Random

> **Step 1.** Formally state your null ($H_0$) and research ($H_1$) hypothesis.
> **Step 2.** Select an appropriate test statistic and the sampling distribution of that test statistic.
> **Step 3.** Select a level of significance (alpha), and determine the critical value and rejection region of the test statistic based on the selected level of alpha.
> **Step 4.** Conduct the test: Calculate the obtained value of the test statistic and compare it to the critical value.
> **Step 5.** Make a decision about your null hypothesis, and interpret this decision in a meaningful way based on the research question.

and independent selection occurs whenever there is a known probability of any element being selected into a sample and the selection of an element into one sample has no effect on the selection of any element into the other sample. In other words, both samples are randomly selected and are independent of one another.

In our example, independence would occur if selecting a male into one sample had no effect on selecting a female into the other sample. The independence assumption is violated in the case of matched or dependent samples, where an element is deliberately selected into a sample or when the same observations are found in both samples. We review the special case of hypothesis testing presented by matched and dependent samples later in this chapter.

In Chapter 9, we used the following $t$ statistic to test a hypothesis about a single population mean:

$$t = \frac{\bar{x} - \mu}{\hat{\sigma}_{\bar{x}}}$$

where

$$\hat{\sigma}_{\bar{x}} = \frac{s}{\sqrt{n-1}} \tag{12.2}$$

In this equation, the $t$ test for a single population mean is computed by subtracting the mean of the sampling distribution ($\mu$) from the sample statistic ($\bar{x}$) and dividing by the estimated standard deviation of the sampling distribution ($\hat{\sigma}_{\bar{x}}$).

This is exactly the statistical test we will conduct here, although with three differences: (1) our sample statistic is not the sample mean but the difference between two sample means ($\bar{x}_1 - \bar{x}_2$); (2) the mean of the sampling distribution is not the population mean but the difference between two population means ($\mu_1 - \mu_2$); and (3) the estimated standard deviation of the sampling distribution is the estimated standard deviation of the sampling distribution of the difference between sample means ($\hat{\sigma}_{\bar{x}_1 - \bar{x}_2}$). The general formula for the $t$ test involving the difference between two sample means, then, is:

$$t_{\text{obt}} = \frac{(\bar{x}_1 - \bar{x}_2) - (\mu_1 - \mu_2)}{\hat{\sigma}_{\bar{x}_1 - \bar{x}_2}} \tag{12.3}$$

Do not be alarmed by the second term in the numerator above ($\mu_1 - \mu_2$). Because we are testing the null hypothesis that the two population means are equal ($\mu_1 = \mu_2$), this term is reduced to zero and can be dropped from the formula. The formula for the $t$ test can now be expressed as:

$$t_{\text{obt}} = \frac{(\bar{x}_1 - \bar{x}_2)}{\hat{\sigma}_{\bar{x}_1 - \bar{x}_2}} \tag{12.4}$$

This $t$ test requires that the two samples be independent random samples, normally distributed populations, and that the dependent variable be measured at the interval or ratio level.

As you can see from Equation 12.4, the $t$ statistic is obtained by dividing the difference between the two sample means by the estimated standard deviation of the sampling distribution (the standard error of the difference). There are, however, two cases of the $t$ test between two means. In one test we can assume that the unknown population standard deviations are equal ($\sigma_1 = \sigma_2$); in the second case we cannot make that assumption ($\sigma_1 \neq \sigma_2$). The importance of this is that our estimate of the standard error of the difference ($\hat{\sigma}_{\bar{x}_1 - \bar{x}_2}$) is different for the two cases. We examine the $t$ test for both of these cases separately.

## Model 1: Pooled Variance Estimate ($\sigma_1 = \sigma_2$)

If we can assume that the two unknown population standard deviations are equal ($\sigma_1 = \sigma_2$), we estimate the standard error of the difference using a pooled variance estimate. As the population standard deviations are not known, the decision as to whether they are equal is made based on the equality of the sample standard deviations ($s_1$ and $s_2$). Something called an $F$ test is the appropriate test for the significance of the difference between the two sample standard deviations. Without going into too much detail here, the $F$ test tests the null hypothesis that $\sigma_1^2 = \sigma_2^2$. If we fail to reject this null hypothesis, we can assume that the population standard deviations are equal. If, however, we are led to reject this hypothesis, we cannot make the assumption that the two population standard deviations are equal and we must estimate the standard error using what is called a *separate variance estimate*, which we discuss later.

We continue under the assumption that $\sigma_1 = \sigma_2$ and demonstrate the use of a *pooled variance estimate of the standard error of the difference*. Recall from Equation 12.1 that the standard error of the difference was:

$$\sigma_{\bar{x}_1 - \bar{x}_2} = \sqrt{\frac{\sigma_1^2}{n_1} + \frac{\sigma_2^2}{n_2}}$$

If we can assume that the two population standard deviations are equal ($\sigma_1 = \sigma_2$), then we would have a common value of $\sigma$. Using the common value of the population standard deviations, we can then rewrite Equation 12.1 as:

$$\sigma_{\bar{x}_1 - \bar{x}_2} = \sqrt{\frac{\sigma_1^2}{n_1} + \frac{\sigma_2^2}{n_2}}$$

$$= \sigma \sqrt{\frac{1}{n_1} + \frac{1}{n_2}}$$

$$= \sigma \sqrt{\frac{n_1 + n_2}{n_1 n_2}}$$

We must, of course, find an estimate of this common standard deviation ($\sigma$). Because we are assuming that the two population standard deviations are equal, we can obtain an estimate of the common variance by pooling or combining the two sample standard deviations. By combining the two sample values, we get a better estimate of the common population standard deviation. In many instances the samples are of unequal size, so we must weight each sample standard deviation by its respective degrees of freedom $(n - 1)$. As we are still using the sample standard deviation to estimate the population value, we continue to employ the degrees of freedom $(n - 1)$ in the denominator. Our pooled sample estimate of the common population standard deviation then becomes:

$$\sigma = \hat{\sigma}$$

$$\hat{\sigma} = \sqrt{\frac{(n_1 - 1)s_1^2 + (n_2 - 1)s_2^2}{n_1 + n_2 - 2}} \tag{12.5}$$

As the formula demonstrates, our estimate of the population standard deviation ($\hat{\sigma}$) uses the weighted average of the two sample standard deviations. More weight is therefore given to larger-size samples. You should also note that our pooled estimate $\hat{\sigma}$ will normally be in between the two sample values of $s_1$ and $s_2$.

Now that we have our estimate of the common population standard deviation ($\hat{\sigma}$), we can multiply it by $\sqrt{\frac{(n_1 + n_2)}{(n_1 n_2)}}$ to obtain our pooled variance estimate of the standard error of the difference:

$$\hat{\sigma}_{\bar{x}_1 - \bar{x}_2} = \sqrt{\frac{(n_1 - 1)s_1^2 + (n_2 - 1)s_2^2}{n_1 + n_2 - 2}} \sqrt{\frac{n_1 + n_2}{n_1 n_2}} \tag{12.6}$$

The formula for our pooled variance $t$ test then becomes:

$$t_{\text{obt}} = \frac{\bar{x}_1 - \bar{x}_2}{\sqrt{\frac{(n_1 - 1)s_1^2 + (n_2 - 1)s_2^2}{n_1 + n_2 - 2}} \sqrt{\frac{n_1 + n_2}{n_1 n_2}}} \tag{12.7}$$

Once we have our obtained value of $t$ ($t_{\text{obt}}$), we compare it to our critical value ($t_{\text{crit}}$) and make a decision about the null hypothesis. The critical value of $t$ is based on our chosen alpha level and is obtained from the $t$ table (Table B.3 of Appendix B). You will remember from Chapter 9 that, before using the $t$ table, we first need to determine the appropriate degrees of freedom. In one-sample cases, the degrees of freedom are equal to $n - 1$. Not surprisingly, when testing the difference between two sample means, the degrees of freedom are equal to $(n_1 - 1) + (n_2 - 1)$. Another way to express this is to say that we have $(n_1 + n_2 - 2)$ degrees of freedom in the two-sample case for the $t$ test. Once we have determined our degrees of freedom, we can go to the $t$ table with our chosen alpha level and find our critical value.

Let's go through an example of a formal hypothesis test using the $t$ test. In this example, we assume that we have conducted our $F$ test and did not reject the null hypothesis. Because we can therefore assume that the population standard deviations are equal, we can use the pooled variance estimate of the standard error of the difference.

Since the days of the Chicago School in the 1920s (Clifford Shaw and Henry McKay), criminologists have long postulated that states of social disorganization within a residential community increase the likelihood of various kinds of social problems and pathologies, including criminal victimization. One indicator that has been used to measure social disorganization within communities is the extent to which people move in and out of the community. Communities wherein very few families move in and move out are considered more stable and more organized than those where there is a great deal of population "turnover." In communities with relatively little turnover, residents live in the same place for a long time, they get to know their neighbors, and, as a result, a sense of community becomes established. It is hypothesized that it is this sense of community and the social relationships between community members that is responsible for the lower crime rates in these kinds of stable neighborhoods. In this hypothesis, the population turnover in a community is the independent variable and rates of crime are the dependent variable.

Suppose that we wanted to investigate the relationship between social disorganization and household crime. To do so, we collect a random sample of residents and ask them whether or not anything has been stolen from or around their home (including their automobile) within the last 6 months. In addition, we ask them how long they have lived at their present address. From this survey, we divide our sample into two groups according to the length of time they have resided at their address: (1) those residing at their current address for less than 1 year (the "transient"), (2) those residing more than 1 year (the "stable"). We then calculate the mean number of times each group experienced a household theft. For this hypothetical example, we obtain the following statistics:

**Less than 1 Year**    **More than 1 Year**

$$\bar{x}_1 = 22.4 \qquad \bar{x}_2 = 16.2$$
$$s_1^2 = 4.3 \qquad s_2^2 = 4.1$$
$$n_1 = 49 \qquad n_2 = 53$$

The steps necessary to test the difference between two means with the $t$ test include: formalizing our null and research hypotheses, adopting a test statistic (in this case the $t$ test), setting the alpha level and obtaining the critical value of $t$ corresponding to this alpha and our degrees of freedom, computing our test statistic based on the sample data, making a decision about our null hypothesis based on this test, and then interpreting this decision in a meaningful way based on our research question.

Because we have some idea about the nature of the relationship between residential stability and risk of household victimization, we adopt a directional (one-tailed) hypothesis test. Because we believe that those who have been residing in an area less than 1 year will be more vulnerable to becoming the victims of household crime, our alternative hypothesis states that the mean number of household victimizations experienced by residents who have been living at their current address less than 1 year will be greater than the mean for those who have been residing in their residences more than 1 year. Both the null and research hypothesis are formally stated as:

$$H_0: \mu_{\text{Less than 1 Year}} = \mu_{\text{More than 1 Year}}$$

$$H_1: \mu_{\text{Less than 1 Year}} > \mu_{\text{More than 1 Year}}$$

For this test, let's select an alpha level of .01. With an alpha of .01 using a directional test and degrees of freedom equal to $(n_1 + n_2 - 2) = (49 + 53 - 2 = 100)$, the critical value of $t$ that defines the rejection region can be found in Table B.3 of Appendix B. Using the degrees of freedom of 120 listed in the table (the closest value), we see that the critical value of $t$ that defines the lower limit of the rejection region is 2.358. To reject the null hypothesis, we must obtain a $t$ value equal to or greater than 2.358. We show the critical value of $t$ and the critical region for this problem in Figure 12.5.

The next step of our hypothesis test is to convert the difference between our sample means into a $t$ value:

$$t_{obt} = \frac{22.4 - 16.2}{\sqrt{\frac{[(49 - 1)(4.3)] + [(53 - 1)(4.1)]}{49 + 53 - 2}} \sqrt{\frac{49 + 53}{(49)(53)}}}$$

$$= \frac{6.2}{\sqrt{\frac{[(48)(4.3)] + [(52)(4.1)]}{100}} \sqrt{\frac{102}{2597}}}$$

$$= \frac{6.2}{\sqrt{\frac{206.4 + 213.2}{100}} \sqrt{.039}}$$

$$= \frac{6.2}{\sqrt{\frac{419.6}{100}} \sqrt{.039}}$$

$$= \frac{6.2}{\sqrt{4.20} \sqrt{.039}}$$

$$= \frac{6.2}{(2.05)(.198)}$$

$$= \frac{6.2}{.406}$$

$$= 15.26$$

FIGURE 12.5. Critical $t$ and critical region for alpha $= .01$ (df $= 120$) and a one-tailed test.

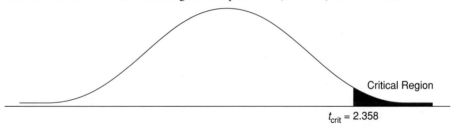

Critical Region

$t_{crit} = 2.358$

Notice that our estimate of the pooled standard deviation ($\hat{\sigma} = 2.05$) is in between the two sample standard deviations of $s_1 = 2.08$ and $s_2 = 2.03$. The $t$ value we obtained of 15.26 is substantially greater than the critical value of $t$ (2.358) needed to reject the null hypothesis. Because $t_{obt} > t_{crit}$, we reject the null hypothesis that the population means are equal. This suggests that the observed sample mean difference is too large to be attributed to chance or sampling variation, and we can therefore assume that the mean rate of household victimization experienced by those who have recently moved is greater than the mean rate experienced by those who have lived in their places of residence for 1 year or more. The results of our statistical test lends support to one of the premises of social disorganization theory; we have found that individuals who have just recently been in a state of transiency (e.g., have moved within the last year) are more likely to become the victims of household crime than are those who have been more residentially stable (e.g., have not moved within the last year).

Let's go through another example. Table 12.2 displays data from correctional facilities for females on the average annual cost to house each inmate. Two additional variables, region and state, are provided in the table as well. Suppose that we are interested in regional differences between the cost of housing female inmates. Let's say that we believe that the average annual cost per female inmate differs in the West and the South. In this scenario, region would be the independent variable (West vs. South) and cost would be the dependent variable.

Because we have no real idea about the nature of the relationship between region and cost, a nondirectional (two-tailed) hypothesis test is appropriate. The null hypothesis ($H_0$) states that the mean annual cost to house female inmates in the West is equal to the mean cost in the South. The research hypothesis ($H_1$) represents our belief that the regional means are not equal to each other:

$H_0$: $\mu_{\text{West}} = \mu_{\text{South}}$

$H_1$: $\mu_{\text{West}} \neq \mu_{\text{South}}$

Let's adopt an alpha level equal to .05. With this level of alpha using a nondirectional test and $(10 + 14 - 2 = 22)$ degrees of freedom, the critical value of $t$ is 2.074 ($t_{crit} = 2.074$). The value of $t$ we obtain from our statistical test must therefore be equal to or greater than 2.074 or equal to or less than $-2.074$ in order to reject the null hypothesis of equal means. This means that we will fail to reject the null hypothesis if $-2.074 < t_{obt} < 2.074$. We show the two critical values and critical regions in Figure 12.6.

FIGURE 12.6. Critical $t$ and critical region for alpha = .05 (df = 22) and a two-tailed test.

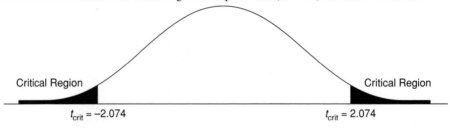

Critical Region        Critical Region

$t_{\text{crit}} = -2.074$          $t_{\text{crit}} = 2.074$

**TABLE 12.2. Average Annual Cost to House Female Inmates for the West and the South by Facility with Sample Statistics for Average Cost Displayed for Both Regions**

| Region | Facility | State | Average Annual Cost ($) |
|--------|----------|-------|-------------------------|
| West | Anchorage | AK | 33580 |
| West | Nome | AK | 46355 |
| West | Chowchilla | CA | 20727 |
| West | Frontera | CA | 20727 |
| West | San Diego | CA | 14600 |
| West | Phoenix | AZ | 16000 |
| West | Hilo | HI | 21900 |
| West | Warm Springs | MT | 16443 |
| West | Carson City | NV | 14000 |
| West | Grants | NM | 28042 |

Sample statistics for West
$\bar{x}_1 = \$23,237$
$s_1^2 = 104,149,768$
$n_1 = 10$

| Region | Facility | State | Average Annual Cost ($) |
|--------|----------|-------|-------------------------|
| South | Pine Bluff | AR | 9066 |
| South | Chattahoochee | FL | 47804 |
| South | Lowell | FL | 14928 |
| South | Marianna | FL | 12625 |
| South | Milan | GA | 17000 |
| South | Lexington | KY | 20000 |
| South | Peuce Valley | KY | 15900 |
| South | Jessup | MD | 14688 |
| South | Black Mountain | NC | 16644 |
| South | Raleigh | NC | 16060 |
| South | Rocky Mount | NC | 23725 |
| South | Greenwood | SC | 14000 |
| South | Nashville | TN | 23389 |
| South | Mountain View | TX | 13052 |

Sample statistics for South
$\bar{x}_2 = \$18,909$
$s_2^2 = 91,621,477$
$n_2 = 14$

*Source: Corrections Compendium* (1992), Lincoln, NE: CEGA Publishing, pp. 12–20.

The calculation of $t_{obt}$ from these sample data follows. As in the previous example, we assume that the population standard deviations are equal and that we can use a pooled variance estimate of the standard error of the difference:

$$t_{obt} = \frac{23,237 - 18,909}{\sqrt{\frac{[(10 - 1)(104,149,768)] + [(14 - 1)(91,621,477)]}{10 + 14 - 2}} \sqrt{\frac{10 + 14}{(10)(14)}}}$$

$$= \frac{4328}{\sqrt{\dfrac{[(9)(104,149,768)] + [(13)(91,621,477)]}{22}} \sqrt{\dfrac{24}{140}}}$$

$$= \frac{4328}{\sqrt{\dfrac{937,347,912 + 1,191,079,201}{22}} \sqrt{.17}}$$

$$= \frac{4328}{\sqrt{\dfrac{2,128,427,113}{22}} \sqrt{.17}}$$

$$= \frac{4328}{\sqrt{96,746,687} \sqrt{.17}}$$

$$= \frac{4328}{(9836)(.41)}$$

$$= \frac{4328}{4033}$$

$$= 1.07$$

The obtained value of $t$ ($t_{obt} = 1.07$) as calculated does not fall in the critical region. The data obtained from our sample, then, do not provide enough evidence for us to reject the null hypothesis that the population means are actually equal. We must conclude that there is no significant relationship between region and annual cost to house female inmates. The results of our test indicate that region, at least the West versus the South, does not affect the cost of incarcerating female offenders.

As a final example of the pooled variance estimate $t$ test, we use data from the Environmental Protection Agency (EPA). In 1991, the EPA released a list of metropolitan areas that failed to meet air quality standards for levels of ozone. Table 12.3 lists the number of days each of these metropolitan areas failed to meet the air quality standards during 1991 in the South and the Northeast. Metropolitan areas in other regions of the country had exceeded the limits, but the number of metropolitan areas in the West and Midwest were really too few to include in a mean difference test. It is worth noting, however, that the worst offending metropolitan areas were in the West. For example, the Los Angeles area exceeded ozone standards 91 out of 365 days in 1991 followed by the San Joaquin Valley, also in California (33.9 days).

Suppose we want to test the extent to which there are mean differences in the number of days metropolitan areas exceed the ozone limits between the northeast and southern regions of the country. The steps necessary to test this nondirectional hypothesis follow:

$H_0$: $\mu_{\text{Northeast}} = \mu_{\text{South}}$

$H_1$: $\mu_{\text{Northeast}} \neq \mu_{\text{South}}$

$df = (26 + 33) - 2 = 57$

Critical value of $t$ with $\alpha = .05 = \pm 2.00$

**TABLE 12.3. Number of Days Metropolitan Areas Failed to Meet National Ambient Air Quality Standards for Ozone, 1991**

| Northern Metropolitan Areas* | State | Days | Southern Metropolitan Areas | State | Days |
|---|---|---|---|---|---|
| Allentown | PA | .00 | Birmingham | AL | .00 |
| Altoona | PA | .00 | Cherokee County | SC | .00 |
| Buffalo | NY | .00 | Edmonson County | KY | .00 |
| Erie | PA | .00 | Greensboro | NC | .00 |
| Harrisburg | PA | .00 | Knoxville | TN | .00 |
| Jefferson County | NY | .00 | Lexington | KY | .00 |
| Johnstown | PA | .00 | Memphis | TN | .00 |
| Lancaster | PA | .00 | Miami | FL | .00 |
| Pittsburgh | PA | .00 | Owensboro | KY | .00 |
| Lewiston | ME | 1.00 | Paducah | KY | .00 |
| Reading | PA | 1.00 | Raleigh | NC | .00 |
| Albany | NY | 1.10 | Richmond | VA | .00 |
| Scranton | PA | 2.00 | Tampa | FL | .00 |
| Atlantic City | NJ | 2.10 | Charleston | WV | 1.00 |
| Poughkeepsie | NY | 2.10 | Charlotte | NC | 1.00 |
| Hancock | ME | 2.50 | Lake Charles | LA | 1.00 |
| Portsmouth | NH | 3.20 | Norfolk | VA | 1.00 |
| Essex County | NY | 3.70 | Parkersburg | WV | 1.00 |
| Portland | ME | 4.80 | Greenbrier County | WV | 1.10 |
| Springfield | MA | 5.70 | Nashville | TN | 1.10 |
| Knox County | ME | 7.00 | Baton Rouge | LA | 2.00 |
| Boston | MA | 7.60 | Detroit | MI | 3.00 |
| Providence | RI | 9.50 | Huntington | WV | 3.10 |
| Philadelphia | PA | 10.30 | Sussex | DE | 3.10 |
| New York | NY | 13.30 | El Paso | TX | 3.20 |
| Hartford | CT | 17.30 | Louisville | KY | 3.40 |
| | | | Atlanta | GA | 4.00 |
| | | | Dallas | TX | 4.82 |
| | | | Beaumont | TX | 6.00 |
| | | | Washington | DC | 6.10 |
| | | | Kent County | MD | 6.30 |
| | | | Baltimore | MD | 8.20 |
| | | | Houston | TX | 16.60 |

Northeast sample statistics

$$\bar{x}_1 = 3.62$$
$$s_1^2 = 21.59$$
$$n_1 = 26$$

Southern sample statistics

$$\bar{x}_2 = 2.31$$
$$s_2^2 = 11.68$$
$$n_2 = 33$$

*Source:* Environmental Protection Agency, press release, tables 370 and 371, June 1992.

*Actual metropolitan areas may contain more than one city or town. The metropolitan area listed here is the first listed in the official listing. For example, Albany, NY, actually represents the Albany-Schenectady-Troy, NY, metropolitan area.

$$t = \frac{3.62 - 2.31}{\sqrt{\dfrac{[(26 - 1)(21.59)] + [(57 - 1)(11.68)]}{26 + 33 - 2}} \sqrt{\dfrac{26 + 33}{(26)(33)}}}$$

$$= \frac{1.31}{\sqrt{\dfrac{539.75 + 654.08}{57}} \sqrt{\dfrac{59}{858}}}$$

$$= \frac{1.31}{\sqrt{\dfrac{1193.83}{57}} \sqrt{.07}}$$

$$= \frac{1.31}{\sqrt{20.9} \sqrt{.07}}$$

$$= \frac{1.31}{(4.58)(.26)}$$

$$= \frac{1.31}{1.19}$$

$$= 1.10$$

The critical values and regions for this hypothesis test are shown in Figure 12.7. We will reject the null hypothesis if our obtained $t$ is either less than or equal to $-2.00$ or greater than or equal to $+2.00$. In other words, the critical regions include $t_{obt}$ scores to the left of $t = -2.00$ and to the right of $t = 2.00$. If $-2.00 < t_{obt} + 2.00$, we will fail to reject the null hypothesis. Our statistical test results in an obtained $t$ value of 1.10. An obtained $t$ of 1.10 does not lie within the critical region. As $t_{obt} > -t_{crit}$ and $t_{obt} < +t_{crit}$, we are not led to reject the null hypothesis. Because we failed to reject the null hypothesis, we must conclude that the mean number of days in which metropolitan areas in the South and the Northeast exceed the standards set for levels of ozone are not significantly different from each other.

### Model 2: Separate Variance Estimate ($\sigma_1 \neq \sigma_2$)

In the previous three examples, we have assumed that the two population standard deviations were equal. Under this assumption, we can take advantage of this equal-

FIGURE 12.7. Critical $t$ and critical regions for alpha $= .05$ (df $= 57$) and a two-tailed test.

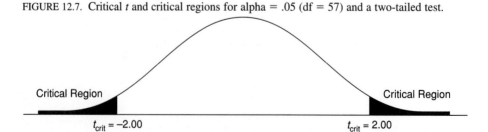

Critical Region                                                    Critical Region

$t_{crit} = -2.00$                                    $t_{crit} = 2.00$

ity and use a common estimate of the population standard deviation ($\sigma$) to calculate a pooled variance estimate for the standard error of the difference ($\sigma_{\bar{x}_1 - \bar{x}_2}$). Of course, it will not always be possible to do this. In many instances, our $F$ test will lead us to reject the null hypothesis that $\sigma_1$ equals $\sigma_2$. When this occurs, we conclude that the two population standard deviations are different. If we cannot maintain the assumption that the two population standard deviations are equal, we cannot use a pooled estimate of that standard deviation. Instead, we must use what is called a *separate variance estimate of the standard error of the difference*. The formula for this estimate is:

$$\sigma_{\bar{x}_1 - \bar{x}_2} = \sqrt{\frac{s_1^2}{n_1 - 1} + \frac{s_2^2}{n_2 - 1}} \tag{12.8}$$

As you can see, unlike the estimated standard error based on a pooled standard deviation, the separate variance estimate is based on just that: contributions from each sample standard deviation separately. This should make sense as we have determined that the two standard deviations are significantly different from each other.

With a separate variance estimate of the standard error of the difference, the formula for our $t$ test becomes:

$$t_{\text{obt}} = \frac{\bar{x}_1 - \bar{x}_2}{\sqrt{\dfrac{s_1^2}{n_1 - 1} + \dfrac{s_2^2}{n_2 - 1}}} \tag{12.9}$$

The steps necessary to conduct a hypothesis test remain the same as before, except for determining the degrees of freedom. The correct degrees of freedom for the separate variance $t$ test are not equal to $n_1 + n_2 - 2$. In fact, the degrees of freedom for a $t$ test using a separate variance estimate are quite a bit more complicated. The following formula has been suggested to obtain the appropriate degrees of freedom for this test (Blalock 1979; Hays 1994):

$$\text{Degrees of Freedom (df)} \simeq \left[ \frac{\left( \dfrac{s_1^2}{n_1 - 1} + \dfrac{s_2^2}{n_2 - 1} \right)^2}{\left( \dfrac{s_1^2}{n_1 - 1} \right)^2 \left( \dfrac{1}{n_1 + 1} \right) + \left( \dfrac{s_2^2}{n_2 - 1} \right)^2 \left( \dfrac{1}{n_2 + 1} \right)} \right] - 2 \tag{12.10}$$

The results should be rounded to the nearest integer to obtain the approximate degrees of freedom. Let's go through two examples using the separate variance estimate approach for the $t$ test.

In 1991, Lawrence Sherman and his colleagues reported the results of a study that examined the effects of time in jail detention on postrelease frequency of domestic assault for suspects arrested for domestic violence. A group of randomly assigned arrestees were placed in short-term detention (approximately 3 hours), while another group of arrestees were placed in longer-term detention (approximately 11 hours). The question that Sherman et al. were investigating was whether the length of time in detention affected the subsequent frequency of domestic violence.

Let's say we replicated their study on a much smaller scale. We randomly assigned arrested domestic violence suspects to either short-term (no more than 3 hours) or long-term (more than 3 hours) detention. We then followed them up for

120 days and recorded the number of arrests for domestic assault during that period. Our hypothetical data are as follows:

| | Short-Term Detention | Long-Term Detention |
|---|---|---|
| Mean number of postdetention assaults | $\bar{x}_1 = 6.4$ | $\bar{x}_2 = 8.1$ |
| Standard deviation | $s_1 = 2.2$ | $s_2 = 3.9$ |
| Sample size | $n_1 = 14$ | $n_2 = 42$ |

In this example, the length of detention (short-term vs. long-term) is the independent variable, and the number of postdetention domestic assaults is the dependent variable. We would like to test the hypothesis that the population mean for the two groups are equal. In saying this, we are suggesting that the length of detention has no effect on the frequency with which domestic violence is committed. Based on an $F$ test, we rejected the null hypothesis that the population standard deviations were equal, and therefore must use the separate variance $t$ test as our statistical test.

Deterrence theory might lead us to predict that a longer period in detention might lead to a decreased rate of future offending. In contrast to this, however, is the review of the empirical literature by Hood and Sparks (1970) who concluded that length of incarceration had no clear effect on postrelease behavior. Moreover, we could even make our own plausible argument that the longer people sit in detention, the angrier they become and, hence, the *more* frequently they will assault their partner when released. In view of these inconsistent suggestions, we are not confident in making a directional research hypothesis. We will therefore conduct the safer nondirectional (two-tailed) research hypothesis that states that the two population means are different. Our null hypothesis states that the two population means are equal:

$H_0$: $\mu_{\text{Short Detention}} = \mu_{\text{Long Detention}}$

$H_1$: $\mu_{\text{Short Detention}} \neq \mu_{\text{Long Detention}}$

As mentioned, our statistical test will be the separate variance $t$ test, and our sampling distribution will be the $t$ distribution. We select an alpha level of .01. To find our critical value of $t$ and the critical region, we first need to determine the appropriate degrees of freedom. Based on Equation 12.10, we can approximate our degrees of freedom as:

$$df \approx \frac{\left(\frac{(2.2)^2}{14-1} + \frac{(3.9)^2}{42-1}\right)^2}{\left(\frac{(2.2)^2}{14-1}\right)^2\left(\frac{1}{14+1}\right) + \left(\frac{(3.9)^2}{42-1}\right)^2\left(\frac{1}{42+1}\right)} - 2$$

$$\approx \frac{\left(\frac{4.84}{13} + \frac{15.21}{41}\right)^2}{\left(\frac{4.84}{13}\right)^2\left(\frac{1}{15}\right) + \left(\frac{15.21}{41}\right)^2\left(\frac{1}{43}\right)} - 2$$

$$\simeq \frac{(.37 + .37)^2}{(.37)^2(.07) + (.37)^2(.02)} - 2$$

$$\simeq \frac{(.74)^2}{.010 + .003} - 2$$

$$\simeq \frac{(.74)^2}{.013} - 2$$

$$\simeq \frac{.55}{.013} - 2$$

$$\simeq 42.3 - 2$$

$$\simeq 40.3$$

$$\simeq 40$$

With 40 degrees of freedom and an alpha of .01 for a two-tailed test, our critical value of $t$ is 2.704 (Table B.3, Appendix B). Our critical region, then, will consist of any $t_{obt}$ less than or equal to $-2.704$ or greater than or equal to 2.704. We will fail to reject the null hypotheses if $-2.704 < t_{obt} < 2.704$. We show the critical values and critical region in Figure 12.8.

We now calculate our obtained value of $t$:

$$t_{obt} = \frac{x_1 - x_2}{\sqrt{\dfrac{s_1^2}{n_1 - 1} + \dfrac{s_2^2}{n_2 - 1}}}$$

$$= \frac{6.4 - 8.1}{\sqrt{\dfrac{(2.2)^2}{14 - 1} + \dfrac{(3.9)^2}{42 - 1}}}$$

$$= \frac{-1.7}{\sqrt{\dfrac{4.84}{13}} + \sqrt{\dfrac{15.21}{41}}}$$

$$= \frac{-1.7}{\sqrt{.37 + .37}}$$

$$= \frac{-1.7}{.86}$$

$$= 1.98$$

Our obtained $t$ statistic is 1.98. Because $-t_{crit} \le t_{obt} \le t_{crit}$, we fail to reject the null hypothesis. Our conclusion, based on our sample results, would be that there is no significant relationship between time in detention and a batterer's propensity to commit acts of violence in the future.

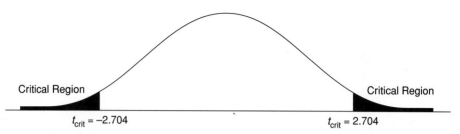

FIGURE 12.8.   Critical $t$ and critical region for alpha $= .01$ (df $= 40$) and a two-tailed test.

As a second example, let's look at the relationship between social class and delinquency. The relationship or lack of relationship between social class and delinquency has generated much controversy in criminology. Some have claimed that there is a consistent and moderately strong inverse relationship between social class and the commission of delinquent acts. These criminologists claim that youths from lower- and working-class families commit more delinquent acts than those from more affluent families. Other criminologists have made the counterclaim that no such relationship exists between delinquency and social class. This argument states that youths from lower- and working-class families are not more delinquent than their counterparts in middle- and upper-class families. You should immediately recognize that the social class of the youth in this scenario is the independent variable and the number of delinquent offenses committed the dependent variable.

Elliott and Ageton (1980) have examined this relationship between social class and delinquency using their data from the National Youth Survey, a nationally representative sample of youth ages 11 to 17 in 1976. For our example, we use the means and standard deviations they report, but substitute our own sample size. They found that the average number of predatory crimes committed by a sample of lower-class youths was $\bar{x}_1 = 12.02$, with a standard deviation of 72.68. The average number of predatory crimes for the sample of middle-class youths was $\bar{x}_2 = 3.32$ with a standard deviation of 11.31. Let's assume that we have a sample of 50 lower-class and 25 middle-class youths. We want to test the hypothesis that the two groups have the same population mean. We assume that based on an $F$ test, we reject the assumption that $\sigma_1 = \sigma_2$ and use the separate variance $t$ test to test our hypothesis. We state what we know about our two samples:

**Lower-Class Sample**   **Middle-Class Sample**

$\bar{x}_1 = 12.02$          $\bar{x}_2 = 3.32$
$s_1 = 72.68$               $s_2 = 11.31$
$n_1 = 50$                  $n_2 = 25$

Let's presume that the formulation of our hypotheses is influenced by the literature from such diverse sources as subcultural theory (Cohen, 1955), strain theory (Cloward and Ohlin, 1960), and conflict theory (Turk, 1969) that argues that lower-class youths are more delinquent than youths from higher social classes. We will then state a directional (one-tailed) research hypothesis that the population mean is greater for lower-class youths than for middle-class youths. The null hypothesis is that the population means are equal, indicating that the frequency of offending is the same for lower- and middle-class youths:

$H_0$: $\mu_{\text{Lower Class}} = \mu_{\text{Middle Class}}$

$H_1$: $\mu_{\text{Lower Class}} > \mu_{\text{Middle Class}}$

Our test statistic is the separate variance $t$ test, and our sampling distribution is the $t$ distribution. We choose an alpha level of .05. Based on Equation 12.10, we determine that the approximate degrees of freedom is 56 (we will not show the work here, but it would be a good idea to compute this for yourself). With 56 degrees of freedom, an alpha of .05, and a one-tailed test, we can see from the $t$ table that our critical $t$ value is 1.671 (actually, this $t$ score corresponds to 60 degrees of freedom, but it is the closest value we have to 56 df in the table). Because we have predicted that the true population mean is greater than that expressed in the null hypothesis, we will reject the null hypothesis if $t_{\text{obt}} \geq 1.671$ and fail to reject the null hypothesis if $t_{\text{obt}} < 1.671$. We show the critical value and the critical region in Figure 12.9.

We now calculate our obtained $t$ value, using the separate variance estimate as shown:

$$t_{\text{obt}} = \frac{12.02 - 3.32}{\sqrt{\dfrac{(72.68)^2}{(50 - 1)} + \dfrac{(11.31)^2}{(25 - 1)}}}$$

$$= \frac{8.7}{\sqrt{107.8 + 5.33}}$$

$$= \frac{8.7}{\sqrt{113.13}}$$

$$= \frac{8.7}{10.64}$$

$$= .82$$

Our obtained $t$ score of .82 is considerably less than the critical $t$ of 1.671. Our decision, then, will be to fail to reject the null hypothesis that there is no difference in the population means. We will conclude that, based on our sample data, there is no

FIGURE 12.9. Critical $t$ and critical region for alpha = .05 (df = 60) and a one-tailed test.

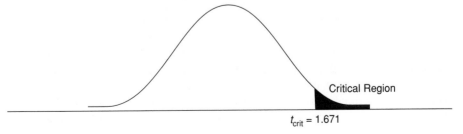

Critical Region

$t_{\text{crit}} = 1.671$

significant relationship between delinquency and social class. The frequency of committing predatory delinquent acts does not appear to be greater for lower-class youths than for middle-class youths.

In this section, we have illustrated the use of two different types of $t$ tests. One, the pooled variance $t$ test, is appropriate when we can assume that the population standard deviations are equal ($\sigma_1 = \sigma_2$). The estimated standard error of the difference ($\sigma_{\bar{x}_1 - \bar{x}_2}$) in this $t$ test is based on a pooled estimate of the common population standard deviation. The second, the separate variance $t$ test, is used whenever we cannot assume that the two population standard deviations are equal ($\sigma_1 \neq \sigma_2$). As the name implies, the standard error of this $t$ test is based on two separate standard deviation estimates. In order not to confuse these two estimates of the standard deviation of the difference between two means and their respective $t$ tests, we provide both formulas and the condition under which each is appropriate:

| Assumption | Estimate of Standard Error of the Difference | Appropriate $t$ test |
|---|---|---|
| $\sigma_1 = \sigma_2$ | Pooled variance estimate | $t_{\text{obt}} = \dfrac{\bar{x}_1 - \bar{x}_2}{\sqrt{\dfrac{n_1 s_1^2 + n_2 s_2^2}{n_1 + n_2 - 2}} \sqrt{\dfrac{n_1 + n_2}{n_1 n_2}}}$ |
| $\sigma_1 \neq \sigma_2$ | Separate variance estimate | $t_{\text{obt}} = \dfrac{\bar{x}_1 - \bar{x}_2}{\sqrt{\dfrac{s_1^2}{n_1 - 1} + \dfrac{s_2^2}{n_2 - 1}}}$ |

So far, we have examined ways in which to compare means across two different samples or groups of cases. In the next section, we look at a procedure called the matched-groups $t$ test, which is used to compare two means within the same or comparable group or sample.

## 12.5 MATCHED-GROUPS OR DEPENDENT-SAMPLES t TEST

In our application of the $t$ test for the difference between two means, we assumed that the two samples were independent of each other. That is, that the selection of the elements of one sample had no effect on the selection of the elements of the other. There are times when this assumption is deliberately violated. One instance of this occurs when we have a "treatment" and a "control" group. To make sure that the two groups are comparable, each observation in one group is "matched" with an observation in the other group on relevant characteristics. Typically, this is done so that the only thing that differentiates them is that one group received a certain type of treatment or was exposed to some phenomena and the other group was not.

For example, one way to determine the effects of counseling on future delinquency would be to collect data from two samples very similar in nature, with the exception that one had received counseling (treatment group) and the other had not (control group). To do this, an 18-year-old minority male who lived in an urban area and who had no prior criminal history might be placed in a sample that received treatment (counseling), whereas another 18-year-old minority male who lived in an urban area and who had no prior criminal history would be "matched" to this treatment male but placed in a sample that received no treatment (no counseling). If the members of the two groups are effectively matched on important characteristics, such as age, criminal history, minority status, and location of residence, then any observed differences between the two groups on the dependent variable (future delinquency) are unlikely to be due to these demographic characteristics and more likely to be due to treatment, which in this example is counseling. The important point here is that, by matching someone in one sample with a counterpart in a second sample, we have violated our assumption that the two samples are independent.

A second common use of matched or dependent samples occurs with "before and after" designs, more generally referred to as "pre and post" designs. In this type of study, there is only one sample, but measures of the dependent variable are taken at two different points in time. An example of this design is when measuring a variable of interest before and after some experimental variable is introduced. In this case, rather than having someone in the experimental group matched with someone in the control group, each person serves as his or her own control. This type of sample also violates our assumption of independence because the same persons appear in both groups.

If we were to use either the matched-sample or pre–post design in a study, we might be tempted to use a difference of means *t* test to determine whether the groups were significantly different on some continuous variable of interest. It should be clear to you, however, that the two previously described *t* tests would not be appropriate because we would not have independent samples. Because the elements of each sample were deliberately selected to be alike, we really only have *n* independent observations. In both the matched-groups and pre–post design, the independent observation is actually a pair of cases, not two independent groups. If we now consider each pair as an independent observation, we can conduct a statistical test based on the difference between the scores for each pair. In other words, we make a pair-by-pair comparison by obtaining a difference score for each pair. Unlike the *t* test for independent samples that tests the difference between two sample means $(\bar{x}_1 - \bar{x}_2)$, the *matched-* or *dependent-groups t test* tests the difference between the scores for each pair $(x_2 - x_1)$.

In the null hypothesis of the *t* test for dependent samples, we assume that the two populations are equal—that the treatment or intervention has no effect. If this is true, the two scores will be equal, so that the difference between them will be zero. If, under the null hypothesis, we take the difference between each pair of observations, each difference will be expected to be zero, and the mean of the differences will be zero. The null hypothesis, then, presumes that the population mean of group differences will be zero. We symbolize the mean of the population of group differences as $\mu_D$, with the subscript *D* indicating that this is the difference between the two populations. The statistical test in a $\mu_D = 0$ dependent-samples $t$ test, then, really is a single-sample test of the hypothesis that $\mu_D = 0$.

Our procedure determines the difference between each sample pair of scores $[x_D = (x_2 - x_1)]$, calculates the mean of these differences ($\bar{x}_D$), and then tests whether this sample mean difference is equal to the expected population mean difference ($\mu_D$) of zero. If the null hypothesis is true, then most of these $x_D$ differences will be close to zero, as will the mean of the differences $\bar{x}_D$. If, however, the null hypothesis is not true, then the two scores will tend to be different and the mean difference score will be greater or less than zero. The greater the difference between the pairs of scores, the greater the mean difference will be, and the more likely we will be to reject the null hypothesis.

The formula for the $t$ test with dependent samples is:

$$t = \frac{x_D - \mu_D}{s_D\sqrt{n-1}} \tag{12.11}$$

Remember that we have analogized the $t$ test for matched samples to a hypothesis test involving a single population mean ($\mu_D$). In the $t$ test in Chapter 10 where we dealt with one-sample problems, we subtracted the population mean from the sample mean and divided by the standard deviation of the sampling distribution. This is exactly what we do in the *matched-groups t test* in Equation 12.11. We subtract the population mean ($\mu_D$) from the sample mean ($\bar{x}_D$), where the sample mean is the mean of the differences between each pair of scores, and divide by the estimated standard deviation of the sampling distribution, which is the standard deviation of the observed difference scores. Notice that the dependent-samples $t$ test is based solely on the difference scores $x_D$ (where, $x_D = x_2 - x_1$), and the standard deviation of the difference scores ($s_D$).

Because the null hypothesis assumes that the population mean is zero ($\mu_D = 0$), the formula for the dependent samples $t$ test can be reduced to:

$$t_{\text{obt}} = \frac{\bar{x}_D}{s_D\sqrt{n-1}} \tag{12.12}$$

where

$$s_D = \frac{\Sigma(x_D - \bar{x}_D)^2}{n}$$

Once we have our obtained $t$ value, we do the same thing as with any $t$ test discussed thus far. We compare $t_{\text{obt}}$ with $t_{\text{crit}}$ and make a decision about our null hypothesis. We go to the same $t$ table as for independent samples $t$ tests (Table B.3 of Appendix B). The difference is that in the case of matched samples, because we only have $n$ pairs of independent observations (rather than $n_1 + n_2$ observations in the case of independent samples), we have $n - 1$ degrees of freedom, where $n$ is equal to the number of *pairs* of observations. A couple of examples will help clarify what is going on here. In each example we conduct a formal hypothesis test.

In 1977, David Farrington published an article in which he examined the effect of a prior court conviction on the number of self-reported juvenile offenses from a sample of London youths. Among his many analyses, Farrington compared the number of self-reported offenses before and after conviction in court. Farrington's original study was guided by labeling theory that hypothesizes that the experience of a formal legal sanction (court conviction) would increase the frequency of post-conviction delinquent acts. He, therefore, would have predicted that for each youth there would be more delinquent acts committed after conviction than before—what labeling theorists call a "deviance amplification" or "secondary deviance" effect. In this example, conviction in court is the independent variable and the number of self-reported offenses is the dependent variable.

Let's presume we have a random sample of 20 youths who are currently appearing in juvenile court for the first time. For each youth we have obtained from the police the number of times they had been arrested in the year before having to appear in court. These arrests for each youth constitute their first score. After their appearance in juvenile court we follow these youths for 1 year when we again get from the police the number of arrests each youth had (we also assume that none were sent to a reformatory school or what the British might call a Borstal). These scores reflect the number of arrests experienced since the youths' appearance in juvenile court and constitute their second score. We would now like to determine what effect the juvenile court appearance had on the second delinquency arrest score. That is, we want to know whether on average the youths' number of arrests increased or decreased after being in court. The fictitious number of arrests at each time are reported for you in the second and third columns of Table 12.4. We are now ready to conduct our hypothesis test.

First, we state our assumptions and the null and research hypothesis. Our null hypothesis is that the mean difference score in the population is equal to zero:

$$H_0: \mu_D = 0$$

This implies that juvenile court appearance has no effect on the youths' number of arrests. Unlike Farrington's research, in stating our research hypothesis, we will not solely be guided by labeling theory. We do think that, consistent with labeling theory, the effect of a juvenile court appearance may be to stigmatize and label these youths. As a result of this experience, they may commit more delinquent offenses after their hearing and experience more arrests as a result of increased offending. We also think, however, that it is possible that these youths may be so frightened by their court appearance (as they are appearing in court for the first time) that they will want to avoid such an experience in the future and commit fewer crimes and have fewer arrests. Consistent with deterrence theory, then, the experience of going to court may deter these youths. In view of these equally compelling but opposite predictions, we state a nondirectional (two-tailed) research hypothesis stating our belief that on average the second scores (posttrial number of arrests) will be different from the first (pretrial number of arrests):

$$H_1: \mu_D \neq 0$$

Second, we state our test statistic and the sampling distribution of that test statistic. Because we have dependent samples, we use the dependent-samples *t* test as the statistical test and the *t* distribution as our sampling distribution.

**TABLE 12.4. Number of Arrests before (first score) and after (second score) Appearance in Juvenile Court and Difference between the Two ($D$) for a Random Sample of 20 Youths**

| Pair Number | First Score ($x_1$) | Second Score ($x_2$) | $X_D$ ($x_2 - x_1$) |
|---|---|---|---|
| 1 | 3 | 4 | 1 |
| 2 | 6 | 9 | 3 |
| 3 | 7 | 5 | −2 |
| 4 | 2 | 6 | 4 |
| 5 | 4 | 5 | 1 |
| 6 | 7 | 7 | 0 |
| 7 | 5 | 9 | 4 |
| 8 | 1 | 6 | 5 |
| 9 | 5 | 2 | −3 |
| 10 | 7 | 6 | −1 |
| 11 | 6 | 9 | 3 |
| 12 | 2 | 4 | 2 |
| 13 | 3 | 3 | 0 |
| 14 | 2 | 7 | 5 |
| 15 | 4 | 5 | 1 |
| 16 | 2 | 1 | −1 |
| 17 | 6 | 8 | 2 |
| 18 | 5 | 5 | 0 |
| 19 | 1 | 5 | 4 |
| 20 | 3 | 6 | 3 |

$\Sigma D = 31$

$\bar{x}_D = \dfrac{31}{20} = 1.55$

Third, we choose our alpha level and determine the critical value and region. We select an alpha level of .01. Because we have 20 pairs of independent observations ($n = 20$), we have $20 - 1$, or 19, degrees of freedom. We go to Table B.3 of Appendix B and find that for a two-tailed hypothesis test, alpha of .01, and 19 degrees of freedom, the critical value of $t$ is ±2.861. We will, therefore, reject the null hypothesis if $t_{obt} \leq -2.861$ or if $t_{obt} \geq 2.861$. The critical region consists of all $t_{obt}$ values greater than or equal to 2.861 or less than or equal to −2.861. We illustrate this for you in Figure 12.10.

In step 4 of our hypothesis testing procedure, we calculate the test statistic and compare it to our critical value. For our first example, we illustrate in detail the calculation of the $t$ test for matched samples. From Equation 12.12 we see that we need to determine the mean of the difference scores and the estimated standard deviation of the difference scores. In Table 12.4, we report that the sum of the difference scores is equal to 31 ($\Sigma D = 31$). Notice how these difference scores are created. For each person, we subtract the second score from the first. For example, the first pair of cases had four arrests after juvenile court and three arrests in the year before they were in court. The difference, then, is $4 - 3 = 1$. We do this for each case, sum across the cases, and then divide by the number of cases to obtain a mean

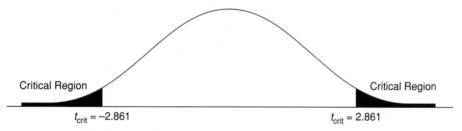

FIGURE 12.10. Critical *t* and critical regions for alpha = .01 (df = 19) and a two-tailed test.

difference score. All scores are added in calculating this mean difference score, including zeros and scores with negative signs. With 20 pairs of scores, the mean difference score for these data is 31/20, or 1.55 ($\bar{x}_D = 1.55$).

We now calculate the estimated standard deviation of the difference scores. This is just like calculating the standard deviation for any other group of scores, except that the raw data are the difference scores and the mean of the difference scores. In this example we use the definitional formula for the standard deviation. First subtract the mean difference score from each difference score, square this difference, sum these squared differences, divide by the number of pairs, and then take the square root. To get the standard deviation of the sampling distribution, divide this result by the square root of the sample size minus 1. The calculations necessary to find this are shown in Table 12.5.

**TABLE 12.5. Standard Deviations of the Sampling Distribution**

| Pair | $(D - \bar{x}_D)$ | | $(D - \bar{x}_D)^2$ |
|------|-------------------|------|---------------------|
| 1 | $(1 - 1.55)$ = | −.55 | .3025 |
| 2 | $(3 - 1.55)$ = | 1.45 | 2.1025 |
| 3 | $(-2 - 1.55)$ = | −3.55 | 12.6025 |
| 4 | $(4 - 1.55)$ = | 2.45 | 6.0025 |
| 5 | $(1 - 1.55$ = | −.55 | .3025 |
| 6 | $(0 - 1.55)$ = | −1.55 | 2.4025 |
| 7 | $(4 - 1.55)$ = | 2.45 | 6.0025 |
| 8 | $(5 - 1.55)$ = | 3.45 | 11.9025 |
| 9 | $(-3 - 1.55)$ = | −4.55 | 20.7025 |
| 10 | $(-1 - 1.55)$ = | −2.55 | 6.5025 |
| 11 | $(3 - 1.55)$ = | 1.45 | 2.1025 |
| 12 | $(2 - 1.55)$ = | .45 | .2025 |
| 13 | $(0 - 1.55)$ = | −1.55 | 2.4025 |
| 14 | $(5 - 1.55)$ = | 3.45 | 11.9025 |
| 15 | $(1 - 1.55)$ = | −.55 | .3025 |
| 16 | $(-1 - 1.55)$ = | −2.55 | 6.5025 |
| 17 | $(2 - 1.55)$ = | .45 | .2025 |
| 18 | $(0 - 1.55)$ = | −1.55 | 2.4025 |
| 19 | $(4 - 1.55)$ = | 2.45 | 6.0025 |
| 20 | $(3 - 1.55)$ = | 1.45 | 2.1025 |
| $n = 20$ | | | $\Sigma = 102.9500$ |

We can place this into our definitional formula for the standard deviation:

$$s = \sqrt{\frac{\Sigma(x_D - \bar{x}_D)^2}{n}}$$

$$= \sqrt{\frac{102.95}{20}}$$

$$= \sqrt{5.1475}$$

$$= 2.2688$$

Before we move on, we would like to show you that you could have obtained this exact same result by using the computational formula for the standard deviation that we learned in Chapter 5. The only change is that the difference scores $D$ are substituted for the $x$s. So, the term $\Sigma x^2$ is obtained by squaring each of the difference scores ($D$) and then adding these squared scores, and $(\Sigma x)^2$ is obtained by first summing the difference scores and then squaring this sum. If you do this, you would get:

$$s = \sqrt{\frac{\Sigma x^2 - \frac{(\Sigma x)^2}{n}}{n}}$$

Just substitute each difference score $D$ for the value of $x$:

$$s = \sqrt{\frac{151 - \frac{961}{20}}{20}}$$

$$= \sqrt{\frac{151 - 48.05}{20}}$$

$$= \sqrt{\frac{102.95}{20}}$$

$$= \sqrt{5.1475}$$

$$= 2.2688$$

Now that we have the standard deviation of the difference scores, we can calculate our test statistic:

$$t_{obt} = \frac{\bar{X}_D}{S_D/\sqrt{n-1}}$$

$$= \frac{\bar{X}_D}{\sqrt{\frac{\Sigma(x_D \bar{x}_D)^2}{n}}/\sqrt{n-1}}$$

$$= \frac{1.55}{\sqrt{\frac{102.95}{20}}/\sqrt{20-1}}$$

$$= \frac{1.55}{\sqrt{5.1475}/\sqrt{19}}$$

$$= \frac{1.55}{2.2688/4.3589}$$

$$= \frac{1.55}{.520}$$

$$= 2.98$$

Finally, we compare our obtained value of $t(2.98)$ with our critical value (2.861) and the critical region. As $t_{obt} > t_{crit}$ (2.98 > 2.861), we reject the null hypothesis that the mean of the differences is equal to zero. We conclude instead that the number of postjuvenile court arrests is greater than the precourt arrests. The experience of appearing in juvenile court for this sample of youth appears to have increased the frequency with which they engaged in delinquent activity. This finding is consistent with labeling rather than deterrence theory. Before moving on to proportions, let's go through one more example of a matched-group $t$ test.

One of the most comprehensive studies undertaken on the causes of delinquent behavior was reported in 1950 by Sheldon and Eleanor Glueck. The Gluecks compared 500 institutionalized chronic delinquents with a matched group of 500 nondelinquents. Among their findings, the Gluecks reported that the delinquent group had a different body build than the nondelinquents (the delinquents were more mesomorphic or muscular) and were more likely to come from broken homes and economically disadvantaged families, to have friends who also were delinquents, and to have parents who were cruel and erratic in their discipline than the group of nondelinquents.

Let's presume that like the Gluecks we have a group of 15 delinquents and a matched group of 15 nondelinquents, who are matched with respect to social class, gender, age, race, and whether both natural parents are in the home. For each youth we also have the number of siblings who they report have been arrested for a crime. What we want to know is whether the delinquent youths have more delinquent siblings than do nondelinquents. The data from the two groups are reported in Table 12.6.

Our null hypothesis is that the number of delinquent siblings is not different between the two groups. In other words, that the population mean for the difference between the pair of scores is zero:

$H_0$: $\mu_D = 0$

Based on our knowledge of the delinquency literature, we make the directional (one-tailed) research hypothesis that the nondelinquent group has fewer delinquent siblings than the delinquent group. Our prediction, therefore, is that the difference scores will generally be negative and that the population mean for the differences will be less than zero.

$H_1$: $\mu_D < 0$

**TABLE 12.6.  Number of Delinquent Siblings for 15 Delinquent Youths and a Matched Group of 15 Nondelinquent Youths**

| | Number of Delinquent Siblings | |
|---|---|---|
| Pair | Delinquent Group | Nondelinquent Group |
| 1 | 3 | 1 |
| 2 | 2 | 0 |
| 3 | 1 | 0 |
| 4 | 4 | 1 |
| 5 | 1 | 2 |
| 6 | 3 | 0 |
| 7 | 2 | 2 |
| 8 | 4 | 1 |
| 9 | 1 | 0 |
| 10 | 2 | 0 |
| 11 | 0 | 0 |
| 12 | 3 | 1 |
| 13 | 2 | 0 |
| 14 | 3 | 1 |
| 15 | 0 | 0 |

Our test statistic is the dependent samples $t$ test, and the sampling distribution is the $t$ distribution. For our hypothesis test, we choose an alpha level of .05. Because our research hypothesis stated that the true population mean was less than zero, our critical region will lie in the left tail of the sampling distribution. With $n - 1$, or 14, degrees of freedom, an alpha of .05, and a one-tailed test, we can find in the $t$ table that $t_{crit} = -1.761$. The critical region consists of all obtained $t$ scores that are equal to or less than $-1.761$. We will, therefore, fail to reject the null hypothesis if $t_{obt} > -1.761$. We show the critical $t$ value and critical region in Figure 12.11.

FIGURE 12.11.  Critical $t$ and critical region for alpha = .05 (df = 14) and a one-tailed test.

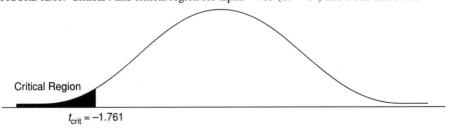

Critical Region

$t_{crit} = -1.761$

In Table 12.7 we provide the necessary calculations to determine both the mean and standard deviation of the difference scores for the data in Table 12.6. The value of $t_{obt}$ is:

$$t_{obt} = \frac{\bar{x}_D}{\sqrt{\dfrac{\Sigma(x_D - x_D)^2}{n}}/\sqrt{n-1}}$$

$$= \frac{-1.47}{\sqrt{\dfrac{21.73}{15}}/\sqrt{14}}$$

$$= \frac{-1.47}{1.45/\sqrt{14}}$$

$$= \frac{-1.47}{1.20/3.74}$$

$$= \frac{-1.47}{.32}$$

$$= -4.59$$

The obtained value of our test statistic is $-4.59$. Because $t_{obt} < t_{crit}$, we are led to reject the null hypothesis that the mean population difference is zero. We would conclude that there is a significant relationship between delinquency and the num-

**TABLE 12.7. Calculations for Matched Samples *t* Test for Data in Table 12.6**

| Pair | Nondelinquent Score | Delinquent Score | $D$ | $(D - \bar{D})$ | $(D - \bar{D})^2$ |
|------|------|------|------|------|------|
| 1 | 1 | 3 | $-2$ | $(-2 - -1.47) = -.53$ | .281 |
| 2 | 0 | 2 | $-2$ | $(-2 - -1.47) = -.53$ | .281 |
| 3 | 0 | 1 | $-1$ | $(-1 - -1.47) = .47$ | .221 |
| 4 | 1 | 4 | $-3$ | $(-3 - -1.47) = -1.53$ | 2.341 |
| 5 | 2 | 1 | 1 | $(1 - -1.47) = 2.47$ | 6.100 |
| 6 | 0 | 3 | $-3$ | $(-3 - -1.47) = -1.53$ | 2.341 |
| 7 | 2 | 2 | 0 | $(0 - -1.47) = 1.47$ | 2.161 |
| 8 | 1 | 4 | $-3$ | $(-3 - -1.47) = -1.53$ | 2.341 |
| 9 | 0 | 1 | $-1$ | $(-1 - -1.47) = .47$ | .221 |
| 10 | 0 | 2 | $-2$ | $(-2 - -1.47) = -.53$ | .281 |
| 11 | 0 | 0 | 0 | $(0 - -1.47) = 1.47$ | 2.161 |
| 12 | 1 | 3 | $-2$ | $(-2 - -1.47) = -.53$ | .281 |
| 13 | 0 | 2 | $-2$ | $(-2 - -1.47) = -.53$ | .281 |
| 14 | 1 | 3 | $-2$ | $(-2 - -1.47) = -.53$ | .281 |
| 15 | 0 | 0 | 0 | $(0 - -1.47) = 1.47$ | 2.161 |
| | | | $\Sigma D = -22$ | | $\Sigma D^2 = 21.73$ |

$\bar{x}_D = -22/15 = -1.47$

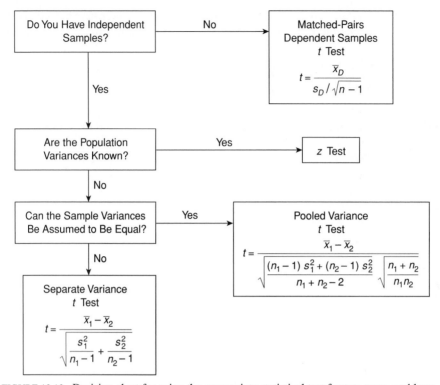

FIGURE 12.12.  Decision chart for using the appropriate statistical test for two mean problems.

ber of delinquent siblings a youth has; nondelinquents have significantly fewer delinquent siblings than delinquents.

In this and the preceding two sections of this chapter, we have examined several different types of statistics to test a hypothesis about two population means. This must present a somewhat bewildering picture to you, and we admit that it might seem a bit overwhelming right now. In selecting the appropriate test statistic for the two-sample mean problem, however, a good deal of confusion can be eliminated if you remember that you need to answer only a few fundamental questions before deciding which test is appropriate for your problem. We have tried to summarize these decisions for you in Figure 12.12. Think of this figure as a road map in deciding which statistical test for two-sample mean problems you should use. In the next section, we examine hypothesis tests about the difference between two sample proportions.

## 12.6 HYPOTHESIS TESTS FOR THE DIFFERENCE BETWEEN TWO PROPORTIONS: LARGE SAMPLES

Up to this point, we have examined the testing of hypotheses that involved the difference between two population means. In this section, we look at a statistical test for the significance of the difference between two population proportions ($p_1$ and

$p_2$). Think of the difference of proportions test as a special case of the difference of means test.

Let's say we have a sample of 100 persons and we ask each of them whether they favor the death penalty for those who commit first-degree murder. We arbitrarily assign a score of 0 for those who say no and 1 for those who say yes. Let's assume that 89 of the 100 said they approved of the death penalty under that circumstance and 11 said that they did not. Because there are only two values (zero "No" and 1 "Yes"), we can treat this variable as being measured at the interval level. We can determine the mean of this variable by counting the number of 1 scores (or 0 scores) and dividing by $n$. Because we have 89 "1" scores, the mean would be 89/100, or .89. As you can see, the mean of a binary variable (0,1) can be calculated exactly like the mean of a continuous variable. The mean for a dichotomized variable (a variable with only two values) that has been coded 0 and 1, then, is the proportion of 1 scores, in this case, the proportion of our sample who were in favor of the death penalty. The mean, therefore, actually is the proportion of "1" scores. Even though the population is dichotomous (it is made up of zeros and ones), we know from the central limit theorem that, with a large enough sample, the distribution of sample means and the difference between two sample means will be approximately normal. Hence, we can use a $z$ test and the $z$ distribution to test hypotheses about the difference between two proportions.

In this chapter, we consider tests appropriate only for data obtained from large independent samples. If $np \geq 5$ and $nq \geq 5$ for each of the two samples (where $p$ is the population proportion and $q = 1 - p$), the sampling distribution of the difference between proportions will be approximately normal, and we can use a $z$ test as our test statistic.

In the $t$ test for two-sample means, we subtracted one sample mean from the other and divided by the standard error of the difference between means. We conduct the same procedure in our test for the difference between two proportions. In our $z$ test for two proportions, we subtract the two sample proportions ($\hat{p}_1 - \hat{p}_2$) and divide by the standard deviation of the sampling distribution of the difference between proportions or the standard error ($\sigma_{p_1 - p_2}$). This standard deviation is also referred to as the *standard error of the difference between proportions*. The $z$ test for the difference between proportions is:

$$z_{obt} = \frac{(\hat{p}_1 - \hat{p}_2) - (p_1 - p_2)}{\sigma_{p_1 - p_2}} \qquad (12.13)$$

where

$\hat{p}_1 =$ the sample proportion for the first sample
$\hat{p}_2 =$ the sample proportion for the second sample
$p_1 =$ the first population proportion
$p_2 =$ the second population proportion
$\sigma_{p_1 - p_2} =$ the standard error of the difference between proportions.

Because the null hypothesis assumes that the population parameters ($p_1$ and $p_2$) are equal, formula 12.13 can be simplified to:

$$z_{obt} = \frac{\hat{p}_1 - \hat{p}_2}{\sigma_{p_1 - p_2}} \qquad (12.14)$$

The two sample proportions ($\hat{p}_1$ and $\hat{p}_2$) are known, so the only remaining unknown is the denominator, the standard error of the difference between two proportions. Because the null hypothesis states that there is no difference between the two population proportions, we can assume that $p_1 = p_2$. We have already seen in Chapter 10 that the standard deviation of a population proportion $\sigma_p = \sqrt{\dfrac{pq}{n}}$. If, by the null hypothesis, $p_1 = p_2$, then it will be true that $\sigma_1 = \sigma_2$ because $\sqrt{p_1 q_1} = \sqrt{p_2 q_2}$. In the difference of proportions test, then, we can assume that the population standard deviations are equal, and we can simplify our hypothesis test by using only a pooled variance estimate for the standard error of the difference between proportions. The formula for the pooled standard error is:

$$\sigma_{p_1 - p_2} = \sigma \sqrt{\frac{n_1 + n_2}{n_1 n_2}} \tag{12.15}$$

where

$$\sigma = \sqrt{pq}$$

However, as the population proportion ($p$) is unknown, we need to estimate the pooled standard deviation ($\sigma = \sqrt{pq}$) by calculating a pooled estimate of $p$ ($\hat{p}$). The formula for our pooled estimate of the population proportion $p$, $\hat{p}$ is:

$$\hat{p} = \frac{n_1 \hat{p}_1 + n_2 \hat{p}_2}{n_1 + n_2}, \tag{12.16}$$

where

$\hat{p} =$ the estimate of pooled population proportion
$\hat{p}_1 =$ the sample proportion for the first sample
$\hat{p}_2 =$ the sample proportion for the second sample

Once we have found $\hat{p}$, we can then determine $\hat{q}$ by subtraction, as $\hat{q} = 1 - \hat{p}$. Our estimate of the standard error of the difference between two proportions can then be calculated from the following formula:

$$\hat{\sigma}_{p_1 - p_2} = \sqrt{\hat{p}\hat{q}} \sqrt{\frac{n_1 + n_2}{n_1 n_2}} \tag{12.17}$$

Our obtained value of $z$ can now be estimated using the following formula:

$$z_{obt} = \frac{\hat{p}_1 - \hat{p}_2}{\sqrt{\hat{p}\hat{q}} \sqrt{\dfrac{n_1 + n_2}{n_1 n_2}}} \tag{12.18}$$

Once we have obtained the test statistic, we compare our $z_{obt}$ with $z_{crit}$ and make a decision about the null hypothesis.

Let's go through an example. Let's say we have independent random samples of 60 arrested property offenders from each of two cities in a state. One city (city A) has a very liberal policy of providing methadone, job and psychological counseling, and other assistance to drug addicts, whereas the second city (city B) provides no such services. Of the 60 arrested property offenders in city A, 38 percent

(.38) tested positively for drugs and 54 percent (.54) did so in city B. We wonder whether the different drug treatment policies of the two cities have any effect on the tendency for addicts to commit property theft. We decide to answer this question with an explicit hypothesis test.

Our null hypothesis is that the two samples came from populations with the same proportions of property offenders who test positively for drugs. That is:

$$H_0: p_1 = p_2$$

Because we do not know enough about the effects of the drug policy of city A to know if it will lead to a reduction or increase in drug-related crime, we test the nondirectional research hypothesis that the two proportions are different:

$$H_1: p_1 \neq p_2$$

To test these hypotheses, we select as our test statistic the $z$ test for a difference of proportions. Because we have a large sample size, the $z$ distribution will be our sampling distribution. We select an alpha level of .01. For a two-tailed test, the critical level of $z$ with an alpha of .01 is, from Table B.2 of Appendix B, $z_{crit} = \pm 2.58$. This is a two-tailed test, so the critical region lies in both tails of the $z$ distribution and consists of all obtained $z$ scores less than or equal to $-2.58$ and greater than or equal to 2.58. We will fail to reject the null hypothesis if $-2.58 < z_{obt} < 2.58$. We illustrate the two critical regions and the critical $z$ values in Figure 12.13.

To make the calculations more manageable, we find our obtained value of $z$ in a series of steps. Step 1: We find the estimated value of the pooled population proportions:

$$\hat{p} = \frac{[(60)(.38)] + [(60)(.54)]}{60 + 60}$$

$$= \frac{22.8 + 32.4}{120}$$

$$= \frac{55.2}{120}$$

$$= .46$$

FIGURE 12.13. Critical $z$ and critical regions for alpha = .01 and a two-tailed test.

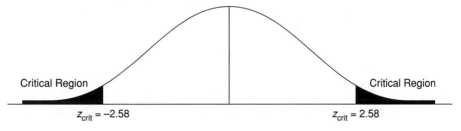

$$\hat{q} = 1 - \hat{p}$$
$$= 1 - .46$$
$$= .54$$

Step 2: We find the estimated standard error of the difference between population proportions:

$$\hat{\sigma}_{p_1 - p_2} = \sqrt{\hat{p}\hat{q}} \sqrt{\frac{n_1 + n_2}{n_1 n_2}}$$

$$= \sqrt{(.46)(.54)} \sqrt{\frac{60 + 60}{(60)(60)}}$$

$$= \sqrt{.2484} \sqrt{\frac{120}{3600}}$$

$$= (.4984)(.1826)$$

$$= .0910$$

Finally, plugging each of these values into our formula, in step 3, we can now calculate the value of our obtained $z$ test:

$$z_{obt} = \frac{\hat{p}_1 - \hat{p}_2}{\sqrt{\hat{p}\hat{q}} \sqrt{\frac{n_1 + n_2}{n_1 n_2}}}$$

$$= \frac{.38 - .54}{\sqrt{(.46)(.54)} \sqrt{\frac{60 + 60}{(60)(60)}}}$$

$$= \frac{.38 - .54}{.0910}$$

$$= \frac{-.16}{.0910}$$

$$= -1.758$$

Our obtained $z$ statistic is $-1.758$. Because $z_{obt}$ does not lie within the critical region $-2.58 < 1.758 < 2.58$, we decide not to reject the null hypothesis. We cannot conclude, based on our sample data, that the proportion of property offenders who test positively for drugs is different in the two cities.

## 12.7 SUMMARY

In this chapter, we discussed techniques used to perform hypothesis tests to determine the difference between two means and two proportions. With unknown population variances, the statistical test for the difference between two means was conducted with a $t$ test. If the test involves two independent random samples, we examined two different kinds of *t* tests. The first type, the pooled variance *t* test, is valid for two sample means when we can assume that the population standard deviations are equal. When we cannot maintain that assumption, the correct *t* test to use is the separate variance *t* test.

In addition to these tests for independent samples, we also studied a *t* test for matched or dependent samples. In this kind of *t* test, we are less interested in the difference between two means than in testing whether the difference between two sets of scores is equal to zero.

Finally, we also learned how to test for the significance of the difference between two proportions and discovered that it was a special instance of the two-sample mean test.

## Key Terms

| | |
|---|---|
| dependent samples | separate variance estimate of the |
| dependent-group *t* test | standard error of the difference |
| dependent variable | sampling distribution of sample |
| independent random samples | mean differences |
| independent random sampling | standard error of the difference |
| independent-samples *t* test | between means |
| independent variable | standard error of the difference |
| matched-groups *t* test | between proportions |
| pooled variance estimate of the | |
| standard error of the difference | |

## Problems

1. Explain the difference between independent and dependent variables. If you think that low self-control affects crime, which is the independent and which the dependent variable?
2. When is it appropriate to use an independent groups *t* test versus a *t* test for dependent samples or matched groups?
3. Thomas Peete and his colleagues (1994) found that the fear of losing the good opinion of others kept people from breaking rules, particularly if the person was very strongly attached to the social group. Let's say that we have two independent random samples of people, those who think that their coworkers would disapprove of them for stealing things from their employer, and those who think that their coworkers would either not care or approve of their stealing from their employer. We ask each person in each group to self-report the number of times that they have stolen from their employer in the past 12 months:

| Would Not Approve of Stealing | Would Approve of Stealing |
|:---:|:---:|
| $n_1 = 40$ | $n_2 = 25$ |
| $\bar{x}_1 = 5.1$ | $\bar{x}_2 = 8.2$ |
| $s_1 = 1.8$ | $s_2 = 1.9$ |

Test the null hypothesis that the two population means are equal against the alternative hypothesis that the group whose coworkers would not approve of stealing has a lower mean rate of theft. In your hypothesis test, assume that the unknown population standard deviations are equal and use an alpha level of .01.

4. The use of monetary fines as a criminal sanction is being considered as one possible solution to the problem of prison overcrowding. Supporters of the use of fines contend that it would be

both an effective deterrent to crime and a way to punish even moderately severe crimes without imprisonment. Critics argue that giving criminal offenders fines only increases their motivation to commit more crimes in order to pay their fine. You want to test the effect of fines versus incarceration on criminal behavior. You take a random sample of 150 convicted offenders who have been given a fine as punishment and follow them up for 3 years. You take a second independent random sample of 110 offenders recently released from prison and follow them up for 3 years. At the end of the 3-year follow-up period you find that 33 percent of those given a fine had been rearrested and 38 percent of those given a prison sentence had been rearrested. Test the null hypothesis that the proportion rearrested in the two groups is equal against the alternative hypothesis that they are different. Use an alpha level of .05.

5. Alissa Worden (1993) has conducted some research on the perceptions that female and male police officers have of their role, the public, and their department. She concluded that female and male police officers do not view their jobs very differently. Let's say that we wanted to continue her work and were interested in how female and male police officers view one component of police work, the handling of domestic disputes. To do this research, we have created a scale that measures how important settling domestic disputes is and whether that is perceived to be a part of "police work." Those who score high on this scale think that the fair settling of domestic disturbances is of high priority and that it should be an important part of a police officer's duties. We have then taken two random samples. One is a sample of 50 male police officers, and a second is an independent random sample of 25 female police officers. We give each officer a questionnaire that includes our domestic dispute scale. The mean score for the male police officers is 18.8 (with a standard deviation of 4.5), and the mean score for female officers is 21.3 (with a standard deviation of 3.0). Test the null hypothesis that the two population means are equal against the alternative hypothesis that the male mean is lower than the female mean. In your hypothesis test *do not* presume that the population standard deviations are equal, and use an alpha level of .05.

6. Capital punishment law is among the most complex bodies of law in our legal system. As a result, judges make frequent errors in capital cases in terms of their rulings regarding a change of venue, the decision to sequester jurors, questions of *voir dire,* suppression of evidence, and so on. When these errors are made, cases are often won on appeal and have to be retried or have a second penalty phase hearing. The Trial Judges Association thinks that only judges who have received special training should sit on capital cases because these judges would commit fewer errors and there would be fewer cases lost on appeal. You decide to test this hypothesis. You take a random sample of 15 judges who have received extensive training in capital punishment law. You match these judges with 15 other judges who have not received such training but are matched in terms of their number of years on the bench, experience as trial lawyers, gender, and age. You want the two groups of judges to be alike in every way except the experience of capital punishment law training. The data on your matched groups of judges are shown:

*Number of Cases Lost on Appeal*

| Judge | Untrained | Trained |
|:-----:|:---------:|:-------:|
| 1 | 3 | 0 |
| 2 | 1 | 3 |
| 3 | 2 | 4 |
| 4 | 7 | 4 |
| 5 | 5 | 2 |
| 6 | 4 | 5 |
| 7 | 6 | 1 |

| | | |
|---|---|---|
| 8 | 2 | 1 |
| 9 | 7 | 0 |
| 10 | 5 | 6 |
| 11 | 3 | 4 |
| 12 | 4 | 2 |
| 13 | 5 | 5 |
| 14 | 6 | 3 |
| 15 | 2 | 1 |

Test the null hypothesis that the mean difference in the number of cases lost on appeal for the two groups of judges is zero against the alternative hypothesis that the untrained judges lose more cases on appeal. Use an alpha level of .01.

7. In a recent book, Adrian Raine (1993) discusses some research in biological criminology that suggests that children with criminal parents are more likely to be criminal themselves than children with noncriminal parents. Suppose you conducted a study on a random sample of 100 delinquent youths confined in a correctional institution with a random sample of 75 nondelinquent youths. You find that 43 percent of the delinquent youths have at least one criminal parent, but only 17 percent of the nondelinquent youths have a criminal parent. Test the null hypothesis that the two population proportions are equal against the alternative that the delinquent group has a higher proportion of criminal parents. Use an alpha level of .01.

8. It is common wisdom to believe that dropping out of high school leads to delinquency. In addition, Travis Hirschi's (1969) control theory also would predict that those with little or no commitment to education are delinquent more often than those with strong educational commitments. In his general strain theory, however, Robert Agnew (1992) would predict that dropping out of school would lower one's involvement in delinquency because it would get youths out of an aversive and painful environment. You want to examine the relationship between dropping out of high school and delinquency. You have a random sample of 11 students. For each student you have the number of delinquent offenses they reported committing in the year before they dropped out of school and the number of offenses they reported in the year after they dropped out of school:

### Number of Delinquent Acts

| Person | Before | After |
|---|---|---|
| 1 | 5 | 7 |
| 2 | 9 | 5 |
| 3 | 2 | 3 |
| 4 | 7 | 7 |
| 5 | 8 | 11 |
| 6 | 11 | 13 |
| 7 | 8 | 4 |
| 8 | 8 | 10 |
| 9 | 5 | 7 |
| 10 | 2 | 1 |
| 11 | 9 | 3 |

Test the null hypothesis that the mean difference between the two sets of scores is zero against the alternative hypothesis that it is different from zero. Use an alpha level of .05.

## Solutions to Problems

1. An independent variable is the variable whose effect or influence you want to measure on the dependent variable. In causal terms, the independent variable is the cause, and the dependent variable is the effect. Low self-control is taken to affect one's involvement in crime, so self-control is the independent variable and involvement in crime is the dependent variable.

2. An independent sample $t$ test should be used whenever the two samples have been selected independently of one another. In an independent sample $t$ test, the sample elements are not related to one another. In a dependent sample or matched groups $t$ test, however, the sample elements are not independent, but are instead related to one another. An example of a dependent sample would be when the same sample elements or persons are measured at two different points in time as in a "before and after" experiment. A second common type of dependent sample is a matched-groups design.

3. The null and alternative hypotheses are:

$H_0$: $\mu_1 = \mu_2$

$H_1$: $\mu_1 < \mu_2$

The correct test is the pooled variance independent-samples $t$ test, and our sampling distribution is the student's $t$ distribution. We reject the null hypothesis if $t_{obt} \leq -2.390$. The obtained value of $t$ is:

$$t_{obt} = \frac{5.1 - 8.2}{\sqrt{\dfrac{[(40 - 1)(1.8)^2] + [(25 - 1)(1.9)^2]}{40 + 25 - 2}} \sqrt{\dfrac{40 + 25}{(40)(25)}}}$$

$$= -6.74$$

Because our obtained value of $t$ is less than the critical value and falls into the critical region, we decide to reject the null hypothesis of equal means. We conclude that those whose coworkers would disapprove of their stealing from their employer steal things less frequently than those whose coworkers are more tolerant of theft.

4. The null and alternative hypotheses are:

$H_0$: $p_1 = p_2$

$H_1$: $p_1 \neq p_2$

Because this problem involves two population proportions, our test statistic is the $z$ test and our sampling distribution is the $z$ or standard normal distribution. Our decision rule is to reject the null hypothesis if $z_{obt} \leq -1.96$ or $z_{obt} \geq 1.96$.
The value of $z_{obt}$ is:

$$z_{obt} = \frac{.33 - .38}{\sqrt{(.35)(.65)} \sqrt{\dfrac{150 + 110}{(150)(110)}}}$$

$$= -.83$$

As $z_{obt}$ is not less than $-1.96$ or greater than 1.96 and does not fall into the critical region, we decide not to reject the null hypothesis. We cannot, therefore, reject the notion that the proportion who are rearrested is not different between those given fines and those given prison sentences.

**5.** $H_0$: $\mu_1 = \mu_2$

$H_1$: $\mu_1 < \mu_2$

The problem instructs you not to presume that the population standard deviations are equal ($\sigma_1 \neq \sigma_2$), so the correct statistical test is the separate variance $t$ test, and the sampling distribution is the student's $t$ distribution. With approximately 60 df and an alpha of .05 for a one-tailed test, the critical value of $t$ is $-1.671$. The value of $t_{obt}$ is:

$$t_{obt} = \frac{18.8 - 21.3}{\sqrt{\frac{(4.5)^2}{50 - 1} + \frac{(3.0)^2}{25 - 1}}}$$

$$= -2.84$$

As $t_{obt} \leq t_{crit}$, we reject the null hypothesis of equal population means. Our conclusion is that the mean score on the domestic disturbance scale is significantly lower for males than females. In other words, males are less likely to see the fair handling of domestic disturbances as an important part of police work.

**6.** The null and alternative hypotheses are:

$H_0$: $\mu_D = 0$

$H_1$: $\mu_D > 0$

Our sample members (the judges) were deliberately matched in order to be comparable, so we have matched samples. The appropriate test statistic, then, is the dependent samples or matched-groups $t$ test, and the sampling distribution is the student's $t$ distribution. Our decision rule is to reject the null hypothesis if $t_{obt} \geq 2.624$. The value of $t_{obt}$ is:

$$t_{obt} = \frac{1.4}{2.55/\sqrt{15 - 1}}$$

$$= 2.06$$

As our $t_{obt}$ (2.06) is not greater than or equal to 2.624, we do not reject the null hypothesis. There is no difference in the number of capital cases lost on appeal between trained and untrained judges.

**7.** $H_0$: $p_1 = p_2$

$H_1$: $p_1 > p_2$

Because this is a difference of proportions problem, the correct test statistic is the $z$ test, and the sampling distribution is the $z$ or standard normal distribution. Our decision rule is to reject the null hypothesis if $z_{obt} \geq 2.33$. The value of $z_{obt}$ is:

$$z_{obt} = \frac{.43 - .17}{\sqrt{(.32)(.68)} \sqrt{\frac{100 + 75}{(100)75}}}$$

$$= 3.71$$

Because our obtained $z$ is greater than the critical value of $z$ (2.33) and $z_{obt}$ falls into the critical region, we reject the null hypothesis. Delinquent children have a significantly higher proportion of criminal parents than do nondelinquent children.

8. $H_0$: $\mu_D = 0$

$H_1$: $\mu_D \neq 0$

Because the two samples are the same youths at two points in time (before and after dropping out), we have dependent samples. The correct test statistic, then, is the dependent-samples or matched-groups $t$ test, and the sampling distribution is the student's $t$ distribution. Our decision rule is to reject the null hypothesis *if* $t_{\text{obt}} \leq -2.228$ or *if* $t_{\text{obt}} \geq 2.228$. The value of $t_{\text{obt}}$ is:

$$z_{\text{obt}} = \frac{.27}{2.93/\sqrt{10}}$$

$$= .29$$

As our critical value of $t$ is not greater than or equal to 2.228 nor less than or equal to $-2.228$ and does not fall into the critical region, we fail to reject the null hypothesis. We cannot reject the assumption that the number of delinquent offenses committed before dropping out is the same as the number committed after dropping out.

# CHAPTER 13

# Hypothesis Tests Involving Three or More Population Means

## Analysis of Variance

*Analysis kills spontaneity. The grain once ground into flour springs and germinates no more.*

—HENRI AMIEL

## 13.1 INTRODUCTION

In the preceding chapter we discussed statistical techniques used to examine the relationship between means from two independent samples. The independent samples *t* tests we learned in that chapter are appropriate when the dependent variable is a continuous (interval or ratio) variable and the independent variable is a dichotomous (two-category) variable. When the categorical variable has more than two levels, however, the *t* test is not the appropriate statistical test.

In this chapter we examine a statistical technique used to analyze the relationship between two variables when (1) the dependent variable is continuous in nature and normally distributed in the population, and (2) the independent variable is categorical and has three or more independent groups or categories. The method we are going to examine is generally referred to as *ANalysis Of VAriance (ANOVA)*. Although there are important differences between the *t* test and the ANOVA, the ANOVA might be thought of as an extension of *t* test.

The analysis of variance procedure determines the extent to which there are significant differences between the means of three or more samples or groups. For example, suppose we were interested in the extent to which there were differences in the length of sentences received by convicted white, African American, Hispanic, and Native American armed robbery offenders. To answer this question we would take an independent random sample of convicted armed robbers from each of the four racial/ethnic groups and calculate the mean sentence lengths received for each of them. We would then have four sample means ($\bar{x}_W$, $\bar{x}_{AA}$, $\bar{x}_H$, $\bar{x}_{AI}$), where the subscript refers to the racial/ethnic group.

Suppose we do this and determine that white armed robbers received a mean sentence length of 36 months, African American armed robbers received a·mean sentence length of 48 months, Hispanic armed robbers received a mean sentence length of 60 months, and Native American armed robbers received a mean sentence length of 72 months. Do these sample differences in means indicate that there are significant differences in the sentence length received for these four racial/ethnic groups in the *population?* By now, we hope that the immediate answer inside your mind is an emphatic "No!" You now know that, because of sampling variation these observed sample differences in means may or may not reflect actual sentence length differences in the population. What our statistical test will help us decide is whether these observed differences are due to sampling variation or real differences in the sentence received by different populations.

In determining whether the observed four sample differences are due to sampling variation or are "statistically significant" differences, you may be tempted to use your *t* test skills from Chapter 12. That is, you might think about calculating a series of *t* tests between each different pair of means. For example, first testing the difference between white and African American defendants, then between white and Hispanic defendants, then between white and Native American defendants, and so on. One obvious disadvantage to this strategy is the amount of work involved. With four groups, you would have to conduct 6 different *t* tests.

Of more concern than the amount of work involved, however is the alpha level of the tests. You will remember that the chosen alpha level is the risk you assume of making a Type I error, which is the probability of rejecting a true null hypothesis. When numerous tests of significance are performed on the same data, as in repeating *t* tests, the actual level of alpha is greater than the chosen level for each individual test. In other words, although you may set alpha at .05 for each of your six individual tests in the example, the combined probability of making a Type I error (the probability of making a Type I error in at least one of the *t* tests), is higher than .05 because the statistical tests are not independent of one another. What the ANOVA test allows you to do is determine whether the sample means are significantly different with a true, single alpha level.

## 13.2 HYPOTHESIS TESTING WITH ANOVA

As with the null hypothesis used for significance testing between two sample means, the null hypothesis used for ANOVA states that there are no differences between more than two population means. Expressed formally as shown, the null hypothesis ($H_0$) states that the population means for each group are equal to each other. The term $k$ refers to the number of group means being compared.

$$H_0: \mu_1 = \mu_2 = \mu_3 = \cdots = \mu_k$$

$$H_1: \mu_1 \neq \mu_2 \neq \mu_3 \neq \cdots \neq \mu_k$$

In the example that involved the length of prison sentences given to four different racial/ethnic groups, the null hypothesis would be:

$H_0$: $= \mu_W = \mu_{AA} = \mu_H = \mu_{AI}$

This null hypothesis states that the mean sentence length for the four racial/ethnic groups are not different from one another.

The research hypothesis ($H_1$) is that there *are* differences between the population means. Unlike the case with our two-sample *t* test, the research hypothesis in an ANOVA does not specify which sample means are different or whether one is greater or less than the other. The research hypothesis in any ANOVA simply is that at least one of the population means is different from at least one other population mean. That is, if we reject the null hypothesis, we only know that one of the means is different from at least one of the others. In our example, the alternative hypothesis would be:

$H_1$: $\mu_W \neq \mu_{AA} \neq \mu_H \neq \mu_{AI}$

The ANOVA does not tell us which mean or means are different. To find this out we have to do some additional analyses that we examine later in this chapter.

## 13.3 THE LOGIC OF ANOVA

When the null hypothesis is expressed as $\mu_1 = \mu_2 = \cdots = \mu_k$, you can see the similarity between the ANOVA and the *t* test for two group means. In addition, many of the assumptions for the *t* test and ANOVA are the same: normal populations, a dependent variable that is normally distributed in the population, independent random samples, and equal population standard deviations. In fact, because you see so much similarity between the two you may be a little confused about the title given to this new statistic, the analysis of variance. You may be thinking to yourself right now, "Well, I understand that we want to test differences between group means, but why is this statistical technique called analysis of variance? I'm interested in group means, not variances!" Well, the reason for the name lies in the fact that we are actually basing our statistical test on the "variability" or variance of our samples.

Although we used the variance and standard deviation of our samples in the *t* test, we certainly did not analyze them. With the *t* test we were concerned only with one type of variance, the variance that existed within each of our two groups (i.e., the variance of the first sample and the variance of the second sample), and one type of mean, the mean of each of our two groups. The variance in our *t* test problem measured how different the scores in a group or sample were from the mean of the sample. It, therefore, reflected the dispersion that exists *within* a group. Unfortunately, when we perform an ANOVA, things get slightly more complicated.

With ANOVA we have two types of variability or variance and two types of means to worry about. One type of variance is like the variance in our *t* test problem in that it reflects the extent to which the cases within a group (or sample) are different from the group's mean. In other words, the first type of variance reflects the *variance within a group*. The mean here, just like in the *t* test, is the mean of the group or sample. The within-group variance, then, is measured as the difference between each score and the mean of the group.

The second type of variance we use in ANOVA measures the extent to which each group mean varies from the other group means and is calculated as the difference between the group means and something called the "grand mean." The grand mean is the mean of all the scores when we add them up (ignoring which group they are in) and divide by the total number of scores. The variation of the group means from this grand mean reflects the *variance between the groups*.

This is probably as clear as mud to you right now, so let's go through an example. In the beginning of this chapter, we presented the hypothetical example of the length of prison sentence given to armed robbers in each of four racial/ethnic groups, white, African American, Hispanic, and Native American. Suppose we took a random sample of 10 convicted armed robbers from each of these four groups and recorded the sentence length they received. Table 13.1 displays these hypothetical data. In this example, race/ethnicity is the independent variable, and sentence length received is the dependent variable. Although in this case the sample sizes are all the same ($n_1 = n_2 = n_3 = n_4 = 10$), this is not always the case. In Table 13.1 we also report the mean and standard deviation for each group and the grand mean ($\bar{x}_G$), which is found by adding up all scores and dividing by 40. We can see that the average sentence given to white armed robbers was 36 months, 48 months for African American armed robbers, 60 months for Hispanic armed robbers, and 72 months for Native American armed robbers. The grand mean, or the mean of all 40 persons, is 54 months.

After looking at the data presented for each group in Table 13.1, would you conclude that there is a significant difference between the sentence length received by these four groups? Notice first that there is little variability within each racial/ethnic group. That is, most of the scores are not much different from their respective group mean. Most of the 10 whites were sentenced close to the group mean of 36 months, most African Americans close to their mean of 48 months, and so on.

**TABLE 13.1. Hypothetical Data on Sentences (in number of months) for Armed Robbery by Race of the Offender**

| Offender | White | African American | Hispanic | Native American | Total |
|---|---|---|---|---|---|
| 1 | 35 | 48 | 60 | 73 | |
| 2 | 35 | 47 | 61 | 71 | |
| 3 | 38 | 46 | 58 | 70 | |
| 4 | 36 | 47 | 59 | 73 | |
| 5 | 38 | 51 | 60 | 72 | |
| 6 | 35 | 48 | 62 | 73 | |
| 7 | 36 | 47 | 59 | 70 | |
| 8 | 34 | 49 | 62 | 72 | |
| 9 | 37 | 47 | 60 | 73 | |
| 10 | 36 | 50 | 59 | 73 | |
| | $\bar{x}_1 = 36$ | $\bar{x}_2 = 48$ | $\bar{x}_3 = 60$ | $\bar{x}_4 = 72$ | $\bar{x}_G = 54$ |
| | $s_1 = 1.33$ | $s_2 = 1.56$ | $s_3 = 1.33$ | $s_4 = 1.25$ | |
| | $n_1 = 10$ | $n_2 = 10$ | $n_3 = 10$ | $n_4 = 10$ | $N = 40$ |

As a result, the sample standard deviations for each of the four groups are quite small (and fairly equal to one another). We know, therefore, that there is little variability within each group (little *"within-group" variability*) and that each sample mean is a good estimate of the score for each group.

Notice also, however, that although the scores within a group do not differ much from their respective group mean, the group means themselves differ from each other and from the grand mean. If we treat the group means as four individual scores and the grand mean as the mean of those four scores, you will find that the estimated standard deviation for the group mean scores is 15.49.[1] There is, then, pronounced variability across the four groups (much *"between-group" variability*).

The data in Table 13.1 indicate that there are great differences in scores across our four racial ethnic groups and a strong similarity of scores within each group. In other words, there is a homogeneity of scores within groups and a heterogeneity of scores across groups. It would appear, then, that there is a distinctive sentence length given to each of the four racial/ethnic groups. White armed robbers are given the least amount of prison time in our example, followed by African Americans, Hispanics, and Native Americans. Moreover, there is no overlap across groups: each white received fewer months than each African American, who received fewer months than each Hispanic, who received less time than each Native American. Findings such as this one would lead us to suspect that our group means are significantly different from one another and that the race/ethnicity of the defendant is an important factor in influencing how much prison time they are sentenced to.

Table 13.2 presents hypothetical data from a second sample of 10 convicted armed robbers from each of the same four racial/ethnic groups. These data are very different from those presented in Table 13.1. In Table 13.2, we see that there is great variability within each group. That is, the sentence length for individuals vary markedly about each group mean. This substantial within-group variability is

**TABLE 13.2. Hypothetical Data on Sentences (in number of months) for Armed Robbery by Race of the Offender**

| Offender | White | African American | Hispanic | Native American | Total |
|----------|-------|------------------|----------|-----------------|-------|
| 1 | 56 | 68 | 39 | 49 | |
| 2 | 43 | 35 | 68 | 33 | |
| 3 | 65 | 57 | 52 | 67 | |
| 4 | 34 | 63 | 73 | 56 | |
| 5 | 70 | 76 | 37 | 71 | |
| 6 | 42 | 45 | 71 | 46 | |
| 7 | 74 | 68 | 39 | 59 | |
| 8 | 45 | 31 | 64 | 73 | |
| 9 | 67 | 49 | 38 | 64 | |
| 10 | 44 | 58 | 49 | 32 | |
| | $\bar{x}_1 = 54$ | $\bar{x}_2 = 55$ | $\bar{x}_3 = 53$ | $\bar{x}_4 = 55$ | $\bar{x}_G = 54.25$ |
| | $s_1 = 14.13$ | $s_2 = 14.79$ | $s_3 = 14.76$ | $s_4 = 14.72$ | |
| | $n_1 = 10$ | $n_2 = 10$ | $n_3 = 10$ | $n_4 = 10$ | $N = 40$ |

reflected in the fact that each of the sample standard deviations is large (though again fairly equal among themselves). In contrast to this great heterogeneity of scores within samples is the homogeneity observed across groups. Although the scores within each group vary a great deal, the group means do not themselves evidence much variability. In fact, if we were to compute a standard deviation with the group means as individual scores and the grand mean as the mean of those four scores, the standard deviation would be only .96. Unlike the case for Table 13.1, in Table 13.2 there is substantial within-group variability and little between-group variability. In Table 13.2 there does not seem to be a distinctive sentence length given to different racial groups. Rather, there seems to be a good deal of overlap in sentence length across the four groups. Findings such as those in Table 13.2 would not lead us to believe that our group means are significantly different. From these data it would appear that the race/ethnicity of the armed robber had no effect on the length of the sentence received.

Our thoughts about whether the group means were significantly different in Tables 13.1 and 13.2 were influenced by how much variability there existed between groups relative to how much variability there existed within groups. In Table 13.1, there was more between-group variability than within-group variability, and we suspected that the group means might be significantly different from one another. In Table 13.2, however, there was more within-group variability than between-group variability, and we did not suspect that the group means might be significantly different from one another.

To illuminate the concepts of between-group variability and within-group variability, let's bring in some help from exploratory data analysis. The two sets of hypothetical data depicted in Tables 13.1 and 13.2 are presented graphically with boxplots in Figures 13.1 and 13.2. What we see in Figure 13.1 illustrates that there is relatively little variability within each racial/ethnic group, but substantial variability across groups. All four boxplots are short, indicating very little dispersion in the data. The medians for each of the groups are, however, very different from one another. The data from Table 13.2, which are displayed in Figure 13.2, clearly demonstrates that there is a high degree of variability within each group but little variability across groups. First of all, compared with those in Figure 13.1, the boxes in Figure 13.2 are very long, indicating a great deal more variability within groups. The whiskers are also much longer in the boxes in Figure 13.2. In addition, unlike in Figure 13.1, the boxes fall almost in a flat line, indicating that the central tendency of the groups is very comparable.

In sum, when conducting an ANOVA to test the null hypothesis of mean equality, we examine both the variability that exists within each group and between each group. More specifically, the ANOVA compares the relative variability that exists between the groups (e.g., from whites to African Americans to Hispanics and Native Americans) to the variability that exists within the groups (among whites, among African Americans, among Hispanics, and among Native Americans). If the group means are significantly different, then the sample means for the groups should be very different (substantial between-group variability), but the scores within a sample should be very similar (very little within-group variability). That is, if the samples are in fact drawn from populations with different means, there

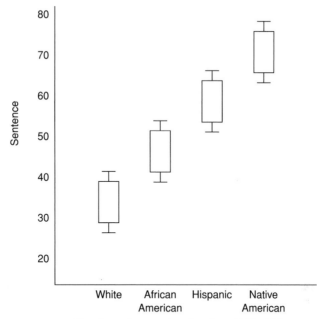

FIGURE 13.1.  Boxplots of sentencing data from Table 13.1.

should be a similarity of scores within each group and pronounced differences across groups. The greater the difference in variability across groups relative to the variability within groups, the more likely it is that the population means are not equal and that we can reject the null hypothesis.

If the logic of ANOVA still seems a little fuzzy to you, let's try to clear things up by briefly going over another example. Suppose we are interested in those factors that are related to one's fear of becoming the victim of a crime. We believe that one characteristic that affects the extent to which individuals are afraid of becoming a crime victim is where they live. More specifically, we think that those persons who live in urban areas will be more fearful of crime than those who live in suburban or rural locations.

To investigate this issue, we randomly select a sample of persons from the population and ask each of them a number of questions concerning their fear of crime and where they currently reside. From this random sample, based on where they live, we divide respondents into one of three groups: urban, suburban, or rural. Based on their responses to our questions concerning their fear of crime, we calculate a fear of crime score for each individual. We presume that this fear of crime scale is measured at the interval level and that the higher the score the greater the fear of crime. In this example the place of residence (urban, suburban, rural) is our independent variable, and fear of crime is our dependent variable. The hypothetical data we obtain are presented in Table 13.3.

In this table notice that the scores within each locality are clustered tightly about their group means. As you can see, the standard deviations for each group are

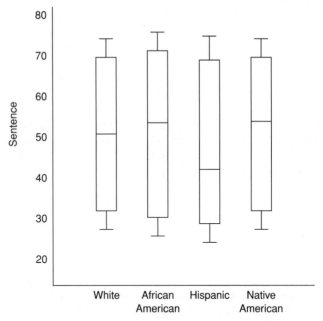

FIGURE 13.2. Boxplots of sentencing data from Table 13.2.

fairly small, indicating that the within-group variation is not substantial. Notice also that the group means are very different from one another. If we treat these group means as individual scores and measure the standard deviation of these scores about the grand mean $(\bar{x}_G)$, we would find it to be 4.2. By just eyeballing the data

**TABLE 13.3. Hypothetical Fear of Crime Scores for a Sample of Urban, Suburban, and Rural Residents**

| Resident | Urban | Suburban | Rural | Total |
|---|---|---|---|---|
| 1 | 22 | 23 | 19 | |
| 2 | 29 | 22 | 24 | |
| 3 | 31 | 26 | 24 | |
| 4 | 28 | 25 | 19 | |
| 5 | 30 | 24 | 20 | |
| 6 | 32 | 25 | 24 | |
| 7 | 32 | 24 | 21 | |
| 8 | 31 | 24 | 17 | |
| 9 | 28 | 27 | 23 | |
| 10 | 30 | 23 | 19 | |
| $\Sigma$ | 293 | 243 | 210 | 746 |
| $\bar{x}$ | 29.3 | 24.3 | 21.0 | $\bar{x}_G = 24.9$ |
| $s$ | 2.9 | 1.5 | 2.6 | |
| $n$ | 10 | 10 | 10 | 30 |

and doing some quick calculations, it appears that there is more variation between the groups than there is within the groups.

In contrast to this are the data in Table 13.4. These hypothetical fear of crime data from randomly selected persons living in urban, suburban, and rural areas are different from the data in Table 13.3. There is substantial variation within each of the three groups, as evidenced by the large group standard deviations. The scores within locality, then, are very different from their respective group means. The group means, however, are not substantially different from each other and, therefore, are not much different from the grand mean. In fact, if we were to calculate the standard deviation of these group means, it would only be .3. For these data, then, it appears that there is substantially more variation within the groups than between them.

What we are telling you about ANOVA is that to determine whether there is a significant difference between group means, we must examine both the variability *within* each group and the variability that exists *between* the group means. In general, because of chance alone (sampling variation), groups will have different means. Of course, the amount of sampling error we have contributes to the variability we observe both within each group and between groups. When the independent variable has a significant influence on the dependent variable, this effect will be reflected *only* in the variability observed between groups. In our fear of crime example, if the locality of residence truly affects the extent to which citizens are afraid of crime, then this should be reflected in the variance we observe between urban, suburban, and rural residents only; it should not affect the variability we observe within each area of residence.

What this means is that if there is no effect of locality of residence on perceived levels of fear, then the variability we observe between the group means should reflect sampling error and sampling error *only*. Because the variability we observe for

**TABLE 13.4. Hypothetical Fear of Crime Scores for a Second Sample of Urban, Suburban, and Rural Residents**

| Resident | Urban | Suburban | Rural | Total |
|---|---|---|---|---|
| 1 | 29 | 26 | 22 | |
| 2 | 23 | 32 | 29 | |
| 3 | 25 | 14 | 33 | |
| 4 | 32 | 25 | 17 | |
| 5 | 21 | 28 | 31 | |
| 6 | 17 | 20 | 24 | |
| 7 | 27 | 29 | 26 | |
| 8 | 28 | 26 | 18 | |
| 9 | 26 | 30 | 30 | |
| 10 | 31 | 23 | 26 | |
| $\Sigma$ | 259 | 253 | 256 | 768 |
| $\bar{x}$ | 25.9 | 25.3 | 25.6 | $\bar{x}_G = 25.6$ |
| $s$ | 4.6 | 5.3 | 5.4 | |
| $n$ | 10 | 10 | 10 | 30 |

the amount of fear within each locality is *just* a reflection of this sampling error (as all persons within each sample have the same locality), then the within- and across-group measures of variability should be approximately equal. If so, then the ratio we obtain by dividing the variability observed between groups from that we observe within groups should be approximately 1.0.

However, if the locality of residence does affect perceived fear of crime, the between-group variability will be greater than the within-group variability. In this case the ratio of between to within variability should be greater than 1.0. However, because both sources of variability are subject to sampling variation and are expected to differ by chance alone, we want to know whether our ratio is so large that we can dismiss the possibility that it is different from 1.0 merely by chance. Fortunately for us, the ratio of between variability to within variability has a known sampling distribution, provided our assumptions are satisfied. We can, then, conduct a statistical test to determine whether our ratio is significantly different from 1.0 or just different because of sampling variation.

Let's extend the logic of this differential variability notion to the null and research hypotheses. If it is the case that all population means are equal and there is no variability across groups (i.e., $\mu_1 = \mu_2 = \mu_3$), the ratio of between-group variability to within-group variability will be zero. When the null hypothesis is true, therefore, we would expect the ratio of between- to within-group variability to be equal to zero. If the ratio of between- to within-group variability is greater than zero but less than 1, we will not be led to question the null hypothesis. This is because a ratio less than 1 indicates that the within-group variability is greater than the between-group variability. Therefore, we will only question the null hypothesis when the ratio of between- to within-group variability is greater than 1. The statistical question, therefore, is whether this ratio is significantly different from 1.

Essentially, then, what ANOVA does is to test the magnitude of the following ratio:

$$\frac{\text{Variability between Groups}}{\text{Variability within Groups}}$$

As mentioned, if our null hypothesis is true and the population means are equal ($\mu_1 = \mu_2 = \mu_3$), this ratio should not be significantly different from zero. In this case, there is no variability across groups and the ratio of between- to within-group variability will be zero. If the variability within groups is greater than that between groups, the ratio will be greater than zero but less than 1. This was illustrated in Table 13.4, where the variability in fear of crime scores within different locality groups was greater than the variability across the three types of locations. We said that we would not have very good evidence from this data set to reject the hypothesis that the population means are equal.

If our null hypothesis is not true and there really are significant differences between the population means, however, the ratio of between to within variability will be greater than 1 because the variability observed between the groups is larger than that observed within each group. This was illustrated in Table 13.3, where the fear of crime scores within locations were much less variable than scores between groups.

If that sound we now hear is your head spinning from all this, do not worry, going through the mechanics of performing this type of analysis will make things brilliantly clear. Before we move on to the calculation procedures of ANOVA, however, there are important assumptions of this statistical test that we must discuss. We mentioned them earlier, but they bear repeating. The first assumption we must make is that the populations are normally distributed. Second, the population variances are assumed to be equal. The final assumption we must make is that we have independent and random samples. A summary of these assumptions follows:

1. The variable distributions within each population or group are assumed to be normally distributed.
2. The population variances are assumed to be equal: $\sigma_1^2 = \sigma_2^2 = \sigma_3^2 = \cdots = \sigma_k^2$
3. The samples or samples have been independently and randomly selected from their respective populations.
4. One variable is a categorical variable measured at the nominal or ordinal level; the second variable is a continuous variable measured at the interval or ratio level.

## 13.4 COMPUTATION OF ANOVA

As discussed, although we want to examine whether there are differences in population means, ANOVA proceeds by examining two different estimates of variation in a given set of scores. Variation will be defined as the sum of squared deviations of a group of scores about a mean $(x - \bar{x})$. Variation, then, refers to the sum of squares of a set of numbers, without dividing by the number of cases involved.

There are three different sum of squares in an ANOVA problem. The first is referred to as the *total sum of squares* (abbreviated as $SS_{Total}$). The total sum of squares measures the total variation in a given set of data and is defined as the sum of each score minus the grand mean, squared. Remember that the grand mean is the sum of all scores (ignoring which group they belong to) divided by the total number of scores. The formula for the total sum of squares, then, is:[2]

$$SS_{Total} = \sum_{i=1}^{N} (x_i - \bar{x}_G)^2 \tag{13.1}$$

where

    $x_i$ = the $i$th score
    $\bar{x}_G$ = the grand mean
    $N$ = the total number of scores (i.e., $n_1 + n_2 + \cdots + n_k$)

To calculate the total sum of squares, then, you first subtract the grand mean from a score and then square this difference. You do this for each score and then sum all of the squared differences.

The total sum of squares measures the total variation of the scores. This total sum of squares is divided into two components, one called the *between-groups sum of squares* (abbreviated $SS_{Between}$) and one called the *within-groups sum of squares* (abbreviated $SS_{Within}$). The between-groups sum of squares measures that part of the total variation that reflects the difference between the group means and the grand mean. The between-groups sum of squares, therefore, measures the dispersion among the different group means, and its formula is:

$$SS_{Between} = \Sigma \, (\bar{x}_k - \bar{x}_G)^2 \tag{13.2}$$

where
   $\bar{x}_k$ = the mean for the $k$th category or group
   $\bar{x}_G$ = the grand mean

To determine the between-groups sum of squares, for each observation you subtract the grand mean from the respective group mean and square the difference. You do this for each observation in each of the $k$ groups and sum across groups.[3]

The within-group sum of squares measures that part of the total variation that is due to the difference between each score and the mean of the group or category. This sum of squares captures the variability that exists within the groups because it is the sum of squared deviations of the individual scores from their own group mean. The formula for the within-sum of squares is:

$$SS_{Within} = \sum_{i} \sum_{k} (x_{ik} - \bar{x}_k)^2 \tag{13.3}$$

where
   $\bar{x}_{ik}$ = the $i$th score in the $k$th group
   $\bar{x}_k$ = the mean for the $k$th group

The formula says to take the first score in the first group $(x_{11})$ and subtract the mean of the group $(\bar{x}_1)$ from that score and then square the difference. Do this for each of the $n$ scores in the first group $(x_{n_1})$, and sum each of the squared differences. Then go to the first score in the second group $(x_{12})$ and subtract the respective mean of the group $(\bar{x}_2)$ from that score and square the difference. Do this for each of the $n$ scores in that group $(x_{n_2})$, and sum each of these squared differences. Continue doing this for each of the $i$ scores in the $k$ groups, and then add all of the sums of the squared differences for each group. In the end, then, you will add the squared differences from the group mean for the first group to the squared differences from the group mean for the second group, and so on for each of the $k$ groups.

There is a definite relationship among the three sources of variance. The total variation in a set of scores is equal to the variation that exists between groups plus the variation within groups:

$$SS_{Total} = SS_{Between} + SS_{Within}$$

With these three sums of squares, we can obtain two estimates of the population variance $(\sigma^2)$ by dividing by the appropriate degrees of freedom.

One estimate of the population variance is based on the weighted average of the variances within each of the groups. This estimate is obtained by dividing the $SS_{Within}$ by its appropriate degrees of freedom. The degrees of freedom associated with $SS_{Within}$ is $N - k$, where $N$ is not the population value but is used here as the symbol for the total number of cases $(N = n_1 + n_2 + \cdots + n_k)$ and $k$ is the number of groups. The variance within samples, then, is defined as:

$$\text{Variance within Samples} = \frac{\text{SS}_{\text{Within}}}{(N - k)} \tag{13.4}$$

where

$$N = (n_1 + n_2 + \cdots + n_k)$$

A second estimate of the population variance is based on the deviations of the group means about the grand mean and therefore involves the $\text{SS}_{\text{Between}}$. To obtain this estimate of the variance, we divide $\text{SS}_{\text{Between}}$ by its appropriate degrees of freedom. The degrees of freedom associated with $\text{SS}_{\text{Between}}$ is $k - 1$, where $k$ is the total number of groups. The variance between samples, then, is defined as:

$$\text{Variance between Samples} = \frac{\text{SS}_{\text{Between}}}{k - 1} \tag{13.5}$$

The total degrees of freedom, associated with $\text{SS}_{\text{Total}}$ is equal to $N - 1$. As a check on your arithmetic you should determine that:

$$\text{df}_{\text{Total}} = \text{df}_{\text{Within}} + \text{df}_{\text{Between}}$$

$$N - 1 = (N - k) + (k - 1)$$

We now have two estimates of the population variance, one based on within-group variability ($\text{SS}_{\text{Within}}/\text{df}_{\text{Within}}$), and one based on between-group variability ($\text{SS}_{\text{Between}}/\text{df}_{\text{Between}}$). Keeping in mind the logic of the ANOVA discussed in the previous section, let's now compute the ratio of the between variance to the within variance. If this ratio is significantly different from 1, that is, if the between variance is greater than the within variance, we will reject the null hypothesis that the population means are equal.

The specific test we perform when calculating an ANOVA is called an $F$ test (after the statistician Sir Ronald Fisher who developed it). The $F$ test that we conduct is simply the ratio of the estimated variance between samples and the estimated variance within samples:

$$F = \frac{\text{Variance between Samples}}{\text{Variance within Samples}} \tag{13.6}$$

$$= \frac{\text{SS}_{\text{Between}}/k - 1}{\text{SS}_{\text{Within}}/N - k}$$

As with the $t$ distribution, when repeated independent random samples are drawn from normal populations with equal variances (or from any population with large sample sizes), this $F$ ratio exhibits a probability distribution known as an $F$ distribution. Like the $t$ distribution, the critical value of $F$ depends on the degrees of freedom. For an $F$ test we have two separate degrees of freedom, corresponding to our two estimates of the variance: the between-groups degrees of freedom ($\text{df}_{\text{Between}} = k - 1$), and the within-groups degrees of freedom ($\text{df}_{\text{Within}} = N - k$).

With these two types of degrees of freedom determined, we can now find the critical value of $F$ we need to reject the null hypothesis that there are no differences between the population means. The $F$ distribution is displayed in Table B.5 of

Appendix B. The top row of the table displays the $df_{Between}$ (the smaller of the two degrees of freedom), and the left column of the table displays the $df_{Within}$. There is one $F$ table for an alpha level of .05 and one for an alpha level of .01. If our obtained value of $F$ is greater than or equal to the critical value (i.e., if $F_{obt} \geq F_{crit}$), we can reject the null hypothesis that the population means are equal.

Unlike the $t$ tests in the preceding chapter, there are no two-tailed $F$ tests and therefore no negative values of $F$. Because we reject the null hypothesis if and only if $F_{obt}$ is significantly greater than one (because $F_{obt}$ will be greater than one only when the between-group variance is greater than the within-group variance), we are interested only in the right tail of the sampling distribution. Our decision rule regarding the null hypothesis with the $F$ test is relatively simple, then: either $F_{obt}$ is greater than or equal to $F_{crit}$ (and we reject $H_0$), or it is not (and we fail to reject $H_0$).

We now know the mechanics necessary to calculate an ANOVA. Before we actually go through the calculations with our fear of crime and residence example, let's review the necessary formulas:

$$SS_{Between} = \Sigma(\bar{x}_k - \bar{x}_G)^2$$

$$SS_{Within} = \sum_i \sum_k (x_{ik} - \bar{x}_k)^2$$

$$df_{Between} = k - 1$$

$$df_{Within} = N - k$$

$$\text{Estimated Variance between Groups} = \frac{SS_{Between}}{df_{Between}}$$

$$\text{Estimated Variance within Groups} = \frac{SS_{Within}}{df_{Within}}$$

$$F_{obt} = \frac{\text{Estimated Variance between Groups}}{\text{Estimated Variance within Groups}}$$

As indicated by its formula, the sum of squares between groups is measured by finding the deviation of each group's mean ($\bar{x}_k$) from the grand mean ($\bar{x}_G$), squaring each of these deviations for each observation in the group and summing over each of the $k$ groups. Similarly, the sum of squares within groups is measured by finding the deviation of each $x$ value from its respective group mean ($\bar{x}_k$), squaring each of these differences, summing the squared differences within each group, and then summing over groups.

Let's now go through an example, using the data relating location of residence (urban, suburban, rural) to perceived fear of crime found in Table 13.3. You may remember that in this table the between-group variability appeared to be much greater than the within-group variability, leading us to suspect that residence was related to fear of crime. We formally test this hypothesis.

First, we state our null and research hypothesis. Our null hypothesis is that the populations from which our residence samples were drawn have equal means on the fear of crime measure:

$$H_0: \mu_{Urban} = \mu_{Suburban} = \mu_{Rural}$$

As in any ANOVA, our research hypothesis is that at least one of the population means is different:

$$H_1: \mu_{\text{Urban}} \neq \mu_{\text{Suburban}} \neq \mu_{\text{Rural}}$$

To test the null hypothesis, we use the $F$ test from an ANOVA, and the sampling distribution will be the $F$ distribution. The critical value of $F$ ($F_{\text{crit}}$) is obtained from Table B.5 of Appendix B. We select an alpha level of .05. Our between-groups degrees of freedom ($df_{\text{Between}}$) is equal to $k - 1$, or 2, and our within-groups degrees of freedom is equal to $N - 3$, or 27. To find the critical value of $F$ with these degrees of freedom, find the table corresponding to an alpha of .05, then locate the number of our $df_{\text{Between}}$ at the top of the table ($df_{\text{Between}} = 2$). Then go down the left column of the table to locate the number of our $df_{\text{Within}}$ ($df_{\text{Within}} = 27$). We can now see from this table that our critical value of $F_{2,27}$ ($F$ with 2 and 27 degrees of freedom) is 3.35 ($F_{\text{crit}} = 3.35$). Our decision rule, then, is to reject the null hypothesis of equal population means if $F_{\text{obt}} \geq 3.35$ and fail to reject the null hypothesis if $F_{\text{obt}} < 3.35$.

We now must determine $F_{\text{obt}}$. We can do this in three easy steps. First, we calculate the sum of squares between groups and then the sum of squares within groups. Second, we obtain an estimated variance between groups by dividing the between-groups sum of squares by its degrees of freedom, and an estimated variance within groups by dividing the within-groups sum of squares by its degrees of freedom. Third, the obtained $F$ statistic is the ratio of estimated between-groups variance to estimated within-groups variance.

In order for you to clearly see how the various estimates were derived we put the calculations in tabular form (Table 13.5). We calculated the between, within, and total sum of squares for you, but you should do them on your own for practice. The $SS_{\text{Between}}$ is equal to 349.3, and the $SS_{\text{Within}}$ is equal to 158.2. When these two sum of squares are added, you can see that they sum to $SS_{\text{Total}}$ (349.3 + 158.2 = 507.5).[4] The basis for our $F$ test is summarized in Table 13.6. The $SS_{\text{Between}}$ is divided by its respective degrees of freedom ($k - 1$) to obtain our estimated variance between groups (174.6). The $SS_{\text{Within}}$ is divided by its degrees of freedom ($N - k$) to obtain our estimated variance within groups (5.9). The $F_{\text{obt}}$ statistic simply is the ratio of these two estimates of the variance:

$$F_{obt} = \frac{\text{Estimated Variance between Groups}}{\text{Estimated Variance within Groups}}$$

$$= \frac{174.6}{5.9}$$

$$= 29.6$$

Our obtained $F$ is 29.6, and the critical value of $F$ is 3.35. Because $F_{\text{obt}} > F_{\text{crit}}$, we reject the null hypothesis of equal means and conclude that at least one of the means is different. It would appear that location of residence and fear of crime are in fact significantly related to each other.

A word of caution. Notice from the alternative hypothesis that we cannot conclude *which* means are different, but only that at least one of them is different from

**TABLE 13.5. Detailed Calculations to Reveal Logic behind Between-Group and Within-Group Variances and Total of Squares from Fear of Crime Data in Table 13.3**

| ID | Locality | Fear | Between $(\bar{x}_k - \bar{x}_G)^2$ | Within $(\bar{x}_i - \bar{x}_k)^2$ | Total $(\bar{x}_i - \bar{x}_G)^2$ |
|---|---|---|---|---|---|
| 1 | Urban | 22 | $(29.3 - 24.9)^2 = 19.36$ | $(22 - 29.3)^2 = 53.29$ | $(22 - 24.9)^2 = 8.41$ |
| 2 | Urban | 29 | $(29.3 - 24.9)^2 = 19.36$ | $(29 - 29.3)^2 = .09$ | $(29 - 24.9)^2 = 16.81$ |
| 3 | Urban | 31 | $(29.3 - 24.9)^2 = 19.36$ | $(31 - 29.3)^2 = 2.89$ | $(31 - 24.9)^2 = 37.21$ |
| 4 | Urban | 28 | $(29.3 - 24.9)^2 = 19.36$ | $(28 - 29.3)^2 = 1.69$ | $(28 - 24.9)^2 = 9.61$ |
| 5 | Urban | 30 | $(29.3 - 24.9)^2 = 19.36$ | $(30 - 29.3)^2 = .49$ | $(30 - 24.9)^2 = 26.01$ |
| 6 | Urban | 32 | $(29.3 - 24.9)^2 = 19.36$ | $(32 - 29.3)^2 = 7.29$ | $(32 - 24.9)^2 = 50.41$ |
| 7 | Urban | 32 | $(29.3 - 24.9)^2 = 19.36$ | $(32 - 29.3)^2 = 7.29$ | $(32 - 24.9)^2 = 50.41$ |
| 8 | Urban | 31 | $(29.3 - 24.9)^2 = 19.36$ | $(31 - 29.3)^2 = 2.89$ | $(31 - 24.9)^2 = 37.21$ |
| 9 | Urban | 28 | $(29.3 - 24.9)^2 = 19.36$ | $(28 - 29.3)^2 = 1.69$ | $(28 - 24.9)^2 = 9.61$ |
| 10 | Urban | 30 | $(29.3 - 24.9)^2 = 19.36$ | $(30 - 29.3)^2 = .49$ | $(30 - 24.9)^2 = 26.01$ |
| 11 | Suburban | 23 | $(24.3 - 24.9)^2 = .36$ | $(23 - 24.3)^2 = 1.69$ | $(23 - 24.9)^2 = 3.61$ |
| 12 | Suburban | 22 | $(24.3 - 24.9)^2 = .36$ | $(22 - 24.3)^2 = 5.29$ | $(22 - 24.9)^2 = 8.41$ |
| 13 | Suburban | 26 | $(24.3 - 24.9)^2 = .36$ | $(26 - 24.3)^2 = 2.89$ | $(26 - 24.9)^2 = 1.21$ |
| 14 | Suburban | 25 | $(24.3 - 24.9)^2 = .36$ | $(25 - 24.3)^2 = .49$ | $(25 - 24.9)^2 = .01$ |
| 15 | Suburban | 24 | $(24.3 - 24.9)^2 = .36$ | $(24 - 24.3)^2 = .09$ | $(24 - 24.9)^2 = .81$ |
| 16 | Suburban | 25 | $(24.3 - 24.9)^2 = .36$ | $(25 - 24.3)^2 = .49$ | $(25 - 24.9)^2 = .01$ |
| 17 | Suburban | 24 | $(24.3 - 24.9)^2 = .36$ | $(24 - 24.3)^2 = .09$ | $(24 - 24.9)^2 = .81$ |
| 18 | Suburban | 24 | $(24.3 - 24.9)^2 = .36$ | $(24 - 24.3)^2 = .09$ | $(24 - 24.9)^2 = .81$ |
| 19 | Suburban | 27 | $(24.3 - 24.9)^2 = .36$ | $(27 - 24.3)^2 = 7.29$ | $(27 - 24.9)^2 = 4.41$ |
| 20 | Suburban | 23 | $(24.3 - 24.9)^2 = .36$ | $(23 - 24.3)^2 = 1.69$ | $(23 - 24.9)^2 = 3.61$ |
| 21 | Rural | 19 | $(21 - 24.9)^2 = 15.21$ | $(19 - 21)^2 = 4$ | $(19 - 24.9)^2 = 34.81$ |
| 22 | Rural | 24 | $(21 - 24.9)^2 = 15.21$ | $(24 - 21)^2 = 9$ | $(24 - 24.9)^2 = .81$ |
| 23 | Rural | 24 | $(21 - 24.9)^2 = 15.21$ | $(24 - 21)^2 = 9$ | $(24 - 24.9)^2 = .81$ |
| 24 | Rural | 19 | $(21 - 24.9)^2 = 15.21$ | $(19 - 21)^2 = 4$ | $(19 - 24.9)^2 = 34.81$ |
| 25 | Rural | 20 | $(21 - 24.9)^2 = 15.21$ | $(20 - 21)^2 = 1$ | $(20 - 24.9)^2 = 24.01$ |
| 26 | Rural | 24 | $(21 - 24.9)^2 = 15.21$ | $(24 - 21)^2 = 9$ | $(24 - 24.9)^2 = .81$ |
| 27 | Rural | 21 | $(21 - 24.9)^2 = 15.21$ | $(21 - 21)^2 = 0$ | $(21 - 24.9)^2 = 15.21$ |
| 28 | Rural | 17 | $(21 - 24.9)^2 = 15.21$ | $(17 - 21)^2 = 16$ | $(17 - 24.9)^2 = 62.41$ |
| 29 | Rural | 23 | $(21 - 24.9)^2 = 15.21$ | $(23 - 21)^2 = 4$ | $(23 - 24.9)^2 = 3.61$ |
| 30 | Rural | 19 | $(21 - 24.9)^2 = 15.21$ | $(19 - 21)^2 = 4$ | $(19 - 24.9)^2 = 34.81$ |
| | | | $SS_{Between} = 349.3$ | $SS_{within} = 158.2$ | $SS_{Total} = 507.5$ |

**TABLE 13.6. Results of One-Way ANOVA for Investigating the Relationship between Locality of Residence and Fear of Crime**

| | | *Estimated Variance* | | |
| | SS | df | SS/df | F |
| --- | --- | --- | --- | --- |
| Between groups | 349.3 | 2 | 174.6 | 29.6 |
| Within groups | 158.2 | 27 | 5.9 | |
| Total | 507.5 | 29 | | |

at least one of the others. That is, we do not know whether the urban residents' fear of crime mean is significantly greater than both the suburban and rural mean, greater than one of them, or whether the suburban mean is greater than the rural mean. All we know is that at least one pair of these means is significantly different. We return to this issue later in the chapter.

Let's now conduct an analysis of variance $F$ test on the data in Table 13.4. This set of hypothetical data also involved location and fear of crime. You will remember, however, that the descriptive statistics indicated that there was more variability within than between groups. That is, for this set of data the fear of crime scores within location of residence seemed to vary more than fear of crime scores across different types of location. We adopt the same alpha level, and, of course, have the same degrees of freedom and critical value of $F$. We can, then, skip right to the calculation of $F_{obt}$. You should do the calculations yourself before looking at the results in Tables 13.7 and 13.8.

We go through the calculations for you in Table 13.7. You can see there that the $SS_{Between}$ is 1.80 and the $SS_{Within}$ is 703.40. As we suspected, there is substantially more variability within groups than there is between groups in this data set. As a check on your calculations, make sure that these two sum of squares sum to the total sum of squares: $SS_{Total} = 1.80 + 703.40 = 705.20$.

In Table 13.8 we report the summary table of our $F$ test for this data set. We obtain the estimated variance between groups by dividing the $SS_{Between}$ by its degrees of freedom ($df_{Between} = 2$), and the estimated variance within groups by dividing $SS_{Within}$ by its degrees of freedom ($df_{Within} = 27$). As before, we calculate $F_{obt}$ by dividing the estimated variance between groups over the estimated variance within groups:

$$F_{obt} = \frac{\text{Estimated Variance between Groups}}{\text{Estimated Variance within Groups}}$$

$$= \frac{.90}{26.03}$$

$$= .03$$

Our obtained $F$ statistic is .03. As $F_{obt}$ is less than the $F_{crit}$ of 3.35, we do not reject the null hypothesis that the population means are equal. Based on the hypothetical data in Table 13.4, where the variability within groups appeared to be greater than

**TABLE 13.7. Detailed Calculations to Reveal Logic behind Between-Group and Within-Group Variances and Total of Squares from Fear of Crime Data in Table 13.4**

| ID | Locality | Fear | Between $(\bar{x}_k - \bar{x}_G)^2$ | Within $(\bar{x}_i - \bar{x}_k)^2$ | Total $(\bar{x}_i - \bar{x}_G)^2$ |
|---|---|---|---|---|---|
| 1 | Urban | 29 | $(25.9 - 25.6)^2 = .09$ | $(29 - 25.9)^2 = 9.61$ | $(29 - 25.6)^2 = 11.56$ |
| 2 | Urban | 23 | $(25.9 - 25.6)^2 = .09$ | $(23 - 25.9)^2 = 8.41$ | $(23 - 25.6)^2 = 6.76$ |
| 3 | Urban | 25 | $(25.9 - 25.6)^2 = .09$ | $(25 - 25.9)^2 = .81$ | $(25 - 25.6)^2 = .36$ |
| 4 | Urban | 32 | $(25.9 - 25.6)^2 = .09$ | $(32 - 25.9)^2 = 37.21$ | $(32 - 25.6)^2 = 40.96$ |
| 5 | Urban | 21 | $(25.9 - 25.6)^2 = .09$ | $(21 - 25.9)^2 = 24.01$ | $(21 - 25.6)^2 = 21.16$ |
| 6 | Urban | 17 | $(25.9 - 25.6)^2 = .09$ | $(17 - 25.9)^2 = 79.21$ | $(17 - 25.6)^2 = 73.96$ |
| 7 | Urban | 27 | $(25.9 - 25.6)^2 = .09$ | $(27 - 25.9)^2 = 1.21$ | $(27 - 25.6)^2 = 1.96$ |
| 8 | Urban | 28 | $(25.9 - 25.6)^2 = .09$ | $(28 - 25.9)^2 = 4.41$ | $(28 - 25.6)^2 = 5.76$ |
| 9 | Urban | 26 | $(25.9 - 25.6)^2 = .09$ | $(26 - 25.9)^2 = .01$ | $(26 - 25.6)^2 = .16$ |
| 10 | Urban | 31 | $(25.9 - 25.6)^2 = .09$ | $(31 - 25.9)^2 = 26.01$ | $(31 - 25.6)^2 = 29.16$ |
| 11 | Suburban | 26 | $(25.3 - 25.6)^2 = .09$ | $(26 - 25.3)^2 = .49$ | $(26 - 25.6)^2 = .16$ |
| 12 | Suburban | 32 | $(25.3 - 25.6)^2 = .09$ | $(32 - 25.3)^2 = 44.89$ | $(32 - 25.6)^2 = 40.96$ |
| 13 | Suburban | 14 | $(25.3 - 25.6)^2 = .09$ | $(14 - 25.3)^2 = 127.69$ | $(14 - 25.6)^2 = 134.56$ |
| 14 | Suburban | 25 | $(25.3 - 25.6)^2 = .09$ | $(25 - 25.3)^2 = .09$ | $(25 - 25.6)^2 = .36$ |
| 15 | Suburban | 28 | $(25.3 - 25.6)^2 = .09$ | $(28 - 25.3)^2 = 7.29$ | $(28 - 25.6)^2 = 5.76$ |
| 16 | Suburban | 20 | $(25.3 - 25.6)^2 = .09$ | $(20 - 25.3)^2 = 28.09$ | $(20 - 25.6)^2 = 31.36$ |
| 17 | Suburban | 29 | $(25.3 - 25.6)^2 = .09$ | $(29 - 25.3)^2 = 13.69$ | $(29 - 25.6)^2 = 11.56$ |
| 18 | Suburban | 26 | $(25.3 - 25.6)^2 = .09$ | $(26 - 25.3)^2 = .49$ | $(26 - 25.6)^2 = .16$ |
| 19 | Suburban | 30 | $(25.3 - 25.6)^2 = .09$ | $(30 - 25.3)^2 = 22.09$ | $(30 - 25.6)^2 = 19.36$ |
| 20 | Suburban | 23 | $(25.3 - 25.6)^2 = .09$ | $(23 - 25.3)^2 = 5.29$ | $(23 - 25.6)^2 = 6.76$ |
| 21 | Rural | 22 | $(25.6 - 25.6)^2 = 0$ | $(22 - 25.6)^2 = 12.96$ | $(22 - 25.6)^2 = 12.96$ |
| 22 | Rural | 29 | $(25.6 - 25.6)^2 = 0$ | $(29 - 25.6)^2 = 11.56$ | $(29 - 25.6)^2 = 11.56$ |
| 23 | Rural | 33 | $(25.6 - 25.6)^2 = 0$ | $(33 - 25.6)^2 = 54.76$ | $(33 - 25.6)^2 = 54.76$ |
| 24 | Rural | 17 | $(25.6 - 25.6)^2 = 0$ | $(17 - 25.6)^2 = 73.96$ | $(17 - 25.6)^2 = 73.96$ |
| 25 | Rural | 31 | $(25.6 - 25.6)^2 = 0$ | $(31 - 25.6)^2 = 29.16$ | $(31 - 25.6)^2 = 29.16$ |
| 26 | Rural | 24 | $(25.6 - 25.6)^2 = 0$ | $(24 - 25.6)^2 = 2.56$ | $(24 - 25.6)^2 = 2.56$ |
| 27 | Rural | 26 | $(25.6 - 25.6)^2 = 0$ | $(26 - 25.6)^2 = .16$ | $(26 - 25.6)^2 = .16$ |
| 28 | Rural | 18 | $(25.6 - 25.6)^2 = 0$ | $(18 - 25.6)^2 = 57.76$ | $(18 - 25.6)^2 = 57.76$ |
| 29 | Rural | 30 | $(25.6 - 25.6)^2 = 0$ | $(30 - 25.6)^2 = 19.36$ | $(30 - 25.6)^2 = 19.36$ |
| 30 | Rural | 26 | $(25.6 - 25.6)^2 = 0$ | $(26 - 25.6)^2 = .16$ | $(26 - 25.6)^2 = .16$ |
| | | | $SS_{Between} = 1.80$ | $SS_{Within} = 703.40$ | $SS_{Total} = 705.20$ |

**TABLE 13.8. Results of One-Way ANOVA for Investigating the Relationship between Locality of Residence and Fear of Crime**

| | SS | df | SS/df | F |
|---|---|---|---|---|
| | | *Estimated Variance* | | |
| Between groups | 1.80 | 2 | .90 | .03 |
| Within groups | 703.4 | 27 | 26.03 | |
| Total | 705.2 | 29 | | |

the variability between groups, we must conclude that the location of residence is not related to one's fear of crime.

There is an easier way to calculate an *F* statistic than with the definitional formulas we have just gone through. As you can see, with these definitional formulas you have to calculate a lot of squared deviation scores. Not only is this quite tedious (which we hope you discovered), but also it creates many opportunities for computational errors. These little errors can frequently lead to a maddening result where the sums of your between and within sum of squares do not sum to the total sum of squares! When that happens, you have to retrace your steps and go through each calculation until you find your error or errors. We examine easier-to-use computational formulas for the sum of squares in the next section. These formulas do not require the calculation of squared deviation scores and are, therefore, both faster and less prone to error.

However, we hope that by now the definitional formulas have helped you understand the concept of the sum of squares. The sum of squares is an integral part of our determination of two estimates of the population variance, the estimated variance between groups, and the estimated variance within groups. The idea of the sum of squares is a basic element of a large body of statistics based on something called the "general linear model." The ANOVA is one such linear model, and in the next chapter we discuss another type of linear model, the regression, or least-squares, model.

## 13.5 COMPUTATIONAL FORMULA FOR ANOVA

The computational formulas for the various ANOVA sum of squares are comparable to the computational formulas we learned for the variance and standard deviation. In fact, the computing formula for the total sum of squares is almost exactly like the computing formula for the variance:

$$SS_{Total} = \Sigma x^2 - \frac{(\Sigma x)^2}{N} \tag{13.7}$$

where

$x$ = each $x$ score

$N$ = the total number of scores (i.e., $n_1 + n_2 \cdots + n_k$)

The computational formula for $SS_{Total}$ is easy if the operations are performed in a series of steps. First, square each score in each group and sum these squared scores ($\Sigma x^2$). This is our first term in Equation 13.7. Second, sum all of the scores across all groups, square this sum, and then divide by the total number of scores (($\Sigma x)^2/N$). This is our second term in Equation 13.7. Third, subtract the second term from the first one.

The computational formula for $SS_{Between}$ also has two terms:

$$SS_{Between} = \Sigma \frac{(\Sigma x_{ik})^2}{n_k} - \frac{(\Sigma x)^2}{N} \tag{13.8}$$

where

   $x_{ik}$ = the $x_i$th score in the $k$th group
   $n_k$ = the sample size for the $k$th group

This equation might look formidable, but it really is not. Again, let's do the operations in a series of steps. The first term tells us first to sum the scores in the first group ($k_1$), square this sum, and then divide by the number of cases in that group. Then sum the scores in the second group ($k_2$), square this sum, and divide by the number of cases in that group. Do this for each of the $k$ groups, and sum the values for each group. That is the first step. The second step is to sum each score (ignoring what group it is in), square this sum, and divide by the total number of cases ($N$). You really do not have to calculate this term, however, because you have already done that in determining the total sum of squares. The final step is to subtract the second term from the first.

Once you have determined $SS_{Total}$ and $SS_{Between}$, you do not have to go through any additional calculations to find the value of $SS_{Within}$. Because we know that $SS_{Total} = SS_{Between} + SS_{Within}$, we can determine $SS_{Within}$ by subtraction:

$$SS_{Within} = SS_{Total} - SS_{Between}$$

When we have determined the within and between sum of squares, we can calculate the estimated variance of each as before by dividing by its respective degrees of freedom. Finally, we can determine our $F_{obt}$ by calculating the ratio of between variance to within variance.

Let's conduct our two hypothesis tests with the location of residence and fear of crime data that we used with our definitional formulas. We adopt the same alpha level, so the critical value of $F$ remains 3.35. We reject the null hypothesis if $F_{obt} \geq 3.35$. We first use the data in Table 13.3. The calculations from the computational formulas are shown in Table 13.9.

As you can see, the necessary calculations with the computational formulas are both less numerous and less tedious than with the computational formulas. In comparing Table 13.9 with Table 13.5, you also should notice that the sum of squares from the computational and definitional formulas are exactly the same. The summary table for the $F$ test from Table 13.9 is illustrated in Table 13.10, and the results of the $F$ test are identical to that conducted earlier. As $F_{obt}$ (29.6) is greater than the critical value ($F_{crit} = 3.35$), we reject the null hypothesis that the population

**TABLE 13.9. Hypothetical Fear of Crime Scores for a Sample of Urban, Suburban, and Rural Residents**

| | Urban | | Suburban | | Rural | |
|---|---|---|---|---|---|---|
| Resident | $x$ | $x^2$ | $x$ | $x^2$ | $x$ | $x^2$ |
| 1 | 22 | 484 | 23 | 529 | 19 | 361 |
| 2 | 29 | 841 | 22 | 484 | 24 | 576 |
| 3 | 31 | 961 | 26 | 676 | 24 | 576 |
| 4 | 28 | 784 | 25 | 625 | 19 | 361 |
| 5 | 30 | 900 | 24 | 576 | 20 | 400 |
| 6 | 32 | 1024 | 25 | 625 | 24 | 576 |
| 7 | 32 | 1024 | 24 | 576 | 21 | 441 |
| 8 | 31 | 961 | 24 | 576 | 17 | 289 |
| 9 | 28 | 784 | 27 | 729 | 23 | 529 |
| 10 | 30 | 900 | 23 | 529 | 19 | 361 |
| $\Sigma$ | 293 | 8663 | 243 | 5925 | 210 | 4470 |

$$SS_{Total} = (8663 + 5925 + 4470) - \frac{(293 + 243 + 210)^2}{30}$$

$$= 19{,}058 - \frac{(746)^2}{30}$$

$$= 19{,}058 - 18{,}550.5$$

$$= 507.5$$

$$SS_{Between} = \frac{(293)^2}{10} + \frac{(243)^2}{10} + \frac{(210)^2}{10} - 18{,}550.5$$

$$= 8584.9 + 5904.9 + 4410.0 - 18{,}550.5$$

$$= 18{,}899.8 - 18{,}550.5$$

$$= 349.3$$

means are the same. It would appear from these data that there are differences in the extent to which urban, suburban, and rural residents are afraid of becoming the victims of crime.

**TABLE 13.10. Results of One-Way ANOVA for Investigating the Relationship between Locality of Residence and Fear of Crime**

| | | Estimated Variance | | |
|---|---|---|---|---|
| | SS | df | SS/df | F |
| Between groups | 349.3 | 2 | 174.6 | 29.6 |
| Within groups | 158.2 | 27 | 5.9 | |
| Total | 507.5 | 29 | | |

## 13.6 ANOTHER ANOVA EXAMPLE: ALCOHOL USE AND WIFE ABUSE

The association between drunkenness and physical aggression has long been established both in the media and in the scholarly literature. As long ago as the 1800s, the Belgian mathematician and criminologist Lambert Adolphe Quetelet documented a relationship between the amount of alcohol consumed and rates of homicide (1968/1842). A similar relationship was found by Wolfgang in his study of criminal homicide (1958). Perhaps the most rigorous attempt to document alcohol's relationship with one specific type of aggression, husband-to-wife violence, has been that of Kantor and Straus (1987). Using data from the National Family Violence Survey for 1985 (Straus and Gelles, 1990), Kantor and Straus developed an index to measure both the quantity and frequency of the respondents' drinking behavior and then examined the relationship between this index and the amount of violence they perpetrated against their wives during a 12-month period. They found a very strong positive relationship between the amount of alcohol consumed by a man and the frequency of violent acts that he committed against his partner.

Let's say we conducted a comparable study between the amount of alcohol consumed by a man and the frequency of violence committed against his wife. Suppose that we have taken a random sample of 45 men and asked them to report the frequency with which they drank in the previous 12 months, the amount they consumed when drinking, and the number of times they have pushed, slapped, or hit their wives over the same period. Based on self-reports of the frequency and amount of their drinking, we were able to classify these 45 men into one of three drinking groups: (1) light drinkers, (2) moderate drinkers, and (3) heavy drinkers. In Table 13.11 we report the number of times each man reported some form of violence against his wife. With these sample data, we want to determine whether there is a relationship between a man's drinking and violence demonstrated against his wife. Toward this end, we conduct a formal hypothesis test.

Our null hypothesis is that there is no relationship between drinking levels and a man's violence against his wife. That is, light, moderate, and heavy drinking men will not differ in the mean number of times they report committing violent acts against their wives:

$$H_0: \mu_{\text{Light Drinking}} = \mu_{\text{Moderate Drinking}} = \mu_{\text{Heavy Drinking}}$$

As always in an ANOVA, our research hypothesis is simply that the means are different from one another, without specifying which specific means are different:

$$H_1: \mu_{\text{Light Drinking}} \neq \mu_{\text{Moderate Drinking}} \neq \mu_{\text{Heavy Drinking}}$$

Our test statistic is the ANOVA $F$ test, and our sampling distribution is the $F$ distribution. We select an alpha level of .01 for our statistical test. To find our critical $F$ we need to determine our $df_{\text{Between}}$ and $df_{\text{Within}}$ for the data in Table 13.11. With three groups, the $df_{\text{Between}}$ is $k - 1$, or $3 - 1 = 2$; with 45 total scores our $df_{\text{Within}}$ is $N - k$, or $45 - 3 = 42$. The $df_{\text{Total}}$ is $N - 1$, or $df_{\text{Between}} + df_{\text{Within}} = 45 - 1$, or 44. To find $F_{\text{crit}}$ we go to the $F$ table (Table 5.B in Appendix B) and find the specific table for $\alpha = .01$. We then find our $df_{\text{Between}}$ of 2 at the top and our $df_{\text{Within}}$ of 44 along

**TABLE 13.11. Number of Violent Acts Committed by Men against Their Wives by the Frequency/Volume of Drinking**

| Subject | Drinking Level | | | Total |
|---|---|---|---|---|
| | Light | Moderate | Heavy | |
| 1 | 1 | 3 | 1 | |
| 2 | 2 | 4 | 3 | |
| 3 | 0 | 2 | 3 | |
| 4 | 1 | 3 | 4 | |
| 5 | 0 | 1 | 2 | |
| 6 | 0 | 0 | 3 | |
| 7 | 1 | 2 | 5 | |
| 8 | 3 | 0 | 4 | |
| 9 | 2 | 0 | 4 | |
| 10 | 1 | 3 | 5 | |
| 11 | 0 | 4 | 2 | |
| 12 | 0 | 0 | 3 | |
| 13 | 0 | 0 | 0 | |
| 14 | 1 | 2 | 5 | |
| 15 | 2 | 3 | 3 | |
| $\Sigma$ | 14 | 27 | 47 | 88 |
| $\bar{x}$ | .93 | 1.80 | 3.13 | 1.96 |
| $s$ | .96 | 1.52 | 1.46 | |
| $n$ | 15 | 15 | 15 | 45 |

the left column (there is no specific 44 degrees of freedom, so we use 40). Our $F_{crit}$ with 2 and 40 degrees of freedom is equal to 5.18. Our decision rule is to reject the null hypothesis if $F_{obt} \geq 5.18$ and to fail to reject the null hypothesis if $F_{obt} < 5.18$. We need now to calculate our $F$ statistic from our sample data and compare it to $F_{crit}$. We use the computational formulas (Equations 13.7 and 13.8) to do this. The calculations for the sum of squares are reported in Table 13.12.

The total sum of squares is 111.9, and the sum of squares between groups is 36.85. By subtraction, we can determine the sum of squares within groups to be:

$$SS_{Within} = SS_{Total} - SS_{Between}$$

$$= 111.9 - 36.85$$

$$= 75.05$$

We can now calculate our two estimates of the variance by dividing $SS_{Between}$ and $SS_{Within}$ by their respective degrees of freedom. We summarize these results in Table 13.13. The between-groups variance is 18.42 (36.85/2), and the within-groups variance is 1.79 (75.05/42). As you can see, there is much greater between-groups than within-groups variance. Not surprisingly, when we take the ratio of between- to within-groups variance, we find that $F_{obt}$ is quite large ($F_{obt} = 10.29$) and is greater than $F_{crit}$ of 5.18. We therefore reject the null hypothesis. We conclude

**TABLE 13.12.  Computation Formula Calculations for Drinking/Violence Data Reported in Table 13.12**

| | Drinking Level | | | | | |
|---|---|---|---|---|---|---|
| | Light | | Moderate | | Heavy | |
| Subject | $x$ | $x^2$ | $x$ | $x^2$ | $x$ | $x^2$ |
| 1 | 1 | 1 | 3 | 9 | 1 | 1 |
| 2 | 2 | 4 | 4 | 16 | 3 | 9 |
| 3 | 0 | 0 | 2 | 4 | 3 | 9 |
| 4 | 1 | 1 | 3 | 9 | 4 | 16 |
| 5 | 0 | 0 | 1 | 1 | 2 | 4 |
| 6 | 0 | 0 | 0 | 0 | 3 | 9 |
| 7 | 1 | 1 | 2 | 4 | 5 | 25 |
| 8 | 3 | 9 | 0 | 0 | 4 | 16 |
| 9 | 2 | 4 | 0 | 0 | 4 | 16 |
| 10 | 1 | 1 | 3 | 9 | 5 | 25 |
| 11 | 0 | 0 | 4 | 16 | 2 | 4 |
| 12 | 0 | 0 | 0 | 0 | 3 | 9 |
| 13 | 0 | 0 | 0 | 0 | 0 | 0 |
| 14 | 1 | 1 | 2 | 4 | 5 | 25 |
| 15 | 2 | 4 | 3 | 9 | 3 | 9 |
| $\Sigma$ | 14 | 26 | 27 | 81 | 47 | 177 |

$$SS_{Total} = (26 + 81 + 177) - \frac{(14 + 27 + 47)^2}{45}$$

$$= 284 - \frac{7744}{45}$$

$$= 284 - 172.09$$

$$= 111.9$$

$$SS_{Between} = \frac{(14)^2}{15} + \frac{(27)^2}{15} + \frac{(47)^2}{15} - 172.09$$

$$= 13.07 + 48.60 + 147.27 - 172.09$$

$$= 208.94 - 172.09$$

$$= 36.85$$

that, based on our sample data, light, moderate, and heavy drinking men do have different mean levels of violence against their wives. Like Quetelet, Wolfgang, Kantor and Straus, and others, we find a positive relationship between drinking alcohol and violence. As levels of drinking increase, so do levels of violence.

The results of the $F$ tests we have performed have allowed us to make only general conclusions regarding the relationships between our means. When we rejected the null hypothesis, our conclusion was only that at least one of the means was sig-

**TABLE 13.13. Results of One-Way ANOVA for Investigating the Relationship between Drinking and Violence towards One's Wife**

| | | | Estimated Variance | |
| --- | --- | --- | --- | --- |
| | SS | df | SS/df | F |
| Between groups | 36.85 | 2 | 18.42 | 10.29 |
| Within groups | 75.05 | 42 | 1.79 | |
| Total | 111.9 | 44 | | |

nificantly different from at least one of the other means. We did not know, however, which specific means were significantly different. For example, we did not know whether light drinkers had significant differences in their mean level of violence from moderate *and* heavy drinkers or whether they were significantly different from only the heavy drinkers. The next section introduces a statistical technique called Tukey's HSD test that allows us to specify just how our group means are different.

## 13.7 TESTING DIFFERENCES BETWEEN MEANS

By simply looking at a set of means in an ANOVA, you can easily determine which mean is the lowest and which is the highest. But can you so easily determine which pair of relationships are significantly different from each other? From our fear of crime data, we know that urban residents had the highest levels of fear, but was this mean fear level significantly different from that of suburban residents or only significantly different from those living in rural locations? We hope by now that you distrust your glancing at the data as far as determining statistical significance is concerned.

To determine which pair of means are significantly different from each other, we must perform additional analyses on our data. In a way, what we are about to do is like testing additional null hypotheses about each pair of means in our study. There are many statistical techniques that we could use to do this. These significance tests include tests such as the Scheffe test, the Newman-Keuls test, or Duncan's multiple test (Hays, 1994). However, for our purposes here, we present only one of the most commonly used methods, called Tukey's honest significant difference (HSD) test.

Let's begin with the fear of crime and location of residence data from Table 13.3. In this study, we were investigating the mean differences in fear of crime among urban, suburban, and rural residents. When we performed an *F* test on this data set, we rejected the null hypothesis that the sample means were equal (see Table 13.6). Unlike the general *F* test, where we tested one null hypothesis, we are now interested in three questions: "Is the mean fear level in the population of urban residents different from the mean fear level in the population of suburban residents?" "Is the mean fear level in the population of suburban residents different from the mean fear level in the population of rural residents?" Finally, "Is the mean fear level in the population of rural residents different from the mean fear level in the population of urban residents?" These questions and their representative hypotheses can be displayed more succinctly in equation form:

$H_0$: $\mu_{Urban} = \mu_{Suburban}$

$H_1$: $\mu_{Urban} \neq \mu_{Suburban}$

$H_0$: $\mu_{Suburban} = \mu_{Rural}$

$H_1$: $\mu_{Suburban} \neq \mu_{Rural}$

$H_0$: $\mu_{Rural} = \mu_{Urban}$

$H_1$: $\mu_{Rural} \neq \mu_{Urban}$

You may be saying to yourself right now, "This looks exactly like the null and research hypotheses we tested with an independent-groups $t$ test in Chapter 12. Why can't we just perform several different $t$ tests to answer these questions?" As we suggested in the introduction to this chapter, however tempting this might be, it is not technically correct to do so because the "separate" significance tests are not independent. As a result, even though we may have a .05 probability of making a Type I error (alpha = .05) on the first statistical test, over the series of pairwise tests this probability does not remain at .05, but increases. Therefore, the cumulative probability of making a Type I error is much higher than .05. By performing the Tukey's HSD test on our separate mean comparisons, however, we are able to maintain our specified alpha level. Here, we ask that you simply believe that we can; if you are eager to understand the mathematical logic of how the HSD test allows us to do this in greater detail, see Tukey (1953), Kirk (1968), Jaccard (1983), or Hays (1994).

The HSD test requires the calculation of something called a *critical difference (CD) score,* which is obtained from:

$$CD = q_\alpha \sqrt{\frac{\text{Estimated Variance within Groups}}{n}} \qquad (13.9)$$

The $n$ in the formula refers to the number of observations or scores in each group. The term $q$ in the formula refers to a value that is obtained from a table listing the $q$ distribution. These critical values of $q$ are actually called "studentized range values." This table is presented in Table B.6 of Appendix B. You obtain a critical value of $q$ with reference to three elements: the alpha level you have selected, your $df_{Within}$, and the number of groups you have in your sample, $k$.

Rather than discuss these notions in the abstract, let's use our fear of crime data in Table 13.3 to examine the necessary calculations for the HSD test. We have calculated all of the components needed to compute our CD score for the HSD test already. We simply have to plug the numbers into the formula. The first step we must take, however, is to determine the critical value of $q$ from Table B.6 in Appendix B. There is one table for alpha = .05 and one for alpha = .01. For each table, the row going across the top is the number of groups we have ($k$), and the column going down the table lists the $df_{Within}$.

Let's find the critical value of $q$ we need for our fear of crime example. Sticking with our selected alpha level from the ANOVA of .05 and going across the table to find three groups and down the table to find the $df_{Within}$, which in our fear of crime data is 27 (we select a value based on 30 degrees of freedom as it is more conservative than one based on 24 degrees of freedom), we obtain a critical value of $q = 3.49$.

Using the values we have already calculated for the $F$ test, then, we can now calculate our critical difference (CD) score as follows:

$$CD = 3.49 \sqrt{\frac{5.9}{10}}$$

$$= 3.49\sqrt{.59}$$

$$= 3.49(.77)$$

$$= 2.69$$

where

5.9 = the estimated within group variance from Table 13.6
10 = the sample size

The CD score we obtain is 2.69. Unlike previous tests where we tested the null hypothesis by comparing our obtained value of a statistic with a critical value, for the HSD test, we compare our obtained CD value with the absolute value of the difference between the group means of interest. If the absolute mean difference between the two means of interest is greater than the CD score, then we can reject the null hypothesis that the two means are equal. Recall that we would actually have three sets of null and research hypotheses to ascertain the relationships between levels of fear for urban, suburban, and rural residents.

Testing the first null hypothesis that mean levels of fear for urban residents is equal to mean levels of fear for suburban residents, we simply calculate the absolute difference between these two group means as follows:

$$(\overline{x}_{Urban} - \overline{x}_{Suburban}) = (29.3 - 24.3) = |5|$$

In this case, 5 does exceed the CD value of 2.69. What conclusion do we make? Because the absolute difference of our sample means is greater than the critical difference we needed, we can reject the null hypothesis that mean levels of fear for urban and suburban residents are equal. It would appear that urban residents are significantly more afraid of becoming the victims of crime than are those who live in suburban areas.

Let's perform the HSD test for the two remaining null hypotheses:

$H_0$: $\mu_{Suburban} = \mu_{Rural}$

$$(24.3 - 21) = |3.3|$$

$H_0$: $\mu_{Urban} = \mu_{Rural}$

$$(29.3 - 21) = |8.3|$$

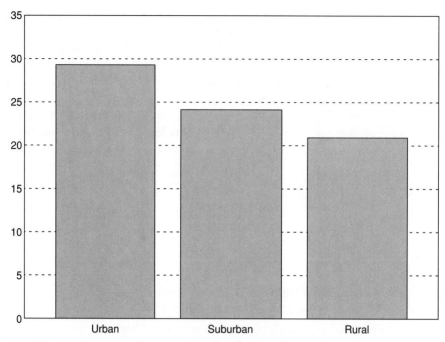

FIGURE 13.3. Mean fear of crime score by location of residence.

Both of these absolute differences exceed the CD value of 2.69. We can now reject the null hypotheses that suburban levels of fear are equal to rural fear levels and that fear of crime among urban residents is equal to those among rural residents. Suburban residents have a significantly greater fear of crime than do rural residents, and urban residents have a significantly greater fear than rural residents. It appears that there are significant differences in the extent to which residents in different areas are fearful of crime. Urban residents are the most fearful, followed by suburban residents, and residents of rural areas are the least afraid of crime.

If you are presenting this information to a nonstatistical audience, this is a good opportunity to incorporate some of the graphical techniques we illustrated in Chapter 5. For example, a bar graph could easily be constructed depicting mean levels of fear by each locality of residence. By looking at a graphic aid, such as that displayed in Figure 13.3, an audience can easily discern the relationships between the variables without having to process the numerical information. By looking at Figure 13.3, even the statistically unsophisticated can see at a glance that those who reside in urban areas are the most afraid of becoming the victims of crime compared to those who reside in either suburban and rural locations and that those who live in rural areas appear to be the least concerned about becoming crime victims.

# 13.8 ANALYSIS OF VARIANCE WITH UNEQUAL SAMPLE SIZES

Up to this point we have assumed that the ANOVA involved groups that were the same size (i.e., $n_1 = n_2 \cdots = n_k$). If at all possible, it is better to have equal sample sizes. It is acceptable to violate some of the ANOVA assumptions (such as equal population variances and normal populations) may be modestly violated if the sample sizes are equal and equal to 10 or more. We are less confident, however, that violations of the ANOVA assumptions are without major consequence if the sample sizes are very unequal. Sometimes, however, we have no choice and have to examine ANOVA techniques data of unequal sample sizes. If the ANOVA assumptions do hold, and the loss of cases from some groups is random, the adjustment you have to make in your calculations for an ANOVA with unequal sample sizes is minor.

If you are using the definitional formulas to calculate the relevant sum of squares, the main difference in the ANOVA with unequal sample sizes is with the total sum of squares. You will remember that $SS_{Total}$ was determined by subtracting the grand mean from each score, squaring the difference, and summing across all scores ($\Sigma[x - \bar{x}_G]^2$). In the ANOVA with equal sample sizes, the grand mean was found by adding each score (ignoring what group the score was in) and dividing by $N$, the total number of scores. In the ANOVA with unequal sample sizes the grand mean is no longer a simple average of all scores, but a weighted average, where each group mean is weighted by its sample size. The formula for the grand mean with unequal sample sizes is:

$$\bar{x}_G = \frac{\Sigma n_k \bar{x}_k}{n_k} \tag{13.10}$$

where
   $n_k$ = the sample size for the $k$th group
   $\bar{x}_k$ = the mean for the $k$th group

To calculate the grand mean with unequal sample sizes, then, simply multiply each group mean by the group sample size and sum over each group, then divide by the sum of the sample sizes. Once the sum of squares are determined, the $F$ test proceeds exactly as before. If you use the computational formulas to determine the sum of squares, the ANOVA with unequal sample sizes involves exactly the same formulas and procedures as with equal sample sizes.

If you reject the null hypothesis of equal population means in the ANOVA, you can then determine which specific means are significantly different using Tukey's HSD test. However, the formula for the HSD is somewhat different when your sample sizes are not equal. With unequal sample sizes, Hays (1994) recommends using $2n_1n_2/(n_1 + n_2)$ in place of $n$ in the numerator of the formula, where $n_1$ is the sample size for the group with the largest mean, and $n_2$ is the size of the sample for the group with the smallest mean.

## 13.9 A MEASURE OF ASSOCIATION WITH ANOVA

When we reject the null hypothesis of equal means using an ANOVA, we are concluding that at least some of the population means are not equal. That is, we are saying that there is a relationship between the categorical independent and continuous dependent variable. In our location and fear of crime example, we concluded that where one lived did seem to influence the amount of fear a person had of becoming the victim of a crime. While the ANOVA can tell us whether there is a significant relationship between two variables, it does not directly tell us anything about the *strength* of that relationship. As in the case of our chi-square statistic, in addition to a statistical test, we also would like to have a measure of association between our two variables.

The lesson we would like to stress is that there is an important difference between the *significance* and the *strength* or *importance* of a relationship. Even if there is only a very slight relationship between two variables, it may be a statistically significant one with a large sample size. Having found that a relationship exists between our independent and dependent variables, then, we would also like some indication of the magnitude or strength of that relationship. Statistics that measure the strength of a relationship are called *measures of association.* For the ANOVA problem, there is a relatively easy measure of association to calculate that is based on the different estimates of the population variance.

You will remember that the total variability in a set of scores is estimated by the total sum of squares. This total variability is comprised of two components, (1) the variability between groups, which measures how different the group scores are, and (2) the variability within groups, which measures how different the individual scores are within a group. As all persons within a group share the same group membership, their scores on the dependent variable should be the same. If they are not, such within-group differences are said to be due to error and are sometimes referred to as unexplained variability. If the independent variable is related to the dependent variable, persons in different groups should have different scores on the dependent variable. These between-group differences are said to be due to group or treatment effects, and such between-group differences are sometimes referred to as explained variability.

If the scores within a group are generally the same whereas the scores across groups are very different, then, the total variability is due to the fact that persons are in different groups. Most of the variability in this case would be explained variability. In other words, the group a person belongs to affects the score attached to the person, and the independent and dependent variables are strongly related. If, however, the scores within a group are very diverse and more diverse than the scores across different groups, then most of the total variability will be due to within-group or unexplained variability. In this case, the group a person is in has very little impact on the person's score, and the two variables are not strongly related.

It would seem, therefore, that one measure of association could be based on how much of the total variability in a given set of scores is due to the variability between groups. Another way to think of this is in terms of the ratio of explained to total variability. The greater the proportion of explained variability to total variability, the stronger the relationship between the independent and dependent variables. This is the idea behind an ANOVA–based measure of association referred to as the *correlation ratio* or *eta squared* $(E^2)_1$, from the Greek letter eta ($\eta$):

$$E^2 = \frac{\text{Explained SS}}{\text{Total SS}} = \frac{SS_{\text{Between}}}{SS_{\text{Total}}} \tag{13.11}$$

The value of the correlation ratio,[5] then, is the ratio of between sum of squares to total sum of squares. Eta squared measures the strength of the relationship between the independent and dependent variables. More specifically, it measures the amount of variance in the dependent variable that is explained by the independent variable. Eta squared can range in magnitude from zero, indicating no relationship, to 1.0, indicating a very strong relationship between the independent and dependent variables. Following Jaccard (1983), as an informal rule of thumb, you might want to consider eta squared values between 0 and .20 as evidence of a "weak" relationship, values between .20 and .50 as evidence of a "moderate" relationship, and values over .50 as evidence of a "strong" relationship.

For our location of residence and fear of crime data in Table 13.6, the $SS_{\text{Total}}$ was 507.5 and the $SS_{\text{Between}}$ was 349.3. For this data set, the sample value of eta squared is:

$$E^2 = \frac{349.3}{507.5}$$

$$= .69$$

This tells us that there is a strong relationship between location of residence and fear of crime. More specifically, that 69 percent of the variance in perceived fear of crime is explained by where the person lives.

Blalock (1979) contends that the sample correlation ratio is a biased estimate of its population value $(E^2)$, and that it is often best (particularly with small samples) to correct for this bias. He suggests an *unbiased* correlation ratio, which is equal to 1 minus the ratio of within-groups variance to total variance. To find the within-groups and total variances, simply divide the within-groups variance and total sum of squares by their respective degrees of freedom:

$$\text{Unbiased } E^2 = 1 - \frac{\text{Estimated Variance within Groups}}{\text{Estimated Total Variance}} \tag{13.12}$$

We have already calculated the within-groups variance with our ANOVA, and the total variance can easily be determined by dividing $SS_{\text{Total}}$ by its degrees of freedom $(N - 1)$. The unbiased correlation ratio also ranges from a minimum of zero to a maximum of 1.0, and the magnitude reflects the amount of variance in the dependent variable explained by the independent variable. This estimate is a more conservative estimate of the strength of the relationship between the two variables.

For our location of residence and fear of crime data, the total variance is 17.5 (507.5/29; see Table 13.6) and the within-groups variance is 5.9. The unbiased correlation ratio between location and fear of crime, then, is:

$$\text{Unbiased } E^2 = 1 - \frac{5.9}{17.5}$$

$$= 1 - .34$$

$$= .66$$

The unbiased correlation is .66. This coefficient indicates that there is a strong relationship between location of residence and fear of crime. Sixty-six percent of the variance in fear of crime is explained by where one lives. Notice that the corrected correlation ratio is slightly smaller in magnitude than the uncorrected one.

## *13.10 SUMMARY*

In this chapter we have examined *analysis of variance (ANOVA)* techniques, which are used to determine the relationship between a dependent variable that is continuous in nature and an independent variable that is categorical and has three or more categories (e.g., groups or three or more samples). We went through the procedures used to calculate an *F ratio,* which is the ratio of the variance observed between our groups ($SS_{Between}$) and the variance observed within each group ($SS_{Within}$).

The results of an ANOVA can lead us to reject or fail to reject the null hypothesis that the population means between our groups or samples are equal ($H_0$: $\mu_1 = \mu_2 = \mu_3$). The *F* test alone cannot tell us which specific means are different from one another. To determine the exact nature of the relationship between each of the population means it is necessary to perform *Tukey's Honest Significant Difference (HSD)* test. This HSD test allows us to maintain our selected level of alpha and perform the number of hypothesis tests necessary to determine exactly which group means are significantly different from one another and which are not.

Finally, we learned a measure of association for an ANOVA. To determine how strongly the two variables in an ANOVA are related, we discussed one type of measure of association, the correlation ratio, or eta squared. Eta squared measures how much of the variance in the dependent variable is explained by the independent variable. The magnitude of this coefficient ranges from zero, for no relationship, to 1.0 for a very strong relationship. As a rule of thumb, we suggested that correlation ratios of 0 to .20 indicate only a very weak relationship, ratios between .20 and .50 indicate a moderate relationship, and ratios over .50 indicate a strong relationship between the independent and dependent variables.

## *Key Terms*

analysis of variance (ANOVA)
between-group sum of squares ($SS_{Between}$)
between-group variability
correlation ratio (Eta squared)
critical difference (CD) score
eta
*F* distribution
*F* ratio measures of association

total sum of squares ($SS_{Total}$)
Tukey's honest significant difference (HSD) test
variance between groups
variance within groups
within-group sum of squares ($SS_{Within}$)
within-group variability

# Problems

1. When is it appropriate to perform an ANOVA with our data? What type of variables do we need?
2. What statistical technique should we use if we have a continuous dependent variable and a categorical independent variable with only two categories?
3. Why do we call this statistical technique an analysis of *variance* when we are really interested in the difference among population *means?*
4. What two types of variability do we use to calculate the $F$ ratio?
5. How do we determine the $df_{Total}$, $df_{Between}$, and $df_{Within}$?
6. In 1995, Robin Ogle and her colleagues (1995) published a paper in which they argued that some women experience great stress (for instance, in physically abusive relationships), and that if this stress is not released in some healthy fashion, they are likely to strike out in violent and homicidal ways. The targets of this aggression, they argue, are likely to be those in close proximity to them, like partners and children. Let's say you want to test this hypothesis. You have a random sample of 30 women with small children living at home. Based on questions about their home life and possible sources of stress, you are able to place them into one of three groups: "high stress," "medium stress," and "low stress." You then ask each of the women how many times they have physically punished their children in the past year. You think that stress might be related to the use of physical punishment. The following are the data from your sample:

### Number of Times Physically Used Punishment Last Year

| | *Level of Stress* | |
|---|---|---|
| High | Medium | Low |
| 4 | 2 | 3 |
| 6 | 4 | 1 |
| 12 | 5 | 2 |
| 10 | 3 | 0 |
| 5 | 0 | 2 |
| 9 | 3 | 2 |
| 8 | 2 | 4 |
| 11 | 5 | 1 |
| 10 | 5 | 0 |
| 8 | 4 | 1 |

With this data set, do the following:

a. Calculate the total, between, and within sum of squares.
b. Determine the correct number of degrees of freedom, calculate the ratio of sum of squares to degrees of freedom, and determine the $F$ ratio.
c. With an alpha of .05, test the null hypothesis that the three population means are equal against the alternative hypothesis that some of them are different.
d. Conduct a mean comparison for each pair of means using Tukey's HSD test.
e. Calculate the value of eta squared and an unbiased estimate of eta squared, and make a conclusion about the strength of the relationship between stress and the rate of physical punishment.

7. One of the most pressing social problems is drunk driving. Drunk driving causes untold human suffering and has profound economic effects. States have tried various things to inhibit drunk driving. Some states have tried to cut down on drunk driving within their borders by "getting tough" with drunk drivers by suspending their driver's license and imposing heavy fines and jail and prison sentences. Other states have tried a moral appeal by mounting public relations campaigns that proclaim the harm and injury produced by drunk driving. You want to determine the effectiveness of these strategies. You calculate the rate of drunk driving per 100,000 residents for each of the 50 states; you also classify each state into one of three categories, a Get Tough state, a Moral Appeal state, or a Control state. The latter states do nothing special to those who get caught drinking and driving. Your summary data looks like the following:

| Get Tough States | Moral Appeal States | Control States |
|---|---|---|
| $n_1 = 15$ | $n_2 = 15$ | $n_3 = 15$ |
| $\bar{x}_1 = 125.2$ | $\bar{x}_2 = 119.7$ | $\bar{x}_3 = 145.3$ |

Part of the summary $F$ table looks like the following:

| | Sum of Squares | df | SS/df | F |
|---|---|---|---|---|
| Between | 475.3 | | | |
| Within | 204.5 | | | |
| Total | 679.8 | | | |

With these summary data, do the following:
a. Determine the correct number of degrees of freedom, calculate the ratio of sum of squares to degrees of freedom, and determine the $F$ ratio.
b. With an alpha of .01, test the null hypothesis that the three population means are equal against the alternative hypothesis that some of them are different.
c. Conduct a mean comparison for each pair of means using Tukey's HSD test.
d. Calculate the value of eta squared and an unbiased estimate of eta squared, and make a conclusion about the strength of the relationship between sanction policy and the rate of drunk driving.

8. In a 1995 article, Fisher and Nasar suggested that some city areas might be characterized as "fear spots." These "fear spots" are defined geographic areas where people feel vulnerable to victimization. As a research project, you wanted to find out why particular areas were feared more than others. You think it is because people's perceptions of their risk of criminal victimization is strongly related to their actual risks of being the victim of a crime. Let's say you identified four geographic areas in your city that varied in terms of how much fear people felt going into those areas ("high fear spot" to "very low fear spot"). You then went into each of those areas and asked a random sample of 50 people how many times they had been the victim of a crime in the last 5 years. You found the following mean number of victimizations for each area:

|         | Very High Fear Spot | High Fear Spot | Medium Fear Spot | Low Fear Spot | Very Low Fear Spot |
|---------|---------------------|----------------|------------------|---------------|--------------------|
| Means   | 14.5                | 14.3           | 14.7             | 13.4          | 13.9               |
| $n$     | 50                  | 50             | 50               | 50            | 50                 |

Part of the summary $F$ table looks like the following:

|         | Sum of Squares | df | SS/df | $F$ |
|---------|----------------|----|-------|-----|
| Between | 12.5           |    |       |     |
| Within  | 616.2          |    |       |     |
| Total   | 628.7          |    |       |     |

With these summary data, do the following:

a. Determine the correct number of degrees of freedom, calculate the ratio of sum of squares to degrees of freedom, and determine the $F$ ratio.

b. With an alpha of .05, test the null hypothesis that the four population means are equal against the alternative hypothesis that some of them are different.

c. Calculate the value of eta squared and an unbiased estimate of eta squared, and make a conclusion about the strength of the relationship between fear spot and number of actual criminal victimizations.

## Solutions to Problems

1. An ANOVA can be performed whenever we have a continuous (interval- or ratio-level) dependent variable that is normally distributed in the population and a categorical variable with three or more levels or categories and we are interested in testing hypothesis about three or more population means.

2. If we have a continuous dependent variable and a categorical independent variable with only two categories or levels, the correct statistical test would be a two-sample $t$ test, assuming that the hypothesis test involved the equality of two population means.

3. It is called the analysis of *variance*, because we make inferences about the differences among population means based on a comparison of the *variance* that exists within each sample, relative to the *variance* that exists across the samples. More specifically, we examine the ratio of variance between the samples to the variance within the samples. The greater this ratio, the more across-sample variance there is relative to within-sample variance. Therefore, as this ratio becomes greater than 1, we are more inclined to believe that the samples were drawn from different populations with different population means.

4. As suggested in the answer to Question 3, the two types of variability we use in the ANOVA $F$ test are the variability between the samples and the variability within the samples.

5. The formulas for the three degrees of freedom are:

$$\mathrm{df}_{\mathrm{Total}} = N - 1$$

$$\mathrm{df}_{\mathrm{Between}} = k - 1$$

$$\mathrm{df}_{\mathrm{Within}} = N - k$$

To check your arithmetic, make sure that $\mathrm{df}_{\mathrm{Total}} = \mathrm{df}_{\mathrm{Between}} + \mathrm{df}_{\mathrm{Within}}$.

**6. a.** The total sum of squares is:

$$SS_{Total} = 924 - \frac{(132)^2}{30}$$

$$= 924 - 580.8$$

$$= 343.2$$

The between-sum of squares is:

$$SS_{Between} = \frac{(83)^2}{10} + \frac{(33)^2}{10} + \frac{(16)^2}{10} - \frac{(132)^2}{30}$$

$$= 688.9 + 108.9 + 25.6 - 580.8$$

$$= 823.4 - 580.8$$

$$= 242.6$$

Now we can obtain the within sum of squares by subtraction:

$$SS_{Within} = SS_{Total} - SS_{Between}$$

$$= 343.2 - 242.6$$

$$= 100.6$$

**b.** $df_{Between} = k - 1 = 3 - 1 = 2$

$df_{Within} = N - k = 30 - 3 = 27$

$df_{Total} = N - 1 = 30 - 1 = 29$

You can see that $df_{Between} + df_{Within} = df_{Total}$.

The ratio of sum of squares to degrees of freedom can now be determined:

$SS_{Between}/df_{Between} = 242.6/2 = 121.30$

$SS_{Within}/df_{Within} = 100.6/27 = 3.72$

The $F$ ratio is:

$F_{obt} = 121.30/3.72 = 32.61.$

**c.** $H_0: \mu_1 = \mu_2 = \mu_3$

$H_1: \mu_1 \neq \mu_2 \neq \mu_3$

Our decision rule will be to reject the null hypothesis if $F_{obt} \geq 3.35$. $F_{obt} = 32.61$. As our obtained value of $F$ is greater than the critical value, we reject the null hypothesis. We conclude that the population means are not equal, and that the frequency of using physical punishment against one's child does vary by the amount of stress the woman feels. Going to the studentized table, you find the value of $q$ to be equal to 3.49. To find the critical difference, you plug these values into your formula:

$$CD = 3.49\sqrt{\frac{3.72}{10}}$$

$$= 3.49\sqrt{.372}$$

$$= 3.49(.610)$$

$$= 2.13$$

The critical difference for the mean comparisons, then, is 2.13. Find the difference between each pair of sample means in the problem:

| High Stress | 8.30 |
|---|---|
| Medium Stress | $-3.30$ |
| | $\lvert 5.00 \rvert$ |

| High Stress | 8.30 |
|---|---|
| Low Stress | $-1.60$ |
| | $\lvert 6.70 \rvert$ |

| Medium Stress | 3.30 |
|---|---|
| Low Stress | $-1.60$ |
| | $\lvert 1.70 \rvert$ |

The difference between the High and Medium Stress groups is greater than 2.13, so these groups are significantly different in the frequency with which they use physical punishment. The difference between the High and Low Stress groups is also greater than 2.13, so these groups are significantly different in their frequency of physical punishment. The Medium and Low Stress groups, however, are not significantly different, the difference between their two means is less than 2.13.

**d.** Eta squared is:

$$E^2 = \frac{242.6}{343.2} = .71$$

The unbiased value of eta$^2$ is:

$$\text{Unbiased } E^2 = 1 - \frac{3.72}{11.83} = 1 - .31 = .69$$

This tells us that there is a moderately strong relationship between a woman's feelings of stress and the frequency with which she uses physical punishment against her children. Specifically, about 70 percent of the variance in the frequency of physical punishment is explained by the mother's feelings of stress.

**7. a.** The correct degrees of freedom for this table are:

$$df_{Between} = k - 1 = 3 - 1 = 2$$

$$df_{Within} = N - k = 45 - 3 = 42$$

$$df_{Total} = N - 1 = 45 - 1 = 44$$

You can see that $df_{Between} + df_{Within} = df_{Total}$. The ratio of sum of squares to degrees of freedom can now be determined:

$$SS_{Between}/df_{Between} = 475.3/2 = 237.65$$

$$SS_{Within}/df_{Within} = 204.5/42 = 4.87$$

The $F$ ratio is:

$F_{obt} = 237.65/4.87 = 48.80$

**b.** $H_0: \mu_1 = \mu_2 = \mu_3$

$H_1: \mu_1 \neq \mu_2 \neq \mu_3$

Our decision rule will be to reject the null hypothesis if $F_{obt} \geq 5.18$. $F_{obt} = 48.80$. As our obtained value of $F$ is greater than the critical value, we reject the null hypothesis. We conclude that the population means are not equal.

**c.** Going to the studentized table, you find the value of $q$ to be 4.37. To find the critical difference, you plug these values into your formula:

$$CD = 4.37\sqrt{\frac{4.87}{15}}$$

$$= 4.37\sqrt{.325}$$

$$= 4.37(.570)$$

$$= 2.49$$

The critical difference for the mean comparisons, then, is 2.49. Find the difference between each pair of sample means in the problem:

| Get Tough | 125.2 |
| Moral Appeal | $-119.7$ |
| | $\lvert 5.5 \rvert$ |

| Get Tough | 125.2 |
| Control | $-145.3$ |
| | $\lvert 20.1 \rvert$ |

| Moral Appeal | 119.7 |
| Control | $-145.3$ |
| | $\lvert 25.6 \rvert$ |

Each pair of differences is greater than 2.49. This means that the Moral Appeal states have a significantly lower level of drunk driving than the Get Tough states, the Get Tough states have a significantly lower level of drunk driving than Control states, and the Moral Appeal states have significantly lower levels of drunk driving than the Control states. It appears, then, that doing *something* about drunk driving is better than doing little or nothing.

**d.** Eta squared is:

$$E^2 = \frac{475.3}{679.8} = .70$$

The unbiased value of eta squared is:

$$\text{Unbiased } E^2 = 1 - \frac{4.87}{15.45} = 1 - .31 = .69$$

This tells us that there is a moderately strong relationship between the state's response to drunk driving and the rate of drunk driving in that state. Specifically, about 70 percent of the variance in levels of drunk driving is explained by the state's public policy.

**8. a.** The correct degrees of freedom for this table are:

$$\text{df}_{\text{Between}} = k - 1 = 5 - 1 = 4$$

$$\text{df}_{\text{Within}} = N - k = 250 - 5 = 245$$

$$\text{df}_{\text{Total}} = N - 1 = 250 - 1 = 249$$

$$\text{SS}_{\text{Between}}/\text{df}_{\text{Between}} = 12.5/4 = 3.125$$

$$\text{SS}_{\text{Within}}/\text{df}_{\text{Within}} = 616.2/245 = 2.51$$

The $F$ ratio is:

$$F_{\text{obt}} = 3.125/2.51 = 1.25$$

**b.** $H_0: \mu_1 = \mu_2 = \mu_3 = \mu_4 = \mu_5$

$H_1: \mu_1 \neq \mu_2 \neq \mu_3 \neq \mu_4 \neq \mu_5$

Our decision rule will be to reject the null hypothesis if $F_{\text{obt}} \geq 2.37$. $F_{\text{obt}} = 1.25$. As our obtained value of $F$ is not greater than or equal to the critical value, our decision is to not reject the null hypothesis. We conclude that different fear spots are not different in terms of their actual risk of victimization.

**c.** The value of eta squared is:

$$E^2 = \frac{12.5}{628.7} = .02.$$

The unbiased estimate of eta squared is:

$$E^2 = 1 - \frac{2.51}{2.52} = 1 - .996 = .004.$$

There is virtually no relationship between a person's fear of a given geographical area and the actual frequency of criminal victimization in that area. About 2 percent of the variance in fear spots is explained by victimization levels.

## *Endnotes*

1. The estimated standard deviation is calculated as:

$$s = \sqrt{\frac{(36 - 54)^2 + (48 - 54)^2 + (60 - 54)^2 + (72 - 54)^2}{(4 - 1)}}$$

$$= \sqrt{\frac{324 + 36 + 36 + 324}{3}}$$

$$= \sqrt{\frac{720}{3}}$$

$$= \sqrt{240}$$

$$= 15.49$$

2. In this formula, capital $N$ does not refer to the population size, but to the sum of all the group sizes, $n_1 + n_2 + \cdots + n_k$. It is, then, the total number of observations or cases in all groups.

3. Instead of subtracting the grand mean from the category mean and squaring for each observation in each category, a somewhat easier formula for $SS_{Between}$ is:

$$SS_{Between} = \Sigma n_k(\bar{x}_k - \bar{x}_G)^2$$

In this formula you subtract the grand mean from the category mean once, square this difference, and then multiply the squared difference by the number of observations in that category.

4. In Table 13.6 we calculated $SS_{Between}$ by subtracting the grand mean from each group mean and then squaring this difference. We did this 10 times for each of the three groups because there were 10 scores in each group. If you use the definitional formulas for the sum of squares, as we suggested in Endnote 3, it might be easier to do this once for each group and then multiply by the number of observations in the group and then adding these together. For example, for the $SS_{Between}$ calculated in Table 13.6 we could have done the following:

$$SS_{Between} = 10(29.3 - 24.9)^2 + 10(24.3 - 24.9)^2 + 10(21.0 - 24.9)^2$$

$$= [(10)(19.36)] + [(10)(.36)] + [(10)(15.21)]$$

$$= 193.6 + 3.6 + 152.10$$

$$= 349.30$$

5. The sample value of the correlation ratio is symbolized as $E^2$, the value of eta squared in the population is $\eta^2$. The symbol $\eta$ is the Greek letter eta.

# CHAPTER 14

# *Bivariate Correlation and Regression*

*If A is a success in life, then A equals x plus y plus z. Work is x; y is play; and z is keeping your mouth shut.*

—ALBERT EINSTEIN

## 14.1 INTRODUCTION

In this chapter we examine the association between two variables measured at the interval or ratio level. Usually whenever there are interval/ratio-level variables the association or relationship between variables is referred to as the *correlation* between two variables *(bivariate correlation).* We adopt this convention here. Our discussion of correlation covers many of the same issues that we have seen when looking at the relationship between other types of variables. That is, we examine issues such as the strength and direction of a relationship, as well as whether the magnitude of the relationship is significantly different from zero. In this chapter we focus on the case where we have one independent variable ($x$) and one dependent variable ($y$). In Chapter 15, we examine more than one independent variable.

## 14.2 SCATTERGRAMS OR SCATTERPLOTS

Throughout this book we have tried to stress the importance and usefulness of displaying data graphically. Let us again remind you that in statistics as in real life "a picture is worth a thousand words." When you are first examining two interval/ratio-level variables, one of the most instructive things you can do is to draw a picture of what the two variables look like when graphed together. The graphic display of two interval/ratio-level variables is called a *scattergram* or *scatterplot* because the picture looks like points scattered across your graph. The idea is that the pattern of the scatter of data points provides you with valuable information about the relationship between the variables.

The first few questions you may have, therefore, are, "How do I construct a scattergram?" and "What can it tell me about the relationship between two interval/

ratio-level variables?" Let's begin this discussion with a simple illustration. In the list that follows we have data on two variables for 10 observations:

| Observation | x Score | y Score |
|:-:|:-:|:-:|
| 1 | 3 | 3 |
| 2 | 5 | 5 |
| 3 | 2 | 2 |
| 4 | 4 | 4 |
| 5 | 8 | 8 |
| 6 | 10 | 10 |
| 7 | 1 | 1 |
| 8 | 7 | 7 |
| 9 | 6 | 6 |
| 10 | 9 | 9 |

We can construct a scattergram for this data set by first drawing a graph with two axes. The first axis of this graph is the horizontal axis or abscissa. The second axis of the graph is formed at a right angle to the first axis and is the vertical axis or ordinate. We label the horizontal axis the x axis and display the data for the x variable on that axis. To do this, simply place the original measurement scale for the x variable at equal intervals along the axis. We label the vertical axis the y axis and display the data for the y variable along that axis. Again, place the measurement scale for the y variable along the vertical axis.

Once you have done this, you can begin to graph your data points. For each observation, find the position of its x score along the horizontal axis. Then, follow in a straight line up from that point until you find the corresponding position of its y score along the vertical axis. Place a dot or point here. For example, for the first observation, go along the x axis until you find 3. Then go straight up from that point until you reach the 3 on the y axis. Place a point here. This point represents the position on the graph for the xy score of the first observation. Continue to do this for each of the 10 observations, placing a point when you have found the intersection of the x and y score. You can see the collection of data points, called the scattergram, in Figure 14.1.

What does this scattergram tell us about the x and y scores? Notice that all the scores fall on a straight line that ascends from the bottom left of the scattergram to the top right because there is a very unique relationship between the x and y scores. The y score is always the same as its corresponding x score. That is, if the x score is 4, the corresponding y score is 4, if x is 6 the y score is 6. Therefore, those observations that have high x scores also have high y scores, and those with low x scores also have low y scores. Notice also that when the x score increases by one unit, the y score also increases by one unit. For example, when the x score changes from 4 to 5, the corresponding score for the y variable changes from 4 to 5, an increase of one unit. Whenever two variables are related in this manner, when high scores on one variable (x) also have high scores on a second variable (y) and an increase in one score is associated with an increase in the other score, we have a *positive correlation* or relationship between x and y.

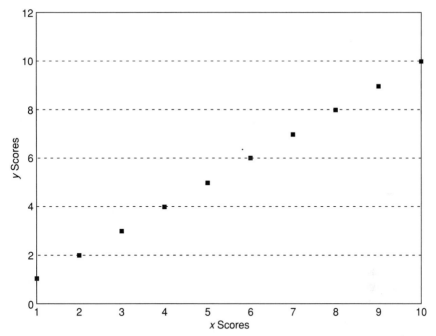

FIGURE 14.1. Positive relationship between $x$ and $y$.

In the list that follows and Figure 14.2 we have a different set of $x$ and $y$ scores for 10 observations:

| Observation | x Score | y Score |
|:---:|:---:|:---:|
| 1 | 2 | 9 |
| 2 | 4 | 7 |
| 3 | 9 | 2 |
| 4 | 7 | 4 |
| 5 | 8 | 3 |
| 6 | 1 | 10 |
| 7 | 5 | 6 |
| 8 | 6 | 5 |
| 9 | 10 | 1 |
| 10 | 3 | 8 |

In this case the data points are still on a straight line, but the pattern is different from that in Figure 14.1. In Figure 14.2, the pattern of the points is one that descends from the top left to the bottom right. This is because those observations that have high scores on the $x$ variable have *low* scores on the $y$ variable. Whenever high scores on one variable ($x$) have low scores on a second variable ($y$), we have a *negative correlation* or relationship between $x$ and $y$.

What we can say about the data in Figures 14.1 and 14.2 is that, when two variables are correlated, their scores vary together; this is termed *covariation* in

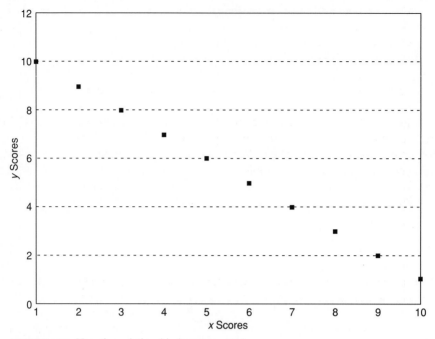

FIGURE 14.2. Negative relationship between *x* and *y*.

statistics. As the scores on the *x* variable change or vary, the scores on the *y* variable change or vary. The direction in which they change is a function of the direction of the correlation. With the positive correlation in Figure 14.1, as the *x* scores increase, the *y* scores increase (similarly, as *x* decreases, *y* decreases). With the negative correlation in Figure 14.2, as the *x* scores increase, the *y* scores decrease (similarly, as *x* decreases, *y* increases). In a positive correlation, then, the two variables covary in the same direction (*x* increases as *y* increases; *x* decreases as *y* decreases). In a negative correlation, the two variables covary in the opposite direction (*x* increases as *y* decreases; *x* decreases as *y* increases).

In the list that follows we have a third set of *x* and *y* scores for 10 observations:

| Observation | *x* Score | *y* Score |
|:---:|:---:|:---:|
| 1 | 6 | 4 |
| 2 | 9 | 4 |
| 3 | 2 | 4 |
| 4 | 7 | 4 |
| 5 | 3 | 4 |
| 6 | 4 | 4 |
| 7 | 1 | 4 |
| 8 | 8 | 4 |
| 9 | 5 | 4 |
| 10 | 10 | 4 |

Figure 14.3 presents the scattergram of these scores. Notice that, unlike the previous two figures, there is no ascending or descending pattern to the scores in this scattergram. In fact, the scores are perfectly horizontal because for different values of $x$, the $y$ score is the same ($y = 4$). In other words, the $x$ variable and the $y$ variable do not seem to covary. As $x$ increases or decreases, the value of $y$ stays the same. To state this one more way, variations in $x$ (increases and decreases) do not seem to result in variations in $y$.

One of the things that we can learn from a scattergram, then, is the *direction* of a relationship between two variables. By direction of a relationship, we mean whether it is positive or negative. When the scattergram looks like Figure 14.1, where the pattern of scores resembles an upward slope, we can conclude that the two variables are positively related. In this case, there is positive covariation. When the scattergram looks like Figure 14.2, where the pattern of scores has a downward slope, we can conclude that the two variables are negatively related. There is negative covariation. Finally, when the scattergram resembles Figure 14.3, and there is no clear upward or downward slope, we can presume that the two variables are not correlated with each other.

In addition to the direction of a relationship, what else can we determine by examining the scattergram of $x$ and $y$ scores? Let's return to the data illustrated in Figure 14.1. Without being too precise, let's draw a straight line that goes through each data point. We have shown this for you in Figure 14.4. In looking at this figure, we can see that, if we were to connect the data points, the straight line would go

FIGURE 14.3. No relationship between $x$ and $y$.

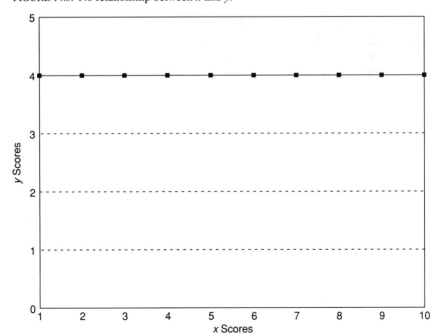

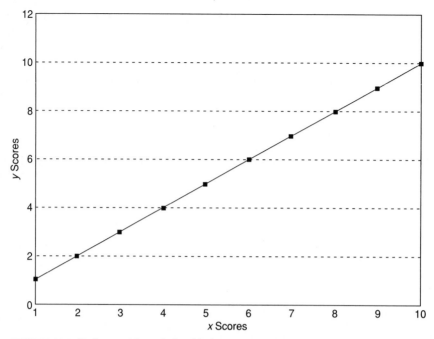

FIGURE 14.4. Perfect positive relationship between *x* and *y*.

through each data point in its upward slope. In other words, each point would fall exactly on that straight upward-moving line. In the following section of this chapter, we have more to say about how to fit this straight line to our data points. For now we simply note that this line is called the *regression line.* The relationship between two variables that can be described by a straight line is a *linear relationship,* and the examination of this relationship is often referred to as linear regression analysis. In the example presented in Figure 14.1, where all the data points fall exactly on a straight upward-sloping line, we can say that the two variables have a *perfect positive correlation*—positive because the regression line slopes upward, and perfect because all the points fall exactly on the line.

Notice that we can also draw a straight line through the data points in Figure 14.2, as shown in Figure 14.5. Here, all the data points lie precisely on this line, but in this case the line slopes downward. This figure illustrates a *perfect negative correlation* between two variables. We have also drawn a line for the data points in Figure 14.3, as shown in Figure 14.6. Notice that this straight line does not have an upward slope (as in Figure 14.4) or a downward slope (as in Figure 14.5), but is instead a flat line that is parallel to the *x* axis. This line has no slope. As we suggested, in this example we have no correlation between *x* and *y*. It might be said that Figure 14.6 presents an example of two variables with absolutely no correlation.

In addition to direction, the second valuable thing we can learn from a scattergram is an indication of the *strength* or *magnitude* of the relationship. The strength of a relationship can be judged by examining the spread of the data points around

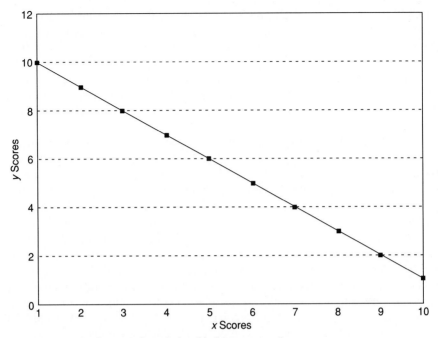

FIGURE 14.5. Perfect negative relationship between *x* and *y*.

FIGURE 14.6. No relationship between *x* and *y*.

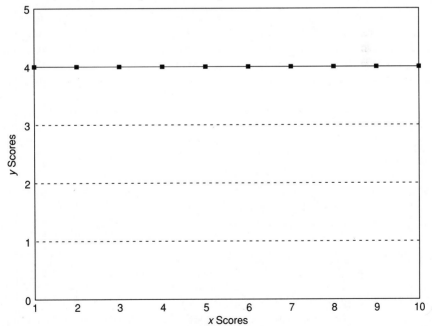

a straight line, called the regression line, that passes through them. The closer the data points are to this line, the stronger the relationship or correlation between the two variables. In a perfect positive or negative relationship, all of the data points will fall exactly on a straight line that passes thorough each data point. The further the data points are from the line, the weaker the correlation between the two variables. When the two variables are not correlated at all (perfect noncorrelation), the points will also cluster around a straight line, but this line will be perfectly horizontal to the $x$ axis.

There is one other very important thing we can learn from a scattergram, how to predict the score on one variable (the $y$ variable) from the score on another variable (the $x$ variable). Figures 14.7 and 14.8 show the previous examples of a perfect positive correlation and no correlation between $x$ and $y$, respectively. In these figures the two axes and the straight regression line have been extended to include additional scores. Let's first look at Figure 14.7. In this figure we want to predict what someone's $y$ score would be if they had an $x$ score of 12. To find the *predicted value of y* (denoted by the symbol $\hat{y}$ to distinguish it from its actual value), we first find the value of $x$ on the $x$ axis ($x = 12$), then draw a straight line up to the regression line and from that point, draw another straight line parallel to the $x$ axis across to the $y$ axis. The predicted value of $y$ ($\hat{y}$) is the value of $y$ where this line touches the $y$ axis. In this case our predicted value of $y$ with $x = 12$ would be 12 ($\hat{y} = 12$). We could follow the same procedure and determine that for $x = 13$, our predicted $y$ score also would be 13.

FIGURE 14.7. Predicting $y$ scores ($\hat{y}$) from $x$ scores with perfect positive correlation.

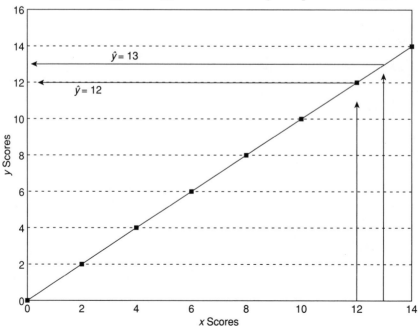

In Figure 14.8, which shows no strong correlation between $x$ and $y$, we also could make predictions about $y$ based on information about $x$, but in this case the predictions would all be the same. That is, no matter what the observed $x$ score, if we draw a straight line up from the $x$ axis to the regression line and then another line over to the $y$ axis, we would have the same predicted $y$ score ($\hat{y} = 4$). With an observed $x$ score of 12, our predicted $y$ would be 4, and with an observed $x$ score of 13 our predicted value of $y$ would also be 4. In the case of no correlation between two variables, it seems that there is no unique predicted score for $y$ at different values of $x$. Instead, no matter what the $x$ score, the predicted $y$ score will always be the same. In the case of no correlation, knowing $x$ does not help us predict the value of $y$.

Relationships or correlations between variables in the real world rarely exhibit such obvious patterns. When real crime data are used, patterns become a little less clear. Let's say, for example, that we are interested in the relationship between two different kinds of crime: murder and armed robbery. More specifically, we want to know if states that have high rates of armed robbery also have a large number of murders. One way to look at this relationship between armed robbery and murder would be to examine the correlation between a state's armed robbery rate (we designate this our $x$, or independent variable) and its murder rate (our $y$, or dependent variable). We would predict that states with high rates of armed robbery also have high murder rates because many armed robberies result in someone getting killed— a positive relationship.

FIGURE 14.8. Predicting $y$ scores ($\hat{y}$) from $x$ scores with no correlation.

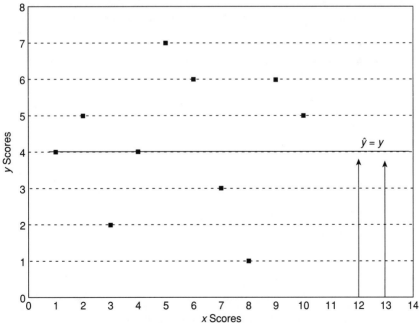

To examine this issue, we take a random sample of 12 states and record the murder rate in the state along with the state's rate of armed robberies. These data are shown for you in Table 14.1. Based on these data, we create the scattergram displayed in Figure 14.9, where each state's data point is indicated by its first letter. By eyeballing the data, we can draw a straight line that we think approximately runs through the data points in Figure 14.9. Unlike our hypothetical data, however, with these real data, the data points do not all fall perfectly on the line. Instead, we will have to draw our line in such a way that it comes as close to all the data points as possible. As before, we use this line to summarize the pattern and strength of the relationship between our two variables.

Based on what we have learned so far in this chapter, we can conclude two things from this scattergram. First, there does seem to be a positive correlation between armed robbery and murder rates. The general pattern of the data points, and the line that runs through them, is an upward slope indicating that as the rate of armed robbery increases (as $x$ increases), the murder rate also increases ($y$ increases). States that have high armed robbery rates, then, also tend to have high rates of murder. Second, the correlation between the two variables is far from perfect. None of the data points fall exactly on the straight line. In fact many of these points lie fairly far below the line (Washington, Delaware, New York) and above it (Louisiana). What we can tell from this scattergram, then, is that we have a nonperfect positive correlation between a state's murder rate and its armed robbery rate. These types of imperfect relationships are more typical of real crime data than the hypothetical data we examined earlier.

In Table 14.2, we have the same random sample of states but two different variables. In this table the $x$ variable is the percent of the population in the state that lives in a nonmetropolitan (rural) area and the $y$ variable is the rate of violent index crime. We examine this relationship because we suspect that there is a correlation

**TABLE 14.1. Murder Rate and Robbery Rate per 100,000 Population for 12 States, 1990**

| State | Robbery Rate ($x$) | Murder Rate ($y$) |
|-------|--------------------|--------------------|
| AL | 144 | 11.6 |
| CA | 377 | 11.9 |
| DE | 165 | 5.0 |
| GA | 263 | 11.8 |
| IN | 101 | 6.2 |
| LA | 270 | 17.2 |
| MD | 364 | 11.5 |
| NY | 625 | 14.5 |
| OK | 122 | 8.0 |
| SC | 152 | 11.2 |
| TN | 191 | 10.5 |
| WA | 130 | 4.9 |

*Source:* Statistical Abstract of the United States—1992. U.S. Department of Commerce, Bureau of the Census, Washington DC: USGPO, 1992.

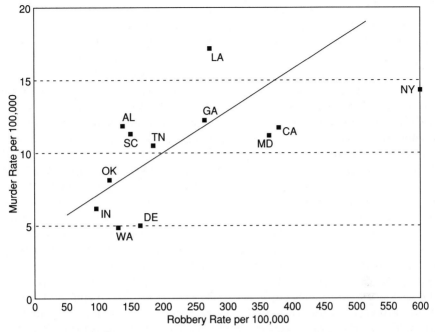

FIGURE 14.9. Armed robbery rate ($x$) and murder rate ($y$) for 12 states.

between how rural or nonmetropolitan a state is and its rate of violent crime. We think that rural states have lower rates of violent crime than urban states because we think they are more cohesive, homogeneous, and less socially disorganized. This is a prediction based on the early Chicago School of crime and social disorganization.

**TABLE 14.2. Percent of the Population Living in a Nonmetropolitan Area and Rate of Violent Crime (per 100,000) for 12 States, 1990**

| State | Percent of Population Living in Nonmetropolitan Area ($x$) | Violent Crime Rate ($y$) |
|-------|------------------------------------------------------------|--------------------------|
| AL | 32.6 | 709 |
| CA | 4.3 | 1045 |
| DE | 33.7 | 655 |
| GA | 35.0 | 756 |
| IN | 31.5 | 474 |
| LA | 30.5 | 898 |
| MD | 7.2 | 919 |
| NY | 8.9 | 1181 |
| OK | 40.6 | 547 |
| SC | 39.4 | 977 |
| TN | 32.3 | 670 |
| WA | 18.3 | 502 |

Figure 14.10 is the scattergram of the data in Table 14.2. Here we see a downward-sloping pattern of data points. This indicates the existence of a negative correlation between rural population and violent crime. States that are more rural, such as Oklahoma and Indiana, have lower rates of violent crime than the less rural states of New York, California, and Maryland. As in the last example, the negative correlation between rural population and violent crime is less than perfect. Not all of the points lie exactly on the regression line. Some states, such as South Carolina and New York, are far above the line while others, such as Washington and Indiana, are far below it.

Let's say we make a third conjecture about our random sample of 12 states. Let's hypothesize that states with high unemployment rates also will have high rates of serious property crimes, such as burglary. In Table 14.3 we record the percent of each state's labor force that is out of work and the burglary rate. We create a scattergram for this data set in Figure 14.11. Unlike the other two scattergrams using the state-level crime data, however, this one has no clear or discernable pattern. That is, it slopes neither upward nor downward. Also, unlike our hypothetical data, these data points do not lie on a perfectly horizontal line. The line that probably best describes this pattern of data would generally be flat, running through the middle of the data somewhere between the data points for Washington and Alabama. Moreover, most data points in this scattergram would be far from the straight line we drew. From this, we would conclude that there probably is very little correlation between these two variables.

FIGURE 14.10. Percent of rural population (*x*) and violent crime rate (*y*) for 12 states.

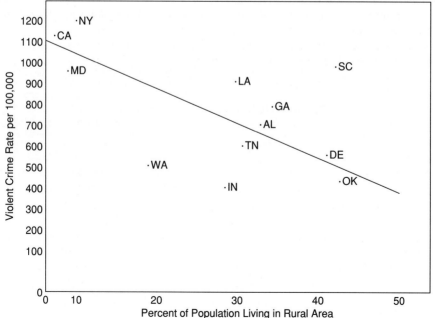

**TABLE 14.3. Percent of the Labor Force that Is Unemployed and Rate of Burglary Crimes per 100,000 Population for 12 States, 1991**

| State | Percent of Labor Force Unemployed ($x$) | Burglary Rate ($y$) |
|---|---|---|
| AL | 7.2 | 1268.6 |
| CA | 7.5 | 1397.8 |
| DE | 6.2 | 1127.6 |
| GA | 5.0 | 1514.7 |
| IN | 5.9 | 977.1 |
| LA | 7.1 | 1411.5 |
| MD | 5.9 | 1157.6 |
| NY | 7.2 | 1132.5 |
| OK | 6.7 | 1478.2 |
| SC | 6.2 | 1454.9 |
| TN | 6.6 | 1365.0 |
| WA | 6.3 | 1235.5 |

*Source:* Statistical Abstract of the United States—1992. U.S. Department of Commerce, Bureau of the Census, Washington DC: USGPO, 1992.

In sum, by graphically representing the relationship between two interval/ratio-level variables, we can learn about both the direction and strength of the relationship or correlation between $x$ and $y$. If the pattern of the data points and a line drawn through them is an ascending one, we can conclude that the correlation between $x$ and $y$ is positive. If the pattern is a descending one, we can conclude that the correlation is negative. If there is no pattern to the data and the line we draw through the data points is almost horizontal, we may conclude that there is very little correlation between the two variables. We can estimate the strength of the relationship by examining the distance between the actual data points and the straight line. The closer the data points cluster to this line, the stronger the correlation between $x$ and $y$. Correlations that are not strong generally have data points that fall far above and below the line.

As with our hypothetical data in Figures 14.7 and 14.8, we also can use regression lines to predict $y$ values from given $x$ values for our state-level crime. For example, using the armed robbery and murder rate data in Figure 14.9, we could locate our observed $x$ score on its axis, draw a straight line up until it touches the drawn regression line and then draw another straight horizontal line across to the $y$ axis. The place where this last line crosses the $y$ axis would be our predicted value of $y$ ($\hat{y}$). Notice, however, that, because we drew the regression line very crudely (remember we "eyeballed" the data and drew a line that seemed to be close to each data point), the predicted value of $y$ would change depending on how accurate our "eyeballing" was. If a somewhat different regression line were drawn, the predicted $y$ values would also be somewhat different. It would be nice if, instead of subjectively drawing a line that looks closest to the data points, there was a way to draw one that would, by more objective criteria, be the "best fitting" line. Fortunately there is, and we discuss it next.

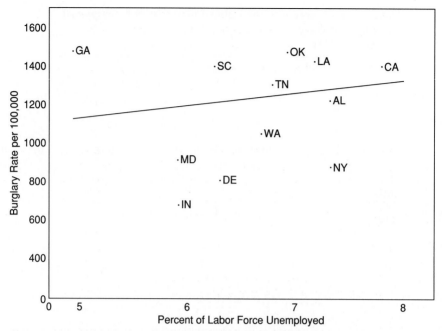

FIGURE 14.11. Percent of unemployment ($x$) and burglary rate ($y$) for 12 states.

## 14.3 THE LEAST-SQUARES REGRESSION LINE

To understand the idea behind the *least-squares regression line*, we first need to discuss how the line is constructed and why it is called the "least-squares" regression line. Let's begin our discussion of the least-squares regression line by looking at the hypothetical data in the following list, which shows the age of a random sample of 20 youths and the number of self-reported acts of delinquency committed by each youth in the previous year. Age is our designated independent ($x$) variable, and the number of self-reported delinquent acts is our dependent ($y$) variable:

| Observation | Age ($x$) | Self-Reported Delinquency ($y$) |
|:-:|:-:|:-:|
| 1 | 12 | 0 |
| 2 | 12 | 2 |
| 3 | 12 | 1 |
| 4 | 12 | 3 |
| 5 | 13 | 4 |
| 6 | 13 | 2 |
| 7 | 13 | 1 |
| 8 | 14 | 2 |
| 9 | 14 | 5 |
| 10 | 14 | 4 |
| 11 | 15 | 3 |
| 12 | 15 | 4 |

| | | |
|---|---|---|
| 13 | 15 | 6 |
| 14 | 15 | 8 |
| 15 | 16 | 9 |
| 16 | 16 | 7 |
| 17 | 16 | 6 |
| 18 | 17 | 8 |
| 19 | 17 | 10 |
| 20 | 17 | 7 |

The first thing to notice is that for any given *x* value, there is more than one value of *y*. This means that there are several youths that have the same age, but they did not commit the same number of delinquent acts. For example, there are four 12-year-old youths in the sample, one who committed no delinquent acts, one who committed one delinquent act, one who committed two acts, and one who committed three delinquent acts. The three 13-year-old youths each committed a different number of delinquent acts as well. For each value of *x*, then, there are a number of different *y* values. Think of these different *y* values at each value of *x* as constituting a distribution of *y* scores. Because there are seven different *x* scores, there are seven different distributions of *y* scores. Another way to say this is that, at every fixed value of *x*, there is a corresponding distribution of *y* scores. In statistics, these distributions of *y* scores are often called *conditional distributions* because the distribution of *y* scores depends on or is conditional on the value of *x*. This is similar to a conditional probability where the probability of one event P(*A*) depends on another event (*B*).

Figure 14.12 is the scattergram illustrating these data. We can tell from "eyeballing" this scattergram that age and self-reported delinquency seem to be positively related to each other and that this relationship looks reasonably strong. The data form an ascending pattern. We would now like to fit a straight line to these data in such a way that the line comes as close to the original data points as possible. Moreover, instead of simply eyeballing the fit of the line to the data, we would like our determination of "the closest fit" to have some objective basis.

Recall from Chapter 4 that we can determine a central score within a distribution of scores that arithmetically varies the least from all other scores in the distribution. This point of minimum variation, you remember, is the mean. The mean is that one score around which the variation of the other scores is the smallest or is minimized. In mathematical terms, the mean satisfies the expression:

$$\Sigma(x - \bar{x})^2 = \text{Minimum Variance}$$

This expression simply means that the sum of the squared differences (deviations) around any mean is the minimum variance that can be defined. Arithmetically, we know that, if any value other than the mean were used in the expression, the variance would be greater. In other words, in any distribution of scores, the mean will be that score that is closest to all of the other scores.

This property of the mean holds true even for a conditional distribution of scores, such as the one we listed. If we calculate a mean of *y* at each value of *x* (called the conditional mean of *y*), this mean is that score which is closest to all

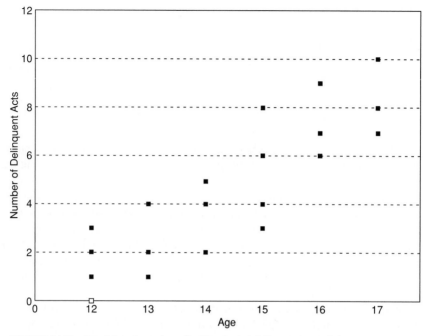

FIGURE 14.12. Age (*x*) and number of self-reported delinquent acts (*y*).

other *y* scores at that given value of *x*. We have calculated each of these conditional *y* means for you and list the results in Table 14.4. These conditional means were calculated like any other mean, by summing all values of *y* at a fixed value of *x*, and then dividing by the total number of these *y* scores. For example, there were four *y* scores (number of self-reported delinquent acts) for those at age 12, 0, 2, 1, and 3. The mean number of self-reported delinquent acts for these four 12-year-old youths is therefore: $(0 + 2 + 1 + 3)/4 = 1.5$. This mean indicates that the 12-year-old youths from this sample reported committing an average of 1.5 delinquent acts. Similarly we can calculate conditional means of *y* for each age, as in Table 14.4. In Figure 14.13 we show the scattergram that includes points for both the original scores and each of the conditional means (shown by $\overline{y}$).

As the conditional means ($\overline{y}$) minimize the variance of the *y* scores for each value of *x*, the regression line that comes the closest to going through each value of $\overline{y}$ is our best-fitting line. By "best-fitting" we mean that it is the line that minimizes the variance of the conditional *y* scores about that line. Because the variance is measured by the squared deviation from the mean $(y - \overline{y})^2$, this regression line is the least-squares regression line, and the estimation procedure is referred to as *ordinary least squares (OLS) regression.* The least-squares regression line, therefore, is the line where the squared deviations of the conditional means for the *y* scores ($\overline{y}$) is the least. Figure 14.14 is the scattergram of the conditional $\overline{y}$ values from Figure 14.13. We have also included the regression line and the distance (drawn with a vertical line) between each conditional mean and the regression line.

**TABLE 14.4. Conditional Means (means of *y* for fixed values of *x*) for the Age and Self-Reported Delinquency Data**

| Age | *y* Scores | Conditional $\bar{y}$ |
|-----|-----------|------------------|
| 12 | 0, 2, 1, 3 | 1.5 |
| 13 | 4, 2, 1 | 2.3 |
| 14 | 2, 5, 4 | 3.7 |
| 15 | 3, 4, 6, 8 | 5.2 |
| 16 | 9, 7, 6 | 7.3 |
| 17 | 8, 10, 7 | 8.3 |

This regression line is the best-fitting line in the sense that it is calculated in such a way that this vertical distance is at a minimum.

Mathematically, the equation that defines this least-squares regression line takes the general linear form:

$$y = \alpha + \beta x \tag{14.1}$$

where

$y$ = the score on the *y* variable
$\alpha$ = the *y* intercept
$\beta$ = the slope of the regression line
$x$ = the score on the *x* variable

FIGURE 14.13. Conditional mean value of *y* at different levels of *x*.

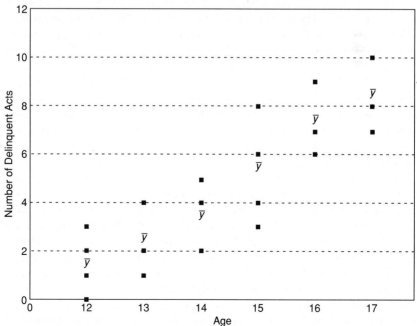

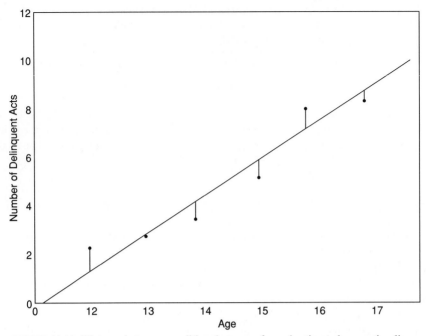

FIGURE 14.14. Distance between conditional means of *y* and estimated regression line.

There are two new terms in this equation, the *intercept* and the *slope,* that must be defined and explained. The *y* intercept ($\alpha$) is the point where the regression line crosses the *y* axis. As you can determine from the equation, it is equal to the value of *y* whenever $x = 0$. The slope of the regression line ($\beta$, also known as the *beta co-efficient* or the *regression coefficient*) measures the amount of change produced in the *y* variable by a one unit change in the *x* variable, and the sign indicates the direction of that change. For example, a slope of 2 indicates that a one-unit change in *x* produces a two-unit increase in *y.* A slope of $-2$ would indicate that a one-unit change in *x* produces a two-unit decrease in *y.* If the slope in our age and delinquency example above were 2, this would indicate that a one-year change in age (a one-unit change in *x*) would increase the number of self-reported delinquent acts by 2 (two-unit changes in *y*). The slope, then, is an important concept because it can be thought of as a measure of the effect of the *x* variable on the *y* variable. The larger the absolute value of the slope, the greater the impact that *x* has on *y* and the more strongly the two variables are related. As suggested, the sign of the slope tells us whether the relationship is negative or positive. A positive sign for the slope indicates a positive relationship between *x* and *y,* and a negative sign indicates a negative relationship. If the two variables are not related to each other, the slope will be zero, indicating that a change in *x* produces no change in *y.* In this case there is no linear relationship between the two variables and the regression line would resemble the flat, horizontal line we saw in Figure 14.3.

In the equation above, alpha is the symbol for the population intercept, and beta signifies the slope of the population. These two values, then, are unknown population parameters. We use sample data to estimate their respective values. The sample intercept is symbolized by the letter $a$, and the slope in the sample is symbolized with the letter $b$. The sample statistic $a$ is an estimate of the unknown population parameter alpha, and $b$ is an estimate of the unknown population parameter beta. The sample *regression equation* can be written as:

$$y = a + bx \tag{14.2}$$

From our sample data, we can determine our regression equation when we know the values of the intercept and slope. Both values are derived from the original data points. We determine the intercept $(a)$ by first estimating the value of the slope $(b)$. The definitional formula for estimating the slope of a regression line is:

$$b = \frac{\Sigma(x - \bar{x})(y - \bar{y})}{\Sigma(x - \bar{x})^2} \tag{14.3}$$

Although this equation looks menacing, it is really comprised of a few components that you should already be familiar with. The numerator of the equation simply is the product of each $x$ score minus its mean and each $y$ score minus its mean. You worked with mean difference scores such as this one when you calculated the standard deviation and variance of a set of scores. Instead of taking the square of this difference, however, we now take the product of the difference for each $x$ and $y$ score. The product of these two mean differences is referred to as the *covariation* between $x$ and $y$. It measures the extent to which $x$ and $y$ vary together, that is, *covary*. If we divide this sum by $n$, what we get is called the *covariance* between $x$ and $y$.

The denominator of Equation 14.3 also should be very familiar to you. It is the squared deviation of each $x$ score about its mean (the sum of squares for $x$). This quantity reflects the amount of variation in $x$, and when divided by $n$ is equal to its *variance*. The slope coefficient, then, can be understood as the ratio of the covariance between $x$ and $y$ to the variance in $x$. Because the $n$ term in both the numerator and the denominator cancel each other out, the equation is written in terms of the ratio of covariation between $x$ and $y$ to the variation in $x$.

Notice that the covariation between $x$ and $y$, the numerator in the formula for $b$, can be either positive or negative. We already know that, when $x$ and $y$ are positively correlated, large values of $x$ $(x > \bar{x})$ also tend to correspond to large values of $y$ $(y > \bar{y})$, and low values of $x$ $(x < \bar{x})$ also are associated with low values of $y$ $(y < \bar{y})$. In the first instance, each term of the product $(x - \bar{x})(y - \bar{y})$ is likely to be positive, as would, of course, the product and the sum of these products. In the second instance, each term of the product $(x - \bar{x})(y - \bar{y})$ is likely to be negative, but the product of two negative terms would be positive, as would the sum of these products. The term describing the covariation, then, would be positive, and the stronger the positive correlation between $x$ and $y$, the greater the magnitude of this covariation.

Correspondingly, when $x$ and $y$ are negatively correlated, high values on $x$ $(x > \bar{x})$ are associated with low values on $y$ $(y < \bar{y})$, and low values on $x$ $(x < \bar{x})$ are associated with high values on $y$ $(y > \bar{y})$. In this case, one term of the product is negative, and one term is positive. With a negative correlation, the product, then, would generally be negative, as would the sum of these products. The term

describing the covariation would be negative, and the stronger the negative correlation between $x$ and $y$, the greater the magnitude of this covariation. When the correlation between $x$ and $y$ is near zero, then approximately half of the products will
be positive, half negative, and the corresponding sum products would be zero. In
this case, the term describing the covariation also would be zero, indicating that $x$
and $y$ do not covary.

Calculating the slope ($b$) from this definitional formula would be a tiresome
(and error-prone) task. It would require that, for each score, we first subtract the
mean from the observed $x$ score, then subtract the mean from the observed $y$ score,
then take the product of these two differences, then sum over all observations. This
would be most unpleasant because it would require so many computations. Fortunately, there is a much easier computational formula for $b$:

$$b = \frac{n\Sigma xy - (\Sigma x)(\Sigma y)}{n\Sigma x^2 - (\Sigma x)^2} \tag{14.4}$$

At first glance this formula looks no easier to use than the definitional formula.
However, we can break this monster up into six component parts that are really
quite simple to compute. After we estimate each of the parts, as shown in the box,
we can then plug them into the formula and solve for $b$: We first illustrate the calculation of $b$ with the hypothetical age and self-reported delinquency data. We then
return to our real state-level data.

The necessary calculations for $b$ for the delinquency data are provided in
Table 14.5. In this table, the component elements of the formula are represented by
separate columns. With this information, we can calculate the slope as:

$$b = \frac{(20)(1409) - (288)(92)}{(20)(4206) - (288)^2}$$

$$= \frac{28,180 - 26,496}{84,120 - 82,944}$$

$$= \frac{1684}{1176}$$

$$= 1.43$$

The slope coefficient in this example is 1.43. It is positive, indicating that there is a
positive relationship between age and the number of self-reported delinquent acts.

---

1. $\Sigma xy$: The sum of the product formed by multiplying each $x$ score by each $y$ score, and
   then summing over all scores.
2. $\Sigma x$: The sum of the $x$ scores.
3. $\Sigma y$: The sum of the $y$ scores.
4. $\Sigma x^2$: The sum of the squared $x$ scores ($x^2_1 + x^2_2 + \cdots + x^2_n$).
5. $(\Sigma x)^2$: The sum of the $x$ scores squared ($x_1 + x_2 + \cdots + x_n)^2$.
6. $n$: The number of observations.

**TABLE 14.5. Calculations for Determining the Slope ($b$) for the Age and Self-Reported Delinquency Data**

| $x$ | $y$ | $x^2$ | $xy$ |
|---|---|---|---|
| 12 | 0 | 144 | 0 |
| 12 | 2 | 144 | 24 |
| 12 | 1 | 144 | 12 |
| 12 | 3 | 144 | 36 |
| 13 | 4 | 169 | 52 |
| 13 | 2 | 169 | 26 |
| 13 | 1 | 169 | 13 |
| 14 | 2 | 196 | 28 |
| 14 | 5 | 196 | 70 |
| 14 | 4 | 196 | 56 |
| 15 | 3 | 225 | 45 |
| 15 | 4 | 225 | 60 |
| 15 | 6 | 225 | 90 |
| 15 | 8 | 225 | 120 |
| 16 | 9 | 256 | 144 |
| 16 | 7 | 256 | 112 |
| 16 | 6 | 256 | 96 |
| 17 | 8 | 289 | 136 |
| 17 | 10 | 289 | 170 |
| 17 | 7 | 289 | 119 |
| $\Sigma x = 288$ | $\Sigma y = 92$ | $\Sigma x^2 = 4206$ | $\Sigma xy = 1409$ |

The value of $b$ is 1.43, indicating that, as age increases by 1 year, the number of self-reported delinquent acts increases by almost one and a half.

Once we have obtained our estimated slope coefficient, we can find the intercept ($a$) in our regression equation. The first step is to find the mean values of both the $x$ and $y$ distributions. We do this by dividing $\Sigma x$ by $n$, and then doing the same for the $y$ scores. For the self-reported acts of delinquency data, $\bar{x} = 14.4$ (288/20) and $\bar{y} = 4.6$ (92/20). Because the regression line always passes through the mean value of both $x$ and $y$ (represented by the data points $(\bar{x}, \bar{y})$) we simply have to substitute these terms into the equation:

$$\bar{y} = a + b\bar{x}$$

Then by substitution, we obtain:

$$a = \bar{y} - b\bar{x}$$

For our example, the solution would be:

$$a = 4.6 - (1.43)(14.4)$$

$$= 4.6 - 20.59$$

$$= -15.99$$

Thus, the regression line crosses the y axis at the point where $y = -15.99$. We can now specify our complete regression equation as:

$$y = a + bx$$
$$= -15.99 + (1.43)x$$

## Using the Regression Line for Prediction

After we have computed the regression equation, we can then use it to determine the predicted values of $y$ ($\hat{y}$) for any value of $x$. For example, using the estimated regression equation for age and self-reported delinquent acts, the expected number of delinquent acts for a 19-year-old youth would be:

$$\hat{y} = -15.99 + (1.43)(19)$$
$$= 11.18$$

This predicted value indicates that we would expect approximately 11 self-reported delinquent acts to be reported by a 19-year-old. In reality, this predicted $y$ value is simply our best guess based on the estimated regression line. It does not mean that every 19-year-old will report 11 delinquent acts. Because age and delinquency are linearly related, however, it does mean that our best guess when using the regression equation is better than guessing the number of delinquent acts without it. The

FIGURE 14.15. Fitting a regression line to the age and delinquency data.

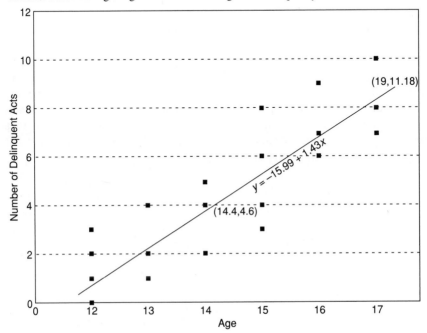

stronger the linear relationship between age and self-reported delinquency, the better or more accurate our guess will be.

We now know two data points that lie exactly on our estimated regression line, the one corresponding to the mean of the $x$ and $y$ values $(\bar{x}, \bar{y}) = (14.4, 4.6)$, and the one corresponding to the predicted value of $y$ when $x = 19$ ($\hat{y} = 11.18$) from our prediction equation. Knowing two data points that lie on our regression line allows us to draw more accurately the regression line without having to "eyeball" the data. We simply can draw a straight line that runs through these two data points. This is shown in Figure 14.15. This line represents the best-fitting regression line that we could obtain to describe the relationship between age and self-reported delinquency.

Let's return now to our state-level data and estimate the value of the slope coefficient for each of the three relationships we examined earlier. In Table 14.1 we reported the armed robbery rate $(x)$ and murder rate $(y)$ for each of the randomly selected 12 states. When we plotted these data in a scattergram (Figures 14.7 and 14.8), we observed an apparent positive relationship between these two variables. Now, we fit a regression line to this data set by first determining the slope $(b)$ and then the intercept $(a)$. The calculations necessary to calculate the slope are provided for you in Table 14.6. With these calculations and Equation 14.4, we can estimate the slope coefficient as:

$$
\begin{aligned}
b &= \frac{n\Sigma xy - (\Sigma x)(\Sigma y)}{n(\Sigma x^2) - (\Sigma x)^2} \\[2mm]
&= \frac{(12)(33{,}924.7) - (2904)(124.3)}{(12)(956{,}850) - (2904)^2} \\[2mm]
&= \frac{407{,}096.4 - 360{,}967.2}{11{,}482{,}200 - 8{,}433{,}216} \\[2mm]
&= \frac{46{,}129.2}{3{,}048{,}984} \\[2mm]
&= .02
\end{aligned}
$$

In this example, the slope coefficient is positive, indicating that there is a positive linear relationship between a state's murder rate and its robbery rate. The magnitude of the slope is .02, which tells us that a one-unit change in the armed robbery rate (1 armed robbery per 100,000) increases the murder rate by approximately .02 per 100,000. Because there are so many more armed robberies than murders, the slope coefficient in this case may be difficult to interpret. One way to understand it better would be to express it in the following terms: an increase of 50 armed robberies per 100,000 will increase the murder rate by 1 per 100,000 (because, if one armed robbery increases the murder rate by .02, 50 armed robberies will increase it by $50 \times .02 = 1$). There is, then, a positive linear relationship between the armed robbery rate in a state and its murder rate.

Knowing the value of $b$ and the mean values of $x$ (armed robbery rate) and $y$ (murder rate), we can now solve for the intercept $(a)$. The mean homicide rate for

**TABLE 14.6. Estimation of Slope Coefficient (*b*) for the Relationship between Murder Rates (*x*) and Armed Robbery Rates (*y*) for 12 States (Table 14.1)**

| State | $x$ | $y$ | $x^2$ | $xy$ |
|---|---|---|---|---|
| AL | 144 | 11.6 | 20,736 | 1670.4 |
| CA | 377 | 11.9 | 142,129 | 4486.3 |
| DE | 165 | 5.0 | 27,225 | 825.0 |
| GA | 263 | 11.8 | 69,169 | 3103.4 |
| IN | 101 | 6.2 | 10,201 | 626.2 |
| LA | 270 | 17.2 | 72,900 | 4644.0 |
| MD | 364 | 11.5 | 132,496 | 4186.0 |
| NY | 625 | 14.5 | 390,625 | 9062.5 |
| OK | 122 | 8.0 | 14,884 | 976.0 |
| SC | 152 | 11.2 | 23,104 | 1702.4 |
| TN | 191 | 10.5 | 36,481 | 2005.5 |
| WA | 130 | 4.9 | 16,900 | 637.0 |
| | $\Sigma x = 2904$ | $\Sigma y = 124.3$ | $\Sigma x^2 = 956,850$ | $\Sigma xy = 33,924.7$ |

these 12 states is 10.4 (124.3/12), and the mean rate of armed robbery is 242 (2904/12). The intercept, then, is:

$a = \bar{y} - b\bar{x}$

$= 10.4 - (.02)(242)$

$= 10.4 - 4.84$

$= 5.56$

The point where the regression line crosses the *y* axis, then, is where *y* = 5.56. We can now write our full regression equation for this example as:

$y = a + bx$

$= 5.56 + (.02)(x)$

With this regression equation, we can now estimate the predicted value of *y* ($\hat{y}$) at any given value of *x*. For example, the predicted murder rate for a state with an armed robbery rate of 246 would be:

$\hat{y} = 5.56 + (.02)(246)$

$= 5.56 + 4.92$

$= 10.48$

Exactly what does this predicted value mean? It means that we would predict that a state with an armed robbery rate of 246 per 100,000 would have a murder rate of 10.48 per 100,000. Keep in mind that this is our predicted value of *y* based on our regression equation estimated from the sample data. It represents our best guess of what $y$ is at a given value of $x$. It does not mean that the $y$ score is that exact value. In fact, let's use the regression equation to get a predicted $y$ score (murder rate) for an $x$ score (armed robbery rate) of 364 per 100,000:

$$\hat{y} = a + bx$$
$$= 5.56 + (.02)(364)$$
$$= 5.56 + 7.28$$
$$= 12.84$$

Thus, if the rate of armed robbery in a state is 364 per 100,000, based on our regression equation, we would predict that its murder rate would be 12.84 per 100,000. Notice in Table 14.1, however, that the state of Maryland has an armed robbery rate of 364 but that its murder rate is 11.5, not 12.84, per 100,000. Our predicted $y$ is not the same as our observed $y$. This means that we have some amount of error in our prediction. Unless all of the sample data points lie exactly on the regression line, which means that our two variables are perfectly correlated, our predicted $y$ values ($\hat{y}$) will be different from our observed $y$ values. In regression analysis, this error in predicting the dependent variable is often called the *residual*. In the case of perfect correlation, we can predict one score from another without error. The closer the data points are to the estimated regression line, therefore, the more accurate our predicted $y$ scores. The further the data points are from the line, the less accurate our predicted $y$ score.

Because we always have errors in prediction we must rewrite the regression equation as:

$$\hat{y} = a + bx + \epsilon$$

where epsilon (symbolized by $\epsilon$, the Greek letter epsilon) is the symbol for the error term. The error term reflects the measurement error in the $y$ variable, the fact that we have a sample of observations and thus sampling error and other factors that explain or account for the $y$ variable besides the $x$ variable we have measured. The latter refers to the fact that there usually are several factors that explain the $y$ variable. If we are examining only one of them, we will not be able to predict $y$ with perfect precision. In other words, in only looking at $x$ and ignoring other factors that influence $y$, our predictions will contain some amount of error. The more $y$ is determined solely by $x$, the less error we will have. We have more to say about this in the next chapter, which is about multiple regression. For now, let's return to our problem.

With our predicted value of $y = 10.48$ for an $x$ score of 246, we now have two data points that fall exactly on our regression line, $(\bar{x}, \bar{y}) = (242, 10.4)$, and $(14.6, \hat{y}) = (246, 10.48)$. Connecting these two points with a straight line gives us our best-fitting regression line that describes the relationship between the murder and armed robbery rate. This is shown in Figure 14.16. Notice that this regression line crosses the $y$ axis at approximately $y = 5.56$. Recall that this is the $y$ intercept, symbolized by the letter $a$ in the regression equation.

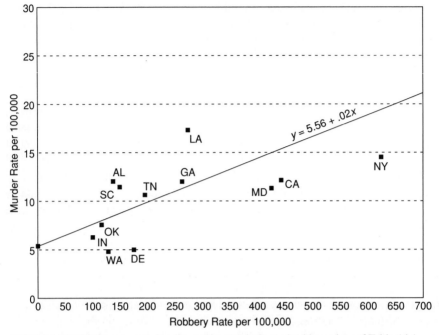

FIGURE 14.16. Fitting a regression line to the murder/armed robbery data of Table 14.1.

Let's go through another example. In Table 14.2 we reported the relationship between the percent of a state's population living in a nonmetropolitan area ($x$) and its rate of violent crime ($y$). In the scattergram we constructed from this data set (Figure 14.10), we observed a negative relationship between these two variables. Now, we fit a regression line to this data set by determining first the slope ($b$) and then the intercept ($a$). The calculations necessary to calculate the slope are provided for you in Table 14.7. With these calculations and Equation 14.4, we can estimate the slope coefficient:

$$b = \frac{(12)(227,117.7) - (314.3)(9333)}{(12)(10,074.6) - (314.3)^2}$$

$$= \frac{2,725,412.4 - 2,933,361.9}{120,895.2 - 98,784.5}$$

$$= \frac{-207,949.5}{22,110.7}$$

$$= -9.41$$

The sign of the slope is negative, indicating a negative relationship between the percentage of the population living in a rural area and a state's rate of violent crime. The magnitude of the slope tells us that for each 1 percent increase in the state's population that is rural, the violent crime rate declines by 9.41 per 100,000. The greater the percentage of a state's population that lives in a rural area, the lower the rate of violent crime.

**TABLE 14.7. Estimation of Slope Coefficient (*b*) for the Relationship between Percent of the Population Living in a Nonmetropolitan Area (*x*) and the Rate of Violent Crime (*y*)**

| State | $x$ | $y$ | $x^2$ | $xy$ |
|---|---|---|---|---|
| AL | 32.6 | 709 | 1062.8 | 23,113.4 |
| CA | 4.3 | 1045 | 18.5 | 4493.5 |
| DE | 33.7 | 655 | 1135.7 | 22,073.5 |
| GA | 35.0 | 756 | 1225.0 | 26,460.0 |
| IN | 31.5 | 474 | 992.3 | 14,931.0 |
| LA | 30.5 | 898 | 930.3 | 27,389.0 |
| MD | 7.2 | 919 | 51.8 | 6616.8 |
| NY | 8.9 | 1181 | 79.2 | 10,510.9 |
| OK | 40.6 | 547 | 1648.4 | 22,208.2 |
| SC | 39.4 | 977 | 1552.4 | 38,493.8 |
| TN | 32.3 | 670 | 1043.3 | 21,641.0 |
| WA | 18.3 | 502 | 334.9 | 9186.6 |
| | $\Sigma x = 314.3$ | $\Sigma y = 9333$ | $\Sigma x^2 = 10{,}074.60$ | $\Sigma xy = 227{,}117.7$ |

Next, we can calculate the mean for the *x* variable (percent nonmetropolitan), 314.3/12 = 26.2, and the mean of *y* (rate of violent crime), 9333/12 = 777.8. With this information, we can determine the intercept:

$$a = 777.8 - (-9.41)(26.2)$$

$$= 777.8 + 246.5$$

$$= 1024.3$$

The point where the regression line crosses the *y* axis when the value of *x* is equal to zero is *y* = 1024.3. We can now write our full regression equation:

$$y = a + bx$$

$$= 1024.3 + (-9.41)x$$

With this regression equation, we can estimate a predicted value of the violent crime rate ($\hat{y}$) for a given value of percent rural population. If the percent of the state that lives in a nonmetropolitan area is 10, our predicted violent crime rate would be:

$$\hat{y} = 1024.3 + (-9.41)(10)$$

$$= 1024.3 + (-94.10)$$

$$= 930.2$$

Given a state with 10 percent of its population living in a rural area, then, we would predict a violent crime rate of 930.2 per 100,000. We now have two data points that lie exactly on the estimated regression line. One of these points is the mean of the *x* and *y* variable ($\bar{x}, \bar{y}$), which is (26.2, 777.8), and the other is our *x* value of 10 and the $\hat{y}$ value of 930.2. We can draw a straight line that runs through both of these points. This line represents the best-fitting regression line that describes the relationship between these data. We have drawn this line for you on the scattergram presented in Figure 14.17.

Our final example involves the relationship between the percent of a state's labor force that is unemployed and its burglary rate (Table 14.3). In our scattergram from this data (Figure 14.11), we could not discern any clear upward or downward linear pattern in the data points. The slope of the line that we drew inspecting these points was almost flat. This suggested to us that the two variables were not very strongly related to each other. Now, we more carefully fit a least-squares regression line to the data.

As in our other examples, we begin by estimating the slope of the regression line ($b$). The necessary calculations are provided for you in Table 14.8. With these calculations we can derive an estimate of $b$ as:

$$b = \frac{(12)(100,699.4) - (77.8)(15,521)}{(12)(509.98) - (77.8)^2}$$

$$= \frac{1,208,032.8 - 1,207,533.8}{6,119.76 - 6,052.8}$$

$$= \frac{499}{66.96}$$

$$= 7.45$$

FIGURE 14.17. Fitting a regression line to the percent of rural and violent crime data from Table 14.2.

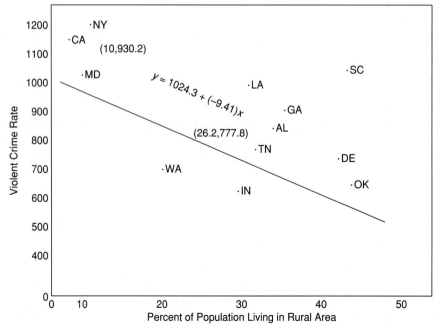

**TABLE 14.8. Estimation of Slope Coefficient (*b*) for the Relationship between Percent of Labor Force that Is Unemployed (*x*) and Burglary Rate (*y*)**

| State | $x$ | $y$ | $x^2$ | $xy$ |
|---|---|---|---|---|
| AL | 7.2 | 1268.6 | 51.8 | 9133.9 |
| CA | 7.5 | 1397.8 | 56.3 | 10,483.5 |
| DE | 6.2 | 1127.6 | 38.4 | 6991.1 |
| GA | 5.0 | 1514.7 | 25.0 | 7573.5 |
| IN | 5.9 | 977.1 | 34.8 | 5764.9 |
| LA | 7.1 | 1411.5 | 50.4 | 10,021.7 |
| MD | 5.9 | 1157.6 | 34.8 | 6829.8 |
| NY | 7.2 | 1132.5 | 51.8 | 8154.0 |
| OK | 6.7 | 1478.2 | 44.9 | 9903.9 |
| SC | 6.2 | 1454.9 | 38.4 | 9020.4 |
| TN | 6.6 | 1365.0 | 43.6 | 9009.0 |
| WA | 6.3 | 1235.5 | 39.7 | 7783.7 |
| | $\Sigma x = 77.8$ | $\Sigma y = 15{,}521.0$ | $\Sigma x^2 = 509.98$ | $\Sigma xy = 100{,}669.4$ |

The sign and magnitude of the slope coefficient indicate that, as the percent unemployed in a state increases by 1 percent, the burglary rate increases by 7.45 per 100,000. There is, then, a positive linear relationship between the amount of unemployment in a state and its corresponding rate of burglary. The mean value of unemployment is 6.48 (77.8/12), and the mean burglary rate is 1268.42 per 100,000 (15,521/12). With these values, the estimated value of the intercept can be determined as:

$$a = \bar{y} - b\bar{x}$$
$$= 1293.42 - 7.45(6.48)$$
$$= 1245.14$$

The point where the regression line crosses the *y* axis (the *y* intercept), then, is where *y* = 1245.14. Our complete regression equation for these data can now be defined as:

$$y = a + bx$$
$$= 1245.14 + 7.45(x)$$

For any value of *x*, we can now estimate a predicted value of *y* ($\hat{y}$). For example, the predicted burglary rate for a state with 8.5 percent unemployment would be:

$$\hat{y} = 1245.14 + 7.45(8.5)$$
$$= 1308.69$$

Thus, if a state's unemployment rate was at 8.5 percent, based on our estimated regression line, we would predict that there would be approximately 1308 burglaries per 100,000 population.

One data point that lies exactly on our regression line is the point $(x, \hat{y} = 8.5, 1307.66)$ estimated from our regression line. The second data point that lies exactly on our regression line is the mean of our $x$ and $y$ distribution, ($\bar{x} = 6.48$, $\bar{y} = 1293.42$). Knowing these two data points, we can create a regression line by drawing a straight line that goes through them (Figure 14.18). Notice that this regression line crosses the $y$ axis where $y = 1244$, the $y$ intercept.

Let's summarize what we know so far about our state-level data. Based on our estimation of the slope coefficients ($b$) from three regression equations, we know that the relationship between a state's murder rate and armed robbery rate is positive ($b = .02$), the relationship between the percent of state's population that lives in a rural area and its rate of violent crime is negative ($b = -9.41$), and that the relationship between the percent unemployed in a state and its rate of burglary is positive ($b = 7.45$). From the signs of these slope coefficients, we can determine the direction of a relationship between our $x$ and $y$ variables. We can interpret the magnitude of the slope coefficient as the expected change in the $y$ variable given a one-unit change in the $x$ variable. For example, we know that an increase of one armed robbery per 100,000 will increase the rate of murder by .02 per 100,000 and that a 1 percent increase in a state's nonmetropolitan population will decrease the rate of violent crime by 9.41 per 100,000.

Notice that the slope coefficient is interpreted in terms of the units of measurement of the variables. That is, an increase of one in the $x$ variable's unit of

FIGURE 14.18. Fitting a regression line to the unemployment and burglary data from Table 14.3.

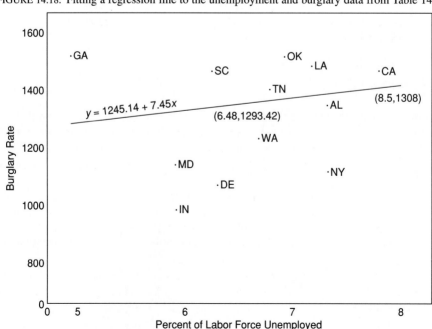

measurement (armed robbery rate, percent rural population, unemployment rate) changes (increases/decreases) the *y* variable by *b* units (murder rate, violent crime rate, burglary rate per 100,000). Beyond this very general interpretation, however, no information conveys the magnitude of the relationship. If, for example, we were to change units of measurement, say from dollars to pennies or rates per 10,000 to rates per 100,000, the magnitude (but not the direction) of our slope coefficient would correspondingly change. That is why we cannot simply assume that a small slope coefficient indicates that the magnitude of the coefficient also is small. Depending on the unit of measurement, a small slope coefficient may carry quite a wallop in terms of how strongly related it is to the dependent variable.

Let's illustrate this important measurement issue with an example. Take a close look at the computing formula for the slope coefficient (Equation 14.4). The numerator in this equation is the product of the mean deviations for both variables, $(x - \bar{x})(y - \bar{y})$. As this numerator increases, of course, the magnitude of the slope will increase. The magnitude of this numerator is, in turn, a partial function of the unit of measurement. Let's say that the *y* variable is measured in units of dollars and the mean for our data happens to be 5. A given *y* score of $7, then, would have a mean deviation of 2 $(7 - 5)$. If the unit of measurement happened to be pennies rather than dollars, however, the mean would be 500 (500 pennies to $5), the same *x* score of $7 would be 700 pennies, and the mean deviation would now be 200 rather than 2. All else equal, the magnitude of the slope coefficient would increase by a factor of 100.

For this reason, the magnitude of the slope coefficient *b* is not a very useful measure of the strength or magnitude of the relationship between two continuous variables. It would be better if we had a measure of association that did not depend on the units of measurement of our variables. Fortunately, there is such a measure of association. It is called the *Pearson correlation coefficient* or *Pearson product–moment correlation coefficient*. We refer to this statistic simply as *Pearson's r*, named after its originator, the statistician, Karl Pearson.

## 14.4 PEARSON CORRELATION COEFFICIENT

Pearson's *r* measures the strength of the *linear correlation* between two continuous- (interval/ratio) level variables. Just as the slope coefficient *b* is a sample estimate of the population parameter beta, the statistic *r* is our sample estimate of the correlation between the two variables in the population. The population correlation coefficient is designated by ρ, the Greek letter rho.

Unlike the slope coefficient, Pearson's correlation coefficient is standardized. By that we mean that the magnitude of *r* does not depend on the natural units of measurement of the *x* and *y* variables. No matter what the unit of measurement is, Pearson's *r* assumes a value of zero whenever there is no correlation between two variables, and attains a maximum value of ±1.0. Figure 14.19 may guide you in interpreting Pearson's *r*. A correlation of ±1.0 occurs when all points fall exactly on a straight regression line. A Pearson correlation coefficient of +1.00 means that there is a perfect positive correlation between two variables (as in Figure 14.1), whereas an *r* of −1.00 means that there is a perfect negative correlation (as in

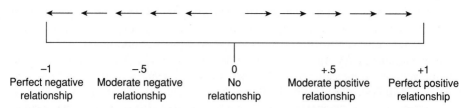

FIGURE 14.19. Pearson's *r* values closer to positive or negative 1 indicate stronger relationships.

Figure 14.2). The closer the data points cluster around the regression line, the stronger the correlation between the two variables, and the higher the absolute value of *r* will be. If there is no linear pattern in data points, the value of *r* will be closer to zero, indicating very little linear relationship between two variables. One of the advantages of Pearson's *r* over the slope coefficient *b*, then, is that it is much easier to interpret.

The calculation of Pearson's *r* is relatively straightforward and involves arithmetic operations you are already very familiar with. As with other statistical formulas, we provide you with both a definitional formula that more clearly defines the foundation of the statistic and a computational formula that is easier to use. The definitional formula for Pearson's *r* is:

$$r = \frac{\Sigma(x - \bar{x})(y - \bar{y})}{\sqrt{[\Sigma(x - \bar{x})^2][\Sigma(y - \bar{y})^2]}} \tag{14.5}$$

The expression in the numerator of the correlation should look very familiar because it is exactly the same as the numerator in the formula for the slope coefficient. The first term of this expression simply is the difference between an *x* score and its mean, and the second is the difference between a *y* score and its mean. In the formula for the correlation coefficient, as for the slope, we multiply these difference scores by each other, do this for each difference score, and then sum over all scores. Because the mean is defined in statistical terms as the *first moment,* the terms $(x - \bar{x})$ and $(y - \bar{y})$ are referred to as the first moments about the mean. The correlation coefficient, then, is based on the product of the first moments about the mean of *x* and *y*; hence it is often referred to as the *product–moment correlation coefficient.*

Remember from our discussion of the formula for the slope that the product of $(x - \bar{x})$ and $(y - \bar{y})$ is the *covariation* between *x* and *y*. That is, it measures the extent to which the *x* and *y* scores vary together, that is, covary. The stronger the relationship between the two variables, the greater the covariance. A covariation of zero implies that the two variables are not correlated, a positive covariation implies positive correlation, and a negative covariation implies negative correlation.

We cannot simply use the size of the covariation as our measure of correlation, however. First of all, remember that the magnitude of the covariation is a function of the measurement units of the variables. For example, other things being equal, we would obtain a much greater covariation if one of our variables was measured in pennies rather than dollars. Second, the covariance can often be greater than 1.0, so we have no clear interpretation for it.

We can, however, standardize the covariation, that is, make its value independent of the units of measurement. We do this by dividing the covariation in *x* and *y* by a term that includes both the variation in $x$ and the variation in $y$. This term is the denominator of the correlation coefficient and should also look very familiar to you. It simply is the product of two terms: the amount of variation in the $x$ variable and the amount of variation in the $y$ variable. The correlation coefficient, then, expresses the ratio of the covariation in $x$ and $y$ to the product of the variation in $x$ and the variation in $y$.

As you can imagine from going over Equation 14.5 in your head, the necessary calculations to estimate $r$ are enough to make you faint. There is, fortunately, a computational formula that involves fewer operations and, therefore, fewer chances of making errors. The computational formula for Pearson correlation coefficient is:

$$r = \frac{n\Sigma xy - (\Sigma x)(\Sigma y)}{\sqrt{[n\Sigma x^2 - (\Sigma x)^2][n\Sigma y^2 - (\Sigma y)^2]}} \tag{14.6}$$

Even this formula may appear forbidding to you, but fear not, we can break it down into five simple elements that we can then plug into the formula and solve. The computational formula requires the following five sums, as outlined in the box. We use this formula to calculate the value of $r$ for the state data in Tables 14.1 to 14.3. In calculating the value of $r$, it will be helpful to first calculate each of the five sums above and then insert them into the formula. A listing of the sums in separate columns will make keeping track of the different components of the formula easier. We have provided the calculations in Tables 14.9 to 14.11, although you should first try to calculate each $r$ yourself.

For the state-level data in Table 14.9 that reports the armed robbery and murder rates for 12 randomly selected states, we calculate the value of $r$ as:

$$r = \frac{(12)(33,924.7) - (124.3)(2904)}{\sqrt{[12(1440.0) - (124.3)^2][12(956,850) - (2904)^2]}}$$

$$= \frac{407,096.4 - 360,967.2}{\sqrt{[17,290.8 - 15,450.5][11,482,200 - 8,433,216]}}$$

$$= \frac{46,129.2}{\sqrt{(1840.3)(3,048,984)}}$$

$$= \frac{46,129.2}{74,906.9}$$

$$= .62$$

---

1. $\Sigma xy$: The sum of each $x$ score times its corresponding $y$ score.
2. $\Sigma x$: The sum of the $x$ scores.
3. $\Sigma y$: The sum of the $y$ scores.
4. $\Sigma x^2$: The sum of the squared $x$ scores ($x^2_1 + x^2_2 + \cdots + x^2_n$).
5. $\Sigma y^2$: The sum of the squared $y$ scores ($y^2_1 + y^2_2 + \cdots + y^2_n$).

**TABLE 14.9. Calculation of Pearson Correlation Coefficient ($r$) for Correlation between State Murder Rate and Rate of Armed Robbery (Table 14.1)**

| State | $x$ | $y$ | $x^2$ | $y^2$ | $xy$ |
|-------|-----|-----|-------|-------|------|
| AL | 144 | 11.6 | 20,736 | 134.6 | 1670.4 |
| CA | 377 | 11.9 | 142,129 | 141.6 | 4486.3 |
| DE | 165 | 5.0 | 27,225 | 25.0 | 825.0 |
| GA | 263 | 11.8 | 69,169 | 139.2 | 3103.4 |
| IN | 101 | 6.2 | 10,201 | 38.4 | 626.2 |
| LA | 270 | 17.2 | 72,900 | 295.8 | 4644.0 |
| MD | 364 | 11.5 | 132,496 | 132.3 | 4186.0 |
| NY | 625 | 14.5 | 390,625 | 210.3 | 9062.5 |
| OK | 122 | 8.0 | 14,884 | 64.0 | 976.0 |
| SC | 152 | 11.2 | 23,104 | 125.4 | 1702.4 |
| TN | 191 | 10.5 | 36,481 | 110.3 | 2005.5 |
| WA | 130 | 4.9 | 16,900 | 24.0 | 637.0 |
| | $\Sigma x = 2904$ | $\Sigma y = 124.3$ | $\Sigma x^2 = 956{,}850$ | $\Sigma y^2 = 1440.9$ | $\Sigma xy = 33{,}924.7$ |

What does this correlation between a state's murder and armed robbery of .62 tell us? Well, the sign of the correlation coefficient informs us that there is a positive correlation between a state's murder and armed robbery rates. Those states with high murder rates also tend to have high rates of armed robbery.

How do we interpret the magnitude of this correlation? Recall that the value of a Pearson correlation coefficient varies between $-1.0$ (a perfect negative correlation) and $+1.0$ (a perfect positive correlation) with 0 indicating no correlation. One thing we can say about our correlation of .62 is that it is much closer to 1.0 than it is to 0 and that it is, therefore, moderately strong. Unfortunately, there are no clear and agreed-upon rules that tell us what constitutes a "weak," "moderate," or "strong" correlation. It is entirely subjective. We provide a more exact interpretation of the magnitude of $r$ in the following section, but for now, we use less precise terms such as "moderately strong" or "weak." We can conclude from this, then, that there is a moderately strong positive correlation between the armed robbery rate in a state and its rate of murder.

Before we go on, we ask you to remember that the regression slope for this relationship was $b = .02$. You may have thought back then that there must not be a very strong relationship between armed robbery and murder rates because the magnitude of the slope was so small. We cautioned you then that, because of the fact that its effect is expressed in terms of the underlying units of measurement, it is virtually impossible to determine the strength of the relationship with the slope coefficient. You have now discovered with this armed robbery and murder data that a seemingly small slope ($b = .02$) may hide a moderately strong correlation between two variables ($r = .62$).

Table 14.10 reports the calculations necessary to estimate the correlation between the percent of a state's population that lives in a nonmetropolitan area and its rate of violent crime. The correlation between these two variables is:

**TABLE 14.10. Calculation of Pearson Correlation Coefficient ($r$) for the Correlation between the Percent of Nonmetropolitan Population and the Rate of Violent Crime (Table 14.2)**

| State | $x$ | $y$ | $x^2$ | $y^2$ | $xy$ |
|---|---|---|---|---|---|
| AL | 32.6 | 709 | 1062.8 | 502,681 | 23,113.4 |
| CA | 4.3 | 1045 | 18.5 | 1,092,025 | 4493.5 |
| DE | 33.7 | 655 | 1135.7 | 429,025 | 22,073.5 |
| GA | 35.0 | 756 | 1225.0 | 571,536 | 26,460.0 |
| IN | 31.5 | 474 | 992.3 | 224,676 | 14,931.0 |
| LA | 30.5 | 898 | 930.3 | 806,404 | 27,389.0 |
| MD | 7.2 | 919 | 51.8 | 844,561 | 6616.8 |
| NY | 8.9 | 1181 | 79.2 | 1,394,761 | 10,510.9 |
| OK | 40.6 | 547 | 1648.4 | 299,209 | 22,208.2 |
| SC | 39.4 | 977 | 1552.4 | 954,529 | 38,493.8 |
| TN | 32.3 | 670 | 1043.3 | 448,900 | 21,641.0 |
| WA | 18.3 | 502 | 334.9 | 252,004 | 9186.6 |
| | $\Sigma x = 314.3$ | $\Sigma y = 9333$ | $\Sigma x^2 = 10{,}074.6$ | $\Sigma y^2 = 7{,}820{,}311$ | $\Sigma xy = 227{,}117.7$ |

$$r = \frac{(12)(227{,}117.7) - (314.3)(9333)}{\sqrt{[12(10{,}074.6) - (314.3)^2][12(7{,}820{,}311) - (9333)^2]}}$$

$$= \frac{2{,}725{,}412.4 - 2{,}933{,}361.9}{\sqrt{(120{,}895.2 - 98{,}784.5)(93{,}843{,}732 - 87{,}104{,}889)}}$$

$$= \frac{-207{,}949.5}{386{,}005.9}$$

$$= -.539$$

This coefficient indicates that there is a moderately strong negative correlation between the percentage of rural population and a state's level of violent crime. States with a higher percentage of its population living in a rural area have lower rates of violent crime than more urbanized states.

Table 14.11 reports the calculations to estimate the correlation between the percent of unemployed in a state and the rate of burglary crimes. The correlation is:

$$r = \frac{(12)(100{,}669.4) - (77.8)(15{,}521)}{\sqrt{[12(509.9) - (77.8)^2][12(20{,}390{,}134) - (15521)^2]}}$$

$$= \frac{1{,}208{,}032.8 - 1{,}207{,}533.8}{\sqrt{(6118.8 - 6052.8)(244{,}681{,}600 - 240{,}901{,}440)}}$$

$$= \frac{499}{\sqrt{(66)(3{,}780{,}167)}}$$

$$= \frac{499}{15{,}795.3}$$

$$= .032$$

**TABLE 14.11. Calculation of Pearson Correlation Coefficient (*r*) for the Correlation between the Percent of Unemployment and the Rate of Burglary (Table 14.3)**

| State | $x$ | $y$ | $x^2$ | $y^2$ | $xy$ |
|---|---|---|---|---|---|
| AL | 7.2 | 1268.6 | 51.8 | 16,093,463.0 | 9133.9 |
| CA | 7.5 | 1397.8 | 56.3 | 1,953,844.8 | 10,483.5 |
| DE | 6.2 | 1127.6 | 38.4 | 1,271,481.8 | 6991.1 |
| GA | 5.0 | 1514.7 | 25.0 | 2,294,316.1 | 7573.5 |
| IN | 5.9 | 977.1 | 34.8 | 954,724.1 | 5764.9 |
| LA | 7.1 | 1411.5 | 50.4 | 1,992,332.3 | 10,021.7 |
| MD | 5.9 | 1157.6 | 34.8 | 1,340,037.8 | 6829.8 |
| NY | 7.2 | 1132.5 | 51.8 | 1,282,556.3 | 8154.0 |
| OK | 6.7 | 1478.2 | 44.9 | 2,185,075.2 | 9903.9 |
| SC | 6.2 | 1454.9 | 38.4 | 2,116,734.0 | 9020.4 |
| TN | 6.6 | 1365.0 | 43.6 | 1,863,225.0 | 9009.0 |
| WA | 6.3 | 1235.5 | 39.7 | 1,526,460.3 | 7783.7 |
| | $\Sigma x = 77.8$ | $\Sigma y = 15,521.0$ | $\Sigma x^2 = 509.9$ | $\Sigma y^2 = 20,390,134.0$ | $\Sigma xy = 100,669.4$ |

How would you interpret this correlation of .032? It is almost zero; this indicates that there is a very weak positive correlation between the percent of a state's population that is unemployed and its rate of burglary. Consistent with the appearance of our scattergram, then, there is not a very strong linear relationship between these two variables.

In our examination of the three relationships, we have found a moderately strong positive correlation between a state's murder rate and its robbery rate, a moderately strong negative correlation between a state's percent of rural population and its rate of violent crime, and a very weak positive correlation between a state's percent of its work force that is unemployed and its burglary rate.

Although we can interpret a perfect positive correlation as +1.0, a perfect negative correlation as −1.0, and no linear correlation at all as .0, what do correlations that fall between these extremes mean? These interpretations are left to a researcher's judgment. However, there is another statistic that allows us to make a more precise interpretation of the strength of the relationship between two variables. This statistic is called the *coefficient of determination*. We examine this statistic in the next section.

## 14.5 INTERPRETING A CORRELATION: THE COEFFICIENT OF DETERMINATION

The *coefficient of determination,* $r^2$, allows us to interpret more definitively the strength of the association between two variables. It is very easy to obtain once we have already calculated the correlation coefficient. As the symbol $r^2$ suggests, the coefficient of determination simply is the square of the Pearson correlation coefficient. It is interpreted as the proportion of the variance in the $y$ variable that is explained by the $x$ variable. When the value of $r^2$ is multiplied by 100 to get a percent, it is interpreted as the *percent of the variance* in the $y$ variable that is explained by the $x$ variable.

For example, our correlation between the armed robbery rate and the murder rate for our 12 states was .62. The coefficient of determination is $.62^2$, or .38, and can be understood as the amount of variance in murder rates that is explained by the rate of armed robbery. In this example, 38 percent of the variance in a state's murder rates is explained by state-level armed robbery rates. The correlation between percent of rural population and the rate of violent crime was $-.54$. The coefficient of determination is $(-.54)^2$, or .29, which indicates that 29 percent of the variance in violent crime rates for these 12 states is explained by the percent of its population that is living in a rural area. Finally, the correlation between percent unemployed and a state's burglary rate is $.03^2$, or .0009. This indicates that less than 1 percent of the variance in burglary rates is explained by the percent of people who are unemployed.

The amount of variance explained varies from 0 percent to 100 percent. The more variance explained, the stronger the association between the two variables. If two variables are perfectly related, the amount of explained variance is 100 percent $(+1.0^2 = -1.0^2 = 1.0)$. If two variables are perfectly unrelated (independent), the amount of variance one variable explains in the other will be 0 percent. The more variance one variable explains in another, the more accurate the predictions of a $y$ variable from an $x$ variable will be.

You can think of the coefficient of determination as a measure of how much we are able to improve our predictions of the $y$ variable by our knowledge of the $x$ variable. In the example concerning murder rates and armed robbery rates, the $r^2$ of .38 indicates that we are able to reduce the amount of error in predicting a state's murder rate from its armed robbery rate by 38 percent. Although knowing the coefficient of determination helps us interpret the correlation coefficient, it is probably not at all clear what the term "explained variance" means or how this relates to minimizing our prediction errors in $y$.

In predicting $y$ scores from the mean, if we wanted to, we could determine how much prediction error we are making by summing the squared difference between each $y$ score and the mean of the $y$ scores. This value, $\Sigma(y - \bar{y})^2$, is referred to as the *total variation* in $y$. We illustrate this in Table 14.12 with the murder and armed robbery data from Table 14.1. This table includes the $x$ (armed robbery rate) and $y$ (murder rate) scores for each of the 12 states. You remember from our discussion earlier in the chapter that, in the absence of other information, the best prediction of a continuous variable is the mean of that variable because the mean is the closest score to all the other scores and the value $\Sigma(y - \bar{y})^2$ is a minimum. If we had no other information, then, the mean of the $y$ scores (12.3) would be our best prediction of the murder rate for each state.

The total variation for these scores, the sum of the squared differences from the mean $\Sigma(y - \bar{y})^2$, is 153.33. Think of this total variation as representing the amount of error we would have if we predicted a state's murder rates by using the mean

**TABLE 14.12. Calculation of Total Variation and Predicted y Scores ($\hat{y}$) for Murder/Armed Robbery Data (Table 14.1)**

| State | x | y | $(y - \bar{y})$ | $(y - \bar{y})^2$ | $\hat{y}$ |
|-------|-----|------|---------------------------|-------|-------|
| AL | 144 | 11.6 | $(11.6 - 10.36) = \quad 1.24$ | 1.54 | 8.44 |
| CA | 377 | 11.9 | $(11.9 - 10.36) = \quad 1.54$ | 2.37 | 13.10 |
| DE | 165 | 5.0 | $(5.0 - 10.36) = -5.36$ | 28.73 | 8.86 |
| GA | 263 | 11.8 | $(11.8 - 10.36) = \quad 1.44$ | 2.07 | 10.82 |
| IN | 101 | 6.2 | $(6.2 - 10.36) = -4.16$ | 17.30 | 7.58 |
| LA | 270 | 17.2 | $(17.2 - 10.36) = \quad 6.84$ | 46.78 | 10.96 |
| MD | 364 | 11.5 | $(11.5 - 10.36) = \quad 1.14$ | 1.30 | 12.84 |
| NY | 625 | 14.5 | $(14.5 - 10.36) = \quad 4.14$ | 17.14 | 18.06 |
| OK | 122 | 8.0 | $(8.0 - 10.36) = -2.36$ | 5.57 | 8.00 |
| SC | 152 | 11.2 | $(11.2 - 10.36) = \quad .84$ | .70 | 8.60 |
| TN | 191 | 10.5 | $(10.5 - 10.36) = \quad .14$ | .02 | 9.38 |
| WA | 130 | 4.9 | $(4.9 - 10.36) = -5.46$ | 29.81 | 8.16 |

$$\Sigma y = 124.3$$
$$\bar{y} = 10.36$$
$$\Sigma(y - \bar{y})^2 = 153.33$$

value of murder rates alone. This error is shown graphically in Figure 14.20 and is represented by the vertical distance between each score and the mean.

The question now is, "How much of this prediction error in murder rates can we reduce by knowing a state's rate of armed robbery?" If the murder rate in a state ($y$) is linearly related to its armed robbery rate ($x$), we should be able to use this information and reduce our prediction errors. To do this, we simply base our prediction of each state's murder rate on our estimated regression line for these data. We have already estimated this regression equation to be:

$$\hat{y} = 5.56 + .02(x)$$

Using this equation, we can predict each state's murder rate ($\hat{y}$) by using its rate of armed robbery ($x$). For example, the first state's (Alabama) armed robbery rate is 144 per 100,000. This gives us a predicted murder rate of:

$$\hat{y} = 5.56 + .02(144)$$
$$= 5.56 + 2.88$$
$$= 8.44$$

The remainder of these predicted y values appear in the last column of Table 14.12. Figure 14.21 presents a scattergram of the $x$ and predicted y ($\hat{y}$) values for the 12 states. These $x$ and $\hat{y}$ data points all fall exactly on the regression line and are not shown by a dot. The data points shown in the scattergram represent the observed values of $x$ and $y$. The vertical lines in this scattergram that run from each observed data point to the regression line represent the amount of prediction error that remains after we use armed robbery rates to predict murder rates using our estimated regression equation.

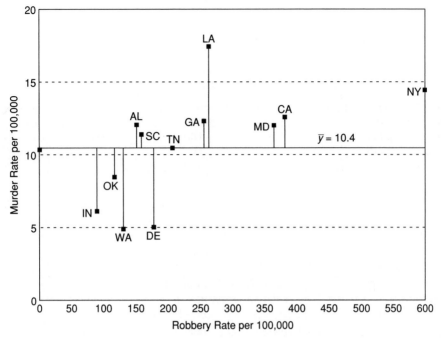

FIGURE 14.20. Predicting *y* values (murder rates) from the mean value of *y*.

FIGURE 14.21. Predicting *y* values (murder) from the regression line.

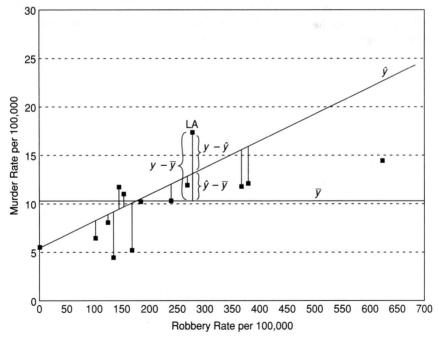

On Figure 14.21 we have highlighted one observed data point for you, which is the state of Louisiana. Louisiana's observed murder rate was 17.2, and the observed armed robbery rate was 270 per 100,000. From the regression equation, the predicted murder rate for the state of Louisiana was 10.96 (see Table 14.12). Because the mean murder rate for the 12 states was 10.36 per 100,000 (see Table 14.12), we have for Louisiana $y = 17.2$, $\hat{y} = 10.96$, $\bar{y} = 10.36$. Remember that in the scattergram, the total variation for our $y$ scores (the murder rate) was defined as the squared distance between the observed value of $y$ (17.2 per 100,000 in this case) and the mean of the $y$'s (10.36 per 100,000). This distance represents the total error made in predicting the murder rate ($y$) without knowledge of the armed robbery rate ($x$). For Louisiana, this total variation is: $(17.2 - 10.36)^2 = (6.84)^2 = 46.79$.

In Figure 14.21 we have separated this total variation into two components. One component is represented by the distance between the predicted $y$ score ($\hat{y} = 10.96$) and the mean of $y$ ($\bar{y} = 10.36$). This corresponds to the increase in accuracy of our prediction of $y$ in using the $\hat{y}$ obtained from our regression equation rather than the mean of $y$. Because the regression equation is based on knowing the robbery rate ($x$), consider this component of the total variation to be the *explained variation* because it is that part of the variation in $y$ that is explained by knowledge of $x$. It is also referred to as the *regression variance* because the value of $\hat{y}$ is based on the regression line. Numerically, the explained variation is defined as $(\hat{y} - \bar{y})^2$. Think of the notion of explained variation this way: instead of using the mean murder rate for the 12 states (10.36) to predict the rate of murders in the state of Louisiana, we instead use the predicted rate (10.96) derived from our knowledge of Louisiana's armed robbery rate.

The second component of the total variation in Figure 14.21 is represented by the distance between the observed $y$ score and the predicted $y$ score from the regression equation ($y - \hat{y}$). We already suggested that this distance represents the amount of prediction error remaining even after we have used our knowledge about $x$ and the regression equation to predict the value of $y$. This means that, even when we use our knowledge about a state's armed robbery rate ($x$) to predict the rate of murders ($y$), we still have some element of inaccuracy or error in our prediction.

This remaining component of the total variation is referred to as the *unexplained variation* or *error variation* because it is that part that is not explained by $x$. Numerically, the unexplained variation is defined as $(y - \hat{y})^2$. For Louisiana, the murder rate predicted from the armed robbery rate was 10.96. The observed rate of murder, however, was 17.2. The amount of unexplained variation, therefore, is $(17.2 - 10.96)^2 = (6.24)^2 = 38.94$.

To recap, the total variation represents the amount of error we have in predicting each $y$ score from the mean of the $y$ scores. It is the difference between the observed $y$ score and the mean of the $y$'s ($\bar{y}$). We can divide this variation into two components. One part, the explained variation, is the improvement we get in predicting $y$ from the regression equation and knowledge of $x$ ($\hat{y}$), rather than the mean. It is the difference between the mean of the $y$ scores and our best prediction from the regression equation ($\hat{y}$). The second component is the remaining error in prediction unaccounted for by $x$. This latter part of the total variation is the difference between our best prediction from the regression line ($\hat{y}$) and the observed $y$ score.

We can represent the relationship between the total, explained, and unexplained variation as follows:

Total Variation = Explained Variation + Unexplained Variation

Numerically, this can be expressed as:

$$\Sigma(y - \bar{y})^2 = \Sigma(\hat{y} - \bar{y})^2 + \Sigma(y - \hat{y})^2$$

Given this equality, you can see that, as the unexplained variance decreases, the amount of explained variance must increase proportionally. As the amount of explained variance increases, then, that component of the total variation due to our knowledge of $x$ increases. We can use this relationship between the explained and total variance to form the ratio:

$$r^2 = \frac{\Sigma(\hat{y} - \bar{y})^2}{\Sigma(y - \bar{y})^2} \qquad (14.7)$$

$$= \frac{\text{Explained Variance}}{\text{Total Variance}}$$

Where the explained variance accounts for a large proportion of our total variance, the $x$ variable is very helpful in predicting the $y$ variable. In the extreme case where all of the variance in $y$ is explained by $x$, the value of $r^2$ is 1.0. In the other extreme case, where all of the total variance is unexplained variance, the numerator of the ratio is zero, as is the magnitude of $r^2$. In this instance, none of the variance in $y$ is explained by $x$. The magnitude of $r^2$, the coefficient of determination, then, is the proportion of variance in $y$ that is explained by $x$. As the amount of explained variance increases, $r^2$ increases. The greater the proportion of total variance that is explained, rather than unexplained, therefore, the stronger the linear relationship between $x$ and $y$.

As you can see, the coefficient of determination ($r^2$) is a very useful measure of association between two continuous variables. Unlike the regression slope ($b$), the coefficient of determination is not dependent on the underlying units of measurement for the $x$ and $y$ variables. Unlike the correlation coefficient ($r$), values of the coefficient of determination between 0 and 1.0 are readily interpretable. $R^2$ values reflect the amount of variance in the $y$ variable explained by the $x$ variable, that is, the improvement in our predictive accuracy.

In our examples, we found that the $r^2$ between a state's murder rate and its rate of armed robbery was $.62^2$, or .38. This coefficient of determination tells us that 38 percent of the variation in murder rates can be explained by armed robbery rates. This means that we reduce our prediction errors of a state's murder rate by 38 percent if we use the predicted values for each state from the regression equation that includes information about the state's armed robbery rate, rather than using the mean murder rate of all states as our prediction. The remaining variance in murder rates, $1 - .38$, or 62 percent, is still unexplained and is due to factors other than the rate of armed robbery.

The $r^2$ between the percent of a state's population that is rural and its rate of violent crime was $-.54^2$, or .29. In words, about one-third of the total variance in violent crime rates is explained by how rural a state is. If we use the regression equation rather than the mean to predict rates of violent crime, we reduce our prediction errors by about 30 percent. Correspondingly, over two-thirds of the variance in violent crime rates is unexplained by how rural a state is, and must, therefore, be due to other factors.

Finally, the $r^2$ between the percent of unemployed in a state and its burglary rate was $.03^2$, or .0009. Less than 1 percent of the variance in burglary rates is explained by unemployment. Knowing the amount of unemployment in a state, then, will not help us predict its burglary rate at all.

## *14.6 COMPARISON OF* b *AND* r

We have discussed two important statistics for continuous variables in this chapter, the slope coefficient ($b$) and the correlation coefficient ($r$), as well as $r^2$, which is based on $r$. You may be wondering at this point why two statistics are necessary. Couldn't we estimate just one with our sample data and be done with it? The quick answer to your question (and you should know by now that there *never* really is a quick answer) is that, even though the two measures have some similar properties, they are not identical. In fact, they are far from identical because they tell us somewhat different things about our continuous variables.

The slope coefficient measures the *form* of the linear relationship between $x$ and $y$. The slope, you will remember, is expressed in terms of the units of measurement of the variables. Even though the correlation coefficient can tell us about the *strength* of the linear relationship between two continuous variables, it tells us nothing about the form or nature of that relationship. We cannot use the value of $r$ to predict $y$ values because we do not know how much of an impact $x$ has on $y$, nor do we know the original measurement units of the variables because the correlation coefficient is standardized.

Remember that, although the numerators for the slope and correlation coefficient are identical (the covariation of $x$ and $y$), the denominators are not. The denominator for the slope reflects the variation in the $x$ variable, and the denominator of the correlation coefficient reflects the product of the variation in both $x$ and $y$. In fact, we can rewrite the correlation coefficient as follows:

$$r_{yx} = b_{yx}\left(\frac{s_x}{s_y}\right)$$ (14.8)

In the $r_{yx}$, the subscript $y$ denotes the dependent variable and comes first, followed by the independent variable $x$.

The important implication of expressing the correlation coefficient as the product of the slope and the ratio of the standard deviation of $x$ to the standard deviation of $y$ is that the value of the correlation coefficient depends not only on the linear relationship between the two variables ($b_{yx}$), but also on a quantity that changes from sample to sample ($s_x/s_y$). We may, then, find relationships with very similar slopes but much different correlation coefficients because the sample standard deviations of *x* and *y* are very different. For this reason, it is important to calculate and report *both* the slope coefficient (*b*) and the correlation coefficient (*r*).

## 14.7 TESTING FOR THE SIGNIFICANCE OF b AND r

Because the slope (*b*) and correlation coefficient (*r*) are only sample estimates of their respective population parameters ($\beta$ and $\rho$), we must test for the statistical significance of *b* and *r*. In our previous examples with state-level data, the question we want to address concerns the relationship between *x* and *y* for the 50 states, not just our sample of 12. The null hypothesis used for the slope and correlation coefficient in the population assumes that there is no linear association between the *x* and *y* variables in the population. Remember that when there is no linear relationship between two variables, both the slope and correlation coefficient are equal to zero. The numerators for the slope and correlation coefficient are identical, so a hypothesis test about the slope also is a hypothesis test about the correlation coefficient. The alternative hypothesis assumes that there is a linear relationship between the *x* and *y* variables in the population and that the slope and correlation coefficient are significantly different from zero. Formally stated, the research and null hypothesis for the slope and regression coefficient would be:

$H_0$: $\beta$ and $\rho = 0$

$H_1$: $\beta$ and $\rho \neq 0$ or

$H_1$: $\beta$ and $\rho > 0$ or

$H_1$: $\beta$ and $\rho < 0$

Before we conduct our hypothesis test, however, we must be sure that our data meet certain assumptions. A few of these assumptions are familiar to you. For example, we must assume that the data were randomly selected. Second, we must assume that both variables are normally distributed. Third, we must assume that the data are continuous, that they are measured at the interval or ratio level. Fourth, we must assume that the nature of the relationship between the two variables is linear.

---

ASSUMPTIONS FOR TESTING HYPOTHESES ABOUT $\beta$ AND $\rho$

1. The observations were randomly selected.
2. Both variables have normal distributions.
3. The two variables are measured at the interval/ratio level.
4. The variables are related in a linear form.
5. The error component is independent of and therefore uncorrelated with the independent or *x* variable, is normally distributed, and has an expected value of zero and constant variance across all levels of *x*.

---

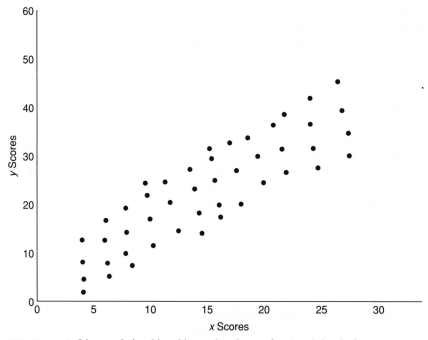

FIGURE 14.22. Linear relationship with equal variance of *y* at each level of *x*.

The fifth assumption really is a set of assumptions about the error term. It is assumed that the error component of a regression equation is independent of and therefore uncorrelated with the independent, or *x*, variable, that it is normally distributed, and has an expected value of zero and constant variance across all levels of *x*. The last assumption is called the assumption of *homoscedasticity*. The assumption of homoscedasticity simply is that the variance of the conditional *y* scores must be the same at each value of *x*.

The assumption of homoscedasticity, as well as the assumption of linearity, may be assessed by examining the scattergrams. In Figure 14.22 the relationship between *x* and *y* is linear, and the assumption of homoscedasticity is met. At each value of *x*, the variance of *y* is the same. In other words, the conditional distribution of the *y* scores at fixed values of *x* shows the same dispersion.

In Figure 14.23, however, the assumption of homoscedasticity is violated. Although the relationship is linear, the variance of the *y* scores is much greater at higher values of *x* than at lower values. This can be seen from the fact that there is a "wedge" pattern in the *y* scores as *x* increases. The spread or dispersion of *y* scores is greater when *x* is greater than 15. When the assumption of linearity is violated, linear-based statistics such as the Pearson correlation or least-squares regression coefficient are not appropriate. When the assumption of homoscedasticity is not supported, you may have to make transformations of your data that are beyond the scope of this book. Whatever the outcome, a careful inspection of your scattergram always is the first order of business because it can warn you of potential problems with your data.

of $y$. When $r$ and $b = 0$, there is no straight line that can fit the data, meaning that there is no *linear relationship* between the two variables.

However, be cautioned that if you do find that $r = b = 0$, this does not necessarily mean that there is no relationship between $x$ and $y$. The two variables may have a very strong *nonlinear relationship,* in which case both the correlation coefficient and slope coefficient would be zero, but the conclusion that no relationship exists would be incorrect. In this case what you would be observing is no linear relationship, but a possibly strong nonlinear relationship. Figure 14.25 illustrates this case.

The relationship between the $x$ and $y$ variables in Figure 14.25 is *curvilinear.* At low levels of $x$ there is a moderate negative relationship with $y$, but at higher $x$ scores this relationship is positive. In this instance the estimated correlation coefficient would be near zero, as would the slope because the best-fitting straight line would go through the middle of the data, as illustrated in the scattergram. With such a flat line, neither $b$ nor $r$ would be significantly different from zero. A much better fitting line would be a curved one shown by the dotted line. The curved line shows that there is actually a very strong relationship between $x$ and $y$, but that the relationship happens to be nonlinear.

Other examples of nonlinear relationships are shown in Figure 14.26. When the relationship between the variables is nonlinear, as in Figures 14.25 and 14.26, linear-based estimation techniques such as those discussed in this chapter are inappropriate. The least-square approaches of this chapter would underestimate the

FIGURE 14.25. Nonlinear relationship between $x$ and $y$.

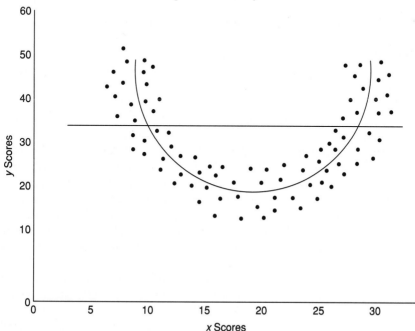

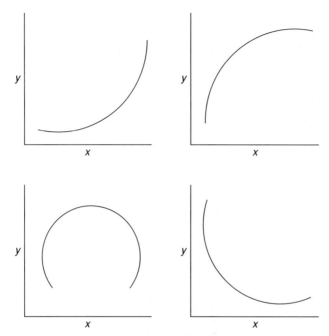

FIGURE 14.26.  Other nonlinear relationships.

strength and nature of the true relationship. Unfortunately, the estimation of non-linear relationships is beyond the scope of this book. Our strong advice for you is that, if you find that $r = b = 0$, do not immediately jump to the conclusion that there is no relationship between your variables. Do not jump to such a conclusion even if your significance test suggests that $\rho = 0$. There may be a nonlinear relationship. To avoid this mistake, we again urge you to scrutinize your scatterplots carefully. If there really is no relationship between the two variables, the scatterplot will show a random scatter of data points (no pattern). In this case the correlation coefficient will correctly be zero. If, however, the scatterplot shows evidence of marked nonlinearity, you should not use the linear statistics of this chapter.

As if these problems were not enough, there is another potential problem out there waiting to fool you. This is the problem posed by *outliers*. Recall from our discussion of EDA techniques that an outlier, as it suggests, is a data point that is "lying out there," far away from the other scores. An outlier is an extreme score, either an extremely low score or an extremely high score. The problem that an outlier poses to the unwary data analyst is that it can unduly influence the value of the slope and correlation coefficient. The presence of one or a few extreme scores may lead you to exaggerate the existence of a linear relationship by inflating the magnitudes of $r$ and $b$.

As an example of this, Table 14.13 reports two pieces of information for our randomly selected 12 states, the rate of violent crime per 100,000 (the $x$ variable), and the incarceration rate per 100,000 (the $y$ variable). The latter variable is the number of state prisoners with a prison sentence of more than one year per 100,000

**TABLE 14.13. Rate of Violent Crime per 100,000 Population (*x*) in 1992 and the Rate of Incarceration per 100,000 Population (*y*) in 1993 for 12 States and the District of Columbia**

| State | Violent Crime Rate | Incarceration Rate |
|-------|--------------------|--------------------|
| AL | 871.1 | 431 |
| CA | 1119.7 | 368 |
| DE | 621.2 | 397 |
| DC | 2832.8 | 1549 |
| GA | 733.2 | 387 |
| IN | 508.5 | 250 |
| LA | 984.6 | 499 |
| MD | 1000.1 | 383 |
| NY | 1122.1 | 354 |
| OK | 622.8 | 506 |
| SC | 944.5 | 489 |
| TN | 746.2 | 250 |
| WA | 534.5 | 196 |

*Source:* Data from Kathleen Maguire and Ann L. Pastore, eds., Sourcebook of Criminal Justice Statistics 1994. U.S. Department of Justice, Bureau of Justice Statistics. Washington DC: USGPO, 1995; and Kathleen Maguire and Ann L. Pastore, eds., Sourcebook of Criminal Justice Statistics 1993. U.S. Department of Justice, Bureau of Justice Statistics. Washington DC: USGPO, 1994.

residents of the state. In this example we are interested in examining whether those states with high rates of serious crime also have high rates of incarceration. We might suspect that the response to high rates of violent crime will be to "lock 'em up." To this 12 sample data set we have added a thirteenth jurisdiction, the District of Columbia. You will note from Table 14.13 that the District of Columbia has both an unusually high rate of violent crime and high rate of incarceration. In fact, the violent crime rate for the District of Columbia is more than twice that of the state with the second highest violent crime rate (New York). In addition, its incarceration rate is more than three times higher than the next highest rate (506 per 100,000 for Oklahoma). The District of Columbia, then, represents an extreme case for these two variables; it is an outlier.

You can see just how far out it lies from the other scores in Figure 14.27, which is a scatterplot of the 13-jurisdiction violent crime and incarceration rate data of Table 14.13. Our familiar 12 states lie in a relatively narrow range of values for both the violent crime rate and incarceration rate. These data points cluster in the bottom left of the scatterplot. The data point representing the District of Columbia lies far out away from these other points in the upper right-hand corner of the scatterplot. You can see from this what we mean when we say that for these data the District of Columbia is an outlier.

The crucial issue, though, is the effect that an outlying score such as this one has on our analysis and interpretation of the data. We have estimated two regression equations, two slopes, and two correlation coefficients from these data,

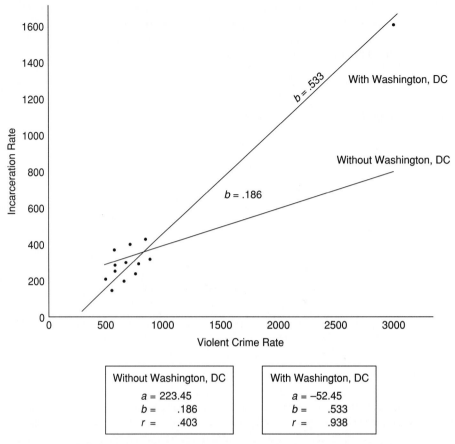

FIGURE 14.27. Effect of an outlier on the regression equation between rates of violent crime and incarceration.

one including the District of Columbia and one excluding it. Based on the regression equations we also have drawn two regression lines in Figure 14.27. Looking at these two lines, you can immediately see the effect that an outlier may have. When the District of Columbia is excluded from the analysis, the slope of the regression line is gently ascending, with a slope coefficient of $b = .186$. The correlation coefficient is $r = .40$, with $r^2 = .16$. This would suggest that the relationship between rates of violent crime and rates of incarceration is positive, although not particularly strong. Only 16 percent of the variance in incarceration rates is explained by the rate of violent crime.

Notice what happens, however, when the District of Columbia is included in the analysis. The regression line that includes the District is ascending much more steeply, as reflected in the fact that the magnitude of the slope coefficient is almost three times higher ($b = .533$) than when it is excluded. The value of Pearson correlation coefficient increases to .938, and the coefficient of determination ($r^2$) is now .88. With the District of Columbia included in the analysis, then, 88 percent of the variance in incarceration rates is explained by the rate of violent crime. We would conclude in this case that there is a very strong positive linear relationship between the two variables.

Not surprisingly, given the dramatic difference in their magnitude, our test of the statistical significance of $r$ and $b$ for the two sets of data would lead us to draw very different conclusions about the significance of the relationship between violent crime and incarceration rates. When the District of Columbia is not included in the data, the null hypothesis that $\rho = \beta = 0$ has an obtained $t$ value of:

$$t_{\text{obt}} = .403\sqrt{\frac{12 - 2}{1 - .162}}$$

$$= .403\sqrt{\frac{10}{.838}}$$

$$= 1.392$$

With 10 $(12 - 2)$ degrees of freedom for a one-tailed hypothesis test, an obtained $t$ value of 1.392 would not be greater than the critical value alpha of .05 $(t_{\text{crit}} = 1.812)$. In this situation, we would fail to reject the null hypothesis. Even though a positive correlation exists in the sample, we would conclude from our hypothesis test that there is no linear relationship in the population between violent crime rates and rates of incarceration.

When we include the District of Columbia in our analysis, however, the obtained $t$ value becomes:

$$t_{\text{obt}} = .938\sqrt{\frac{13 - 2}{1 - .88}}$$

$$= .938\sqrt{\frac{11}{.12}}$$

$$= 8.981$$

With 11 $(13 - 2)$ degrees of freedom, an obtained $t$ value of 8.981 would be significant at an alpha of .05, .01, or .001 for a one-tailed test. In this circumstance, we would reject the null hypothesis and conclude that there is a positive linear relationship between rates of violent crime and rates of incarceration in the population.

The lesson to be learned from this is that extreme scores, or *outliers,* may have a very pronounced effect on $r$ and $b$ and its associated significance test. In the case of outliers, like the one in our example, it might be advisable to report the analysis both with and without the outlying score or scores. In detecting outliers and other possible problems, we would once again urge you carefully to examine your scattergram before rushing into any analysis. If you have not yet grasped a very important theme of this book, let us now unequivocally state it: *There is probably nothing more important than a very slow and careful inspection of your data, complete with descriptive statistics and graphic displays, before proceeding with your statistical analyses.*

## *14.9 SUMMARY*

In this chapter we have been concerned with the relationship between two continuous-(interval/ratio) level variables. This relationship often is expressed in terms of the correlation between them. In examining the correlation between two continuous variables it is helpful to look at their *scatterplot.* From the pattern of these data points you can discern whether the relationship between your variables is *linear* (a pattern resembling a straight line), *nonlinear* (a pattern resembling a curved line) or whether there is no relationship between them (no pattern, but a random scatter of points).

If the relationship is linear, you can estimate a *least-squares regression line.* The slope of this regression line will tell you the effect of a one-unit change in the independent variable on the dependent variable. Unfortunately, because the magnitude of the slope coefficient is in terms of the natural units of measurement of the *x* and *y* variable, it is not a very convenient measure of association. A standardized measure of association for continuous variables is the *Pearson correlation coefficient (r).* The value of the correlation coefficient is that its upper limit is unity, so that, as the relationship between *x* and *y* gets stronger, the magnitude of *r* gets closer to $\pm 1.0$. The squared value of $r$ ($r^2$), the *coefficient of determination,* is interpreted as the amount of variance in the *y* variable that is explained by the *x* variable.

Finally, in this chapter, we hope that we have convinced you of the importance of carefully examining a scattergram of your data before estimating correlation and regression coefficients. The fact that $r = b = 0$ should not uncritically lead you to the conclusion that there is no relationship between *x* and *y*. It may be that, although there is no linear relationship between the two, they have a very strong nonlinear relationship. Furthermore, the value of our correlation and regression coefficients may be dramatically affected by the presence of one or more extreme scores, that is, *outliers,* in our data. By examining the scattergram we can determine whether we have a nonlinear relationship between *x* and *y* or whether some extreme scores might be leading us astray.

## *Key Terms*

beta coefficient
bivariate correlation
coefficient of determination ($r^2$)
conditional distribution
conditional means of *y*
correlation
correlation coefficient
covariation
curvilinear relationship
epsilon
error variance
explained variation
homoscedasticity
intercept
least-squares regression line
linear correlation
linear relationship
negative correlation

nonlinear relationship
ordinary least-squares (OLS) regression
outlier
Pearson correlation coefficient
Pearson's *r*
positive correlation
predicted value of *y* ($\hat{y}$)
product–moment correlation coefficient
regression analysis
regression coefficient
regression equation
regression line
regression variance
residual
scattergram/scatterplot
slope
total variation
unexplained variation

## Problems

1. Interpret the following scatterplots:

**a.**

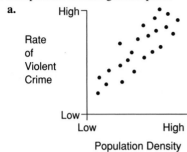

**b.**

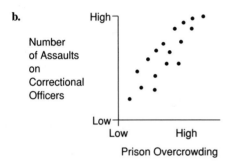

**c.**

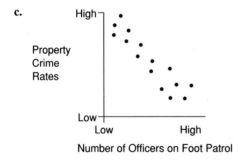

**d.**

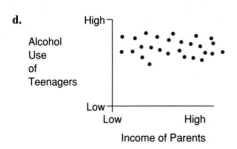

**e.**

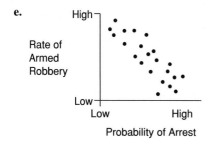

**f.**

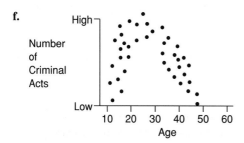

2. Interpret the following Pearson correlation coefficients:
   **a.** An $r$ of $-.55$ between the crime rate in a neighborhood and median income level per household.
   **b.** An $r$ of .17 between the number of hours spent working after school and self-reported delinquency.
   **c.** An $r$ of .74 between the number of prior arrests and length of sentence received for most recent conviction.
   **d.** An $r$ of $-.12$ between number of jobs held when 15 to 17 years old and number of arrests as an adult.
   **e.** An $r$ of $-.03$ between the divorce rate and a state's rate of violent crime.
3. Square each correlation coefficient in Problem 2, and interpret the coefficient of determination.
4. Interpret the following regression slope coefficients:
   **a.** A $b$ of $-.017$ between the dollar fines given a federal court for white-collar crimes and the number of citations for price fixing.
   **b.** A $b$ of .715 between the percent of unemployed and property crime rates.
   **c.** A $b$ of 1444.53 between the number of years of education and a police officer's salary.
5. In their 1993 research, Grasmick and his colleagues found a moderately strong relationship between a low self-control scale and self-reported acts of crime. Persons with low self-control admitted committing more criminal acts. Let's say you wanted to replicate this study. With the following data for self-control ($x$): assume that high scores on this scale mean low self-control and self-reported delinquency ($y$), do the following:
   **a.** Draw a scattergram of your data points.
   **b.** Calculate what the slope of the regression line would be.
   **c.** Determine what the $y$ intercept is.
   **d.** What is the predicted number of self-reported offenses ($\hat{y}$) when the self-control scale is 70?
   **e.** Calculate the value of $r$, and test for its significance with an alpha level of .01.

**f.** How much of the variance in self-reported delinquency is explained by self-control?

**g.** What would you conclude about the relationship between self-control and delinquency? Are your findings consistent with those reported by Grasmick and colleagues?

| Self Control (x) | Self-Reported Delinquency (y) |
|---|---|
| 45 | 5 |
| 63 | 10 |
| 38 | 2 |
| 77 | 23 |
| 82 | 19 |
| 59 | 7 |
| 61 | 17 |
| 88 | 24 |
| 52 | 14 |
| 67 | 20 |

**6.** Kohfeld and Sprague (1990) found that the faster the police respond to crime (x), the lower the crime rate (y) may be in a given community. The following data list the average time it takes the police to respond to a call by a citizen for help in a community and that community's rate of crime. With these data, do the following exercises:

**a.** Draw a scattergram of your data points.

**b.** Calculate what the slope of the regression line would be.

**c.** Determine what the y intercept is.

**d.** What is the predicted rate of crime ($\hat{y}$) when the police response time is 11 minutes?

**e.** Calculate the value of r, and determine whether it is significantly greater than zero with an alpha level of .05.

**f.** How much of the variance in the rate of crime is explained by police response time?

**g.** What would you conclude about the relationship between police response rate and crime?

| Police Response Time (x) (in minutes) | Community Rate of Crime per 1000 (y) |
|---|---|
| 14 | 82.9 |
| 3 | 23.6 |
| 5 | 42.5 |
| 6 | 39.7 |
| 5 | 63.2 |
| 8 | 51.3 |
| 7 | 58.7 |
| 4 | 44.5 |
| 10 | 61.2 |
| 12 | 73.5 |

**7.** A group of citizens has filed a complaint with the police commissioner of a large city. In this complaint they allege that poor neighborhoods receive significantly less protection than more affluent neighborhoods. The commissioner asks you to examine this issue, and you have the following data on the percent of the population in the neighborhood that is on welfare (x) and the number of hours of daily police patrols ($y$) in a sample of 12 communities in the city. With these data in mind, do the following:

a. Draw a scattergram of the data points.

b. Calculate what the slope of the regression line would be.

c. Determine what the $y$ intercept is.

d. What is the predicted number of hours of foot patrol ($\hat{y}$) when the percent of unemployed is 30 percent?

e. Calculate the value of $r$, and determine whether it is significantly less than zero with an alpha of .01.

f. How much of the variance in the number of hours of police patrol is explained by the percent of the population on welfare?

g. What would you conclude about the relationship between the percent on welfare and the number of police patrols?

h. Calculate the value of $b$ and $r$ again, but this time leave out community numbers 11 and 12. What do you conclude now? What causes these very different findings? Draw a scattergram of this data set, and compare it with the one in part $a$.

| Community Number | Percent on Welfare ($x$) | Hours of Daily Police Patrol ($y$) |
|---|---|---|
| 1 | 40 | 20 |
| 2 | 37 | 15 |
| 3 | 32 | 20 |
| 4 | 29 | 20 |
| 5 | 25 | 15 |
| 6 | 24 | 20 |
| 7 | 17 | 15 |
| 8 | 15 | 20 |
| 9 | 12 | 10 |
| 10 | 8 | 20 |
| 11 | 4 | 40 |
| 12 | 2 | 50 |

## Solutions to Problems

1. a. There is a positive linear relationship between population density and the rate of violent crime.

   b. There is a positive linear relationship between prison overcrowding and the number of assaults on correctional officers.

   c. There is a negative linear relationship between the number of officers on foot patrol and rates of property crime.

   d. There is no relationship between the income level of parents and the frequency of alcohol use by teenage children.

   e. There is a negative linear relationship between the probability of being arrested for armed robbery and the rate of armed robbery.

   f. There is a curvilinear relationship between age and the number of criminal acts.

2. a. There is a moderately strong negative linear relationship between the median income level in a neighborhood and its rate of crime.

**b.** There is a weak positive linear relationship between the number of hours spent working after school and self-reported delinquency.

**c.** There is a strong positive linear relationship between the number of prior arrests and the length of current sentence.

**d.** There is a weak negative linear relationship between the number of jobs held between the ages of 15 and 17 and the number of arrests as an adult.

**e.** There is no linear relationship between the divorce rate and a state's rate of violent crime.

**3. a.** $(-.55)^2 = .30$. Thirty percent of the variance in neighborhood crime rates is explained by the median income level of the neighborhood.

   **b.** $(.17)^2 = .03$. Three percent of the variance in self-reported delinquency is explained by the number of hours a youth works after school.

   **c.** $(.74)^2 = .55$. Fifty-five percent of the variance in sentence length is explained by the number of prior arrests.

   **d.** $(-.12)^2 = .01$. One percent of the variance in the number of arrests as an adult is explained by the number of jobs held between 15 and 17 years of age.

   **e.** $(-.03)^2 = .0009$. Less than 1 percent of the variance in a state's violent crime rate is explained by its divorce rate.

**4. a.** A \$1 increase in the fine imposed decreases the number of price fixing citations by .017.

   **b.** An increase of 1 percent in unemployment increases the rate of property crime by .715.

   **c.** One additional year of education increases a police officer's salary by \$1,444.53.

**5. a.**

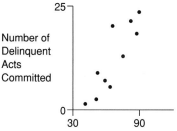

**b.** The value of the regression coefficient $b$ is:

$$b = \frac{10(9890) - (632)(141)}{10(42,230) - (632)^2}$$

$$= \frac{98,900 - 89,112}{422,300 - 399,424}$$

$$= .428$$

The value of the slope coefficient is .428. This tells us that a one-score increase on the low self-control scale increases the number of self-reported criminal acts by .428.

**c.** The value of the $y$ intercept is:

$$14.1 = a + .428(63.2)$$

$$14.1 = a + 27.05$$

$$14.1 - 27.05 = a$$

$$-12.95 = a$$

The value of the $y$ intercept, or $a$, is $-12.95$.

**d.** The value of $\hat{y}$ is:

$$\hat{y} = -12.95 + .428(70)$$

$$= -12.95 + 29.96$$

$$= 17.01$$

The predicted number of offenses, therefore, is 17.01.

**e.** The value of $r$ is:

$$r = \frac{10(9890) - 632(141)}{\sqrt{[10(42,230) - (632)^2][10(2529) - (141)^2]}}$$

$$= \frac{98,900 - 89,112}{\sqrt{(422,300 - 399,424)(25,290 - 19,881)}}$$

$$= \frac{9788}{11,123.68}$$

$$= .88$$

There is a strong positive correlation between low self-control and the number of self-reported criminal offenses.

Our null hypothesis is that $r = 0$, and our alternative hypothesis is that $r > 0$. Our decision rule is to reject the null hypothesis if $t_{obt} \geq 2.896$. Now, we calculate our $t$ statistic:

$$t = .88\sqrt{\frac{10 - 2}{1 - (.88)^2}}$$

$$= .88\sqrt{\frac{8}{1 - .77}}$$

$$= .88(5.90)$$

$$= 5.19$$

As $5.19 > 2.896$, we reject the null hypothesis. There is a significant positive correlation between low self-control and self-reported crime.

**f.** Our $r$ was .88, $.88^2 = .77$, so 77 percent of the variance in self-reported crime is explained by low self-control.

**g.** Based on our results, we would conclude that there is a significant positive linear relationship between low self-control and self-reported offending.

**6. a.**

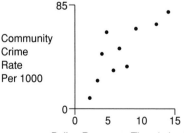

**b.** The value of the regression coefficient is:

$$b = \frac{(10)(4491.4) - (74)(541.1)}{(10)(664) - (74)^2}$$

$$= \frac{4872.6}{1164}$$

$$= 4.19$$

The value of the slope coefficient is 4.19. This tells us that a 1-minute increase in police response time increases the crime rate by 4.19 per 1000.

**c.** The value of the *y* intercept is:

$$54.11 = a + 4.19(7.4)$$

$$54.11 = a + 31.01$$

$$54.11 - 31.01 = a$$

$$23.1 = a$$

The value of the *y* intercept, or *a*, is 23.1.

**d.** The value of $\hat{y}$ is:

$$\hat{y} = 23.1 + 4.19(11)$$

$$= 23.1 + 46.09$$

$$= 69.19$$

The predicted crime rate, therefore, is 69.19 crimes per 1000 population.

**e.** The value of *r* is:

$$r = \frac{10(4491.4) - (74)(541.1)}{\sqrt{[10(664) - (74)^2][10(32,011.27) - (541.1)^2]}}$$

$$= \frac{4872.6}{5,639.55}$$

$$= .86$$

There is a strong positive correlation between police response time and the crime rate.

We now want to conduct a hypothesis test about *r*. Our null hypothesis is that $r = 0$, and our alternative hypothesis is that $r > 0$. Our decision rule is to reject the null hypothesis if $t_{obt} \geq 1.86$. Now we calculate our $t_{obt}$:

$$t_{obt} = .86\sqrt{\frac{10 - 2}{1 - (.86)^2}}$$

$$= .86\sqrt{\frac{8}{1 - .74}}$$

$$= .86(5.55)$$

$$= 4.77$$

As 4.77 > 1.86, we decide to reject the null hypothesis. There is a significant positive correlation between the length of police response time and community crime rates.

**f.** Our $r$ was .86, $.86^2 = .74$, so 74 percent of the variance in community crime rates is explained by police response time.

**g.** Based on our results, we would conclude that there is a significant positive linear relationship between police response time and community crime rates.

**7. a.**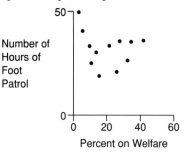

**b.** The value of the regression coefficient is:

$$b = \frac{(12)(4525) - (245)(265)}{(12)(6777) - (245)^2}$$

$$= \frac{54,300 - 64,925}{81,324 - 60,025}$$

$$= -.499$$

The value of the slope coefficient is $-.499$. This tells us that a 1 percent increase in the percent of the population that is on welfare decreases the hours of daily police patrol by $-.499$ (about one-half hour).

**c.** The value of the $y$ intercept is:

$$22.1 = a + (-.499)(20.4)$$

$$22.1 = a + (-10.18)$$

$$22.1 = a - (10.18)$$

$$22.1 + 10.18 = a$$

$$32.28 = a$$

The value of the $y$ intercept, or $a$, then, is 32.28.

**d.** The value of $\hat{y}$ is:

$$\hat{y} = 32.28 + (-.499)(30)$$

$$= 32.28 - 14.97$$

$$= 17.31$$

The predicted number of hours of police patrol is 17.31 hours.

**e.** The value of $r$ is:

$$r = \frac{(12)(4525) - (245)(265)}{\sqrt{[(12)(6777) - (245)^2][(12)(7275) - (265)^2]}}$$

$$= \frac{-10,625}{\sqrt{(21,299)(17,075)}}$$

$$= \frac{-10,625}{\sqrt{363,680,425}}$$

$$= -.56$$

There is a moderately strong negative correlation between the percent of the community on welfare and the number of daily hours of police patrol.

We now want to conduct a hypothesis test about $r$. Our null hypothesis is that $r = 0$, and our alternative hypothesis is that $r < 0$. Our decision rule is to reject the null hypothesis if $t_{\text{obt}} \leq 1.812$:

$$t_{\text{obt}} = -.56\sqrt{\frac{12 - 2}{1 - (-.56)^2}}$$

$$= -.56\sqrt{\frac{10}{1 - .31}}$$

$$= -.56\sqrt{14.49}$$

$$= -.56(3.81)$$

$$= -2.13$$

We have a $t_{\text{obt}}$ of $-2.13$. As $-2.13 \leq -1.812$, we decide to reject the null hypothesis. There is a significant negative correlation between the percent of a neighborhood that is receiving public assistance and the number of hours of daily police patrol.

**f.** Our $r$ was $-.56$, $-.56^2 = .31$, so 31 percent of the variance in the number of hours of police patrol is explained by the percent of the neighborhood that is on welfare.

**g.** Based on our results, we would conclude that there is a significant negative linear relationship between the affluence of a neighborhood and the number of hours that the police patrol it per day.

**h.** The values of $b$ and $r$ without community numbers 11 and 12 are:

$$b = \frac{(10)(4265) - (239)(175)}{(10)(6757) - (239)^2}$$

$$= \frac{42,650 - 41,825}{67,570 - 57,121}$$

$$= \frac{825}{10,449}$$

$$= .079$$

$$r = \frac{(10)(4265) - (239)(175)}{\sqrt{[(10)(6757) - (239)^2][(10)(3175) - (175)^2]}}$$

$$= \frac{42,650 - 41,825}{\sqrt{(67,570 - 57,121)\,(31,750 - 30,625)}}>$$

$$= \frac{825}{\sqrt{(10,449)(1125)}}$$

$$= \frac{825}{\sqrt{(11,755,125)}}$$

$$= \frac{825}{3428.57}$$

$$= .24$$

When the last two observations are deleted, the value of *b* becomes .079, and the correlation coefficient indicates a weak *positive* correlation between the affluence of a neighborhood and the number of hours of daily police patrols. Without the last two observations the slope of the data points changes. These last two data points are very unusual. They are unusually affluent neighborhoods, and they receive an unusually high number of hours of police patrols. These two neighborhoods are, then, outliers, and as outliers they can distort your conclusions.

# CHAPTER 15

# *Multiple Regression and Partial Correlation*

*I always avoid prophesying before-hand, because it is a much better policy to prophesy after the event has already taken place.*

—SIR WINSTON CHURCHILL

## *15.1 INTRODUCTION*

In the preceding chapter we examined the effect of a single independent variable on a dependent variable by learning about the least-squares regression model and correlation coefficient. An implicit assumption behind this simple regression model was that the dependent variable is adequately explained by one independent variable and an error component (see Figure 15.1). When there is only one independent variable, the regression model often is referred to as a bivariate model and the correlation coefficient as a bivariate correlation.

It is rare, however, that one independent variable sufficiently explains the dependent variable because in reality there usually are several factors that jointly influence the dependent variable (see Figure 15.2). We need, therefore, to build on our knowledge of the bivariate regression model by adding more independent variables. When we examine the effect of more than one independent variable on a dependent variable, we employ what is called a *multivariate regression model*. As the name implies, in the *multi*variate model, we have more than one independent variable whose effects on the dependent variable we wish to gauge. An implicit assumption of the multivariate regression model, therefore, is that there is more than one variable that explains the dependent variable. The corresponding correlation coefficient is called the *partial correlation coefficient*. In this chapter, we hope to introduce you to some of the most important features of the multivariate regression model and partial correlation.

FIGURE 15.1. A bivariate model.

**489**

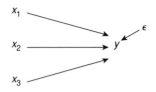

FIGURE 15.2. A multivariate model.

## 15.2 THE MULTIPLE REGRESSION EQUATION

As suggested, the *multiple regression* model or equation simply is a straightforward extension of the bivariate regression model. One of the most important differences between the bivariate and multiple regression models is that the latter has more than one independent variable. In the case of multiple regression, we aim to estimate the effect of several independent variables on a dependent variable. Because there are several independent variables, there will be more than one slope coefficient to estimate. Formally, the multiple regression model specifies the dependent variable ($y$) as a linear function of more than one independent variable ($x_1$, $x_2$, and so on) plus an error term that encompasses various omitted factors:

$$y = \alpha + \beta_1 x_1 + \beta_2 x_2 + \cdots + \beta_k x_k + \epsilon \tag{15.1}$$

where
  $k$ = the number of exploratory variables
  $\epsilon$ = the error term

There are several similarities between this model and the bivariate regression model of Chapter 14. The $\alpha$ and $\beta$ are population parameters estimated by sample data. The corresponding sample estimates are $a$ and $b$. As before, the multivariate regression equation estimates the "best-fitting" regression line to the data. It is best fitting according to the same principle of least squares—it minimizes the sum of the squared deviations between the predicted $y$ values and the observed $y$ values. As with bivariate regression, then, the goal of multiple regression is to provide the best-fitting line between a continuous dependent variable and several continuous independent variables.

In spite of these similarities, however, the multivariate regression model in Equation 15.1 contains some new concepts and different meanings for some old concepts. The multivariate regression model from sample data is represented as:

$$y = a + b_1 x_1 + b_2 x_2 + \cdots + b_k x_k + e \tag{15.2}$$

The intercept ($a$) in this multivariate equation is the predicted value of $y$ when all independent variables equal zero. The interpretation of the slope coefficients ($b$), which are identified by subscripts, is somewhat different from the way it is with the bivariate case. Technically, slope coefficients estimated with multiple regression equations are referred to as *partial slope coefficients,* or *partial regression coefficients.* The first slope coefficient in Equation 15.2, $b_1$, is the partial slope of the linear relationship between the first independent variable and the dependent variable, $y$. The second slope coefficient, $b_2$, is the partial slope of the linear relationship between the second independent variable and $y$. If you were using five independent variables to predict a dependent variable, there would be 5 partial slope coefficients, each denoted by its subscript ($b_1$, $b_2$, $b_3$, $b_4$, $b_5$).

Each slope coefficient indicates the change in the mean of the $y$ variable associated with a one-unit change in a given independent variable, *when all other independent variables in the model are held constant.* This last component of the interpretation, "when all other independent variables are held constant," is important. It is this statistical control that allows us to separate the effect of one independent variable from those of other independent variables. In other words, the partial slope coefficient measures the effect of one independent variable on the dependent variable when the effect of all the other independent variables on the dependent variable has been considered.

The final term in the multiple regression equation is the error term, $e$. As in the bivariate model, the error component in the multiple regression model reflects elements such as measurement error and explanatory variables that are excluded from the model. We should note that the order in which the independent variables are listed does not matter in a regular multiple regression analysis.[1] What does matter are the potential explanatory variables that are explicitly included in the model as $x$ variables and that are left out and implicitly included in the error term.

The practice of good regression analysis consists of including in the model those explanatory variables that are most strongly related to the dependent variable and are unrelated to one another. Although the multiple regression equation can be estimated with a large number of independent variables, for ease of presentation, in this chapter we concentrate on equations using only two independent variables. The extension to more than two independent variables is relatively straightforward, and the interested reader is encouraged to examine other sources.[2]

The assumptions behind the multiple regression model are identical to those in the one independent variable case. It is assumed that (1) the data were randomly selected, (2) the dependent variables are normally distributed in the population, (3) the data are continuous (that they are measured at the interval or ratio level), (4) the nature of the relationship between the dependent and each of the independent variables is linear, and (5) the error term ($\epsilon$) is independent of, and therefore uncorrelated with, each of the independent or $x$ variables, that it is normally distributed, and has an expected value of zero and constant variance across all levels of $x$.

There is one very important new assumption in the multivariate regression model. This assumption is that the independent variables are independent of or uncorrelated with one another. That was the point we were making in the preceding paragraph when we noted that the ideal way of doing good regression analysis is to select independent variables that are strongly related to the dependent variable and weakly or unrelated to one another. This problem did not arise in the case of one independent variable, but it is a constant concern as we add to the list of independent variables in our model. Why is it so important that the independent variables be uncorrelated with one another?

To answer this question, think carefully about what we want to do in our multiple regression problem. We have a dependent variable whose variation we are trying to explain. We have at least two independent variables that we think explains this variation in the dependent variable. What we would like to know from our multiple regression analysis are two important things: (1) how much of the variance in the dependent variable are we explaining by our two independent variables together?, and (2) how much of this combined explained variance can we say is uniquely due to each of the independent variables? The first question asks how much variance we can explain in the dependent variable. The second asks how much of what we explain is due to the unique contribution of each of our independent variables. It is this second question that is difficult to answer when the independent variables are correlated.

Think of two independent variables as lying on a continuum from being completely unique variables having nothing in common to being identical to one another and having everything in common. At one end of this continuum are two variables that are completely unique. These variables are not correlated, that is, the correlation between them is zero ($r = 0$). When two variables are correlated, however, it means that they share something in common. The lower the correlation, the more unique the variables are and the less they have in common. The higher the correlation, however, the less unique they are and the more they have in common. At the other end of the continuum, the two variables are indistinguishable, they have nothing unique, and one variable may be used in place of the other because they are essentially the same variable. In this extreme case, the two independent variables are perfectly correlated ($r = 1.0$).

When two independent variables are completely uncorrelated, we are able to separate their combined explained variance of the dependent variable into separate and unique components. For example, we can specify that of the 60 percent of explained variance in the dependent variable ($y$), two-thirds is due to $x_1$ and the other one-third is due to $x_2$. As two independent variables become correlated, however, some of the explained variance to the dependent variable cannot be uniquely attributed to one or the other variable. That is, some of the explained variance cannot be said to be due to $x_1$ or $x_2$, but can be said to be due only to their shared influence. The stronger the correlation between the two independent variables, the less of the explained variance we can attribute to the unique effect of each variable, the more we must attribute to the explained variance that they share. When the two variables are very highly correlated, we can attribute no unique explained variance to them, and all of the explained variance in the dependent variable is shared between the two.

The problem of having independent variables that are correlated is referred to as the problem of *multicollinearity*. When the independent variables in a regression equation are correlated with one another, they are said to be *collinear*. This means that there is a linear relationship among the independent variables. The problem of multicollinearity is something you want to avoid in multiple regression analysis. As stated, you want your independent variables to be strongly correlated with the dependent variable, but uncorrelated with each other.

You can detect problems of multicollinearity in your data. If you have only two independent variables, the easiest way to identify multicollinearity is to examine the correlation between them. The higher the correlation, the greater the problem of multicollinearity. Although this is not a hard-and-fast rule, be suspicious of multicollinearity when the correlation between two independent variables is .70 or higher. With more than two independent variables, detecting multicollinearity is more of a problem and is beyond the scope of this text. One simple way to detect multicollinearity, however, would be to inspect the standard error of your regression coefficients. Multicollinearity frequently manifests itself in high standard errors for two or more coefficients. If one variable is dropped from the model, and the standard error of the other is substantially decreased, multicollinearity frequently is the source. Another way to detect multicollinearity is to regress each independent variable on the other independent variables. In this analysis each independent variable becomes the dependent variable and the other independent variables serve as independent variables for it. If multicollinearity is not a problem, the amount of explained variance will be quite low.

We may have gotten a little ahead of ourselves with this detailed discussion of multicollinearity. It was important, however, for you fully to understand this very important assumption of the multiple regression model. Now let's return to the multiple regression model described in Equation 15.2, and consider some data to illustrate and give meaning to the concepts we have discussed thus far. Table 15.1 presents murder rates per 100,000 (murder), the percent of the population below the poverty level (poverty), and the number of people per household (density), for a random sample of 14 cities. From this data set, we are going to estimate the effect that both poverty and household density have on murder rates. For the sake of this

TABLE 15.1. Murder Rate per 100,000 Population (1991), Percent of all Persons below the Poverty Level (1989), and Number of Persons per Household (1990), for a Sample of 14 Cities

| Case | City | Murder Rate $y$ | Poverty Rate $x_1$ | Household Density $x_2$ |
|------|------|------|------|------|
| 1 | New York, NY | 29.3 | 19.3 | 2.67 |
| 2 | Los Angeles, CA | 28.9 | 18.9 | 2.91 |
| 3 | Chicago, IL | 32.9 | 21.6 | 2.72 |
| 4 | Houston, TX | 36.5 | 20.7 | 2.75 |
| 5 | Philadelphia, PA | 27.6 | 20.3 | 2.66 |
| 6 | San Diego, CA | 14.7 | 13.4 | 2.69 |
| 7 | Detroit, MI | 59.3 | 32.4 | 2.67 |
| 8 | Phoenix, AZ | 12.9 | 14.2 | 2.59 |
| 9 | Denver, CO | 18.4 | 17.1 | 2.46 |
| 10 | Seattle, WA | 8.1 | 12.4 | 2.45 |
| 11 | Boston, MA | 19.7 | 18.7 | 2.61 |
| 12 | Atlanta, GA | 50.9 | 27.3 | 2.64 |
| 13 | Oklahoma City, OK | 12.5 | 15.9 | 2.53 |
| 14 | Cleveland, OH | 34.3 | 8.5 | 2.56 |
| | | $\bar{x}_Y = 27.57$ | $\bar{x}_1 = 18.62$ | $\bar{x}_2 = 2.64$ |
| | | $s_Y = 18.62$ | $s_1 = 6.07$ | $s_2 = .12$ |

*Source:* Murder and poverty rate, Statistical Abstract of the United States (1993), pp. 194 and 472 respectively; Household Density Rate, Statistical Abstract of the United States (1993), p. 50.

example, let's say that we believe that both are positively related to murder rates. Cities with high rates of poverty and greater household density, we believe, also have high murder rates. Poverty is positively related to murder rates because of the frustration and anger it may produce among those who experience it. One manifestation of this anger and resentment is a high rate of homicide. The number of people per household is also presumed to be positively related to the murder rate. Because a large number of homicides involve family members, as the density in the home increases, so does both the motivation and opportunity to commit murder (Galle et al., 1972; Gove et al., 1979). In this example, the murder rate in the city is our dependent variable ($y$), and poverty ($x_1$) and the number of people in the household ($x_2$) are our two independent variables. It is also probably true that household density and poverty are not strongly correlated. We might expect a weak positive correlation between the two, as less affluent families tend to be larger than more affluent ones, but we do not expect multicollinearity to be a problem. Our two-variable regression model, then, looks like the following:

Murder Rates $= a + b_1$ (Poverty) $+ b_2$ (Household Density) $+ \epsilon$

The mean and the standard deviation of each variable are presented at the bottom of each column in Table 15.1.

Just as we did with the bivariate regression model in Chapter 14, the first step we need to take in computing our multiple regression equation is to calculate each partial slope. The formula used for calculating partial slope coefficients follows.

$$b_1 = \left(\frac{s_y}{s_{x_1}}\right)\left(\frac{r_{yx_1} - (r_{yx_2})(r_{x_1x_2})}{1 - r^2_{x_1x_2}}\right) \qquad (15.3)$$

$$b_2 = \left(\frac{s_y}{s_{x_2}}\right)\left(\frac{r_{yx_2} - (r_{yx_1})(r_{x_1x_2})}{1 - r^2_{x_1x_2}}\right) \qquad (15.4)$$

where
  $b_1 =$ the partial slope of $x_1$ on $y$
  $b_2 =$ the partial slope of $x_2$ on $y$
  $s_y =$ the standard deviation of $y$
  $s_1 =$ the standard deviation of the first independent variable ($x_1$)
  $s_2 =$ the standard deviation of the second independent variable ($x_2$)
  $r_{y_1} =$ the bivariate correlation between $y$ and $x_1$
  $r_{y_2} =$ the bivariate correlation between $y$ and $x_2$
  $r_{1\,2} =$ the bivariate correlation between $x_1$ and $x_2$

Notice that you need not only the bivariate correlation coefficient between the independent variable and each of the dependent variables, but also the bivariate correlation between the two independent variables. That is, to obtain a partial slope coefficient for each independent variable, the equation takes into account the bivariate relationship between that variable and the dependent variable ($r_{yx_1}$), between the other independent variable and the dependent variable ($r_{yx_2}$), and between both independent variables ($r_{x_1x_2}$).

In this first example of the multiple regression model, we go through the calculations of each component of the partial slope formula, including the computation of each bivariate correlation. In the remainder of the chapter, we provide you with the bivariate correlation coefficients. However, for this example let's compute each of the bivariate correlations to sharpen our skills. Recall from the previous chapter the formula used to obtain a bivariate correlation coefficient was:

$$r_{xy} = \frac{n\Sigma xy - (\Sigma x)(\Sigma y)}{\sqrt{[n\Sigma x^2 - (\Sigma x)^2][n\Sigma y^2 - (\Sigma y)^2]}} \tag{15.5}$$

To find the correlation coefficient for the relationship between our two independent variables, you would simply substitute the subscripts $x_1$ and $x_2$ in place of the $x$ and $y$ subscripts in *formula* Equation 15.5 as follows:

$$r_{x_1x_2} = \frac{n\Sigma x_1x_2 - (\Sigma x_1)(\Sigma x_2)}{\sqrt{[n\Sigma x_1^2 - (\Sigma x_1)^2][n\Sigma x_2^2 - (\Sigma x_2)^2]}} \tag{15.6}$$

Tables 15.2 through 15.4 provide each of the elements needed to calculate bivariate correlation coefficients for the relationship between murder and poverty, murder and household density, and poverty and household density for the sample of 14 cities. These calculations are illustrated for you, but you should perform them on your own with the data provided in Tables 15.2 through 15.4 before moving on.

**TABLE 15.2. Calculations Necessary to Compute the Bivariate Correlation Coefficient between Murder and Poverty Rates in 14 States (Table 15.1)**

| Case | City | Murder Rate $y$ | Poverty Rate $x_1$ | $y^2$ | $x_1^2$ | $x_1y$ |
|------|------|------|------|------|------|------|
| 1 | New York, NY | 29.3 | 19.3 | 858.49 | 372.49 | 565.49 |
| 2 | Los Angeles, CA | 28.9 | 18.9 | 835.21 | 357.21 | 546.21 |
| 3 | Chicago, IL | 32.9 | 21.6 | 1082.41 | 466.56 | 710.64 |
| 4 | Houston, TX | 36.5 | 20.7 | 1332.25 | 428.49 | 755.55 |
| 5 | Philadelphia, PA | 27.6 | 20.3 | 761.76 | 412.09 | 560.28 |
| 6 | San Diego, CA | 14.7 | 13.4 | 216.09 | 179.56 | 196.98 |
| 7 | Detroit, MI | 59.3 | 32.4 | 3516.49 | 1049.76 | 1921.32 |
| 8 | Phoenix, AZ | 12.9 | 14.2 | 166.41 | 201.64 | 183.18 |
| 9 | Denver, CO | 18.4 | 17.1 | 338.56 | 292.41 | 314.64 |
| 10 | Seattle, WA | 8.1 | 12.4 | 65.61 | 153.76 | 100.44 |
| 11 | Boston, MA | 19.7 | 18.7 | 388.09 | 349.69 | 368.39 |
| 12 | Atlanta, GA | 50.9 | 27.3 | 2590.81 | 745.29 | 1389.57 |
| 13 | Oklahoma City, OK | 12.5 | 15.9 | 156.25 | 252.81 | 198.75 |
| 14 | Cleveland, OH | 34.3 | 8.5 | 1176.49 | 72.25 | 291.55 |
| Total | | 386.0 | 260.7 | 13,484.92 | 5334.01 | 8102.99 |

**TABLE 15.3. Calculations Necessary to Compute the Bivariate Correlation Coefficient between Murder and Household Density in 14 States (Table 15.1)**

| Case | City | Murder Rate $y$ | Household Density $x_2$ | $y^2$ | $x_2^2$ | $x_2 y$ |
|------|------|------|------|------|------|------|
| 1 | New York, NY | 29.3 | 2.67 | 858.49 | 7.13 | 78.23 |
| 2 | Los Angeles, CA | 28.9 | 2.91 | 835.21 | 8.47 | 84.10 |
| 3 | Chicago, IL | 32.9 | 2.72 | 1082.41 | 7.40 | 89.49 |
| 4 | Houston, TX | 36.5 | 2.75 | 1332.25 | 7.56 | 100.38 |
| 5 | Philadelphia, PA | 27.6 | 2.66 | 761.76 | 7.08 | 73.42 |
| 6 | San Diego, CA | 14.7 | 2.69 | 216.09 | 7.24 | 39.54 |
| 7 | Detroit, MI | 59.3 | 2.67 | 3516.49 | 7.13 | 158.33 |
| 8 | Phoenix, AZ | 12.9 | 2.59 | 166.41 | 6.71 | 33.41 |
| 9 | Denver, CO | 18.4 | 2.46 | 338.56 | 6.05 | 45.26 |
| 10 | Seattle, WA | 8.1 | 2.45 | 65.61 | 6.00 | 19.84 |
| 11 | Boston, MA | 19.7 | 2.61 | 388.09 | 6.81 | 51.42 |
| 12 | Atlanta, GA | 50.9 | 2.64 | 2590.81 | 6.97 | 134.38 |
| 13 | Oklahoma City, OK | 12.5 | 2.53 | 156.25 | 6.40 | 31.62 |
| 14 | Cleveland, OH | 34.3 | 2.56 | 1176.49 | 6.55 | 87.81 |
| | Total | 386.0 | 36.91 | 13,484.92 | 97.50 | 1027.23 |

Bivariate correlation between murder and poverty:

$$r_{yx_1} = \frac{(14)(8102.99) - (260.7)(386)}{\sqrt{[(14)(5334.01) - (260.7)^2][(14)(13,484.92) - (386)^2]}}$$

$$= \frac{12,811.66}{\sqrt{(6711.65)(39,792.88)}}$$

$$= \frac{12,811.66}{16,342.46}$$

$$= .78$$

Bivariate correlation between murder and household density:

$$r_{yx_2} = \frac{(14)(1027.23) - (36.91)(386)}{\sqrt{[(14)(97.5) - (36.91)^2][(14)(13,484.92) - (386)^2]}}$$

$$= \frac{133.96}{\sqrt{(2.65)(39,792.88)}}$$

$$= \frac{133.96}{324.73}$$

$$= .41$$

**TABLE 15.4.  Calculations Necessary to Compute the Bivariate Correlation Coefficient between Poverty and Household Density in 14 States (Table 15.1)**

| Case | City | Poverty Rate $x_1$ | Household Density $x_2$ | $x_1^2$ | $x_2^2$ | $x_1 x_2$ |
|---|---|---|---|---|---|---|
| 1 | New York, NY | 19.3 | 2.67 | 372.49 | 7.13 | 51.53 |
| 2 | Los Angeles, CA | 18.9 | 2.91 | 357.21 | 8.47 | 55.00 |
| 3 | Chicago, IL | 21.6 | 2.72 | 466.56 | 7.40 | 58.75 |
| 4 | Houston, TX | 20.7 | 2.75 | 428.49 | 7.56 | 56.92 |
| 5 | Philadelphia, PA | 20.3 | 2.66 | 412.09 | 7.08 | 54.00 |
| 6 | San Diego, CA | 13.4 | 2.69 | 179.56 | 7.24 | 36.05 |
| 7 | Detroit, MI | 32.4 | 2.67 | 1049.76 | 7.13 | 86.51 |
| 8 | Phoenix, AZ | 14.2 | 2.59 | 201.64 | 6.71 | 36.78 |
| 9 | Denver, CO | 17.1 | 2.46 | 292.41 | 6.05 | 42.07 |
| 10 | Seattle, WA | 12.4 | 2.45 | 153.76 | 6.00 | 30.38 |
| 11 | Boston, MA | 18.7 | 2.61 | 349.69 | 6.81 | 48.81 |
| 12 | Atlanta, GA | 27.3 | 2.64 | 745.29 | 6.97 | 72.07 |
| 13 | Oklahoma City, OK | 15.9 | 2.53 | 252.81 | 6.40 | 40.23 |
| 14 | Cleveland, OH | 8.5 | 2.56 | 72.25 | 6.55 | 21.76 |
| Total | | 260.7 | 36.91 | 5334.01 | 97.50 | 690.86 |

Bivariate correlation between poverty and household density:

$$r_{x_1 x_2} = \frac{(14)(690.86) - (260.7)(36.91)}{\sqrt{[(14)(5334.01) - (260.7)^2][(14)(97.5) - (36.91)^2]}}$$

$$= \frac{49.60}{\sqrt{(6711.65)(2.65)}}$$

$$= \frac{49.60}{\sqrt{17,785.87}}$$

$$= .37$$

All of the correlation coefficients we calculated indicate that the relationship between each pair of variables is positive. Both poverty ($r_{yx_1} = .78$) and household density ($r_{yx_2} = .41$) are positively related to the murder rate in these cities, and poverty and household density are positively related to each other ($r_{x_1 x_2} = .37$). These correlation coefficients suggest that cities with high rates of poverty and of household density also tend to have higher murder rates, and that cities with high rates of poverty also have high rates of household density. The correlation between our two independent variables ($r = .37$) is not very high, so we do not have to worry about the problem of multicollinearity.

With these correlation coefficients, the standard deviation of each of the variables, and Equations 15.3 and 15.4, for each independent variable we can calculate the partial slope coefficient. From these partial slope coefficients we will be able to ascertain the effect of each independent variable on the dependent variable while holding the other independent variable *constant*. These calculations are shown.

Partial slope coefficient for the effect of poverty on murder rates:

$$b_1 = \left(\frac{14.79}{6.07}\right)\left(\frac{.78 - (.41)(.37)}{1 - (.37)^2}\right)$$

$$= (2.44)\left(\frac{.78 - .15}{1 - .14}\right)$$

$$= (2.44)\left(\frac{.63}{.86}\right)$$

$$= 1.78$$

Partial slope coefficient for the effect of household density on murder rates:

$$b_2 = \left(\frac{14.79}{.12}\right)\left(\frac{.41 - (.78)(.37)}{1 - (.37)^2}\right)$$

$$= (123.25)\left(\frac{.41 - .29}{1 - .14}\right)$$

$$= (123.25)\left(\frac{.12}{.86}\right)$$

$$= 17.20$$

The partial slope coefficient for the effect of poverty on the murder rate ($b_1$) is 1.78. This indicates that, on average, murder rates increase by 1.78 per 100,000 with every 1 percent increase in the poverty rate while holding household density constant. Similarly, the partial slope coefficient for the effect of household density on the murder rate ($b_2$) is 17.20. This indicates that, on average, murder rates increase by 17.20 per 100,000 for each increase in one person per household while holding levels of poverty constant.

Now that we have obtained the partial slopes ($b_1$ and $b_2$) for the independent variables of poverty and household density, we can compute the final unknown element in the least-squares regression equation, the intercept ($a$). This is done in the same way in which we obtained the intercept in the bivariate regression equation, by substituting the mean of the dependent variable ($\bar{x}_y$) and the means of the two independent variables ($\bar{x}_1$ and $\bar{x}_2$) into the equation and solving for $a$:

$$a = \bar{y} - b_1\bar{x}_1 - b_2\bar{x}_2$$

$$= 27.57 - (1.78)(18.62) - (17.2)(2.64)$$

$$= 27.57 - (33.14) - (45.41)$$

$$= -50.98$$

The intercept value in the equation indicates that, when both independent variables are equal to zero, the average value of $y$ is $-50.98$. Now that we have solved for the intercept ($a$) and both partial regression slopes, our multiple regression equation for murder rates can now be expressed as:

$$\hat{y} = a + b_1x_1 + b_2x_2$$
$$= -50.98 + 1.78(x_1) + 17.20(x_2)$$
$$= -50.98 + 1.78(\text{Poverty}) + 1.70(\text{Household Density})$$

As with the bivariate regression equation we examined in Chapter 14, this least-squares multiple regression equation provides us with the best-fitting line for our data. However, we can no longer represent the equation graphically with a simple straight line fitted to a two-dimensional ($x,y$) scattergram. In a two-independent variable multiple regression, we have to use our imagination to visualize the fitting of a regression plane to a three-dimensional scatter of points that is defined by each of coefficients ($a$, $b_1$, $b_2$). As you can imagine, this exercise in imagery becomes even more complex as more independent variables are brought into the equation. With $k$ independent variables, the regression equation is represented by a plane in $k$-dimensional space.

As was also true for the bivariate equation, we can use this multivariate equation to predict scores on our dependent variable, murder rates, from scores on the independent variables of poverty and household density. For example, our best prediction of the murder rate ($\hat{y}$) for a city with a 15 percent poverty rate and an average household density of 2.8 persons would be obtained by substituting these two $x$ values into the least-squares regression formula:

$$\hat{y} = -50.98 + (1.78)(15) + (17.2)(2.8)$$
$$= -50.98 + 26.70 + 48.16$$
$$= 23.88$$

Our multiple regression equation predicts that a city with a poverty rate of 15 percent and an average household density of 2.8 persons would have a predicted murder rate of 23.88 per 100,000. Let's predict what the murder rate would be for a city with a 21.6 percent poverty rate and an average household density of 2.72 persons. Using our regression equation, the predicted murder rate would be:

$$\hat{y} = -50.98 + (1.78)(21.6) + (17.20)(2.72)$$
$$= -50.98 + 38.45 + 46.78$$
$$= 34.25$$

The predicted murder rate for a city with these characteristics would be 34.25 per 100,000. Notice that the city of Chicago has a poverty rate of 21.6 percent and a household density of 2.72 persons. Its observed murder rate is 32.9. Our regression equation permitted us to make a good prediction of Chicago's murder rate, but as in the bivariate case, our predictions of $y$ will not be perfectly accurate. There will be some error in our prediction.

We have found in our example that the slope coefficient for percent poverty on the murder rate was 1.78 while holding household density constant, and that the slope coefficient for household density on the murder rate was 17.20 while holding percent poverty constant. We would caution you not to conclude from this that the effect of household density on the rate of murders is almost 17 times greater than the effect of percent poverty. In other words, you cannot conclude on the basis of the size of these partial slope coefficients that household density is a more important (more powerful) explanatory variable than percent poverty. *In a multiple regression analysis you cannot determine which independent variable has the strongest effect on the dependent variable by comparing partial slope coefficients.*

Remember from our discussion in Chapter 14 that the slope coefficient is measured in terms of the unit of measurement of the $x$ variable, that is, a one-unit change in $x$ produces a $b$ change in the $y$ variable. The size of the partial slope coefficient, then, reflects the underlying units of measurement. As a result, the magnitude of the slope coefficient is not a good indicator of the strength of the variable.

In the bivariate model we solved this problem by calculating a standardized coefficient that did not depend on the independent variable's unit of measurement, the correlation coefficient. We have a similar *standardized regression coefficient;* it is called the *standardized partial slope.* They are also referred to as *beta weights* (not to be confused with the beta, the population parameter for the slope coefficient). We examine beta weights next.

## 15.3 BETA WEIGHTS

To compare the effects of two independent variables on a dependent variable, it is necessary to remove differences in the relative magnitudes of the slopes that are solely the function of differences in the units of measurement (e.g., dollars compared to cents, years compared to months). One way of doing this is to convert all of the variables in the equation to a common scale. For example, we could standardize all of our original variable distributions by converting our scores on the independent variables into $Z$ scores. If we did this, each variable distribution would have a mean of 0 and a standard deviation of 1. Comparisons across independent variables, then, would be much more meaningful because differences in size would reflect differences in effect and not the underlying unit of measurement.

To obtain slope coefficients in this way, first we have to convert all of our original data points for each variable into $z$ scores and then to recompute the partial slopes and the $Y$ intercept from these new $z$ distributions. This would not only require a great deal of work, but we would also lose the value of the original partial slope coefficient that was specific to each variable's original measurement unit. There is a way, however, to compute a standardized partial slope coefficient (a beta weight) easily from the obtained partial slope coefficient. If we do this, we have two partial slope coefficients for each independent variable, one standardized (the beta weight), and one in the original measurement scale.

The formulas used to obtain standardized partial slopes or beta weights, symbolized as $b^*$, from a multiple regression equation with two independent variables are shown in equation (15.7).

$$b^{*}_{x_1} = b_{x_1}\left(\frac{s_{x_1}}{s_y}\right) \tag{15.7}$$

$$b^{*}_{x_2} = b_{x_2}\left(\frac{s_{x_2}}{s_y}\right)$$

As the formula indicates, the computation of the beta weight involves multiplying the partial slope coefficient ($b_1$) obtained for an independent variable by the ratio of the standard deviation of that variable ($s_{x_1}$) to the standard deviation of the dependent variable ($s_y$). The interpretation of a beta weight is relatively straightforward. Like a partial slope coefficient, beta coefficients can be either positive or negative. A positive beta coefficient indicates a positive linear relationship between the independent and dependent variable, and a negative beta weight indicates a negative relationship. The standardized partial slope always has the same sign as the unstandardized slope. As with the interpretation of a correlation coefficient, the larger the beta weight, the stronger the relationship between the independent and dependent variable. More specifically, the beta weights show the expected change in a standardized score on the dependent variable for a one-unit change in a standardized score of the independent variable while holding the other independent variable constant. If we want to know the relative importance of two variables, then we can compare the magnitude of their respective beta weights. The variable with the larger beta weight (absolute value) has the stronger effect on the dependent variable.

Let's go through an example using the city-level murder, poverty, and household density data. Recall that the partial slope coefficient for poverty ($b_1$) was 1.78 and that the partial slope coefficient for household density ($b_2$) was 17.20. The standard deviations for each of the variable distributions are presented in Table 15.1. To determine the beta weights for each independent variable, we simply plug these values into Equation 15.7:

$$\text{Beta}_{x_1} = (1.78)\left(\frac{6.07}{14.79}\right)$$

$$= (1.78)(.41)$$

$$= .73$$

$$\text{Beta}_{x_2} = (17.20)\left(\frac{.12}{14.79}\right)$$

$$= (17.20)(.008)$$

$$= .14$$

The value of the beta weights (in parentheses) and the partial slope coefficients for our two variable multiple regression model of murder rates for 14 cities are shown in Figure 15.3. Using these beta weights, we can compare the effect of one independent variable on the dependent variable with the effect of the other, without our comparison being distorted by a variable's unit of measurement. From the beta weights displayed in Figure 15.3, we can immediately ascertain that the percent of persons living below the poverty level in a city has a much stronger relationship with murder rates ($b^*_{x_1} = .73$) than does household density ($b^*_{x_1} = .14$). You should now see that, even though the partial slope coefficient for the effect of household density ($b_{x_2} = 17.2$) was substantially greater than that for percent poverty ($b_{x_1} = 1.78$), this difference was due to the different units of measurement for the two variables. When we examine the standardized coefficients, we can see that the variable that is more important in explaining murder rates in these 14 cities is the percent of the population living below the poverty level.

There are two other ways of assessing the relative importance of independent variables in a multiple regression analysis. One method with which you are already familiar from our treatment of bivariate regression, is to calculate correlation coefficients and coefficients of determination. The second way is by comparing the absolute value of the magnitude of the obtained $t$ value for each independent variable from a hypothesis test that the slope coefficient is equal to zero. We explore the multivariate equivalent of correlation coefficients and coefficients of determination in the next section and hypothesis tests for the significance of partial slope coefficients in the section following that.

## 15.4 PARTIAL CORRELATION COEFFICIENTS

Another way of addressing the relative effects of our independent variables is to compute *partial correlation coefficients*. With partial correlation coefficients, we can also compute the *multiple coefficient of determination* ($R^2$). Both of these coefficients allow us to investigate the question of the relative importance of independent variables, although they do so in somewhat different ways. The interpretation of the partial correlation coefficient and multiple coefficient of determination, however, is analogous to their bivariate equivalents, so you should have no problem with this section! We begin our discussion with the partial correlation coefficient.

The magnitude of a partial correlation coefficient indicates the correlation or strength of the relationship between a given independent variable and the dependent variable when the linear effect of another independent variable is held constant or removed. In the example we are currently using, the partial correlation between

FIGURE 15.3. Partial slope coefficients (and beta weights) for the relationship between percent poverty, household density, and murder rates.

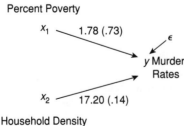

poverty and murder in cities would measure the relationship between these two variables when the linear effect of household density has been removed.

In referring to the partial correlation coefficient, we continue with the same subscripts we have used throughout this chapter with one additional twist. We use the partial correlation symbol $r_{yx_1 \cdot x_2}$ to show the correlation between the dependent variable ($y$), and the first independent variable ($x_1$) while controlling for the second independent variable ($x_2$). The subscript to the right of the dot indicates the variable whose effect is being controlled. The formulas used to obtain partial correlation coefficients for two independent variables with a dependent variable is shown in equation 15.8.

$$r_{yx_1 \cdot x_2} = \frac{r_{yx_1} - (r_{yx_2})(r_{x_1x_2})}{\sqrt{1 - r^2_{yx_2}} \sqrt{1 - r^2_{x_1x_2}}}$$

$$= \frac{r_{yx_2} - (r_{yx_1})(r_{x_1x_2})}{\sqrt{1 - r^2_{yx_1}} \sqrt{1 - r^2_{x_1x_2}}}$$

(15.8)

We now have all the values we need to calculate this coefficient for our murder rate, poverty, and household density example. Recall that the bivariate correlation between poverty and murder for the city level data was $r_{yx_1} = .78$, the correlation between murder and household density was $r_{yx_2} = .41$, and the correlation between poverty and household density was $r_{x_1x_2} = .37$. With this information, we can compute the partial correlation coefficients for both independent variables.

Partial correlation coefficient for poverty and murder controlling for household density:

$$r_{yx_1 \cdot x_2} = \frac{.78 - (.41)(.37)}{\sqrt{1 - (.41)^2} \sqrt{1 - (.37)^2}}$$

$$= \frac{.78 - .15}{\sqrt{1 - .17} \sqrt{1 - .14}}$$

$$= \frac{.63}{.85}$$

$$= .74$$

Partial correlation coefficient for household density and murder controlling for poverty:

$$r_{yx_2 \cdot x_1} = \frac{.41 - (.78)(.37)}{\sqrt{1 - (.78)^2} \sqrt{1 - (.37)^2}}$$

$$= \frac{.41 - .29}{\sqrt{1 - .61} \sqrt{1 - .14}}$$

$$= \frac{.12}{.58}$$

$$= .21$$

The partial correlations between each independent and the dependent variable, along with the bivariate correlation between the two independent variables, are shown for you in Figure 15.4. The partial correlation between poverty and the murder rate in these cities is .74, when controlling for household density. The partial correlation between population density and the murder rate is .21 when controlling for poverty. Because the partial correlation for poverty (.74) is greater than the partial correlation for household density (.21), poverty has the stronger effect on murder rates. This is consistent with the conclusion we reached when we used beta weights. In general, the relative explanatory power of two independent variables can be determined by comparing their partial correlation coefficients. The variable with the largest partial correlation coefficient has the strongest relationship with the dependent variable.

Note that the partial correlation coefficients for both independent variables is less than their respective bivariate correlation because, as the two independent variables are themselves positively correlated ($r_{x_1x_2} = .37$), they share a certain amount of the total explanatory power or explained variance. Think of it this way. Four sources explain murder rates: (1) that which is due uniquely to the effect of poverty, (2) that which is due uniquely to the effect of household density, (3) that which is due to the joint effect of poverty and household density, and (4) that which is due to all other factors not explicitly included in the model but whose effect is manifested through the error term ($\epsilon$). What the partial correlation (and partial slope) coefficients reflect is the unique effect of each independent variable on the dependent variable. That is, the effect of each independent variable that is not shared with the other independent variable. The greater the correlation between the two independent variables ($r_{x_1x_2}$), the weaker the first two sources and the stronger the joint effect.

Another way to disentangle the separate effects of the independent variables on the dependent variable is to compute the increase in the amount of explained variance when each independent variable is added separately to the regression model. With two independent variables ($x_1$, $x_2$), this requires a series of steps. First, estimate what is called a full model that contains both independent variables and determine the amount of variance explained ($R^2_{Full}$). Second, estimate two reduced models. In one reduced model, only the constant and one independent variable ($x_1$) is included. In the second reduced model, only the constant and the second independent variable ($x_2$) is included. Determine the amount of variance explained in each of these reduced models ($R^2_{Reduced}$). The next step is to subtract the $R^2$ of each

FIGURE 15.4. Partial correlation coefficients for the relationship between percent poverty, household density, and murder rates.

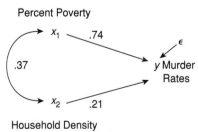

Percent Poverty

Household Density

reduced model from the full model. This gives you the amount of variance that is explained uniquely by that independent variable ($R^2_{\text{Full}} - R^2_{\text{Reduced}}$).

To do this, of course, requires knowing how much of the variance in the dependent variable is explained by both independent variables together. We obtain this value by computing what is termed the *multiple coefficient of determination,* symbolized by a capital $R^2$ to differentiate it from the bivariate coefficient of determination $r^2$. The multiple coefficient of determination indicates the proportion of variance in the dependent variable that is explained by both independent variables combined. You might think of the multiple coefficient of determination as an indicator of how well your model fits the data in terms of the combined ability of the independent variables to explain the dependent variable. The range of $R^2$ is from 0 percent, which indicates that the independent variables explain no variance in the dependent variable, to a maximum of 100 percent, which indicates that the independent variables explain all of the variance. As the independent variables explain a larger amount of the variance (i.e., as $R^2$ approaches 100 percent), the estimated regression model is providing a better fit to the data.

To obtain the multiple coefficient of determination, we cannot simply add together the separate bivariate coefficients of determination. Why? Because the independent variables are also correlated with one another. If the independent variables in a multiple regression equation are correlated, the estimated value of $R^2$ reflects both the amount of variance that each variable uniquely explains and that which they share through their joint correlation. As a result, there will be a joint effect on the dependent variable that cannot be attributed to one variable alone. Again, the amount of this joint effect is a function of the extent to which the two independent variables are correlated themselves.[3]

For a two–independent variable regression equation, the multiple coefficient of determination is found with the following formula:

$$R^2 = r^2_{yx_1} + (r^2_{yx_2 \cdot x_1})(1 - r^2_{yx_1}) \tag{15.9}$$

where

$R^2$ = the multiple coefficient of determination

$r^2_{yx_1}$ = the bivariate correlation between $x_1$ and $y$, the quantity squared

$r^2_{yx_2 \cdot x_1}$ = the partial correlation of $x_2$ and $y$ while controlling for $x_1$, the quantity squared

$r^2_{yx_1}$ = the bivariate correlation between $x_1$ and $y$, the quantity squared

Before we explain the different components of this formula, let's compute the multiple coefficient of determination with our city-level data on murder rates, poverty, and household density. We have already calculated all of the values we need, so we can simply plug them into Equation 15.9:

$$R^2 = (.78)^2 + (.21)^2[1 - (.78)^2]$$

$$= (.61) + (.04)(1 - .61)$$

$$= (.61) + (.04)(.39)$$

$$= .61 + .02$$

$$= .63$$

This $R^2$ indicates the proportion of variance explained in the dependent variable by both independent variables in the regression equation. The obtained $R^2$ of .63 indicates that, combined, rates of poverty and household density together explain 63 percent of the variation in murder rates across cities.

How can we disentangle the contribution of each independent variable to this total explained variance? Notice what the formula for the multiple coefficient of determination (Equation 15.9) does. It first lets one independent variable do all the explaining in the dependent variable it can. That is the first expression after the equals sign ($r^2_{yx_1}$). The value of this term is simply the square of the bivariate correlation coefficient between the first independent variable and the dependent variable. After the first independent variable has done all its explanation, the second variable is then given the chance to explain what it can of the remaining unexplained variation. That is the second term in the expression. This term is the squared partial correlation coefficient between the second independent variable and the dependent variable (controlling for the first independent variable), multiplied by the proportion of variance that the first variable cannot explain:

$$R^2 = r^2_{yx_1} + [(r^2_{yx_2 \cdot x_1})(1 - r^2_{yx_1})]$$

| $\begin{pmatrix} \text{Proportion Explained} \\ \text{by Both} \\ \text{Independent Variables} \end{pmatrix}$ | $\begin{pmatrix} \text{Proportion Explained} \\ \text{by the First} \\ \text{Independent Variable} \end{pmatrix}$ | $\begin{pmatrix} \text{Proportion Explained} \\ \text{by the Second} \\ \text{Independent Variable} \end{pmatrix}$ | $\begin{pmatrix} \text{Proportion Unexplained} \\ \text{by the First} \\ \text{Independent Variable} \end{pmatrix}$ |

The magnitude of the $R^2$ will be the same no matter which of the two independent variables appears first. The following two formulas, then, produce identical results:

$$R^2 = r^2_{yx_1} + (r^2_{yx_2 \cdot x_1})(1 - r^2_{yx_1})$$
$$= r^2_{yx_2} + (r^2_{yx_1 \cdot x_2})(1 - r^2_{yx_2})$$

In the first formula, we first let $x_1$ explain all the variance it can in the dependent variable, and then we let $x_2$ explain what it can of the remaining variance. In the second formula, we first let $x_2$ do all the explaining it can in the dependent variable, then we let $x_1$ explain what remains. The combined explanatory power of the two variables always is the same. However, although the value of $R^2$ is the same no matter which variable is considered first, the amount of explained variance that is attributed to a given variable differs, depending on the order in which it appears. The first variable considered explains more variance, unless the two independent variables are not correlated. If there is a substantial correlation between the two independent variables, the first variable considered will be "given credit" for the explained variance that they share. In this circumstance, the variance explained by the second variable that is not already explained by the first is small. It is, therefore, a good idea to estimate $R^2$ with each variable appearing first to see how much additional variance the second-considered variable can explain above that explained by the first-considered variable.

As you can now perhaps see, the expression for the multiple coefficient of determination can give us some idea of the contribution to the total explained variance made by each variable. To see this perhaps more clearly, we can rewrite our two expressions for the multiple coefficient of determination as follows.

$$R^2 - r^2_{yx_1} = (r^2_{yx_2 \cdot x_1})(1 - r_{yx_1})^2 \qquad\qquad (15.10)$$

$$R^2 - r^2_{yx_2} = (r^2_{yx_1 \cdot x_2})(1 - r_{yx_2})^2$$

In the first formula, the expression on the left-hand side of the equals sign is the difference between the total amount of explained variance and the variance that is explained by the first variable if it alone appeared in the regression equation. You can see that the latter is just the squared bivariate correlation between the first independent variable and the dependent variable. The expression to the right of the equals sign reflects the amount of variance explained by the second variable that is left unexplained by the first. This latter component of the total explained variance often is referred to as the $R^2$ *change* because it reflects the change in the amount of variance explained when the second variable is entered into the regression model. If the change in variance explained is substantial, it tells us that the second variable is able to give us information about the dependent variable that we do not get from the first independent variable.

The second formula is a corollary formula for the $R^2$ change. The expression on the left-hand side of the equals sign is the difference between the total amount of explained variance and the variance that is explained by the second variable if it alone appeared in the regression equation. The $r_{yx_2}$ term is just the squared bivariate correlation between the second independent variable and the dependent variable. The expression to the right of the equals sign reflects the amount of variance explained by the first independent variable that is left unexplained by the second. This formula measures the change in explained variance that we can uniquely attribute to the first independent variable because it reflects the amount of variance it explains over and above that explained by the second independent variable. We illustrate the $R^2$ change term with our murder rate data.

In the calculation of the multiple coefficient of determination for the murder rate, the percent poverty was the independent variable considered first. It explained 61 percent of the total 63 percent explained variance in murder rates. Household density explained the remaining 2 percent. It would appear, then, that percent poverty is much more important in explaining crime rates than household density. In fact, once the percent poverty in a city is considered, household density does not really add much new information.

In the following calculation, household density appears first. It is given the opportunity to explain all it can in murder rates, and then poverty is entered to explain the remaining variance left unexplained by density:

$$R^2 = (.41)^2 + (.74)^2[1 - (.41)^2]$$

$$= .17 + (.5476)(.8319)$$

$$= .17 + .46$$

$$= .63$$

The combined variance explained is still 63 percent, thus, regardless of which variable is considered first the total amount of explained variance remains the same. We find here that household density explains only 17 percent of the variance when considered first, whereas percent poverty explains 46 percent of the variance above and beyond that explained by the density variable. Again, we would conclude that the percent of the population below the poverty level is a more important variable in explaining murder rates among these cities than the number of persons per household.

You should also note here that 37 percent of the variance in murder rates remains unexplained by poverty and household density $(1 - R^2 = .37$, or 37 percent). This gives us a clue that there are factors other than poverty and household density that explain why some cities have higher murder rates than other cities. This would lead us on a search for suitable other independent variables to add to our regression model. Maybe because murder is committed by young males, a good independent variable would be the percent of each city's population that is male and between 18 and 25 years of age. We suggested earlier that in general a good independent variable would be one that is strongly correlated with the dependent variable, but weakly correlated with other independent variables already in the model. What we would do next is to bring these other independent variables explicitly into our model and estimate a regression equation with three or more independent variables.

The next questions we need to address are whether there is a significant relationship between (1) the combination of independent variables and the dependent variable, and (2) between each of the independent variables and the dependent variable. We discuss issues of hypothesis testing with multiple regression in the next section.

## 15.5 HYPOTHESIS TESTING IN MULTIPLE REGRESSION

So far in this chapter, we have focused on calculating and interpreting the various coefficients associated with multiple regression analysis. However, because we are really interested in knowing if the total amount of variance explained is significantly different from zero and in estimating the value of the population partial slope coefficients $(\beta_1, \beta_2)$ from the sample coefficients $(b_1$ and $b_2)$, we must now examine issues of hypothesis testing. In multiple regression analysis we are interested in testing hypotheses about the multiple coefficient of determination and the partial slope coefficients. We examine each of these in turn.

The first null hypothesis of interest states that all slope coefficients in the regression equation are equal to zero. This is the same as saying that the multiple coefficient of determination $R^2$ is equal to zero. The alternative hypothesis states that the slopes for all independent variables when used together are not equal to zero. This can be expressed as:

$H_0$: $\beta_1, \beta_2, \beta_3, \cdots, \beta_k = 0$     or $R^2 = 0$

$H_1$: $\beta_1, \beta_2, \beta_3, \cdots, \beta_k \neq 0$     or $R^2 \neq 0$

To reject the null hypothesis, only one of the partial slope coefficients need to be different from zero.

An $F$ test is used to test this null hypothesis. This $F$ test is very comparable to the $F$ test we conducted with the analysis of variance. It is based on two sources of variability in our data, explained and unexplained variability. These correspond to two estimates of the population variance, explained/regression variance and unexplained/residual variance. You should be familiar with these terms from the previous chapter on bivariate regression models.

The regression variance is the variance in the data we can explain from our regression equation. Hence, this is often referred to as "explained variance." It is estimated as the ratio of the regression sum of squares to its degrees of freedom. The regression sum of squares is the sum of the squared differences between the predicted value of $y$ ($\hat{y}$) based on the regression equation and the mean of $y$ ($\bar{y}$). The number of degrees of freedom for the regression sum of squares is equal to $k$, where $k$ equals the number of independent variables in the regression model. This ratio of regression sum of squares to degrees of freedom is one estimate of the population variance. In Figure 15.5, this estimate of the variance is labeled as the regression "mean square."

The residual variance is the variance in our data unexplained by the regression equation. It is estimated as the ratio of the residual sum of squares to its degrees of freedom. The residual sum of squares is the sum of the squared differences between the observed value of $y$ and the predicted value ($\hat{y}$). The number of degrees

FIGURE 15.5. Multiple regression results for poverty and household density regressed on rates of murder in 15 cities.

```
                          MULTIPLE REGRESSION

  Equation Number 1   Dependent Variable..   MURDER

  Block Number 1.   Method: Enter   DENSITY   POVERTY

  Variable(s) Entered on Step Number
        1..   POVERTY
        2..   DENSITY

  Multiple R            .79504
  R Square              .63201
  Adjusted R Square     .56520
  Standard Error       9.75011

  Analysis of Variance

                       df      Sum of Squares      Mean Squares
  Regression            2         1796.63837         898.31919
  Residual             11         1045.71020          95.06456

  F =         9.44957

  Signif F = .0041
```

|  | | Variables in the Equation | | | | |
|---|---|---|---|---|---|
| Variable | B | SE B | Beta | T | Sig T |
| DENSITY | 17.62532 | 24.35257 | .14270 | .724 | .4843 |
| POVERTY | 1.77901 | .48009 | .73062 | 3.706 | .0035 |
| (Constant) | −52.02420 | 61.48027 |  | −.846 | .4155 |

of freedom for the residual sum of squares is equal to $n - k$. This ratio of residual sum of squares to degrees of freedom is the second estimate of the population variance, and in Figure 15.5 it is labeled as the residual "mean square."

The $F$ test for the significance of $R^2$ is based on the ratio of these two estimates of variance or mean squares, shown as follows.

$$F = \frac{\text{Regression Variance}}{\text{Residual Variance}}$$

$$F = \frac{\text{Mean Square for the Regression}}{\text{Mean Square for the Residual}}$$

The obtained value of $F$ can be directly compared with a critical $F$ at a chosen alpha level with $k$ and $n - k$ degrees of freedom. If $F_{\text{obt}} \geq F_{\text{crit}}$, your decision is to reject the null hypothesis. Again, many computer software programs report only the exact probability of the $F$ statistic, under the assumption that the null hypothesis is true and $R^2 = 0$. If this exact probability is equal to or less than your chosen alpha level, your decision is to reject the null hypothesis. If the reported exact probability is greater than your alpha level, you fail to reject the null hypothesis.

In Figure 15.5, we report the results of an $F$ test for our murder rate, poverty, and household density example. Before we begin, we should formally state our null and alternative hypotheses:

$H_0$: $b_{\text{Poverty}}$ and $b_{\text{Density}} = 0$ \qquad or $R^2_{\text{Poverty, Density}} = 0$

$H_1$: $b_{\text{Poverty}}$ and $b_{\text{Density}} \neq 0$ \qquad or $R^2_{\text{Poverty, Density}} \neq 0$

Let's first conduct this hypothesis test by going to the $F$ table (Table B.5 of Appendix B) to find a critical value of $F$. We select an alpha level of .05. With $k = 2$ and $n = 14$, we have 2 and 11 degrees of freedom, and our critical value of $F$ is 3.98. Our decision rule, then, is to reject the null hypothesis if $F_{\text{obt}} \geq 3.98$, and fail to reject if $F_{\text{obt}} < 3.98$. As shown in Figure 15.5, the $F$ value obtained from the regression equation utilizing both poverty and household density to predict rates of murder is 9.45. Because this is greater than the critical $F$ value of 3.98, we would reject the null hypothesis that $R^2 = 0$.

Figure 15.5 also reports the exact probability of our obtained $F$, and it is .0041. This tells us that the probability of obtaining an $F$ value of 9.45 if the null hypothesis was true is .0041. This probability is well below an alpha of .05, so we can safely reject the null hypothesis that both of the slope coefficients when used together to predict the dependent variable are equal to zero. We can instead conclude that there is a significant linear relationship between the independent variables of poverty and household density used together to explain rates of murder within cities.

The $F$ test for the significance of the $R^2$ can also be made directly from the $R^2$ value itself, without computing the various sum of squares and mean squares. The formula is as follows.

$$F = \frac{R^2}{1 - R^2} \frac{n - k - 1}{k} \tag{15.11}$$

No matter how it is calculated, the $F$ test has $k$ and $n - k - 1$ degrees of freedom. For our data in Figure 15.5, the value of $F_{\text{obt}}$ with this formula would be:

$$F_{\text{obt}} = \frac{.63}{1 - .63} \cdot \frac{14 - 2 - 1}{2}$$

$$= \left(\frac{.63}{.37}\right)\left(\frac{11}{2}\right)$$

$$= (1.703)(5.5)$$

$$= 9.37$$

This value of $F_{\text{obt}}$ is very comparable to that found from the mean square formula. Our decision would still be to reject the null hypothesis that $R^2 = 0$.

If we reject the null hypothesis that $R^2 = 0$, we know only that at least one of the partial slope coefficients is significantly different from zero. If we want to know which specific partial slopes are significant, we must perform hypothesis tests on our individual slope coefficients. The hypothesis tests associated with partial slopes are very similar to the tests we conducted in Chapter 14 for bivariate slope coefficients. Specifically, we want to determine whether each partial slope coefficient is significantly different from zero. The null hypothesis in this case would state that the true population parameter for each independent variable, $\beta_i$, is zero.

Just as we did with the bivariate slope hypothesis tests in Chapter 14, we use the $t$ statistic and sampling distribution to test this hypothesis. The calculations for the $t$ statistic in the multiple regression case are, however, much more complicated. The $t$ statistic we use for our partial slope coefficient hypothesis test simply is the ratio of the partial slope to the standard error of the slope:

$$t = \frac{b_i}{s_{bi}} \tag{15.12}$$

The sampling distribution used for the $t$ statistic is the student's $t$ with $(n - k - 1)$ degrees of freedom, where $k$ is the number of independent variables in the regression equation.

The formula may look easy, but the complicated part is in estimating the denominator, the standard error of the partial slope. For a two-variable multiple regression problem $(x_1, x_2)$, the estimate for the standard error of the slope can be derived from the formulas

$$s_{byx_1 \cdot x_2} = \sqrt{\frac{\text{Residual Mean Square}}{\Sigma x_1^2 (1 - r^2_{x_1 x_2})}}$$

$$s_{byx_2 \cdot x_1} = \sqrt{\frac{\text{Residual Mean Square}}{\Sigma x_2^2 (1 - r^2_{x_1 x_2})}} \tag{15.13}$$

where
$\Sigma x_1^2 =$ the sum of squares for $x_1$
$\Sigma x_2^2 =$ the sum of squares for $x_2$
$R^2_{x_1 x_2} =$ the squared correlation coefficient between $x_1$ and $x_2$

Fortunately, we do not require you to calculate the standard error of the partial slope coefficient or any other statistics from a multiple regression analysis necessary to do hypothesis tests. Most of the time, you can rely on statistical software programs (like SPSS, SAS, BMDP, MINITAB, or STATA) to do the calculations for you. In the remainder of this chapter, therefore, we simply report the results of the calculations and work through the interpretation.

For the sake of illustration, let's go through the steps of testing the significance of the partial regression slopes with our example of murder rates, poverty, and household density. The necessary information to make this hypothesis test is shown in Figure 15.5.[4]

First, we direct your attention to the portion of the table that says, "Variables in the Equation." Under this heading, you find the partial slopes ($B$), the standard error of each slope, the beta coefficients (beta weights or standardized partial slopes), the resulting $t$ values obtained for each slope, and the *exact* significance level (two-tailed) that corresponds to each $t$ value. Because these are two-tailed probabilities, you will have to divide the reported value by 2 if you are testing a one-tailed alternative hypothesis. The row displaying the "Constant" refers to the $y$ intercept from the equation.

We are interested in testing the null hypothesis associated with each partial slope coefficient that there is no linear relationship between rates of poverty and murder and that there is no linear relationship between household density and murder. That is, we are testing the null hypothesis that the population parameters, $\beta_{x_1}$ *and* $\beta_{x_2}$, are both equal to zero. The alternative hypotheses state that the slope coefficients in the population are not equal to zero. These null and research hypotheses for each partial slope can be expressed as follows:

$H_0$: $\beta_{\text{Poverty}} = 0$
$H_1$: $\beta_{\text{Poverty}} \neq 0$

$H_0$: $\beta_{\text{Density}} = 0$
$H_1$: $\beta_{\text{Density}} \neq 0$

The next step in our hypothesis test is to select an alpha level with the appropriate degrees of freedom and to determine what the critical value of $t$ is. You can now select an alpha level (let's use an alpha of .05) and go to the $t$ table (Table B.3) in Appendix B with $n - k - 1$ degrees of freedom and find the critical value of $t$. For this example, with $n = 14$ and $k = 2$, we have $14 - 2 - 1$, that is, 11, degrees of freedom. The critical value of $t$ with an alpha of .05 for a two-tailed hypothesis test and 11 degrees of freedom is 2.201. If our obtained $t$ is greater than or equal to 2.201 or less than or equal to $-2.201$, we will reject the null hypothesis.

Many computer software programs that do multiple regression analysis do not print the critical value of $t$ for you because the program does not know if you are conducting a one- or a two-tailed test and what particular alpha level you have chosen. What they do usually print for you, however, is the exact probability of each $t$ statistic (two-tailed) under the assumption that the null hypothesis is true. This exact probability is displayed for you in Figure 15.5 under the column labeled "Sig $T$" (for the significance of $t$). The reported probability is the probability of getting the partial regression slope you did if the null hypothesis was true and the population partial slope coefficient was equal to zero. Your decision to reject the null hypothesis is the same as before. If this reported probability is less than or equal to your chosen alpha level, your decision is to reject the null hypothesis. If the reported probability is greater than your selected alpha level, your decision is to fail to reject the null hypothesis. To conduct our hypothesis test, all we need now is the obtained $t$ statistic for each partial slope coefficient. We report these for you in Figure 15.5 under the heading $T$. We now proceed with our test.

We can see from Figure 15.5 that the partial slope coefficient for the effect of household density on murder rates is 17.62 and that the obtained $t$ value for that partial slope coefficient is .724. The critical value of $t$ we got from the $t$ table with an alpha of .05 was ±2.201. Because $-t_{crit} < t_{obt} < t_{crit}$ we would not reject the null hypothesis that this partial slope coefficient is equal to zero. Under the heading "Sig $T$," you can also see that the exact probability of a sample slope coefficient this large if the population coefficient was actually zero is .4843. Remember that we will reject the null hypothesis that the slope coefficient is zero only if the obtained $t$ is very unlikely. By "very unlikely," we have in previous chapters meant that it would occur by chance with a probability equal to .05 or .01 or .001. By this decision rule, .4843 is not very unlikely, and we fail to reject the null hypothesis. We would conclude, therefore, that there is no significant linear effect of household density on murder rates once percent poverty is controlled.

The partial slope coefficient for percent poverty is 1.78, and the obtained $t$ value is 3.706. With our critical $t$ of ±2.201, we would reject the null hypothesis that the population slope coefficient is equal to zero ($t_{obt} > t_{crit}$; 3.706 > 2.201). If we look at the exact probability, we can see that the probability of getting a $t$ that large if the null hypothesis is true is only .0035. Because the exact probability is less than .05 (.0035 < .05), we reject the null hypothesis. Let us put this another way. If the partial slope coefficient in the population was actually zero, we would obtain a sample value of 1.78 by chance alone less than four times out of 1000. Because this is a very unlikely event, we reject the null hypothesis that the slope coefficient in the population is equal to zero. Instead, we conclude that there is a significant positive linear effect of percent poverty on murder rates even after controlling for the number of people in the household.

We suggested to you earlier that, in addition to their use in conducting hypothesis tests, the obtained $t$ statistic can also be used to compare the relative effects of two independent variables on the dependent variable. If you want to know which independent variable has the stronger effect, simply compare the absolute value of each variable's obtained $t$ statistic. For a given regression equation, the greater the $t_{obt}$, the stronger the effect the variable has on the dependent variable.[5] In our example, the obtained $t$ of the partial slope for household density was .724, and the $t_{obt}$ for percent poverty was 3.706. Because the absolute value of 3.706 is greater than .724, we would conclude that poverty has a stronger effect on murder rates than does household density. This conclusion is consistent with our earlier findings.

Let's move on to another example from the criminological literature. For the remainder of the chapter, we place more emphasis on the interpretation of multiple regression analysis, rather than on the calculation of these coefficients.

## *15.6 ANOTHER EXAMPLE: PRISON DENSITY, STAFFING, AND RATES OF INMATE-TO-INMATE ASSAULT*

Several researchers have examined the effect of prison overcrowding on the frequency with which inmates assault one another. Results of this research have remained equivocal, however, with some researchers finding a significant positive relationship between prison overcrowding and assaults between inmates (Gaes, 1985; Nacci et al., 1977) and others report finding no relationship (Innes, 1986; Sechrest, 1991).

Let's set up a hypothetical study investigating the extent to which prison overcrowding is related to the rate of inmate-to-inmate assault. To do this, we select a sample of prisons and collect data for three variables: inmate-to-inmate assault rates, prison density, which we use as our measure of overcrowding, and the mean age of inmates in the facility. We operationalize overcrowding by a "prison density index" computed by dividing a prison's inmate population by the prison's official rated inmate capacity. For example, if a prison had a population of 500 and a rated capacity of 400, it would yield a density index of 1.25, indicating that the facility was 25 percent over capacity, that is, that the prison was overcrowded by 25 percent. We suspect that the rate of inmate assault is positively related to the extent to which the prison is overcrowded. We collect information on age because previous research has found that, compared to facilities with older populations, prisons with younger inmates tend to have higher rates of inmate-to-inmate assault.

The hypothetical data we obtain from a random sample of 30 correctional facilities is presented in Table 15.5. Also reported in Table 15.5 are each of the component values necessary to calculate the bivariate correlation coefficients between each of the variables in addition to the correlation coefficients themselves. We do not go through the labor of computing these correlation coefficients by hand here, but it would be a good exercise for you to do so on your own before moving on.

The bivariate correlation coefficients shown in Table 15.5 indicate that both independent variables have moderately strong relationships with the dependent variable. The relationship between overcrowding (prison density) and inmate-to-inmate assault rates is moderate and positive ($r = .62$), indicating that overcrowding in prisons tends to increase the number of assaults between inmates. The correlation between the mean age of inmates and inmate-to-inmate assault rates is negative and moderately strong ($r = -.76$), indicating that prisons with a younger inmate population tend to have higher assault rates than prisons with older inmate populations. The correlation between our two independent variables is $-.56$. Although not small, the $R^2$ value is only .31, indicating that only 31 percent of the variance in one independent variable is explained by the other. The correlation is not large enough to create a problem of multicollinearity for us.

With these bivariate correlation coefficients and the respective standard deviations of each variable, we can calculate the partial slope coefficients from Equations 15.3 and 15.4.

Partial slope coefficient for prison overcrowding regressed on inmate assault rates:

$$b_1 = \left(\frac{3.78}{.28}\right)\left(\frac{.62 - (-.76)(-.56)}{1 - (-.56)^2}\right)$$

$$= (13.5)\left(\frac{.62 - .42}{1 - .31}\right)$$

$$= (13.5)\left(\frac{.2}{.69}\right)$$

$$= 3.92$$

Partial slope coefficient for mean age of prison inmate population regressed on inmate assault rates:

$$b_2 = \left(\frac{3.78}{4.2}\right)\left(\frac{-.76 - (.61)(-.56)}{1 - (-.56)^2}\right)$$

$$= (.9)\left(\frac{-.76 - -.34}{1 - .31}\right)$$

$$= (.9)\left(\frac{-.42}{.69}\right)$$

$$= -.549$$

The partial slope coefficient for overcrowding, $b_1$, indicates that on average, inmate-to-inmate assault rates increase by 3.92 with every 1 percent increase in prison overcrowding while holding the mean age of the inmate population constant. The partial slope coefficient for mean inmate age, $b_2$, indicates that on average, assault rates between inmates decrease by $-.549$ with every 1-year increase in mean age while holding prison density constant.

These partial slopes help us determine the form of the linear effect for a given independent variable. However, because their magnitude is affected by the underlying units of measurement, they are not very useful in comparing relative effects across independent variables. This is why it is necessary to calculate other statistics such as the standardized partial slope coefficient or beta weights ($b^*$). Before we do this, however, we solve the multiple regression equation for this model:

$$y = a + b_1 x_1 + b_2 x_2$$

$$= a + (3.92)x_1 + (-.549)x_2$$

Now that we have obtained the partial slopes for overcrowding ($b_1$) and age ($b_2$), we can compute the intercept value by substituting the mean of the dependent variable and the means of the two independent variables (Table 15.5) into the equation as follows:

$$a = \bar{x}_y - b_1\bar{x}_1 - b_2\bar{x}_2$$

$$= 10.94 - (3.92)(1.29) - (-.549)(29.26)$$

$$= 10.94 - 5.06 - (-16.06)$$

$$= 21.94$$

**TABLE 15.5. Hypothetical Inmate-to-Inmate Assault Rates per 100 Inmate Population, Prison Density Index, and Mean Age of Inmates for a Random Sample of 30 Prisons**

| Case | Prison | Assault Rate $y$ | Density Index $x_1$ | Mean Age $x_2$ |
|---|---|---|---|---|
| 1 | Prison A | 10.20 | 1.50 | 25.80 |
| 2 | Prison B | 8.20 | 1.00 | 32.10 |
| 3 | Prison C | 11.30 | 1.60 | 26.20 |
| 4 | Prison D | 9.20 | 1.20 | 29.60 |
| 5 | Prison E | 5.30 | .98 | 34.50 |
| 6 | Prison F | 8.50 | 1.10 | 27.50 |
| 7 | Prison G | 8.60 | 1.30 | 30.20 |
| 8 | Prison H | 7.50 | .88 | 33.20 |
| 9 | Prison I | 15.30 | 1.90 | 27.20 |
| 10 | Prison J | 10.50 | 1.50 | 26.30 |
| 11 | Prison K | 12.50 | 1.50 | 28.30 |
| 12 | Prison L | 5.40 | 1.10 | 32.30 |
| 13 | Prison M | 10.50 | 1.40 | 23.50 |
| 14 | Prison N | 15.40 | 1.40 | 24.50 |
| 15 | Prison O | 12.80 | 1.20 | 24.50 |
| 16 | Prison P | 13.50 | 1.30 | 27.50 |
| 17 | Prison Q | 17.50 | 1.80 | 25.80 |
| 18 | Prison R | 11.50 | 1.60 | 32.60 |
| 19 | Prison S | 19.00 | 1.40 | 21.20 |
| 20 | Prison T | 14.20 | 1.20 | 26.50 |
| 21 | Prison U | 11.40 | 1.60 | 32.00 |
| 22 | Prison V | 9.80 | 1.10 | 29.90 |
| 23 | Prison W | 6.60 | .85 | 36.20 |
| 24 | Prison X | 8.90 | .95 | 35.00 |
| 25 | Prison Y | 10.60 | 1.10 | 29.80 |
| 26 | Prison Z | 12.50 | 1.20 | 25.60 |
| 27 | Prison AA | 7.40 | 1.10 | 33.50 |
| 28 | Prison BB | 3.30 | 1.20 | 38.20 |
| 29 | Prison CC | 17.50 | 1.70 | 25.20 |
| 30 | Prison DD | 13.20 | .90 | 33.10 |

$$\Sigma_y = 328.10 \quad \Sigma x_1 = 38.56 \quad \Sigma x_2 = 877.80$$
$$\bar{x}_y = 10.94 \quad \bar{x}_{x_1} = 1.29 \quad \bar{x}_{x_2} = 29.26$$
$$s_y = 3.78 \quad s_{x_1} = .28 \quad s_{x_2} = 4.2$$
$$\Sigma y^2 = 4002.10 \quad \Sigma x_1^2 = 51.85 \quad \Sigma x_2^2 = 2,6193.2$$

$$\Sigma y x_1 = 440.6 \quad \Sigma y x_2 = 9,250.9 \quad \Sigma x_1 x_2 = 1,109.2$$
$$r_{y x_1} = .62 \quad r_{y x_2} = -.76 \quad r_{x_1 x_2} = -.56$$

The intercept value we obtained from this equation indicates that, when both independent variables are equal to zero, the average value of $y$, our inmate assault rate, will be 21.94.

Now that we have solved for the intercept and both partial slope coefficients, the multiple regression equation for this model can be expressed as:

$$y = 21.94 + (3.92)x_1 + (-.549)x_2$$

This least-squares regression equation represents the best linear model we could obtain using our sample data to predict inmate-to-inmate assaults using what we know about overcrowding and the mean age of the inmate population in prisons. With this equation, we can predict inmate-to-inmate assault rates in prisons. For example, our best prediction of a prison's inmate assault rate ($\hat{y}$) for a prison with an overcrowding index score of 1.6 and a mean age of 24 would be obtained by substituting these $x$ values into the regression equation as follows:

$$\hat{y} = 21.94 + (3.92)(1.6) + (-.549)(24)$$

$$= 21.94 + 6.27 + -13.18$$

$$= 15.03$$

As shown, our least-squares multiple regression equation predicts that a prison with an overcrowding index of 1.6 and a mean inmate age of 24 would have an inmate-to-inmate assault rate of 15.03. Remember that the predictions we make using this regression equation are not perfect and that we continue to have error in our regression equation and our predictions from that equation.

Now let's return to the issue of comparing the relative magnitude of effects for our two independent variables. Recall that standardized partial slope coefficients, called beta weights ($b^*$), are one way to achieve this end. Using Equation 15.7, let's compute the beta weights for overcrowding and mean age:

$$b_1^* = 3.7\left(\frac{.28}{3.78}\right)$$

$$= (3.7)(.074)$$

$$= .274$$

$$b_2^* = (-.54)\left(\frac{4.19}{3.78}\right)$$

$$= (-.54)(1.108)$$

$$= -.598$$

The obtained absolute value of the beta weight for age is almost double that of the beta weight for prison overcrowding ($-.598$ vs. $.274$). This indicates that mean inmate age in prison settings has a much stronger effect on inmate-to-inmate assaults than does overcrowding.

Another way of assessing the relative importance of the independent variables in predicting the dependent variable is through the partial correlation coefficients and a partitioning of the multiple coefficient of determination. Using Equation 15.9, let's compute $r_{yx_1 \cdot x_2}$ and $r_{yx_2 \cdot x_1}$.

Partial correlation coefficient for overcrowding and assault controlling for age:

$$r_{yx_1 \cdot x_2} = \frac{.62 - (-.76)(-.56)}{\sqrt{1 - (-.76)^2} \sqrt{1 - (-.56)^2}}$$

$$= \frac{.62 - .426}{\sqrt{1 - .58} \sqrt{1 - .31}}$$

$$= .359$$

Partial correlation coefficient for age and assaults controlling for overcrowding:

$$r_{yx_2 \cdot x_1} = \frac{-.76 - (.62)(-.56)}{\sqrt{1 - (.62)^2} \sqrt{1 - (.56)^2}}$$

$$= \frac{-.76 - -.35}{\sqrt{1 - .38} \sqrt{1 - .31}}$$

$$= -.625$$

The partial correlation coefficient between age and assault when controlling for prison overcrowding is $-.625$. Its absolute value is greater than the partial correlation between overcrowding and assault when controlling for inmate age ($.359$). This would lead us to conclude that age is more important than overcrowding in explaining inmate assault rates.

With these partial correlation coefficients, we can calculate the multiple coefficient of determination. Using Equation 15.9, we would obtain this coefficient by:

Multiple coefficient of determination for overcrowding and age on assault:

$$R^2_{yx_1 x_2} = (.62)^2 + (-.63)^2(1 - (.62)^2)$$

$$= (.38) + (.40)(1 - .38)$$

$$= .63$$

The obtained $R^2_{yx_1 x_2} = .63$ indicates that both overcrowding and mean age, when used together, explain 63 percent of the variance in inmate-to-inmate assault rates in prisons.

With the multiple coefficient of determination calculated, we can now determine the relative contribution in explained variance made by each independent variable. Recall that we do this by subtracting the bivariate coefficient of determination for each variable from the multiple coefficient of determination. For example, to determine the relative contribution that age has in explaining assault rates, we simply subtract the bivariate coefficient of determination for overcrowding on inmate assaults $(r_{yx_1})^2$ by the multiple coefficient of determination. This will give us the proportion of explained variance added to the total when mean age is added to the model explaining inmate assault rates.

In the calculated multiple coefficient of determination, we found that prison density by itself explains 38 percent of the variance in inmate assault rates. When age is considered, it contributes an additional 25 percent to the total explained variance over and above that explained by prison density. The $R^2$ change value for age, then, is 25 percent (63%–38%). This indicates that age contributes unique information about the dependent variable of assault rates that is not available through data on overcrowding.

When age is the first variable considered we find the following:

$$R^2_{yx_1x_2} = (-.76) + (.36)^2 [1 - (-.76)^2]$$

$$= (.58) + (.13)(.42)$$

$$= .58 + .05$$

$$= .63$$

By itself, age explains 58 percent of the total variance, and prison overcrowding explains only 5 percent additional variance beyond that explained by age. It would appear, then, that, although both variables contribute to the total explained variance, the age of the inmates gives us more information about assault rates than does the extent of overcrowding.

After having examined the issue of the relative effects of the two variables, we need to perform hypothesis tests to determine whether the multiple coefficient of determination and each partial regression slope are significantly different from zero. The information pertaining to these tests is provided for you in Figure 15.6. Before we proceed to the hypothesis tests, however, we would like to discuss a term referred to in Figure 15.6 as the "Adjusted $R$ square."

The *adjusted* $R^2$ is often used in multiple regression problems because in some instances the unadjusted value gives an inflated estimate of how much variance is explained, and, therefore, how good a particular regression model fits the data. The estimated $R^2$ is at times inflated because, in calculating it, sample correlation coefficients are used to estimate population values. These sample coefficients, which vary from sample to sample, are treated as if they were error free. In fact, the sample estimates are positively biased, inflating the sample estimate of $R^2$. Because of this bias, it is a good idea to examine the adjusted $R^2$ of your multiple regression model. Formally, the equation used to obtain the Adjusted $R^2$ is as displayed as follows.

$$R^2_{\text{Adjusted}} = R^2 - \frac{k(1 - R^2)}{n - k - 1} \tag{15.14}$$

where
  $k$ = the number of independent variables

Even though the adjusted value of $R^2$ is already displayed for you in Figure 15.6, you can see that if we plugged the appropriate values into the equation, we would obtain the same result:

$$R^2_{\text{Adjusted}} = .63216 - \frac{(2)(1 - .63216)}{30 - 2 - 1}$$

$$= .63216 - \frac{(2)(.3678)}{27}$$

$$= .6049$$

```
                        MULTIPLE REGRESSION

Equation Number 1   Dependent Variable..   ASSAULT

Block Number 1.   Method: Enter   AGE   DENSITY

Variable(s) Entered on Step Number
       1..   DENSITY
       2..   AGE

Multiple R            .79509
R Square              .63216
Adjusted R Square     .60491
Standard Error       2.37419

Analysis of Variance

                    df      Sum of Squares      Mean Squares
Regression           2          261.55637         130.77819
Residual            27          152.19329           5.63679

F =          23.20083

Signif F = .00001
```

```
----------------------------Variables in the Equation-----------------------------

Variable          B          SE B         Beta          T        Sig T
AGE          −.547323      .126790      −.606939      −4.317      .0002
DENSITY      3.721021     1.890986       .276668       1.968      .0594
(Constant)  22.168592     5.469280                     4.053      .0004
```

FIGURE 15.6. Multiple regression results for prison overcrowding and mean age of inmate population regressed on rates of inmate-to-inmate assault rates in 30 prisons.

In this example, the unadjusted $R^2$ value is .63, and its adjusted value is .60, so the shrinkage in the amount of explained variance in this particular regression model is slight.

The coefficient of determination ($R^2$) always increases some or stays the same when additional independent variables are added into the equation. For this reason, some statisticians believe that the adjusted $R^2$ is a more appropriate indicator of explained variance than its unadjusted value. The amount of the adjustment or shrinkage depends on the ratio of the number of independent variables in the model to sample size. If there are many independent variables relative to the sample size, the adjustment will be large and the adjustment will amount to a substantial reduction in $R^2$. In larger samples with fewer independent variables, however, the adjustment makes less difference. Some statisticians have recommended as a rule of thumb that there be 30 observations for each one independent variable. When using multiple regression, however, you should always examine both the unadjusted and the adjusted $R^2$ values.

Let's move on to testing the significance of our partial slope coefficients and the entire multiple regression equation. We first want to address the extent to which there is a significant linear relationship between the dependent variable, the number of inmate assaults, and our two independent variables, prison overcrowding and inmate age, considered in combination. The null and research hypotheses for this test can be expressed as follows:

$H_0$: $\beta_{\text{Overcrowding}}$, $\beta_{\text{Age}} = 0$

$H_1$: $\beta_{\text{Overcrowding}}$, $\beta_{\text{Age}} \neq 0$

As stated, this hypothesis test really determines whether the $R^2$ value is significantly different from zero. If we reject this null hypothesis, we can conclude that at least one of the partial slope coefficients is significantly different from zero. Our next set of hypothesis tests, then, is to determine which specific slopes are significantly different from zero.

We use the $F$ statistic and sampling distribution to test the null hypothesis about $R^2$. We adopt an alpha level of .01 for this test and find $F_{\text{crit}}$ with the appropriate degrees of freedom. As before, however, we also provide the exact probability level of $F_{\text{obt}}$. With a sample size of 30 and two independent variables, our $F$ test has 2 and 27 degrees of freedom. For an alpha level of .01 with 2 and 27 degrees of freedom, our critical value of $F$ is 5.49. Our decision rule, then, is to reject the null hypothesis if $F_{\text{obt}} \geq 5.49$ and fail to reject if $F_{\text{obt}} < 5.49$.

All of the information necessary to make a decision about the null hypothesis is provided in the top portion of Table 15.7. The obtained value of $F$ for the entire equation is 23.2. Because an $F_{\text{obt}}$ of 23.2 is greater than the critical $F$ of 5.49, our decision is to reject the null hypothesis. Table 15.7 shows that, if the null hypothesis was true and the population $R^2$ was really zero, the probability level of observing a sample $R^2$ of .63 by chance is less than 1 in 10,000. The exact probability level of .00000 is much less than our chosen alpha level of .01, so again we would be led to reject the null hypothesis. We can conclude that there is a significant linear relationship between prison overcrowding and the mean age of the inmate population when used together to predict rates of inmate-to-inmate assault.

Next we determine exactly which independent variable(s) is significant in predicting the dependent variable. The null hypotheses we are testing is that the population parameters, $\beta_1$ and $\beta_2$, are each equal to zero. The research hypotheses state that the slope coefficients for the effect of inmate age and prison overcrowding on inmate assaults in the population are not equal to zero. These can be formally expressed as follows:

$H_0$: $\beta_{\text{Overcrowding}} = 0$
$H_1$: $\beta_{\text{Overcrowding}} \neq 0$

$H_0$: $\beta_{\text{Age}} = 0$
$H_1$: $\beta_{\text{Age}} \neq 0$

The next step in our hypothesis test is to select an alpha level, determine our degrees of freedom, and identify the critical value of our test statistic. Let's continue with an alpha of .01. The statistic we use to test our null hypothesis is the student's $t$, and the sampling distribution is the $t$ distribution with $n - k$ degrees of freedom. Our critical value of $t$ with an alpha of .01, a two-tailed hypothesis test, and 28 degrees of freedom is $\pm 2.763$. Our decision rule will be to reject the null hypothesis if $t_{\text{obt}} \geq 2.763$ or if $t_{\text{obt}} \leq -2.763$, and to fail to reject the null hypothesis if

$-2.763 < t_{obt} < 2.763$. We also conduct this hypothesis test with the exact probability of $t_{obt}$.

From Figure 15.6 you can see that the partial slope coefficient for the effect of age on inmate assaults is $-.547$ and that the $t$ statistic is $-4.317$. Because this $t$ statistic is lower than the critical $t$ of $-2.763$, we reject the null hypothesis that the slope coefficient in the population is zero. You can see that the exact probability (two-tailed) of this $t_{obt}$ is .0002. Because this probability is lower than our critical alpha of .01, we are again led to reject the null hypothesis. We conclude that the age of the inmate population is significantly related to the rate of inmate-to-inmate assaults. As the mean age of the inmate population increases, rates of assault between inmates decrease. In other words, our sample data indicate that prisons with younger inmate populations tend to have significantly higher rates of assault between inmates than prisons with older inmate populations. The slope coefficient for the effect of prison density on inmate assaults is 3.72, with a $t$ value of 1.968. Because the obtained value of $t$ is not greater than the critical $t$ of 2.763, we fail to reject the null hypothesis stating that the slope coefficient in the population for prison overcrowding is equal to zero. We conclude that there is no significant linear relationship between overcrowding and rates of inmate-to-inmate assault within prisons. Finally, notice that the absolute value of $t_{obt}$ for age (4.317) is greater than that for prison density (1.968). This would also lead us to believe that inmate age has more of an effect on the rate of inmate assaults than does prison density.

## 15.7 SUMMARY

In this chapter we have examined techniques of *multiple regression analysis.* The multiple regression model is really a straightforward extension of the bivariate, or one-variable, model. The slope coefficient in the multiple regression model, the *partial slope coefficient,* reflects the change in the dependent variable for a one-unit change in one independent variable while holding all other independent variables constant. The relative explanatory power of independent variables can be assessed by *partial correlation coefficients,* the value of $R^2$ *change,* and the absolute value of the $t$ ratios. In deciding which explanatory variables to include in a multiple regression model, the optimal strategy is to include those variables that are strongly correlated with the dependent variable but uncorrelated with other independent variables.

## Key Terms

| | |
|---|---|
| adjusted $R^2$ | multivariate regression model |
| beta weight | partial correlation coefficient |
| constant | partial slope (or regression) coefficient |
| multicollinearity | $R^2_{change}$ |
| multiple coefficient of determination ($R^2$) | standardized partial slope |
| multiple regression | standardized regression coefficient |

# Problems

1. Suppose we were interested in the extent to which rates of divorce and mean age of the population within states affected state-level rates of violent crime. To examine these relationships, we take a random sample of 35 states and obtain the divorce rate per 100,000 population for each, the mean age in each state, and rates of violent crime per 100,000. Assume that this is the multiple regression output you obtained:

```
                        MULTIPLE REGRESSION

Dependent Variable..   VIOLENT CRIME

Multiple R              .79527
R Square                .63245
Adjusted R Square       .60948

Analysis of Variance

                    df      Sum of Squares      Mean Squares
Regression          2          324.53830          162.26915
Residual           32          188.60456            5.89389

F =         27.53175

Signif F = .00052
```

| ------------------------------ | Variables in the Equation ------------------------------- |

| Variable | B | SE B | Beta | T | Sig T |
|---|---|---|---|---|---|
| DIVORCE | .871106 | .119850 | .594392 | 4.268 | .0001 |
| AGE | −.146392 | .158443 | −.133410 | −3.110 | .0011 |
| (Constant) | 19.642352 | 2.736158 | | .600 | .5526 |

From this output, answer the following questions.
a. Specify the exact least-squares multiple regression equation.
b. Interpret both partial slope coefficients and the intercept value.
c. Using this output, how would you examine the relative importance of each independent variable?
d. What is the total variance explained?
e. Conduct a hypothesis test using the obtained output, both for the entire regression model and for the independent slope coefficients. Use an alpha level of .01 for both tests. What are your formal hypothesis statements? What do you conclude based on the $F$ test and the two $t$ tests?

2. Suppose that we are interested in the reasons why escapes occur in local jails. To investigate this issue, we take a random sample of 30 jails. We ask the jail manager how many escapes they had from their facility in the past year. This is our dependent variable. Based on our knowledge of the literature, we also know that work-related morale and the extent to which facilities are understaffed affects parameters such as supervision and motivation to identify and solve problems. To measure the level of morale, we ask jail employees to respond to a number of questions regarding their morale (e.g., "I think my supervisors appreciate my work," "I feel secure in my job," "I like the people I work with"). With their responses we compute a morale index with high scores indicating high morale and low scores indicating low morale.

To determine the extent that the institution is understaffed, we construct a jail staff-to-inmate ratio. Again, high scores indicate a large number of staff relative to inmates and low scores indicate a small number of jail staff relative to inmates.

| | Number of Escapes | Morale Score | Staff-to-Inmate Ratio |
|---|---|---|---|
| 1 | 12.00 | 3.00 | .22 |
| 2 | 10.00 | 7.00 | .41 |
| 3 | 3.00 | 14.00 | .66 |
| 4 | 7.00 | 8.00 | .45 |
| 5 | 9.00 | 9.00 | .32 |
| 6 | 13.00 | 5.00 | .33 |
| 7 | 17.00 | 2.00 | .10 |
| 8 | 12.00 | 5.00 | .30 |
| 9 | 15.00 | 4.00 | .20 |
| 10 | 9.00 | 5.00 | .50 |
| 11 | 3.00 | 7.00 | .60 |
| 12 | 5.00 | 3.00 | .40 |
| 13 | 11.00 | 2.00 | .20 |
| 14 | 14.00 | 5.00 | .50 |
| 15 | 7.00 | 8.00 | .40 |
| 16 | 10.00 | 5.00 | .20 |
| 17 | 14.00 | 3.00 | .30 |
| 18 | 15.00 | 2.00 | .40 |
| 19 | 17.00 | 2.00 | .10 |
| 20 | 6.00 | 8.00 | .20 |
| 21 | 9.00 | 4.00 | .20 |
| 22 | 3.00 | 10.00 | .50 |
| 23 | 2.00 | 11.00 | .60 |
| 24 | 4.00 | 7.00 | .30 |
| 25 | 13.00 | 2.00 | .30 |
| 26 | 11.00 | 8.00 | .50 |
| 27 | 14.00 | 4.00 | .30 |
| 28 | 9.00 | 4.00 | .30 |
| 29 | 5.00 | 11.00 | .40 |
| 30 | 4.00 | 14.00 | .50 |

The statistics necessary to calculate the slope coefficients are:

$\Sigma y = 283$      $\Sigma x_1 = 182$      $\Sigma x_2 = 10.7$
$s_y = 4.49$      $s_{x1} = 3.47$      $s_{x2} = .15$
$\bar{y} = 9.43$      $\bar{x}_{x1} = 6.07$      $\bar{x}_{x2} = .36$

$\Sigma y^2 = 3255$      $\Sigma x^2_{x1} = 1454$      $\Sigma x^2_{x2} = 4.44$

$$r_{yx_1} = -.76$$
$$r_{yx_2} = -.63$$
$$r_{x_1x_2} = .67$$

$r_{yx_1 \cdot x_2} = -.59$      $r_{yx_2 \cdot x_1} = -.245$

a. What would the values of $b_1$ and $b_2$ be from these sample statistics? Interpret these coefficients.
b. From your calculated partial slope coefficients and sample means, solve for the value of the intercept ($a$). What is the complete multiple regression equation?
c. Using the above multiple regression equation, predict the value of $Y$ (number of escapes) from a morale score of 8 and a staff ratio score of .3?
d. Calculate the beta weights for each of the partial slope coefficients above. What do they tell you about the relative importance of each independent variable?
e. Calculate the multiple coefficient of determination from these sample statistics. What does this coefficient indicate?

3. In a 1994 article, Harold Grasmick and Anne McGill conducted a study on the religious beliefs and attitudes toward punishing criminal offenders. They found that those people who were religiously conservative saw the character of the offender rather than environmental factors as a cause of crime and were more punitive in their response to crime. You want to conduct a similar study. You first develop three attitude scales; one that measures Punitiveness toward the Criminal (PUN), one that measures Religious Conservatism (REL), and one that measures persons' belief that environmental factors are responsible for crime (ENV). Those who score high on the punitiveness scale want to punish convicted criminals severely, those who score high on the religious conservatism scale take a strict interpretation of the Bible, those who score high on the environmental factors scale think that social factors are to blame for crime rather than the evil character of the offender. Based on the Grasmick and McGill study, you expect that religious conservatism will be positively related to punitiveness and that a belief in environmental causes of crime will be negatively related to punitiveness. You take a random sample of 15 persons who respond to a questionnaire that contains your attitude scales. You conduct a multiple regression analysis on your data, and here are the results.

| MULTIPLE REGRESSION | | | | | |
|---|---|---|---|---|---|
| Dependent Variable.. | PUN | | | | |
| Multiple $R$ | .81179 | | | | |
| $R$ Square | .65901 | | | | |
| Adjusted $R$ Square | .60218 | | | | |

| | df | Sum of Squares | | Mean Squares | |
|---|---|---|---|---|---|
| Regression | 2 | 481.34136 | | 240.67068 | |
| Residual | 12 | 249.05864 | | 20.75489 | |

$F =$ 11.59586

Signif $F = .0016$

----------------------------Variables in the Equation----------------------------

| Variable | B | SE B | Beta | T | Sig T |
|---|---|---|---|---|---|
| ENV | −1.467559 | .443083 | −.608892 | −3.312 | .0062 |
| REV | 1.075656 | .570909 | .346367 | 1.884 | .0840 |
| (Constant) | 16.245121 | 5.514051 | | 2.946 | .0122 |

With this output, answer the following questions.
a. Specify the exact least-squares multiple regression equation.
b. Interpret both partial slope coefficients and the intercept value.

c. How would you examine the relative importance of each independent variable?

d. What is the total variance explained?

e. Conduct a hypothesis test using the obtained output, both for the entire regression model and for the independent slope coefficients. Use an alpha level of .01 for both tests. What are your formal hypothesis statements? What do you conclude based on the $F$ test and the two $t$ tests?

f. Using the multiple regression equation, predict the punitiveness score for a person who has a religious conservatism score of 8 and an environmental factor score of 2.

## Solutions to Problems

**1. a.** The least-squares regression equation for this problem is:

$$y = a + b_1x_1 + b_2x_2$$

$$= 19.64 + (.871)\text{Divorce Rate} + (-.146)\text{Age}$$

**b.** The partial slope coefficient for the variable DIVORCE indicates that, as the divorce rate per 100,000 population increases by 1, the rate of violent crime per 100,000 increases by .871, controlling for the mean age of the state's population. The partial slope coefficient for the variable AGE indicates that, as the mean age of the state's population increases by 1 year, the rate of violent crime per 100,000 decreases by .146, controlling for the divorce rate. The intercept is 19.64. This tells us that when both the divorce rate and mean age are equal to 0, the rate of violent crime is 19.64 per 100,000.

**c.** The standardized regression coefficient for DIVORCE is .594, and that for AGE is $-.133$. Based on this, then, we would conclude that the divorce rate is more influential in explaining state violent crime rates than is the mean age of the population. A second way to look at the relative strength of the independent variables is to compare the absolute value of their respective $t$ ratios. The $t$ ratio for DIVORCE is 4.268, and that for AGE is $-3.110$. Based on this, we would conclude that the divorce rate is more influential in explaining rates of violence than the mean age of a state's population.

**d.** The divorce rate and mean age together explain approximately 63 percent of the variance in rates of violent crime. The adjusted $R^2$ value is .61, indicating that 61 percent of the variance is explained.

**e.** The null and alternative hypotheses are:

$$H_0: \beta_1, \beta_2 = 0, \text{ or } R^2 = 0$$

$$H_1: \beta_1 \text{ or } \beta_2 \neq 0; \text{ or } R^2 \neq 0.$$

$F_{\text{obt}} = 27.53$. The probability of an $F$ of 27.53, if the null hypothesis was true, is .00052. Because this probability is lower than our alpha of .01, our decision is to reject the null hypothesis that all the slope coefficients are equal to zero.

$$H_0: \beta_{\text{Divorce}} = 0$$

$$H_1: \beta_{\text{Divorce}} > 0$$

$t_{\text{obt}} = 4.268$. The probability of obtaining a $t$ this size if the null hypothesis was true is .0001/2, or .00005. Because this probability is less than our alpha level of .01, we decide to reject the null hypothesis. We conclude that the population partial slope coefficient is greater than 0.

$$H_0: \beta_{\text{Age}} = 0$$

$$H_1: \beta_{\text{Age}} < 0$$

$t_{obt} = -3.11$. The probability of obtaining a $t$ statistic this low if the null hypothesis is true is .0011/2, or .00055. Because this is lower than .01, we reject the null hypothesis.

**2. a.** $b_{Morale} = \left(\dfrac{4.49}{3.47}\right)\left(\dfrac{(-.76) - (-.63)(.67)}{1 - (.67)^2}\right)$

$\qquad = 1.29\left(\dfrac{(-.76) - (-.42)}{1 - .45}\right)$

$\qquad = -.800$

$b_{Staff} = \left(\dfrac{4.49}{.15}\right)\left(\dfrac{(-.63) - (-.76)(.67)}{1 - (.67)^2}\right)$

$\qquad = 29.93\left(\dfrac{(-.63) - (-.51)}{1 - .45}\right)$

$\qquad = -6.585$

The partial slope coefficient for employee morale is $-.800$. This tells us that, as the score on our measure of employee morale increases by 1, the number of jail escapes decreases by .800, controlling for the staff-to-inmate ratio. The partial slope coefficient for the staff-to-inmate ratio is $-6.585$. This indicates that as the staff-to-inmate ratio increases by 1 unit, the number of jail escapes decreases by 6.585.

**b.** $\qquad \bar{y} = a + b_1\bar{x}_1 + b_2\bar{x}_2$

$\qquad 9.43 = a + (-.800)(6.06) + (-6.585)(.36)$

$\qquad 9.43 = a - 7.227$

$\qquad 9.43 + 7.227 = a$

$\qquad 16.657 = a$

The value of the intercept is 16.657, and the full regression equation is:

$y = 16.657 + (-.800)x_1 + (-6.585)x_2$

**c.** $\hat{y} = 16.657 + (-.800)(8) + (-6.585)(.3)$

$\qquad = 16.657 + (-6.400) + (-1.975)$

$\qquad = 16.657 + (-8.375)$

$\qquad = 8.282$

With a staff morale score of 8 and a staff to inmate ratio of .3, we would predict that there would be approximately eight escapes a year.

**d.** The beta weights are:

$b^*_{Morale} = (-.800)\left(\dfrac{3.47}{4.49}\right)$

$\qquad = -.616$

$b^*_{Staff} = (-6.585)\left(\dfrac{.15}{4.49}\right)$

$\qquad = -.197$

The beta weight for staff morale is $-.616$, and the beta weight for the staff-to-inmate ratio is $-.197$. Because the beta weight for morale is greater than that for the staff-to-inmate ratio, it has a stronger effect on the number of jail escapes.

**e.** $R^2 = (-.76)^2 + (-.245)^2[(1 - (-.76)^2]$

$= .58 + (.06)(.42)$

$= .58 + .03$

$= .61$

Together, staff morale and the staff-to-inmate ratio explain approximately 61 percent of the variance in jail escapes.

**3. a.** The least-squares regression equation from the supplied output would be:

$\hat{y} = 16.245 + (-1.467)\,\text{ENV} + 1.076(\text{REL})$

**b.** The partial slope coefficient for the environmental factors variable is $-1.467$. This tells us that, as a person's score on the environmental causes of crime scale increases by 1, his or her score on the punitiveness scale decreases by 1.467, controlling for religious conservatism. The partial slope coefficient for the religious conservatism scale is 1.076. As a person's score on religious conservatism increases by one unit, his or her score on the punitiveness scale increases by 1.076, controlling for the score on environmental factors as a cause of crime. The value of the intercept is 16.245. When both independent variables are zero, a person's score on the punitiveness scale is 16.245.

**c.** The beta weight for ENV is $-.609$. The beta weight for REL is .346. A one-unit change in the ENV variable produces almost twice the change in the dependent variable than the REL variable. Comparing these beta weights would lead us to conclude that the environmental factors scale is more important in explaining punitiveness scores than the religious conservatism variable.

The $t$ ratio for ENV is $-3.312$, and that for REL is only 1.884. We would again conclude that ENV has the greater influence on the dependent variable.

**d.** The adjusted $R^2$ coefficient indicates that, together, the environmental factors and religious conservatism scales explain approximately 60 percent of the variance in the punitiveness measure.

**e.** $H_0$: $\beta_{\text{ENV}}$, $\beta_{\text{REL}} = 0$; or $R^2 = 0$

$H_1$: $\beta_{\text{ENV}}$ or $\beta_{\text{REL}} \neq 0$; or $R^2 \neq 0$

The probability of an $F$ of 11.59, if the null hypothesis was true, is .0016. Because this probability is lower than our chosen alpha of .01, our decision is to reject the null hypothesis that all the slope coefficients are equal to zero.

$H_0$: $\beta_{\text{ENV}} = 0$

$H_1$: $\beta_{\text{ENV}} < 0$

The output gives you an obtained $t$ value of $-3.312$, and the probability of obtaining a $t$ this size if the null hypothesis was true is .0062. Because this is a two-tailed $p$ value, the correct probability for our one-tailed test is .0062 divided by 2, or .0031. Because this probability is lower than our chosen alpha level of .01, we decide to reject the null hypothesis. We conclude that the population partial slope coefficient is less than 0.

$H_0$: $\beta_{\text{REL}} = 0$

$H_1$: $\beta_{\text{REL}} > 0$

The $t$ ratio for the variable ENV is $t_{obt} = 1.884$. The probability of obtaining a $t$ statistic of this magnitude if the null hypothesis is true is .0840. Again, because we are conducting a one-tailed test, our probability is .0840 divided by 2, or .04. Because this probability is greater than .01, our decision is to fail to reject the null hypothesis. The partial slope coefficient between religious conservatism and punitiveness toward criminal offenders is not significantly different from zero in the population, once a belief in environmental causes of crime are controlled.

**f.** $\hat{y} = 16.245 + (-1.467)$ ENV $+ (1.076)$REL

$= 16.245 + (-1.467)(2) + (1.076)(8)$

$= 16.245 + (-2.934) + 8.608$

$= 21.92$

The predicted value of $y$ is 21.92.

## *Endnotes*

1. The order of variables does not matter because in regular multiple regression models the variables are entered into the equation all at once. There is a type of multiple regression analysis called "stepwise" regression, where the order in which variables appear in the equation matters. In stepwise regression, variables are entered one at a time, with successive variables explaining the variance that previously entered variables left unexplained. We do not consider the more detailed stepwise regression model in this book.

2. Excellent and detailed treatments of multiple regression analysis can be found in Greene (1990); Cohen and Cohen (1983); Hanushek and Jackson (1977); and Draper and Smith (1981).

3. The multiple coefficient of determination equals the sum of the two coefficients of determination only in the limited instance when the correlation between the two independent variables is zero:

$$R^2 = r^2_{yx_1} + r^2_{yx_2}$$

when

$$r_{x_1 x_2} = 0$$

4. Because of rounding error the values in this figure are slightly different from those we obtained from our hand calculations.

5. This is true only for a given regression equation. You cannot compare $t$ values across different regression equations to determine the relative effects of different independent variables.

## CHAPTER 16

# Nonparametric or Distribution-Free Statistical Tests

*There's no such thing as a free lunch.*

—ANONYMOUS

## 16.1 INTRODUCTION

Most of the hypothesis tests we have conducted up to this point have been of a particular kind. Often, we were interested in using sample data to test hypotheses about some unknown population parameter, such as a mean ($\mu$), the difference between two or more means ($\mu_1 - \mu_2$), or the linear correlation between two variables ($\rho$). The sample statistics we used to conduct these hypothesis tests, such as means and correlation coefficients, as well as the statistical tests we performed, such as our various $t$, $z$, and $F$ tests, presumed that our data were measured at the interval/ratio level. In using our sample data to test hypotheses about population parameters, we have also had to make some rather restrictive assumptions about the distribution of the population. We assumed that the population was normally distributed or that our sample size was large enough so that this assumption could be relaxed. The statistical tests we have been concerned with thus far, then, have involved hypothesis tests about population parameters, interval- or ratio-level data, and an assumption that the population was normally distributed. These kinds of statistical tests are often referred to as *parametric statistics.*

There are, however, a great many occasions in our research when we cannot make the assumptions necessary to use the parametric statistics we have studied thus far. Sometimes our population is not normal and our samples are too small to enable us to take advantage of the central limit theorem and assume that the sampling distribution is normal. In other instances our data are not measured at the interval/ratio level, but consist of rank-ordered scores, with only ordinal properties. With rank-ordered data, we cannot calculate such statistics as means and standard deviations. In those instances where a normal population cannot be assumed and data are measured at the ordinal level, parametric statistical tests such as the $t$, $z$, or

**530**

*F* tests for mean differences cannot be used any more than can Pearson correlation or ordinary least-squares regression statistics.

Unfortunately, even when we cannot presume a normal population or when we have only rank-ordered data, we are often still interested in the same kinds of issues as when we have interval- or ratio-level data. We still want to know, for example, whether the central tendency of two populations can be presumed to be the same or whether two variables are correlated. Although we cannot use parametric statistical methods on these occasions, there is a set of statistical techniques that we can rely on that are very comparable to our familiar parametric tests. These statistical tests do not require us to make an assumption about normal populations and do not require interval- or ratio-level data. This class of statistical techniques is called *nonparametric*, or *distribution-free* statistical tests.

Nonparametric and distribution-free statistics do not require that populations be normal and that the data be at the interval/ratio level. Their name does not mean that the populations are distribution free or that the distributions involved have no parameters, nor does it mean that we are not interested in making inferences about unknown population parameters. Rather, nonparametric statistics simply have assumptions that are less demanding than the assumption of a normal population. The assumptions of nonparametric statistics are, thus, weaker than those necessary for parametric statistics.

Nonparametric and distribution-free statistics, though often combined under the former name in most statistics texts, are actually two somewhat different types of statistical procedures (Daniel, 1990). True nonparametric statistics do not involve estimating population parameters. Such true nonparametric statistics involve goodness-of-fit tests and tests for randomness. Distribution-free statistics, however, are concerned with hypothesis tests about some unknown population parameter. Sometimes this parameter is a location parameter, a measure of central tendency. In the case of parametric statistics, the location parameter is the mean. In the case of distribution-free statistics, the population location parameter of interest usually is the median. Moreover, unlike their parametric counterparts, these distribution-free statistics do not assume that the sampling distribution is normal. They, therefore, have a much more relaxed set of assumptions than do parametric statistics. Recognizing these differences, in this chapter we continue the tradition of referring to both true nonparametric and distribution-free tests as nonparametric statistics.

The fact that nonparametric statistical tests require weaker assumptions does not mean that they are not very useful for us. Quite the contrary. There are diverse nonparametric statistical tests that cover almost all of our research needs. As we will see, there is a nonparametric equivalent for such parametric statistical tests as the independent- and dependent-samples *t* test for the difference between two population means and the analysis of variance (ANOVA) *F* test. There also is a nonparametric correlation coefficient for ranked data comparable to the Pearson correlation coefficient.

We begin this chapter with a discussion of a one-sample estimation problem involving a proportion. We then proceed with two sample problems for independent and dependent samples and with nonparametric equivalents to the ANOVA *F* test and Pearson correlation coefficient.

## 16.2 A ONE-SAMPLE ESTIMATION PROBLEM

### The Binomial Test

You should recognize the term "binomial" because we examined the binomial distribution in an earlier chapter (remember that "friend" who flipped a coin to see who was going to pay for our outings in Chapter 7). A frequent application of the *binomial test* occurs when we want to make an inference about a population proportion from a sample proportion, and we only have a small sample. In this case, we want to know if our sample proportion ($\hat{p}$) is equal to some population proportion ($p$). The null hypothesis is that $\hat{p} = p$.

You may remember that we worked with one-sample proportion problems such as this in an earlier chapter (Chapter 10), where we wanted to determine whether a sample proportion was equal to some unknown population proportion. In that chapter, however, we used the $z$ test as our test statistic and the $z$ distribution as our sampling distribution. We were able to use the standard normal distribution instead of the binomial distribution because we had large samples. When our sample size is large, the central limit theorem states that the theoretical sampling distribution of proportions is approximately normal. Because the central limit theorem does not apply to smaller samples, we must use the binomial sampling distribution for small sample tests. Let's go through an example of testing a hypothesis about a population proportion from a small sample.

Suppose that in a given criminal court jurisdiction about three-fourths of all accused property crime suspects released on bail appear in court and that one-fourth fail to appear. Our population values in this example, then, would be $p = .75$ and $q = .25$. Remember that $q = 1 - p$, and in this example, $q$ refers to the proportion of property suspects who failed to appear in court. Let's say you wanted to replace the traditional bail system for property offenders with a release on recognizance (ROR) system that does not require cash bail. Before you can do this, however, you must convince the chief judge that under your ROR plan, the rate at which suspects appear in court will be no lower than under the cash bail plan (.75). You are given permission to try your plan out on the next 10 property offenders coming before the court for trial. Of these 10 property crime suspects whom you have released on their own recognizance, only two failed to appear in court for their trial. In the sample data, then, we have $\hat{p} = .80$ and $\hat{q} = .20$. You now want to test the hypothesis that $\hat{p} = p$.

Try to conceive of this as a binomial problem. There are 10 independent "trials" (each trial is whether an accused suspect appears in court), and there are two and only two outcomes (appeared at trial/failed to appear at trial). In the population, the probability of a "success" is .75 and the probability of a "failure" is .25. You want to know if your sample proportion of .80 came from a population where the probability of success is .75.

To conduct a formal hypothesis test, we must first state our null and research hypotheses. The null hypothesis is that the sample proportion is equal to the population proportion:

$H_0$: $\hat{p} = p$

As our proposed policy of ROR will be acceptable only if the proportion appearing at trial is no more than under the old bail system, our research hypothesis will be the directional alternative:

$H_1: \hat{p} < p$

Second, we must select an appropriate test statistic and sampling distribution. Given our small sample size ($n = 10$), we will use the binomial test and the binomial distribution. Unlike the $z$ distribution, there is no one binomial distribution. The binomial distribution depends on the number of trials ($n$) and the probability of success ($p$). If we let $r$ be the number of successes we observe in our sample, we can then use the binomial formula to compute the exact probability of observing that many successes given a population proportion of $p$. In our example, where $p = .75$ and where we observed 8 successes out of 10 trials, the probability of observing 8 successes is determined by the following formula:

$$P(r) = \binom{n}{r} p^r q^{n-r} \tag{16.1}$$

where

$$\binom{n}{r} = \frac{n!}{r!\,(n-r)!}$$

The binomial formula above will give us the probability that we would observe 8 successes from a random sample of 10 trials when the population proportion is .75.

Then we select our alpha level. We choose an alpha level of .05 for this example. The critical value of the binomial coefficient is equal to this selected alpha level. Our critical value, then, is .05. If the probability that we would get 8 successes in a random sample of 10 trials from a population where $p = .75$ is less than .05, we will reject the null hypothesis that the true population proportion is equal to .75.

We can now conduct the test, determining our obtained probability from Equation 16.1:

$$P(r) = \left[ \frac{n!}{(r!)(n-r)!} \right] p^r q^{n-r}$$

where

   $r$ = the number of observed successes
   $n$ = the number of trials
   $p = .75$
   $q = .25$

$$P(8) = \left[ \frac{10!}{(8!)(10-8)!} \right] (.75)^8 (.25)^2$$

$$= \left[ \frac{10 \times 9 \times 8 \times 7 \times 6 \times 5 \times 4 \times 3 \times 2 \times 1}{(8 \times 7 \times 6 \times 5 \times 4 \times 3 \times 2 \times 1)(2 \times 1)} \right] (.1001)(.0625)$$

$$= (45)(.1001)(.0625)$$

$$= .2816$$

If the population proportion was indeed .75, the probability that a random sample of 10 would contain 8 successes is .2816. Notice that unlike with previous hypothesis tests, we did not consult an entire sampling distribution, so we did not define a critical region. Instead, with the binomial formula, we have the exact probability of observing the sample data. Now what we need to do is to make a decision regarding the null hypothesis. As our decision rule was to reject the null hypothesis that $p = .75$ if our obtained probability was less than .05, we must fail to reject the null hypothesis ($p_{obt} > p_{crit}$; .282 > .05). Based on our hypothesis test, we must conclude that our ROR plan for property suspects is not different from the original bail system. Both programs appear to be equally successful in getting suspects to appear for their trial.

Had we so desired, we could have calculated the complete probability distribution by determining the probability of observing seven or fewer successes and nine or more successes. All we had to do was to follow the same procedure substituting different values for $r$ ($p$, $q$, and $n$ would remain the same at .75, .25, and 10, respectively). This would give us the full probability distribution of observing $r$ successes from 10 random trials. We have done these calculations for you and report them:

| Number of Successes | Probability |
|:---:|:---:|
| 0 | .0000 |
| 1 | .0000 |
| 2 | .0004 |
| 3 | .0031 |
| 4 | .0162 |
| 5 | .0584 |
| 6 | .1460 |
| 7 | .2503 |
| 8 | .2816 |
| 9 | .1877 |
| 10 | .0563 |

With this complete probability distribution, we can use our chosen alpha level of .05 to define a critical region. With an alpha of .05 the critical region would consist of any number of successes that has a probability lower than .05. Looking down the column of probabilities, we can see that this would consist of four or fewer successes. The probability of observing four successes in 10 trials from a population where $p = .75$ is .0162. As this is lower than .05, observing only four successes would lead us to reject the null hypothesis. We would also reject the null hypothesis if we observed only three, two, one, or zero successes because each of these probabilities is lower than .05 as well. In other words, had we observed four or fewer successes in our sample of 10 trials, we would have rejected the null hypothesis that $p = .75$. Our critical region, then, would include $rs \leq 4$.

Fortunately, if you ever need to use the binomial formula with small samples, you probably will not have to do the calculations yourself because many statistics books have binomial tables already calculated for you to use.

# 16.3 TWO-SAMPLE PROBLEMS: INDEPENDENT SAMPLES

## *Mann-Whitney* U *Test*

One of the most frequently used nonparametric tests for two independent samples is the *Mann-Whitney* U *Test* (an identical test is called the Wilcoxon Rank-Sum test). For the sake of brevity, we will just call this the U test. The U test is comparable to the t test for the significance of the difference between two independent sample means. It is, therefore, a test that compares the central tendency for two randomly selected independent samples. Rather than computing sample means, however, the U test is based on the *ranks* of the sample scores.

Let's say that we believe there is a relationship between a city's location and its rate of crime. More specifically, we believe that cities that are warm, "sunbelt cities," are experiencing rapid population and economic growth and consequently, all the attendant social problems associated with such quick expansion. These "sunbelt" cities would include places in Florida, Arizona, New Mexico, and California. We think that crime in these rapidly changing cities is higher than in those U.S. cities that are experiencing population loss such as in the "rust belt" of the old industrial Northeast and Midwest (e.g., New York, Pennsylvania, Ohio, and Indiana). We test our hypothesis by gathering some crime data for 18 U.S. cities, nine in each of the two areas.

Table 16.1 reports the total index crime rate (ICR) per 100,000 population for each of the 18 cities. Let's ignore for the moment that the crime rate is an interval- or ratio-level variable. We will work only with the rank order of the cities rather than the raw crime rate score. We want to know whether there is a difference between the two areas in their overall level of crime, the total ICR. Because the data are in the form of ordered ranks (ordinal-level data), we cannot calculate a mean or run a t test for the difference between two means. What we can do, however, is to test the hypothesis of equal medians by using the Mann-Whitney U test.

**TABLE 16.1. Total ICR for Nine Sunbelt and Nine Rustbelt Cities per 100,000 Population—1992**

| Sunbelt Cities | ICR | Rustbelt Cities | ICR |
|---|---|---|---|
| Albuquerque, NM | 7556.3 | Akron, OH | 4924.9 |
| Ft. Lauderdale, FL | 8526.2 | Baltimore, MD | 7382.3 |
| Ft. Myers, FL | 6311.6 | Flint, MI | 7416.2 |
| Miami, FL | 12,336.4 | Gary, IN | 5989.7 |
| Phoenix, AZ | 7464.6 | Hartford, CT | 5344.5 |
| San Diego, CA | 6605.5 | Indianapolis, IN | 5987.8 |
| Sarasota–Bradenton, FL | 7479.8 | Cleveland, OH | 4330.1 |
| Tampa–St. Petersburg, FL | 7940.1 | Pittsburgh, PA | 3281.8 |
| Tucson, AZ | 8340.6 | Toledo, OH | 6442.2 |

*Source:* Federal Bureau of Investigation, Uniform Crime Reports for the United States—1992. U.S. Department of Justice, Washington, DC: USGPO, 1993.

The first step in calculating the $U$ statistic is to combine the two samples into one group and rank-order the scores assigning the lowest raw score a rank of 1, the second lowest raw score a rank of 2, and so on until you get to the highest raw score, which is assigned a rank of $n$ (where $n$ is the number of observations in the combined group). (Please note that you could also calculate the $U$ statistic by assigning the *highest* raw score a rank of 1, the second highest a rank of 2, and so on until you get to the lowest score, which would be assigned a rank of $n$, where $n$ is the number of observations in the group. However you assign ranks, the result of your $U$ test will be exactly the same.) The ranks of the 18 cities from Table 16.1 are shown in Table 16.2. Note that in assigning ranks you ignore the fact that the scores came from two different samples. You combine the two samples, then proceed by assigning the lowest score the rank of 1 and so on.

In assigning ranks, if there are two or more observations with the same raw score, you simply assign the average of the ranks they would have if they had not been tied. For example, if there were two other cities that happened to share with Miami the highest crime rate we would assign all three cities the rank of 17 because it is the average of the highest three ranks ($18 + 17 + 16/3 = 51/3 = 17$). If two cities were tied for the lowest crime rate they would be assigned the same rank of 1.5 because it is the average of the two lowest ranks ($1 + 2/2 = 3/2 = 1.5$).

**TABLE 16.2. Total ICR (per 100,000) and Rank Order of Total Crime Rate for the 18 Rustbelt and Sunbelt Cities of Table 16.1**

| City | ICR | Rank |
|---|---|---|
| Pittsburgh, PA | 3281.8 | 1 |
| Cleveland, OH | 4330.1 | 2 |
| Akron, OH | 4924.9 | 3 |
| Hartford, CT | 5344.5 | 4 |
| Indianapolis, IN | 5987.8 | 5 |
| Gary, IN | 5989.7 | 6 |
| Ft. Myers, FL | 6311.6 | 7 |
| Toledo, OH | 6442.2 | 8 |
| San Diego, CA | 6605.5 | 9 |
| Baltimore, MD | 7382.3 | 10 |
| Flint, MI | 7416.2 | 11 |
| Phoenix, AZ | 7464.6 | 12 |
| Sarasota–Bradenton, FL | 7479.8 | 13 |
| Albuquerque, NM | 7556.3 | 14 |
| Tampa–St.Petersburg, FL | 7940.1 | 15 |
| Tucson, AZ | 8340.6 | 16 |
| Ft. Lauderdale, FL | 8526.2 | 17 |
| Miami, FL | 12,336.4 | 18 |

| | Sunbelt Cities | Rustbelt Cities |
|---|---|---|
| Sum of ranks | 121 | 50 |
| Mean rank | 121/9 = 13.44 | 50/9 = 5.55 |

Notice that if the two samples come from the same population with the same population median, the ranks should be comparable. That is, both samples should have approximately the same number of high and low ranks. If, however, the median crime rate for the sunbelt cities is higher than that for rustbelt cities, the ranks of the sunbelt cities should be higher than those for the sample of rustbelt cities, which is the same thing as saying that the rustbelt cities come from a different population with a different median. We can examine this phenomenon by summing the ranks for each type of city (bottom of Table 16.2).

In looking at the rankings in Table 16.2, it appears as if sunbelt cities are ranked considerably higher than the rustbelt cities. In fact, the highest seven ranks are held by sunbelt cities, and the lowest six ranks are held by rustbelt cities. A way to determine if this difference in ranks is statistically significant is to use the $U$ test.

In calculating the $U$ test, we first determine which of the two samples is the smaller. The smaller sample is designated as the second sample, the larger sample is designated as the first. In our example the sample sizes are the same, so it makes no difference. To distinguish the two sets of cities, let's call the rustbelt cities sample 2 and the sunbelt cities sample 1. The $U$ statistic is calculated by taking each score in the second sample and counting the number of scores in the first sample that have higher ranks. After doing this for each score in the second sample, we then sum the results to get the value of $U$.

Let's go through the calculations for our city example. Taking the city in sample 2 (rustbelt cities) that has the lowest rank, Pittsburgh, we see that there are nine sunbelt cities that have higher ranks. For Cleveland, there are also nine sunbelt cities that have higher ranks. This is also true for Akron, Hartford, Indianapolis, and Gary. For Toledo, there are eight sunbelt cities with higher ranks (only Ft. Myers is lower), and for Baltimore and Flint there are seven sunbelt cities with higher ranks. The value of $U$ is then: $9 + 9 + 9 + 9 + 9 + 9 + 8 + 7 + 7 = 76$. We could have obtained the value of $U$ a little more easily with the following formula:

$$U = n_1 n_2 + \frac{n_1(n_1 + 1)}{2} - R_1 \qquad (16.2)$$

where

$n_1$ = the number of observations in sample 1
$n_2$ = the number of observations in sample 2
$R_1$ = the sum of the ranks for sample 1

Using our city data, the value of $U$ would be:

$$U = (9)(9) + \frac{(9)(9 + 1)}{2} - 50$$

$$= 81 + \frac{90}{2} - 50$$

$$= 76$$

We now calculate a second value of $U$, which we will call $U'$ ($U$ prime) by determining how many rustbelt cities have higher ranks than the sunbelt cities. As Miami, Ft. Lauderdale, Tucson, Tampa-St. Petersburg, Albuquerque, Sarasota-Bradenton, and Phoenix have no rustbelt cities with higher ranks, San Diego has two rustbelt cities with higher ranks, and Ft. Myers has three with higher ranks, the value of $U'$ is: $0 + 0 + 0 + 0 + 0 + 0 + 0 + 2 + 3 = 5$. We can also obtain $U'$ by using the following formula:

$$U' = n_1 n_2 + \frac{(n_2)(n_2 + 1)}{2} - R_2$$

where

$n_1$ = the number of observations in group 1
$n_2$ = the number of observations in group 2
$R_2$ = the sum of the ranks for group 2

Using this formula, we can compute $U'$ as follows:

$$U' = (9)\,(9) + \frac{(9)(9 + 1)}{2} - 121$$

$$= 81 + \frac{90}{2} = 121$$

$$= 5$$

After we have dragged you through both of these calculations, we must now tell you that it is not necessary to calculate both $U$ and $U'$. Once you have calculated one value, the value of the other can easily be determined by the following formulas:

$$U' = n_1 n_2 - U \qquad \text{or} \qquad U = n_1 n_2 - U' \tag{16.4}$$

For our example, as $U$ was 76, we can calculate $U'$ as $(9)(9) - 76 = 5$. We hope that you now understand why the $U$ test can be considered a difference-of-summed-ranks test.

Either $U$ or $U'$ can be used as the test statistic, but the tables of the sampling distribution of $U$ have been established in terms of the smaller $U$ value. For this reason, the value of $U$ we use is always the lesser of the two: $U$ or $U'$. This means that, unlike our other hypothesis tests, the null hypothesis will be rejected whenever our obtained value of $U$ is *less than our critical value*. So, remember this: smaller values of $U$ lead us to reject the null hypothesis.

Once we have calculated our two $U$ values and determined which is the smaller, we are ready to conduct our significance test. Let's go through the hypothesis test procedures. First we state the null and alternative hypothesis:

$H_0$: There is no difference in the crime rates between sunbelt and rustbelt cities.

$H_1$: Crime rates in sunbelt cities will be greater than those in rustbelt cities.

Second, we select our appropriate test statistic (Mann-Whitney $U$ Test) and our alpha level ($\alpha = .05$ for a one-tailed test). We then go to our sampling distribution table of $U$ (Table B.7 of Appendix B) and find the critical value of $U$ with an alpha of .05 and a one-tailed test. Different $U$ tables correspond to different levels of alpha. The number of observations in the first sample/group is at the top of the table, and the number of observations in the second sample/group is down the left margin. Using these sample sizes in the table which corresponds to our selected level of alpha, we can find the critical values of $U$ in the body of the table. In this case, as we have $n_1 = n_2 = 9$, we look for the table corresponding to an alpha level of .05. Because we have a one-tailed alternative hypothesis, we find that the critical value of $U$ is 21. Therefore, we need to obtain a $U$ of 21 or *smaller* in order to reject the null hypothesis.

Third, we calculate the obtained value of our test statistic, which we know is $U = 5$, and compare it to the critical value. Because our obtained $U$ (5) is smaller than the critical value (21), we reject the null hypothesis and conclude that the crime rates in the two types of cities are not the same. Again, do not forget that with the Mann-Whitney test, the null hypothesis is rejected when our obtained value of $U$ is *smaller* than the critical value.

If both sample sizes are greater than 20, we can safely assume that the sampling distribution of $U$ is approximately normal and has a mean ($\mu_U$) and a standard deviation ($\sigma_U$) that are equal to the following quantities:

$$\mu_U = \frac{n_1 n_2}{2}$$

$$\sigma_U = \sqrt{\frac{(n_1 n_2)(n_1 + n_2 + 1)}{12}}$$
(16.5)

The luxury of being able to make this assumption is that we can use the familiar $z$ test as our test statistic. Once we calculate our value of $U(U_{\text{obt}})$, the obtained value of $z$ can be found from the following formula:

$$z = \frac{U_{\text{obt}} - \mu_U}{\sigma_U}$$
(16.6)

In the case of the normal approximation, it makes no difference if you use $U$ or $U'$ in the formula. The difference, however, is that instead of using the cumbersome $U$ tables, we can now use the standard normal ($z$) distribution as our sampling distribution and the critical value of $z$ as our test statistic. You then carry out the hypothesis test just as we have done when performing other $z$ tests.

In spite of the fact that our samples are too small for the normal approximation, let's go through the calculation of the $z$ test for practice. From Equation 16.5 we can calculate the mean and standard deviation of the sampling distribution of $U$ to be:

$$\mu_U = \frac{(9)(9)}{2} = \frac{81}{2} = 40.5$$

$$\sigma_U = \sqrt{\frac{(9)(9)(9 + 9 + 1)}{12}} = \sqrt{\frac{81(19)}{12}} = 11.32$$

Now, using either $U$ or $U'$, we can calculate the value of $z_{\text{obt}}$:

$$z_{\text{obt}} = \frac{5 - 40.5}{11.32} = \frac{-35.5}{11.32} = -3.14$$

$$z_{\text{obt}} = \frac{76 - 40.5}{11.32} = \frac{30.5}{11.32} = 3.14$$

With a $z_{obt}$ of $\pm 3.14$ and an alpha of .01, we would reject the null hypothesis that the rustbelt and sunbelt cities come from the same population.

The Mann-Whitney $U$ test is fairly easy to calculate and is a very powerful alternative to the parametric difference-of-means $t$ test. In fact, it is almost as powerful as the $t$ test in being able to reject a false null hypothesis. Its one disadvantage, however, is that it becomes quite unwieldy whenever there are a large number of scores with tied ranks. Recall that when we are confronted with tied ranks, we simply assign the tied scores the average of the ranks they would have had if they had not been tied. As you can imagine, with a large number of tied scores, this process would become quite time-consuming. Even the "correction factor" that statisticians have developed to deal with this problem is not easy or quick to calculate. For this reason, in the presence of a large number of tied ranks, we suggest you abandon the Mann-Whitney $U$ test and opt for another nonparametric test called the *Kolmogorov-Smirnov two-sample test.*

## Kolmogorov-Smirnov Two-Sample Test

The Kolmogorov-Smirnov two-sample test, or the $K$-$S_2$ test, evaluates the difference between two independent samples that are arranged into a cumulative frequency distribution of $k$ rank-ordered categories. The null hypothesis assumes that the two samples came from the same population. If this is true, then we would expect the two cumulative frequency distributions to be comparable. In words, the $K$-$S_2$ test is based on the maximum difference between the two samples on any of the $k$ categories. If the maximum difference is greater than we would expect by chance alone under the null hypothesis, we would reject the null hypothesis and conclude that the two samples were drawn from different populations.

Let's say that we were interested in the relationship between the number of delinquent peers a youth has and their evaluations of "how wrong" it is to commit a delinquent offense. In his theory of differential association, Edwin Sutherland (1973) argued that in our interactions with others, we learn "definitions favorable to the violation of the law." One such definition that favors violation of the law is the belief that breaking the law is not morally wrong. Let's say we suspect that one of the ways we learn such definitions is from our friends who have themselves violated the law. Based on this suspicion, we hypothesize that there is a relationship between having delinquent friends and believing that it is not wrong to commit delinquent acts.

In Table 16.3, we present some data collected by Delbert Elliott and his colleagues (1985) as part of the National Youth Survey. In this table, 15- and 16-year-old males are divided into two groups, those who reported that none of their friends drink liquor and those who reported that at least some of their friends drink liquor. We can consider these two groups as being independent samples selected from the larger population of American youths with no and some delinquent peers, respectively. We also report in that table the responses of these boys to the question, "How wrong do you think it is to drink liquor?" Our expectation is that those with no drinking friends are more likely to think that drinking is wrong than those with at least one friend who drinks alcohol. Because the variable measuring moral beliefs about drinking is measured at the ordinal level (we have rank-ordered categories

**TABLE 16.3. Data from the National Youth Survey on the Number of Friends Who Drink Liquor and a Person's Moral Beliefs about Drinking ("How wrong is it to drink liquor?")**

| | No Drinking Friends | | | | | One or More Drinking Friends | | | | |
|---|---|---|---|---|---|---|---|---|---|---|
| | Number of Respondents | f | cf | cp | D | Number of Respondents | f | cf | cp | D |
| Very wrong | 20 | 20 | 20 | 20/35 | .57 | 20 | 20 | 20 | 20/184 | .11 | .46 |
| Wrong | 10 | 10 | 30 | 30/35 | .86 | 59 | 59 | 79 | 79/184 | .43 | .43 |
| A little wrong | 5 | 5 | 35 | 35/35 | 1.00 | 71 | 71 | 150 | 150/184 | .82 | .18 |
| Not wrong at all | 0 | 0 | 35 | 35 | 1.00 | 34 | 34 | 184 | 184/184 | 1.00 | — |
| Total | 35 | | | 35 | | 184 | | | | |

*Source:* D. Elliot et al. (1985).

from "very wrong" to "not wrong at all"), we use a nonparametric statistical test, the Kolmogorov-Smirnov two-sample test.

As always, we now go through the procedures for a hypothesis test. First we state the null and alternative hypotheses:

$H_0$: The two samples come from the same population. This is the same as saying that there is no difference between the boys with no and at least one drinking friend in the extent to which they think that drinking liquor is morally wrong.

$H_1$: The sample with no drinking friends is more likely to report that drinking liquor is wrong than the sample that reports having at least one drinking friend.

Second, we select our test statistic (Kolmogorov-Smirnov two-sample test, $D$) and our level of significance ($\alpha = 0.5$ for a one-tailed test). We then determine what our critical value of $D$ is. In Table B.8 of Appendix B we can see that for an alpha level of .05 and a one-tailed hypothesis test we use the following formula:

$$D = 1.22\sqrt{\frac{n_1 + n_2}{n_1 n_2}}$$

$$= 1.22\sqrt{\frac{35 + 184}{(35)(184)}}$$

$$= (1.22)(.184)$$

$$= .225$$

The critical value of $D$ for this problem, then, is .225. Our obtained value of $D$ must be equal to or greater than .225 for us to reject the null hypothesis.

Now let's calculate our test statistic. The test statistic is based on the difference between the cumulative proportions for each of the categories. The first thing we need to do for the K-S$_2$ test, then, is to compute the cumulative frequencies and cumulative proportions for each sample. In the column labeled $D$, we have calculated the difference between the cumulative proportions for each category. For example, the first value of $D$ is found by subtracting the cumulative proportion of those who thought it was "very wrong" to drink among those with no drinking friends ($p = .57$) from those who had at least one drinking friend ($p = .11$). This difference is $.57 - .11 = .46$. We then calculate this difference for each of the $k$ categories. The largest difference is .46, which was found for the first category. This value, is then, our critical value of $D$.

Remember that we are predicting the direction of our alternative hypothesis by stating that those without drinking friends should report that drinking was "very wrong." In this case, then, we need to examine our difference scores and make sure that they are consistent with our prediction. Because a higher proportion of the youths with no drinking friends are in the "very wrong" and "wrong" categories than those with at least one drinking friend, the frequency distributions do correspond to the prediction of our alternative hypothesis. As you can see, we are interested in the largest positive difference between the two cumulative frequency distributions. If we had not predicted the direction of our alternative hypothesis, that is, if we had conducted a two-tailed test, we would be interested in the largest absolute value of the differences. The obtained value of $D$, .46, constitutes our test statistic, which we then compare to our critical value.

The critical value of $D$ actually corresponds to a critical proportion that the observed $D$ must equal or exceed to be statistically significant at that probability level. Because our obtained value of .46 exceeds the critical value of .225, we can reject the null hypothesis. We can therefore conclude that youths without friends who drink are more likely to think that drinking is morally wrong that those who have drinking friends.

Both the Mann-Whitney $U$ test and the Kolmogorov-Smirnov $D$ test are useful nonparametric equivalents for the parametric independent-samples $t$ test for the difference between means. Both the Mann-Whitney and Kolmogorov-Smirnov statistical tests concern location problems of central tendency. They are appropriate under different circumstances, however. The Mann-Whitney $U$ test is appropriate whenever there are only a few scores that are tied, and the Kolmogorov-Smirnov $D$ test is more appropriate with categorical data that involve a large proportion of tied scores.

## Wald-Wolfowitz Runs Test

There are times in our research when we are less interested in central tendency than we are in the dispersion of a group of scores. That is, we may hypothesize that two samples come from populations that are comparable with respect to central tendency but differ markedly with respect to dispersion. For this type of problem neither the $U$ nor the $D$ tests are particularly powerful. There is, as you may suspect, another nonparametric statistical test that is very powerful in detecting differences of dispersion between two samples, the *Wald-Wolfowitz runs test*. We call this statistical test the runs test and examine it next.

In his research on the social climate in prisons and other correctional institutions, Rudolf Moos (1975) developed the Correctional Institutions Environment Scale (CIES). Part of the CIES measures the extent to which the correctional institution is oriented toward treatment rather than custody or control. We call these questions on the CIES the treatment subscale. Let's say that as a hypothetical research project, we asked a random sample of 10 employees and 10 inmates from a correctional institution to take the CIES. We were curious to see whether staff and inmates have the same perceptions about the climate and atmosphere of the institution. Table 16.4 represents their scores (those who score high on the subscale believe that the prison is oriented toward treatment rather than strict custody).

As we are not willing to assume that the treatment subscale of the CIES is measured at the interval level (the difference between a score of 10 and 11, for example, is not the same as the difference between 22 and 23), we make the less demanding assumption that the data are ordinal. We can, therefore, rank-order the scores, but cannot compute a mean.

Let's calculate the sum of the ranks for these scores, just as we did for the Mann-Whitney test. Remember first to pool the data into one group and then assign the ranks by giving the lowest score a rank of 1, the next lowest a rank of 2, and so on. We have calculated the rank of each score and have included it next to the raw score for each person. The sum of the ranks for the two groups are identical ($\Sigma R = 105$), suggesting that the central tendencies of the two groups are comparable. In fact, if we calculate the $U$ statistic, we find that $U = U' = 55$. With $n_1 = n_2 = 10$, and an alpha of .05 for a two-tailed test, the critical value of $U$ would be 23. On the basis of the Mann-Whitney $U$ test, then, we could not reject the null hypothesis (remember, we reject $H_0$ with values of $U_{obt}$ that are *smaller* than the critical value).

Clearly, however, the two sample scores are quite different. In examining the ranks, the scores for the inmate sample are much more variable than those for the prison staff. Half of the inmate scores are lower than all of the staff scores, and the other half are higher. Let's let the letter $I$ represent the inmate scores and the letter $S$ represent the staff scores. Starting with the lowest rank, list the order in which sample scores appear. For example, the lowest rank comes from the inmate sample

**TABLE 16.4. Hypothetical CIES Scores of Staff and Inmates of a Correctional Institution**

|  | Staff | | Inmates | |
|---|---|---|---|---|
|  | Score | Rank | Score | Rank |
| Person 1 | 13 | 7 | 9 | 4 |
| Person 2 | 15 | 8 | 7 | 2 |
| Person 3 | 18 | 10 | 8 | 3 |
| Person 4 | 11 | 6 | 5 | 1 |
| Person 5 | 17 | 9 | 10 | 5 |
| Person 6 | 23 | 14 | 25 | 16 |
| Person 7 | 22 | 12.5 | 26 | 17 |
| Person 8 | 21 | 11 | 30 | 20 |
| Person 9 | 22 | 12.5 | 29 | 19 |
| Person 10 | 24 | 15 | 28 | 18 |

($I$), the second lowest rank also comes from the inmate sample ($I$), so does the third, fourth, and fifth lowest ranks, the next ranks in order come from the staff sample ($S$). If we do this for each score, we can then display the rank order of scores from lowest to highest according to the sample from which it comes:

$$\underline{I\ I\ I\ I\ I}\ \underline{\underline{S\ S\ S\ S\ S\ S\ S\ S\ S\ S}}\ \underline{I\ I\ I\ I\ I}$$

This is a list of runs in the data. In the list above, there are three runs: one run of five $I$s, followed by one run of 10 $S$s, followed by another run of 5 $I$s. These scores are not very well mixed. The $I$s are bunched together, as are the $S$s. If the two samples came from the same population as assumed by the null hypothesis, we would expect the rank of the two groups of scores to be better mixed, something like this:

$$\underline{I\ I}\ \underline{\underline{S\ S}}\ \underline{I}\ \underline{\underline{S}}\ \underline{I}\ \underline{\underline{S}}\ \underline{I\ I}\ \underline{\underline{S\ S\ S}}\ \underline{I\ I}\ \underline{\underline{S\ S}}\ \underline{I}\ \underline{\underline{S}}\ \underline{I}$$

As you can see, even though the two distributions are similar in terms of central tendency, they are very different in terms of dispersion. In the first there is a long run of cases from the inmate sample, then a long run from the staff sample, followed by another long run from the inmate sample. In the second distribution there are no long runs from either sample, the two groups are well mixed in terms of their ranks.

One way we can determine whether the two samples come from the same population is to see how well they mix together when ranked. That is, we can count the number of *runs* that occur in the rank-ordered scores. To repeat, then, a run is defined as any sequence of scores from the same sample. In the first example above, there are only three runs; there is one run of five $I$s, followed by one run of 10 $S$s, followed by another run of five $I$s. Remember that a run refers to a sequence of scores from a sample, not the number of scores from the sample, so there are only three runs in our first distribution.

In the second distribution of scores there are 13 runs; a run of two $I$s, a run of two $S$s, a run of a single $I$, followed by a run of a single $S$, then another run of a single $I$ and a run of a single $S$, a run of two $I$s, a run of three $S$s, a run of two $I$s, a run of two $S$s, a run of a single $I$, then a single $S$, and ending with a run of a single $I$. There are, then, a total of 13 runs. The number of runs for the two distributions are underlined once if the score comes from the inmate sample and twice if it comes from the staff sample so you can more easily count them yourself.

From these two examples, you can see that if the number of runs is large, this indicates that the two samples are mixed very well, and we probably cannot reject the null hypothesis that the two samples come from the same population. If, however, the number of runs is quite small, we may be led to reject the null hypothesis and instead conclude that the two samples come from different populations. We can use the known sampling distribution of the number of runs, $r$, to test this hypothesis. This is the idea behind the Wald-Wolfowitz runs test.

The test statistic of the runs test simply is the number of runs in the set of scores. Our obtained $r$, then, is determined by counting the number of runs. With our staff and inmate data from the treatment subscale of the CIES, there were three runs. If both $n_1$ and $n_2$ are less than or equal to 20, the exact sampling distribution of $r$ can be found in Table B.9 of Appendix B. In these instances we can get our critical value of $r$ from the provided table. For sample sizes greater than 20 the sampling distribution of $r$ is approximately normal with mean ($\mu_r$) and standard deviation ($\sigma_r$) equal to:

$$\mu_r = \frac{2n_1n_2}{n_1 + n_2} + 1$$

$$\sigma_r = \sqrt{\frac{(2n_1n_2)(2n_1n_2 - n_1 - n_2)}{(n_1 + n_2)^2(n_1 + n_2 - 1)}}$$

$$(16.7)$$

With the population mean and standard deviation so defined, we can calculate the well-known $z$ test:

$$z = \frac{r - \mu_r}{\sigma_r} \tag{16.8}$$

Let's now conduct our hypothesis test for the CIES data with the by now quite familiar refrain: First we state the null and alternative hypothesis:

$H_0$: The two samples come from the same population.

$H_1$: The two samples come from different populations (a two-tailed alternative).

Second, we choose the appropriate test statistic and significance level. In this case we have chosen the Wald-Wolfowitz runs test ($r$) because we suspect that the samples come from populations that differ with respect to their dispersion. We select an alpha level of .05 for a two-tailed test. Because both samples are less than 20, we cannot use the normal approximation for our test and must use the $r$ distribution.

With $n_1 = n_2 = 10$, $\alpha = .05$ (two-tailed), we can go to the exact sampling distribution of $r$ in Table B.9 of Appendix B and find our critical value. We locate the critical value of $r$ by going down the column until we find $n_1 = 10$ and across the top until we find $n_2 = 10$. We go to the body of the table and find that the critical value of $r$ is 6. Because a small number of runs is indicative that the populations from which the samples were drawn are different, we need an obtained value of $r$ less than or equal to the critical value in order to reject the null hypothesis.

Third, we calculate the obtained value of our test statistic $r$ and compare it to our critical value. In our example the obtained value of $r$ was 3. Because this is less than the critical value of 6, we reject the null hypothesis that the two samples come from the same population. We can conclude that the inmate and staff samples come from different populations.

Although not appropriate in this case because of our small sample size, just for practice, let's conduct the same hypothesis test with the normal approximation. The test statistic is the $z$ test from Equation 16.8. We calculate:

$$\text{Mean} = \mu_r = \frac{[(2)(10)](10)}{10 + 10} + 1$$

$$= 11$$

$$\text{Standard Deviation} = \sigma_r = \sqrt{\frac{[(2)(10) \times (10)]\{[(2)(10) \times (10)] - 10 - 10\}}{(10 + 10)^2(10 + 10 - 1)}}$$

$$= \sqrt{\frac{36,000}{7600}}$$

$$= 2.18$$

The $z$ test, then, is:

$$z = \frac{r - \mu_r}{\sigma_r}$$

$$= \frac{3 - 11}{2.18}$$

$$= -3.67$$

With an alpha of .05 for a two-tailed test, the critical value of $z$ is $\pm 1.97$. The interpretation of the $z_{obt}$ and $z_{crit}$ value is the same as for any $z$ test. The obtained $z$ of $-3.67$ is less than the critical value of $z$ $(-1.97)$ so we would reject the null hypothesis that the two samples come from the same population. This also was our conclusion when we used the exact sampling distribution of $r$.

## 16.4 TWO-SAMPLE PROBLEMS: DEPENDENT SAMPLES

In this section, as in the preceding, we continue to be concerned with two-sample problems. Unlike the previous section, however, where the two samples were selected independent of one another, in this section the samples are dependent, or "matched," samples. For example, this is the type of problem that we encounter when we have "before" and "after" scores for the same group of persons or a "matched" group of experimental and control subjects. In this type of problem, then, the two samples are not independent but are selected to be as similar as possible. In the parametric case, we calculated our test statistic (the $t$ test for matched or dependent samples) based on the difference between each pair of cases in the two samples. We now learn nonparametric equivalents to this paired difference test.

### Sign Test

One of the simplest of the nonparametric tests for matched or dependent samples is called the *sign test*. The sign test is comparable to a test for the equality between two medians. The logic of the sign test is very simple: If a pair of scores comes from the same population with the same median, then the number of times one pair is higher than the other pair should be approximately the same as the number of times one pair is lower than the other. If, however, the two sets of scores come from different populations with a different central tendency, then, one of the pairs will be consistently higher (or lower) than the other pair.

Let's take the hypothetical data in Table 16.5 as an example. These scores represent the scores received by a group of 10 police officers serving in a domestic violence unit on a conflict resolution test before and after receiving an intensive course in interpersonal relations and conflict management. We assume that a higher score represents the ability to resolve family disputes without conflict, which was the purpose of the training course. If the second score is higher than the first score, we have placed a plus sign in the sign column and a minus sign if the second score is lower than the first. If the scores were tied, we would have placed a zero in the sign column and excluded this score from further analysis. The sample size is then the number of untied scores.

You can see from examining the last column in Table 16.5 that, in eight instances, the second score was higher than the first (hence, eight plus signs). In two instances, the second score was lower, so there are two "−" signs. The sign test is based on the number of less frequently occurring signs. The test statistic is symbolized by the letter $m$. In the example above, the less frequent sign is the minus sign, and there are two of them, so $m = 2$. The sign test, $m$, then, is a simple count of the number of signs that occurs less often. If our sample size is less than 25, we can find the critical value of $m$ in Table B.10 of Appendix B at various significance levels for one- and two-tailed tests. When our sample size exceeds 25, the sampling distribution of $m$ is approximately normally distributed and we can use a $z$ test with the formula:

$$z = \frac{2m - n}{\sqrt{n}} \tag{16.9}$$

**TABLE 16.5. Hypothetical Scores for 10 Police Officers before and after Completing a Conflict Resolution Course**

| Officer No. | Before Score | After Score | Sign |
|---|---|---|---|
| 1 | 24 | 26 | + |
| 2 | 19 | 22 | + |
| 3 | 25 | 21 | − |
| 4 | 32 | 33 | + |
| 5 | 30 | 28 | − |
| 6 | 28 | 31 | + |
| 7 | 27 | 29 | + |
| 8 | 25 | 30 | + |
| 9 | 24 | 26 | + |
| 10 | 30 | 31 | + |

where

    $m$ = the sum of the less frequent signs
    $n$ = the number of pairs of untied scores

We now test the null hypothesis that the two sets of scores on the conflict resolution test come from the same population:

    $H_0$: There is no difference between the before and after scores on the conflict resolution test.

We expected that the intensive training course would increase the officers' score on the test, so our alternative is the one-tailed hypothesis that:

    $H_1$: Police officers will score higher on the conflict resolution test after having taken the training course.

Because our sample size is below 25, the appropriate test statistic is the sign test ($m$). We conduct our hypothesis with an alpha of .01. With a sample of 10 ($n$ is the number of pairs of scores, so $n = 10$), and an alpha level of .01 for a one-tailed test, the critical value of $m$, as found in Table B.10 of Appendix B, is zero. Our obtained value of $m$ must be less than or equal to the critical value in order to reject the null hypothesis. As the $m_{obt}$ of 2 is greater than the critical value, we fail to reject the null hypothesis. We must therefore conclude that there is no difference between the before and after scores on the conflict resolution test.

For practice, even though our sample size is below 25, let's test the same hypothesis at the same alpha level using the normal approximation:

$$z = \frac{(2)(2) - 10}{\sqrt{10}}$$

$$= -1.90$$

The critical value of $z$ with a one-tailed test and an alpha of .01, is $-2.33$. With an obtained $z$ of $-1.90$, we would still fail to reject the null hypothesis.

One of the disadvantages of the sign test is that it does not take into account the *magnitude* of the difference between each pair of scores. When we calculate the sign test, it does not matter if the second score is substantially lower or higher than the first, the only thing we count is the number of pluses and minuses. There is another nonparametric test for two dependent samples that does take into account the magnitude of the difference between paired samples, the *Wilcoxon Signed-Ranks Test.*

## Wilcoxon Signed-Ranks Test

The Wilcoxon signed-ranks test, like the sign test, is very easy to calculate. As our example, we continue to use our hypothetical data of the 10 police officers' scores on a conflict resolution test before and after a training session. These data are redisplayed for our purposes in Table 16.6.

**TABLE 16.6. Calculation of Wilcoxon Signed-Ranks Test for the Data in Table 16.5**

| Officer No. | Before Score | After Score | Sign and Magnitude of Difference | Absolute Value of Difference | Rank of Difference | Signed Ranks |
|---|---|---|---|---|---|---|
| 1 | 24 | 26 | +2 | 2 | 4.5 | + 4.5 |
| 2 | 19 | 22 | +3 | 3 | 7.5 | + 7.5 |
| 3 | 25 | 21 | −4 | 4 | 9.0 | − 9.0 |
| 4 | 32 | 33 | +1 | 1 | 1.5 | + 1.5 |
| 5 | 30 | 28 | −2 | 2 | 4.5 | − 4.5 |
| 6 | 28 | 31 | +3 | 3 | 7.5 | + 7.5 |
| 7 | 27 | 29 | +2 | 2 | 4.5 | + 4.5 |
| 8 | 25 | 30 | +5 | 5 | 10.0 | +10.0 |
| 9 | 24 | 26 | +2 | 4 | 4.5 | + 4.5 |
| 10 | 30 | 31 | +1 | 1 | 1.5 | + 1.5 |

To calculate the Wilcoxon signed-ranks test, we first subtract the first score from the second score and record both the sign and the magnitude of this difference score (*D*) (fourth column of Table 16.6). Then, *ignoring the sign,* we rank-order the difference score assigning the rank of one to the lowest score, the rank of two to the next lowest score, and so on. In other words, we assign ranks to the *absolute value* of the difference scores. In the case of tied ranks, we assign to each tied score the average of the rank they would be assigned if they were not tied. For example, in Table 16.6 the smallest difference is 1, and there are two of these. Both differences would be assigned the rank of $1 + 2/2 = 1.5$. The next smallest difference is 2 and there are four of these (three are +2, and one is −2, but these are treated the same because we are interested in the absolute value of the difference). These difference scores would all be assigned the average of the 3rd, 4th, 5th, and 6th ranks or $3 + 4 + 5 + 6/4 = 4.5$. As for the sign test, if the two scores are tied, we just place a zero in the difference column and exclude the score from consideration (remember that *n* is then the number of *untied pairs*).

After assigning ranks to each of the absolute difference values, we go back and record the sign for each rank, noting whether the original sign is negative or positive. This is done in the last column of Table 16.6. After recording the correct sign, we simply sum the ranks for both the negative and positive signs. The sum of the positive ranks for this data set is:

$$\Sigma+ = 4.5 + 7.5 + 1.5 + 7.5 + 4.5 + 10.0 + 4.5 + 1.5 = 41.5$$

The sum of the negative ranks for this data set is:

$$\Sigma- = 9.0 + 4.5 = 13.5$$

The value of the Wilcoxon signed-rank test statistic, symbolized by the letter *T*, is the *smaller* of these two sums. The null hypothesis for this test also is that the two samples come from the same population. If this is correct, the sum of the positive ranks should be approximately the same as the sum of the negative ranks. The statistical test determines whether the observed difference is statistically significant or not. For the data in Table 16.6, $T = 13.5$. If $n \leq 30$, the exact sampling distribution of $T$ can be found in Table B.11 of Appendix B. For sample sizes greater than 30, we can take advantage of the normal approximation and calculate a $z$ test where:

$$z = \frac{\Sigma T - \dfrac{(n)(n + 1)}{4}}{\sqrt{\dfrac{(n)(n + 1)(2n + 1)}{24}}} \tag{16.10}$$

With the data in Table 16.6 we now conduct our formal hypothesis test:

$H_0$: The two samples come from the same population. In other words, the "after" scores are no different from the "before" scores.

$H_1$: The two samples come from two different populations. The "after" scores are significantly higher than the "before" scores.

Our test statistic is the Wilcoxon matched-pairs signed-ranks test $(T)$. We keep the same alpha level as for the sign test above, $\alpha = .01$ for a one-tailed test. We next go to Table B.11 of Appendix B and find the critical value of $T$ with $n = 10$ and an alpha of .01 (one-tailed). The critical value of $T$ is 5. As $T$ always is the smaller of the two sums of ranks, we need an obtained value of $T$ equal to or smaller than the critical value in order to reject the null hypothesis. Our obtained value of $T$ (13.5) is much greater than the critical value, so we would fail to reject the null hypothesis. Using the normal approximation (for practice only), we would have an obtained $z$ value of:

$$z = \frac{13.5 - \dfrac{(10)(10 + 1)}{4}}{\sqrt{\dfrac{(10)(10 + 1)[(2)(10 + 1)]}{24}}}$$

$$= \frac{-14.00}{10.04}$$

$$= -1.39$$

With a critical $z$ of $-2.33$ ($\alpha = .01$, one-tailed), we would also fail to reject the null hypothesis.

## 16.5 k INDEPENDENT SAMPLE PROBLEMS

In the previous two sections, we have examined problems involving two samples. We mentioned that these two-sample problems were analogous to the parametric $t$ test problems. In this section we have more than two independent samples, and the null hypothesis is that each of the $k$ independent samples (where $k \geq 3$) comes from the same population. The type of statistic we examine in this section is analogous to the parametric one-way ANOVA test we learned about in Chapter 13.

Because each of our samples is independent, this $k$-sample problem is an extension of the two-sample Mann-Whitney $U$ test.

## Kruskal-Wallis H test

Unlike the parametric one-way ANOVA, the nonparametric Kruskal-Wallis test does not require normally distributed populations and can be used with ordinal-level data. Think of the *Kruskal-Wallis H test,* then, as parallel to the ANOVA $F$ test, except that we have ordinal level data.

As our example, let's examine some research by Harold Grasmick and his colleagues (1993). As part of their study, Grasmick et al. created an attitude scale that was designed to measure a trait called "self-control." Self-control was the time-stable individual attribute believed by Gottfredson and Hirschi (1990) in their book *A General Theory of Crime* to be one of the most important factors in the generation of all types of crime/delinquency as well as other inappropriate behaviors (sexual promiscuity, unemployment, substance abuse). It was thought that persons lacking in self-control are impulsive, self-centered, quick-tempered, physical, and unable to defer gratification. These people, it is believed, are thus very easily involved in crime.

The self-control scale developed by Grasmick et al. was comprised of 24 questionnaire items. Let's suppose that we administered this self-control scale to three randomly selected groups of persons: a group of incarcerated adult males, a group of males at a residential drug abuse clinic, and a group of males selected from the local Rotary Club. The scores for each person in the three groups are shown in Table 16.7. We only assume that the self-control scale is an ordinal-level measure, where a higher score indicates greater self-control. Because the self-control scale is assumed to be only an ordinal measure, we can rank persons as higher or lower than another, but the difference between any two adjacent scores is not the same. Our null hypothesis is that the three samples come from the same population. The statistical test of this hypothesis is based on the Kruskal-Wallis $H$ test.

In calculating the $H$ test, we first pool the scores from all of the samples together and rank-order them from low to high, assigning the rank of 1 to the lowest score, the rank of 2 to the next lowest score, and so on. (Again, you could assign the rank of 1 to the *highest* score, the rank of 2 to the next highest score, and so on. It makes no difference.) As before, if there are tied ranks, we assign the average of the ranks each score would have if they were not tied. In Table 16.7, we report each person's score and rank (in parentheses). After pooling the data and assigning ranks, we then sum the ranks for each sample separately. That is, we add the ranks for the first sample and obtain a sum, then we add the ranks for the second sample and obtain a sum, doing this until the last, or $k$th, sample ranks are summed.

If the null hypothesis is true and the three samples come from the same population, the sum of the ranks for each sample should approximately be the same. If this is not true, the sum of the ranks will be different. The statistical test $H$ determines if any observed differences among the ranks of the samples is due to chance or is so large that the more likely alternative is that the populations are different. At the bottom of Table 16.7 we also report the sum of the ranks [$\Sigma(R)$] for each group.

**TABLE 16.7. Hypothetical Score on Self-Control Scale for Three Samples, Incarcerated Adults, Clients in a Drug Treatment Clinic, and Members of a Rotary Club**

| Incarcerated Group ($n_1 = 7$) | | Drug Clinic Group ($n_2 = 8$) | | Rotary Club Group ($n_3 = 10$) | |
|---|---|---|---|---|---|
| Score | Rank | Score | Rank | Score | Rank |
| 85 | 3 | 92 | 7 | 117 | 24 |
| 102 | 16 | 81 | 2 | 109 | 19 |
| 93 | 8 | 98 | 12 | 114 | 21.5 |
| 88 | 5 | 103 | 17 | 97 | 11 |
| 79 | 1 | 99 | 13 | 114 | 21.5 |
| 95 | 10 | 87 | 4 | 111 | 20 |
| 100 | 14 | 90 | 6 | 115 | 23 |
| | | 94 | 9 | 101 | 15 |
| | | | | 107 | 18 |
| | | | | 118 | 25 |
| $\Sigma(R_1) = 57$ | | $\Sigma(R_2) = 70$ | | $\Sigma(R_3) = 198$ | |

Once we have determined the sum of the ranks for each group, we can calculate the test statistic $H$ using the following general formula:

$$H = \frac{12}{(N)(N + 1)}\left(\frac{R_1^2}{n_1} + \frac{R_2^2}{n_2} + \cdots + \frac{R_k^2}{n_k}\right) - 3(N + 1) \qquad (16.11)$$

where

$N$ = the total number of observations in all samples combined ($N = n_1 + n_2 \cdots + n_k$)

$R_1$ = the sum of ranks for the first sample

$R_2$ = the sum of ranks for the second sample

$R_k$ = the sum of ranks for the $k$th sample

$k$ = the number of samples or groups

For our example with the data in Table 16.7 where $k = 3$, we can calculate the obtained value of $H$ as:

$$H_{obt} = \frac{12}{25(25 + 1)}\left[\left(\frac{(57)^2}{7} + \frac{(70)^2}{8} + \frac{(198)^2}{10}\right)\right] - (3)(25 + 1)$$

$$= (.01846)\,[(464.1) + (612.5) + (3920.4)] - (78)$$

$$= 14.24$$

The obtained value of $H$ then, is 14.24. We now need to obtain our critical value. When each sample has five or more observations, the sampling distribution of $H$ is approximately a chi-square distribution with $k - 1$ degrees of freedom. We can find our $H_{crit}$ from the chi-square distribution in Table B.4 of Appendix B.

Before doing this, let's formally state what our null and alternative hypotheses are:

$H_0$: The three samples come from the same population. For Table 16.7, the three groups are equal self-control.

$H_1$: The three samples come from different populations. The groups are not equal in self-control.

The test statistic is the Kruskal-Wallis $H$ test. With an alpha of .05 and 2 degrees of freedom $(k - 1)$, the critical $H$ from the chi-square distribution is 5.991. As $H_{obt}$ (14.24) is greater than $H_{crit}$ (5.991), we can reject the null hypothesis that the three groups come from the same population. We can therefore conclude that the incarcerated, addict, and Rotary Club males are different in their level of self-control.

Like the one-way ANOVA's $F$ test, the Kruskal-Wallis $H$ test tells us whether *any* group is statistically different from any other. If we reject the null hypothesis, however, we do not know which specific groups are significantly different from each other. In the one-way ANOVA we tested for the difference between pairs of sample means with the Tukey Honest Significant Difference (HSD) test. Unfortunately, there is no nonparametric equivalent for this test. The samples must be compared, two at a time, with the Mann-Whitney $U$ test. As we warned you in the ANOVA chapter about repeated pairwise $t$ tests, these multiple significance tests are not independent. The true alpha level is therefore not the same for each test.

## 16.6 A CORRELATION COEFFICIENT FOR RANK-ORDERED DATA

In Chapter 14 we examined the Pearson product–moment correlation coefficient as a measure of the association between two interval/ratio-level variables. You will remember that the Pearson correlation $(r)$ ranged in magnitude from $-1.0$ to $+1.0$, with a high correlation corresponding to a strong association between two variables and 0 indicating a lack of relationship. We also discussed a significance test for the Pearson correlation so we could determine the extent to which the correlation was significantly different from zero. The Pearson correlation required interval- or ratio-level data, so we cannot use this very valuable statistic when our data are only ordinal. Fortunately, we do have a nonparametric correlation coefficient that we can use with rank-ordered data that we discuss next.

### The Spearman Rank-Order Correlation Coefficient ($r_s$)

*Spearman's rank-order correlation coefficient* $(r_s)$ is appropriate whenever both variables are measured at the ordinal level or one is ordinal and the other interval/ratio. Think of Spearman's $r_s$ as the nonparametric counterpart to the parametric Pearson's $r$. Recall that with Pearson's $r$, the issue was whether the two variables were linearly related. With Spearman's $r_s$, we examine whether a person's *rank* on one variable is related to his or her rank on a second variable.

Like Pearson's $r$, Spearman's $r_s$ ranges in value from $-1.0$ for a perfect negative relationship to $+1.0$ for a perfect positive relationship, with 0 indicating the absence of any relationship between the two variables. To avoid any confusion between the two, the Spearman rank-order correlation always is shown with the subscript $s$ ($r_s$).

As an example, let's say we were interested in the relationship between the quality of the neighborhood in which people live and the level of crime in that neighborhood. The Chicago or Ecological School would argue that communities that are poor, inhabited by a highly mobile and transient population, and that have few community organizations suffer from "social disorganization." The Chicago School theorists have claimed that neighborhoods that are socially disorganized have higher crime rates than those that are not disorganized.

Let's assume that we have developed a community rating scale that measures how disorganized a neighborhood is. It includes such items as the number of community clubs and the number of owner-occupied residences. With this scale we rate a random sample of 15 neighborhoods in a given city. We also get a count from the local police of the number of crimes committed in each of these neighborhoods during a 12-month period. What we want to know is the correlation or the strength of the association between neighborhood organization and the neighborhood levels of crime. Because our community rating scale only measures at the ordinal level (we can only state that some communities are more disorganized than others but cannot state that the difference between any two ratings is constant), we will determine the correlation between the two variables with the Spearman rank-order correlation coefficient. The community rating and number of crimes for each of the 15 communities are reported in Table 16.8.

In order to estimate $r_s$ (which is the sample estimate for $p_s$, the population rank-order correlation coefficient) we need to rank-order both sets of raw scores. Unlike our assignment of ranks with the Mann-Whitney $U$ or Wilcoxon $T$ statistic, we do not first pool the data before assigning ranks. In computing $r_s$, the ranks for the two variables should be assigned separately. In this way, we can determine the extent to which the rankings on one variable are correlated with rankings on the other variable. So, we first rank-order the scores on one variable by assigning a rank of 1 to the lowest score, a rank of 2 to the next lowest score, and so on (or assign a rank of 1 to the *highest* score, a rank of 2 to the next highest score, etc.; it does not matter). Then we do the same for the second variable. As before, tied ranks are assigned the average of the ranks each score would receive if they were not tied. For example, there are two communities with the same community rating score of 4.6. This corresponds to the two ranks of 3 and 4. In this case, then, each community gets the average of $3 + 4/2 = 3.5$. The ranks for the two variables are also reported in Table 16.8.

The formula for Spearman's rank-order correlation coefficient ($r_s$) is:

$$r_s = 1 - \frac{6\Sigma D^2}{n(n^2 - 1)} \tag{16.12}$$

where
  $\Sigma D^2$ = the sum of the differences in ranks, squared

**TABLE 16.8. Raw Score and Rank on Community Rating Scale and Number of Crimes Committed in the Community for Random Sample of 15 Neighborhoods**

| Community Number | Community Rating | | Number of Crimes | | Difference between Ranks D | $D^2$ |
|---|---|---|---|---|---|---|
| | Score | Rank | Score | Rank | | |
| 1 | 4.6 | 3.5 | 41 | 5 | −1.5 | 2.25 |
| 2 | 7.8 | 8 | 66 | 9 | −1 | 1.00 |
| 3 | 3.1 | 1 | 25 | 1 | 0 | 0 |
| 4 | 6.9 | 6 | 46 | 6 | 0 | 0 |
| 5 | 8.6 | 11 | 80 | 11 | 0 | 0 |
| 6 | 9.1 | 12 | 95 | 13 | −1 | 1.00 |
| 7 | 7.2 | 7 | 35 | 3 | 4 | 16.00 |
| 8 | 11.1 | 14 | 112 | 14 | 0 | 0 |
| 9 | 8.3 | 9 | 75 | 10 | −1 | 1.00 |
| 10 | 3.2 | 2 | 32 | 2 | 0 | 0 |
| 11 | 10.3 | 13 | 92 | 12 | 1 | 1.00 |
| 12 | 4.6 | 3.5 | 36 | 4 | −.5 | .25 |
| 13 | 8.5 | 10 | 62 | 8 | 2 | 4.00 |
| 14 | 6.7 | 5 | 58 | 7 | −2 | 4.00 |
| 15 | 11.7 | 15 | 125 | 15 | 0 | 0 |
| | | | | | $\Sigma = 0$ | $\Sigma = 30.5$ |

To calculate the rank-order correlation, then, we need to find the difference between the two ranks, which we will label $D$. Once we find this difference by subtracting the second score from the first, we square it to obtain $D^2$. In subtracting the two ranks to arrive at $D$, be advised that the sum of $D$ will always be zero ($\Sigma D = 0$). That is, the sum of the negative differences in rank always equals the sum of the positive differences. You can use this as a check on your arithmetic.

Spearman's rank-order correlation coefficient is based on the sum of the squared differences of the ranks between two variables. This is comparable to what we did for the Pearson product–moment correlation coefficient with raw scores. You can think of Spearman's correlation coefficient as a product–moment correlation between the ranks of two variables. You can also see that $D$ and $D^2$ will be equal to one when the two rankings are exactly equal—when the highest rank on $x$ is also the highest rank on $y$. In this case $r_s = 1.0$.

Our interpretation of the Spearman correlation is also comparable to that for the Pearson correlation. When $r_s$ is $+1.0$, the two variables are perfectly positively correlated. That is, the ranks for the two variables are in the same order; the lowest rank on one variable is the lowest rank on the other. When $r_s$ is $-1.0$, the two variables are perfectly negatively correlated. There is perfect disagreement between the two ranks; the lowest rank on one variable is the highest rank on the other. When $r_s = \pm 1.0$, then, we can predict without error the rank of one variable based on our knowledge of the rank on the other. When $r_s = 0$, knowledge of the ranks on one variable provides no help in predicting the rank on the other.

Spearman's correlation when squared also has a proportionate reduction in error interpretation, as did Pearson's $r^2$. The value of $r^2_s$ represents the proportional reduction in error when predicting the rank of one variable from the rank of another. If an obtained $r_s$ was .75, for example, we could reduce our errors in predicting rank by $.75^2$, that is, 56 percent.

Let's calculate the value of $r_s$ for the data in Table 16.8:

$$r_s = 1 - \frac{(6)(30.5)}{15(15^2 - 1)}$$

$$= 1 - .05$$

$$= .95$$

The correlation between a community's ranking on a social disorganization rating scale and its ranking on crime is .95. The positive association tells us that, consistent with the theory of the Chicago School, communities that are ranked high in social disorganization also rank high in crime. If we square the obtained Spearman correlation coefficient, we learn that we can reduce our errors in predicting community crime ranks by 90 percent if we know the community's social disorganization rank.

As was true for the Pearson correlation, we also want to know if our obtained Spearman correlation is significantly different from zero in the population. The null hypothesis in this case states that the correlation in the population is equal to zero. Because we hypothesized that there would be a positive correlation between social disorganization rank and crime rank, our alternative hypothesis is directional:

$H_0: \rho_s = 0$

$H_1: \rho_s > 0$

This statistical test is relatively easy to conduct. When $n \leq 30$, the exact sampling distribution of $p_s$ can be found in Table B.12 of Appendix B, with corresponding values of $n$ and alpha. When $n > 30$, the sampling distribution of $\rho_s$ is approximately normal, and the statistical test is the $z$ test with the formula:

$$z = \frac{r_s}{\left(\dfrac{1}{\sqrt{n-1}}\right)} \tag{16.13}$$

The critical value of $z$ can be found in the standard normal table with the selected alpha level.

For $n < 30$ in Table 16.8, we can test the significance of $r_s$ by going to the exact sampling distribution of $\rho_s$ in Table B.12 of Appendix B. With an alpha of .01 (one-tailed) and $n = 15$, the critical value of $r_s$ is .623. Our obtained value of $r_s$ must be larger than the critical value to reject the null hypothesis. As $r_{s\,obt}$ is .95, we can reject the hypothesis that $\rho_s = 0$. We can therefore conclude that a neighborhood's social disorganization rank and crime rank are positively correlated in the population. If we were to use the normal approximation, our obtained value of $z$ would be:

$$z = \frac{.92}{\left(\dfrac{1}{\sqrt{15 - 1}}\right)}$$

$$= \frac{.92}{\left(\dfrac{1}{3.74}\right)}$$

$$= 3.44$$

With an alpha of .01 for a one-tailed test, our critical value of $z$ would be 2.33. As the obtained value of $z$ is greater than $z$ the critical value, we can reject the null hypothesis that $\rho_s = 0$. Had we not predicted the direction of our alternative hypothesis, that is, had we conducted a two-tailed hypothesis test, our critical $z$ value would have been $\pm 2.58$. As our obained $z$ value of 3.44 is greater than our critical $z$ value, we would have rejected the null hypothesis for a two-tailed test as well.

## 16.7 SUMMARY

Very often in criminological research, because we have small sample sizes and ordinal-level data, we cannot conduct parametric statistical hypothesis tests such as $t$ tests, $z$ tests, or ANOVA $F$ tests, nor can we estimate measures of association such as the Pearson correlation coefficient. In research situations where parametric statistics cannot be used, however, we can employ equivalent *nonparametric statistics*. Although nonparametric tests are less powerful than their parametric counterparts, we can, nonetheless, test many of the same hypotheses, and nonparametric statistics often are much easier to calculate by hand.

**TABLE 16.9. Parametric Statistical Tests and Their Corresponding Nonparametric Tests**

| Number of Samples | Parametric Test | Nonparametric Test |
|---|---|---|
| One | $z$ test | Binomial test |
| Two independent samples | Independent-samples $t$ test | Mann-Whitney $U$ test; two-sample Kolmogorov-Smirnov test; Wald-Wolfowitz runs test |
| Two dependent samples | Dependent or matched-samples $t$ test | Sign test; Wilcoxon matched-pairs signed-rank test |
| $k$ Independent samples | One-way analysis of variance | Kruskal-Wallis $H$ test |
| Correlation | Pearson product–moment correlation coefficient $r$ | Spearman's rank-order correlation $r$ |

**TABLE 16.10. Decision Rules for Rejecting the Null Hypothesis with Common Nonparametric Tests**

| Statistical Test | Reject $H_0$ if |
|---|---|
| Mann-Whitney $U$ test | $U_{obt} \leq U_{crit}$ |
| Kolmogorov-Smirnov two-sample test | $KS_{obt} \geq KS_{crit}$ |
| Wald-Wolfowitz runs test | $r_{obt} \leq r_{crit}$ |
| Sign test | $m_{obt} \leq m_{crit}$ |
| Wilcoxon signed-rank test | $T_{obt} \leq T_{crit}$ |
| Kruskal-Wallis test | $H_{obt} \geq \chi^2_{crit}$ |
| Spearman rank-order correlation coefficient | $-r_{obt} \leq -r_{crit}$ or $r_{obt} \geq r_{crit}$ |

In this chapter we studied the nonparametric analogs to several of the most popular parametric statistical tests. These include one- and two-sample independent-sample $t$ tests, a dependent-sample $t$ test, and a one-way ANOVA. We also examined the nonparametric correlation coefficient for rank-ordered data. To help you match the parametric statistic with its equivalent nonparametric counterpart, we have put both types of statistical tests for your review in Table 16.9. In addition, because with some nonparametric statistical tests you reject the null hypothesis when the obtained test statistic is less than the critical value, whereas with others you reject $H_0$ when the test statistic is greater than the critical value, we have provided a table (Table 16.10) that lists the conditions under which the null hypothesis is rejected for the most frequently used nonparametric tests. We hope that by now the nonparametric statistical tests examined in this chapter are important tools in your statistical arsenal.

## Key Terms

binomial test

distribution-free tests

Kolmogorov-Smirnov two-sample test ($K$-$S_2$)

Kruskal-Wallis $H$ test

Mann-Whitney $U$ test

nonparametric statistics

parametric statistics

sign test

Spearman rank-order correlation coefficient ($r_s$)

Wald-Wolfowitz runs test

Wilcoxon signed-ranks test

## Problems

**1.** It has been suggested in the literature on criminal violence that males who have an extra $Y$ chromosome (so-called $XYY$ males) are more likely to be violent than those males with only one $Y$ chromosome (Hook, 1973). To test this suggestion, you go to an adult penitentiary and take a random sample of 7 inmates who were convicted of homicide. You test them, and discover that 2 out of the 7 are $XYY$. The probability of any male in the population being $XYY$ is only .005. Test the null hypothesis that the probability of being $XYY$ for the population of murderers is .005, against the alternative hypothesis that it is greater than .005. Use an alpha level of .001.

**2.** You suspect that white citizens may be more satisfied with the police services they receive than nonwhite citizens. To test your hypothesis you develop a Police Satisfaction Scale. You believe this scale to be measured at the ordinal level. Scores on the scale range from 0 to 20, with higher scores indicating greater satisfaction with police services. You then take a random sample of 10 white citizens who live in a predominately white neighborhood and a second, independent random sample of 8 nonwhite citizens who live in a predominately minority neighborhood. The following data are the scores on the Police Satisfaction Scale for your two samples:

| White Citizens | Nonwhite Citizens |
|:---:|:---:|
| 10 | 20 |
| 6 | 8 |
| 5 | 15 |
| 18 | 14 |
| 11 | 19 |
| 12 | 7 |
| 4 | 3 |
| 17 | 16 |
| 13 | |
| 9 | |

Use the Mann-Whitney $U$ test to test the null hypothesis that the two samples were drawn from the same population against the alternative that the white citizen population is more satisfied with their police services. Use an alpha level of .05.

3. In their book *Crime and Human Nature*, James Q. Wilson and Richard J. Herrnstein (1985) claim that criminals are more impulsive in their temperament than noncriminals. You think that as a group criminals are also more diverse in how impulsive they are than noncriminals. To test this claim you take a psychological test of impulsivity called the Porteus Maze Test and administer it to a random sample of 12 convicted criminals and an independent random sample of 12 male members of the local chamber of commerce. Scores on the Maze test can be assumed to be measured at the ordinal level, with higher scores indicating more impulsivity. You obtain the following data.

*Porteus Maze Test Scores*

| Criminals | Noncriminals |
|:---:|:---:|
| 16 | 29 |
| 24 | 21 |
| 42 | 14 |
| 15 | 34 |
| 10 | 47 |
| 28 | 36 |
| 31 | 38 |
| 40 | 23 |
| 25 | 32 |
| 22 | 19 |

Using the Wald-Wolfowitz runs test, test the null hypothesis that the two samples were drawn from the same population against the alternative hypothesis that criminals are more impulsive. Use an alpha level of .025.

4. In a 1993 article, the British criminologist David Farrington suggested that kids who were bullies when young are more likely to be violent in the future. You suspect that one of the causes of bullying is a lack of parental supervision. To test your hypothesis you take a random sample of 12 single-parent families and a matched sample of 12 two-parent families. The parents are matched on race, age of child, income, and education. In both samples there is only one child in the home. You devise a behavioral instrument that measures bullying, with high scores indicating that a child is more of a bully. You are confident that this instrument measures at the ordinal level. You then score each child on the bullying instrument, and you obtain the following data.

| Single-Parent Families | Two-Parent Families |
|---|---|
| 15 | 11 |
| 18 | 13 |
| 25 | 10 |
| 32 | 36 |
| 19 | 12 |
| 27 | 15 |
| 21 | 24 |
| 14 | 19 |
| 26 | 20 |
| 39 | 14 |
| 27 | 20 |
| 23 | 16 |

Using the sign test, test the null hypothesis that the two samples were drawn from the same population, against the alternative that the population children in single-parent families have higher bullying scores.

5. With the data from Problem 4, test the same null and alternative hypotheses, but this time with the Wilcoxon signed-ranks test. Are your conclusions the same? If not, why not?

6. You want to do a study to see whether the strength of the evidence in a criminal case is related to the case outcome. You devise a scale that measures the quality and strength of evidence in a criminal case. This scale includes such things as the presence of eyewitnesses or expert witnesses, physical evidence, and other factors. The scale produces a single score reflecting the strength of the case. High scores on this ordinal scale reflect a stronger case. You then take a random sample of 10 cases that recently resulted in an acquittal, 8 that resulted in a conviction of a lesser charge, and 11 that resulted in a conviction on the original charge. You then read the cases and score each on the evidence measure. You obtain the following data:

| Acquitted | Convicted of Lesser Charge | Convicted of Original Charge |
|---|---|---|
| 19 | 36 | 31 |
| 25 | 28 | 46 |
| 21 | 40 | 50 |
| 10 | 33 | 27 |
| 32 | 45 | 39 |
| 14 | 18 | 47 |
| 12 | 43 | 34 |
| 17 | 15 | 30 |
| 20 | 37 | 22 |
| 29 | 33 | 49 |

With an alpha of .01, test the null hypothesis that all three samples were drawn from the same population against the alternative that there are different populations.

7. As the director of research for a state police academy, you want to replace the civil service exam, which all new recruits must take, with a police academy entrance exam. The superintendent of the academy will allow you to replace the civil service exam only if you can demonstrate that those who score high on the police academy exam also score high on the civil service exam. Both exams are measured at the ordinal level. To make your case, you give your police academy entrance exam to a random sample of 13 new recruits to the academy who have already taken the civil service exam. Here are your results for the two exams:

| Recruit | Civil Service Exam Score | Police Academy Exam Score |
|---|---|---|
| 1 | 65 | 4 |
| 2 | 88 | 15 |
| 3 | 97 | 19 |
| 4 | 75 | 5 |
| 5 | 82 | 16 |
| 6 | 77 | 8 |
| 7 | 80 | 10 |
| 8 | 78 | 9 |
| 9 | 69 | 6 |
| 10 | 92 | 12 |
| 11 | 81 | 7 |
| 12 | 96 | 20 |
| 13 | 83 | 17 |

Calculate the correlation between these two ordinal variables, and determine whether the obtained correlation coefficient is significantly different from zero. Use an alpha of .01.

## Solutions to Problems

1. You should recognize this as a binomial problem. Our null and alternative hypotheses are:

$H_0: p = .005$

$H_1: p > .005$

The probability of observing two out of seven men with an *XYY* chromosome combination is:

$$p = \frac{7!}{2!\,5!}(.005)^2\,(.995)^5$$

$$= \frac{5040}{240}(.000025)\,(.975)$$

$$= 21\,(.000024)$$

$$= .0005$$

This is less than .001, so we reject the null hypothesis. The probability of having an *XYY* chromosome set for those convicted of murder is greater than .005.

**2.** Our hypotheses are:

$H_0$: The population of white and nonwhite citizens are no different in their level of satisfaction with the police services they receive.

$H_1$: White citizens are more satisfied with their police services than nonwhite citizens.

The test statistic is the Mann-Whitney $U$ test. Our decision rule is to reject the null hypothesis if $U_{obt} \leq 20$. Letting the sample of nonwhites be the second sample, and using our computational formulas, we can determine the values of $U$ and $U'$ to be:

$$U = \left((10)(8) + \frac{(8)(9)}{2}\right) - 86$$

$$= (80 + 36) - 86$$

$$= 30$$

$$U' = (10)(8) - 30$$

$$= 80 - 30$$

$$= 50$$

The smaller of these two values is $U$, so our value of $U_{obt}$ is 30. Because this is not less than the critical value of $U$, we do not reject the null hypothesis. White and nonwhite citizens are not different in their satisfaction with police services.

**3.** Our hypotheses are:

$H_0$: The two samples were drawn from the same population. In other words, criminals and noncriminals are not different in terms of their impulsivity.

$H_1$: The two samples come from different populations. Criminals are more impulsive than noncriminals.

The test statistic is the Wald-Wolfowitz runs test. Our decision rule is to reject the null hypothesis if $r_{obt} \leq 6$. The list of runs would be:

| 1 | 2 | 3 | 4 | 5 | 6 | 7 | 8 | 9 | 10 | 11 | 12 |
|---|---|---|---|---|---|---|---|---|---|---|---|
| C | N | CC | NN | C | N | CCC | N | C | NNNN | CC | N |

As you can see, there are 12 runs in the data.

$r_{obt} = 12$. As $r_{obt} > r_{crit}$ (12 > 6), we decide not to reject the null hypothesis. We cannot reject the assumption that criminals and noncriminals have the same level or degree of impulsivity.

**4.** The hypotheses are:

$H_0$: There is no difference between the children of single- and two-parent families in terms of their tendency to bully.

$H_1$: Children from single-parent families are more of a bully than children from two-parent families.

The critical value of $m$ is 0. Our decision rule, therefore, is to reject the null hypothesis if $m_{obt}$ is less than or equal to 0.

There are 9 minus signs and 3 plus signs. The less frequently occurring sign, therefore, is the plus sign. Because there are three of them, $m_{obt}$ is 3. This is greater than the critical value of $m$ ($m_{crit} = 0$), so we fail to reject the null hypothesis. Children in single-parent families are not more of a bully than those in two-parent families.

5. Our hypotheses are the same. The statistical test for the Wilcoxon signed-ranks test is $T$. Our decision rule is to reject the null hypothesis if $T_{obt} \leq 10$. The sum of the negative ranks is 70, and the sum of the positive ranks is equal to 8. The value of $T_{obt}$ is the lesser of these two sums, so $T_{obt} = 8$. As this is less than the critical value of 10, our decision is to reject the null hypothesis. Children in single-parent families are more of a bully than children in two-parent families. The reason why this conclusion differs from that with the sign test is that the Wilcoxon signed-ranks test takes into account the *magnitude* of the difference between the matched scores, whereas the sign test only takes into account the *direction* of the difference.

6. The hypotheses are:

   $H_0$: All three samples were selected from the same population.

   $H_1$: The samples have been drawn from different populations.

   The test statistic is the Kruskal-Wallis $H$ test. Our decision rule is to reject the null hypothesis if $H_{obt} \geq 9.210$.

   $H_{obt}$ is equal to:

$$H_{obt} = \frac{12}{(29)(29 + 1)} \left( \frac{85^2}{10} + \frac{166^2}{8} + \frac{214^2}{11} \right) - (3)(29 + 1)$$

$$= \frac{12}{870} (722.5 + 3444.5 + 4163.3) - 90$$

$$= 116.6 - 90$$

$$= 26.6$$

   Our value of $H_{obt}$ is 26.0, whereas that for $H_{crit}$ is 9.210. As our obtained value is greater than the critical value, we decide to reject the null hypothesis. Cases that result in acquittal, conviction on reduced charges, and conviction on original charges do differ in terms of the strength of the evidence.

7. The sum of the squared difference scores ($\Sigma D^2$) is 34. We can now calculate our correlation coefficient with the formula for $r_s$:

$$r_s = 1 - \left( \frac{6(34)}{13(13^2 - 1)} \right)$$

$$= 1 - \left( \frac{204}{2184} \right)$$

$$= .91$$

   There is a very high positive correlation between the two variables. High ranks on the civil service exam are correlated with high ranks on the police academy exam.

   To determine whether our sample correlation coefficient $r_s$ is significantly different from zero, we can test the hypotheses that:

   $H_0$: $\rho = 0$

   $H_1$: $\rho > 0$

   Our decision rule is to reject the null hypothesis if $r_{obt} \geq .673$. As our obtained value of $r_s$ is .91, we decide to reject the null hypothesis. Scores on the civil service exam and police academy exam are positively correlated in the population.

CHAPTER 17

# Regression Analysis with a Dichotomous Dependent Variable: Logit and Probit Models

*Enjoy yourself, drink, call the life you live today your own, but only that, the rest belongs to chance.*

—EURIPIDES

## 17.1 INTRODUCTION

In Chapters 14 and 15, we examined the linear bivariate and multivariate regression model, respectively. In this model, a set of explanatory (independent) variables was presumed to be linearly related to a dependent variable that was measured at the interval/ratio level. We learned in those two chapters that the ordinary least-squares (OLS) regression model is a very good and very general tool in analyzing the relationship between one or more independent variables and a dependent variable. Unfortunately, however, the linear regression model is not so general that it is the only technique we need to learn to analyze the effect of one or more independent variables on a dependent variable because the model is appropriate only when our dependent variable is continuous and normally distributed in the population.

There are many times when the dependent variable we wish to explain or understand is not a continuously measured variable with interval- or ratio-level properties. In a great many instances in criminological and criminal justice research our dependent variable is a *dichotomous dependent variable*. By dichotomous we mean that there are only two different values for the outcome or dependent variable. Examples include whether a victim reports their victimization ("No," "Yes"), the type of charge filed by a prosecutor (capital, noncapital), whether someone has committed an offense ("Yes," "No"), the type of sentence imposed by a jury (life in prison, death), and whether a pretrial defendant appears for trial (appears, absconds) or tests positively for drugs (positive, negative). When a variable is assigned a value

564

of 0,1 (i.e., 0 = "No," 1 = "Yes"), it is often referred to as a *binary variable* or a *dummy variable*. As you can perhaps see, there are numerous cases where our outcome or dependent variable consists of a dichotomy. In these cases, we cannot examine our data with the OLS regression model. We must instead use another technique.

In this chapter, we briefly examine two other types of regression models; one is called a *logistic regression model* and the other a *probit regression model*. These models are the appropriate statistical procedures to use when the outcome variable is a dichotomy. We see that the logistic and probit regression models, like their OLS counterpart, estimate a coefficient that measures the effect of one or more independent variables on a dichotomous dependent variable. Also, like the OLS coefficient, we can test for the statistical significance of the estimated logistic and probit regression coefficient and determine how well our model fits the data. Before we examine these models, however, we need to understand why we cannot estimate OLS equations if we have a dichotomous dependent variable.

## 17.2 ESTIMATING ORDINARY LEAST-SQUARES REGRESSION MODELS WITH DICHOTOMOUS DEPENDENT VARIABLES

We use the hypothetical data in Table 17.1 as our example in this section. These data are the age of a random sample of 40 youths, and each youth's self-reported involvement in some type of alcohol use. Age is, therefore, our independent variable, and self-reported alcohol use is the dependent variable. Notice that, although the independent variable, age, is measured as a continuous variable, the dependent variable, self-reported alcohol use, has only two outcomes, "No" and "Yes." Rather than the frequency of alcohol consumption, then, we have measured whether these youths ever used alcohol.

In Table 17.1, we coded the "No" answers as 0 and the "Yes" answers as 1. Our outcome or dependent variable, then, is what is called a binary or a dummy dependent variable, which take on the values of 0 or 1 only. It appears from briefly examining Table 17.1 that there is a relationship between age and alcohol use, as few youths of young ages get 1s whereas most of those ages 15–17 do. If both of the variables were continuous, one of the first things we would do is to construct a scatterplot of the two variables to determine the strength and the nature of the relationship between them. Figure 17.1 shows the scatterplot of these two variables. Notice that all of the data points fall on one of two lines parallel to the $x$ axis. These lines correspond to the two observed values of $y$ (0 and 1), for those not using and those using alcohol, respectively. We can see from this scatterplot that most of the 0 values cluster at the younger ages and most of the 1 values cluster near the older ages. This supports our earlier hunch that age is related to alcohol consumption.

If we were to describe the relationship between age and alcohol use with an OLS regression model, it would take the following form:

$$y = a + bx + \epsilon \tag{17.1}$$

**TABLE 17.1. Data on Age and Alcohol Use for a Hypothetical Random Sample of 40 Youths**

| Age | Used Alcohol?* | Age | Used Alcohol?* |
|-----|-----|-----|-----|
| 10 | 0 | 14 | 0 |
| 10 | 0 | 14 | 0 |
| 10 | 0 | 14 | 1 |
| 10 | 0 | 14 | 1 |
| 10 | 1 | 14 | 1 |
| 11 | 0 | 15 | 0 |
| 11 | 0 | 15 | 1 |
| 11 | 0 | 15 | 1 |
| 11 | 0 | 15 | 1 |
| 11 | 1 | 15 | 1 |
| 12 | 0 | 16 | 0 |
| 12 | 0 | 16 | 1 |
| 12 | 0 | 16 | 1 |
| 12 | 1 | 16 | 1 |
| 12 | 1 | 16 | 1 |
| 13 | 0 | 17 | 1 |
| 13 | 0 | 17 | 1 |
| 13 | 1 | 17 | 1 |
| 13 | 1 | 17 | 1 |
| 13 | 1 | 17 | 1 |

*Coded as 0 if no alcohol use was reported, coded as 1 if alcohol was used at least once.

where

$a$ = the intercept

$x$ = the youth's age

$y$ = 0 if the youth reported no alcohol use; 1 if the youth reported using alcohol

$\epsilon$ = a term that reflects measurement errors and other factors that influence alcohol use in addition to age

FIGURE 17.1. Relationship between age and alcohol use.

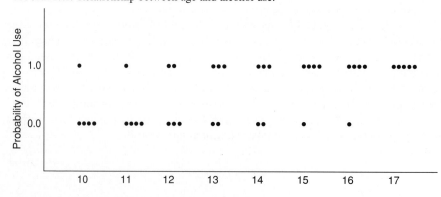

In this equation, observed values of $y$ would be restricted to either 0 or 1. As the expected value of $y$ is limited to 0 and 1, Equation 17.1 represents the effect of age on the *probability* of using alcohol. Because we are estimating the effect of an independent variable on the probability of the dependent variable occurring, models like the one in Equation 17.1 are often referred to as *linear probability regression models* because the probability of the dependent variable is expressed as a linear function of the independent variable or variables. Our regression equation, then, describes the probability that a youth will use alcohol, given his or her age. The regression coefficient, $b$, measures the effect on the probability of alcohol use with each unit (year) change in age.

Had our explanatory or independent variable been the dichotomous or binary coded (i.e., 0,1) variable and the dependent variable been continuous, we could easily have estimated an OLS regression model. However, we cannot use our OLS procedures to estimate the model illustrated in Equation 17.1 when it is the *dependent variable* that is binary coded. Why?

To answer this question, let's keep a few things in mind. First, let's remember that when the problem we wish to understand involves a dependent variable that only takes on the values of 0 and 1, as in Equation 17.1, we are actually examining the probability of the dependent variable occurring. As such, the observed (and expected) values of the dependent variable are bounded between 0 and 1, because we cannot have a probability that is less than 0 or greater than 1. Second, let's keep in mind that one of the assumptions we had to make before we could use the OLS estimation procedure was that the error term ($\epsilon$) be normally distributed at each value of $x$ (the assumption of *homoscedasticity*). This assumption really means that the epsilons are independent or unrelated to the independent variable. Let's now see what happens to these two ideas when we use our OLS to estimate a regression equation with a dichotomous dependent variable.

If we use the data in Table 17.1 to estimate an OLS regression model, we obtain the following equation:

$$\hat{y} = -1.00 + .116667x$$

The $y$ intercept is $-1.00$, so that when $x = 0$, the predicted value of $y$ is $-1.0$. The slope coefficient is .116667. The sign and magnitude of the slope coefficient tells us that a 1-year increase in age increases the probability of alcohol use by .116667. With this equation, we can determine that the predicted probability of alcohol use for a 12-year-old would be:

$$\hat{y} = -1.0 + (.116667)(12) \qquad = -1.0 + 1.40 \qquad = .40$$

The predicted probability of alcohol use for a 16-year-old would be:

$$\hat{y} = -1.0 + (.116667)(16) \qquad = -1.0 + 1.87 \qquad = .87$$

The probability that a 12-year-old will use alcohol is .40. The expected probability increases to .87 for a 16-year-old. This corresponds to our belief that age and the probability of alcohol use are positively correlated.

From this estimated OLS regression equation, let's now predict the probability of alcohol use for an 8-year-old youth:

$$\hat{y} = -1.0 + (.116667)(8) \qquad = -1.0 + .93 \qquad = -.07$$

The predicted probability is $-.07$, which is impossible, because a probability can never be less than 0. Let's predict the probability of alcohol use for a 20-year-old:

$$\hat{y} = -1.0 + (.116667)(20) \quad = -1.0 + 2.33 \quad = 1.33$$

The predicted probability that a 20-year-old will use alcohol is 1.33, which also is impossible, because a probability can never be greater than 1.0. You may now see one of the problems in using OLS to estimate a regression equation when the dependent variable is binary. Unless restrictions are placed on the values of the independent ($x$) variable, the predicted probability of the dependent variable may at times take on impossible values (less than 0 and greater than 1).

The reason why predicted values for the probability of $y$ can lie outside the limiting values of 0 and 1 is because an OLS model assumes that the best line that fits the data is a straight line. Thus, a unit increase in the $x$ or independent variable produces a $b$ change in the dependent variable (where $b$ is the value of the slope coefficient) *at all values of x*. The fitted straight line assumes that the relationship between the $x$ and $y$ variable is linear *across all x values*. In our example, this means that the probability that someone will use alcohol is a linear function of their age, and that a one-unit increase in age will have a $b$-unit change in the probability of committing alcohol use at any age.

The actual functional form of the relationship with a dichotomous dependent variable, however, may not be linear. Let us illustrate. We now have enough data coordinates to fit a straight line to the age and alcohol use data. We show this scatterplot and the best-fitting OLS line in Figure 17.2. In the top part of Figure 17.2, you can see that the predicted values of the probability of $y$ from the linear prediction line can exceed 0 and 1. High values of $x$ will result in predicted probability values of $y$ that are greater than 1.0, and low values of $x$ will result in predicted probability values of $y$ that are less than 0. In the bottom part of Figure 17.2, it appears from examining the data points that the expected change in $y$ for a one-unit increase in $x$ becomes smaller as $y$ approaches 0 or 1.

The poor fit of the linear regression line and an examination of the scatterplot would suggest to us that the effect of a one-unit change in age is greater for the values in the middle of the observed distribution of age than at either of its two ends. It appears that the best line to fit the data in Figure 17.2 is not a straight line, but an *S*-shaped curve. This is shown in Figure 17.3. This *S*-shaped curve indicates that the underlying relationship between the $x$ and $y$ variable is decidedly nonlinear.

One of the problems in using OLS to estimate the probability of a dichotomous dependent variable, then, is that predicted probabilities may exceed the two limiting values of 0 and 1. A second problem concerns the error term in the OLS model. One of the assumptions of the OLS regression model is that the error term is normally distributed and independent of any $x$ variable. With our estimated OLS regression equation, we can calculate a predicted value of $y$ ($\hat{y}$) for each age. We can then determine the value of the error term by subtracting the predicted from the observed value ($y - \hat{y}$). We have calculated these error terms, and the results are reported in Table 17.2.

A 12-year-old youth has a predicted probability of .17 of using alcohol. Because the outcome variable can take only two values (0,1), the error component can

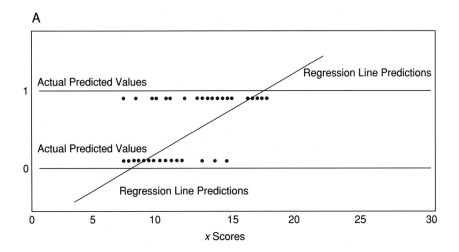

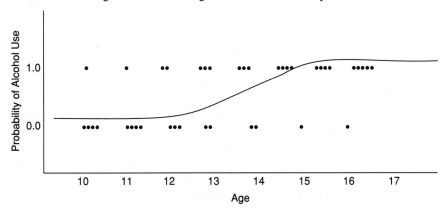

FIGURE 17.2. Fitting a straight line to the age and alcohol use data.

FIGURE 17.3. Fitting an *S*-curve to the age and alcohol use scatterplot.

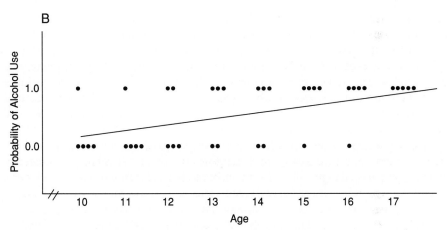

**TABLE 17.2.  Predicted Probability of *y* (*ŷ*) and
Value of the Error Term (*y* − *ŷ*) for Age and
Alcohol Use (data from Table 17.1)**

| Age | *ŷ* | ($y - ŷ$) for | |
|---|---|---|---|
| | | *y* = 0 | *y* = 1 |
| 10 | .17 | .83 | −.17 |
| 11 | .28 | .72 | −.28 |
| 12 | .40 | .60 | −.40 |
| 13 | .52 | .48 | −.52 |
| 14 | .63 | .37 | −.63 |
| 15 | .75 | .25 | −.75 |
| 16 | .87 | .13 | −.87 |
| 17 | .98 | .02 | −.98 |

take only two values, .83 when the observed value of *y* is 1 and −.17 when the observed value of *y* is 0. As you can see from Table 17.2, because *y* takes on only two values (0,1), the error term can assume only two values for any given value of *x*. This means that the error term is not normally distributed, but has a binomial distribution. You may remember from one of our earlier discussions that the variance of a proportion (*p*) is estimated as $\sqrt{pq/n}$ (where $q = 1 - p$). The variance of a proportion has a maximum value when $p = .5$ and declines as *p* approaches 0 and 1.

An implication of this, therefore, is that the variance of the binomially distributed error term is not constant, but depends on the predicted value of *y*. Observations where the predicted value of *y* are closer to 0 and 1 will have small variances, whereas observations where the predicted value of *y* is closer to .5 will have higher variances. Because the error terms do not have constant variance, they are said to be *heteroscedastic,* in violation of the OLS assumption of homoscedasticity. As a consequence of heteroscedasticity, hypothesis tests about estimated parameters such as the regression coefficient *b* will be incorrect.

When the dependent variable is a dichotomy (0,1), then, the OLS procedure cannot be used to estimate the linear probability model (Equation 17.1) because (1) unless there are restrictions placed on the values of the *x* variables, predicted values of *y* may not fall within the probability limits of 0 and 1, and (2) the error terms will not have constant variance. Because OLS cannot be used to estimate the effect of age on the probability of alcohol use, what other estimation strategies can we use? In short, the objective of our statistical modeling is to arrive at an understanding of the underlying processes that generated the empirical data. To the extent that nonlinear processes are at work and they are depicted as linear, we are not being faithful to our major objective.

One solution to this problem is to use a different type of linear estimation strategy, called a *generalized least-squares* model instead of the OLS model. A discussion of the generalized least-squares model is far beyond the scope of this book. In addition, the generalized least-squares approach may not be the best solution to our problem because this procedure still tries to fit a straight line to what appears to be nonlinear data points. The real problem, then, is that the relationship between our two variables may be nonlinear, necessitating a nonlinear estimation solution. In the sections that follow, we examine two nonlinear alternatives to the linear probability model that are appropriate with dichotomous dependent variables. These two models are the logistic and probit regression models.

Before we begin our discussion, however, let's first determine the shape or functional form of our model that best describes the relationship between age and the probability of alcohol use. With reference to the scatterplot of our age and alcohol use data (Figure 17.3), we noted that the best-fitting line was not a straight one but an *S*-shaped curve. There are two common distributions that take the *S*-shaped pattern of Figure 17.3, the cumulative logistic *(logit)* distribution and the cumulative normal *(probit)* distribution. These two distributions are shown in Figure 17.4. Although a detailed discussion of the logit and probit distributions is also beyond the scope of this book, we want to provide you with the basics of conducting a statistical analysis when you are confronted with a dichotomous dependent variable. Just think of both distributions as probability distributions that range from 0 to 1. As you can see from Figure 17.4, the logit and probit distributions are very comparable.

Using these two probability distributions gives rise to two somewhat different types of regression models, the logistic and probit regression model. For both models, the relationship between the independent variable or variables and the probability of $y$ is nonlinear, rather than linear, as in the OLS model. In addition, the logit and probit models do not require the assumption of constant variance, which we

FIGURE 17.4. Probit and logit distributions.

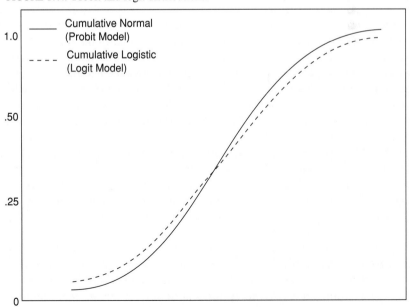

know is a requirement of the OLS model. There are, however, some basic similarities between OLS and logit/probit regression models. For example, both assume the following: that the dependent variable is a function of a set of one or more independent variables, that the data are randomly selected and independent observations, and that no two independent variables are perfectly correlated. In the sections that follow, we review the logit and probit regression models. As with OLS regression we examine logit and probit models first with one and then with more than one independent variable.

## 17.3 A LOGIT MODEL WITH ONE INDEPENDENT VARIABLE

The logistic regression model is based on something called the *cumulative logistic probability function.* In the logistic regression model we directly estimate the probability of an event occurring. In the case of one independent variable the logistic regression model is:

$$\text{Prob (Event)} = \frac{1}{1 + e^{-(\beta_0 + \beta_1 x)}} \qquad (17.2)$$

where

$\beta_0$ = the constant for the model estimated from the data
$\beta_1$ = the slope coefficient estimated from the data
$x$ = the independent variable and
$e$ = the base of the natural logarithms, which is approximately equal to 2.718

In the linear regression model, the constant and slope coefficients were estimated using the principle of least squares. In the least-squares method we estimated values of $\beta_0$ and $\beta_1$ that minimized the sum of the squared differences between the observed $y$ values and those predicted from the regression equation ($\hat{y}$). In the one-independent variable logistic regression model, the constant ($\beta_0$) and regression coefficient ($\beta_1$) are estimated according to the principle of maximum-likelihood. In *maximum-likelihood estimation* (MLE), the coefficients are estimated so as to maximize the probability or likelihood of obtaining the observed data. In other words, values for the unknown coefficients are chosen to make the observed data "most likely." In understanding the distinction between OLS and MLE methods, remember that they differ in terms of the criterion used to derive the estimates of the model. In OLS estimation, the procedure selects estimates that minimize $(y - \hat{y})^2$. In MLE, the procedure selects estimates that are most likely to be correct, given the data.

To use this method, we first construct something called a likelihood function, which expresses the probability of the observed data as a function of the unknown regression parameters ($\beta_0, \beta_1$). The MLEs of these parameters ($b_0, b_1$) are selected as values that maximize this likelihood function. It is in this sense that the estimated coefficients are those that make the observed data "most likely." The questions before us now are how we estimate these coefficients, how we interpret them, and how we assess how well our logistic regression model fits the data.

Put your mind at rest if you were already panicking at the prospect of having to hand-calculate a logistic or probit regression model. As in the preceding chapter, our goal here is for you to be able to understand and interpret logit and probit regression models. To achieve this end, we use models estimated with computer programs and concentrate our efforts on interpretation rather than calculation. Although the specific output you get varies with different statistical packages, most give you the following information: (1) the estimated logistic regression coefficient for each independent variable (*b*), (2) the standard error of the coefficient, (3) a Wald, or *t*, test for the significance of the estimated *b* and the significance level of the test statistic, and (4) various measures of the model's goodness of fit.

We report the generated results of an estimated logistic regression equation for the age and alcohol use data from Table 17.1 in Table 17.3.

**TABLE 17.3. Results of Logistic Regression Model for Age and Alcohol Use (data from Table 17.1)**

| Variable | Beta | Standard Error | Wald Statistic | df | Sig. |
|---|---|---|---|---|---|
| Age | .5979 | .1966 | 9.2460 | 1 | .0024 |
| Constant | −7.6397 | 2.6038 | 8.6084 | 1 | .0033 |

Initial log likelihood function (constant only in the model)
 −2 log likelihood = 54.548

With age in model
 −2 log likelihood = 41.553

| | Chi-Square | df | Sig. |
|---|---|---|---|
| Model chi-square | 12.995 | 1 | .0003 |

**Classification Table**

| | Predicted y Value | | |
|---|---|---|---|
| Observed y Value | 0 | 1 | Total |
| 0 | 11 | 6 | 17 |
| 1 | 4 | 19 | 23 |
| Total | 15 | 25 | 40 |

All cases predicted correctly   30/40 = 75.0%
0 cases predicted correctly   11/17 = 64.7%
1 case predicted correctly   19/23 = 82.6%

Percent predicted by chance   23/40 = 57.5%
Improvement over chance      = 17.5%

Before we begin interpreting these results, however, let's reintroduce the logit regression model with one independent variable:

$$\text{Prob (Event)} = \frac{1}{1 + e^{-(\beta_0 + \beta_1 x)}}$$

We can express the equation a little differently so that it looks more like the regression equation we are familiar with. We will let $P$ be the symbol for the probability of an event (alcohol use in our example). We then multiply both sides of the equation by $1 + e^{-(\beta_0 + \beta_1 x)}$ to get:

$$(1 + e^{-(\beta_0 + \beta_1 x_1)})P = 1$$

We then divide this expression by $P$, and subtract 1 to get:

$$e^{-(\beta_0 + \beta_1 x)} = \frac{1}{P} - 1 = \frac{1 - P}{P}$$

As by definition $e^{-(\beta_0 + \beta_1 x)} = 1/e^{(\beta_0 + \beta_1 x)}$, we can rewrite the expression as:

$$e^{\beta_0 + \beta_1 x_1} = \frac{P}{1 - P}$$

By taking the natural logarithm of both sides we obtain the following regression equation:

$$\beta_0 + \beta_1 x = \ln\left(\frac{P}{1 - P}\right)$$

$$\ln\left(\frac{P}{1 - P}\right) = \beta_0 + \beta_1 x \qquad (17.3)$$

We now have our familiar regression model, with a constant and a regression coefficient on the right-hand side of the equation. Because the odds of an event occurring are defined as the probability of the event occurring ($P$) over the probability of the event not occurring ($1 - P$), this equation indicates that the dependent variable in a logistic regression analysis ($\ln [P/(1 - P)]$) is the natural logarithm of the odds that an event will occur.[1] In the example we have been working with, the dependent variable is the natural log of the odds that a person used alcohol.

Because the dependent variable in a logistic regression equation is the natural log of the odds that an event will occur, the regression coefficient is interpreted as the change in the natural log of the odds of the dependent variable associated with a one-unit change in the independent variable. For example, a logistic regression coefficient of .58 tells us that a one-unit increase in the independent variable increases the log of the odds of the dependent variable by .58. A logistic regression coefficient of −.79 tells us that a one-unit increase in the independent variable decreases the log of the odds of the dependent variable by .79.

Because it is somewhat easier to think in terms of the odds of an event occurring rather than the log of the odds, we can take the *antilog* of the estimated logistic coefficient $b$.[2] The antilog of a coefficient can be obtained by most hand calculators. If $b$ is positive, this value will be greater than 1, indicating that the odds are higher; if *b* is negative, this value will be less than 1, indicating that the odds are lower. When the coefficient is zero, the antilog is equal to 1, indicating that when *x* increases by one unit, the odds of the dependent variable are not changed. For example, the antilog of a logistic regression coefficient of .58 is 1.79, telling us that when the independent variable is increased by one unit, the odds of the dependent variable occurring increase by a factor of 1.79. The antilog of a logistic regression coefficient of −.79 is .45, telling us that when the independent variable is increased by one unit, the odds of the dependent variable occurring decreases by a factor of .45.

Because even the odds of an event occurring is a somewhat difficult concept to understand for some, we suggest other ways to interpret the logit regression coefficient. From Table 17.3, we can see that the logistic regression coefficient for the effect of age on the probability of alcohol use is .5979. The sign of the coefficient tells us that the relationship between age and alcohol use is positive, and the magnitude tells us that a 1-year increase in age increases the log odds of alcohol use occurring by .5979. The antilog of .5979 is 1.82, indicating that when age increases 1 year, the odds that the youth has used alcohol increases by 1.82. What the antilog of a logistic regression coefficient tells us, then, is the increase (or decrease if the coefficient is negative) in the *odds* of the dependent variable occurring with a one-unit change in the independent variable. This does not mean, however, that the probability of a 15-year-old using alcohol is 1.82 times greater than the probability for a 14-year-old because the antilog of a logit coefficient does not express the probability of an event, but is really the *ratio of two odds ratios*. Let's explain and suggest a more understandable interpretation for the logit regression coefficient.

## Predicted Probabilities in Logit Models

Although the logit coefficient is not directly expressed as a probability, we can use the results of our logit analysis to estimate the probability of an event occurring. From Equation 17.2, the probability that *y* is 1 can be estimated by finding $\hat{p}$ for any given *x* value:

$$\hat{p} = \frac{1}{1 + e^{-(b_0 + b_1 x_1)}}$$

Following Roncek (1991), we can multiply the right side of this equation by 1.0 in the form of $e^{(b_0 + b_1 x_1)}/e^{(b_0 + b_1 x_1)}$ so that we have a formula for the probability (*P*) that does not have a negative sign for *e* in the denominator:

$$\hat{p} = \frac{e^{(b_0 + b_1 x_1)}}{1 + e^{(b_0 + b_1 x_1)}} \tag{17.4}$$

To find the predicted probability of a given *x* value, this formula tells us to choose a particular value of the independent variable, multiply it by the obtained logistic regression coefficient, add the value of the constant, and then exponentiate the sum. This result is the numerator of the estimated probability; the denominator is 1 plus the numerator. Let's go through an entire example with the logistic regression equation estimated from our age and alcohol use data.

From the results of our logistic regression model reported in Table 17.3, we can determine that the log odds that a 14-year-old youth would have used alcohol is:

$$\ln \frac{\hat{p}}{1 - \hat{p}} = -7.6397 + (.5979)(14)$$

$$= -7.6397 + 8.3706$$

$$= .7309$$

The estimated probability for a 14-year-old is:

$$\hat{p} = \frac{e^{.7309}}{1 + e^{.7309}}$$

$$= \frac{2.076949}{1 + 2.076949}$$

$$= \frac{2.076949}{3.076949}$$

$$= .675003$$

Because the probability that a 14-year-old used alcohol is .675, the probability that alcohol was not used is .325 (1 − .675). The odds of a 14-year-old using alcohol, then, is estimated as:[3]

$$\text{Odds} = \frac{\text{Prob Event}}{\text{Prob No Event}}$$

$$= \frac{.675}{.325}$$

$$= 2.08$$

Now, let's increase age (our independent variable) by one unit (1 year) and estimate the probability of alcohol use by a 15-year-old youth. From the regression equation we can calculate the log odds that a 15-year-old will use alcohol:

$$\ln \frac{\hat{p}}{1 - \hat{p}} = -7.6397 + (.5979)(15)$$

$$= -7.6397 + 8.96850$$

$$= 1.3288$$

The log odds that a 15-year-old will use alcohol is 1.3288. By increasing age by 1 year (from 14 to 15), we have increased the log odds of alcohol use by .5979 (1.3288 − .7309). Notice that this is precisely the value of the logistic regression coefficient for age (see Table 17.3). You can now perhaps see more clearly that the logistic regression coefficient reflects the change in the natural logarithm of the odds of the dependent variable for a one-unit change in an independent variable.

The probability that a 15-year-old used alcohol is:

$$\hat{p} = \frac{e^{1.3288}}{1 + e^{1.3288}}$$

$$= \frac{3.776509}{1 + 3.776509}$$

$$= \frac{3.776509}{4.776509}$$

$$= .790642$$

The estimated probability of alcohol use for a 15-year-old is .791, so the probability of no alcohol use is .209 (1 − .791). The odds of a 15-year-old using alcohol, then, are equal to 3.78 (.791/.209). Notice that, by increasing age by 1 year, we have increased the probability of alcohol use from .675 to .791. The probability that a 15-year-old used alcohol is .116, or 11.6 percent, higher than the probability for a 14-year-old.

Please observe that the difference in probabilities (.116) is *not* the value of the logistic regression coefficient ($b_{age} = .5979$). This coefficient, therefore, does not tell us the increase (or decrease) in the probability of the dependent variable for a one-unit change in $x$. Notice also that, by increasing age by 1 year, we increased the odds of alcohol use from 2.08 to 3.78. The odds increased by a factor of approximately 1.82 (3.78/2.08), which is the value of the antilog of the logistic regression coefficient for age ($e^{.5979} = 1.82$). As stated, then, the antilog of the logistic regression coefficient is the ratio of two ratios: (1) the odds ratio for 15-year-old youths (.791/.209 = 3.78), and (2) the odds ratio for 14-year-old youths (.675/.325 = 2.08) and cannot be directly interpreted as an increase in the probability of the dependent variable occurring.

Although the logistic regression coefficient cannot be interpreted directly in probability terms, we can use it to estimate the probability of $y$ at different values of $x$, and from that, determine the exact change in the predicted probability between any two values. Using Equation 17.4 we have calculated the probability of alcohol use for ages 10 to 17 from the data in Table 17.1 and report these probabilities in Table 17.4. From these probabilities you can discern several things. First, the relationship between age and alcohol use is positive. With each 1-year increase in age, the estimated probability of using alcohol increases. The probability of alcohol use increases from approximately .16 for 10-year-olds to more than .90 for 17-year-olds.

Second, this positive relationship between age and the probability of using alcohol is nonlinear. The numerical value of the increase in the probability of using alcohol varies depending on the age. Stated in more general terms, the effect of a given explanatory or $x$ variable on the dependent variable depends on the specific value of $x$. The effect of $x$ is greatest when the predicted probability is near .5 and diminishes at both higher and lower probabilities. Reflecting the fact that the slope

**TABLE 17.4. Probability of Theft and Changes in Probability for Ages 10–17 (data in Table 17.1)**

| Age | Estimated Probability | Change in Probability |
|-----|----------------------|----------------------|
| 10  | .159668              | —                    |
| 11  | .256775              | .097107              |
| 12  | .385824              | .129049              |
| 13  | .533201              | .147377              |
| 14  | .675003              | .141802              |
| 15  | .790642              | .115639              |
| 16  | .872884              | .082242              |
| 17  | .925848              | .052964              |

of the line for the *S*-shaped curve describing this relationship (see Figure 17.3) is steepest in the middle, an increase in 1 year of age has its greatest effect where the predicted probability is close to .5. There is a much smaller effect of age on the probability of alcohol use at both high and low values of the age distribution. For example, a change in 1 year from 13 to 14 increases the probability of alcohol use by approximately .142, but a change in 1 year from 16 to 17 increases the probability by only .052.

Now that we have the probability of alcohol use for each age, we can determine the odds of alcohol use, where the odds are equal to $\hat{p}/(1 - \hat{p})$ as shown in Table 17.5. The odds that a 12-year-old youth will have used alcohol is .628 and 1.142 for a 13-year-old. The ratio of the odds for a 13-year-old to the odds for a 12-year-old, then, is 1.142/.628, or 1.82. Because this value is derived by taking the ratio of two odds, it is often called the *odds ratio*. It is also referred to as the *odds multiplier* because it reflects how much higher (or lower) the odds of the dependent variable are by a change in the independent variable.

The odds of drinking, but not the probability, are 1.82 times higher for a 13-year-old than for a 12-year-old. The odds of a 17-year-old drinking alcohol are 12.486, whereas the odds of a 16-year-old are 6.867. The ratio of these two odds is

**TABLE 17.5. Predicted Probability ($\hat{p}$) and Odds of Alcohol Use by Age (data from Table 17.1)**

| Age | $\hat{p}$ | $1 - \hat{p}$ | Odds ($\hat{p}/[1 - \hat{p}]$) |
|-----|-----------|---------------|-------------------------------|
| 10  | .159668   | .840322       | .190                          |
| 11  | .256775   | .743235       | .345                          |
| 12  | .385284   | .614716       | .627                          |
| 13  | .533201   | .466799       | 1.142                         |
| 14  | .675003   | .324997       | 2.077                         |
| 15  | .790642   | .205398       | 3.849                         |
| 16  | .872884   | .127116       | 6.867                         |
| 17  | .925848   | .074152       | 12.486                        |

12.486/6.867, or 1.82. The odds of drinking for a 17-year-old, then, are 1.82 times higher than those for a 16-year-old. Thus, no matter which two ages you choose, a 1-year increase in age increases the odds of drinking by 1.82 or by a value approximately equal to $e^{b_{Age}}$ ($e^{.5979}$). Thus, a 1-year increase in age almost doubles the odds of drinking, although it does not have a comparable effect on the probability of drinking. The difference in the probability of drinking depends on the ages being compared.

There are two important points to keep in mind. One is that with a continuous independent variable, the logit regression coefficient cannot be directly interpreted in probability terms. Second, because the relationship between the independent variable is nonlinear, so that the effect of $x$ on the probability of $y$ depends on the value of $x$, the logistic regression coefficient cannot be interpreted in the same manner as an OLS regression coefficient. When the relationship between the variables is nonlinear, there is no constant effect of $x$ on $y$.

## Significance Testing for Logit Coefficients

The slope coefficient from our logistic regression model ($b$) is an estimate of an unknown population parameter ($\beta$). As with an OLS regression coefficient, we can conduct a statistical test that a given logistic regression coefficient is significantly different from zero in the population. The null hypothesis is that the coefficient is equal to zero ($H_0$: $\beta = 0$). The research hypothesis would be either the nondirectional alternative that the logistic regression coefficient is different from zero ($H_1$: $\beta \neq 0$) or the directional alternative that it is greater than zero ($H_1$: $\beta > 0$) or less than zero ($H_1$: $\beta < 0$).

Depending on the statistical software or package that you use, this hypothesis test will be either a $t$ statistic or a *Wald statistic*. Many computer programs report the standard error of the coefficient along with the estimated logistic regression coefficient. The $t$ statistic simply is the ratio of the estimated logistic regression coefficient to its standard error ($t = b/\text{SE}$). The $t$ statistic is distributed according to the Student's $t$ distribution with $n - k$ degrees of freedom. In this case, $k$ refers to the number of parameters to be estimated (the constant counts as 1). Thus, in the model with one independent variable, then, there are two unknown parameters that are estimated ($\beta_0$ and $\beta_1$; the constant and the logistic regression coefficient) and $n - 2$ degrees of freedom.

A comparable hypothesis test that $\beta$ equals zero can be conducted with the Wald statistic. This statistic has a chi-square distribution, so observed values are compared with critical values from a chi-square table at a given alpha level and degrees of freedom (unless the computer package you use prints the exact probability level, which most do). The degrees of freedom for the Wald test depend on the level of measurement of the independent variable(s). If you have a continuous independent variable, the degrees of freedom are equal to 1. Categorical independent variables with more than one level or groups have $k - 1$ (in this case $k$ refers to groups) degrees of freedom. For example, a categorical independent variable such as social class with three levels (lower, middle, and upper class) would have 2 ($3 - 1 = 2$) degrees of freedom.[4] When a variable has 1 degree of freedom, the

Wald statistic simply is the square of the ratio of the logistic regression coefficient to its standard error:

Wald $= t^2 = (b/\text{SE})^2$

Let's return to the output displayed in Table 17.3. Let's test the null hypothesis that the coefficient for age is equal to zero against the one-tailed alternative that the coefficient is greater than zero. Our research hypothesis, then, is that there is a significant positive relationship between age and alcohol use.

We will first test this hypothesis with the Wald statistic. From Table 17.3 you can see that the Wald statistic is 9.246 [approximately $(3.04)^2$]. The critical value of chi-square with 1 degree of freedom and an alpha of .05 is 3.841. Because the obtained value of Wald is greater than the critical value, we would reject the null hypothesis that the coefficient for age is equal to zero. Most computer programs will also give you the exact two-tailed probability values. To obtain the one-tailed values, simply divide the two-tailed probability by 2. These two-tailed values are shown in Table 17.3 under the heading "Sig." The exact probability of obtaining the Wald statistic we did for age given a true null hypothesis is .0024. The one-tailed probability is .0024 divided by 2, or .0012. As this is less than .05, we would reject the null hypothesis that $\beta_{\text{Age}}$ is equal to zero.

We could also test this hypothesis with the $t$ test by simply calculating the $t$ statistic ($b/\text{SE}$) from the coefficient for age. If we did this, we would obtain a $t$ statistic equal to 3.04 (.5979/.1966). With 38 degrees of freedom ($40 - 2$) and an alpha of .05, the critical value of $t$ necessary to reject the null hypothesis is 1.684 for a one-tailed test. As our obtained $t$ of 3.04 is greater than the critical value, we will reject the null hypothesis. Our conclusion would still be that age is significantly related to alcohol use.

## Model Goodness-of-Fit Measures

In addition to conducting significance tests for our independent variables, we would also like to assess how good of a model we have. It would be nice if we had a measure like the $R^2$ coefficient in OLS regression, where the magnitude of the coefficient reflected the amount of variance explained. Although statisticians have developed a few measures for logit and probit regression models that are comparable to the OLS $R^2$, none are exactly like it and not many have gained wide acceptance. Nevertheless, there are a few different tests we can use to evaluate the goodness of fit of our logistic and probit regression models.

One way to assess how well our model fits the data is based on how accurately we can predict the dependent variable. With a dichotomous dependent variable (coded as 0 or 1), we will have to predict which category of the dependent variable (0 or 1) each case falls into. Remember from our discussion that with an estimated logistic regression equation we can predict the probability of an event occurring (i.e., being a 1 rather than a 0 on a binary coded dependent variable). With these predicted probabilities, we can determine a cutoff point at which we assign cases to one category or the other of our dependent variable. For example, we might adopt the prediction rule that if the estimated probability of the dependent variable derived from the logistic regression equation ($\hat{y}$) is greater than .5, then we will predict that the value of $y$ for the dependent variable will be 1. In our example, the 1 would be those who used alcohol. If the estimated probability is less than or equal to .5, our prediction rule will be that the value of $y$ will be zero. In our example, the zero would be those who did not use alcohol. Our prediction or classification table in this instance, therefore, is based on the following prediction rule:

If $\hat{p} \leq .5$, $\hat{y} = 0$.
If $\hat{p} > .5$, $\hat{y} = 1$.

Because approximately .50 of our cases are in the 1 category of the dependent variable (23/40, or .575, to be exact), this is a reasonable prediction rule.

What we have, then, are observed values of $y$ for each observation, and predicted values of $y$ ($\hat{y}$) based on the logistic regression equation. One assessment of how well our model fits the data is the extent to which it correctly predicts observed values of the dependent variable. In Figure 17.5, we illustrate the predicted probabilities for each age group, the location of our cutoff point ($\hat{p} = .5$), and the two predicted values of $y$. All cases that fall to the left of the cutoff point are predicted to have a $y$ value of zero, whereas those to the right have a predicted $y$ value of 1.

In Table 17.6, we report for each of the 40 observations in our age and alcohol use data the age of the respondent, the predicted probability of $y$, the predicted value of $y$, the observed value of $y$, and whether the predicted value is correct. As you can see, if the predicted probability of $y$ is less than or equal to .5, the predicted value of $y$ is zero, and if the predicted probability of $y$ is greater than .5, the predicted value of $y$ is 1. We then compare the predicted with the observed value of $y$ and note with a plus sign correct predictions and incorrect predictions with a minus sign.

For example, the first observation has a predicted probability of .160. Because this value is lower than .5, we would predict that this observation would fall into the 0 category on the dependent variable (no alcohol use). In fact, the first respondent reported no alcohol use, so our model made a correct prediction, and we note that correct prediction with a plus. The fifth respondent also has a predicted probability

FIGURE 17.5. Observed $y$ values at each predicted probability value.
*Denotes an error in prediction.

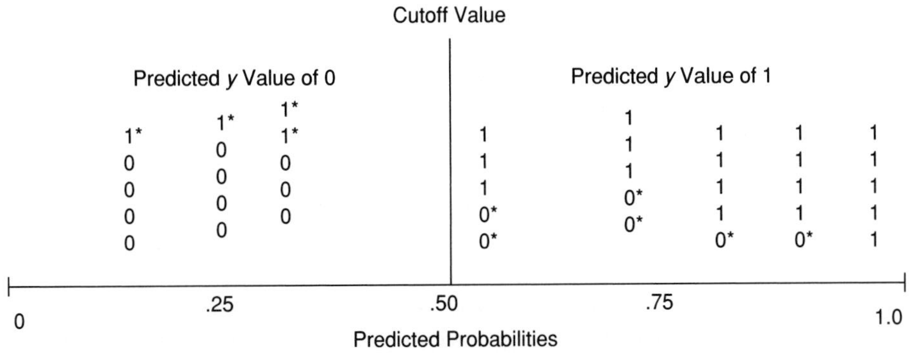

**TABLE 17.6. Estimated Probability, Predicted and Observed $y$ Value, and the Correctness of the Prediction Data for Age and Alcohol Use (data from Table 17.1)**

| Observation Number | Age | Estimated Probability | Predicted $y$ Value | Observed $y$ Value | Correct $(+)$ or Incorrect $(-)$ Prediction |
|:---:|:---:|:---:|:---:|:---:|:---:|
| 1 | 10 | .160 | 0 | 0 | + |
| 2 | 10 | .160 | 0 | 0 | + |
| 3 | 10 | .160 | 0 | 0 | + |
| 4 | 10 | .160 | 0 | 0 | + |
| 5 | 10 | .160 | 0 | 1 | − |
| 6 | 11 | .257 | 0 | 0 | + |
| 7 | 11 | .257 | 0 | 0 | + |
| 8 | 11 | .257 | 0 | 0 | + |
| 9 | 11 | .257 | 0 | 0 | + |
| 10 | 11 | .257 | 0 | 1 | − |
| 11 | 12 | .386 | 0 | 0 | + |
| 12 | 12 | .386 | 0 | 0 | + |
| 13 | 12 | .386 | 0 | 0 | + |
| 14 | 12 | .386 | 0 | 1 | − |
| 15 | 12 | .386 | 0 | 1 | − |
| 16 | 13 | .533 | 1 | 0 | − |
| 17 | 13 | .533 | 1 | 0 | − |
| 18 | 13 | .533 | 1 | 1 | + |
| 19 | 13 | .533 | 1 | 1 | + |
| 20 | 13 | .533 | 1 | 1 | + |
| 21 | 14 | .675 | 1 | 0 | − |
| 22 | 14 | .675 | 1 | 0 | − |
| 23 | 14 | .675 | 1 | 1 | + |
| 24 | 14 | .675 | 1 | 1 | + |
| 25 | 14 | .675 | 1 | 1 | + |
| 26 | 15 | .791 | 1 | 0 | − |
| 27 | 15 | .791 | 1 | 1 | + |
| 28 | 15 | .791 | 1 | 1 | + |
| 29 | 15 | .791 | 1 | 1 | + |
| 30 | 15 | .791 | 1 | 1 | + |
| 31 | 16 | .873 | 1 | 0 | + |
| 32 | 16 | .873 | 1 | 1 | + |
| 33 | 16 | .873 | 1 | 1 | + |
| 34 | 16 | .873 | 1 | 1 | + |
| 35 | 16 | .873 | 1 | 1 | + |
| 36 | 17 | .926 | 1 | 1 | + |
| 37 | 17 | .926 | 1 | 1 | + |
| 38 | 17 | .926 | 1 | 1 | + |
| 39 | 17 | .926 | 1 | 1 | + |
| 40 | 17 | .926 | 1 | 1 | + |

of .160 and a predicted value of zero. The observed value, however, was 1, because this person reported using alcohol. In this case the model made an incorrect prediction, which we note with a minus. To assess how well our model fits the data, we can compare the predicted with the observed *y* values and determine how often we make correct predictions.

In Table 17.3, we report the classification table that shows the observed and predicted values of alcohol use. The rows correspond to observed values of the dependent variable, and the columns refer to the predicted values. Note that in the observed data there were 17 observations with a *y* value of zero (no alcohol use) and 23 with a *y* value of 1 (alcohol use). The model predicted that 15 cases would have a *y* value of 0 and 25 would have a value of 1. The cells in the table show the number of correct and incorrect predictions. For example, of the 40 cases, the model predicted that 15 persons would not have used alcohol. Of these 15, 11 actually did not use alcohol, so there were 11 correct predictions and 4 incorrect predictions. The model also predicted that 25 of the 40 cases would have used alcohol. Of these 25, 6 actually did not use alcohol, so there were 19 correct predictions and 6 incorrect predictions.[5]

The classification table reveals that 30 of the 40 cases, or 75 percent, of the total were correctly predicted. Approximately 65 percent (11/17) of the 0 cases were predicted correctly, as were 83 percent (19/23) of those cases that fell into the 1 category of the dependent variable. We can say, then, that with our logistic regression model, we are able to predict correctly which category of the dependent variable the case falls into 75 percent of the time. This 75 percent prediction accuracy, however, must be viewed against how well we could predict our cases without the model. If we know the percent of the cases that would be correctly predicted without the regression model by chance alone, we can discern how much we have improved our prediction with the model.

If we attempted to predict the dependent variable knowing only from our observed data that 17 cases fell into the 0 category and 23 cases fell into the 1 category, our best prediction would be that all 40 cases would be 1's because the 1 category is the mode. If we were to do this, we would make 23 correct predictions (because 23 cases actually did fall into the 1 category) and 17 incorrect predictions. Without our logistic regression model, therefore, we will accurately predict 23/40, or 57.5 percent, of the cases. With our regression model, we correctly predicted 75 percent of the cases. Our improvement in prediction with the regression model, then, is 75 percent minus 57.5 percent, that is, 17.5 percent. We have improved our prediction by 17.5 percent, a modest improvement over chance (see Table 17.3). Keep in mind, however, the fact that, even when we use a person's age to predict whether they use alcohol, we continue to have some errors in prediction. This should suggest to us the possibility that other factors in addition to age may be useful in predicting alcohol use and should be directly incorporated into our logistic regression model.

In our example, our prediction rule was that, if the predicted probability of *y* was greater than .5, we would predict a 1 (alcohol use) on the dependent variable, and if the predicted probability of *y* was less than or equal to .5, we would predict a zero (no alcohol use) on the dependent variable. Most computer programs that estimate logistic regression models use the predicted probability value of .5 for *y* to compute their prediction tables. This .5 value is chosen mainly because of convention rather than any sound mathematical or statistical properties. When the proportion of cases in the two categories of the dependent variable are approximately .5, a cutoff value of .5 will provide a very reasonable prediction strategy. There may be times, however, when you might want to use a different prediction rule. As the proportion of cases in the two categories deviates farther from an even split, you will probably want to change your predicted cutoff value.

One procedure to use if your intention is to minimize misspredictions of both 0 and 1 cases is first to estimate the probability of the dependent variable occurring for each case. Then, rank-order these probabilities from high to low, and calculate a cumulative frequency distribution. Next, determine the proportion or percent of cases that fall into the 1 category of the dependent variable. Finally, go down the cumulative frequency distribution and make your cutoff threshold so that the proportion of predicted 1 cases from the estimated probability distribution is equal to the proportion of observed 1 cases.

For example, suppose that for a given dependent variable 15 percent (.15) of your cases are 1s. To minimize misspredictions of both 0 and 1 cases, calculate an estimated probability for each case in your sample. Construct a cumulative frequency distribution from these estimated probabilities where the scores are ranked from high to low. Then draw your cutoff line so that the highest 15 percent of the estimated probability scores will have a score of 1. In this way, 15 percent of your estimated probabilities will be predicted to be 1s, and 15 percent of your observed scores will be 1s.

In other instances your cutoff point will be dictated by substantive concerns, rather than trying to maximize your general accuracy of prediction. That is, in some instances, you may want to minimize your errors in predicting cases that are 1s on the dependent variable (and are less interested in minimizing prediction errors for 0 cases). Given this interest, it will make more sense to you to adopt a decision rule that tells you only whether, if the predicted probability of $y$ exceeds some high value, say .75, the prediction of the dependent variable will be 1. What happens if you increase the value of the predicted probability of $y$? What you are saying is that you want to be very sure before you make the prediction that a particular case falls into the 1 category of the dependent variable. By doing this, you will avoid the error of predicting someone to be a 1 when in fact he or she scores a 0 (what is called a false-positive error). In other words, you may miss some of the 1 cases, but those that you do predict to be 1s will have a high probability of being correct. For other substantive problems, it may be better to lower the prediction cutoff value (say to .25) to make sure you capture more of the 1 cases, at the expense of overpredicting. In this scenario, you will predict many more 1 cases than actually exist.

The more general and perhaps most important point is that, even though many computer statistical programs adopt a .5 cutoff by default, you do not have to follow this rule automatically. There is no one "optimal" prediction strategy or cutoff value that is appropriate in all circumstances. Your decision as to the predicted probability of the cutoff value should be guided by your knowledge of the problem and the various costs of making over- or underpredictions.

In our alcohol use data, for example, we could have chosen the following prediction rule:

If $\hat{p} \leq .75$, $\hat{y} = 0$.
If $\hat{p} > .75$, $\hat{y} = 1$.

Had we adopted this decision strategy, we would have predicted that everyone under the age of 15 would have no alcohol use ($\hat{y} = 0$), and everyone 15 to 17 years of age would have used alcohol ($\hat{y} = 1$). We illustrate this new prediction strategy in Figure 17.6, and the classification table reported in Table 17.7. Using the cutoff of .75, we would have a lower overall prediction rate than what we had when we used .50 as our cutoff point (70 percent correctly predicted as opposed to 75 percent). Notice, however, that in the first prediction table we predicted that 25 cases were 1s, but only 19 were. We made six errors in predicting the 1 cases. In the prediction table above using the cutoff of .75, we predicted that only 15 cases would be 1s. Of these 15 predicted to be 1s, 13 were 1s, so we made only two errors of this type. Our accuracy in predicting one cases is now 88 percent. The lesson you should draw from this is that, when deciding on a prediction rule, the various costs of accurate and inaccurate predictions must be carefully weighed. In sum, your cutoff value and prediction rule should depend on your data and specific substantive problem at hand and not the default value of some computer statistical program.

Determining how well the regression model predicts cases on the dependent variable is one way to assess how well the model fits the data. Another way is to test the null hypothesis that all the coefficients in the model (except for the constant) are equal to zero. This is comparable to what we did with the $F$ test in OLS regression. In the case of logistic regression, we determine the *likelihood* of a model, which we have said before is the probability of the observed results given the coefficient estimates. Because the likelihood is a number smaller than 1, it has become convention to use $-2$ times the natural logarithm of the likelihood (often referred to as $-2LL$, or the *likelihood ratio statistic*) as an expression of how well a given model fits the data. A good model, one wherein the probability of the observed results is high, is one with a small value of $-2LL$. If the model has a perfect fit to the data, the likelihood would equal 1 and $-2LL$ would equal zero.

To determine how well a model with a given number of independent variables fits the data, we first estimate a model that includes only the constant. This model, then, has no independent variables in it. From this model, let's call it the baseline or constant-only model, we determine the value of $-2LL$, which measures how

FIGURE 17.6. Observed y values at each predicted probability value.
*Denotes an error in prediction.

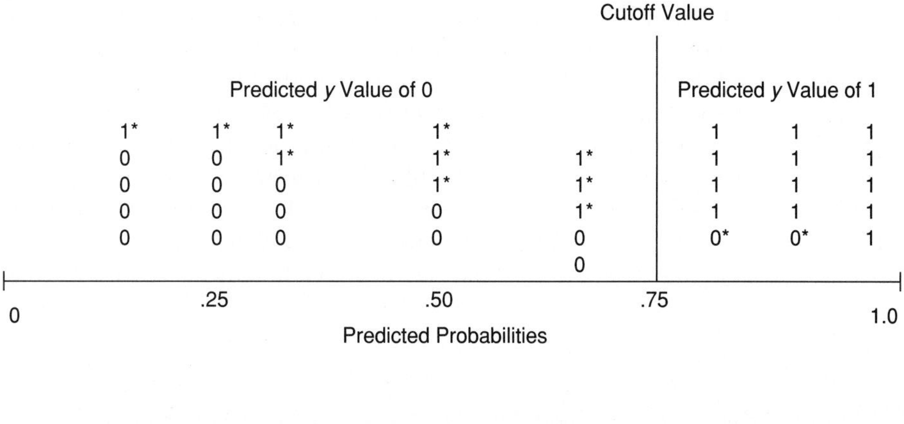

**TABLE 17.7.  Predicted and Observed Alcohol Use**

**Classification Table**

|  | Predicted y Value | | |
| --- | --- | --- | --- |
| Observed y Value | No Alcohol Use | Alcohol Use | Total |
| No Alcohol Use | 15 | 2 | 17 |
| Alcohol Use | 10 | 13 | 23 |
| Total | 25 | 15 | 40 |
| All cases predicted correctly | 28/40 = 70.0% | | |
| 0 cases predicted correctly | 15/17 = 88.2% | | |
| 1 case predicted correctly | 13/23 = 56.5% | | |

likely the observed results are with no independent variables. We then estimate our model with both the constant and independent variable (or variables) included and determine the value of $-2LL$ for this model. If the independent variable(s) explain the dependent variable, the fit of this model to the data will be better than our baseline model, and this improvement in fit will be seen in a lower $-2LL$ value. (Remember that a good model is one with a low value of $-2LL$.) The difference between $-2LL$ for the baseline model and $-2LL$ for the independent variable model is a chi-square statistic. The number of degrees of freedom is equal to the difference in the degrees of freedom between the two models. We can, then, conduct a chi-square test that all of the logistic coefficients in the independent variables model are equal to zero. As we said, this is comparable to our OLS overall $F$ test.

In Table 17.3, we report the value of $-2LL$ for the constant-only (baseline) model. It is equal to 54.548.[6] The number of degrees of freedom for a logistic regression model are $n - k$, where $k$ is the number of parameters to be estimated in the model. With only the constant in the baseline model, there is only one parameter to estimate ($\beta_0$), so there are $40 - 1$, or 39, degrees of freedom. The value of $-2LL$ for the model that includes age is 41.553. We have another parameter to estimate in this model ($\beta_1$) in addition to the constant, so there are $n - 2$, or 38, degrees of freedom. The difference in $-2LL$ between the two models is $54.548 - 41.553 = 12.995$, and the difference in the degrees of freedom is 1 ($39 - 38 = 1$).

The test that all of the independent variable coefficients in the model (in this example there is only one independent variable, the coefficient for age) are zero is a chi-square test, where the obtained chi-square value is 12.995 with 1 degree of freedom. We then conduct a hypothesis test that $\beta_{Age}$ is zero with an alpha of .01. The critical chi-square value with 1 degree of freedom is 6.635. Because our obtained chi-square value of 12.995 is greater than the critical value, we reject the null hypothesis and conclude that the coefficient in the model is significantly different from zero. It would appear from our model diagnostics, then, that our model that includes ages provides a better fit to the data than one that includes only the constant.

## Another Logit Regression Example

Before we discuss the probit model with one independent variable, let's go through another example of a one-independent variable logistic regression equation. In this case, however, the independent variable as well as the dependent variable are dichotomous and coded as 0,1. In this example, the independent variable is the race of the victim in a murder (0 = African American victim, 1 = white victim), and the dependent variable is the decision of the prosecutor to seek a death sentence (0 = life sentence, 1 = death sentence). The data for this example are shown for you in Table 17.8. From this data set, we create a contingency table, which is displayed in Table 17.9.

**TABLE 17.8. Race of Victim and Decision of the Prosecutor to Seek the Death Sentence for 29 Hypothetical Cases**

| Number of Case | Race of Victim* | Prosecutor's Decision† |
|---|---|---|
| 1 | 0 | 0 |
| 2 | 0 | 0 |
| 3 | 0 | 0 |
| 4 | 0 | 0 |
| 5 | 0 | 0 |
| 6 | 0 | 0 |
| 7 | 0 | 0 |
| 8 | 0 | 0 |
| 9 | 0 | 0 |
| 10 | 0 | 0 |
| 11 | 1 | 0 |
| 12 | 1 | 0 |
| 13 | 0 | 1 |
| 14 | 0 | 1 |
| 15 | 0 | 1 |
| 16 | 1 | 1 |
| 17 | 1 | 1 |
| 18 | 1 | 1 |
| 19 | 1 | 1 |
| 20 | 1 | 1 |
| 21 | 1 | 1 |
| 22 | 1 | 1 |
| 23 | 0 | 0 |
| 24 | 0 | 0 |
| 25 | 0 | 0 |
| 26 | 1 | 1 |
| 27 | 0 | 1 |
| 28 | 1 | 0 |
| 29 | 0 | 0 |

*Coded as 0 if victim was African American and 1 if white.
†Coded as 0 if prosecutor sought life sentence and 1 if prosecutor sought death sentence.

**TABLE 17.9. Relationship between Race of Victim and Prosecutor's Decision to Seek a Death Sentence (data from Table 17.8)**

| Prosecutor's Decision | Race of Victim | | Total |
|---|---|---|---|
| | African American | White | |
| Life | 14 | 3 | 17 |
| Death | 4 | 8 | 12 |
| Total | 18 | 11 | 29 |

In Table 17.9 you can see that the prosecutor sought the death penalty in 8 white victim cases and 4 African American victim cases, and sought a life sentence for 3 white victim and 14 African American victim cases. We can easily determine, then, that the probability of a death sentence rather than a life sentence is much greater for those cases that involve a white murder victim .727 (8/11) than for those with an African American victim .222 (4/18). This would lead us to suspect a relationship between race of the victim and the decision of the prosecutor to seek a death sentence.

To examine this relationship further, we estimate a logistic regression model. In this model the decision of the prosecutor to seek a life (coded 0) or death sentence (coded 1) is the dependent variable, and the race of the victim (coded 0 for African American victims and 1 for white victims) is the independent variable. As you can see, both the dependent and independent variables are dichotomous and binary coded. The results for this logistic regression model are reported in Table 17.10.

The estimated regression model is:

$$\ln \left( \frac{\text{Prob of Death Sentence}}{\text{Prob of No Death Sentence}} \right) = -1.2528 + (2.2336)(x_1)$$

You can see that the logistic regression coefficient for the race of the victim is 2.2336. From what we have learned about logistic coefficients, we know that this means that a one-unit change in the independent variable (i.e., going from the case of an African American victim to that of a white victim) increases the log of the odds of a death sentence by 2.2336.

If we were to test the significance of the regression coefficient for victim's race, we could use the $t$ test and take the ratio of the race of victim coefficient to its estimated standard error (2.2336/.8830). The $t$ statistic would be 2.53. With $n - 2$, that is, 27, degrees of freedom and a one-tailed alpha of .05, the critical value of $t$ would be 1.703. Because the obtained $t$ value is greater than the critical $t$ value, we would reject the null hypothesis that $\beta_{\text{Race of Victim}}$ equals zero. It would appear that the race of the victim is significantly related to the prosecutor's decision to seek the death sentence. Prosecutors are significantly more likely to seek a death sentence when the victim is white rather than African American.

We could also conduct the hypothesis test that $\beta_{\text{Race of Victim}}$ equals zero with our Wald statistic. The Wald statistic for the race of the victim is 6.3980 (remember, the Wald is the square of the obtained $t$ statistic). Because the Wald statistic has a

**TABLE 17.10. Results of Logistic Regression Model for Race of Victim and Prosecutor's Decision (data from Table 17.8)**

| Variable | Beta | Standard Error | Wald Statistic | df | Sig. |
|---|---|---|---|---|---|
| Victim's race | 2.2336 | .8830 | 6.3980 | 1 | .0114 |
| Constant | −1.2528 | .5669 | 4.8826 | 1 | .0271 |

Initial log likelihood function (constant only in the model)
  −2 log likelihood = 39.336

With race of victim in model
  −2 log likelihood = 31.960

| | Chi-Square | df | Sig. |
|---|---|---|---|
| Model chi-square | 7.376 | 1 | .0066 |

**Classification Table**

| | Predicted y Value | | |
|---|---|---|---|
| Observed y Value | 0 | 1 | Total |
| 0 | 14 | 3 | 17 |
| 1 | 4 | 8 | 12 |
| Total | 18 | 11 | 29 |

| | |
|---|---|
| All cases predicted correctly | 22/29 = 75.9% |
| 0 cases predicted correctly | 14/17 = 82.4% |
| 1 case predicted correctly | 8/12 = 66.7% |
| Percent predicted by chance | 17/29 = 58.6% |
| Improvement over chance | = 17.3% |

chi-square distribution, if we went to our chi-square table with 1 degree of freedom and our previous .05 alpha level, we would find a critical chi-square of 3.841. Because our Wald statistic is greater than this value, we would reject the hypothesis that $\beta_{\text{Race of Victim}}$ equals zero. From Table 17.10 we can see that the exact probability (two-tailed) of our Wald statistic for the race of the victim is .0114; the one-tail value is less than our selected alpha of .05, so we would reject the null hypothesis.

To learn more about the logistic regression coefficient, we would like to demonstrate that we could have estimated the regression model by hand calculations directly from the data in Table 17.9. Let's begin with the logistic regression coefficient for the effect of the race of the victim on the decision of the prosecutor to seek a death sentence. Keeping in mind that the logistic regression coefficient measures the log of the odds of the dependent variable occurring, let's express this relationship with the following equation:

$$b_{\text{Race of Victim}} = \ln \left( \frac{\text{Odds of Death Sentence for White Victim Case}}{\text{Odds of Death Sentence for African American Victim Case}} \right)$$

$$(17.5)$$

Remember that the odds of an event are equal to the ratio of the probability that the event will occur over the probability that it will not occur (Odds = Prob (Event)/Prob (No Event)). With this, we can determine from Table 17.9 the odds that a death sentence will be sought in a white and African American victim case:

$$\text{Odds of a Death Sentence for a White Victim Case} = \frac{8/11}{3/11}$$

$$= \frac{.727}{.273}$$

$$= 2.66$$

$$\text{Odds of a Death Sentence for an African American Victim Case} = \frac{4/18}{14/18}$$

$$= \frac{.222}{.778}$$

$$= .285$$

From Equation 17.5, we can find the value of the logistic regression coefficient for the race of the victim by taking the natural log of these two ratios:

$$b_1 = \ln\left(\frac{2.66}{.285}\right)$$

$$= \ln 9.33$$

$$= 2.234$$

As you can see from this solution, the logistic regression coefficient for victim's race simply is the natural log of the ratio of the odds that a death sentence will be sought in a white victim case to the odds that a death sentence will be sought in an African American victim case. The log of the odds is higher in white victim cases by a factor of 2.234.

If we take the antilog of the logistic regression coefficient for the victim's race ($e^{2.2336} = 9.33$), we arrive at something we earlier called the odds ratio, or odds multiplier. Notice that, as before, the odds ratio simply is the ratio of two odds, the odds of the dependent variable occurring in one category of the independent variable to the odds of its occurring in the other category of the independent variable. The odds of a death sentence in a white victim case is 2.66 (.727/.273), and the odds of a death sentence in an African American victim case is .285 (.222/.778). The ratio of these two odds is the odds ratio or odds multiplier (2.66/.285 = 9.33). Again, we remind you that the *probability* of a death sentence in white victim cases is not over nine times higher, but the *odds* are. The odds ratio of 9.33 in our example indicates that the odds of a death sentence being sought by the prosecutor are 9.33 times higher for murders that involve a white victim than for those that involve an African American victim.

Finally, let's examine how well the model we have estimated fits the observed data. One way to do this is to use our estimated logistic regression equation to predict the value of the dependent variable and then compare the predicted with the observed values. Using the familiar logit formula for predicted probabilities:

$$\hat{p} = \frac{e^{b_0 + b_1 x_1}}{(1 + e^{(b_0 + b_1 x_1)})}$$

we can predict the probability of a death sentence for white and African American victim cases. For white victim cases ($x_1 = 1$), the predicted probability is:

$$\hat{p} = \frac{e^{-1.253 + 2.234}}{(1 + e^{(-1.253 + 2.234)})}$$

$$= \frac{e^{.981}}{(1 + e^{.981})}$$

$$= \frac{2.667}{3.667}$$

$$= .727$$

And for African American victim cases ($x_1 = 0$) the predicted probability is:

$$\hat{p} = \frac{e^{-1.253 + 0}}{(1 + e^{(-1.253 + 0)})}$$

$$= \frac{e^{-1.253}}{(1 + e^{-1.253})}$$

$$= \frac{.286}{1.286}$$

$$= .222$$

Using the prediction rule that:

If $\hat{p} \leq .5$, $\hat{y} = 0$,

If $\hat{p} > .5$, $\hat{y} = 1$,

we would predict that the prosecutor would seek a sentence of death in all 11 of the white victim cases and none of the 18 African American victim cases. Comparing the predicted with the observed value of $y$, we can create a prediction or classification table, which we show in Table 17.10. We can see that, overall, the model correctly predicts 22 of the 29 cases, for a correct prediction rate of 75.9 percent.

Although the overall prediction rate was 75.9 percent, to understand better the usefulness of our prediction rate we need to determine how much our predictions with the model are improved over chance. With no knowledge of the independent variable, we would predict that all 29 cases would be life sentence cases (because a life sentence is the modal category of the dependent variable). If we did this, we would make 12 prediction errors, because there are 12 death sentence cases observed. Our prediction rate by chance alone, then, would be 17/29, or 58.6 percent. Our prediction rate when we used our knowledge of the victim's race was 75.9 percent, so we have improved our prediction rate by 17.3 percent. In other words, when we use our logistic regression equation, we are able to reduce our prediction errors by almost 20 percent.

We also can assess the fit of our model by examining the improvement in the likelihood function when we compare the baseline (constant-only) model to one that includes the victim's race. From Table 17.10 we can see that with no independent variables in our model, the value of $-2LL$ is 39.336. With the race of the victim in the model the value of $-2LL$ is down to 31.960. The difference between the two values (the improvement in the model) is 7.376. We know that the difference has a chi-square distribution with 1 degree of freedom, so we can test the hypothesis that all independent variable coefficients in the model are equal to zero by comparing this with a critical value of chi-square at a given alpha level. Again, let us remind you that this is similar to the OLS $F$ test. We select an alpha level of .01. With 1 degree of freedom and an alpha of .01, we can see from the chi-square table that the critical chi-square value is 6.635. Because our obtained chi-square value is 7.376, we would reject the null hypothesis that all βs ($\beta_{\text{Race of Victim}}$ in this model) are equal to zero. From Table 17.10, we can see that the exact significance level (two-tailed) of obtaining the value of chi-square we did given a true null hypothesis would be .0066 (remember, for a one-tailed test, divide this reported probability by 2). We could have also based our hypothesis decision on this.

## 17.4 PROBIT MODELS WITH ONE INDEPENDENT VARIABLE

In looking at the scatterplot of the raw data in our age and alcohol use example in Figure 17.1, you may have noticed that the shape of the distribution looks a lot like a cumulative probability distribution. The probit model is based on the assumption that the distribution of the probabilities of a given dependent variable follows the cumulative normal probability function. This means that the predicted probabilities in a probit regression model correspond to the area under the normal curve.

The logit model, you will remember, is based on the assumption that the distribution of the probabilities of a dependent variable follows the logistic probability function. As we demonstrated in Figure 17.4, the logit and probit probability distributions are quite similar, differing only at the tails. This would lead us to suspect that the results from a given logistic regression model will be very similar to those from a probit regression, and our suspicions would be correct.[7] With a dichotomous dependent variable, then, the choice between a logit or probit regression model is based on personal preference and software availability.

To understand better the probit regression model, think of an unobserved, theoretical dependent variable that is measured as a continuous variable. For example, think of the alcohol use variable as measuring a theoretical construct like the intent to use alcohol. This unobserved dependent variable, which we will call $z$, is a function of a single independent variable $x$ in this one–independent variable model. In our example, intent to use alcohol is a function of one's age. We can write this as a regression model:

$$z = \beta_0 + (\beta_1 x_1) \tag{17.6}$$

Keep in mind that we do not actually observe the construct $z$ (intent to use alcohol). What we observe is data on a dependent variable $y$ coded 0 or 1. In our example, the observed dependent variable is 0 whenever a person has not used alcohol and 1 whenever they have used it at least one time. For each person, there also is an unobserved threshold value $z_i^*$ (the subscript $i$ refers to the observation number), which, when reached, will translate into a decision to drink or not drink alcohol:

$y = 0$ if $z \le z_i^*$.

$y = 1$ if $z > z_i^*$.

The probit model assumes that the unobserved $z^*$ is a standard normal variable with a mean of zero and standard deviation of 1.

Although it is not a pretty sight, we will show you the derived standard normal probability function:

$$P_i = F(z_i) = \frac{1}{\sqrt{2\pi}} \int_{-\infty}^{z_i} e^{-s^2/2} ds$$

where

   $s$ = a random variable that is normally distributed with a mean of 0 and a variance of 1

$P_i$ is the probability that an event will occur (that $y$ will equal 1; in our example, that a person will have used alcohol). The higher the value of $z_i$, the higher the probability that the event will occur. To estimate the unobserved variable $z^*$ (and obtain our familiar-looking regression equation), we take the inverse of the standard normal cumulative distribution function:

$$z = F^{-1}(P_i) = \beta_0 + (\beta_1 x_1)$$

Where $\beta_0$ and $\beta_1$ are estimated probit coefficients. As with the logit regression equation, the probit coefficients are estimated by the MLE method. Also, as was true with logistic regression, there are readily available computer programs that do the estimation for you. We examine the results of a probit regression model for our two examples of age and alcohol use and race of victim and prosecutor's decision to seek the death penalty.

## Predicted Probabilities in Probit Models

Table 17.11 reports the results of a probit regression analysis of the age and alcohol use data. The estimated probit equation is:

$$z_i = -4.597 + (.3596)(\text{Age})$$

**TABLE 17.11. Results of Probit Regression Model for Age and Participation in Theft (data from Table 17.1)**

| Variable | Beta | Standard Error | t Ratio |
|---|---|---|---|
| Age | .3596 | .1094 | 3.286 |
| Constant | −4.5970 | 1.4600 | −3.149 |

Initial log likelihood function (constant only in the model)
  −2 log likelihood = 54.548

With age in model
  −2 log likelihood = 41.478

| | Chi-Square | df |
|---|---|---|
| Model Chi-square | 13.07 | 1 |

**Classification Table**

| | Predicted y Value | | |
|---|---|---|---|
| Observed y Value | 0 | 1 | Total |
| 0 | 11 | 6 | 17 |
| 1 | 4 | 19 | 23 |
| Total | 15 | 25 | 40 |

| | |
|---|---|
| All cases predicted correctly | 30/40 = 75.0% |
| 0 cases predicted correctly | 11/17 = 64.7% |
| 1 case predicted correctly | 19/23 = 82.6% |
| Percent predicted by chance | 23/40 = 57.5% |
| Improvement over chance | = 17.5% |

The value of the probit coefficient for age is .3596. Unlike the logit coefficient, this probit regression coefficient has no intuitive interpretation. We can say that it reflects the change in standard deviation units in the unobserved standard normal variable ($z^*$) for a unit change in the independent variable. This, however, does not make a lot of intuitive sense! We can estimate the predicted probability of alcohol use for each age by simply substituting for age in the equation and then go to the standard normal ($z$) table (Table B.2 of Appendix B) to find our predicted probability.

For example, the probit prediction that a 10-year-old youth will drink alcohol is:

$$\hat{z}_{10} = -4.597 + (.3596)(10)$$

$$= -4.597 + 3.596$$

$$= -1.001$$

This is the predicted value of a standard normal variable. To find the predicted probability, we simply go to our $z$ table and find the area under the normal curve that

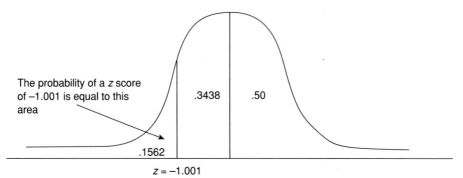

FIGURE 17.7. Determining the probability of a *z* score.

corresponds to this *z* score. Figure 17.7 shows the standard normal curve, and our *z* score of −1.001. Looking at the table of *z* scores, we can see that the area under the curve from the mean to a score of −1.001 is .3438. Because the total area of the curve to the left of the mean is .50, we can subtract .3438 from .50. This is equal to .1562 and corresponds to the probability of a *z* score of −1.001. The probability that a 10-year-old youth would have used alcohol, then, is .1562.

In Table 17.12 we report the probit probabilities (and the earlier estimated logit probabilities) for each age. As you can see, the probit model tells much the same story as the logit regression model. There is a positive relationship between age and alcohol use. Although the probability of alcohol use is less than 2 chances in 10 for those 10 years of age, the estimated probability is greater than .90 that a 17-year-old youth will have used alcohol. Moreover, the estimated probabilities from the probit and logit models at each age are very comparable. Also notice that, as was true for the logit model, the predicted probit probabilities increase more in the middle of the distribution of *x* scores, where the slope of the *S* is steepest. This reinforces the idea that the relationship between age and alcohol use is nonlinear.

**TABLE 17.12.  Probit and Logit Probabilities for Alcohol Use at Different Ages (data from Table 17.1)**

| Age | Probit Probability | Logit Probability |
|-----|--------------------|--------------------|
| 10 | .16 | .17 |
| 11 | .26 | .28 |
| 12 | .39 | .40 |
| 13 | .53 | .52 |
| 14 | .67 | .63 |
| 15 | .79 | .75 |
| 16 | .88 | .87 |
| 17 | .94 | .98 |

## Significance Testing for Probit Coefficients

As we did for the logit coefficient, we can test whether the probit regression coefficient is significantly different from zero. The hypothesis that the probit $\beta$ is equal to zero can be tested with the $t$ statistic, which is defined as the ratio of the estimated coefficient to its standard error. As was true for the logit model, this $t$ statistic has a student's $t$ distribution, with $n - k$ degrees of freedom (where $k$ is the number of parameters estimated in the model). The estimated standard error and $t$ ratio for the probit age coefficient are reported in Table 17.11. From our logit example, we know that the critical value of $t$ for a one-tailed test and an alpha of .05 is 1.703. Because our obtained value of $t$ is 3.286, which is greater than 1.703, we would reject the null hypothesis that the $b$ for age is zero. Age is significantly related to alcohol use.

## Model Goodness-of-Fit Measures

To determine the goodness of fit of our probit model, we can construct a prediction table as we did for our logit model. This prediction table would compare the observed value of the dependent variable ($y$) with the value predicted from the probit regression equation ($\hat{y}$). In the probit regression model, a common prediction rule is:[8]

$$z^* = \beta_0 + \beta_1$$

If $z^* \leq 0, \hat{y} = 0,$

if $z^* > 0, \hat{y} = 1.$

In our model, the threshold at which a youth is predicted to decide to drink occurs when $z^*$, the unobserved construct we referred to as the intent to drink, is greater than zero. With the results from Table 17.11, we can, then, derive a predicted value of $y$ for each age in our age and alcohol use example. Substituting the estimated values for the constant ($\beta_0$), slope coefficient ($\beta_1$), and $x$ (age), we can solve for each $z^*$ (each age):

$$\hat{z} = -4.597 + [(.3596)(10)]$$

$$= -4.597 + 3.596$$

$$= -1.001 = \text{Predicted } y \text{ Value of } 0$$

$$\hat{z} = -4.597 + [(.3596)(11)]$$

$$= -4.597 + 3.956$$

$$= -.641 = \text{Predicted } y \text{ Value of } 0$$

$$\hat{z} = -4.597 + [(.3596)(12)]$$

$$= -4.597 + 4.315$$

$$= -.282 = \text{Predicted } y \text{ Value of } 0$$

$\hat{z} = -4.597 + [(.3596)(13)]$

$= -4.597 + 4.675$

$= .078 =$ Predicted $y$ Value of 1

$\hat{z} = -4.597 + [(.3596)(14)]$

$= -4.597 + 5.034$

$= .437 =$ Predicted $y$ Value of 1

$\hat{z} = -4.597 + [(.3596)(15)]$

$= -4.597 + 5.394$

$= .797 =$ Predicted $y$ Value of 1

$\hat{z} = -4.597 + [(.3596)(16)]$

$= -4.597 + 5.754$

$= 1.157 =$ Predicted $y$ Value of 1

$\hat{z} = -4.597 + [(.3596)(17)]$

$= -4.597 + 6.113$

$= 1.516 =$ Predicted $y$ Value of 1

Based on the probit model, then, we would predict that youths age 10 to 12 would have a $y$ value of 0, whereas those 13 to 17 would have a $y$ value of 1. We can compare these predicted values with the observed values in Table 17.1. We can see from Table 17.1 that we have four youths between the ages of 10 and 12 who reported drinking alcohol (they are coded 1), so we have made four prediction errors here. There are six youths between the ages of 13 and 17 who reported no alcohol use (they are coded 0), so we have made six additional prediction errors here. In Table 17.11, we report the classification table of predicted and observed $y$ values. With our probit regression model we have correctly predicted 30 of 40 cases, for a prediction accuracy rate of 75 percent. This is about 17 percent better than we would have predicted by chance alone.[9]

We also can assess the model by testing how well it performs next to a model that includes only the constant. This is the same test we applied in the logit model where we took the difference in $-2LL$ (likelihood ratio statistic) for the baseline (constant-only) model and the model we were examining. From Table 17.11, you can see that the value of $-2LL$ for the constant-only model is 54.548. This is down to 41.478 when we estimate our probit regression with age as an independent variable. The difference in these two values is 13.07, which has a chi-square distribution with 1 degree of freedom. The test that all coefficients in the model are equal to zero is a chi-square test with 1 degree of freedom. We know from our logit example that the critical value of chi-square with an alpha of .01 and 1 degree of freedom is 6.635. Because our obtained chi-square of 13.07 is greater than 6.635, we would reject the null hypothesis that $\beta_{age}$ is zero.

## Another Probit Example

We now go through an example of a probit regression model when both the independent and dependent variable are dichotomized. We use the race of victim and prosecutor's decision data in Table 17.8. Let us remind you that in this data set, the race of the victim is coded 0 for murders involving an African American victim and 1 for those involving a white victim, and the prosecutor's decision is coded 0 if a life sentence is sought and 1 if a death sentence is sought. In Table 17.13, we report the results of a probit regression analysis for this data set.

The estimated probit regression equation is:

$$\hat{z} = -.7647 + (1.3693)(x_1)$$

We can solve for this equation by substituting the value of the $x$, or independent, variable (race of victim). For African American victims ($x = 0$), the probit value is:

$$\hat{z} = -.7647 + (1.3693)(0)$$

$$= -.7647$$

**TABLE 17.13. Results of Probit Regression Model for Race of Victim and Prosecutor's Decision to Seek the Death Penalty (data from Table 17.8)**

| Variable | Beta | Standard Error | t Ratio |
|---|---|---|---|
| Race of victim | 1.3693 | .5211 | 2.628 |
| Constant | -.7647 | .3290 | -2.324 |

Initial log likelihood function (constant only in the model)
 $-2$ log likelihood = 39.336

With race of victim in model
 $-2$ log likelihood = 31.960

| | Chi-square | df |
|---|---|---|
| Model chi-square | 7.38 | 1 |

**Classification Table**

| | Predicted y Value | | |
|---|---|---|---|
| Observed y Value | 0 | 1 | Total |
| 0 | 14 | 3 | 17 |
| 1 | 4 | 8 | 12 |
| Total | 18 | 11 | 29 |

| | |
|---|---|
| All cases predicted correctly | 22/29 = 75.9% |
| 0 cases predicted correctly | 14/17 = 82.4% |
| 1 case predicted correctly | 8/12 = 66.7% |
| Percent predicted by chance | 17/29 = 58.6% |
| Improvement over chance | = 17.3% |

Because the value of the unobserved construct $\hat{z}$ is less than zero, the predicted value of $y$ for African American victim cases is 0 (a life sentence). With a $\hat{z}$ score of $-.7647$, we can go to the $z$ table and find that the predicted probability that a death sentence will be sought by the prosecutor in African American murder victims, is .2236. The predicted logit probability, you will remember, was .222.

For white murder victims ($x = 1$), the probit value is:

$$\hat{z} = -.7647 + (1.3693)(1)$$

$$= .6046$$

Because the value of the unobserved construct is greater than zero, the predicted value of $y$ for white murder victim cases is 1 (a death sentence). With a $\hat{z}$ score of .6046, we can go to the $z$ table and find that the predicted probability that a death sentence will be sought by the prosecutor in white victim cases is .7291. The predicted probability of a death sentence from the logit model was .727.

The probit coefficient for the race of the victim is 1.3693. Because white victim cases were coded 1 and African American victim cases were coded 0, the probit coefficient tells us that a one-unit change in the independent variable increases the standard deviation of the standard normal variable $z^*$ by 1.3693 standard deviation units. As you can see, the probit coefficient is not as readily interpretable as the logit coefficient.

The test for the significance of the probit coefficient in this case also is the $t$ statistic. The obtained value of $t$ is the ratio of the probit coefficient to its estimated standard error. In Table 17.13, you can see that the $t$ ratio for the race of the victim is 2.628. We know that this $t$ statistic has a student's $t$ distribution with $n - k$ degrees of freedom (where $k$ is the number of parameters estimated in the model). We conduct the hypothesis test that $\beta_{\text{Race of Victim}}$ equals zero, with an alpha of .01. The critical value of $t$ with 27 degrees of freedom ($29 - 2$) and a one-tailed alpha of .01 is 2.473. Because our obtained $t$ value is greater than our critical $t$ value, we reject the null hypothesis that $\beta_{\text{Race of Victim}}$ equals zero. The race of the victim is significantly related to the prosecutor's decision to seek a death sentence.

We can assess how well our probit model fits the data by examining the extent to which it makes correct predictions on the dependent variable. We noted that our probit model would predict that the prosecutor would seek a life sentence in all African American victim cases and would seek a death sentence in all white victim cases. When we compare these predictions with the observed results (see Table 17.9), we can create a classification table of predicted and observed $y$ values (Table 17.13). You can see that our predictions with the probit model are identical to those with the logit model (Table 17.10). We correctly predict nearly 76 percent of the cases and can improve our prediction over chance by 17 percent.

As a final check on our model, we can examine the improvement in the likelihood ratio statistic ($-2LL$). In Table 17.13, you can see that the value of $-2LL$ for our baseline model with only the constant is 39.336. When we add the race of the victim to the model, the likelihood ratio statistic is reduced to 31.960. The improvement in models is 7.38, which we know is distributed as a chi-square with 1 degree of freedom. We test the null hypothesis that all $\beta$s in the model are equal to zero. With an alpha of .01 and 1 degree of freedom, the critical value of chi-square is 6.635. Because our obtained chi-square value is greater than our critical chi-square value, we would reject the null hypothesis.

## 17.5 LOGISTIC REGRESSION MODELS WITH TWO INDEPENDENT VARIABLES

In the logit regression models we discussed in Section 17.3, we considered only one independent variable. Most of the time, however, we are interested in the effect of more than one independent variable on a given dichotomous dependent variable. In this case, we want to estimate a logistic regression model that contains more than one independent variable. As was true in the case of OLS regression, when there is more than one independent variable in the logistic regression model we determine the effect of one independent variable on the dependent variable while holding the other independent variables constant. In this section we briefly introduce a second independent variable to our previous examples. The extension to more than two independent variables is straightforward.

Before we proceed, however, we might well want to ask ourselves, "why do we need to add another variable to our logistic equation"? The answer is that, by adding another independent variable, we hope to be better able to explain, understand, and predict our dependent variable. The fact that we cannot accurately predict the dependent variable for all of our observations gives us a hint that we need more than one independent variable.

Once this is understood, the next question might be which independent variable we add to our model. This question, however, is not really a statistical one, but a substantive one that requires you to know your subject matter thoroughly. There is no "program" or "option" in your computer software that can tell you what new independent variable to add. You should choose an independent variable that you think, based on your knowledge of the subject, explains or "accounts for" the dependent variable, and one that is not the same as the variable or variables already in the model. In other words, you should choose additional independent variables that you think are strongly correlated with the dependent variable but not correlated with the independent variable or variables. If any two independent variables are too highly correlated, you have the same problem of *multicollinearity* that you had with the OLS regression model.

Let's say that in addition to the effect of age, we also wanted to know the effect of gender on participation in alcohol use. Gender is a good independent variable to add to our original one independent variable model because it probably is related to alcohol use and unrelated to age. In this new example we have two independent variables, age and gender, and a dichotomous dependent variable, alcohol use (coded 0 for no and 1 for yes). The data for this example are given to you in Table 17.14. They are the same as those in Table 17.1, except that we have added the gender of each youth, where females are coded 0 and males are coded 1.

We can now expand our logistic regression Equation 17.3 to include two independent variables:

$$\ln \frac{p}{1-p} = \beta_0 + \beta_1 x_1 + \beta_2 x_2$$

$$\ln \frac{\hat{p}}{1-\hat{p}} = b_0 + b_1(\text{Age}) + b_2(\text{Gender})$$

(17.7)

This tells us that the dependent variable in our example, the log of the odds of using alcohol, is affected by age and gender. As in the one–independent variable model, the unknown parameters of this two–independent variable model ($\beta_0$, $\beta_1$, and $\beta_2$) are estimated according to the MLE principle. When we use our computer software to estimate this model, the results we get are reported for you in Table 17.15, and the equation obtained from this model is presented:

$$\ln \frac{\hat{p}}{1-\hat{p}} = -9.8268 + (.6431)(\text{Age}) + (3.2445)(\text{Gender})$$

From our logistic regression equation we can see that alcohol use is positively related to both age and gender. Because gender is coded 0 for females and 1 for males, this indicates that older youths and males are more likely to have used alcohol than younger youths and females. More specifically, a one-unit (1-year) increase in age increases the log of the odds of alcohol use by .6431, while holding

**TABLE 17.14. Data on Age, Gender, and Alcohol Use for a Hypothetical Random Sample of 40 Youths**

| Age | Used Alcohol* | Gender† | Age | Used Alcohol* | Gender† |
|-----|-----|-----|-----|-----|-----|
| 10 | 0 | 0 | 14 | 0 | 1 |
| 10 | 0 | 0 | 14 | 0 | 0 |
| 10 | 0 | 0 | 14 | 1 | 0 |
| 10 | 0 | 1 | 14 | 1 | 1 |
| 10 | 1 | 1 | 14 | 1 | 1 |
| 11 | 0 | 0 | 15 | 0 | 0 |
| 11 | 0 | 0 | 15 | 1 | 1 |
| 11 | 0 | 0 | 15 | 1 | 1 |
| 11 | 0 | 0 | 15 | 1 | 1 |
| 11 | 1 | 1 | 15 | 1 | 0 |
| 12 | 0 | 0 | 16 | 0 | 0 |
| 12 | 0 | 0 | 16 | 1 | 1 |
| 12 | 0 | 1 | 16 | 1 | 1 |
| 12 | 1 | 1 | 16 | 1 | 1 |
| 12 | 1 | 1 | 16 | 1 | 1 |
| 13 | 0 | 0 | 17 | 1 | 0 |
| 13 | 0 | 0 | 17 | 1 | 1 |
| 13 | 1 | 0 | 17 | 1 | 1 |
| 13 | 1 | 1 | 17 | 1 | 1 |
| 13 | 1 | 1 | 17 | 1 | 1 |

*Coded as 0 if no alcohol use was reported; coded as 1 if alcohol was used at least once.
†Coded as 0 for females and 1 for males.

**TABLE 17.15. Results of Logistic Regression Model for Age, Gender and Alcohol Use (data from Table 17.14)**

| Variable | Beta | Standard Error | Wald Statistic | df | Sig. |
|---|---|---|---|---|---|
| Age | .6431 | .2582 | 6.2013 | 1 | .0128 |
| Gender | 3.2445 | 1.0476 | 9.59151 | 1 | .0020 |
| Constant | −9.8268 | 3.6346 | 7.3099 | 1 | .0069 |

Initial log likelihood function (constant only in the model)
  −2 log likelihood = 54.548

With age and gender in model
  −2 log likelihood = 27.922

| | Chi-Square | df | Sig. |
|---|---|---|---|
| Model chi-square | 26.626 | 2 | .0000 |

**Classification Table**

| Observed y Value | Predicted y Value | | Total |
|---|---|---|---|
| | 0 | 1 | |
| 0 | 14 | 3 | 17 |
| 1 | 4 | 19 | 23 |
| Total | 18 | 22 | 40 |

| | |
|---|---|
| All cases predicted correctly | 33/40 = 82.5% |
| 0 cases predicted correctly | 14/17 = 82.4% |
| 1 case predicted correctly | 19/23 = 82.6% |
| Percent predicted by chance | 23/40 = 57.5% |
| Improvement over chance | = 25.0% |

gender constant. A unit change in gender (being male rather than female) increases the log of the odds of alcohol use by 3.2445, while holding age constant.

With this logistic regression model, we can estimate the predicted probability of alcohol use for some substantively interesting cases. For example, the estimated probability of alcohol use for a 16-year-old male would be:

$$\hat{p} = \frac{e^{b_0 + b_1(\text{Age}) + b_2(\text{Gender})}}{(1 + e^{b_0 + b_1(\text{Age}) + b_2(\text{Gender})})}$$

$$= \frac{e^{-9.8268 + (.6431)(16) + (3.2445)(1)}}{(1 + e^{-9.8268 + (.6431)(16) + (3.2445)(1)})}$$

$$= \frac{e^{3.7073}}{(1 + e^{3.7073})}$$

$$= \frac{40.73}{41.73}$$

$$= .976$$

The estimated probability that a 16-year-old male will have used alcohol, then, is .98. The corresponding probability for a 16-year-old female is:

$$\hat{p} = \frac{e^{-9.8268+(.6431)(16)+(3.2445)(0)}}{(1 + e^{-9.8268+(.6431)(16)+(3.2445)(0)})}$$

$$= \frac{e^{.4628}}{(1 + e^{.4628})}$$

$$= \frac{1.59}{2.59}$$

$$= .61$$

The probability that a same-aged female would have used alcohol is only .61. The probability of alcohol use for a 16-year-old male, therefore, is over one and a half times that for a similar-age female. The estimated probability that a 15-year-old male will have used alcohol is:

$$\hat{p} = \frac{e^{-9.8268+(.6431)(15)+(3.2445)(1)}}{(1 + e^{-9.8268+(.6431)(15)+(3.2445)(1)})}$$

$$= \frac{e^{3.0642}}{(1 + e^{3.0642})}$$

$$= \frac{21.42}{22.42}$$

$$= .955$$

The expected probability of a 15-year-old male is .955. Just as we have done here, you can calculate the estimated probability for any combination of age and gender in your data set.

The significance of the logistic coefficients for age and gender can be tested with a $t$ test (coefficient/standard error) or the Wald statistic [(coefficient/standard error)$^2$]. We use a $t$ test here. The null hypotheses are that $\beta_{Age}$ and $\beta_{Gender}$ equal zero, the two research hypotheses are that the coefficients are greater than zero. The obtained $t$ ratios are 2.49 for age and 3.10 for gender. With $40 - 3$, or 37, degrees of freedom, the critical value of $t$ (one-tailed alpha of .01) is 2.423. Because both obtained $t$ values are higher than the critical $t$ values, we would reject the null hypotheses that $\beta_{Age}$ or $\beta_{Gender}$ equals 0. We would conclude that age has a significant effect on alcohol use while holding gender constant, and that gender has a significant effect on alcohol use when holding age constant. Even when gender is added to our model, then, the age of the youth has a significant positive effect on the decision to drink alcohol.

Because both independent variables are significantly related to our dependent variable, we may want to assess the *relative* effect of each, that is, which variable is more important in explaining the dependent variable. There are a number of ways to look at the relative importance of variables. One very simple way is to compare the $t$ ratios for the two coefficients. In comparing two coefficients, the one with the larger $t$ or Wald statistic has the greater impact. For example, in our age, gender, and alcohol use model, the $t$ statistic for age is 2.49 (.6431/.2582), but it is 3.10 for gender. We would conclude from this that gender has a stronger effect on alcohol use than age.

Another way to examine the relative importance of a given independent variable is to compare the likelihood ratio statistics ($-2LL$) for two models: (1) one that includes every variable, and (2) one that includes every variable except the one whose importance you are examining. The difference between the likelihood ratio statistics between the two models can then be compared for different independent variables. The variable that, after being removed, results in a more substantial deterioration in the fit of the model, has the stronger effect.

For example, our two variable logistic regression model has a likelihood ratio statistic of 27.922 (see Table 17.15). When gender is not in the model, the likelihood ratio statistic is 41.553 (Table 17.3). The model without gender, then, gives us a worse fit, and the difference between the two models is 13.63. When age is not in the model, the likelihood ratio statistic is 36.594, and the difference between this value and that for the two-variable model is 8.67. Because the drop in the likelihood ratio statistic is greater when gender is removed (13.63) than when age is removed (8.67), indicating a worse fit between the model and our data, gender has more of an effect on the dependent variable than does age.[10] This is consistent with our conclusion when we compared $t$ ratios.

As we did in our one–independent variable logistic regression model, we can use the likelihood ratio statistic to determine the overall goodness of fit of the model. The null hypothesis that all of the coefficients in the model are equal to zero (all $\beta$'s = 0), is tested by taking the difference in the likelihood ratio statistic between the model that contains only the constant and the model that contains both independent variables. This difference has a chi-square distribution where the degrees of freedom are equal to the difference in degrees of freedom between the two models. You will remember that this hypothesis test is comparable to an $F$ test for the overall goodness of fit for an OLS regression model.

In Table 17.15, you can see that the likelihood ratio statistic for the baseline model (constant only) is 54.548. This model has only one parameter to estimate, so there are $n - k = 40 - 1$, or 39, degrees of freedom. When age and gender are added to the model, the likelihood ratio statistic drops to 27.922. This model has three parameters to estimate, so there are 37 ($n - k = 40 - 3$) degrees of freedom. The difference between the two models, therefore, is 26.626, with 2 degrees of freedom. Let's test the null hypothesis that all $\beta$'s equal zero with an alpha of .01. From the table of chi-square values, you can see that the critical value of chi-square with an alpha of .01 and 2 degrees of freedom is 9.210. Because our obtained chi-square of 26.626 is higher than the critical value, we reject the null hypothesis that the two coefficients are both equal to zero.

Finally, let's examine the fit of the two-variable model by looking at the derived prediction or classification table in Table 17.15. With a prediction cutoff value of $\hat{p} = .5$, we can correctly predict 82.5 percent of the cases correctly. This is an improvement of approximately 7 percent over the model that contained only age (see Table 17.3) and a 25 percent improvement over chance. In looking at the classification tables in Table 17.3 (one-variable model) and Table 17.15 (two-variable model), you can see that our improvement in prediction comes about by reducing the number of errors in predicting 0 cases (those who did not drink) by 3. Our accuracy in predicting those who did drink remained the same.

We now return to our logistic regression model that involved the effect of the race of the victim on the prosecutor's decision to seek a life or death sentence. In that regression model, we found that the race of the victim was a significant factor in influencing when a death sentence was sought as opposed to a life sentence. More specifically, we found that the odds of a death sentence were nine times greater for those cases that involved the killing of a white compared to those that involved the killing of an African American.

Although this finding may suggest that the prosecutor's decision to seek a death sentence is based on race, and therefore, discriminatory, we cannot yet be confident in that conclusion. It may be that death sentences are sought more often in white victim cases not because of race and any feelings of discrimination, but because murders of whites are more brutal than murders of African American victims. If this were true, once the brutality of the homicide is controlled, the effect of victim's race would be greatly diminished and may even disappear completely.

To examine this possibility, let's say that we were able to measure how brutally a homicide was perpetrated (our measure of brutality included such things as the number of victims, whether the victim was tortured or bound and gagged, etc.) for each of our 29 hypothetical cases. We coded nonbrutal homicides 0, and those with at least one element of brutality as 1. Keep in mind that the victim's race is coded 0 for black victims and 1 for white victims. These data are reported in Table 17.16. We would now like to estimate a logistic regression model for this data set. In this model the dependent variable is the prosecutor's decision to seek a life (coded 0) or death (coded 1) sentence, and the independent variables are the victim's race, and whether or not the homicide involved brutality. The results from this regression analysis are reported in Table 17.17.

The two-variable logistic regression equation for the prosecutor's decision to seek a death sentence is:

$$\ln \frac{\hat{p}}{1 - \hat{p}} = b_0 + b_1 x_1 + b_2 x_2$$

$$= -2.6841 + (2.7975)(\text{Victim's Race}) + (3.2334)(\text{Brutality})$$

Both logistic regression coefficients are positive, as we would expect. Compared with African American victim homicides, the log of the odds of a death sentence are increased by 2.7975 in white victim cases. Even when the brutality of the homicide is controlled, then, prosecutors are more likely to seek a death sentence if a white is killed than if an African American is killed. The presence of brutality, then, does not completely explain the effect of race that we have found. Controlling for victim's race, the log odds of a death sentence are increased by 3.2334 for those homicides that involve an element of brutality. Prosecutors are more likely to seek a death sentence if the homicide involved some element of brutality.

**TABLE 17.16. Race of Victim, Brutality of the Homicide, and Decision of the Prosecutor to Seek a Death Sentence for 29 Hypothetical Cases**

| Case Number | Race of Victim* | Prosecutor's Decision† | Brutality Present?‡ |
|:---:|:---:|:---:|:---:|
| 1 | 0 | 0 | 0 |
| 2 | 0 | 0 | 0 |
| 3 | 0 | 0 | 0 |
| 4 | 0 | 0 | 0 |
| 5 | 0 | 0 | 0 |
| 6 | 0 | 0 | 0 |
| 7 | 0 | 0 | 0 |
| 8 | 0 | 0 | 0 |
| 9 | 0 | 0 | 1 |
| 10 | 0 | 0 | 0 |
| 11 | 1 | 0 | 0 |
| 12 | 1 | 0 | 0 |
| 13 | 0 | 1 | 0 |
| 14 | 0 | 1 | 1 |
| 15 | 0 | 1 | 1 |
| 16 | 1 | 1 | 0 |
| 17 | 1 | 1 | 1 |
| 18 | 1 | 1 | 1 |
| 19 | 1 | 1 | 1 |
| 20 | 1 | 1 | 1 |
| 21 | 1 | 1 | 0 |
| 22 | 1 | 1 | 0 |
| 23 | 0 | 0 | 1 |
| 24 | 0 | 0 | 0 |
| 25 | 0 | 0 | 0 |
| 26 | 1 | 1 | 1 |
| 27 | 0 | 1 | 1 |
| 28 | 1 | 0 | 0 |
| 29 | 0 | 0 | 0 |

*Coded as 0 if victim was African American and 1 if white.
†Coded as 0 if prosecutor sought life sentence and 1 if prosecutor sought death sentence.
‡Coded as 0 if the cases did not contain an element of brutality and 1 if at least one element of brutality was present.

If we take the antilog of these coefficients, we can see that the odds that the prosecutor will seek a death sentence are 16 times greater in white victim cases than in African American victim cases ($e^{2.7975} = 16.40$), with brutality controlled. The effect of brutality is even stronger. The odds of a death sentence being sought by the prosecutor are more than 25 times greater ($e^{3.2334} = 25.36$) if the murder was committed with some degree of brutality, with the race of the victim controlled.

With the coefficient values from our logistic regression equation, we can estimate the probability that the prosecutor will seek a death sentence in four kinds of cases: (1) African American victim cases that do not involve brutality, (2) white

**TABLE 17.17. Results of Logistic Regression Model for Race of Victim, Homicide Brutality, and the Prosecutor's Decision (data from Table 17.16)**

| Variable | Beta | Standard Error | Wald Statistic | df | Sig. |
|---|---|---|---|---|---|
| Victim's race | 2.7975 | 1.2351 | 5.1299 | 1 | .0235 |
| Brutality | 3.2334 | 1.2766 | 6.4153 | 1 | .0113 |
| Constant | −2.6841 | 1.0488 | 6.5493 | 1 | .0105 |

Initial log likelihood function (constant only in the model)
  −2 log likelihood = 39.336

With race and brutality in model
  −2 log likelihood = 22.523

|  | Chi-square | df | Sig. |
|---|---|---|---|
| Model chi-square | 16.813 | 2 | .0002 |

**Classification Table**

| | Predicted y Value | | |
|---|---|---|---|
| Observed y Value | 0 | 1 | Total |
| 0 | 12 | 5 | 17 |
| 1 | 1 | 11 | 12 |
| Total | 13 | 16 | 29 |

| | |
|---|---|
| All cases predicted correctly | 23/29 = 79.3% |
| 0 cases predicted correctly | 12/17 = 70.6% |
| 1 case predicted correctly | 11/12 = 91.7% |
| Percent predicted by chance | 17/29 = 58.6% |
| Improvement over chance | = 20.7% |

victim cases that do not involve brutality, (3) African American victim cases that involve brutality, and (4) white victim cases that involve brutality. These estimated probabilities are:

Probability for African American victim cases with no brutality:

$$\hat{p} = \frac{e^{-2.6841+(2.7975)(0)+(3.2334)(0)}}{1 + e^{-2.6841+(2.7975)(0)+(3.2334)(0)}}$$

$$= \frac{e^{-2.6841}}{1 + e^{-2.6841}}$$

$$= \frac{.068}{1.068}$$

$$= .06$$

Probability for white victim cases with no brutality:

$$\hat{p} = \frac{e^{-2.6841+(2.7975)(1)+(3.2334)(0)}}{1 + e^{-2.6841+(2.7975)(1)+(3.2334)(0)}}$$

$$= \frac{e^{-2.6841+2.7975}}{1 + e^{-2.6841+2.7975}}$$

$$= \frac{1.120}{2.120}$$

$$= .53$$

Probability for African American victim cases with brutality:

$$\hat{p} = \frac{e^{-2.6841+(2.7975)(0)+(3.2334)(1)}}{1 + e^{-2.6841+(2.7975)(0)+(3.2334)(1)}}$$

$$= \frac{e^{-2.6841+3.2334}}{1 + e^{-2.6841+3.2334}}$$

$$= \frac{1.73}{2.73}$$

$$= .63$$

Probability for white victim cases with brutality:

$$\hat{p} = \frac{e^{-2.6841+(2.7975)(1)+(3.2334)(1)}}{1 + e^{-2.6841+(2.7975)(1)+(3.2334)(1)}}$$

$$= \frac{e^{-2.6841+2.7975+3.2334}}{1 + e^{-2.6841+2.7975+3.2334}}$$

$$= \frac{28.41}{29.41}$$

$$= .96$$

These estimated probabilities will help us understand the relationship between the race of the victim, the brutality of the homicide, and the prosecutor's decision to seek a death sentence. The decision to seek a death sentence is least likely in African American victim cases that involve no brutality ($\hat{p} = .06$) and most likely in white victim cases that involve some element of brutality ($\hat{p} = .96$). The effect of brutality is the strongest for African American victim homicides. If the victim is African American, the probability that a death sentence will be sought is over 10 times greater if there is some brutality in the murder ($.63/.06 = 10.5$). For white victim cases, however, the presence of brutality increases the probability by only a factor less than 2 ($.96/.53 = 1.8$). The effect of race is the strongest, then, when there is no brutality present. The probability of a death sentence is only slightly greater (1.5 times) in white victim cases if there is some brutality present. For more serious crimes (those that involve brutality), white victim and African American victim cases are, for the most part, treated comparably by the prosecutor. When there is no brutality present, however, the probability of a death sentence is over eight times greater in white victim cases than in African American victim cases (.53/.06 = 8.8).

We can test the significance of the coefficients for race of victim and brutality in this model with either a $t$ test or the Wald statistic. One null hypothesis is that the coefficient for victim's race is zero, when holding brutality constant. The $t$ statistic for the race of victim is 2.265 (2.7975/1.2351), and the Wald statistic is 5.1299. A second null hypothesis is that the coefficient for brutality is zero, when holding constant the race of the victim. The $t$ statistic for brutality is 2.53, and the Wald statistic is 6.41.

We test these hypotheses with an alpha of .05 (one-tailed). With 26 degrees of freedom (df = $n - k = 29 - 3$), the critical value of $t$ is 1.706, and with 1 degree of freedom for the Wald statistic, the critical chi-square value is 3.841. Because both the obtained $t$ and Wald statistics for the race of the victim are greater than the critical values, we would reject the null hypothesis that $\beta_{\text{Race of Victim}}$ equals zero when controlling for brutality. Similarly, because the obtained $t$ and Wald statistic for brutality are greater than the critical values, we would reject the null hypothesis that $\beta_{\text{Brutality}}$ equals zero when controlling for race. From this, we would conclude that both variables have a significant effect on the prosecutor's decision to seek a death sentence, when controlling for the other.

We can examine the overall goodness of fit for our two variable probit model by examining the difference in the likelihood ratio statistic between the baseline (constant-only) model and one that includes both race of victim and brutality. To refresh your memory, the difference between the two models' $-2LL$ has a chi-square distribution with degrees of freedom equal to the difference in degrees of freedom between the two models. The likelihood ratio statistic for the baseline model is 39.336 and is 22.523 when the two independent variables are included (see Table 17.17). The difference between these two likelihood ratio statistics is 16.813 with 2 degrees of freedom. We test the null hypothesis that $b_1 = b_2 = 0$, with an alpha of .05. The critical value of chi-square with 2 degrees of freedom and an alpha of .05 is 5.991. Because our obtained chi-square value (16.813) is greater than the critical chi-square value (5.991), we reject the null hypothesis that all $\beta$s equal zero.

Looking at the classification table in Table 17.17, we can see that our model predicts approximately 80 percent of the cases correctly. This is about a 20 percent improvement over chance and a 5 percent improvement over the model that only had the victim's race as an independent variable (see Table 17.10). Perhaps more important, we are able to predict more than 90 percent of the cases in which a death sentence was sought.

If we wanted to examine the relative explanatory power of our two independent variables, a comparison of their respective $t$ ratios would lead us to conclude that the brutality of the offense ($t = 2.53$) has slightly more of an impact on the prosecutor's decision to seek a death sentence than the race of the victim ($t = 2.26$). Another way to look at this is to see what happens to the fit of our two-variable model when each independent variable is removed. The likelihood ratio for the two-variable model was 22.523. When the brutality variable is removed, the likelihood ratio statistic is 31.960, a difference of 9.437. When the race of the victim variable is removed, the likelihood ratio statistic becomes 29.564, a difference of 7.04. Because the fit of the model gets worse when the brutality variable is removed, we can conclude that it has a stronger influence on the prosecutor's decision than the race of the victim.

## 17.6 PROBIT REGRESSION MODELS WITH TWO INDEPENDENT VARIABLES

We would like to conclude this chapter with a brief discussion of probit models that contain more than one independent variable. With what you have learned thus far, you should be convinced that the probit and logit models are very comparable. Just as our one independent variable probit regression models led us to conclusions similar to our logit models, the results of a two–independent variable probit model will be similar to a comparable logit regression model. Thus, we repeat our observation that the choice between the two is really a matter of personal preference and computer software availability.

The two independent variable probit model takes the following general form:

$$z = \beta_0 + \beta_1 x_1 + \beta_2 x_2 \tag{17.8}$$

where $z$ is an unobserved, standard normal variable. We estimate probit models for the two examples we have discussed thus far in this chapter. In Table 17.18, we report the results of a probit regression of the age, gender, and alcohol use data.

The estimated probit regression equation for this data set is:

$$\hat{z} = -5.7716 + (.3766)(\text{Age}) + (1.8844)(\text{Gender})$$

Both age and gender have a positive effect on alcohol use; older youths and males are more likely to have used alcohol than younger youths and females. Again, these probit regression coefficients have no intuitive interpretation. They simply indicate that a one-unit change in age (1 year) increases the unobserved standard normal dependent variable by .3766 standard deviation units, controlling for gender, and that a one-unit change in gender (being male rather than female) increases the standard normal dependent variable by 1.88 standard deviation units, controlling for age. As we did with the logit equation, we can estimate the probability of alcohol use for various combinations of values of the independent variables. For example, the probit prediction for a 16-year-old male is:

$$\hat{z} = -5.7716 + (.3766)(16) + (1.8844)(1)$$

$$= -5.7716 + 6.0256 + 1.8844$$

$$= 2.14$$

The probit prediction, then, is $\hat{z} = 2.14$, and is the predicted value of a standard normal variable. To convert this to a probability, we simply go to our standard normal ($z$) table and find that the predicted probability is approximately .98.[11] The probability that a 16-year-old male will have used alcohol is .98. This is the same as the

**TABLE 17.18. Results of Probit Regression Model for Age, Gender, and Alcohol Use (data from Table 17.1)**

| Variable | Beta | Standard Error | *t* Ratio |
|----------|------|----------------|-----------|
| Age | .3766 | .1449 | 2.599 |
| Gender | 1.8844 | .5621 | 3.353 |
| Constant | −5.7716 | 2.0150 | −2.864 |

Initial log likelihood function (constant only in the model)
  −2 log likelihood = 54.548

With age and gender in model
  −2 log likelihood = 27.618

|  | Chi-Square | df |
|--|------------|-----|
| Model chi-square | 26.93 | 2 |

**Classification Table**

| | Predicted y Value | | |
|---|---|---|---|
| Observed y Value | 0 | 1 | Total |
| 0 | 14 | 3 | 17 |
| 1 | 4 | 19 | 23 |
| Total | 18 | 22 | 40 |

| | |
|--|--|
| All cases predicted correctly | 33/40 = 82.5% |
| 0 cases predicted correctly | 14/17 = 82.4% |
| 1 case predicted correctly | 19/23 = 82.6% |
| Percent predicted by chance | 23/40 = 57.5% |
| Improvement over chance | = 25.0% |

predicted logit probability. The probit prediction that a 16-year-old female will have used alcohol is:

$$\hat{z} = -5.7716 + (.3766)(16) + (1.8844)(0)$$

$$= -5.7716 + 6.0256$$

$$= .254$$

which corresponds to a predicted probability of .5987. The logit predicted probability was .61.

We can test the null hypotheses that $\beta_{Age}$ equals 0 and $\beta_{Gender}$ equals 0 with our *t* statistic. This *t* test has $n - k$, or 37, degrees of freedom. With an alpha of .01 (one-tailed), the critical value of *t* is 2.423. The *t* ratio for age is 2.599 and 3.352 for gender. Both of these *t* ratios are greater than the critical value, so we can reject both null hypotheses. Age has a significant positive effect on alcohol use when controlling for gender, and gender has a significant positive effect on alcohol use when controlling for age.

The magnitude of the respective $t$ ratios would lead us to conclude that gender ($t = 3.352$) has a more pronounced effect on alcohol use than age ($t = 2.559$). We would also come to this conclusion by looking at the likelihood ratio statistics from a number of different models. When both age and gender are in the model, the likelihood ratio statistic is 27.618. When gender is excluded and only age is in the model, the likelihood ratio statistic becomes 41.478, a difference of 13.86. When age is excluded and only gender is in the model, the likelihood ratio becomes 36.594, a difference of 8.976. Excluding gender produces a worse fit than excluding age, so we can deduce that gender has a greater effect on alcohol use than age.

Finally, the general fit of the model can be examined. First, the difference in likelihood ratio statistics between the baseline (constant-only) model and the model with both age and gender in it is 26.93 (see Table 17.18). With 2 degrees of freedom, this chi-square is significantly different from zero at any conventional alpha level. Second, we can examine the classification table between observed and predicted $y$ values (see Table 17.18). This two-variable probit model correctly predicts 82.5 percent of the cases correctly, a 25 percent improvement over chance.

As a final exercise, let's estimate a probit regression model for our data on the race of the victim, the brutality of the homicide, and the prosecutor's decision to seek a death sentence. The results from that probit model are reported in Table 17.19. The estimated probit regression equation is:

$$\hat{z} = -1.5101 + (1.5911)(\text{Victim's Race}) + (1.8635)(\text{Brutality})$$

The model indicates that both the race of the victim and the presence of brutality increase the probability that a prosecutor will seek a death sentence. A death sentence is more likely to be sought when a white, rather than an African American, is killed, and when the homicide involves an element of brutality.

With this probit equation we can compute the estimated standard normal variable and predicted probability that the prosecutor would seek a death sentence for our four combinations of cases, (1) African American victim/no brutality, (2) white victim/no brutality, (3) African American victim/brutality, and (4) white victim/ brutality. These calculations are presented in Table 17.20.

You can see that the predicted probabilities from the probit model are very similar to those from the logistic regression model. The probability that the prosecutor will seek a death sentence is very small for African American victim cases if there is not special brutality involved in the killing. When there is brutality, the probability that death will be sought is only slightly lower for African American victim cases than for white victim cases.

The hypothesis test that $\beta_{\text{Victim's Race}}$ equals zero and $\beta_{\text{Brutality}}$ equals zero can be tested with the $t$ statistic. With $n - k$ (29 − 3), or 26, degrees of freedom, with an alpha of .05 (one-tailed), the critical value of $t$ is 1.706. Because the $t$ ratio for victim's race is 2.442 and the $t$ ratio for brutality is 2.751, we would reject both null hypotheses. The race of the victim has a significant effect on the prosecutor's decision to seek a death sentence with brutality controlled, and brutality has a significant effect with the race of the victim controlled. A comparison of the $t$ ratios would lead us to believe that the brutality of the offense is more important than the victim's race in influencing the prosecutor's decision.

**TABLE 17.19. Results of Probit Regression Model for Race of Victim, Brutality of the Homicide, and Prosecutor's Decision to Seek the Death Penalty (data from Table 17.16)**

| Variable | Beta | Standard Error | $t$ Ratio |
|---|---|---|---|
| Race of victim | 1.5911 | .6516 | 2.442 |
| Brutality | 1.8635 | .6516 | 2.751 |
| Constant | −1.5101 | .4998 | −3.021 |

Initial log likelihood function (constant only in the model)
  −2 log likelihood = 39.336

With race of victim and brutality in model
  −2 log likelihood = 22.444

| | Chi-Square | df |
|---|---|---|
| Model chi-square | 16.892 | 2 |

**Classification Table**

| | Predicted y Value | | |
|---|---|---|---|
| Observed y Value | 0 | 1 | Total |
| 0 | 12 | 5 | 17 |
| 1 | 1 | 11 | 12 |
| Total | 13 | 16 | 29 |

All cases predicted correctly  23/29 = 79.3%
0 cases predicted correctly  12/17 = 70.6%
1 case predicted correctly  11/12 = 91.7%

Percent predicted by chance  17/29 = 58.6%
Improvement over chance  = 20.7%

**TABLE 17.20. Predicted Probability (from the probit model) that a Prosecutor Will Seek the Death Penalty Based on a Victim's Race and the Presence of Brutality**

| Case Characteristics | Probit Equation | Probit Prediction | Predicted Probability |
|---|---|---|---|
| African American victim/no brutality | −1.5101 + 1.5911(0) + 1.8635(0) = | −1.51 | .066 |
| White victim/no brutality | −1.5101 + 1.5911(1) + 1.8635(0) = | .08 | .532 |
| African American victim/Brutality | −1.5101 + 1.5911(0) + 1.8635(1) = | .35 | .637 |
| White victim/Brutality | −1.5101 + 1.5911(1) + 1.8635(1) = | 1.94 | .974 |

Finally, the overall fit of the model can be determined by testing the null hypothesis that all βs in the model are equal to zero. The likelihood ratio statistic is 39.336 for the baseline (constant-only) model and 22.444 for the model with both independent variables included. The difference is 16.892, and this chi-square value is significant at an alpha of .05 with 2 degrees of freedom, so we would reject the null hypothesis. Our prediction/classification table indicates that we can accurately predict nearly 80 percent of the cases with the two variable model, an improvement of almost 21 percent over chance.

## 17.7 SUMMARY

In this chapter we have examined regressionlike models when we have a *dichotomous dependent variable*. Although we might like to apply our well-known OLS methods to such problems, we found out that the linear probability model is not well suited to the task. If we use OLS methods to estimate a regression model with a dichotomous dependent variable, we find that our probability predictions may not be bounded by zero and 1 and that the assumption of constant variances cannot be maintained. Because the OLS model is inappropriate, we examined two other regression models for dichotomous dependent variables, the *logit* and the *probit regression model*.

The logit model is based on the *cumulative logistic distribution*. The dependent variable in a logistic distribution is the natural *logarithm* of the *odds* of the dependent variable occurring. The logit model allows us to estimate a regressionlike equation that contains coefficients that reflect the effect of each independent variable on the dependent variable. In addition, we can estimate probabilities for the dependent variable.

The probit model is based on the *cumulative normal distribution*. The probit model estimates an unobserved standard normal variable. It, too, has coefficients that reflect the effect of the independent variables. Like the logit model, we can use the probit equation to estimate the probability of the dependent variable occurring based on characteristics of the independent variable.

## Key Terms

| | |
|---|---|
| antilog | logistic regression model |
| binary variable | logit |
| cumulative logistic probability function | maximum-likelihood estimation (MLE) |
| dummy variable | multicollinearity |
| dichotomous dependent variable | odds of an event |
| heteroscedasticity | odds ratio |
| homoscedasticity | probit |
| likelihood ratio statistic | probit regression model |
| linear probability regression model | Wald statistic |
| logarithm | |

## Problems

1. Why is an OLS regression model inappropriate to use when you are analyzing a dichotomous dependent variable?
2. What is the dependent variable in a logistic regression analysis? What is the dependent variable in a probit regression analysis?

3. Give an example of a research question in which logistic or probit regression models would be more appropriate than OLS procedures.
4. Out of a group of 700 criminal defendants:
   a. If 250 test positive for drugs, what is the probability that any one defendant randomly chosen will have tested positively? What are the odds?
   b. If 500 have at least one prior arrest, what is the probability that any one defendant chosen randomly will have a prior arrest? What are the odds?
   c. If 630 have a juvenile record, what is the probability that any one defendant chosen randomly will have a juvenile record? What are the odds?
   d. If 180 eventually get sentenced to prison, what is the probability that any one defendant chosen randomly will be sent to prison? What are the odds?
5. Presented below are the results from a hypothetical logit regression analysis using gender of the defendant (Def. Gender: female = 0, male = 1) as the independent variable to predict guilty verdicts (not guilty = 0, guilty = 1) in 52 randomly selected cases involving homicides committed by one spouse against another.

| Variable | Beta | Standard Error | Wald | df | Sig. |
|---|---|---|---|---|---|
| Def. Gender | .3278 | .1369 | 5.736 | 1 | .0166 |
| Constant | .0561 | .1105 | .2576 | 1 | .6117 |

   a. Interpret the regression coefficient
   b. Test the null hypothesis that the logistic regression coefficient for Def. Gender in the population is zero against the alternative hypothesis that it is different than zero. Use an alpha of .05.
   c. Compute the probabilities of a guilty verdict for both male and female defendants from the above equation. What are their respective odds of a guilty verdict?
   d. We present the hypothetical classification table for the above equation of gender predicting guilty verdicts.

| | | Predicted y Value | | |
|---|---|---|---|---|
| | | 0 | 11 | Total |
| Observed y Value | 0 | 22 | 7 | 29 |
| | 1 | — 2 | — 21 | — 23 |
| Total | | 24 | 28 | 52 |

   Assuming that the percent of correct predictions by chance alone is 55.8 percent, calculate the percent of correct predictions that resulted from knowing the independent variable (gender) using the classification table.
6. The following table reports the results of a two–independent variable logistic regression model. The dependent variable is the decision of the police to arrest a suspect (0 = no, 1 = yes). One independent variable is the expressed desire of the victim (Desire) that the suspect be arrested (0 = no, 1 = yes), and the second independent variable is the age of the victim (Age). The sample size is 50.

| Variable | Coefficient | Standard Error | t Ratio |
|----------|-------------|----------------|---------|
| Desire | .81477 | .9385 | .868 |
| Age | .15930 | .0410 | 3.889 |
| Constant | −7.2461 | | |

Initial log likelihood function (constant only in the model)
   −2 log likelihood 66.406

With Desire and Age in the model
   −2 log likelihood 34.586

| | Chi-Square | df |
|---|-----------|-----|
| Model chi-square | 31.821 | 1 |

With this table, answer the following questions:
**a.** What is the equation for the two–independent variable logistic regression model?
**b.** Interpret the two regression coefficients.
**c.** What is the predicted probability of arrest for a victim who expresses that an arrest should be made and who is 50 years old? What are the odds of an arrest?
**d.** Using an alpha of .05, test the null hypothesis that the population regression coefficients are zero against the null hypothesis that they are both greater than zero.
**e.** Which variable is more important in understanding the police decision to make an arrest? What are your conclusions from this model?

**7.** The following below reports the results of a one–independent variable probit regression model. The dependent variable is the probability of rearrest after release from a prison boot camp (0 = not arrested, 1 = arrested). The independent variable is whether the person has a stable job on release (0 = no, 1 = yes). The sample size is 50.

| Variable | Coefficient | Standard Error | t Ratio |
|----------|-------------|----------------|---------|
| Job | −1.0941 | .3880 | −2.820 |
| Constant | .63364 | | |

Initial log likelihood function (constant only in the model)
   −2 log likelihood 69.324

With Job in the model
   −2 log likelihood 60.886

| | Chi-Square | df |
|---|-----------|-----|
| Model chi-square | 8.438 | 1 |

With this table, answer the following questions:
**a.** What is the equation for the one–independent variable probit model?
**b.** Interpret the regression coefficient.
**c.** What is the predicted probability of rearrest for a defendant with no job after release? For a defendant with a job after release?

**d.** Using an alpha of .01, test the null hypothesis that the population regression coefficient for Job is zero against the alternative hypothesis that it is less than zero.

**8.** We have taken the probit regression model from Problem 7 and added a second independent variable, the number of prior arrests the person has (Priors). We now think that having a job on release and the number of prior arrests are related to the likelihood that a person will be re-arrested following release from a prison boot camp. We show you below the results for this two independent variable probit model. The sample size is 50.

| Variable | Coefficient | Standard Error | *t* Ratio |
|----------|-------------|----------------|-----------|
| Job | −1.0186 | .4297 | −2.371 |
| Priors | .18247 | .0620 | 3.031 |
| Constant | −.25823 | | |

Initial log likelihood function (constant only in the model)
−2 log likelihood 69.324

With Job and Priors in the model
−2 log likelihood 49.044

| | Chi-Square | df |
|---|-----------|-----|
| Model chi-square | 20.191 | 2 |

With this table, answer the following questions:

**a.** What is the equation for the two–independent variable probit model?

**b.** Interpret the regression coefficients.

**c.** What is the predicted probability of rearrest for a person with no job after release and five prior arrests? For a person with a job after release and one prior arrest?

**d.** Using an alpha of .05, test the null hypothesis that the population probit coefficients for Job and Priors are zero against the alternative hypothesis that they are both different from zero.

## Solutions to Problems

**1.** There are two problems in using OLS regression when you have a binary or dichotomized dependent variable. One occurs because the predicted probabilities from an OLS model may exceed the lower (0) and upper (1) limits of a probability. A second problem concerns the error term. OLS regression assumes that the error term is normally distributed and independent of any given $x$ value. When OLS is used to predict probabilities, however, the error terms are correlated with $x$; that is, there is heteroscedasticity.

**2.** In a logistic regression analysis, the dependent variable is the natural log of the odds that the event will occur ($\ln P/(1 - P)$, where $P$ is the probability of the event occurring). The dependent variable in a probit regression model is an unobserved continuous index $z$ that is presumed to be normally distributed with a mean of zero and standard deviation of 1. In neither the logit nor the probit regression model, therefore, is the dependent variable the probability of an event. We can, however, obtain estimates of those probabilities with both types of models.

**3.** A logistic or probit regression model would be appropriate whenever the dependent variable is a dichotomy. For example, whether or not someone is arrested or rearrested, whether or not someone is convicted, commits or refrains from committing a criminal act, makes bail or fails to make bail, is sentenced to probation or a prison term, appears at trial or absconds. Anytime you are interested in a dependent variable that has only two outcomes, the logistic and probit regression models would be appropriate. Remember that you can use continuous (interval/ratio) independent variables in logistic and probit regression and that you can have dichotomized independent variables in OLS regression.

**4. a.** Probability = 250/700 = .36
Odds = .36/.64 = .56
**b.** Probability = 500/700 = .71
Odds = .71/.29 = 2.45
**c.** Probability = 630/700 = .90
Odds = .90/.10 = 9.00
**d.** Probability = 180/700 = .26
Odds = .26/.74 = .35

**5. a.** The logistic regression coefficient is .3278. This tells us that the log of the odds of a guilty verdict is .3278 higher for males than for females. The antilog of .3278 is $e^{.3278} = 1.39$. This tells us that the odds of a guilty verdict for males is 1.39 times higher than for females.

**b.** There are three ways we can determine the significance of the logistic regression coefficient. One way simply is to look at the significance level provided in the table. This significance level is .0166. This tells us that, if the null hypothesis is true, $\beta$ equals zero, the probability that we would observe a sample $b$ of .3278 is .0166. Because this is less than our selected alpha of .05, we would reject the null hypothesis. Another way would be to conduct a $t$ test. In our problem, $t = .3278/.1369 = 2.39$. With a two-tailed alpha of .05 and $52 - 2 = 50$ degrees of freedom, our critical value of $t$ from the $t$ table is $\pm 2.00$. As our $t$ ratio is 2.39, we would reject the null hypothesis that $\beta$ equals zero. Yet another way to test the null hypothesis is with the Wald statistic, which is shown in the table. The Wald statistic is the square of the $t$ ratio and has a chi-square distribution. With 1 degree of freedom and an alpha of .05, the critical value of chi-square is 3.841. As our Wald statistic is 5.736, we would reject the null hypothesis.

**c.** The predicted log odds that a male would plead guilty is:

$$\ln \frac{\hat{p}}{1 - \hat{p}} = .0561 + (.3278)(1)$$

$$= .0561 + .3278$$

$$= .3839$$

The predicted probability of a guilty plea for a male is:

$$\hat{p} = \frac{e^{.3839}}{1 + e^{.3839}}$$

$$= \frac{1.468}{2.468}$$

$$= .595$$

The predicted log odds that a female would enter a guilty plea is:

$$\ln \frac{\hat{p}}{1 - \hat{p}} = .0561 + (.3278)(0)$$

$$= .0561$$

The predicted probability of a guilty verdict for a female is:

$$\hat{p} = \frac{e^{.0561}}{1 + e^{.0561}}$$

$$= \frac{1.058}{2.058}$$

$$= .514$$

For males the odds are $.595/.405 = 1.47$. The odds of a guilty plea for a female are $.514/.486 = 1.06$.

    **d.** Using the independent variable, we have $22 + 21$, or 43, correct predictions out of 52 cases. This is equal to 82.7 percent.

**6. a.** The equation for this model is:

$$b_0 + b_1x_1 + b_2x_2 = -7.2461 + (.81477)(\text{Desire}) + (.1593)(\text{Age})$$

    **b.** A one-unit increase in the desire of the victim to have an arrest made increases the log of the odds of an arrest by .81477, when holding the age of the victim constant. The log of the odds of an arrest increases by .15930 when age increases by 1 year, holding constant the expressed desire of the victim for an arrest.

    **c.** The predicted probability that an arrest will be made is:

$$\hat{p} = \frac{e^{1.53}}{1 + e^{1.53}}$$

$$= \frac{4.618}{5.618}$$

$$= .82$$

The odds of an arrest in this case are $.82/.18 = 4.55$.

    **d.** The $t$ ratio for Desire is .868. We cannot reject the null hypothesis that the population regression coefficient for Desire is zero. The $t$ ratio for Age is 3.889. We can reject the null hypothesis that the population regression coefficient for Age is zero.

    **e.** The coefficient for Desire is not significant once Age is controlled. The coefficient for Age is significant even with Desire controlled. On the basis of this, we would conclude that the age of the victim has more of an effect on the log odds of an arrest than the desire of the victim that an arrest be made.

**7. a.** The probit equation is:

$$z = .63364 + (-1.0941)(\text{Job})$$

    **b.** A change of one unit on Job decreases the unmeasured variable $z$ by 1.0941 standard deviation units.

    **c.** First we obtain the predicted $z$ score:

$$z = .63364 + (-1.0941)(0)$$

$$= .63364$$

The predicted probability is .73.

To find the predicted probability for someone with a job, first we find the $z$ score:

$z = .63364 + (-1.0941)(1)$

$\quad = -.46$

The predicted probability of rearrest for someone with a job on release is .32.
   **d.** Our decision is to reject the null hypothesis if the $t$ ratio for Job is less than or equal to $-2.423$. As the obtained $t$ ratio is $-2.820$, we decide to reject the null hypothesis.
**8. a.** The probit equation is:

$z = -.25823 + (-1.0186)(\text{Job}) + (.18247)(\text{Priors})$

   **b.** The coefficient for Job tells us that a increase of one unit on Job decreases the unmeasured variable $z$ by 1.0186 standard deviation units, controlling for the number of prior arrests. The coefficient for Priors tells us that a change of one arrest increases the unmeasured variable $z$ by .18247 standard deviation units, controlling for the existence of a job after release.
   **c.** To determine the predicted probability of rearrest for someone with no job after release and five prior arrests, first we obtain the predicted $z$ score:

$z = -.25823 + (-1.0186)(0) + (.18247)(5)$

$\quad = -.25823 + .91235$

$\quad = .65412$

The predicted probability is .74. The predicted probability of rearrest for someone with a job on release and one prior arrest is approximately .14.
   **d.** We decide to reject the null hypothesis if the $t$ ratio for Job and Priors is either greater than or equal to 2.021 or less than or equal to $-2.021$. As the $t$ ratio for Job is $-2.371$ and that for Priors is 3.031, we decide to reject the null hypothesis for both coefficients.

## Endnotes

1. The term $P/(1 - P)$ refers to the odds of an event occurring. It is expressed as the ratio of the probability of the event occurring to the probability that it will not occur. The odds of an event occurring, therefore, are not the same as its probability. For example, in our age and alcohol use data 23 persons reported using alcohol and 17 persons did not. The odds that someone used alcohol, then, is the ratio of the probability that alcohol was used ($23/40 = .575$) to the probability that alcohol was not used ($17/40 = .425$), that is, 1.35 ($.575/.425$).
2. Taking the antilog of a given value is the same thing as exponentiating it. For example, the antilog of 1.23 is $e^{1.23}$, or 3.42.
3. Another way to determine this is as follows. Because the log of the odds of a 14-year-old using alcohol is .7309, the odds are equal to $e^{.7309}$, or 2.08.
4. This is because you would actually have two variables for social class. One variable would be coded 1 for lower-class cases and 0 for all other cases, the second variable would be coded 1 for middle-class cases and 0 for all other cases. Upper-class cases would be coded 0 on both variables, and would represent what is called the reference category. The choice as to which value would be the reference category is arbitrary. In this example, you would have two estimated logistic regression coefficients for the effect of social class. The first (with lower class coded 1) would represent the effect of being in the lower class on the log odds of the dependent variable, compared with upper-class cases. The second (with middle class coded 1) would represent the effect of being in the middle class on the log odds of the

dependent variable, compared with upper-class cases. The effect of being in the upper class on the log odds of the dependent variable will be zero. With more than two levels of a categorical variable, then, your statements about effects must always be in comparison to some other reference category.

5. From Table 17.6, we can see and count which specific cases were correctly and incorrectly predicted. For example, of those cases predicted to fall into the zero category of the dependent variable (no alcohol use), observations number 1,2,3,4,6,7,8,9,11,12, and 13 were correctly predicted (a total of 11) and numbers 5,10,14, and 15 were incorrectly predicted (a total of 4). Of those cases predicted to fall into the 1 category of the dependent variable (alcohol use), observations number 18,19,20,23,24,25,27,28,29,30,32,33,34,35,36,37,38,39, and 40 were correctly predicted (a total of 19) and numbers 16,17,21,22,26, and 31 were incorrectly predicted (a total of 6).

6. The value of the likelihood function and $-2LL$, or the likelihood ratio statistic for the baseline (constant-only), model can be obtained from one of three sources: (1) some computer programs automatically provide you with the likelihood ratio statistic for the baseline model (constant only included), (2) you can estimate a model with your statistical computer package that only has a constant term, or (3) you can estimate the value of $-2LL$ for any baseline model from the following equation:

$$-2LL_0 = -2\{[n[P \ln P + (1 - P) \ln (1 - P)]\}$$

where $P$ is the proportion of observations in the data with $y = 1$. For example, in the age and alcohol use data, 23 of 40 youths reported alcohol use, so that $P = 23/40$, or .575. The estimated value of $-2LL$ for the baseline model would be:

$$-2LL_0 = -2[40[.575 \ (\ln .575) + .425 \ (\ln .425)]]$$

$$= -2[40 \ [.575(-.553) + .425(-.856)]]$$

$$= -2[40[-.318 + -.364]]$$

$$= -2[40(-.682)]$$

$$= -2(27.28)$$

$$= 54.56$$

This is comparable to the value of 54.54 reported in Table 17.3.

7. The substantive results will be comparable, however, as we will see, but the values of the coefficient estimates will not.

8. As was true for our prediction rule with the logistic regression equation, this probit prediction rule will generally give you reasonable results when the proportion of cases in the two categories of the dependent variable is .5. Moreover this is the default prediction rule in most computer programs. As we have tried to stress, there may be times when, for substantive reasons, you will want to adopt a different cutoff or threshold value for your prediction strategy.

9. Notice that the predictions made for the probit and logit regression models are exactly the same.

10. Another way to look at this is to compare the baseline (constant-only) model with a model that contains only age and one that contains only gender. The difference between the baseline model and each of these one-variable models will indicate how much better the model fits when each independent variable is added. The more improvement we see in the baseline

model, the stronger the influence of the independent variable. For our alcohol use example, the likelihood ratio statistic for the baseline model was 54.548. When age is added to the model, the likelihood ratio statistic improves to 41.553, an improvement of 12.995. When gender is added to the model by itself, the likelihood ratio statistic improves to 36.594, an improvement of 17.954. Because the model shows greater improvement when gender is added to the model than when age is added, it has a stronger effect on the dependent variable.

11. We offer you some help in translating a $\hat{z}$ score of 2.14 into a probability. To do this, go to the $z$ table and find the area of the curve to the right of the mean corresponding to a $z$ score of 2.14. You will find that it is .4838. The area to the left of the mean is .50, so we simply add the two proportions, .4838 + .50 = .9838. This means that .98 of the normal curve is to the left of a $z$ score of 2.14 and that the predicted probability of this $\hat{z}$ score is .98.

# APPENDIX A

# *Review of Basic Mathematical Operations*

*I never did very well in math—I could never seem to persuade the teacher that I hadn't meant my answers literally.*

—Calvin Trillin

*A man has one hundred dollars and you leave him with two dollars, that's subtraction.*

—Mae West

## INTRODUCTION

Many of you undoubtedly have avoided taking a statistics class because you believed that the mathematics involved would be too difficult for your meager skills. After many years of teaching undergraduate statistics courses, we have probably heard all the stories. Some students protest, "I'm not very good at math, so how can I ever hope to pass a statistics course! Statistics is nothing but math!" Others are more pessimistic, "I've *never* been good at math, I did lousy in junior high, high school, and college. I just have a mental block against doing math"! Others are only slightly more optimistic, claiming that they are simply rusty, "I haven't had a math course since high school, I've forgotten everything since then!"

This anxiety you brought with you to the course was probably only made worse when you thumbed through the chapters of this book, seeing all the equations, formulas, and strange symbols. Even letters in a different alphabet! "God," you thought, "I am sunk, maybe I should change my major or start planning for summer school"! Put your mind at rest, you need do none of those things. The study of statistics does require some mathematical skills, but they are no more than the ability to add, subtract, multiply, and divide. Let us assure you that, if you can do these simple mathematical operations, you can do statistics.

In this statistical text, we have emphasized the conceptual and logical dimension of statistical analyses of crime data. Most complex statistical analyses are now performed by computer programs. You will undoubtedly learn one of these programs in this or some other course. The computer workbook that is a companion to this text introduces you to one such statistical software program called SPSS-PC.

This stands for the *S*tatistical *P*ackage for the *S*ocial *S*ciences for the *P*ersonal *C*omputer. This is only one such statistical package that will do the calculations for you for the statistics described in this book. There are many others available, and all of them perform high-speed and accurate calculations of simple and complex statistics.

Although computer software programs can perform the calculations for us much quicker than we could by hand and with far greater accuracy, we need to know some basics about statistics so that we know which statistical analyses to perform in which situations. We also need to know how to interpret and diagnose the mass of statistical information most computer programs spit out for us. In other words, no matter how fast, accurate, or sophisticated the statistical computer package you use, *you still need to know what you are doing.* Therefore, in this statistics course you need to learn how to hand-calculate the various statistical procedures.

The hand calculation of statistics is not that daunting a task. Again, all you need to know how to do mathematically, is to add, subtract, multiply, and divide. The task will be made simpler by two things we have provided in each chapter of the text:

1. Clear and simplified examples
2. A step-by-step approach in which even the most difficult statistical procedures are broken down into simple steps

In addition, you will probably find it necessary to use a hand calculator to do the numerical operations for you. There are a great many kinds of calculators on the market now. Some of these calculators seem as complex as personal computers, with graphic screens and everything! Others, in addition to basic mathematical operations, actually calculate some of the statistics in this book for you, such as standard deviations and correlation coefficients.

We would recommend that you use a calculator for your calculations. You do not, however, need a very fancy or expensive one. All you really need is a calculator that, in addition to mathematical operations such as adding and subtracting, has a square root key ($\sqrt{\phantom{x}}$) and a square key ($x^2$). The square key will enable you to square (multiply by itself) any number. A simple calculator that does these things is all you really need to work the problems described in this text.

Before we describe some simple mathematical operations, we would like to show you some common symbols used in statistics. Mathematical operations involve many symbols in their own right; as if this were not difficult enough, many statistics are symbolized by a Greek letter. To help you through the symbolism, the following are some common math symbols and Greek letters you will find in this text:

## COMMON MATHEMATICAL SYMBOLS

| | | | |
|---|---|---|---|
| + | Addition | > | Greater than |
| − | Subtraction | ≥ | Greater than or equal to |
| * | Multiplication | ≈ | Approximately equal to |

| / or ÷ | Division | $x^2$ | The number $x$ squared |
|---|---|---|---|
| = | Equals | $\sqrt{x}$ | The square root of the number $x$ |
| ≠ | Is not equal to | $\ln x$ | The natural log of the number $x$ |
| ± | Plus or minus | $\log x$ | The common log of the number $x$ |
| < | Less than | $|x|$ | The absolute value of the number $x$ |
| ≤ | Less than or equal to | | |

## COMMON GREEK LETTERS USED IN STATISTICS

| Uppercase | Lowercase | |
|---|---|---|
| A | α | alpha |
| B | β | beta |
| Γ | γ | gamma |
| Δ | δ | delta |
| E | ε | epsilon |
| Λ | λ | lambda |
| M | μ | mu |
| P | ρ | rho |
| Σ | σ | sigma |
| T | τ | tau |
| Φ | φ | phi |
| X | χ | chi |

## MATHEMATICAL OPERATIONS

Most of you are familiar with the four basic mathematical operations: addition, subtraction, multiplication, and division. In this text, the operations of addition and subtraction are shown with their common symbols, + and − . In the text, the operations of multiplication and division are shown with several different symbols. For example, the operation of multiplying $x$ by $y$ may be shown as $xy$, $x \times y$, $x*y$, $x \cdot y$, or $(x)(y)$. The operation of dividing $x$ by $y$ may be shown as $x/y$, $x \div y$, or $x/y$.

In addition to the standard operations of addition, subtraction, multiplication, and division, there are three other very frequent mathematical operations in statistics. One of these is the squaring of a number. A number squared is symbolized by the number being squared shown with a superscript of 2. For example, 4 squared is shown as $4^2$, and 7 squared is shown as $7^2$. When you square a number, you multiply that number by itself, so that 4 squared is equal to $4 \times 4 = 16$, and 7 squared is equal to $7 \times 7 = 49$. These expressions tell us that 4 squared is equal to 16 and 7 squared is equal to 49. One squared is equal to 1, because $1^2 = 1 \times 1 = 1$. When calculating the square of fractions, it is probably easier to first convert the fraction to a decimal and then square. For example, the square of one-half $(\frac{1}{2})^2$ would be equal to $.50^2$, or $(.50)(.50) = .25$. The square of one-third $(\frac{1}{3})^2$ would be equal to $.33^2$, or $(.33)(.33) = .1089$.

A second frequent mathematical operation in statistics is taking the square root of a number. This is symbolized by placing the number we want the square root of within something called a radical sign ($\sqrt{\phantom{x}}$). For example, the square root of 2 is shown as $\sqrt{2}$, and the square root of 9 is shown as $\sqrt{9}$. The square root of a number is the value that, when squared, results in the original number. For example, the square root of 9 is 3 ($\sqrt{9} = 3$) because when 3 is squared we obtain 9 ($3^2 = 3 \times 3 = 9$). The square root of 25 is 5 ($\sqrt{25} = 5$) because when 5 is squared, we obtain 25 ($5^2 = (5)(5) = 25$). As with the squaring of fractions, it will probably be easier to convert a fraction into a decimal before taking the square root. For example, the square root of one-half ($\sqrt{1/2}$) is equal to $\sqrt{.5}$, which is equal to .707 because $.707^2 = .5$. The square root of a negative number, $\sqrt{-x}$, is not defined because there is no number $x$ that, when squared (multiplied by itself), results in a negative number. This is because the multiplication of two negative numbers always results in a positive product.

The third other operation that you will frequently see in this text is the summation operation. This is actually an addition operation, but because it appears with its own symbol we need to call special attention to it. The operation of summation is symbolized by the uppercase Greek letter sigma ($\Sigma$). The summation sign stands for "the sum of," and the operation requires you to add a series of scores for a given variable. For example, presuming that there are five scores for the variable Age (itself symbolized as $x$), the ages of five persons might be as follows:

$x_1 = 13 \quad x_4 = 20$
$x_2 = 18 \quad x_5 = 17$
$x_3 = 25$

The operation $\Sigma x$ instructs you to sum or add each of these $x$ scores or ages. That is, instead of stating that you should take the first person's age and add it to the second person's age, and then add this sum to the third person's age, and so on, a formula will simply state sum all the $x$ scores or $\Sigma x$. In this example, then, $\Sigma x = 13 + 18 + 25 + 20 + 17 = 93$. Think of the symbol $\Sigma$, then, as a mathematical operation that says "add all of the $x$ scores up and determine the sum."

## ORDER OF OPERATIONS

Many statistical formulas require you to perform several mathematical operations at once. At times these formulas may seem very complex, requiring addition, division, squaring, square roots, and summation. Your task of comprehending statistical formulas would not be so difficult if it did not matter how all the calculations were performed, so long as they were all completed. Unfortunately, however, statistical formulas require not only that all mathematical operations be conducted, but also that they be conducted in the right order, because you will get different results depending on the order in which the operations are performed!

For example, take the very simple equation below that requires you to add and divide a few numbers:

$15 + 10 \div 5$

Notice that you will get completely different results depending on whether you complete the addition before dividing or do the dividing first:

$(15 + 10) \div 5$      $15 + (10 \div 5)$

$25 \div 5 = 5$        $15 + 2 = 17$

As you can see, the order in which you perform your mathematical operations does make a substantial difference, and must, therefore, be correctly followed. Fortunately, there are some standard rules that tell you the order in which operations should be performed. In addition, we would like to emphasize that even the most complex formula or mathematical expression can be simplified by solving it in sequential steps. We now illustrate these rules of operation and our recommended step-by-step approach for solving mathematical expressions.

The first rule is that any operation that is included in parentheses should be performed before operations not included in parentheses. For example, for the following expression

$15 + (10 \div 5) \times (7 \times 2)$

the order of operations would be to first divide 10 by 5 and multiply 7 by 2. We now have simplified the expression

$15 + 2 \times 14$

How do we solve the remainder of this? Do we first add $15 + 2$ and then multiply by 14 to get 238? Or do we first multiply 2 by 14 and then add 15 to get 43?

The second rule of the order of operations is that you should first obtain all squares and square roots first, then multiplication and division, and last complete the addition and subtraction. Because in the expression just listed we have no squares or square roots to calculate, we know that we should first multiply the 2 and 14 to get 28.

$15 + 28$

After this we should add this to 15 to get the final sum of 43.

To summarize, the rules of operation for solving mathematical expressions are, in order:

- Solve all expressions in parentheses.
- Determine the value of all squares and square roots.
- Perform division and multiplication operations.
- Perform all addition and subtraction operations.

We will practice these rules with some exercises momentarily, but first, we need to illustrate the parentheses rule in combination with the rule of squares.

The rules are to perform all operations within parentheses first, then squares and square roots, multiplication and division, and then addition and subtraction. As an example, assume that we have the following six scores: 46, 29, 61, 14, 33, and 25. With these scores, examine the two expressions, $\Sigma x^2$ and $(\Sigma x)^2$. These two expressions look virtually identical because they both require a summation of scores and that a number be squared. Notice, however, that in the first expression there are no parentheses. We know that the summation sign tells us that we have to add the six scores. Before we do this, however, following the correct order of operations, we must first square each $x$ score, and then sum them:

$$\Sigma x^2 = 46^2 + 29^2 + 61^2 + 14^2 + 33^2 + 25^2$$

$$= 2116 + 841 + 3721 + 196 + 1089 + 625$$

$$= 8588$$

In this first expression, then, we have followed the order of operations by first squaring each $x$ score and then taking the sum (squaring before addition).

Notice that in the second expression we have a parentheses $(\Sigma x)^2$. As the order of operations is to conduct all calculations within parentheses first, this expression tells us to first sum the six scores and then square the sum:

$$(\Sigma x)^2 = (46 + 29 + 61 + 14 + 33 + 25)^2$$

$$= 208^2$$

$$= 43{,}264$$

To reiterate the point made above, $\Sigma x^2$, called the sum of the $x$ squares, is obtained by first squaring each $x$ score and then adding all squared numbers. This is different from the expression, $(\Sigma x)^2$, called the sum of the $x$s, squared, which is obtained by first adding up all the $x$ scores and then squaring the sum.

## OPERATIONS WITH NEGATIVE NUMBERS AND FRACTIONS IN DENOMINATORS

In many statistical calculations you have both positive and negative scores. Positive scores are shown with no sign at all, so that a positive 10 appears as 10. Negative numbers are shown with a minus sign in front of them, so that a negative 10 appears as $-10$. Negative numbers are less than zero, and positive numbers are greater than zero. It is important to keep track of the signs of numbers because it makes a substantial difference for the final result of a mathematical operation.

For example, when a positive number is added to a positive number, nothing special happens, and the sum of the two numbers can be obtained directly: $10 + 14 = 24$. When a negative number is added to a positive number, however, it has the same effect as a subtraction. For example, adding a negative 14 to 10 is the same thing as subtracting 14 from 10: $10 + (-14) = 10 - 14 = (-4)$. When a positive number is subtracted from another positive number, nothing special happens, and the difference between the two numbers can be obtained directly: $25 - 10 = 15$. When a negative number is subtracted from either a positive or negative number, the sign changes to a positive number, so that $25 - (-10) = 25 + 10 = 35$; $(-10) - (-7) = (-10) + 7 = (-3)$. Remember, then, that the subtraction of a negative number changes the sign of the number from negative to positive.

When two positive numbers are multiplied, nothing special happens, and the product of the two numbers can be obtained directly: $6 \times 3 = 18$. When two numbers are multiplied and one is positive and the other negative, the resulting product is negative. For example: $25 \times (-3) = -75$; $(-14) \times 5 = -70$. When two negative numbers are multiplied, the resulting product is always positive: $(-23) \times (-14) = 322$. So, the rule is that the multiplication of either two positive or two negative numbers results in a positive product, whereas the multiplication of one positive and one negative number results in a negative product.

The same pattern occurs when the operation is division rather than multiplication. When two positive numbers are divided, nothing special happens, and the result (the *quotient*) is positive: $125 \div 5 = 25$; $10 \div 20 = .5$. When two numbers are divided and one is positive and the other negative, the quotient is negative: $250 \div (-25) = (-10)$; $(-33) \div 11 = -3$. When two negative numbers are divided, the quotient always is positive: $(-16) \div (-4) = 4$. So, the rule is that the division of either two positive or two negative numbers results in a positive quotient, whereas the division of one positive and one negative number has a negative quotient.

## *ROUNDING NUMBERS OFF*

Whenever you are working with statistical formulas, you need to decide how precise you want your answer to be. For example, should your answer be correct to the tenth decimal place? the fifth? the third? It is also important to decide when to round up and when to round down. For example, having decided that we want to be accurate only to the second decimal place, should the number 28.355 be rounded up to 28.36 or rounded down to 28.35? It is important to make these decisions explicit, because two people may get different answers to the same statistical problem simply because they employed different rounding rules.

Unfortunately, any rule as to when to round off cannot always be hard and fast. When we are dealing with large numbers, we can frequently do our calculations with whole numbers (integers). In this case, we would not gain much precision by carrying out our calculations to one or two decimal places. When we are dealing with much smaller numbers, however, it may be necessary, in order to be as precise as possible, to take a number out to three or four decimal places in our calculations. With smaller numbers, there is a substantial gain in precision by including more decimal places in our calculations. Whenever possible, however, we have tried to limit our precision to two decimal places. This means that most of the time numbers will include only two decimal places. We warn you, however, that this will not always be the case.

The question as to how to round can be answered a little more definitively. When rounding, the following convention should be applied. When deciding how to round, look at the digit to the right of the last digit you want to keep. If we are rounding to the second decimal place, then, look at the third digit to the right of the decimal point. If this digit is larger than 5, you should round up. For example, 123.148 becomes 123.15, and 34.737 becomes 34.74. If this digit is less than 5, you should round down. For example, 8.923 becomes 8.92, and 53.904 becomes 53.90.

What do you do in the case where the third digit is a 5, 34.675, for example? Do you round up or round down? You cannot simply say that you should always round up or always round down because there will be systematic bias to your rounding decision. Your decision rule will be consistent to be sure, but it will be biased because numbers are always being overestimated (if rounded up) or underestimated (if rounded down). You would like your decision rule to be consistent, but consistently fair, that is, never in the same direction. This way, sometimes the 5 will be rounded up and sometimes it will be rounded down, and the number of times it is rounded up and down will be approximately the same. One way to ensure this is to adopt the following rounding rule: if the third digit is a 5, then look at the digit immediately *before* the 5; if that digit (the second decimal place) is an even number, then round up, if it is an odd number, then round down. For example, the number 34.675 should be rounded down to 34.67 because the number immediately before the 5 is an odd number. The number 164.965 should be rounded up to 164.97 because the number before the 5 is an even number. Notice that the number of occasions you will decide to round up (if the immediately preceding digit is an even number 0,2,4,6, or 8) is the same as the number of occasions when you will decide to round down (if the immediately preceding digit is an odd number 1,3,5,7,9). Because even numbers should appear in our calculations as frequently as odd numbers there is no bias to our rounding decision rule.

## EXAMPLES

Let's go through a few examples step by step to make sure that we understand all the rules and procedures. We will begin by solving the following problem:

$$25 + 192 - (3 + 5)^2$$

Following the rules of operation, we first solve within the parentheses:

$$25 + 192 - (8)^2$$

Then square the 8:

$$25 + 192 - 64$$

Now we can solve for the final answer either by adding 25 to 192 and then subtracting 64, or subtracting 64 from 192 and then adding 25. Either way, we get the same result:

$$217 - 64 = 153 \qquad 25 + 128 = 153$$

Now let's solve a more complicated-looking problem. Please note that this problem is only more complicated looking. When we solve it step by step, you will see that it is very manageable and that all you really need to know is addition, subtraction, multiplication, and division:

$$((32 + 17)^2/10) + (\sqrt{16}/(10 - 6)^2)$$

First, we solve within parentheses:

$$((49)^2/10) + (\sqrt{16}/(4)^2)$$

Then, calculate all squares and square roots:

$$(2401/10) + (4/16)$$

Then, do the division:

$$240.1 + .25$$

Finally, do the addition:

$$240.35$$

One more problem that is probably as difficult as any you will have to face in the book:

$$\sqrt{\frac{(116 - 27)^2 + 21}{\sqrt{15 + 1}}} - \frac{(212 - 188)}{2}$$

Following the rules of operations, we first want to solve within all parentheses first:

$$\sqrt{\frac{(89)^2 + 21}{\sqrt{15 + 1}}} - \frac{24}{2}$$

Then, calculate all squares and square roots. Notice, however, that in the denominator of the first term we first have to use addition ($15 + 1$) before taking the square root of the sum. Notice also that we cannot take the square root of the entire first term until we solve for all that is under the square root sign:

$$\sqrt{\frac{7921 + 21}{4}} - 12$$

Now, we will continue to solve that part of the problem within the square root by first completing the numerator (by addition) and then dividing:

$$\sqrt{\frac{7942}{4}} - 12$$

$$\sqrt{1985.5} - 12$$

Finally, now that we have completed all the operations within the square root sign, we can complete that:

$$44.56 - 12$$

Notice that the result for the first expression was 44.558. Because the third decimal place is greater than 5, we round the second digit up, so that 44.558 becomes 44.56. Then we complete the problem by subtracting 12:

$$32.56$$

We hope that you now feel greater confidence in solving math equations. As long as things are performed in a step-by-step manner, in accordance with the rules of operations, everything in any equation can be solved relatively easily. To make sure that you comprehend these rules, as well as to brush up on your math skills, complete the following exercises. We have provided answers for you at the end of the section. If you can do these problems, you are ready to tackle any of the statistics problems in this text. If some of the problems in the exercises below give you difficulty, simply review that section of this appendix or consult a mathematics book for some help.

## Practice Problems

1. Calculate each of the following:
   a. $5^2 + 3$
   b. $(35/7) - 4$
   c. $\sqrt{64} + 7 - (4/2)$
   d. $[(35)(.3)]/10 + 15$
2. Calculate each of the following:

   a. $45 + \sqrt{\dfrac{125}{15 - (3)^2}}$

   b. $18 + (12 * 10) - \sqrt{150 - 50}$
   c. $(18 + 12) * 10 - \sqrt{150 - 50}$
   d. $[(23 + 17) - (5 * 4)]/(8 + 2)^2$
   e. $(-5) * 13$
   f. $(-5) * (-13)$
   g. $[18 + (-7)] * [(-4) - (-10)]$
   h. $125/ - 5$
   i. $450 - [(-125/ - 10)/2]$
3. With these 10 scores, 7, 18, 42, 11, 34, 65, 30, 27, 6, 29, perform the following operations:
   a. $\Sigma x$
   b. $(\Sigma x)^2$
   c. $\Sigma x^2$
4. Round the following numbers off to two places to the right of the decimal point:
   a. 118.954
   b. 65.186
   c. 156.145
   d. 87.915
   e. 3.212
   f. 48.565
   g. 48.535

## Solutions to Problems

1. a. 28
   b. 1 (remember to do the division before the subtraction)
   c. 13
   d. 16.05
2. a. 49.56
   b. 128
   c. 290

**d.** .20 (remember to do all operations within parentheses first, starting with the innermost parentheses).

**e.** $-65$

**f.** 65

**g.** 66

**h.** $-25$

**i.** 443.75 (following the rules of operation, you should have divided the two negative numbers ($-125$ and $-10$) first, then divided by 2, finally subtracted that quotient from 450).

**3. a.** This expression says to sum all $x$ scores: $7 + 18 + 42 + 11 + 34 + 65 + 30 + 27 + 6 + 29 = 269$.

**b.** Notice the parentheses in this expression. It tell you to first sum all the $x$ scores and then square the sum: $(7 + 18 + 42 + 11 + 34 + 65 + 30 + 27 + 6 + 29)^2 = (269)^2 = 72{,}361$.

**c.** Following the order of operations, first square each $x$ score, and then sum these squared scores: $7^2 + 18^2 + 42^2 + 11^2 + 34^2 + 65^2 + 30^2 + 27^2 + 6^2 + 29^2 = 49 + 324 + 1764 + 121 + 1156 + 4225 + 900 + 729 + 36 + 841 = 10{,}145$.

**4. a.** 118.95

**b.** 65.19

**c.** 156.15 (round up because the number to the left of the 5 is an even number).

**d.** 87.91 (round down because the number to the left of the 5 is an odd number).

**e.** 3.21

**f.** 48.57

**g.** 48.53

# *Statistical Tables*

## TABLE B.1. Table of Random Numbers

| | | | | | | | | | | | | | | | |
|---|---|---|---|---|---|---|---|---|---|---|---|---|---|---|---|
| 10480 | 15011 | 01536 | 02011 | 81647 | 91647 | 69179 | 14194 | 62590 | 36207 | 20969 | 99570 | 91291 | 90700 |
| 22368 | 46573 | 25595 | 85393 | 30995 | 73258 | 27982 | 53402 | 93965 | 34095 | 52666 | 19174 | 39615 | 99505 |
| 24130 | 48360 | 22527 | 97265 | 76393 | 03469 | 15179 | 24830 | 49340 | 32081 | 30680 | 19655 | 63348 | 58629 |
| 42167 | 93093 | 06243 | 61680 | 07856 | 29718 | 39440 | 53537 | 71341 | 57004 | 00849 | 74917 | 97758 | 16379 |
| 37570 | 39975 | 81837 | 16656 | 06121 | 45938 | 60468 | 81305 | 49684 | 60672 | 14110 | 06927 | 01263 | 54613 |
| | | | | | | | | | | | | | |
| 77921 | 06907 | 11008 | 42751 | 27756 | 14663 | 18602 | 70659 | 90655 | 15053 | 21916 | 81825 | 44394 | 42880 |
| 99562 | 72905 | 56420 | 69994 | 98872 | 53633 | 71194 | 18738 | 44013 | 48840 | 63213 | 21069 | 10634 | 12952 |
| 96301 | 91977 | 05463 | 07972 | 18876 | 43514 | 94595 | 56869 | 69014 | 60045 | 18425 | 84903 | 42508 | 32307 |
| 89579 | 14342 | 63661 | 10281 | 17453 | 38588 | 57740 | 84378 | 25331 | 12566 | 58678 | 44947 | 05585 | 56941 |
| 85475 | 36857 | 53342 | 53988 | 53060 | 71568 | 38867 | 62300 | 08158 | 17983 | 16439 | 11458 | 18593 | 64952 |
| | | | | | | | | | | | | | |
| 28918 | 69578 | 88231 | 33276 | 70997 | 79936 | 56865 | 05859 | 90106 | 31595 | 01547 | 85590 | 91610 | 78188 |
| 63553 | 40961 | 48235 | 03427 | 49626 | 69445 | 18663 | 72695 | 52180 | 20847 | 12234 | 90511 | 33703 | 90322 |
| 09429 | 93969 | 52636 | 92737 | 88974 | 33488 | 36320 | 17617 | 30015 | 08272 | 84115 | 27156 | 30613 | 74952 |
| 10365 | 61129 | 87529 | 85689 | 48237 | 52267 | 67689 | 93394 | 01511 | 26358 | 85104 | 20285 | 29975 | 89868 |
| 07119 | 97336 | 71048 | 08178 | 77233 | 13916 | 47564 | 81056 | 97735 | 85977 | 29372 | 74461 | 28551 | 90707 |
| | | | | | | | | | | | | | |
| 51085 | 12765 | 51821 | 51259 | 77452 | 16308 | 60756 | 92144 | 49442 | 53900 | 70960 | 63990 | 75601 | 40719 |
| 02368 | 21382 | 52404 | 60268 | 89368 | 19885 | 55322 | 44819 | 01188 | 65255 | 64835 | 44919 | 05944 | 55157 |
| 01011 | 54092 | 33362 | 94904 | 31273 | 04146 | 18594 | 29852 | 71585 | 85030 | 51132 | 01915 | 92747 | 64951 |
| 52162 | 53916 | 46369 | 58586 | 23216 | 14513 | 83149 | 98736 | 23495 | 64350 | 94738 | 17752 | 35156 | 35749 |
| 07056 | 97628 | 33787 | 09998 | 42698 | 06691 | 76988 | 13602 | 51851 | 46104 | 88916 | 19509 | 25625 | 58104 |
| | | | | | | | | | | | | | |
| 48663 | 91245 | 85828 | 14346 | 09172 | 30168 | 90229 | 04734 | 59193 | 22178 | 30421 | 61666 | 99904 | 32812 |
| 54164 | 58492 | 22421 | 74103 | 47070 | 25306 | 76468 | 26384 | 58151 | 06646 | 21524 | 15227 | 96909 | 44592 |
| 32639 | 32363 | 05597 | 24200 | 13363 | 38005 | 94342 | 28728 | 35806 | 06912 | 17012 | 64161 | 18296 | 72851 |
| 29334 | 27001 | 87637 | 87308 | 58731 | 00256 | 45834 | 15398 | 46557 | 41135 | 10367 | 07684 | 36188 | 18510 |
| 02488 | 33062 | 28834 | 07351 | 19731 | 92420 | 60952 | 61280 | 50001 | 67658 | 32586 | 86679 | 50720 | 94953 |

(Continued)

| | | | | | | | | | | | | | |
|---|---|---|---|---|---|---|---|---|---|---|---|---|---|
| 81525 | 72295 | 04839 | 96423 | 24878 | 82651 | 66566 | 14778 | 76797 | 14780 | 13300 | 87074 | 79666 | 95725 |
| 29676 | 20591 | 68086 | 26432 | 46901 | 20849 | 89768 | 81536 | 86645 | 12659 | 92259 | 57102 | 80428 | 25280 |
| 00742 | 57392 | 39064 | 66432 | 84673 | 40027 | 32832 | 61362 | 98947 | 96067 | 64760 | 64584 | 96096 | 98253 |
| 05366 | 04213 | 25669 | 26422 | 44407 | 44048 | 37937 | 63904 | 45766 | 66134 | 75470 | 66520 | 34693 | 90449 |
| 91921 | 26418 | 64117 | 94305 | 26766 | 25940 | 39972 | 22209 | 71500 | 64568 | 91402 | 42416 | 07844 | 09018 |
| 00582 | 04711 | 87917 | 77341 | 42206 | 35126 | 74087 | 99547 | 81817 | 42607 | 43808 | 76655 | 62028 | 76630 |
| 00725 | 69884 | 62797 | 56170 | 86324 | 88072 | 76222 | 36086 | 84637 | 93161 | 76038 | 65855 | 77919 | 88006 |
| 69011 | 65795 | 95876 | 55293 | 18988 | 27354 | 26575 | 08625 | 40801 | 59920 | 29841 | 80150 | 12777 | 48501 |
| 25976 | 57948 | 29888 | 88604 | 67917 | 48708 | 18912 | 82271 | 65424 | 69774 | 33611 | 54262 | 85963 | 03547 |
| 09763 | 83473 | 73577 | 12908 | 30883 | 18317 | 28290 | 35797 | 05998 | 41688 | 34952 | 37888 | 38917 | 88050 |
| 91567 | 42595 | 27958 | 30134 | 04024 | 86385 | 29880 | 99730 | 55536 | 84855 | 29080 | 09250 | 79656 | 73211 |
| 17955 | 56349 | 90999 | 49127 | 20044 | 59931 | 06115 | 20542 | 18059 | 02008 | 73708 | 83517 | 36103 | 42791 |
| 46503 | 18584 | 18845 | 49618 | 02304 | 51038 | 20655 | 58727 | 28168 | 15475 | 56942 | 53389 | 20562 | 87338 |
| 92157 | 89634 | 94824 | 78171 | 84610 | 82834 | 09922 | 25417 | 44137 | 48413 | 25555 | 21246 | 35509 | 20468 |
| 14577 | 62765 | 35605 | 81263 | 39667 | 47358 | 56873 | 56307 | 61607 | 49518 | 89656 | 20103 | 77490 | 18062 |
| 98427 | 07523 | 33362 | 64270 | 01638 | 92477 | 66969 | 98420 | 04880 | 45585 | 46565 | 04102 | 46880 | 45709 |
| 34914 | 63976 | 88720 | 82765 | 34476 | 17032 | 87589 | 40836 | 32427 | 70002 | 70663 | 88863 | 77775 | 69348 |
| 70060 | 28277 | 39475 | 46473 | 23219 | 53416 | 94970 | 25832 | 69975 | 94884 | 19661 | 72828 | 00102 | 66794 |
| 53976 | 54914 | 06990 | 67245 | 68350 | 82948 | 11398 | 42878 | 80287 | 88267 | 47363 | 46634 | 06541 | 97809 |
| 76072 | 29515 | 40980 | 07391 | 58745 | 25774 | 22987 | 80059 | 39911 | 96189 | 41151 | 14222 | 60697 | 59583 |
| 90725 | 52210 | 83974 | 29992 | 65831 | 38857 | 50490 | 83765 | 55657 | 14361 | 31720 | 57375 | 56228 | 41546 |
| 64364 | 67412 | 33339 | 31926 | 14883 | 24413 | 59744 | 92351 | 97473 | 89286 | 35931 | 04110 | 23726 | 51900 |
| 08062 | 00358 | 31662 | 25388 | 61642 | 34072 | 81249 | 35648 | 56891 | 69352 | 48373 | 45578 | 78547 | 81788 |
| 95012 | 68379 | 93526 | 70765 | 10592 | 04542 | 76463 | 54328 | 02349 | 17247 | 28865 | 14777 | 62730 | 92277 |
| 15664 | 10493 | 20492 | 38391 | 91132 | 21999 | 59516 | 81652 | 27195 | 48223 | 46751 | 22923 | 32261 | 85653 |

**TABLE B.1. Table of Random Numbers (Continued)**

| | | | | | | | | | | | | |
|---|---|---|---|---|---|---|---|---|---|---|---|---|
| 16408 | 81899 | 04153 | 53381 | 79401 | 21438 | 83035 | 92350 | 36693 | 31238 | 59649 | 91754 | 72772 |
| 18629 | 81953 | 05520 | 91962 | 04739 | 13092 | 97662 | 24822 | 94730 | 06496 | 35090 | 04822 | 86774 |
| 73115 | 35101 | 47498 | 87637 | 99016 | 71060 | 88824 | 71013 | 18735 | 20286 | 23153 | 72924 | 35165 |
| 57491 | 16703 | 23167 | 49323 | 45021 | 33132 | 12544 | 41035 | 80780 | 45393 | 44812 | 12515 | 98931 |
| 30405 | 83946 | 23792 | 14422 | 15059 | 45799 | 22716 | 19792 | 09983 | 74353 | 68668 | 30429 | 70735 |
| 16631 | 35006 | 85900 | 98275 | 32388 | 52390 | 16815 | 69298 | 82732 | 38480 | 73817 | 32523 | 41961 |
| 96773 | 20206 | 42559 | 78985 | 05300 | 22164 | 24369 | 54224 | 35083 | 19687 | 11052 | 91491 | 60383 |
| 38935 | 64202 | 14349 | 82674 | 66523 | 44133 | 00697 | 35552 | 35970 | 19124 | 63318 | 29686 | 03387 |
| 31624 | 76384 | 17403 | 53363 | 44167 | 64486 | 64758 | 75366 | 76554 | 31601 | 12614 | 33072 | 60332 |
| 78919 | 19474 | 23632 | 27889 | 47914 | 02584 | 37680 | 20801 | 72152 | 39339 | 34806 | 08930 | 85001 |
| 03931 | 33309 | 57047 | 74211 | 63445 | 17361 | 62825 | 39908 | 05607 | 91284 | 68833 | 25570 | 38818 |
| 74426 | 33278 | 43972 | 10119 | 89917 | 15665 | 52872 | 73823 | 73144 | 88662 | 88970 | 74492 | 51805 |
| 09066 | 00903 | 20795 | 95452 | 92648 | 45454 | 09552 | 88815 | 16553 | 51125 | 79375 | 97596 | 16296 |
| 42238 | 12426 | 87025 | 14267 | 20979 | 04508 | 64535 | 31355 | 86064 | 29472 | 47689 | 05974 | 52468 |
| 16153 | 08002 | 26504 | 41744 | 81959 | 65642 | 74240 | 56302 | 00033 | 67107 | 77510 | 70625 | 28725 |
| 21457 | 40742 | 29820 | 96783 | 29400 | 21840 | 15035 | 34537 | 33310 | 06116 | 95240 | 15957 | 16572 |
| 21581 | 57802 | 02050 | 89728 | 17937 | 37621 | 47075 | 42080 | 97403 | 48626 | 68995 | 43805 | 33386 |
| 55612 | 78095 | 83197 | 33732 | 05810 | 24813 | 86902 | 60397 | 16489 | 03264 | 88525 | 42786 | 05269 |
| 44657 | 66999 | 99324 | 51281 | 84463 | 60563 | 79312 | 93454 | 68876 | 25471 | 93911 | 25650 | 12682 |
| 91340 | 84979 | 46949 | 81973 | 37949 | 61023 | 43997 | 15263 | 80644 | 43942 | 89203 | 71795 | 99533 |
| 91227 | 21199 | 31935 | 27022 | 84067 | 05462 | 35216 | 14486 | 29891 | 68607 | 41867 | 14951 | 91696 |
| 50001 | 38140 | 66321 | 19924 | 72163 | 09538 | 12151 | 06878 | 91903 | 18749 | 34405 | 56087 | 82790 |
| 65390 | 05224 | 72958 | 28609 | 81406 | 39147 | 25549 | 48542 | 42627 | 45233 | 57202 | 94617 | 23772 |
| 27504 | 96131 | 83944 | 41575 | 10573 | 08619 | 64482 | 73923 | 36152 | 05184 | 94142 | 25299 | 84387 |
| 37169 | 94851 | 39117 | 89632 | 00959 | 16487 | 65536 | 49071 | 39782 | 17095 | 02330 | 74301 | 00275 |

| | | | | | | | | | | | | |
|---|---|---|---|---|---|---|---|---|---|---|---|---|
| 11508 | 70225 | 51111 | 38351 | 19444 | 66499 | 71945 | 05422 | 13442 | 78675 | 84081 | 66938 | 93654 |
| 37449 | 30362 | 06694 | 54690 | 04052 | 53115 | 62757 | 95348 | 78662 | 11163 | 81651 | 50245 | 34971 |
| 46515 | 70331 | 85922 | 38329 | 57015 | 15765 | 97161 | 17869 | 45349 | 61796 | 66345 | 81073 | 49106 |
| 30986 | 81223 | 42416 | 58353 | 21532 | 30502 | 32305 | 86482 | 06174 | 07901 | 54339 | 58861 | 74818 |
| 63798 | 64995 | 46583 | 09785 | 44160 | 78128 | 83991 | 42865 | 92520 | 83531 | 80377 | 35909 | 81250 |
| 82486 | 84846 | 99254 | 67632 | 43218 | 50076 | 21361 | 64816 | 51202 | 88124 | 41870 | 52689 | 51275 |
| 21885 | 32906 | 92431 | 09060 | 64297 | 51674 | 64126 | 62570 | 26123 | 05155 | 59194 | 52799 | 28225 |
| 60336 | 98782 | 07408 | 53458 | 13564 | 59089 | 26445 | 29789 | 85205 | 41001 | 12535 | 12133 | 14645 |
| 43937 | 46891 | 24010 | 25560 | 86355 | 33941 | 25786 | 54990 | 71899 | 15475 | 95434 | 98227 | 21824 |
| 97656 | 63175 | 89303 | 16275 | 07100 | 92063 | 21942 | 18611 | 47348 | 20203 | 18534 | 03862 | 78095 |
| 03299 | 01221 | 05418 | 38982 | 55758 | 92237 | 26759 | 86367 | 21216 | 98442 | 08303 | 56613 | 91511 |
| 79626 | 06486 | 03574 | 17668 | 07785 | 76020 | 79924 | 25651 | 83325 | 88428 | 85076 | 72811 | 22717 |
| 85636 | 68335 | 47539 | 03129 | 65651 | 11977 | 02510 | 26113 | 99447 | 68645 | 34327 | 15152 | 55230 |
| 18039 | 14367 | 61337 | 06177 | 12143 | 46609 | 32989 | 74014 | 64708 | 00533 | 35398 | 58408 | 13261 |
| 08362 | 15656 | 60627 | 36478 | 65648 | 16764 | 53412 | 09013 | 07832 | 41574 | 17639 | 82163 | 60859 |
| 79556 | 29068 | 04142 | 16268 | 15387 | 12856 | 66227 | 38358 | 22478 | 73373 | 88732 | 09443 | 82558 |
| 92608 | 82674 | 27072 | 32534 | 17075 | 27698 | 98204 | 63863 | 11951 | 34648 | 88022 | 56148 | 34925 |
| 23982 | 25835 | 40055 | 67006 | 12293 | 02753 | 14827 | 23235 | 35071 | 99704 | 37543 | 11601 | 35503 |
| 09915 | 96306 | 05908 | 97901 | 28395 | 14186 | 00821 | 80703 | 70426 | 75647 | 76310 | 88717 | 37890 |
| 59037 | 33300 | 26695 | 62247 | 69927 | 76123 | 50842 | 43834 | 86654 | 70959 | 79725 | 93872 | 28117 |
| 42488 | 78077 | 69882 | 61657 | 34136 | 79180 | 97526 | 43092 | 04098 | 73571 | 80799 | 76536 | 71255 |
| 46764 | 86273 | 63003 | 93017 | 31204 | 36692 | 40202 | 35275 | 57306 | 55543 | 53203 | 18098 | 47625 |
| 03237 | 45430 | 55417 | 63282 | 90816 | 17349 | 88298 | 90183 | 36600 | 78406 | 06216 | 95787 | 42579 |
| 86591 | 81482 | 52667 | 61582 | 14972 | 90053 | 89534 | 76036 | 49199 | 43716 | 97548 | 04379 | 46370 |
| 38534 | 01715 | 94964 | 87288 | 65680 | 43772 | 39560 | 12918 | 86537 | 62738 | 19636 | 51132 | 25739 |

*Source:* Adapted with permission from Byer, W. H. (Ed.). 1991. *CRC Standard Probability and Statistics: Tables and Formulae, XII.3.* Boca Raton, Florida: CRC Press.

## TABLE B.2.  Area under the Standard Normal Curve (z Distribution)*

| z | .00 | .01 | .02 | .03 | .04 | .05 | .06 | .07 | .08 | .09 |
|---|---|---|---|---|---|---|---|---|---|---|
| 0.0 | .0000 | .0040 | .0080 | .0120 | .0160 | .0199 | .0239 | .0279 | .0319 | .0359 |
| 0.1 | .0398 | .0438 | .0478 | .0517 | .0557 | .0596 | .0636 | .0675 | .0714 | .0753 |
| 0.2 | .0793 | .0832 | .0871 | .0910 | .0948 | .0987 | .1026 | .1064 | .1103 | .1141 |
| 0.3 | .1179 | .1217 | .1255 | .1293 | .1331 | .1368 | .1406 | .1443 | .1480 | .1517 |
| 0.4 | .1554 | .1591 | .1628 | .1664 | .1700 | .1736 | .1772 | .1808 | .1844 | .1879 |
| 0.5 | .1915 | .1950 | .1985 | .2019 | .2054 | .2088 | .2123 | .2157 | .2190 | .2224 |
| 0.6 | .2257 | .2291 | .2324 | .2357 | .2389 | .2422 | .2454 | .2486 | .2517 | .2549 |
| 0.7 | .2580 | .2611 | .2642 | .2673 | .2704 | .2734 | .2764 | .2794 | .2823 | .2852 |
| 0.8 | .2881 | .2910 | .2939 | .2967 | .2995 | .3023 | .3051 | .3078 | .3106 | .3133 |
| 0.9 | .3159 | .3186 | .3212 | .3238 | .3264 | .3289 | .3315 | .3340 | .3365 | .3389 |
| 1.0 | .3413 | .3438 | .3461 | .3485 | .3508 | .3531 | .3554 | .3577 | .3599 | .3621 |
| 1.1 | .3643 | .3665 | .3686 | .3708 | .3729 | .3749 | .3770 | .3790 | .3810 | .3830 |
| 1.2 | .3849 | .3869 | .3888 | .3907 | .3925 | .3944 | .3962 | .3980 | .3997 | .4015 |
| 1.3 | .4032 | .4049 | .4066 | .4082 | .4099 | .4115 | .4131 | .4147 | .4162 | .4177 |
| 1.4 | .4192 | .4207 | .4222 | .4236 | .4251 | .4265 | .4279 | .4292 | .4306 | .4319 |
| 1.5 | .4332 | .4345 | .4357 | .4370 | .4382 | .4394 | .4406 | .4418 | .4429 | .4441 |
| 1.6 | .4452 | .4463 | .4474 | .4484 | .4495 | .4505 | .4515 | .4525 | .4535 | .4545 |
| 1.7 | .4554 | .4564 | .4573 | .4582 | .4591 | .4599 | .4608 | .4616 | .4625 | .4633 |
| 1.8 | .4641 | .4649 | .4656 | .4664 | .4671 | .4678 | .4686 | .4693 | .4699 | .4706 |
| 1.9 | .4713 | .4719 | .4726 | .4732 | .4738 | .4744 | .4750 | .4756 | .4761 | .4767 |
| 2.0 | .4772 | .4778 | .4783 | .4788 | .4793 | .4798 | .4803 | .4808 | .4812 | .4817 |
| 2.1 | .4821 | .4826 | .4830 | .4834 | .4838 | .4842 | .4846 | .4850 | .4854 | .4857 |
| 2.2 | .4861 | .4864 | .4868 | .4871 | .4875 | .4878 | .4881 | .4884 | .4887 | .4890 |
| 2.3 | .4893 | .4896 | .4898 | .4901 | .4904 | .4906 | .4909 | .4911 | .4913 | .4916 |
| 2.4 | .4918 | .4920 | .4922 | .4925 | .4927 | .4929 | .4931 | .4932 | .4934 | .4936 |
| 2.5 | .4938 | .4940 | .4941 | .4943 | .4945 | .4946 | .4948 | .4949 | .4951 | .4952 |
| 2.6 | .4953 | .4955 | .4956 | .4957 | .4959 | .4960 | .4961 | .4962 | .4963 | .4964 |
| 2.7 | .4965 | .4966 | .4967 | .4968 | .4969 | .4970 | .4971 | .4972 | .4973 | .4974 |
| 2.8 | .4974 | .4975 | .4976 | .4977 | .4977 | .4978 | .4979 | .4979 | .4980 | .4981 |
| 2.9 | .4981 | .4982 | .4982 | .4983 | .4984 | .4984 | .4985 | .4985 | .4986 | .4986 |
| 3.0 | .4987 | .4987 | .4987 | .4988 | .4988 | .4989 | .4989 | .4989 | .4990 | .4990 |

*Source:* Adapted with permission from Frederick Mosteller and Robert E. K. Rourke. 1973. *Sturdy Statistics,* Table A-1. Reading, MA: Addison-Wesley.
*Proportion of the area under the normal curve corresponding to the distance between the mean (0) and a point that is z standard deviation units away from the mean.

## TABLE B.3.  The *t* Distribution

| df | Level of Significance for a One-Tailed Test | | | | | |
|---|---|---|---|---|---|---|
|  | .10 | .05 | .025 | .01 | .005 | .0005 |
|  | Level of Significance for Two-Tailed Test | | | | | |
|  | .20 | .10 | .05 | .02 | .01 | .001 |
| 1 | 3.078 | 6.314 | 12.706 | 31.821 | 63.657 | 636.619 |
| 2 | 1.886 | 2.920 | 4.303 | 6.965 | 9.925 | 31.598 |
| 3 | 1.638 | 2.353 | 3.182 | 4.541 | 5.841 | 12.941 |
| 4 | 1.533 | 2.132 | 2.776 | 3.747 | 4.604 | 8.610 |
| 5 | 1.476 | 2.015 | 2.571 | 3.365 | 4.032 | 6.859 |
| 6 | 1.440 | 1.943 | 2.447 | 3.143 | 3.707 | 5.959 |
| 7 | 1.415 | 1.895 | 2.365 | 2.998 | 3.499 | 5.405 |
| 8 | 1.397 | 1.860 | 2.306 | 2.896 | 3.355 | 5.041 |
| 9 | 1.383 | 1.833 | 2.262 | 2.821 | 3.250 | 4.781 |
| 10 | 1.372 | 1.812 | 2.228 | 2.764 | 3.169 | 4.587 |
| 11 | 1.363 | 1.796 | 2.201 | 2.718 | 3.106 | 4.437 |
| 12 | 1.356 | 1.782 | 2.179 | 2.681 | 3.055 | 4.318 |
| 13 | 1.350 | 1.771 | 2.160 | 2.650 | 3.012 | 4.221 |
| 14 | 1.345 | 1.761 | 2.145 | 2.624 | 2.977 | 4.140 |
| 15 | 1.341 | 1.753 | 2.131 | 2.602 | 2.947 | 4.073 |
| 16 | 1.337 | 1.746 | 2.120 | 2.583 | 2.921 | 4.015 |
| 17 | 1.333 | 1.740 | 2.110 | 2.567 | 2.898 | 3.965 |
| 18 | 1.330 | 1.734 | 2.101 | 2.552 | 2.878 | 3.922 |
| 19 | 1.328 | 1.729 | 2.093 | 2.539 | 2.861 | 3.883 |
| 20 | 1.325 | 1.725 | 2.086 | 2.528 | 2.845 | 3.850 |
| 21 | 1.323 | 1.721 | 2.080 | 2.518 | 2.831 | 3.819 |
| 22 | 1.321 | 1.717 | 2.074 | 2.508 | 2.819 | 3.792 |
| 23 | 1.319 | 1.714 | 2.069 | 2.500 | 2.807 | 3.767 |
| 24 | 1.318 | 1.711 | 2.064 | 2.492 | 2.797 | 3.745 |
| 25 | 1.316 | 1.708 | 2.060 | 2.485 | 2.787 | 3.725 |
| 26 | 1.315 | 1.706 | 2.056 | 2.479 | 2.779 | 3.707 |
| 27 | 1.314 | 1.703 | 2.052 | 2.473 | 2.771 | 3.690 |
| 28 | 1.313 | 1.701 | 2.048 | 2.467 | 2.763 | 3.674 |
| 29 | 1.311 | 1.699 | 2.045 | 2.462 | 2.756 | 3.659 |
| 30 | 1.310 | 1.697 | 2.042 | 2.457 | 2.750 | 3.646 |
| 40 | 1.303 | 1.684 | 2.021 | 2.423 | 2.704 | 3.551 |
| 60 | 1.206 | 1.671 | 2.000 | 2.390 | 2.660 | 3.460 |
| 120 | 1.289 | 1.658 | 1.980 | 2.358 | 2.617 | 3.373 |
| ∞ | 1.282 | 1.645 | 1.960 | 2.326 | 2.576 | 3.291 |

*Source:* Table B.3 is adapted with permission from Table III of Fisher and Yates, *Statistical Tables for Biological, Agricultural and Medical Research* (6th ed.). Published by Longman Group UK Ltd., 1974.

## TABLE B.4. The Chi-Square ($\chi^2$) Distribution

| | | | | | Area to the Right of the Critical Value | | | | | |
|---|---|---|---|---|---|---|---|---|---|---|
| df | 0.995 | 0.99 | 0.975 | 0.95 | 0.90 | 0.10 | 0.05 | 0.025 | 0.01 | 0.005 |
| 1 | — | — | 0.001 | 0.004 | 0.016 | 2.706 | 3.841 | 5.024 | 6.635 | 7.879 |
| 2 | 0.010 | 0.020 | 0.051 | 0.103 | 0.211 | 4.605 | 5.991 | 7.378 | 9.210 | 10.597 |
| 3 | 0.072 | 0.115 | 0.216 | 0.352 | 0.584 | 6.251 | 7.815 | 9.348 | 11.345 | 12.838 |
| 4 | 0.207 | 0.297 | 0.484 | 0.711 | 1.064 | 7.779 | 9.488 | 11.143 | 13.277 | 14.860 |
| 5 | 0.412 | 0.554 | 0.831 | 1.145 | 1.610 | 9.236 | 11.071 | 12.833 | 15.086 | 16.750 |
| 6 | 0.676 | 0.872 | 1.237 | 1.635 | 2.204 | 10.645 | 12.592 | 14.449 | 16.812 | 18.548 |
| 7 | 0.989 | 1.239 | 1.690 | 2.167 | 2.833 | 12.017 | 14.067 | 16.013 | 18.475 | 20.278 |
| 8 | 1.344 | 1.646 | 2.180 | 2.733 | 3.490 | 13.362 | 15.507 | 17.535 | 20.090 | 21.955 |
| 9 | 1.735 | 2.088 | 2.700 | 3.325 | 4.168 | 14.684 | 16.919 | 19.023 | 21.666 | 23.589 |
| 10 | 2.156 | 2.558 | 3.247 | 3.940 | 4.865 | 15.987 | 18.307 | 20.483 | 23.209 | 25.188 |
| 11 | 2.603 | 3.053 | 3.816 | 4.575 | 5.578 | 17.275 | 19.675 | 21.920 | 24.725 | 26.757 |
| 12 | 3.074 | 3.571 | 4.404 | 5.226 | 6.304 | 18.549 | 21.026 | 23.337 | 26.217 | 28.299 |
| 13 | 3.565 | 4.107 | 5.009 | 5.892 | 7.042 | 19.812 | 22.362 | 24.736 | 27.688 | 29.819 |
| 14 | 4.075 | 4.660 | 5.629 | 6.571 | 7.790 | 21.064 | 23.685 | 26.119 | 29.141 | 31.319 |
| 15 | 4.601 | 5.229 | 6.262 | 7.261 | 8.547 | 22.307 | 24.996 | 27.488 | 30.578 | 32.801 |
| 16 | 5.142 | 5.812 | 6.908 | 7.962 | 9.312 | 23.542 | 26.296 | 28.845 | 32.000 | 34.267 |
| 17 | 5.697 | 6.408 | 7.564 | 8.672 | 10.085 | 24.769 | 27.587 | 30.191 | 33.409 | 35.718 |
| 18 | 6.265 | 7.015 | 8.231 | 9.390 | 10.865 | 25.989 | 28.869 | 31.526 | 34.805 | 37.156 |
| 19 | 6.844 | 7.633 | 8.907 | 10.117 | 11.651 | 27.204 | 30.144 | 32.852 | 36.191 | 38.582 |
| 20 | 7.434 | 8.260 | 9.591 | 10.851 | 12.443 | 28.412 | 31.410 | 34.170 | 37.566 | 39.997 |
| 21 | 8.034 | 8.897 | 10.283 | 11.591 | 13.240 | 29.615 | 32.671 | 35.479 | 38.932 | 41.401 |
| 22 | 8.643 | 9.542 | 10.982 | 12.338 | 14.042 | 30.813 | 33.924 | 36.781 | 40.289 | 42.796 |
| 23 | 9.260 | 10.196 | 11.689 | 13.091 | 14.848 | 32.007 | 35.172 | 38.076 | 41.638 | 44.181 |
| 24 | 9.886 | 10.856 | 12.401 | 13.848 | 15.659 | 33.196 | 36.415 | 39.364 | 42.980 | 45.559 |
| 25 | 10.520 | 11.524 | 13.120 | 14.611 | 16.473 | 34.382 | 37.652 | 40.646 | 44.314 | 46.928 |
| 26 | 11.160 | 12.198 | 13.844 | 15.379 | 17.292 | 35.563 | 38.885 | 41.923 | 45.642 | 48.290 |
| 27 | 11.808 | 12.879 | 14.573 | 16.151 | 18.114 | 36.741 | 40.113 | 43.194 | 46.963 | 49.645 |
| 28 | 12.461 | 13.565 | 15.308 | 16.928 | 18.939 | 37.916 | 41.337 | 44.461 | 48.278 | 50.993 |
| 29 | 13.121 | 14.257 | 16.047 | 17.708 | 19.768 | 39.087 | 42.557 | 45.722 | 49.588 | 52.336 |
| 30 | 13.787 | 14.954 | 16.791 | 18.493 | 20.599 | 40.256 | 43.773 | 46.979 | 50.892 | 53.672 |
| 40 | 20.707 | 22.164 | 24.433 | 26.509 | 29.051 | 51.805 | 55.758 | 59.342 | 63.691 | 66.766 |
| 50 | 27.991 | 29.707 | 32.357 | 34.764 | 37.689 | 63.167 | 67.505 | 71.420 | 76.154 | 79.490 |
| 60 | 35.534 | 37.485 | 40.482 | 43.188 | 46.459 | 74.397 | 79.082 | 83.298 | 88.379 | 91.952 |
| 70 | 43.275 | 45.442 | 48.758 | 51.739 | 55.329 | 85.527 | 90.531 | 95.023 | 100.425 | 104.215 |
| 80 | 51.172 | 53.540 | 57.153 | 60.391 | 64.278 | 96.578 | 101.879 | 106.629 | 112.329 | 116.321 |
| 90 | 59.196 | 61.754 | 65.647 | 69.126 | 73.291 | 107.565 | 113.145 | 118.136 | 124.116 | 128.299 |
| 100 | 67.328 | 70.065 | 74.222 | 77.929 | 82.358 | 118.498 | 124.342 | 129.561 | 135.807 | 140.169 |

*Source:* Donald Owen, *Handbook of Statistical Tables,* ©1962 by Addison-Wesley Publishing Company, Inc. Reprinted by permission of Addison-Wesley Publishing Company, Inc.

**TABLE B.5. The *F* Distribution**

p = .05

| $n_2$ \ $n_1$ | 1 | 2 | 3 | 4 | 5 | 6 | 8 | 12 | 24 | ∞ |
|---|---|---|---|---|---|---|---|---|---|---|
| 1 | 161 | 200 | 216 | 225 | 230 | 234 | 239 | 244 | 249 | 254 |
| 2 | 18.51 | 19.00 | 19.16 | 19.25 | 19.30 | 19.33 | 19.37 | 19.41 | 19.45 | 19.50 |
| 3 | 10.13 | 9.55 | 9.28 | 9.12 | 9.01 | 8.94 | 8.84 | 8.74 | 8.64 | 8.53 |
| 4 | 7.71 | 6.94 | 6.59 | 6.39 | 6.26 | 6.16 | 6.04 | 5.91 | 5.77 | 5.63 |
| 5 | 6.61 | 5.79 | 5.41 | 5.19 | 5.05 | 4.95 | 4.82 | 4.68 | 4.53 | 4.36 |
| 6 | 5.99 | 5.14 | 4.76 | 4.53 | 4.39 | 4.28 | 4.15 | 4.00 | 3.84 | 3.67 |
| 7 | 5.59 | 4.74 | 4.35 | 4.12 | 3.97 | 3.87 | 3.73 | 3.57 | 3.41 | 3.23 |
| 8 | 5.32 | 4.46 | 4.07 | 3.84 | 3.69 | 3.58 | 3.44 | 3.28 | 3.12 | 2.93 |
| 9 | 5.12 | 4.26 | 3.86 | 3.63 | 3.48 | 3.37 | 3.23 | 3.07 | 2.90 | 2.71 |
| 10 | 4.96 | 4.10 | 3.71 | 3.48 | 3.33 | 3.22 | 3.07 | 2.91 | 2.74 | 2.54 |
| 11 | 4.84 | 3.98 | 3.59 | 3.36 | 3.20 | 3.09 | 2.95 | 2.79 | 2.61 | 2.40 |
| 12 | 4.75 | 3.88 | 3.49 | 3.26 | 3.11 | 3.00 | 2.85 | 2.69 | 2.50 | 2.30 |
| 13 | 4.67 | 3.80 | 3.41 | 3.18 | 3.02 | 2.92 | 2.77 | 2.60 | 2.42 | 2.21 |
| 14 | 4.60 | 3.74 | 3.34 | 3.11 | 2.96 | 2.85 | 2.70 | 2.53 | 2.35 | 2.13 |
| 15 | 4.54 | 3.68 | 3.29 | 3.06 | 2.90 | 2.79 | 2.64 | 2.48 | 2.29 | 2.07 |
| 16 | 4.49 | 3.63 | 3.24 | 3.01 | 2.85 | 2.74 | 2.59 | 2.42 | 2.24 | 2.01 |
| 17 | 4.45 | 3.59 | 3.20 | 2.96 | 2.81 | 2.70 | 2.55 | 2.38 | 2.19 | 1.96 |
| 18 | 4.41 | 3.55 | 3.16 | 2.93 | 2.77 | 2.66 | 2.51 | 2.34 | 2.15 | 1.92 |
| 19 | 4.38 | 3.52 | 3.13 | 2.90 | 2.74 | 2.63 | 2.48 | 2.31 | 2.11 | 1.88 |
| 20 | 4.35 | 3.49 | 3.10 | 2.87 | 2.71 | 2.60 | 2.45 | 2.28 | 2.08 | 1.84 |
| 21 | 4.32 | 3.47 | 3.07 | 2.84 | 2.68 | 2.57 | 2.42 | 2.25 | 2.05 | 1.81 |
| 22 | 4.30 | 3.44 | 3.05 | 2.82 | 2.66 | 2.55 | 2.40 | 2.23 | 2.03 | 1.78 |
| 23 | 4.28 | 3.42 | 3.03 | 2.80 | 2.64 | 2.53 | 2.38 | 2.20 | 2.00 | 1.76 |
| 24 | 4.26 | 3.40 | 3.01 | 2.78 | 2.62 | 2.51 | 2.36 | 2.18 | 1.98 | 1.73 |
| 25 | 4.24 | 3.38 | 2.99 | 2.76 | 2.60 | 2.49 | 2.34 | 2.16 | 1.96 | 1.71 |
| 26 | 4.22 | 3.37 | 2.98 | 2.74 | 2.59 | 2.47 | 2.32 | 2.15 | 1.95 | 1.69 |
| 27 | 4.21 | 3.35 | 2.96 | 2.73 | 2.57 | 2.46 | 2.30 | 2.13 | 1.93 | 1.67 |
| 28 | 4.20 | 3.34 | 2.95 | 2.71 | 2.56 | 2.44 | 2.29 | 2.12 | 1.91 | 1.65 |
| 29 | 4.18 | 3.33 | 2.93 | 2.70 | 2.54 | 2.43 | 2.28 | 2.10 | 1.90 | 1.64 |
| 30 | 4.17 | 3.32 | 2.92 | 2.69 | 2.53 | 2.42 | 2.27 | 2.09 | 1.89 | 1.62 |
| 40 | 4.08 | 3.23 | 2.84 | 2.61 | 2.45 | 2.34 | 2.18 | 2.00 | 1.79 | 1.51 |
| 60 | 4.00 | 3.15 | 2.76 | 2.52 | 2.37 | 2.25 | 2.10 | 1.92 | 1.70 | 1.39 |
| 120 | 3.92 | 3.07 | 2.68 | 2.45 | 2.29 | 2.17 | 2.02 | 1.83 | 1.61 | 1.25 |
| ∞ | 3.84 | 2.99 | 2.60 | 2.37 | 2.21 | 2.09 | 1.94 | 1.75 | 1.52 | 1.00 |

*(Continued)*

**TABLE B.5.** *(Continued)*

<table>
<tr><th colspan="11" style="text-align:center">p = .01</th></tr>
<tr><th>$n_1$<br>$n_2$</th><th>1</th><th>2</th><th>3</th><th>4</th><th>5</th><th>6</th><th>8</th><th>12</th><th>24</th><th>∞</th></tr>
<tr><td>1</td><td>4052</td><td>4999</td><td>5403</td><td>5625</td><td>5764</td><td>5859</td><td>5981</td><td>6106</td><td>6234</td><td>6366</td></tr>
<tr><td>2</td><td>98.49</td><td>99.01</td><td>99.17</td><td>99.25</td><td>99.30</td><td>99.33</td><td>99.36</td><td>99.42</td><td>99.46</td><td>99.50</td></tr>
<tr><td>3</td><td>34.12</td><td>30.81</td><td>29.46</td><td>28.71</td><td>28.24</td><td>27.91</td><td>27.49</td><td>27.05</td><td>26.60</td><td>26.12</td></tr>
<tr><td>4</td><td>21.20</td><td>18.00</td><td>16.69</td><td>15.98</td><td>15.52</td><td>15.21</td><td>14.80</td><td>14.37</td><td>13.93</td><td>13.46</td></tr>
<tr><td>5</td><td>16.26</td><td>13.27</td><td>12.06</td><td>11.39</td><td>10.97</td><td>10.67</td><td>10.27</td><td>9.89</td><td>9.47</td><td>9.02</td></tr>
<tr><td>6</td><td>13.74</td><td>10.92</td><td>9.78</td><td>9.15</td><td>8.75</td><td>8.47</td><td>8.10</td><td>7.72</td><td>7.31</td><td>6.88</td></tr>
<tr><td>7</td><td>12.25</td><td>9.55</td><td>8.45</td><td>7.85</td><td>7.46</td><td>7.19</td><td>6.84</td><td>6.47</td><td>6.07</td><td>5.65</td></tr>
<tr><td>8</td><td>11.26</td><td>8.65</td><td>7.59</td><td>7.01</td><td>6.63</td><td>6.37</td><td>6.03</td><td>5.67</td><td>5.28</td><td>4.86</td></tr>
<tr><td>9</td><td>10.56</td><td>8.02</td><td>6.99</td><td>6.42</td><td>6.06</td><td>5.80</td><td>5.47</td><td>5.11</td><td>4.73</td><td>4.31</td></tr>
<tr><td>10</td><td>10.04</td><td>7.56</td><td>6.55</td><td>5.99</td><td>5.64</td><td>5.39</td><td>5.06</td><td>4.71</td><td>4.33</td><td>3.91</td></tr>
<tr><td>11</td><td>9.65</td><td>7.20</td><td>6.22</td><td>5.67</td><td>5.32</td><td>5.07</td><td>4.74</td><td>4.40</td><td>4.02</td><td>3.60</td></tr>
<tr><td>12</td><td>9.33</td><td>6.93</td><td>5.95</td><td>5.41</td><td>5.06</td><td>4.82</td><td>4.50</td><td>4.16</td><td>3.78</td><td>3.36</td></tr>
<tr><td>13</td><td>9.07</td><td>6.70</td><td>5.74</td><td>5.20</td><td>4.86</td><td>4.62</td><td>4.30</td><td>3.96</td><td>3.59</td><td>3.16</td></tr>
<tr><td>14</td><td>8.86</td><td>6.51</td><td>5.56</td><td>5.03</td><td>4.69</td><td>4.46</td><td>4.14</td><td>3.80</td><td>3.43</td><td>3.00</td></tr>
<tr><td>15</td><td>8.68</td><td>6.36</td><td>5.42</td><td>4.89</td><td>4.56</td><td>4.32</td><td>4.00</td><td>3.67</td><td>3.29</td><td>2.87</td></tr>
<tr><td>16</td><td>8.53</td><td>6.23</td><td>5.29</td><td>4.77</td><td>4.44</td><td>4.20</td><td>3.89</td><td>3.55</td><td>3.18</td><td>2.75</td></tr>
<tr><td>17</td><td>8.40</td><td>6.11</td><td>5.18</td><td>4.67</td><td>4.34</td><td>4.10</td><td>3.79</td><td>3.45</td><td>3.08</td><td>2.65</td></tr>
<tr><td>18</td><td>8.28</td><td>6.01</td><td>5.09</td><td>4.58</td><td>4.25</td><td>4.01</td><td>3.71</td><td>3.37</td><td>3.00</td><td>2.57</td></tr>
<tr><td>19</td><td>8.18</td><td>5.93</td><td>5.01</td><td>4.50</td><td>4.17</td><td>3.94</td><td>3.63</td><td>3.30</td><td>2.92</td><td>2.49</td></tr>
<tr><td>20</td><td>8.10</td><td>5.85</td><td>4.94</td><td>4.43</td><td>4.10</td><td>3.87</td><td>3.56</td><td>3.23</td><td>2.86</td><td>2.42</td></tr>
<tr><td>21</td><td>8.02</td><td>5.78</td><td>4.87</td><td>4.37</td><td>4.04</td><td>3.81</td><td>3.51</td><td>3.17</td><td>2.80</td><td>2.36</td></tr>
<tr><td>22</td><td>7.94</td><td>5.72</td><td>4.82</td><td>4.31</td><td>3.99</td><td>3.76</td><td>3.45</td><td>3.12</td><td>2.75</td><td>2.31</td></tr>
<tr><td>23</td><td>7.88</td><td>5.66</td><td>4.76</td><td>4.26</td><td>3.94</td><td>3.71</td><td>3.41</td><td>3.07</td><td>2.70</td><td>2.26</td></tr>
<tr><td>24</td><td>7.82</td><td>5.61</td><td>4.72</td><td>4.22</td><td>3.90</td><td>3.67</td><td>3.36</td><td>3.03</td><td>2.66</td><td>2.21</td></tr>
<tr><td>25</td><td>7.77</td><td>5.57</td><td>4.68</td><td>4.18</td><td>3.86</td><td>3.63</td><td>3.32</td><td>2.99</td><td>2.62</td><td>2.17</td></tr>
<tr><td>26</td><td>7.72</td><td>5.53</td><td>4.64</td><td>4.14</td><td>3.82</td><td>3.59</td><td>3.29</td><td>2.96</td><td>2.58</td><td>2.13</td></tr>
<tr><td>27</td><td>7.68</td><td>5.49</td><td>4.60</td><td>4.11</td><td>3.78</td><td>3.56</td><td>3.26</td><td>2.93</td><td>2.55</td><td>2.10</td></tr>
<tr><td>28</td><td>7.64</td><td>5.45</td><td>4.57</td><td>4.07</td><td>3.75</td><td>3.53</td><td>3.23</td><td>2.90</td><td>2.52</td><td>2.06</td></tr>
<tr><td>29</td><td>7.60</td><td>5.42</td><td>4.54</td><td>4.04</td><td>3.73</td><td>3.50</td><td>3.20</td><td>2.87</td><td>2.49</td><td>2.03</td></tr>
<tr><td>30</td><td>7.56</td><td>5.39</td><td>4.51</td><td>4.02</td><td>3.70</td><td>3.47</td><td>3.17</td><td>2.84</td><td>2.47</td><td>2.01</td></tr>
<tr><td>40</td><td>7.31</td><td>5.18</td><td>4.31</td><td>3.83</td><td>3.51</td><td>3.29</td><td>2.99</td><td>2.66</td><td>2.29</td><td>1.80</td></tr>
<tr><td>60</td><td>7.08</td><td>4.98</td><td>4.13</td><td>3.65</td><td>3.34</td><td>3.12</td><td>2.82</td><td>2.50</td><td>2.12</td><td>1.60</td></tr>
<tr><td>120</td><td>6.85</td><td>4.79</td><td>3.95</td><td>3.48</td><td>3.17</td><td>2.96</td><td>2.66</td><td>2.34</td><td>1.95</td><td>1.38</td></tr>
<tr><td>∞</td><td>6.64</td><td>4.60</td><td>3.78</td><td>3.32</td><td>3.02</td><td>2.80</td><td>2.51</td><td>2.18</td><td>1.79</td><td>1.00</td></tr>
</table>

Values of $n_1$ and $n_2$ represent the number of degrees of freedom associated with the between and within estimates of variance, respectively.

*Source:* R. P. Runyon and A. Haber. *Fundamentals of Behavioral Statistics,* 6th ed. New York: McGraw-Hill. Table D (pp. 463–465). 1987. Reprinted with permission from McGraw-Hill.

**TABLE B.6. Studentized Range Statistic, $q$**

$q$ Value When Alpha = .05

| $v$ \ $k$ | 2 | 3 | 4 | 5 | 6 | 7 | 8 | 9 | 10 | 11 | 12 | 13 | 14 | 15 | 16 | 17 | 18 | 19 | 20 |
|---|---|---|---|---|---|---|---|---|---|---|---|---|---|---|---|---|---|---|---|
| 1 | 18.0 | 27.0 | 32.8 | 37.1 | 40.4 | 43.1 | 45.4 | 47.4 | 49.1 | 50.6 | 52.0 | 53.2 | 54.3 | 55.4 | 56.3 | 57.2 | 58.0 | 58.8 | 59.6 |
| 2 | 6.09 | 8.3 | 9.8 | 10.9 | 11.7 | 12.4 | 13.0 | 13.5 | 14.0 | 14.4 | 14.7 | 15.1 | 15.4 | 15.7 | 15.9 | 16.1 | 16.4 | 16.6 | 16.8 |
| 3 | 4.50 | 5.91 | 6.82 | 7.50 | 8.04 | 8.48 | 8.85 | 9.18 | 9.46 | 9.72 | 9.95 | 10.15 | 10.35 | 10.52 | 10.69 | 10.84 | 10.98 | 11.11 | 11.24 |
| 4 | 3.93 | 5.04 | 5.76 | 6.29 | 6.71 | 7.05 | 7.35 | 7.60 | 7.83 | 8.03 | 8.21 | 8.37 | 8.52 | 8.66 | 8.79 | 8.91 | 9.03 | 9.13 | 9.23 |
| 5 | 3.64 | 4.60 | 5.22 | 5.67 | 6.03 | 6.33 | 6.58 | 6.80 | 6.99 | 7.17 | 7.32 | 7.47 | 7.60 | 7.72 | 7.83 | 7.93 | 8.03 | 8.12 | 8.21 |
| 6 | 3.46 | 4.34 | 4.90 | 5.31 | 5.63 | 5.89 | 6.12 | 6.32 | 6.49 | 6.65 | 6.79 | 6.92 | 7.03 | 7.14 | 7.24 | 7.34 | 7.43 | 7.51 | 7.59 |
| 7 | 3.34 | 4.16 | 4.68 | 5.06 | 5.36 | 5.61 | 5.82 | 6.00 | 6.16 | 6.30 | 6.43 | 6.55 | 6.66 | 6.76 | 6.85 | 6.94 | 7.02 | 7.09 | 7.17 |
| 8 | 3.26 | 4.04 | 4.53 | 4.89 | 5.17 | 5.40 | 5.60 | 5.77 | 5.92 | 6.05 | 6.18 | 6.29 | 6.39 | 6.48 | 6.57 | 6.65 | 6.73 | 6.80 | 6.87 |
| 9 | 3.20 | 3.95 | 4.42 | 4.76 | 5.02 | 5.24 | 5.43 | 5.60 | 5.74 | 5.87 | 5.98 | 6.09 | 6.19 | 6.28 | 6.36 | 6.44 | 6.51 | 6.58 | 6.64 |
| 10 | 3.15 | 3.88 | 4.33 | 4.65 | 4.91 | 5.12 | 5.30 | 5.46 | 5.60 | 5.72 | 5.83 | 5.93 | 6.03 | 6.11 | 6.20 | 6.27 | 6.34 | 6.40 | 6.47 |
| 11 | 3.11 | 3.82 | 4.26 | 4.57 | 4.82 | 5.03 | 5.20 | 5.35 | 5.49 | 5.61 | 5.71 | 5.81 | 5.90 | 5.99 | 6.06 | 6.14 | 6.20 | 6.26 | 6.33 |
| 12 | 3.08 | 3.77 | 4.20 | 4.51 | 4.75 | 4.95 | 5.12 | 5.27 | 5.40 | 5.51 | 5.62 | 5.71 | 5.80 | 5.88 | 5.95 | 6.03 | 6.09 | 6.15 | 6.21 |
| 13 | 3.06 | 3.73 | 4.15 | 4.45 | 4.69 | 4.88 | 5.05 | 5.19 | 5.32 | 5.43 | 5.53 | 5.63 | 5.71 | 5.79 | 5.86 | 5.93 | 6.00 | 6.05 | 6.11 |
| 14 | 3.03 | 3.70 | 4.11 | 4.41 | 4.64 | 4.83 | 4.99 | 5.13 | 5.25 | 5.36 | 5.46 | 5.55 | 5.64 | 5.72 | 5.79 | 5.85 | 5.92 | 5.97 | 6.03 |
| 15 | 3.01 | 3.67 | 4.08 | 4.37 | 4.60 | 4.78 | 4.94 | 5.08 | 5.20 | 5.31 | 5.40 | 5.49 | 5.58 | 5.65 | 5.72 | 5.79 | 5.85 | 5.90 | 5.96 |
| 16 | 3.00 | 3.65 | 4.05 | 4.33 | 4.56 | 4.74 | 4.90 | 5.03 | 5.15 | 5.26 | 5.35 | 5.44 | 5.52 | 5.59 | 5.66 | 5.72 | 5.79 | 5.84 | 5.90 |
| 17 | 2.98 | 3.63 | 4.02 | 4.30 | 4.52 | 4.71 | 4.86 | 4.99 | 5.11 | 5.21 | 5.31 | 5.39 | 5.47 | 5.55 | 5.61 | 5.68 | 5.74 | 5.79 | 5.84 |
| 18 | 2.97 | 3.61 | 4.00 | 4.28 | 4.49 | 4.67 | 4.82 | 4.96 | 5.07 | 5.17 | 5.27 | 5.35 | 5.43 | 5.50 | 5.57 | 5.63 | 5.69 | 5.74 | 5.79 |
| 19 | 2.96 | 3.59 | 3.98 | 4.25 | 4.47 | 4.65 | 4.79 | 4.92 | 5.04 | 5.14 | 5.23 | 5.32 | 5.39 | 5.46 | 5.53 | 5.59 | 5.65 | 5.70 | 5.75 |
| 20 | 2.95 | 3.58 | 3.96 | 4.23 | 4.45 | 4.62 | 4.77 | 4.90 | 5.01 | 5.11 | 5.20 | 5.28 | 5.36 | 5.43 | 5.49 | 5.55 | 5.61 | 5.66 | 5.71 |
| 24 | 2.92 | 3.53 | 3.90 | 4.17 | 4.37 | 4.54 | 4.68 | 4.81 | 4.92 | 5.01 | 5.10 | 5.18 | 5.25 | 5.32 | 5.38 | 5.44 | 5.50 | 5.54 | 5.59 |
| 30 | 2.89 | 3.49 | 3.84 | 4.10 | 4.30 | 4.46 | 4.60 | 4.72 | 4.83 | 4.92 | 5.00 | 5.08 | 5.15 | 5.21 | 5.27 | 5.33 | 5.38 | 5.43 | 5.48 |
| 40 | 2.86 | 3.44 | 3.79 | 4.04 | 4.23 | 4.39 | 4.52 | 4.63 | 4.74 | 4.82 | 4.91 | 4.98 | 5.05 | 5.11 | 5.16 | 5.22 | 5.27 | 5.31 | 5.36 |
| 60 | 2.83 | 3.40 | 3.74 | 3.98 | 4.16 | 4.31 | 4.44 | 4.55 | 4.65 | 4.73 | 4.81 | 4.88 | 4.94 | 5.00 | 5.06 | 5.11 | 5.16 | 5.20 | 5.24 |
| 120 | 2.80 | 3.36 | 3.69 | 3.92 | 4.10 | 4.24 | 4.36 | 4.48 | 4.56 | 4.64 | 4.72 | 4.78 | 4.84 | 4.90 | 4.95 | 5.00 | 5.05 | 5.09 | 5.13 |
| $\infty$ | 2.77 | 3.31 | 3.63 | 3.86 | 4.03 | 4.17 | 4.29 | 4.39 | 4.47 | 4.55 | 4.62 | 4.68 | 4.74 | 4.80 | 4.85 | 4.89 | 4.93 | 4.97 | 5.01 |

(Continued)

**TABLE B.6.**  (*Continued*)

*q Value When Alpha = .01*

| v \ k | 2 | 3 | 4 | 5 | 6 | 7 | 8 | 9 | 10 | 11 | 12 | 13 | 14 | 15 | 16 | 17 | 18 | 19 | 20 |
|---|---|---|---|---|---|---|---|---|---|---|---|---|---|---|---|---|---|---|---|
| 1 | 90.0 | 135 | 164 | 186 | 202 | 216 | 227 | 237 | 246 | 253 | 260 | 266 | 272 | 277 | 282 | 286 | 290 | 294 | 298 |
| 2 | 14.0 | 19.0 | 22.3 | 24.7 | 26.6 | 28.2 | 29.5 | 30.7 | 31.7 | 32.6 | 33.4 | 34.1 | 34.8 | 35.4 | 36.0 | 36.5 | 37.0 | 37.5 | 37.9 |
| 3 | 8.26 | 10.6 | 12.2 | 13.3 | 14.2 | 15.0 | 15.6 | 16.2 | 16.7 | 17.1 | 17.5 | 17.9 | 18.2 | 18.5 | 18.8 | 19.1 | 19.3 | 19.5 | 19.8 |
| 4 | 6.51 | 8.12 | 9.17 | 9.96 | 10.6 | 11.1 | 11.5 | 11.9 | 12.3 | 12.6 | 12.8 | 13.1 | 13.3 | 13.5 | 13.7 | 13.9 | 14.1 | 14.2 | 14.4 |
| 5 | 5.70 | 6.97 | 7.80 | 8.42 | 8.91 | 9.32 | 9.67 | 9.97 | 10.24 | 10.48 | 10.70 | 10.89 | 11.08 | 11.24 | 11.40 | 11.55 | 11.68 | 11.81 | 11.93 |
| 6 | 5.24 | 6.33 | 7.03 | 7.56 | 7.97 | 8.32 | 8.61 | 8.87 | 9.10 | 9.30 | 9.49 | 9.65 | 9.81 | 9.95 | 10.08 | 10.21 | 10.32 | 10.43 | 10.54 |
| 7 | 4.95 | 5.92 | 6.54 | 7.01 | 7.37 | 7.68 | 7.94 | 8.17 | 8.37 | 8.55 | 8.71 | 8.86 | 9.00 | 9.12 | 9.24 | 9.35 | 9.46 | 9.55 | 9.65 |
| 8 | 4.74 | 5.63 | 6.20 | 6.63 | 6.96 | 7.24 | 7.47 | 7.68 | 7.87 | 8.03 | 8.18 | 8.31 | 8.44 | 8.55 | 8.66 | 8.76 | 8.85 | 8.94 | 9.03 |
| 9 | 4.60 | 5.43 | 5.96 | 6.35 | 6.66 | 6.91 | 7.13 | 7.32 | 7.49 | 7.65 | 7.78 | 7.91 | 8.03 | 8.13 | 8.23 | 8.32 | 8.41 | 8.49 | 8.57 |
| 10 | 4.48 | 5.27 | 5.77 | 6.14 | 6.43 | 6.67 | 6.87 | 7.05 | 7.21 | 7.36 | 7.48 | 7.60 | 7.71 | 7.81 | 7.91 | 7.99 | 8.07 | 8.15 | 8.22 |
| 11 | 4.39 | 5.14 | 5.62 | 5.97 | 6.25 | 6.48 | 6.67 | 6.84 | 6.99 | 7.13 | 7.25 | 7.36 | 7.46 | 7.56 | 7.65 | 7.73 | 7.81 | 7.88 | 7.95 |
| 12 | 4.32 | 5.04 | 5.50 | 5.84 | 6.10 | 6.32 | 6.51 | 6.67 | 6.81 | 6.94 | 7.06 | 7.17 | 7.26 | 7.36 | 7.44 | 7.52 | 7.59 | 7.66 | 7.73 |
| 13 | 4.26 | 4.96 | 5.40 | 5.73 | 5.98 | 6.19 | 6.37 | 6.53 | 6.67 | 6.79 | 6.90 | 7.01 | 7.10 | 7.19 | 7.27 | 7.34 | 7.42 | 7.48 | 7.55 |
| 14 | 4.21 | 4.89 | 5.32 | 5.63 | 5.88 | 6.08 | 6.26 | 6.41 | 6.54 | 6.66 | 6.77 | 6.87 | 6.96 | 7.05 | 7.12 | 7.20 | 7.27 | 7.33 | 7.39 |
| 15 | 4.17 | 4.83 | 5.25 | 5.56 | 5.80 | 5.99 | 6.16 | 6.31 | 6.44 | 6.55 | 6.66 | 6.76 | 6.84 | 6.93 | 7.00 | 7.07 | 7.14 | 7.20 | 7.26 |
| 16 | 4.13 | 4.78 | 5.19 | 5.49 | 5.72 | 5.92 | 6.08 | 6.22 | 6.35 | 6.46 | 6.56 | 6.66 | 6.74 | 6.82 | 6.90 | 6.97 | 7.03 | 7.09 | 7.15 |
| 17 | 4.10 | 4.74 | 5.14 | 5.43 | 5.66 | 5.85 | 6.01 | 6.15 | 6.27 | 6.38 | 6.48 | 6.57 | 6.66 | 6.73 | 6.80 | 6.87 | 6.94 | 7.00 | 7.05 |
| 18 | 4.07 | 4.70 | 5.09 | 5.38 | 5.60 | 5.79 | 5.94 | 6.08 | 6.20 | 6.31 | 6.41 | 6.50 | 6.58 | 6.65 | 6.72 | 6.79 | 6.85 | 6.91 | 6.96 |
| 19 | 4.05 | 4.67 | 5.05 | 5.33 | 5.55 | 5.73 | 5.89 | 6.02 | 6.14 | 6.25 | 6.34 | 6.43 | 6.51 | 6.58 | 6.65 | 6.72 | 6.78 | 6.84 | 6.89 |
| 24 | 3.96 | 4.54 | 4.91 | 5.17 | 5.37 | 5.54 | 5.69 | 5.81 | 5.92 | 6.02 | 6.11 | 6.19 | 6.26 | 6.33 | 6.39 | 6.45 | 6.51 | 6.56 | 6.61 |
| 30 | 3.89 | 4.45 | 4.80 | 5.05 | 5.24 | 5.40 | 5.54 | 5.65 | 5.76 | 5.85 | 5.93 | 6.01 | 6.08 | 6.14 | 6.20 | 6.26 | 6.31 | 6.36 | 6.41 |
| 40 | 3.82 | 4.37 | 4.70 | 4.93 | 5.11 | 5.27 | 5.39 | 5.50 | 5.60 | 5.69 | 5.77 | 5.84 | 5.90 | 5.96 | 6.02 | 6.07 | 6.12 | 6.17 | 6.21 |
| 60 | 3.76 | 4.28 | 4.60 | 4.82 | 4.99 | 5.13 | 5.25 | 5.36 | 5.45 | 5.53 | 5.60 | 5.67 | 5.73 | 5.79 | 5.84 | 5.89 | 5.93 | 5.98 | 6.02 |
| 120 | 3.70 | 4.20 | 4.50 | 4.71 | 4.87 | 5.01 | 5.12 | 5.21 | 5.30 | 5.38 | 5.44 | 5.51 | 5.56 | 5.61 | 5.66 | 5.71 | 5.75 | 5.79 | 5.83 |
| ∞ | 3.64 | 4.12 | 4.40 | 4.60 | 4.76 | 4.88 | 4.99 | 5.08 | 5.16 | 5.23 | 5.29 | 5.35 | 5.40 | 5.45 | 5.49 | 5.54 | 5.57 | 5.61 | 5.65 |

*Source:* H. L. Hartner, "Table of Range and Studentized Range," *The Annals of Mathematical Statistics*, Vol. 31, No. 4. 1960. Reprinted with permission from the Institute of Mathematical Statistics.

## TABLE B.7. Critical Values of the Mann-Whitney $U$ Test*

Alpha = .05

In each cell the lightface value is given first, the boldface value second.

| $n_2$, Number of Observations in Second Group | $n_1$, Number of Observations in First Group | | | | | | | | | | | | | | | | | | | |
|---|---|---|---|---|---|---|---|---|---|---|---|---|---|---|---|---|---|---|---|---|
| | 1 | 2 | 3 | 4 | 5 | 6 | 7 | 8 | 9 | 10 | 11 | 12 | 13 | 14 | 15 | 16 | 17 | 18 | 19 | 20 |
| 1 | — | — | — | — | — | — | — | — | — | — | — | — | — | — | — | — | — | — | 0 | 0 |
| 2 | — | — | — | — | 0 | 0 | 0 | 1 **0** | 1 **0** | 1 **0** | 1 **0** | 2 **1** | 2 **1** | 2 **1** | 3 **1** | 3 **1** | 3 **2** | 4 **2** | 4 **2** | 4 **2** |
| 3 | — | — | 0 | 0 | 1 **0** | 2 **1** | 2 **1** | 3 **2** | 3 **2** | 4 **3** | 5 **3** | 5 **4** | 6 **4** | 7 **5** | 7 **5** | 8 **6** | 9 **6** | 9 **7** | 10 **7** | 11 **8** |
| 4 | — | — | 0 | 1 **0** | 2 **1** | 3 **2** | 4 **3** | 5 **4** | 6 **4** | 7 **5** | 8 **6** | 9 **7** | 10 **8** | 11 **9** | 12 **10** | 14 **11** | 15 **11** | 16 **12** | 17 **13** | 18 **13** |
| 5 | — | 0 | 1 **0** | 2 **1** | 4 **2** | 5 **3** | 6 **5** | 8 **6** | 9 **7** | 11 **8** | 12 **9** | 13 **11** | 15 **12** | 16 **13** | 18 **14** | 19 **15** | 20 **17** | 22 **18** | 23 **19** | 25 **20** |
| 6 | — | 0 | 2 **1** | 3 **2** | 5 **3** | 7 **5** | 8 **6** | 10 **8** | 12 **10** | 14 **11** | 16 **13** | 17 **14** | 19 **16** | 21 **17** | 23 **19** | 25 **21** | 26 **22** | 28 **24** | 30 **25** | 32 **27** |
| 7 | — | 0 | 2 **1** | 4 **3** | 6 **5** | 8 **6** | 11 **8** | 13 **10** | 15 **12** | 17 **14** | 19 **16** | 21 **18** | 24 **20** | 26 **22** | 28 **24** | 30 **26** | 33 **28** | 35 **30** | 37 **32** | 39 **34** |
| 8 | — | 1 **0** | 3 **2** | 5 **4** | 8 **6** | 10 **8** | 13 **10** | 15 **13** | 18 **15** | 20 **17** | 23 **19** | 26 **22** | 28 **24** | 31 **26** | 33 **29** | 36 **31** | 39 **34** | 41 **36** | 44 **38** | 47 **41** |
| 9 | — | 1 **0** | 3 **2** | 6 **4** | 9 **7** | 12 **10** | 15 **12** | 18 **15** | 21 **17** | 24 **20** | 27 **23** | 30 **26** | 33 **28** | 36 **31** | 39 **34** | 42 **37** | 45 **39** | 48 **42** | 51 **45** | 54 **48** |
| 10 | — | 1 **0** | 4 **3** | 7 **5** | 11 **8** | 14 **11** | 17 **14** | 20 **17** | 24 **20** | 27 **23** | 31 **26** | 34 **29** | 37 **33** | 41 **36** | 44 **39** | 48 **42** | 51 **45** | 55 **48** | 58 **52** | 62 **55** |
| 11 | — | 1 **0** | 5 **3** | 8 **6** | 12 **9** | 16 **13** | 19 **16** | 23 **19** | 27 **23** | 31 **26** | 34 **30** | 38 **33** | 42 **37** | 46 **40** | 50 **44** | 54 **47** | 57 **51** | 61 **55** | 65 **58** | 69 **62** |
| 12 | — | 2 **1** | 5 **4** | 9 **7** | 13 **11** | 17 **14** | 21 **18** | 26 **22** | 30 **26** | 34 **29** | 38 **33** | 42 **37** | 47 **41** | 51 **45** | 55 **49** | 60 **53** | 64 **57** | 68 **61** | 72 **65** | 77 **69** |
| 13 | — | 2 **1** | 6 **4** | 10 **8** | 15 **12** | 19 **16** | 24 **20** | 28 **24** | 33 **28** | 37 **33** | 42 **37** | 47 **41** | 51 **45** | 56 **50** | 61 **54** | 65 **59** | 70 **63** | 75 **67** | 80 **72** | 84 **76** |
| 14 | — | 2 **1** | 7 **5** | 11 **9** | 16 **13** | 21 **17** | 26 **22** | 31 **26** | 36 **31** | 41 **36** | 46 **40** | 51 **45** | 56 **50** | 61 **55** | 66 **59** | 71 **64** | 77 **67** | 82 **74** | 87 **78** | 92 **83** |
| 15 | — | 3 **1** | 7 **5** | 12 **10** | 18 **14** | 23 **19** | 28 **24** | 33 **29** | 39 **34** | 44 **39** | 50 **44** | 55 **49** | 61 **54** | 66 **59** | 72 **64** | 77 **70** | 83 **75** | 88 **80** | 94 **85** | 100 **90** |
| 16 | — | 3 **1** | 8 **6** | 14 **11** | 19 **15** | 25 **21** | 30 **26** | 36 **31** | 42 **37** | 48 **42** | 54 **47** | 60 **53** | 65 **59** | 71 **64** | 77 **70** | 83 **75** | 89 **81** | 95 **86** | 101 **92** | 107 **98** |
| 17 | — | 3 **2** | 9 **6** | 15 **11** | 20 **17** | 26 **22** | 33 **28** | 39 **34** | 45 **39** | 51 **45** | 57 **51** | 64 **57** | 70 **63** | 77 **67** | 83 **75** | 89 **81** | 96 **87** | 102 **93** | 109 **99** | 115 **105** |
| 18 | — | 4 **2** | 9 **7** | 16 **12** | 22 **18** | 28 **24** | 35 **30** | 41 **36** | 48 **42** | 55 **48** | 61 **55** | 68 **61** | 75 **67** | 82 **74** | 88 **80** | 95 **86** | 102 **93** | 109 **99** | 116 **106** | 123 **112** |
| 19 | 0 | 4 **2** | 10 **7** | 17 **13** | 23 **19** | 30 **25** | 37 **32** | 44 **38** | 51 **45** | 58 **52** | 65 **58** | 72 **65** | 80 **72** | 87 **78** | 94 **85** | 101 **92** | 109 **99** | 116 **106** | 123 **113** | 130 **119** |
| 20 | 0 | 4 **2** | 11 **8** | 18 **13** | 25 **20** | 32 **27** | 39 **34** | 47 **41** | 54 **48** | 62 **55** | 69 **62** | 77 **69** | 84 **76** | 92 **83** | 100 **90** | 107 **98** | 115 **105** | 123 **112** | 130 **119** | 138 **127** |

*(Continued)*

# TABLE B.7.  Critical Values of the Mann-Whitney $U$ Test*(Continued)

Alpha = .01

Each cell is shown as *one-tailed* / **two-tailed**. One-tailed values are in lightface type, two-tailed values are in **bold type**. A dash (—) indicates no critical value.

| $n_2$ (Second Group) \ $n_1$, Number of Observations in First Group | 1 | 2 | 3 | 4 | 5 | 6 | 7 | 8 | 9 | 10 | 11 | 12 | 13 | 14 | 15 | 16 | 17 | 18 | 19 | 20 |
|---|---|---|---|---|---|---|---|---|---|---|---|---|---|---|---|---|---|---|---|---|
| 1 | — | — | — | — | — | — | — | — | — | — | — | — | — | — | — | — | — | — | — | — |
| 2 | — | — | — | — | — | — | — | — | — | — | — | — | 0/— | 0/— | 0/— | 0/— | 0/— | 0/— | 1/**0** | 1/**0** |
| 3 | — | — | — | — | — | — | 0/— | 0/— | 1/**0** | 1/**0** | 1/**0** | 2/**1** | 2/**1** | 2/**1** | 3/**2** | 3/**2** | 4/**2** | 4/**2** | 4/**3** | 5/**3** |
| 4 | — | — | — | — | 0/— | 1/**0** | 1/**0** | 2/**1** | 3/**1** | 3/**1** | 4/**2** | 5/**3** | 5/**3** | 6/**4** | 7/**5** | 7/**5** | 8/**6** | 9/**6** | 9/**7** | 10/**8** |
| 5 | — | — | — | 0/— | 1/**0** | 2/**1** | 3/**1** | 4/**2** | 5/**3** | 6/**3** | 7/**5** | 8/**6** | 9/**7** | 10/**7** | 11/**8** | 12/**9** | 13/**10** | 14/**11** | 15/**12** | 16/**13** |
| 6 | — | — | — | 1/**0** | 2/**1** | 3/**2** | 4/**3** | 6/**4** | 7/**5** | 8/**6** | 9/**7** | 11/**9** | 12/**10** | 13/**11** | 15/**12** | 16/**13** | 18/**15** | 19/**16** | 20/**17** | 22/**18** |
| 7 | — | — | 0/— | 1/**0** | 3/**1** | 4/**3** | 6/**4** | 7/**6** | 9/**7** | 11/**8** | 12/**10** | 14/**12** | 16/**13** | 18/**15** | 19/**16** | 21/**18** | 23/**19** | 24/**21** | 26/**22** | 28/**24** |
| 8 | — | — | 0/— | 2/**1** | 4/**2** | 6/**4** | 7/**6** | 9/**7** | 11/**9** | 13/**11** | 15/**13** | 17/**15** | 20/**17** | 22/**18** | 24/**20** | 26/**22** | 28/**24** | 30/**26** | 32/**28** | 34/**30** |
| 9 | — | — | 1/**0** | 3/**1** | 5/**3** | 7/**5** | 9/**7** | 11/**9** | 14/**11** | 16/**13** | 18/**16** | 21/**18** | 23/**20** | 26/**22** | 28/**24** | 31/**27** | 33/**29** | 36/**31** | 38/**33** | 40/**36** |
| 10 | — | — | 1/**0** | 3/**1** | 6/**3** | 8/**6** | 11/**8** | 13/**11** | 16/**13** | 19/**16** | 22/**18** | 24/**21** | 27/**24** | 30/**26** | 33/**29** | 36/**31** | 38/**34** | 41/**37** | 44/**39** | 47/**42** |
| 11 | — | — | 1/**0** | 4/**2** | 7/**5** | 9/**7** | 12/**10** | 15/**13** | 18/**16** | 22/**18** | 25/**21** | 28/**24** | 31/**27** | 34/**30** | 37/**33** | 41/**36** | 44/**39** | 47/**42** | 50/**45** | 53/**48** |
| 12 | — | — | 2/**1** | 5/**3** | 8/**6** | 11/**9** | 14/**12** | 17/**15** | 21/**18** | 24/**21** | 28/**24** | 31/**27** | 35/**31** | 38/**34** | 42/**37** | 46/**41** | 49/**44** | 53/**47** | 56/**51** | 60/**54** |
| 13 | — | 0/— | 2/**1** | 5/**3** | 9/**7** | 12/**10** | 16/**13** | 20/**17** | 23/**20** | 27/**24** | 31/**27** | 35/**31** | 39/**34** | 43/**38** | 47/**42** | 51/**45** | 55/**49** | 59/**53** | 63/**56** | 67/**60** |
| 14 | — | 0/— | 2/**1** | 6/**4** | 10/**7** | 13/**11** | 18/**15** | 22/**18** | 26/**22** | 30/**26** | 34/**30** | 38/**34** | 43/**38** | 47/**42** | 51/**46** | 56/**50** | 60/**54** | 65/**58** | 69/**63** | 73/**67** |
| 15 | — | 0/— | 3/**2** | 7/**5** | 11/**8** | 15/**12** | 19/**16** | 24/**20** | 28/**24** | 33/**29** | 37/**33** | 42/**37** | 47/**42** | 51/**46** | 56/**51** | 61/**55** | 66/**60** | 70/**64** | 75/**69** | 80/**73** |
| 16 | — | 0/— | 3/**2** | 7/**5** | 12/**9** | 16/**13** | 21/**18** | 26/**22** | 31/**27** | 36/**31** | 41/**36** | 46/**41** | 51/**45** | 56/**50** | 61/**55** | 66/**60** | 71/**65** | 76/**70** | 82/**74** | 87/**79** |
| 17 | — | 0/— | 4/**2** | 8/**6** | 13/**10** | 18/**15** | 23/**19** | 28/**24** | 33/**29** | 38/**34** | 44/**39** | 49/**44** | 55/**49** | 60/**54** | 66/**60** | 71/**65** | 77/**70** | 82/**75** | 88/**81** | 93/**86** |
| 18 | — | 0/— | 4/**2** | 9/**6** | 14/**11** | 19/**16** | 24/**21** | 30/**26** | 36/**31** | 41/**37** | 47/**42** | 53/**47** | 59/**53** | 65/**58** | 70/**64** | 76/**70** | 82/**75** | 88/**81** | 94/**87** | 100/**92** |
| 19 | — | 1/**0** | 4/**3** | 9/**7** | 15/**12** | 20/**17** | 26/**22** | 32/**28** | 38/**33** | 44/**39** | 50/**45** | 56/**51** | 63/**56** | 69/**63** | 75/**69** | 82/**74** | 88/**81** | 94/**87** | 101/**93** | 107/**99** |
| 20 | — | 1/**0** | 5/**3** | 10/**8** | 16/**13** | 22/**18** | 28/**24** | 34/**30** | 40/**36** | 47/**42** | 53/**48** | 60/**54** | 67/**60** | 73/**67** | 80/**73** | 87/**79** | 93/**86** | 100/**92** | 107/**99** | 114/**105** |

*Source:* Adapted with permission from R. E. Kirk. 1978. *Introductory Statistics.* Pacific Grove, CA: Brooks/Cole.

*One-tailed values are in lightface type, two-tailed values are in **bold type.**

## TABLE B.8. Critical Values of $D$ for the Kolmogorov-Smirnov Two-Sample Test ($K$-$S_2$): Large Sample Approximation

| .10 (one tail) | .05 (one tail) | .025 (one tail) | .01 (one tail) | .005 (one tail) |
|---|---|---|---|---|
| .20 (two tails) | .10 (two tails) | .05 (two tails) | .02 (two tails) | .01 (two tails) |
| $1.07\sqrt{\dfrac{n_1 + n_2}{n_1 n_2}}$ | $1.22\sqrt{\dfrac{n_1 + n_2}{n_1 n_2}}$ | $1.36\sqrt{\dfrac{n_1 + n_2}{n_1 n_2}}$ | $1.52\sqrt{\dfrac{n_1 + n_2}{n_1 n_2}}$ | $1.63\sqrt{\dfrac{n_1 + n_2}{n_1 n_2}}$ |

*Source:* F. J. Massey, Jr. "Distribution Table for the Deviation between Two Sample Cumulations," *The Annals of Mathematical Statistics,* Vol. 23, No. 3. 1952. Reprinted with permission from the Institute of Mathematical Statistics.

## TABLE B.9. Critical Values of $r$ for the Wald-Wolfowitz Runs Test (two-tailed test with $\alpha = .05$)*

| $n_1$ \ $n_2$ | 2 | 3 | 4 | 5 | 6 | 7 | 8 | 9 | 10 | 11 | 12 | 13 | 14 | 15 | 16 | 17 | 18 | 19 | 20 |
|---|---|---|---|---|---|---|---|---|---|---|---|---|---|---|---|---|---|---|---|
| 4 |  |  | 2 |  |  |  |  |  |  |  |  |  |  |  |  |  |  |  |  |
| 5 |  | 2 | 2 | 3 |  |  |  |  |  |  |  |  |  |  |  |  |  |  |  |
| 6 |  | 2 | 3 | 3 | 3 |  |  |  |  |  |  |  |  |  |  |  |  |  |  |
| 7 |  | 2 | 3 | 3 | 4 | 4 |  |  |  |  |  |  |  |  |  |  |  |  |  |
| 8 | 2 | 2 | 3 | 3 | 4 | 4 | 5 |  |  |  |  |  |  |  |  |  |  |  |  |
| 9 | 2 | 2 | 3 | 4 | 4 | 5 | 5 | 6 |  |  |  |  |  |  |  |  |  |  |  |
| 10 | 2 | 3 | 3 | 4 | 5 | 5 | 6 | 6 | 6 |  |  |  |  |  |  |  |  |  |  |
| 11 | 2 | 3 | 3 | 4 | 5 | 5 | 6 | 6 | 7 | 7 |  |  |  |  |  |  |  |  |  |
| 12 | 2 | 3 | 4 | 4 | 5 | 6 | 6 | 7 | 7 | 8 | 8 |  |  |  |  |  |  |  |  |
| 13 | 2 | 3 | 4 | 4 | 5 | 6 | 6 | 7 | 8 | 8 | 9 | 9 |  |  |  |  |  |  |  |
| 14 | 2 | 3 | 4 | 5 | 5 | 6 | 7 | 7 | 8 | 8 | 9 | 9 | 10 |  |  |  |  |  |  |
| 15 | 2 | 3 | 4 | 5 | 6 | 6 | 7 | 8 | 8 | 9 | 9 | 10 | 10 | 11 |  |  |  |  |  |
| 16 | 2 | 3 | 4 | 5 | 6 | 6 | 7 | 8 | 8 | 9 | 10 | 10 | 11 | 11 | 11 |  |  |  |  |
| 17 | 2 | 3 | 4 | 5 | 6 | 7 | 7 | 8 | 9 | 9 | 10 | 10 | 11 | 11 | 12 | 12 |  |  |  |
| 18 | 2 | 3 | 4 | 5 | 6 | 7 | 8 | 8 | 9 | 10 | 10 | 11 | 11 | 12 | 12 | 13 | 13 |  |  |
| 19 | 2 | 3 | 4 | 5 | 6 | 7 | 8 | 8 | 9 | 10 | 10 | 11 | 12 | 12 | 13 | 13 | 14 | 14 |  |
| 20 | 2 | 3 | 4 | 5 | 6 | 7 | 8 | 9 | 9 | 10 | 11 | 11 | 12 | 12 | 13 | 13 | 14 | 14 | 15 |

*For the two-sample runs test any value of $r$ equal to or less than that shown in the body of the table is significant at the .05 level with direction not predicted, or at the .025 level with direction predicted.
*Source:* F. S. Swed and C. Eisenhart. "Tables for Testing Randomness of Grouping in a Sequence of Alternatives," *The Annals of Mathematical Statistics,* Vol. 14, No. 1. 1943. Reprinted with permission from the Institute of Mathematical Statistics.

**TABLE B.10. Critical Values for the Sign Test**

| | $\alpha$ | | | |
|---|---|---|---|---|
| $n$ | .005 (one tail) .01 (two tails) | .01 (one tail) .02 (two tails) | .025 (one tail) .05 (two tails) | .05 (one tail) .10 (two tails) |
| 1 | • | • | • | • |
| 2 | • | • | • | • |
| 3 | • | • | • | • |
| 4 | • | • | • | • |
| 5 | • | • | • | 0 |
| 6 | • | • | 0 | 0 |
| 7 | • | 0 | 0 | 0 |
| 8 | 0 | 0 | 0 | 1 |
| 9 | 0 | 0 | 1 | 1 |
| 10 | 0 | 0 | 1 | 1 |
| 11 | 0 | 1 | 1 | 2 |
| 12 | 1 | 1 | 2 | 2 |
| 13 | 1 | 1 | 2 | 3 |
| 14 | 1 | 2 | 2 | 3 |
| 15 | 2 | 2 | 3 | 3 |
| 16 | 2 | 2 | 3 | 4 |
| 17 | 2 | 3 | 4 | 4 |
| 18 | 3 | 3 | 4 | 5 |
| 19 | 3 | 4 | 4 | 5 |
| 20 | 3 | 4 | 5 | 5 |
| 21 | 4 | 4 | 5 | 6 |
| 22 | 4 | 5 | 5 | 6 |
| 23 | 4 | 5 | 6 | 7 |
| 24 | 5 | 5 | 6 | 7 |
| 25 | 5 | 6 | 7 | 7 |

*Source:* Mario F. Triola, *Elementary Statistics,* © Addison-Wesley Publishing Company, Inc. Reprinted by permission of Addison-Wesley Publishing Company, Inc.

**TABLE B.11. Critical Values of *T* for the Wilcoxon
Matched-Pairs Signed-Ranks Test**

| *n* | .025 (one tail) .05 (two tails) | .01 (one tail) .02 (two tails) | .005 (one tail) .01 (two tails) |
|---|---|---|---|
| 6 | 0 | — | — |
| 7 | 2 | 0 | — |
| 8 | 4 | 2 | 0 |
| 9 | 6 | 3 | 2 |
| 10 | 8 | 5 | 3 |
| 11 | 11 | 7 | 5 |
| 12 | 14 | 10 | 7 |
| 13 | 17 | 13 | 10 |
| 14 | 21 | 16 | 13 |
| 15 | 25 | 20 | 16 |
| 16 | 30 | 24 | 20 |
| 17 | 35 | 28 | 23 |
| 18 | 40 | 33 | 28 |
| 19 | 46 | 38 | 32 |
| 20 | 52 | 43 | 38 |
| 21 | 59 | 49 | 43 |
| 22 | 66 | 56 | 49 |
| 23 | 73 | 62 | 55 |
| 24 | 81 | 69 | 61 |
| 25 | 89 | 77 | 68 |

*Source:* Courtesy of Lederle Laboratories Division of American Cyanamid Company, Madison, NJ.

**TABLE B.12. Critical Values of $r_s$ for the Spearman Rank-Order Correlation Coefficient**

| $n$ | .05 (one tail)<br>.10 (two tails) | .025 (one tail)<br>.05 (two tails) | .01 (one tail)<br>.02 (two tails) | .005 (one tail)<br>.01 (two tails) |
|---|---|---|---|---|
| 5 | .900 | — | — | — |
| 6 | .829 | .886 | .943 | — |
| 7 | .714 | .786 | .893 | .929 |
| 8 | .643 | .738 | .833 | .881 |
| 9 | .600 | .700 | .783 | .833 |
| 10 | .564 | .648 | .745 | .794 |
| 11 | .536 | .618 | .709 | .818 |
| 12 | .497 | .591 | .703 | .780 |
| 13 | .475 | .566 | .673 | .745 |
| 14 | .457 | .545 | .646 | .716 |
| 15 | .441 | .525 | .623 | .689 |
| 16 | .425 | .507 | .601 | .666 |
| 17 | .412 | .490 | .582 | .645 |
| 18 | .399 | .476 | .564 | .625 |
| 19 | .388 | .462 | .549 | .608 |
| 20 | .377 | .450 | .534 | .591 |
| 21 | .368 | .438 | .521 | .576 |
| 22 | .359 | .428 | .508 | .562 |
| 23 | .351 | .418 | .496 | .549 |
| 24 | .343 | .409 | .485 | .537 |
| 25 | .336 | .400 | .475 | .526 |
| 26 | .329 | .392 | .465 | .515 |
| 27 | .323 | .385 | .456 | .505 |
| 28 | .317 | .377 | .448 | .496 |
| 29 | .311 | .370 | .440 | .487 |
| 30 | .305 | .364 | .432 | .478 |

*Source:* E. G. Olds. "The 5% Significance Levels for Sums of Squares of Rank Differences and a Correction," *The Annals of Mathematical Statistics,* Vol. 20, No. 1. 1949. Reprinted with permission from the Institute of Mathematical Statistics.

# Glossary

**absolute value**   the magnitude or value of a number without regard to its sign. The absolute value of a number usually is symbolized by placing the number between two vertical lines. The absolute value of $-3$, then, is written as $|-3|$ and is equal to 3.

**addition rule of probabilities**   for mutually exclusive events $A$ and $B$, the probability of either event $A$ occurring or event $B$ occurring is equal to the sum of their separate probabilities: $P(A$ or $B) = P(A) + P(B)$. For nonmutually exclusive events $A$ and $B$, the probability of either event $A$ occurring or event $B$ occurring is equal to the sum of their separate probabilities minus the probability of their joint occurrence: $P(A$ or $B) = P(A) + P(B) - P(A$ and $B)$. The addition rule of probabilities is often referred to as the "or" rule because it is used to determine the probability of one event *or* another occurring. See Multiplication Rule of Probabilities.

**adjacent values**   in a box-and-whisker plot, the adjacent values are the most extreme scores in a distribution that do not fall outside of the inner and outer fences. There is a low adjacent value and a high adjacent value. The low adjacent value is the lowest score in the distribution that does not fall outside the low inner fence; the high adjacent value is the highest score in the distribution that does not fall outside the high inner fence. The low and high adjacent values are used in the construction of the whiskers for the box-and-whisker plot.

**adjusted $R^2$**   in a multiple regression analysis, the adjusted $R^2$ is the value of the multiple coefficient of determination that is adjusted by taking into account the number of independent variables. It is smaller in value than the unadjusted $R^2$ and gives a truer estimate of the percent of the variance in the dependent variable explained by the independent variables. See Multiple Coefficient of Determination.

**alpha level ($\alpha$)**   the probability that a researcher is willing to take in rejecting a null hypothesis that is actually true. The alpha level in a statistical test, then, is the determined probability of making a Type I error. It is also referred to as the level of significance. The smaller the alpha level, the less likely we are to reject a true null hypothesis. We run a smaller risk of a Type I error with an alpha level of .01, therefore, than we do with one of .05. See Level of Significance, Type I Error.

**alphanumeric data**   data that take the form of letters and words rather than numbers. For example, you could have as a nominal-level variable State; the values of this variable would be the names of the states, Alabama, Arizona, Arkansas, . . ., Wyoming. In this case, our data take the form of names or letters rather than numbers. See Numeric Data.

**653**

**alternative hypothesis**   the alternative to the null hypothesis in a hypothesis test, symbolized by $H_1$. The alternative hypothesis is also called the research hypothesis and is the conclusion we adopt when the null hypothesis is rejected. The alternative hypothesis may be either directional or nondirectional.

**analysis of variance (ANOVA)**   a statistical test that involves the significance of the difference among three or more sample means. An analysis of variance is used to examine the relationship between one or more categorical independent variables and a continuous dependent variable. It is a logical extension of the $t$ test, which examines the difference between two sample means. An ANOVA extends this to a comparison of three or more sample means.

**antilog**   the inverse of the logarithm (common or natural) of a number. For example, the common logarithm of 100 is 2 because $10^2 = 100$. The inverse of this is that the common antilog of 2 is 100. The natural logarithm of 100 is 4.6052 because $2.71828^{4.6052} = 100$. The inverse of this is that the natural antilog of 4.6052 is 100. See Logarithm.

**asymmetric measure of association**   a measure of association between two variables that assumes a different value depending on which is the independent and which is the dependent variable. Lambda is an example of an asymmetric measure of association. See Symmetric Measure of Association.

**availability sample**   a type of nonprobability sample wherein elements of the sample are selected because they happen to be readily available or close at hand to be selected. It is also known as an accidental sample.


**bar graph**   a way to display graphically the frequency distribution of a variable in which the frequency of each value is represented by the length of a rectangular bar. Bar charts may be constructed with the bars displayed vertically or horizontally. In either case the bars have equal width and the length is proportionate to the frequency of the value. Unlike histograms, the bars of a bar chart are separated by a space, indicating that the values of the represented variable are discrete, not continuous.

**basic counting rule**   in probability theory, the basic counting rule is a rule that determines the number of possible outcomes for $N$ trials. The rule is: If any one of $K$ mutually exclusive and exhaustive events can occur on each of $N$ trials, there are $K^N$ different outcomes that may occur.

**Bernoulli process events**   in probability theory, events with two outcomes and their probabilities. Also called a Bernoulli trial.

**Bernoulli trial**   in probability theory, a trial or event that has only two outcomes, such as flipping a coin. One of the outcomes is referred to as a "success" and the other is designated as a "failure." The probability of a success is designated as $p$, and the probability of a failure is designated as $q$. It will always be true that $p + q = 1$, and $q = 1 - p$. The Bernoulli trial is named after the Swiss mathematician Jacques Bernoulli.

**beta coefficient ($\beta$)**   the population value for the estimated unstandardized slope or partial slope coefficient *(b)* in a regression analysis. See Regression Coefficient.

**beta weight (standardized partial slopes)**   in multiple regression analysis, it measures the linear relationship, measured in standard normal units, between one $x$ variable and a $y$ variable when all other $x$ variables are held constant. The standardized slope is the slope coefficient we would obtain from a multiple regression analysis if we first created standardized *(z)* scores for all our variables. The standardized slopes, therefore, measure the effect on the dependent variable of a standard normal independent variable, controlling for all other independent variables. As all explanatory variables have a common measurement metric (unlike unstandardized partial slopes), the standardized slopes can be directly compared to assess the relative effect of various independent variables. See Regression Coefficient, Standardized Regression Coefficient.

**between-groups sum of squares ($SS_{Between}$)**   in an analysis of variance, the between-groups sum of squares reflects the variation between the group means. It is measured by the squared difference between each group mean and the overall or grand mean. It measures the amount of dispersion that exists across group or sample means and, therefore, is defined by the following formula: $SS_{Between} = \sum(\bar{x}_k - \bar{x}_G)^2$, where $\bar{x}_k$ equals the mean of the $k$th group and $\bar{x}_G$ equals the grand mean.

**between-groups variability**   in an analysis of variance, the between-groups variability is the variation or dispersion that exists between the different groups or samples. It is reflected in the difference between each group mean and the overall mean of all scores. This between-group variability, therefore, reflects the differences between the groups on the dependent variable.

**bimodal distribution**   a frequency distribution that has two distinct modes.

**binary dependent variable**   a dichotomous (two-category) dependent variable that is coded 0 and 1. See binary variable, dummy variable.

**binary variable**   a dichotomous variable in which the two values are coded 0 and 1. For example, the variable gender could be a binary variable if males are coded 0 and females are coded 1. See Binary Dependent Variable, Dummy Variable.

**binomial coefficient**   the expression for the number of ways for selecting $r$ objects from $n$ distinct objects, without regard to their order. The formula for the binomial coefficient is
$$\binom{n}{r} = \frac{n!}{r!\,(n-r)!}.$$

**binomial distribution**   a theoretical probability distribution for a variable that has only two distinct outcomes, such as the flip of a coin (head/tails) or the results of a drug test (positive/negative). It is also called a Bernoulli distribution.

**binomial test**   a nonparametric statistical test used when testing a hypothesis about a small sample proportion ($H_0: \hat{p} = p$).

**bivariate correlation**   a correlation or measure of association that reflects the relationship between two variables.

**bounding rule of probabilities**   the probability of an event $A$ must always be greater than or equal to zero and less than or equal to 1. The probability of an event $A$, then, is bounded by 0 and 1: $0 \leq P(A) \leq 1$.

**boxplot/box-and-whisker plot**   a graphical display of the shape and characteristics of a frequency distribution. It contains a box, that is the length of the interquartile range, and whiskers that extend to specified values at the two tails of the distribution. From a box-and-whisker plot you can determine the shape of a distribution, its median, and the position of outliers. A box-and-whisker plot is one of a class of statistics called Exploratory Data Analysis (EDA). See Stem and Leaf Display, Exploratory Data Analysis.

**categorical variable**   a variable whose values take the form of a limited number of discrete (mutually exclusive, nonoverlapping) categories or groups. An example of a categorical variable would be Type of Offense Committed measured as Property, Violent, Drug, or Other. See Qualitative Variable.

**cell**   in a contingency table, a cell is the joint occurrence of two categories from two variables. It is the intersection between a row and a column variable in a contingency table. For example, in a contingency table of gender (male vs. female) and number of delinquent acts (none vs. one or more) there are four cells corresponding to the four possible joint occurrences: (1) males who are nondelinquents, (2) females who are nondelinquents, (3) males who are delinquents, and (4) females who are delinquents.

**central limit theorem**  an important theorem in statistics that says that, regardless of the shape of the population distribution, the sampling distribution of a statistic from that population will be approximately normal as sample size increases. In other words, with large sample sizes, the sampling distribution of a statistic will be approximately normal. What constitutes a "large sample" depends somewhat on the shape of the population distribution. If the distribution of the population is only slightly nonnormal, a sample size of 30 or more will result in a normal sampling distribution. If the population distribution departs radically from normality, then larger sample sizes are necessary to assume a normal sampling distribution.

**chi-square ($\chi^2$) goodness-of-fit test**  a nonparametric statistical test about the distribution of a single nominal-level variable. In this test, we compare the observed distribution of a categorical variable with some expected or theoretical distribution. The greater the difference between the observed and expected distribution, the more likely it is that the two distributions are significantly different from one another, the higher the value of our chi-square statistic, and the more likely we are to reject the null hypothesis.

**chi-square ($\chi^2$) test of independence**  a nonparametric statistical test of the null hypothesis that the distributions of two variables are independent. The alternative hypothesis is that the distributions of the two variables are related and that an association exists between the two variables. The chi-square test of independence measures the extent to which the observed frequencies in a contingency table are significantly different from the frequencies we would expect if the two variables were unrelated. Large differences between the observed and expected frequencies will lead us to reject the null hypothesis.

**class intervals**  the categories or groups of a grouped frequency distribution. For example, in a grouped frequency distribution of number of prior offenses, one possible class interval would be 0–3, indicating an interval from zero prior offenses to three prior offenses. For clarity of presentation, the number of class intervals in a grouped frequency distribution should be limited to approximately 10 to 15.

**coefficient of determination ($r^2$)**  the squared value of the Pearson product–moment correlation coefficient. It measures the strength of the bivariate linear relationship between two continuous variables. The coefficient of determination ranges from $-1.0$, which indicates a perfect negative linear relationship, to $+1.0$, which indicates a perfect positive linear relationship. A value of 0.0 indicates no linear relationship (although there may be a nonlinear relationship between the two variables). When the coefficient of determination is multiplied by 100 to get a percent, we have a measure of association that reflects the percent of the variance in one variable that is explained by the other. For example, an $r^2$ value of .65 would indicate that 65 percent of the variance in one variable is explained by the other. The more variance one variable explains in another, the stronger the relationship. It also has an improvement in prediction interpretation. An $r^2$ of .65 would indicate that we can reduce our prediction errors in one variable by 65 percent if we know its value on the other variable. See Correlation Coefficient.

**coefficient of variation**  a measure of the amount of variability or dispersion in a variable. It is determined by taking the ratio of a variable's standard deviation to its mean $(s/\bar{x})$. The higher the coefficient of variation, the more dispersion there is in the data. Because the standard deviation of a variable is multiplied by its mean, the coefficient of variation is a "standardized" measure of dispersion. The coefficients of variation for two variables measured in different units of measurement, therefore, can be directly compared. The variable with the larger coefficient of variation is more disperse.

**column marginal**   in a contingency table, the column marginal is the number of observations or frequency in that column category. See Row Marginal.

**combination**   the way of selecting a subset of objects *(r)* from a distinct set of other objects *(n)*, where $r < n$, in which the ordering of events does not matter. The number of combinations of *r* events from *n* events, without regard to order, is determined by the binomial coefficient $\left( \dfrac{n!}{[r! \, (n - r)!]} \right)$. See Permutation.

**complement of an event**   the mutually exclusive and exhaustive set of all possibilities of an event not occurring. The complement of an event *(A)* often is referred to as *(non-A)*. If the probability of an event is defined as *p*, then the complement of this event is defined by $1 - p$. The complement of the event "the respondent is a male," is "the respondent is a female." These two events are both mutually exclusive and exhaustive.

**conditional distribution**   the distribution of one variable at fixed levels of another. It reflects, then, the distribution of a variable given the value of another variable. For example, if we have data on the number of delinquent acts committed by 20 youths who were 13 years old, 25 youths who were 14 years old, and 40 youths who were 15 years old, we actually have three distributions of delinquent acts. We have one distribution of delinquent acts given the fact that a youth was 13 years old ($n = 20$), another distribution given the fact that a youth was 14 years old ($n = 25$), and a third distribution given the fact that a youth was 15 years old ($n = 40$). Each of these three distributions of delinquent acts is conditioned on age. See Conditional Means of *y*.

**conditional means of *y***   in a correlation/regression analysis, these are the mean values of one variable (the *y*, or dependent, variable) at fixed values of another variable (the *x*, or independent, variable). The statistical procedure of least-squares regression estimates a straight line that minimizes the squared distance of each conditional mean from the estimated line.

**conditional probability**   the probability of an event occurring, given that another event has occurred. The notation for the conditional probability of *A* given *B* is P(*A*|*B*). For example, in a draw from a deck of cards, the conditional probability of selecting a jack given that a spade was first drawn is equal to 1/13, or .076, because there are 13 spades, only one of which can be a jack.

**confidence interval**   the interval within which a parameter has a known probability of lying. For example, in a 95% confidence interval for a mean, there is a 95 percent probability that an infinite number of confidence intervals will contain the true population value. The confidence interval is estimated from sample data. Other things being equal, the higher the level of confidence (90% vs. 95% vs. 99% vs. 99.9%), the wider the confidence interval because the price of being more confident that the estimated interval contains the true population value is a wider interval. Other things being equal, the larger the sample size, the smaller the confidence interval because with a larger sample size the standard error of the sampling distribution is smaller. With a larger sample, the sample statistic is a more accurate estimate of the unknown population parameter.

**confidence level**   the degree to which we are confident that our estimated interval contains the true population value. With a 95% confidence interval, our confidence level is 95 percent because we are 95 percent certain that an infinite number of confidence intervals with the same sample size will contain the true population value.

**confidence limits**   the lower and upper values of an estimated confidence interval.

**constant**   a characteristic of your sample or population that does not take on different values or does not vary but is the same from one element to the next. For example, if your sample contained all males, gender would be a constant because it does not vary. It also refers to the

$y$ intercept in a regression analysis, and reflects the predicted value of $y$ when all independent variables are equal to zero. See $y$ Intercept.

**contingency table**    a table that shows the joint distribution of two or more categorical variables. The number of categories of the variables determines the number of rows and columns of the contingency table. The size of a contingency table, therefore, is determined by the number of rows and columns it has. For example, a table with 2 rows and 2 columns is a $2 \times 2$ contingency table.

**continuous variable**    a variable whose values are theoretically infinite. An example of a continuous variable would be the rate of auto theft per 100,000 population for a given sample of cities. Theoretically, the rate of auto thefts could range from 0 to $+\infty$ (infinity). See Quantitative Variable.

**correlation**    the extent to which two or more variables are related. A positive correlation means that the two variables covary in the same direction. That is, those with high scores (low scores) on one variable have high scores (low scores) on the other. A negative correlation means that the two variables covary in opposite directions. Those with high scores (low scores) on one variable have low scores (high scores) on the other. Usually correlation coefficients range from $-1.0$, indicating a perfect negative correlation, to $+1.0$, indicating a perfect positive correlation. Correlations of 0.0 indicate no correlation or relationship between the two variables. See Pearson and Spearman correlation coefficients.

**correlation coefficient**    a number whose magnitude shows how strongly two or more variables are correlated or related to one another.

**correlation ratio (eta squared—$E^2$)**    a measure of the strength of the association between a categorical independent variable and a continuous dependent variable in an analysis of variance. The correlation ratio is defined as the ratio of explained variability to total variability $(E^2 = \dfrac{\text{Explained SS}}{\text{Total SS}} = \dfrac{\text{SS}_{\text{Between}}}{\text{SS}_{\text{Total}}})$. The correlation ratio can range in value from 0.0, indicating no relationship between the independent and dependent variable, to 1.0, indicating a very strong relationship between the two. A small sample unbiased Eta squared is calculated as $1 - \dfrac{(\text{Variance Within Groups})}{\text{Total Variance}}$. See Eta.

**count**    the number of occurrences of a value for a given variable. It is also commonly referred to as a frequency or frequency count.

**covariance**    when the values of two variables fluctuate or vary together. The covariance of two variables reflects the extent to which they are related to each other. When they are completely independent, their covariance is equal to zero. For example, if $y$ increases when $x$ increases, they are said to covary. In this example, their covariance is positive.

**critical difference (CD)**    in Tukey's test of honest significant differences from the analysis of variance, the critical difference is the absolute value the difference between two means must be in order to reject the null hypothesis that the two means are equal.

**critical region**    the area in the theoretical sampling distribution that leads to the rejection of the null hypothesis. That is, if the obtained test statistic falls into the critical region, one would reject the null hypothesis. The critical region, therefore, contains unlikely sample outcomes, given that the null hypothesis is true. The size of the critical region depends on the alpha level of the hypothesis test, and the location of the critical region depends on whether there is a one- or two-tailed hypothesis test. See Region of Rejection.

**critical value**    the value of the test statistic (such as a $z$ or $t$ test) that determines whether the null hypothesis is rejected. It is the value that defines the beginning of the critical region.

The critical value of a test statistic depends on the selected alpha level and on whether the hypothesis test is a one- or two-tailed test.

**cumulative frequency distribution**   a tabular display of a frequency distribution in which the reported frequency value represents the frequency with which a variable's value is less than or equal to a particular value. It is often symbolized in a table as cf. In the following cumulative frequency distribution, there are 18 persons who are 26 years old or younger:

| Age | Frequency | cf |
|-----|-----------|-----|
| 25 | 10 | 10 |
| 26 | 8 | 18 |
| 27 | 45 | 63 |
| Total | 63 | |

**cumulative frequency polygon**   the graphical display of a cumulative frequency distribution in which the values of the variable are represented by a dot over each score or value (or a dot over the midpoint of each interval if class intervals are used), where the height of each dot reflects the cumulative frequency of the value. The dots are then connected by a straight line. Because the distribution represents a cumulative frequency, the line in a cumulative frequency polygon never drops; it either goes up or stays flat.

**cumulative logistic probability function**   an $S$-shaped probability curve that has a minimum value of zero and a maximum value of 1. The slope of the logistic distribution is greatest at $p = .50$, indicating that changes in the independent variables will have their greatest effect on the probability of the dependent variable at the middle of the probability curve. At either tail, large changes in the independent variable are necessary to produce a modest change in the probability of the dependent variable.

**cumulative percent distribution**   a tabular display of a percent distribution in which the reported percent represents the percent with which a variable's value is less than or equal to a particular value. It is often symbolized in a table as cp. In the following cumulative percent distribution, 29 percent of the persons are 26 years old or younger:

| Age | Frequency | Percent | cp (%) |
|-----|-----------|---------|--------|
| 25 | 10 | 16 | 16 |
| 26 | 8 | 13 | 29 |
| 27 | 45 | 71 | 100 |
| Total | 63 | 100 | |

**cumulative percent polygon**   the graphical display of a cumulative percent distribution in which the values of the variable are represented by a dot over each score or value (or a dot over the midpoint of each interval if class intervals are used), where the height of each dot reflects the cumulative percent of the value. The dots are then connected by a straight line. Because the distribution represents a cumulative percent, the line in a cumulative percent polygon never drops; it either goes up or stays flat.

**cumulative proportion distribution**   a tabular display of a proportion distribution in which the reported proportion represents the proportion with which a variable's value is less than or equal to a particular value. The following is an example of a cumulative proportion distribution:

| Age | Frequency | Proportion | Cumulative Proportion |
|---|---|---|---|
| 25 | 10 | .16 | .16 |
| 26 | 8 | .13 | .29 |
| 27 | 45 | .71 | 1.00 |
| Total | 63 | | 1.00 |

The table shows that .29 of the persons are 26 years old or younger. See Cumulative Relative Frequency Distribution.

**cumulative proportion polygon**   the graphical display of a cumulative proportion distribution in which the values of the variable are represented by a dot over each score or value (or a dot over the midpoint of each interval if class intervals are used), where the height of each dot reflects the cumulative proportion of the value. The dots are then connected by a straight line. Because the distribution represents a cumulative proportion, the line in a cumulative proportion polygon never drops; it either goes up or stays flat.

**cumulative relative frequency distribution**   a tabular display of a relative frequency distribution in which the reported relative frequency represents the relative frequency with which a variable's value is less than or equal to a given value. It is the same thing as a cumulative proportion distribution. The following table illustrates a relative frequency and a cumulative relative frequency distribution:

| Number of Prior Arrests | Frequency | Relative Frequency | Cumulative Relative Frequency |
|---|---|---|---|
| 0 | 30 | 30/75 (.40) | 30/75 (.40) |
| 1 | 13 | 13/75 (.17) | 43/75 (.57) |
| 2 | 5 | 5/75 (.07) | 48/75 (.64) |
| 3 | 8 | 8/75 (.11) | 56/75 (.75) |
| 5 or more | 19 | 19/75 (.25) | 75/75 (1.00) |

You can see that .75 of the persons committed three or fewer offenses. A cumulative relative frequency distribution is another name for a cumulative proportion distribution. The cumulative relative frequency distribution should sum to 1.0.

**cumulative relative frequency polygon**   See Cumulative Proportion Polygon.

**curvilinear relationship**   a nonlinear relationship between two or more continuous variables. One example of a curvilinear relationship is when one variable is inversely related to a second variable at low levels of that variable but positively related to that variable at high levels. The form of this relationship is described by a curved line, rather than a straight or linear one. See Nonlinear Relationship.

**degrees of freedom**   the number of values that are free to vary when calculating a test statistic. The degrees of freedom are often denoted by the symbol df. The degrees of freedom are used with the $t$, chi-square, and $F$ distributions.

**dependent samples**   two random samples whose elements are not independent from each other. One type of dependent sample occurs when we look at the same persons before and after some experimental manipulation. Because the same subjects make up the before and after sample, the two samples were not independently selected. See Matched Groups or Pairs, Independent Random Samples.

**dependent-samples *t* test**   a *t* test for the difference between two means used whenever the samples are not independent random samples but are dependent or matched samples. See Matched Groups or Pairs.

**dependent variable**   the variable that is being affected or influenced by another variable. It is often denoted as *y*. In a causal analysis the dependent variable is caused by the independent variable. See Outcome Variable, Independent Variable.

**descriptive statistics**   the branch of statistics that is concerned with describing, displaying, and summarizing data. Descriptive statistics are distinguished from inferential statistics, which concern the making of inferences about population characteristics from sample characteristics. See Inferential Statistics.

**directional hypothesis test**   a hypothesis test in which the research or alternative hypothesis states that the sample was selected from a population with a higher (or lower) population value than that expressed in the null hypothesis. For example, if the null hypothesis is $H_0$: $\mu = 25$, a directional hypothesis test would be that the population mean is greater than 25: $H_1$: $\mu > 25$. A directional hypothesis test also is referred to as a one-tailed test because the test is conducted with reference to one tail of the sampling distribution. See Nondirectional Hypothesis Test, One-Tailed Significance Test.

**distribution**   a listing of all the values or outcomes for a particular variable. A distribution often takes the form of a frequency distribution or a percentile distribution.

**distribution-free statistics**   another term for nonparametric statistical tests. They are called distribution-free tests because they do not make assumptions about the form of the population from which a sample was drawn. See Parametric Statistics.

**dummy variable**   a dichotomous variable that has been coded 0 and 1. For example, if gender is coded as 0 for females and 1 for males, it is referred to as a dummy or dummy coded variable. It is also called a binary or binary coded variable. See Binary Variable.

**element**   A single member of a population.

**empirical distribution**   a list of the different values for a variable and the number of times each value appears in your data. It is also referred to as a frequency distribution. See Frequency Distribution.

**empirical probability distribution**   See Probability Distribution, Empirical.

**epsilon (ε)**   the error component or error term in a regression analysis. It exists because even with several independent variables included in our model, we have inevitably left out some variables that help explain the dependent variable (omitted variables), and the independent variables we have included are often imperfectly measured (measurement error). See Regression Analysis.

**error variance**   in a regression equation, it is the squared difference between the observed score on the dependent variable and the predicted score based on the regression equation $(y - \hat{y})^2$. It represents the error in prediction remaining after knowledge of the independent variable is used. It also is referred to as the error or residual sum of squares. See Unexplained Variation.

**eta**   a measure of the nonlinear correlation between a categorical independent variable and a continuous dependent variable. Eta is calculated by taking the square root of Eta Squared: eta $= \sqrt{\text{Eta}^2}$. Eta ranges in value from $-1.0$ to $+1.0$, with 0 indicating the absence of a correlation.

**eta squared ($E^2$)**   a measure of association between a categorical independent variable and a continuous dependent variable in an analysis of variance. Eta squared is the ratio of the between sum of squares and total sum of squares. It is interpreted in terms of how much variance in the dependent variable is explained by the independent variable. Eta squared, also referred to as the correlation ratio, can range in value from 0 to 1.0. The higher the value, the more variance explained and the stronger the association. See Correlation Ratio.

**event**   in probability, it is the outcome of a trial which may or may not occur.

**expected frequencies**   in a chi-square test, the expected frequencies are the cell frequencies we would expect to find if the distributions of the two variables were independent. The cell frequencies we would expect under the null hypothesis of independence. See Observed Frequencies.

**experiment**   an operation that results in the generation of observations or data. Flipping a coin, selecting a card from a deck, administering a questionnaire, or conducting an interview are examples of experiments. See Trial.

**explained variation**   in a correlation/regression analysis, the explained variation is that part of the variation in the dependent or $y$ variable that is attributable to the independent or $x$ variable. Numerically, the explained variation is the squared distance between the value of $y$ predicted by the regression equation ($\hat{y}$) and the mean of $y$: explained variation $= (\hat{y} - \bar{y})^2$. See Regression Variance.

**exploratory data analysis (EDA)**   a class of statistical/graphical techniques designed to illustrate visually and numerically the major properties of a data distribution, such as its shape, skew, and central tendency. Exploratory data analysis tools include stem-and-leaf displays and box-and-whisker plots. See Box-and-Whisker Plot, Stem-and-Leaf Display.

**$F$ distribution**   a theoretical distribution used to study population variances. It is the distribution of the $F$ ratio in an analysis of variance.

**$F$ ratio**   the statistical test in an analysis of variance. It is the ratio of the variance between samples and the variance within samples ($F = \dfrac{(\text{SS}_{\text{Between}}/k - 1)}{(\text{SS}_{\text{within}}/N - k)}$). The $F$ statistic has an $F$ distribution, with $k - 1$ and $N - k$ degrees of freedom.

**failure**   in probability theory, a failure is when an event does not occur. If you were interested in the number of heads from three flips of a coin, the occurrence of a tail would be a failure. See Success.

**fences**   components of a box-and-whisker plot. There are four fences; low inner fence, lower outer fence, high inner fence, higher outer fence. The low inner fence marks a value that is one and one-half times the interquartile range less than the median. The lower outer fence marks a value that is three times the interquartile range less than the median. The high inner fence marks a point that is one and one-half times the interquartile range greater than the median. The higher outer fence marks a point that is three times the interquartile range greater than the median.

**frequency**   See Frequency Count.

**frequency count**   in a frequency distribution, the frequency count is the number of times (frequency) that a particular value appears in your data. For example, in a sample that contains 10 persons 18 years old, the frequency count of 18-year-olds is 10.

**frequency distribution**   a distribution of the values of a variable and the number of times each value occurs in the data. See Empirical Distribution.

**frequency polygon**   a graphical display of the frequency distribution for a quantitative variable in which the values of the variable are represented by a dot over each score or value (or a dot over the midpoint of each interval if class intervals are used) where the height of each dot reflects the frequency of the value. The dots are then connected by a straight line.

**gamma (γ)**   a proportionate reduction in error measure of association between two ordinal-level variables. Values of gamma range between 0 and ±1.0.

**gap**   in a distribution of data, a gap refers to the fact that some values may not appear in your distribution, thus creating a gap in the listing of values. Let's say, for example, in a distribution of ages for a sample of 10 youths, you have three youths who were 15 years old, four who were 16 years old, and three who were 18 years old. In this distribution, you would have a gap in between the ages of 16 and 18 because no one was 17 years old.

**Goodman and Kruskal's tau$_{yx}$**   a measure of association between two nominal-level variables. It is appropriate for any size contingency table and has a proportionate reduction in error interpretation. Goodman and Kruskal's tau ranges in value from 0 to 1.0, with larger values of tau$_{yx}$ indicating a stronger relationship between the two variables.

**grouped frequency distribution**   a tabular display of the frequencies for a variable in which the values are collapsed into groups or a range of values. An example of a grouped frequency distribution of property crime rates would be as follows:

| Property Crimes (per 100,000) | Frequency |
|:---:|:---:|
| 0–100 | 17 |
| 101–200 | 23 |
| 201–300 | 46 |
| 301–400 | 73 |
| 401–500 | 41 |
| 501–600 | 15 |
| 601–700 | 7 |

**heteroscedasticity**   in regression analysis, heteroscedasticity occurs when the variance of $y$ scores are different at different levels of $x$. Heteroscedasticity violates one of the assumptions of regression. See Homoscedasticity.

**histogram**   a way to display graphically the frequency distribution (or grouped frequency distribution) of a quantitative variable in which the frequency of each value is represented by the length of a rectangular bar. Histograms may be constructed with the bars displayed vertically or horizontally; in either case the width of the bars are equal and the length is proportionate to the frequency of the value. Unlike bar charts, the rectangular bars of a histogram have no space between them, indicating that the values of the represented variable are continuous.

**homoscedasticity**   the assumption in ordinary least-squares regression analysis that the variance of the $y$ scores are the same at each value of the $x$ scores. If the variance of the $y$ scores are different at different values of $x$, the data are said to be heteroscedastic. See Heteroscedasticity.

**honest significant difference test (HSD)**   see Tukey's Honest Significant Difference Test.

**hypothesis testing**   when we test a hypothesis we use statistical theory to determine the truthfulness of a statement about our sample data. For example, let's assume that we have data from two different samples and that the sample means are very different from each other. We may want to test a hypothesis that these means are different solely because of chance or sampling variation against an alternative hypothesis that the two samples come from different populations with different means. The first hypothesis is our null hypothesis. It states that any difference between our two sample means is due to chance. Our test of this null hypothesis essentially asks this question, "If the population means were equal, what is the probability that we would observe sample mean differences of the magnitude we have?" As this probability becomes smaller (determined by our alpha level), we are led to question the truth of our null hypothesis.

**independent random samples**   two or more samples where the elements of one sample are independent from the elements of all other samples. Independent random samples are randomly chosen in such a way that the selection of one element into a sample has no effect on the probability of selecting another element. The selection of a sample of males and a second sample of females from some population would be one example of independent random samples.

**independent random sampling**   the process of selecting independent random samples.

**independent-samples $t$ test**   a two-sample $t$ test that is used when the two samples whose means are being compared come from independent random samples.

**independent variable**   the explanatory variable or variable whose effect you wish to measure. Often denoted as the $x$ variable. In a causal analysis, the independent variable is the cause of the dependent variable. See Dependent Variable.

**index of qualitative variation (IQV)**   a measure of dispersion for categorical-level variables. The index of qualitative variation measures the percent of maximum variation in the data. It is the ratio of the amount of observed heterogeneity in the data to the maximum amount of heterogeneity that can exist in the data multiplied by 100. The formula is:

$$\text{IQV} = \left( \frac{\text{Observed Heterogeneity}}{\text{Maximum Heterogeneity}} \right) \times 100.$$

**inferential statistics**   the branch of statistics that is concerned with making inferences from sample data to populations through hypothesis testing. See Descriptive Statistics.

**intercept**   the point at which a regression line crosses the $y$ axis. See $y$ Intercept.

**interquartile range (IQR)**   a measure of dispersion for continuous-level variables. The interquartile range is calculated by subtracting the score at the 25th percentile (the first quartile, or $Q_1$) from the score at the 75th percentile (the third quartile, or $Q_3$). The formula for the interquartile range, therefore, is $Q_3 - Q_1$.

**interval-level variable**   a continuous, quantitative variable where the distance between values is both known and constant. Unlike a ratio variable, however, the zero point for an interval-level variable is arbitrary. An example of an interval-level variable would be IQ score as measured by the Stanford-Binet Intelligence Test. On this test, a one-point difference in IQ is the same at a score of 69–70 as it is at 110–111, and an IQ score of 0 does not mean a complete lack of intelligence.

**interval width**   the width of a class interval in a grouped frequency distribution. The width of the interval is determined by subtracting the lower real limit from the upper real limit. For example, if a class interval is 101–200, the true limits of the interval are 100.5–200.5, and the interval width is 200.5–100.5, or 100.

**joint probability**   the probability of two or more events occurring simultaneously. The notion for the joint probability of two events, A and B, is given by P(A and B) and is calculated by the multiplication rule of probabilities: P(A and B) = P(A) · P(B|A).

**Kendall's tau$_b$**   a measure of association between two ordinal-level variables. It has a proportionate reduction in error interpretation and ranges in value from 0.0 to $\pm1.0$. Values of 0.0 indicate no relationship between the two variables. Tau$_b$ is an appropriate measure of association when the number of rows in the contingency table is equal to the number of columns ($r = c$) in the contingency table.

**Kendall's tau$_c$**   a measure of association between two ordinal-level variables. Unlike tau$_b$, Kendall's tau$_c$ does not have a proportionate reduction in error interpretation. It ranges in value from 0.0 to $\pm1.00$ and is equal to 0.0 when the two variables are unrelated. Tau$_c$ is an appropriate measure of association when the number of rows in the contingency table do not equal the number of columns ($r \neq c$).

**Kolmogorov-Smirnov two-sample test (K-S$_2$)**   a nonparametric statistical test concerning the distribution of two randomly selected independent samples. The null hypothesis is that the two independent samples were selected from the same population. In the K-S$_2$ test, we compare the cumulative frequency distributions of the two samples. If they are statistically different, we reject the null hypothesis that the two samples come from the same population. The K-S$_2$ test is a nonparametric equivalent to the parametric independent-samples $t$ test in that it involves a question of central tendency.

**Kruskal-Wallis H test**   a nonparametric statistical test of the null hypothesis that three or more samples were all selected from the same population. Like the parametric analysis of variance test, it is a statistical test of central tendency.

**lambda ($\lambda$)**   a proportionate reduction in error measure of association for nominal-level variables. Lambda may be calculated for any $r \times c$ table. It ranges in value from 0 to 1, with higher values of lambda indicating a stronger relationship between the two variables.

**least squares**   in regression analysis, the principle of least squares is a criteria for determining the "best-fitting" line to the data. The method of least-squares estimates a regression line in which the squared distance of each y score from the conditional mean of the y's ($(y - \bar{y})^2$) is at a minimum. The least-squares regression line, therefore, is the estimated line through the data where the squared deviations of the conditional means for the y scores is the least. See Ordinary Least Squares, Regression Analysis.

**level of measurement**   the mathematical properties of your variable. This is determined by the precision of your measurement of the variable. Different levels of measurement include the nominal, ordinal, interval, and ratio level.

**level of significance**   the probability at which we decide to reject the null hypothesis. Therefore, it can also be thought of as the probability of rejecting a true null hypothesis in a significance test. The level of significance is the probability of a type I error and is determined by the selected alpha level. See Type I Error.

**likelihood ratio statistic (−2LL)**    in a logistic and probit regression model, the likelihood ratio statistic is −2 times the natural logarithm of the likelihood function. The likelihood ratio statistic is used to assess the fit of a logistic/probit regression model. If the model has a perfect fit to the data, the likelihood ratio statistic would be equal to 0. In logistic and probit regression analysis the likelihood ratio statistic is used to test the null hypothesis that all regression coefficients are equal to zero. This is done by subtracting the likelihood ratio statistic from a model that includes at least one independent variable from the likelihood ratio statistic from a baseline model that includes only the intercept. The difference in the two likelihood ratio statistics is a chi-square test of the null hypothesis that all $b$'s equal zero. This test is comparable to the overall $F$ test in an ordinary least-squares regression.

**linear probability model**    a least-squares regression model in which the dependent variable is binary coded (0,1) and is the probability of some event occurring. The probability of the dependent variable is expressed as a linear function of a set of independent or explanatory variables.

**linear regression analysis**    a way to analyze the relationship between one or more independent variables and a dependent variable. In a linear regression model, the dependent variable is presumed to be a linear, additive function of the independent variables. See Regression Analysis, Regression Equation.

**linear relationship**    a relationship between two continuous variables in which increasing (decreasing) values of one variable are related to increasing (decreasing) values of the other. A linear relationship can be described by a straight line that slopes upward for a positive linear relationship, and downward for a negative linear relationship. The mathematical form of a linear relationship is $y = a + bx$, where $y$ is the dependent variable, $a$ is the $y$ intercept, $b$ is the slope, and $x$ is the independent variable.

**logarithm**    an exponent of some base number indicating the power to which that number must be raised to produce another number. If the base number is 10, the log is referred to as a *common log;* if the base number is 2.71828 (the universal constant, $e$), the log is referred to as a *natural log.* The common log of 100 is 2 because $10^2 = 100$. Because 10 is the base, 10 must be raised to the power of 2 to equal 100. The natural log of 100 is approximately 4.6052 because $2.71828^{4.6052} = 100$. In the case of a natural log, the base is the universal constant 2.71828, and 2.71828 must be raised to the power of 4.6052 to equal 100.

**logistic regression model**    a regression model that involves a dichotomous dependent variable that is binary coded (0 and 1). In a logistic regression model the dependent variable is the log of the odds of the dependent variable occurring. The probability of the dependent variable can be determined by the formula: $\text{Prob (Event)} = \dfrac{[e^{(\beta_0 + \beta_1 x_1)}]}{[1 + e^{(\beta_0 + \beta_1 x_1)}]}$ where the coefficients $\beta_0$ and $\beta_1$ are estimated by the method of maximum likelihood.

**logit**    the natural logarithm of the odds of an event. For example, let us assume that based upon an estimated logistic regression model we estimate that the probability that a criminal suspect will appear for trial if released on her own recognizance is .80. The probability that she will not appear is $1 - .80$ or .20. The odds of appearing for trial, therefore, are .80/.20, or 4.0. The natural logarithm of this odds, or logit, is 1.386.

**Mann-Whitney U test**    a nonparametric statistical test for two independent samples. The $U$ test is a statistical test about the central tendency of two variables and is the nonparametric analog to the parametric $t$ test. Rather than sample means, however, the $U$ test is based on the ranks of the two sample scores. This test is identical to the Wilcoxon rank-sum test, another nonparametric statistical test regarding the central tendency of two randomly selected independent samples.

**marginal frequencies**   the column and row frequencies in a contingency table. There are, then, column and row marginals. In addition, the total number of observations in the table is expressed as a total marginal. They are called marginal frequencies because they are found in the "margins" of the table. See Column Marginal, Row Marginal.

**matched groups or pairs**   a type of dependent sample. With matched groups, the cases in one sample are deliberately selected so that they are comparable to the cases in another sample on some set of characteristics. In this sense, the cases in one sample are "matched with" the cases in another. The two samples are as alike as possible with respect to the matched characteristics. See Dependent Samples.

**maximum likelihood estimation**   a method for estimating the population parameters in a logistic and probit regression analysis. The goal of maximum likelihood estimation is to estimate the population parameters that make the observed sample data most likely.

**mean**   a measure of central tendency. The mean is the arithmetic average of a group of scores. The formula for the mean is $\bar{x} = \Sigma x/n$. It is calculated by adding each score and dividing by the number of scores. As a measure of central tendency, the mean is sometimes distorted. Because it takes into account every score, it is affected by extremely low and extremely high scores.

**mean deviation**   a measure of dispersion for continuous data. In a distribution of scores, the mean deviation is the average absolute difference of each score from the mean of the scores. It measures, then, the average distance of each score from the mean. It is calculated by summing the absolute value of the difference between each score and the mean, and then dividing by the total number of scores. The formula is: $MD = \Sigma(|x - \bar{x}|)/n$

**measure of association**   a statistic that indicates the strength of the relationship between two or more variables. The appropriate measure of association depends on the level of measurement of the variables involved.

**measure of central tendency**   descriptive statistics that reflect the most typical or representative score in a distribution of scores. The appropriate measure of central tendency depends on both the level of measurement and the dispersion of the data.

**measure of dispersion**   descriptive statistics that reflect the amount of variability there is in a distribution of scores. These measures reveal how different the scores are from one another. The appropriate measure of dispersion depends on both the level of measurement and whether or not there are extreme scores or outliers in the data. When the magnitude of the measure of dispersion is large, it means that the scores are very different from one another and there is a substantial amount of variability in the data.

**median**   the score that is the exact middle score in a distribution of ranked scores. It is, therefore, the score at the 50th percentile. In a rank-ordered distribution of scores, the position of the median can be found with the formula $(n + 1)/2$, where $n$ is the number of scores.

**midpoint**   See Midpoint of a Class Interval.

**midpoint of a class interval**   The midpoint is the middle score of a class interval in a grouped frequency distribution. The midpoint is exactly midway between the lower and upper class limits and is determined by adding the upper and lower limits (stated or true limits) and dividing by 2. The midpoint of the class interval 100-200 would be $(100 + 200)/2 = 150$.

**mode**   a measure of central tendency. The mode is the most frequent score in a distribution of scores or most frequently occurring interval in a grouped frequency distribution.

**model**   a graphical and/or mathematical representation of the relationship among several variables. Usually, a model describes, either visually or mathematically, some presumed set of theoretical relationships. For example, the following are models of Hirschi's theory of social control. One model is visual, the other is based on a set of linear equations:

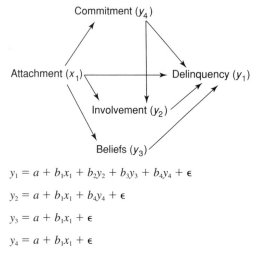

$$y_1 = a + b_1x_1 + b_2y_2 + b_3y_3 + b_4y_4 + \epsilon$$

$$y_2 = a + b_1x_1 + b_4y_4 + \epsilon$$

$$y_3 = a + b_1x_1 + \epsilon$$

$$y_4 = a + b_1x_1 + \epsilon$$

**mu (μ)**   the symbol for the population mean.

**multicollinearity**   in a multivariate analysis, multicollinearity occurs when two or more independent variables are highly correlated with one another. When multicollinearity occurs among the independent variables, it is difficult to disentangle the independent effect each has on the dependent variable.

**multiple coefficient of determination ($R_2$)**   a measure in a multiple regression analysis that reflects the amount of variance explained in the dependent variable by a set of independent variables. The multiple coefficient of determination ranges from 0.0, which indicates that the independent variables explain no variance in the dependent variable, to 1.0, which indicates that the independent variables explain all of the variance. As the included set of independent variables explains more of the variance in $y$, the estimated regression model is providing a better fit to the data.

**multiple peaks**   in a distribution of values, if you have some values with very high frequencies relative to other values, it will take the form of peaks in a bar chart or histogram. These multiple peaks correspond to multiple modes. See Bimodal Distribution, Trimodal Distribution.

**multiple regression**   a multivariate statistical procedure that measures the relative linear effect of a set of independent or explanatory variables on an interval/ratio dependent variable. From an estimated multiple regression equation, we can (1) determine the relative effects of two or more independent variables, (2) estimate predicted values of the dependent variable given particular values of the independent variables, (3) determine how well the independent variables as a group explain the dependent variable. The multiple regression equation can be written as: $y = a + b_1x_1 + b_2x_2 + \cdots + \epsilon$, where $a$ is the $y$ intercept, $b_1$ is the partial slope coefficient for the independent variable $x_1$, $b_2$ is the partial slope coefficient for the independent variable $x_2$, and $\epsilon$ is an error term that includes all explanatory variables not included in the model and measurement error in the variables. See Regression Analysis, Regression Equation.

**multiplication rule of probabilities**   in probability theory, the probability of two or more events occurring simultaneously (events $A$ and $B$ occurring at the same time). For statistically independent events, the probability of both *A* and *B* is determined by the product of their separate probabilities: P(*A* and *B*) = P(*A*) $\times$ P(*B*). For statistically dependent events, the probability of both *A* and *B* is equal to the probability of *A* times the conditional probability of *B* given *A:* P(*A* and *B*) = P(*A*) $\times$ P(*B*|*A*). See Addition Rule of Probabilities.

**multistage cluster sample**   a type of probability sample that involves several stages. In the first stage, aggregates of elements or clusters are first randomly selected (such as the random selection of a sample of schools from all schools in a given city). In the second stage, individual elements from these clusters (students within the schools) are then randomly selected for inclusion into the final sample.

**multivariate regression model**   See Multiple Regression.

**mutually exclusive events**   two or more events that cannot occur at the same time. The joint probability of mutually exclusive events is, therefore, equal to zero. For example, the events of rolling both a 2 and a 4 on a single roll of a die are mutually exclusive because you cannot get both a 2 and a 4 on a single roll.

**N!**   *N* factorial, an operation that means $N \times N - 1 \times N - 2 \times \cdots \times 1$. For example, 5! is $5 \times 4 \times 3 \times 2 \times 1 = 120$.

**negative correlation**   a correlation or association between two variables wherein the scores covary in opposite direction: high scores on one variable are related to low scores on the second variable and low scores on one variable are related to high scores on the other. On a scatterplot, a negative correlation is shown as a downward-sloping line.

**negative skew**   See Negatively Skewed Distribution.

**negatively skewed distribution**   a distribution where the probability of a value above the mean is greater than the probability of a value below the mean. In a negatively skewed distribution the mean is less than the median because there are some unusually low values.

**nominal-level variable**   a qualitative, categorical variable. It is, therefore, a variable whose values take on a limited number of different category values that differ only in terms of quality or kind. Examples of a nominal variable would include gender, race, or political party preference.

**nondirectional hypothesis test**   a hypothesis test in which the research or alternative hypothesis states that the sample was selected from a population with a different population value than that expressed in the null hypothesis. In a nondirectional hypothesis test, the alternative hypothesis simply states that the true population value is different than that expressed in the null hypothesis, not that it is greater than or less than. For example, if the null hypothesis is that two population means are equal: $H_0$: $\mu_1 - \mu_2 = 0$, a nondirectional hypothesis test would be that the population means are different from one another: $H_1$: $\mu_1 - \mu_2 \neq 0$. A nondirectional hypothesis test also is referred to as a two-tailed test, because the test is conducted with reference to both tails of the sampling distribution. See Directional Hypothesis Test.

**nonlinear relationship**   a relationship between two variables that, when the variables are plotted, does not take the shape of a straight line. An example of a nonlinear relationship is a curvilinear one, where the data points form a curve. See Curvilinear Relationship.

**nonparametric statistics**   often called distribution-free tests because they are statistical tests that do not assume that the population distribution is normal. Nonparametric tests do not require interval- or ratio-level data. Examples of nonparametric tests include the binomial test, the Mann-Whitney *U* test, and the signs test. See Distribution-Free Statistics, Parametric Statistics.

**nonprobability sample** a type of sampling procedure in which each element of the population has an unknown probability of being included in the sample. Because the probability of being selected is unknown, nonprobability samples cannot be used to make inferences from sample values to population characteristics. There are different types of nonprobability samples, such as quota, purposive, or availability samples.

**normal distribution or normal curve** a theoretical probability distribution that is symmetric and has one mode that is centered at the mean. In a normal distribution, the mean, median, and mode are the same. There are many normal distributions, each with a different mean and standard deviation. No matter what the shape of a specific normal distribution, there is a fixed proportion of cases within a given number of standard deviation units away from the mean. A special normal distribution is the standard normal distribution. The standard normal, or $z$ distribution, is a normal distribution with a mean of zero and a standard deviation of 1. See $z$ Distribution.

**null hypothesis** the hypothesis of no difference or no association that is the object of a hypothesis test. The null hypothesis is tested against the alternative or research hypothesis, and it is the one that we reject or fail to reject in favor of the alternative. In a one-sample test, the null hypothesis usually is that the sample was drawn from a particular population. For a two- or more sample test, the null hypothesis is that the samples all came from the same population. For measures of association, the null hypothesis is usually that the association between the variables in the population is equal to zero. The null hypothesis commonly is referred to with the symbol $H_0$. The null hypothesis that two population means are equal, for example, would be described as: $H_0$: $\mu_1 = \mu_2$. See Alternative Hypothesis.

**numeric data** data that take the form of numbers. For example, age is numeric data because it usually takes the form of the number of years old someone is. See Alphanumeric Data.

**observed frequencies** in a chi-square test, the observed frequencies are the cell frequencies that we actually observe or find in our data. See Expected Frequencies, Table of Observed Frequencies.

**odds of an event** the odds of an event occurring is the ratio of the probability of the event occurring to the probability of the event not occurring: Odds of $A$ = Prob of $A/(1 -$ Prob of $A$). For example, if the probability that a released offender will commit another crime is equal to .66, the odds are equal to: (1.9) (.66/.34).

**odds ratio** the ratio of two odds. For example, suppose that the odds that a released male offender will be rearrested is .65, and the odds that a released female offender will be rearrested is .30. The odds ratio of a male to a female being rearrested is, then, 2.17 (.65/.30). The odds of rearrest for males is over twice as great as the odds of rearrest for females. In logistic regression analysis the odds ratio is the antilog of the logistic regression coefficient.

**one-tailed significance test** a hypothesis test where the probability of a type I error resides entirely in one tail of the sampling distribution of the test statistic. It is, then, a directional hypothesis test. See Directional Hypothesis Test, Two-Tailed Significance Test.

**ordinal-level variable** a quantitative, categorical variable whose values take the form of mutually exclusive and rank-ordered categories. Unlike nominal-level variables, the categories of an ordinal-level variable can be rank-ordered in terms of "less than" or "more than." An example of an ordinal-level variable would be family income measured as: $0–$10,000, $10,001–$30,000, $30,001–$50,000, more than $50,001.

**ordinary least squares (OLS)** a statistical principle for estimating the straight line in a regression equation. According to the principle of least squares, the estimated regression line will be determined so as to minimize the squared difference between a *y* score and the conditional mean of *y* at a given *x* score. See Least Squares.

**outcome variable**   another name for the dependent variable. See Dependent Variable.

**outlier**   an extremely high or low score in a distribution of scores. In a box-and-whisker plot, a mild outlier is a score that lies in between the inner and outer fences, and an extreme outlier is a score than lies outside the outer fences.

**parameter**   an unknown or known characteristic of a population, rather than a sample. An example of a parameter would be the population mean, $\mu$; another example would be the population standard deviation, $\sigma$. Parameters are usually symbolized with Greek letters.

**parametric statistics**   statistical tests that assume that the underlying population distribution is normal or approximately normal and that the data are measured at the interval/ratio level. It also refers to a set of statistics used to test hypotheses about population parameters. Examples of parametric statistics are the *t* test, *F* test, and *z* test. See Nonparametric Statistics.

**partial correlation coefficient**   a measure of the linear association between two interval/ratio-level variables, when controlling for the effect of one or more other interval/ratio-level variables. The partial correlation coefficient ranges from $-1.0$ to 1.0. A partial correlation of $-1.0$ indicates a perfect negative relationship between two variables when specified other variables are held constant. A partial correlation of 1.0 indicates a perfect positive relationship between two variables when specified other variables are held constant. The partial correlation coefficient $r_{yx1.x2}$ is the partial correlation between $x_1$ and $y$ when $x_2$ is held constant.

**partial slope coefficient**   in a multiple regression analysis, the coefficient that reflects the effect of a given independent variable on the dependent variable when controlling for all other independent variables in the model. It is the multiple regression analog to the slope coefficient in a bivariate (one–independent variable) regression analysis.

**Pearson correlation coefficient (*r*)**   a measure of the linear relationship between two interval/ratio-level variables. The population Pearson correlation value is symbolized by the Greek letter rho ($\rho$), and the sample value is symbolized by *r*. The Pearson correlation ranges in value from $-1.0$, which indicates a perfect negative linear relationship, to $+1.0$, which indicates a perfect positive linear relationship. A value of 0.0 indicates no *linear* relationship, but not necessarily no relationship. Pearson correlation values in between the two extremes are not easy to interpret. It is a common practice to square the value of *r* to obtain the coefficient of determination. Unlike the slope coefficient, *b,* the Pearson correlation coefficient is standardized. No matter what the underlying unit of measurement, the correlation coefficient assumes a value of 0.0 when there is no linear relationship between the two variables and attains a maximum value of 1.0 or $-1.0$ with a perfect correlation. See Correlation Coefficient.

**percent**   a descriptive statistic obtained by dividing the frequency of a subset of events by the total number of events and dividing by 100. For example, if there are 50 property crimes out of a total of 75 crimes, the percent of property crimes is 50/75, or 66.7 percent, of the total. See Proportion.

**permutation**   the arrangement of *r* objects from any *n* distinct objects when the order of the objects matters. The number of permutations of *r* objects from *n* distinct objects can be found with the formula $n!/(n - r)!$. See Combination.

**phi coefficient ($\phi$)**   a measure of association between two nominal-level variables that each have two categories or levels. It is an appropriate measure of association, therefore, for a $2 \times 2$ contingency table. The phi coefficient is comparable to the Pearson correlation coefficient. It ranges in value from 0 to 1.0. The larger the value of the phi coefficient, the stronger the relationship between the two nominal-level variables. The phi coefficient is calculated directly from the observed chi-square value: $\phi = \sqrt{\chi^2/n}$. The phi coefficient does not have a proportionate reduction in error interpretation, but its squared value does.

**phi coefficient squared ($\phi^2$)**   the value of the phi coefficient squared ($\phi^2 = \chi^2/n$). The phi coefficient squared is a measure of association between two nominal-level variables that each have two categories or levels. It is an appropriate measure of association for a 2 × 2 contingency table. It has a proportionate reduction in error interpretation and ranges in value from 0 to 1.0. The larger the value, the more the variation in one variable is explained by the other.

**pie chart**   a circular diagram divided into parts or slices that are proportionate to the frequency (percentage) of the values for a given variable. A pie chart is most effective in summarizing data for a qualitative variable that has five or fewer categories.

**point estimate**   the sample statistic that is used to estimate an unknown population parameter. A sample mean ($\bar{x}$) is used as the point estimate of the population mean ($\mu$). The point estimate is a single value, unlike a confidence interval, which is a range of values. See Confidence Interval.

**pooled variance estimate of the standard error of the difference**   an estimate of the standard error of the difference ($\sigma_{\bar{x}_1 - \bar{x}_2}$) that is obtained by pooling or combining the values of the standard deviation from the two independent samples. The formula for the pooled variable estimate is:

$$\hat{\sigma}_{\bar{x}_1 - \bar{x}_2} = \sqrt{\frac{(n_1 - 1)s_1^2 + (n_2 - 1)s_2^2}{n_1 + n_2 - 2}} \sqrt{\frac{n_1 + n_2}{n_1 n_2}}$$

The pooled variance estimate may be used whenever it can be assumed that the two population standard deviations are equal. If the two population standard deviations are significantly different, the separate variance estimate of the standard error of the difference must be used.

**population**   the entire collection or universe of objects, events, or people that a researcher is actually interested in and from which a sample is drawn. The population often is referred to as the universe of cases.

**positive correlation**   a correlation or association between two variables wherein the scores covary in the same direction: high scores on one variable are related to high scores on the second variable and low scores on one variable are related to low scores on the other. On a scatterplot, a positive correlation is shown as an upward-sloping line.

**positive skew**   See Positively Skewed Distribution.

**positively skewed distribution**   a distribution where the probability of a value below the mean is greater than the probability of a value above the mean. In a positively skewed distribution the mean is greater than the median because there are some unusually high values.

**predicted y value**   the predicted value of the dependent variable derived from a regression equation. The predicted value of y is often symbolized by $\hat{y}$.

**probability**   a measure of the likelihood or chance of an event. The probability of an event $A$ [symbolized as P($A$)] is defined as the ratio of the number of occurrences of $A$ to the total possible number of occurrences:

$$P(A) = \frac{\text{Number of Occurrences of } A}{\text{Total Number of Possible Occurrences}}$$

**probability distribution, empirical**   a listing of the outcomes and probability of each outcome in a particular trial or experiment.

**probability distribution, theoretical**   a distribution of the probability of a given outcome if the trial or experiment were repeated an infinite number of times. Examples of probability distributions include the standard normal ($z$) distribution, Student's $t$ distribution, and the chi-square distribution.

**probability sample**   a type of sampling procedure in which each element of the population has a known probability of being included in the sample. The probability sample is distinguished from the nonprobability sample. There are many different kinds of probability samples, including simple random samples, cluster samples, stratified random samples. Only with a probability sample can a researcher be assured that a given sample will be representative of the population from which it was drawn.

**probit regression model**   a regression model that involves a dichotomous dependent variable that is binary coded (0 and 1). In a probit regression model the dependent variable is an unobserved standard normal variable. The probability of the dependent variable can be determined by the formula: $Z = \beta_0 + \beta_1 x_1$, where $Z$ is a standard normal variable and the coefficients $\beta_0$ and $\beta_1$ are estimated by the method of a maximum likelihood.

**product–moment correlation coefficient**   See Pearson Correlation Coefficient.

**proportion**   a descriptive statistic that is obtained by dividing the frequency of a subset of events by the total number of events. For example, in a sample of 75 females and 125 males, the proportion of females is $75/(75 + 125)$, or .375. See Percent, Relative Frequency.

**proportionate reduction in error (PRE)**   a property of a measure of association. If a measure of association has a PRE measure, we compare the number of prediction errors we would make without knowledge of the independent variable to the number of prediction errors we would make with knowledge of the independent variable. The magnitude of a PRE measure, then, tells us how much better we can predict the occurrence of one variable with the information we have about another variable. The basic form of a PRE measure of association is the following ratio:

$$\frac{\text{Prediction Errors without a Variable} - \text{Prediction Errors with a Variable}}{\text{Prediction Errors without a Variable}}$$

**purposive/judgment sample**   a type of nonprobability sample wherein elements of the sample are selected based on the researcher's own knowledge of the population and subject matter of the particular research.

**qualitative variable**   a variable whose values differ in quality and kind rather than quantity. With a qualitative variable you can say that one value is different from another, but mathematical expressions such as "more than" or "less than" are meaningless. An example of a qualitative variable would be gender. Males are different than females, but we cannot say that males have "more gender" than females. See Nominal-Level Variable, Categorical Variable.

**quantitative variable**   a variable whose values differ in quantity. With a quantitative variable, you can make distinctions based on arithmetic properties, such as "more than" or "less than." An example of a quantitative variable would be the number of prior arrests a convicted offender has. A person with one prior arrest has fewer than a person with three prior arrests. In fact, the latter person has three times as many prior arrests. See Interval-Level Variable, Ratio-Level Variable, Continuous Variable.

**quartile deviation**   a measure of dispersion for continuous data based on the interquartile range. The quartile deviation is defined as one-half the distance between the first and third quartiles. The formula is: $(Q_3 - Q_1)/2$. See Interquartile Range.

**quota sample**   a type of nonprobability sample in which elements are selected into the sample in such a way that the proportion of the sample with certain specified characteristics is the same as the corresponding proportion in the population. For example, if a given population is 75 percent white/25 percent nonwhite; 45 percent male/55 percent female; and 70 percent under the age of 40/30 percent over the age of 40, we can select a quota sample that will contain the same proportion of whites, males, and persons under the age of 40.

**$R^2$ change**   in a multiple regression analysis, it reflects the increment in the amount of variance that is explained in the dependent variable when another variable is included in the model. It measures, therefore, the change in the multiple coefficient of determination ($R^2$) when another variable is considered. For any given variable, the amount of $R^2$ *Change* tells us the amount of variance in the dependent variable that is uniquely explained by that variable. That is, it reflects the proportion of the variance explained by a variable above and beyond that explained by variables already in the model. If the increase in the amount of explained variance is substantial, then, it tells us that the added variable is able to give us information about the dependent variable that we do not get from the variables already included in the regression model. If the increase in the amount of explained variance is small, it tells us that the added variable is not providing any new information above and beyond that provided by the variables already in the model. See Multiple Coefficient of Determination.

**random selection**   a way of ensuring that the sample selected is representative of the population from which it was drawn. In random selection, each element of the population has a known, nonzero, independent, and equal chance of being selected into the sample.

**range**   a measure of dispersion. With continuous data, the range is the difference between the highest score and the lowest score. With rank-ordered categorical data, the range is defined as the difference between the midpoints of the highest and lowest class intervals.

**rate**   a ratio of the number of occurrences or frequency of an event to the total possible number of elements. For example, if there were 1725 robberies in a community with a population of 25,000 residents, the robbery rate would be 1725/25,000, which is .069. Frequently, a rate, such as a crime rate, is expressed in terms of a standard unit of population (per 1000 persons or per 100,000 persons). In this case, the estimated rate is then multiplied by the selected base unit of population. For example, the robbery rate per 1000 persons in the community would be .069 × 1000 = 69 robberies per 1000 persons. See Ratio.

**ratio**   the relation between two numbers that indicates their relative size. The ratio of $x$ to $y$ is determined by dividing $x$ by $y$. For example, the ratio of 12 to 6 is 2 because 12/6 = 2. This indicates that 12 is twice as large as 6.

**ratio-level variable**   a continuous, quantitative variable where the distance between values is both known and equal. Unlike an interval-level variable, a ratio-level variable has an absolute or true zero point, which implies the complete absence of the characteristic. An example of a ratio-level variable would be a robbery victimization rate per 100,000 for persons between the ages of 20 and 40.

**real class limits**   the upper and lower class limits of a class interval in a grouped frequency distribution. Real class limits are reported to reflect the fact that the underlying distribution of the variable is continuous. The real class limits are determined by dividing the distance between any two class intervals by 2 and then subtracting this from the lower stated limit of each interval and adding it to the upper stated limit of each interval. For example, with stated class limits like the following:

**Stated Limits**

13–15
16–18
19–21

you would find the real limits by dividing the distance between intervals (which is 1) by 2, and then subtracting this value (.5) from each lower stated limit and adding it to each upper stated limit. The true limits, then, would be:

**True Limits**

12.5–15.5
15.5–18.5
18.5–21.5

**region of rejection**   the area in the tail or tails of a sampling distribution that leads to the rejection of the null hypothesis. For a one-tailed significance test there is only one region of rejection, for a two-tailed test there are two regions of rejection. The critical region is defined by the critical value of the test statistic. See Critical Region.

**regression analysis**   a statistical technique for describing the linear relationship between one or more independent variables and a continuous dependent variable. From the estimated regression equation, predicted values of the dependent variable can be derived from assumed values of the independent variable.

**regression coefficient**   a measure of the linear effect of a given independent variable on a dependent variable in a regression analysis. The magnitude of an unstandardized bivariate regression coefficient reflects the predicted change in the dependent variable for a one-unit change in the independent variable. The magnitude of an unstandardized multivariate regression coefficient reflects the predicted change in the dependent variable for a one-unit change in the independent variable, after all other independent variables in the model are held constant. The magnitude of a standardized bivariate regression coefficient reflects the predicted change in standard deviation units on the dependent variable for a one-unit change in the independent variable. The magnitude of a standardized multivariate regression coefficient reflects the predicted change in standard deviation units on the dependent variable for a one-unit change in the independent variable, after all other independent variables in the model are held constant. See Beta Coefficient, Slope, Partial Slope Coefficient, Beta Weight, Regression Analysis.

**regression equation**   an equation that expresses a continuous dependent variable as a linear function of one or more independent variables. An example of a regression equation is: $\hat{y} = a + b_1x_1 + b_2x_2 + b_3x_3$, where $\hat{y}$ is the predicted value of the dependent variable, $a$ is the constant or $y$ intercept, the $b$'s represent regression coefficients, and the $x$'s are the independent variables. See Regression Analysis.

**regression line**   the best-fitting straight line that describes the linear relationship between two variables. The best-fitting regression line often is estimated according to the principle of least squares. When the regression line slopes upward, it indicates a positive relationship between the two variables. When the line slopes downward, it indicates a negative relationship between the two variables. See Regression Analysis.

**regression variance**   the sum of the squared difference between the value of the dependent variable predicted from the regression equation and the mean value of the dependent variable $(\hat{y} - \bar{y})^2$. It is also called the explained variation in regression analysis because it is that part of the variation in the dependent variable that is due to knowing the independent variable. It also is referred to as the regression sum of squares. See Explained Variation.

**relative frequency**   the number of times a given value occurs relative to the total number of cases. For example, if there are 10 persons who are 30 years old in a sample of 100 persons, the relative frequency of 30-year-old persons is .10 (10/100). It is another name for a proportion. See Proportion.

**research hypothesis ($H_1$)**   another name for the alternative hypothesis in a hypothesis test. See Alternative Hypothesis.

**residual**   in regression analysis, the difference between the observed value of the dependent variable and that predicted by the regression equation $(y - \hat{y})$.

**residual variance**   another name for the unexplained variation or error variance in regression analysis. It is the sum of the squared difference between the observed value of the dependent variable and that predicted by the regression equation $(y - \hat{y})^2$. See Error Variance, Unexplained Variation.

**row marginal**   in a contingency table, the row marginal is the total number of observations or frequency in that category of the row variable. See Column Marginal, Marginal Frequencies.

**sample**   a subset of objects, events, or people selected from a population. A sample is selected to estimate values or characteristics (parameters) of the population or to test hypotheses about the population.

**sample space**   the total number of possible outcomes or events of a trial. For example, in selecting a card from a deck of cards, the sample space is 52 because there are 52 possible cards to choose.

**sampling distribution**   a theoretical probability distribution of a sample statistic of a particular sample size from a given population. A sampling distribution is derived by selecting an infinite number of samples of size $n$ from a population and then graphing the distribution of a given sample statistic. The theoretical sampling distribution has a known shape. An example of a sampling distribution (the sampling distribution of sample means) would be a distribution of estimated means from taking an infinite number of samples of size 100 ($n = 100$) from a population. The shape of this sampling distribution would be normal (according to the central limit theorem), it would have a mean equal to the population mean ($\mu$) and a standard deviation equal to $\sigma/\sqrt{n}$. See Probability Distribution, Theoretical.

**sampling distribution of the mean**   a theoretical sampling distribution of means from an infinite number of samples of size $n$. The mean of the sampling distribution of means is equal to the population mean ($\mu$). The standard deviation of the sampling distribution (the standard error of the mean or $\sigma_{\bar{x}}$) is equal to $\sigma/\sqrt{n}$ if the population standard deviation is known. If $\sigma$ is not known, $\sigma_{\bar{x}}$ can be estimated with the sample standard deviation ($\hat{\sigma}_{\bar{x}} = s/\sqrt{n-1}$).

**sampling distribution of sample mean differences**   a theoretical sampling distribution that is made up of mean differences ($\bar{x}_1 - \bar{x}_2$) from an infinite number of samples of size $n$. The mean of the sampling distribution of mean differences is equal to the difference between population means ($\mu_1 - \mu_2$), and the standard deviation is equal to the standard error of the difference ($\sigma_{\bar{x}_1 - \bar{x}_2}$).

**sampling variation**   refers to the fact that statistics from different samples drawn from the same population will differ from each other simply because of differences in sample composition. For example, take as the population all citizens of the United States. If we were to take a census and ask each citizen how many times they had ever been arrested, we could determine the population mean ($\mu$). Now let's assume that we take a random sample of 200 citizens and ask each of them how many times they had ever been arrested. The sample mean would be ($\bar{x}_1$). Let's assume we take a second random sample of 200 citizens and calculate another mean number of arrests ($\bar{x}_2$), a third sample ($\bar{x}_3$), and so on. If we were to do this, each sample mean would most likely differ from each of the others because a different 200 citizens with different arrest histories would be included in each sample. The difference in sample means is due to sampling variation.

**scattergram/scatterplot**   a graph that displays the relationship between two continuous variables. From an examination of the scatterplot we can determine whether the relationship between the two variables is linear or nonlinear, whether there are any outliers in the data, and whether we can make a reasonable determination as to the strength of the relationship.

**separate variance estimate of the standard error of the difference**   an estimate of the standard error of the difference ($\sigma_{\bar{x}_1-\bar{x}_2}$) that is obtained by using the two separate sample estimates of the standard deviation. The formula for the separate variance estimate is:

$$\hat{\sigma}_{\bar{x}_1-\bar{x}_2} = \sqrt{\frac{s_1^2}{n_1-1} + \frac{s_2^2}{n_2-1}}.$$

The separate variance estimate of the standard error of the difference must be used if the two sample standard deviations are significantly different. If they are not significantly different, the pooled variance estimate can be employed. See Pooled Variance Estimate of the Standard Error of the Difference.

**sigma ($\sigma$)**   the symbol for the population standard deviation. See Standard Deviation.

**sigma squared ($\sigma^2$)**   the symbol for the population variance. See Variance.

**sign test**   a nonparametric statistical test for two matched or dependent samples. The sign test is comparable to a test for the equality of two medians and is similar to the parametric matched-groups or dependent-samples $t$ test. The null hypothesis is that the two samples were selected from the same population.

**significance level**   the probability of rejecting a true hypothesis and making a type I error. It is the alpha level selected by the researcher. See Alpha Level, Type I Error.

**simple random sample**   a type of probability sample in which each element of the population has a known and equal probability of being included in the sample.

**skewed distribution**   a distribution where the mean and median do not coincide, such that the distribution is nonsymmetrical. In a skewed distribution there is no equal probability for scores above and below the mean. A skewed distribution can be either positively skewed or negatively skewed. In a positively skewed distribution, the infrequent scores are on the right side of the distribution (toward higher scores). In a negatively skewed distribution, the infrequent scores are on the left side of the distribution (toward lower scores). See Negatively Skewed Distribution and Positively Skewed Distribution.

**slope**   the slope of the regression line measures the amount of change in the $y$ variable produced by a one-unit change in the $x$ variable. The slope coefficient is symbolized by $b$. The magnitude of the slope measures the amount of change, and the sign of the slope measures the direction of the change. If the slope is positive, the relationship between the two variables is positive, if the slope is negative, the relationship between the two variables is negative. For example, a slope of 5 would indicate that a one-unit change in $x$ is related to a five-unit change in $y$. The magnitude of the slope coefficient reflects the underlying units of measurement of the $x$ and $y$ variable, so that two slope coefficients cannot be directly compared. See Regression Coefficient.

**smoothing or smoothed score**   a transformed score in a time-series plot to remove irregularities from the data, making trends easier to discern. A smoothed score is created by taking the average of a series of scores. For example, in smoothing a set of scores by taking a moving span of 3, one would take the value for a given time period (say 1 year) and add together the values for the previous and subsequent time periods (the year before and the year after) and then divide by 3. The resulting score is an average of 3 years of scores.

**Somers' *d***   a proportionate reduction in error measure of association for two ordinal-level variables. Somers' *d* is an asymmetric measure of association, so it makes a difference which variable is designated as the independent variable ($d_{x_1x_2} \neq d_{x_2x_1}$). Somers' *d* ranges in value from 0.0 to $\pm 1.0$, with higher values indicating a stronger relationship between the two variables.

**Spearman rank-order correlation coefficient ($r_s$)**   a measure of association for ordinal-level variables. Its magnitude reflects the correlation between the ranks of the two variables, a high value indicates that one's rank order on one variable is related to the rank on the other variable. It is the nonparametric counterpart to the Pearson correlation coefficient. Spearman's *r* ranges from $-1.0$, indicating a perfect negative relationship, to 1.0, indicating a perfect positive relationship. A value of 0.0 indicates that the ranks on the two variables are unrelated. The population symbol for Spearman's correlation coefficient is $\rho_s$. See Pearson Correlation Coefficient.

**standard deviation**   a measure of dispersion. The standard deviation is the square root of the average squared distance of each score from the mean. It is, then, the square root of the variance. With ungrouped data, the definitional formula for the standard deviation is: $\sqrt{\Sigma(x - \bar{x})^2/n}$, and a handy computational formula is:

$$\sqrt{\dfrac{\Sigma x^2 - \dfrac{(\Sigma x)^2}{n}}{n}}$$

See Measure of Dispersion, Variance.

**standard error**   the standard deviation of a sampling distribution. For example, the standard deviation of the sampling distribution of means ($\sigma_{\bar{x}}$, the standard error of the mean) is the standard deviation of a distribution of an infinite number of sample means of size *n* drawn from some population. With a known population standard deviation ($\sigma$), the standard error of the mean is equal to $\sigma/\sqrt{n}$. The standard error of the proportion is the standard deviation of the sampling distribution of proportions (an infinite number of sample proportions of size *n*). The standard error of the proportion is equal to $\sqrt{pq/n}$. The standard error is a measure of sampling error, sample-to-sample variability in our estimate of some population parameter.

**standard error of the difference between means**   the standard deviation of the sampling distribution of mean differences. The population value of the standard error of the difference is symbolized by $\sigma_{\bar{x}_1-\bar{x}_2}$. It is, therefore, the standard deviation of a sampling distribution of an infinite number of differences between two sample means ($\bar{x}_1 - \bar{x}_2$), with sample sizes $n_1$ and $n_2$. The formula for the standard error of the difference between means is $\sigma_{\bar{x}_1-\bar{x}_2} = \sqrt{(\sigma^2_1)/n_1 + (\sigma^2_2)/n_2}$.

**standard error of the difference between proportions**   the standard deviation of the sampling distribution of differences between proportions. The population value of the standard error of the difference between proportions is symbolized by $\sigma_{p_1-p_2}$. It is, therefore, the standard deviation of a sampling distribution of an infinite number of differences between two sample proportions ($p_1 - p_2$) with sample sizes $n_1$ and $n_2$. The formula for the standard error of the difference between proportions is $\sqrt{pq} \sqrt{(n_1 + n_2)/n_1n_2}$.

**standard error of the mean**   the standard deviation of the sampling distribution of the mean. The population value of the standard error of the mean is symbolized by $\sigma_{\bar{x}}$. It is, therefore, the standard deviation of a sampling distribution of an infinite number of sample means of sample size $n$. The formula for the standard error of the mean (with a known population standard deviation) is $\sigma_{\bar{x}} = \sigma/\sqrt{n}$.

**standard error of the proportion**  the standard deviation of the sampling distribution of the proportion. The population value of the standard error of the proportion is symbolized by $\sigma_p$. It is, therefore, the standard deviation of a sampling distribution of an infinite number of sample proportions of sample size $n$. The formula for the standard error of the proportion is $\sigma_p = \sqrt{[p\,(1-p)]/n}$. Because the population proportion $p$ is almost never known, $\sigma_p$ must be estimated. One estimate is based on using the sample proportion to estimate the population proportion: $\sigma_{\hat{p}} = \sqrt{[\hat{p}\,(1-\hat{p})]/n}$. A second, more conservative estimate is to always use .5 as the estimate of the population proportion: $\sigma_{\hat{p}} = \sqrt{(.5)(.5)/n}$.

**standardized partial slope coefficient**  a partial regression coefficient that has been standardized by multiplying the partial slope coefficient by the ratio of its standard deviation to the standard deviation of the dependent variable ($b^* = b\,(s_x/s_y)$). The standardized partial slope coefficient will show the amount of change in the standardized score of $y$ for a 1 unit change in the standardized score of $x$, controlling for all other independent variables.

**standard normal distribution**  a normally distributed sampling distribution that has a mean of zero, a standard deviation of 1, and a total area of 1.0. It is also referred to as the $z$ distribution. See $z$ Distribution.

**standard score**  a score obtained by transforming a variable into another score whose distribution has known characteristics. The most common standard score is the $z$ score, which is obtained by subtracting the mean from a raw score and dividing by the standard deviation. The $z$ score is distributed as a normal variable with a mean of zero and a standard deviation of 1. See $z$ Score.

**standardized regression coefficient**  a regression coefficient that indicates the change in standard deviation units of the dependent variable for a one-unit change in the independent variable. Because the effect on the dependent variable is measured in a common metric (standard deviation units), the relative effects of independent variables in a regression analysis can be determined by comparing the magnitude of their standardized coefficients. See Beta Weight, Regression Coefficient.

**stated class limits**  the upper and lower class limits of a class interval in a grouped frequency distribution. See Class Intervals.

**statistic**  a sample characteristic that is an estimate of a population characteristic or parameter. The mean of a sample ($\bar{x}$) is a sample statistic, as is the standard deviation of a sample ($s$). Sample statistics are usually symbolized with a roman letter or letters. See Parameter.

**statistical independence**  two events ($A$ and $B$) are statistically independent if the probability of one is not conditioned by the other. That is, $A$ and $B$ are independent if the probability of $A$ is equal to the probability of $A$ given $B$: $P(A) = P(A|B)$.

**stem-and-leaf display**  a graphical display of a frequency distribution used in exploratory data analysis. From a stem-and-leaf display you can determine the shape of a distribution, the median score, and identify any outliers in the data. See Exploratory Data Analysis, Box-and-Whisker Plot.

**Student's $t$ distribution**  See $t$ distribution.

**success**  in probability theory, the success of an event is when the event occurs. For example, if one were interested in the probability of obtaining at least three heads on six flips of a coin, the occurrence of a head would be a success. See Failure.

**sum of the differences**  the sum arrived at by subtracting each score in a distribution by the mean of the distribution. The formula for the sum of the differences is $\Sigma(x - \bar{x})$.

**symmetric distribution**  a distribution that is normally or approximately normally distributed. A symmetric distribution has no negative nor positive skew. See Negatively Skewed Distribution and Positively Skewed Distribution.

**symmetric measure of association**  a measure of association that has the same value no matter which variable is designated as the dependent and which as the independent variable. The Pearson correlation coefficient is an example of a symmetric measure of association. See Asymmetric Measure of Association.

**systematic random sample**  a type of probability sample in which the first element is randomly selected from an unordered population and every $k$th element is chosen thereafter (where $k$ is a nonzero integer).

*t* **distribution**  the Student's $t$ distribution is a theoretical sampling distribution that is flatter than the standard normal ($z$) distribution and is appreciably flatter as the sample size becomes small. The $t$ distribution has a mean of 0 and a standard deviation that becomes smaller as the sample size increases. With large samples, the $t$ distribution approximates the $z$ distribution. It is the sampling distribution for the $t$ test.

**table of expected frequencies**  this is the joint distribution of frequencies in a contingency table that you would expect to find if the null hypothesis was true and the two variables in the table were independent. In calculating a chi-square statistic, the expected frequencies are compared with the observed frequencies. Large differences between observed and expected frequencies leads you to reject the null hypothesis. See Expected Frequencies, Table of Observed Frequencies.

**table of observed frequencies**  this is the observed frequencies for the joint distribution two variables that you find in your data. In calculating a chi-square statistic, the observed frequencies are compared with the expected frequencies. Large differences between observed and expected frequencies leads you to reject the null hypothesis. See Observed Frequencies, Table of Expected Frequencies.

**theoretical probability distribution**  See Probability Distribution, Theoretical.

**time plot**  a graphical technique that shows how a given variable changes over time. An example would be the plot of victimization rates for a given city over the years 1970–1990.

**total sum of squares ($SS_{Total}$)**  in an analysis of variance, the total sum of squares reflects the total variation in a group of scores. It is measured by the squared difference between each individual score and the overall or grand mean and is defined by the following formula: $SS_{Total} = \Sigma(x_i = \bar{x}_G)^2$, where $x_i$ equals the $x_i$th score, and $\bar{x}_G$ equals the grand mean.

**total variation**  in a regression analysis, it reflects the sum of the squared difference between each $y$ score and the mean of $y$: $\Sigma(y - \bar{y})^2$. The total variation is equal to the sum of the explained and unexplained variation. See Explained Variation, Unexplained Variation.

**trial**  also referred to as an experiment in probability theory. A trial is any operation that results in the collection of observations or data. Examples of trials include the selection of one card from a deck of cards or the act of rolling a die and observing what number comes up. See Experiment.

**trimodal distribution**  a frequency distribution that has three distinct modes.

**truncated median position**  the position of the median with the decimal place dropped. For example, if the position of the median is the 16.5th score (in between the 16th and 17th scores), the truncated median position is 16, because the decimal place (.5) is omitted.

**Tukey's honest significant difference (HSD) test**  a test for the significance of the difference between pairs of sample means in an analysis of variance. The test was developed by John Tukey. Because a significant $F$ ratio in an analysis of variance only tells us that at least two of the sample means are significantly different from each other, the HSD tests will allow us to determine specifically which sample means are significantly different.

**two-tailed significance test**  a hypothesis test where the probability of a Type I error resides in both tails of the sampling distribution of the test statistic. It is, then, a nondirectional hypothesis test. See Nondirectional Hypothesis test.

**type I error**  an error made by rejecting a null hypothesis that happens to be true. The probability of a Type I error is determined by the set alpha level. See Alpha Level, Level of Significance.

**type II error**  an error made by not rejecting a null hypothesis that happens to be false. Type I and Type II errors are inversely related. By minimizing the risk of one type of error, you increase the risk of making the other type of error.

**unexplained variation**  in a regression analysis, the unexplained variation is the proportion of the total variation in the $y$ variable that is not explained by the $x$ variable. It is reflected in the squared distance of each $y$ score from the value of $y$ predicted from the regression equation: $\Sigma(y - \hat{y})^2$. It also is called the error or residual sum of squares. See Error Variance, Explained Variation.

**ungrouped frequency distribution**  a tabular display of the frequencies of a variable in which each value of the variable is listed along with its corresponding frequency. The following is an example of an ungrouped frequency distribution of the variable, age:

| Age | Frequency |
| --- | --- |
| 10 | 4 |
| 11 | 13 |
| 12 | 54 |
| 13 | 120 |
| 14 | 76 |
| 15 | 29 |
| 16 | 10 |

**unimodal distribution**  a frequency distribution that has only one mode.

**unit of analysis**  refers to the level of aggregation of the objects of our research. Sometimes our unit of analysis is comprised of individuals (persons), at other times it is collectivities such as families, communities, cities, states, or even nations. The unit of analysis is the level at which we collect and analyze our data.

**variable**  an attribute or characteristic that can change or vary. In a sample of males and females, gender is a variable.

**variance**  a measure of dispersion. The variance is the average squared difference of each score from the mean. The variance is the square of the standard deviation. With ungrouped data, the definitional formula for the variance is: $\Sigma(x - \bar{x})^2/n$, and an easier computational formula is: $[\Sigma x^2 - ((\Sigma x)^2)/n)]/n$. See Measure of Dispersion, Standard Deviation.

**variance between samples**    in an analysis of variance, it reflects one measure of the population variance. It is measured by the ratio of the sum of squares between groups ($SS_{Between}$) to the degrees of freedom between groups ($k - 1$): Variance between Samples $= SS_{Between}/(k - 1)$.

**variance within samples**    in an analysis of variance, it reflects one measure of the population variance. It is measured by the ratio of the sum of squares within groups ($SS_{Within}$) to the degrees of freedom within groups ($N - k$): Variance within Samples $= SS_{Within}/(N - k)$.

**variation ratio**    a measure of dispersion for qualitative, categorical data. The variation ratio measures the extent to which the cases are not concentrated in the modal category. The higher the value of the variation ratio, the greater the dispersion of cases in categories other than the modal category. The formula for the variation ratio is: $1 - \dfrac{f_{modal}}{n}$, where $f_{modal}$ is the frequency of cases in the modal category.

**Wald statistic**    a statistical test that a logistic or probit regression coefficient is significantly different from zero. It is equal to the square of the ratio of the regression coefficient to its standard error: Wald $= (b/se)^2$. The Wald statistic has a chi-square distribution.

**Wald-Wolfowitz runs test**    a nonparametric statistical test that examines differences in the dispersion of two independent samples. The null hypothesis is that the two samples were selected from the same population. The Wald-Wolfowitz test is appropriate when we suspect that the difference between two populations is one of dispersion of the distribution rather than central tendency.

**weighted mean**    a mean calculated by taking the sum of several subgroup means where each subgroup mean is first multiplied (weighted) by the number of scores in the subgroup, with the result divided by the total number of scores. The formula for a weighted mean is:

$$\bar{x} = \sum_{i=1}^{k} n_i \bar{x}_i / N$$

where $n_i$ is the number of observations in the $n$th group, $\bar{x}_i$ is the mean of the $i$th group, and $N$ is the total number of cases in all the groups. If the mean for 125 persons in group 1 is 12.3, the mean for 65 persons in group 2 is 8.4, and the mean for 40 persons in group 3 is 10.2, the weighted mean would be:

$$\frac{125(12.3) + 65(8.4) + 40(10.2)}{125 + 65 + 40} = \frac{2491.5}{230} = 10.83.$$

See Mean.

**weighted sample**    a type of probability sample in which each element of the population has a known but unequal probability of being selected. In this type of sample, some elements have a higher probability of being selected than others in order to ensure that they appear in the sample.

**Wilcoxon signed-ranks test**    a nonparametric test about the central tendency of two matched or dependent samples. It is one of the nonparametric analogs to the matched groups or dependent samples $t$ test. The null hypothesis is that the two samples were selected from the same population.

**within-group sum of squares ($SS_{Within}$)**    in an analysis of variance, the within-group sum of squares reflects the variation within a group of scores. It is measured by the squared difference between each individual score and the group mean and is defined by the following formula: $SS_{Within} = \Sigma(x_i - \bar{x}_k)^2$, where $x_i$ is the $x_i$th score, and $\bar{x}_k$ is the mean for the $k$th group.

**within-group variability**   in an analysis of variance, the within-group variability is the variation or dispersion that exists within each group or sample. It is reflected in the difference between each score and the group or sample mean. This within-group variability, therefore, reflects the differences within each group on the dependent variable.

*x* **axis**   the horizontal axis on a graph. It also is referred to as the abscissa.

$\bar{x}$ (*x* **bar**)   the symbol for a sample mean.

*x* **variable**   the independent variable in an analysis.


*y* **axis**   the vertical axis on a graph. It also is referred to as the ordinate.

$\hat{y}$ (*y*-**hat**)   the predicted value of the dependent variable in a regression analysis.

*y* **intercept**   the point where the regression line crosses the *y* axis. It is the predicted value of *y* when the *x* variable or variables equal zero. See Constant.

**Yule's Q**   a measure of association for two categorical variables that each have two categories or levels. It is an appropriate measure of association in a $2 \times 2$ contingency table. Yule's *Q* has a proportionate reduction in error interpretation. It ranges in value from $-1.0$ to $1.0$, with $0.0$ indicating no relationship between the two variables.

*y* **variable**   the dependent variable in an analysis.

*z* **distribution**   a theoretical probability distribution that is normally distributed with a mean of zero and a standard deviation of 1. It also is called the standard normal distribution.

*z* **score**   a transformed score that is determined by subtracting the mean of a distribution of scores from a raw score and dividing by the standard deviation of the distribution: $z = (x - \bar{x})/s$. The transformed *z* score, then, represents the deviation of a particular score from the mean, expressed in standard deviation units. For example, a *z* score of 1.7 is 1.7 standard deviation units greater than (to the right of) the mean. This *z* score is normally distributed, with a mean of zero and standard deviation of 1.

# References

Abel, G., J. Becker, M. Mittolman, J. Cunningham-Rathner, J. Rouleau, and W. Murphy. 1987. "Self-Reported Sex Crimes of Nonincarcerated Paraphiliacs." *Journal of Interpersonal Violence* 2:3–25.

Agnew, Robert. 1992. "Foundation for a General Strain Theory of Crime." *Criminology* 30:47–87.

Akers, Ronald L. 1992. *Drugs, Alcohol, and Society: Social Structure, Process and Policy.* Belmont, CA: Wadsworth.

Bachman, Ronet. 1992. *Death and Violence on the Reservation: Homicide, Suicide and Family Violence in American Indian Populations.* Westport, CT: Auburn House.

Bachman, Ronet. 1994. *Violence Against Women: A National Crime Victimization Report.* Bureau of Justice Statistics, U.S. Department of Justice. Washington, DC.

Bachman, Ronet, Raymond Paternoster, and Sally Ward. 1992. "The Rationality of Sexual Offending: Testing a Deterrence/Rational Choice Conception of Sexual Assault." *Law and Society Review* 26:343–372.

Bailey, W. C. 1984. "Poverty, Inequality, and City Homicide Rates: Some Not So Unexpected Results." *Criminology* 22:531–550.

Bayley, David H., and James Garofalo. 1989. "The Management of Violence by Patrol Officers." *Criminology* 27:1–25.

Benoit, J. L., and Kennedy, W. A. 1992. "The Abuse History of Male Adolescent Sex Offenders." *Journal of Interpersonal Violence* 7:543–548.

Blalock, Hubert M. 1979. *Social Statistics, 2nd Ed.* New York: McGraw-Hill.

Blau, Judith R., and Peter M. Blau. 1982. "The Cost of Inequality: Metropolitan Structure and Violent Crime." *American Sociological Review* 47:114–129.

Bowers, William J. 1984. *Legal Homicide.* Boston: Northeastern University Press.

Box, G. E., and S. L. Anderson. 1955. "Permutation Theory in the Derivation of Robust Criteria and the Study of Departures from Assumption." *Journal of the Royal Statistical Society, Series B* 17:1–26.

Bureau of Justice Statistics, U.S. Department of Justice. 1976. *Criminal Victimization in the United States, 1973.* Washington, DC.

Bureau of Justice Statistics, U.S. Department of Justice. 1977. *Criminal Victimization in the United States, 1974.* Washington, DC.

Bureau of Justice Statistics, U.S. Department of Justice. 1977. *Criminal Victimization in the United States, 1975.* Washington, DC.

Bureau of Justice Statistics, U.S. Department of Justice. 1977. *Criminal Victimization in the United States, 1976.* Washington, DC.

Bureau of Justice Statistics, U.S. Department of Justice. 1979. *Criminal Victimization in the United States, 1977.* Washington, DC.

Bureau of Justice Statistics, U.S. Department of Justice. 1980. *Criminal Victimization in the United States, 1978.* Washington, DC.

Bureau of Justice Statistics, U.S. Department of Justice. 1981. *Criminal Victimization in the United States, 1979.* Washington, DC.

Bureau of Justice Statistics, U.S. Department of Justice. 1982. *Criminal Victimization in the United States, 1980.* Washington, DC.

Bureau of Justice Statistics, U.S. Department of Justice. 1983. *Criminal Victimization in the United States, 1981.* Washington, DC.

Bureau of Justice Statistics, U.S. Department of Justice. 1984. *Criminal Victimization in the United States, 1982.* Washington, DC.

Bureau of Justice Statistics, U.S. Department of Justice. 1985. *Criminal Victimization in the United States, 1983.* Washington, DC.

Bureau of Justice Statistics, U.S. Department of Justice. 1986. *Criminal Victimization in the United States, 1984.* Washington, DC.

Bureau of Justice Statistics, U.S. Department of Justice. 1987. *Criminal Victimization in the United States, 1985.* Washington, DC.

Bureau of Justice Statistics, U.S. Department of Justice. 1988. *Criminal Victimization in the United States, 1986.* Washington, DC.

Bureau of Justice Statistics, U.S. Department of Justice. 1989. *Criminal Victimization in the United States, 1987.* Washington, DC.

Bureau of Justice Statistics, U.S. Department of Justice. 1990. *Criminal Victimization in the United States, 1988.* Washington, DC.

Bureau of Justice Statistics, U.S. Department of Justice. 1991. *Criminal Victimization in the United States, 1989.* Washington, DC.

Bureau of Justice Statistics, U.S. Department of Justice. 1991. *Criminal Victimization in the United States, 1990.* (Special Report NCJ-134126). Washington, DC.

Bureau of Justice Statistics, U.S. Department of Justice. 1992. *Criminal Victimization in the United States, 1991.* (Special Report NCJ-139563). Washington, DC.

Bureau of Justice Statistics, U.S. Department of Justice. 1992. *Criminal Victimization in the United States, 1973–90 Trends.* (Special Report NCJ-138564). Washington, DC.

Bureau of Justice Statistics, U.S. Department of Justice. 1994. *Criminal Victimization in the United States, 1973–92 Trends.* (Special Report NCJ-147006). Washington, DC.

Bureau of Justice Statistics, U.S. Department of Justice. 1994. *Highlights from Twenty Years of Surveying Crime Victims: The National Crime Victimization Survey, 1973–92.* Washington, DC.

Cohen, Jacob, and Patricia Cohen. 1983. *Applied Multiple Regression/Correlation Analysis for the Behavioral Sciences.* Hillsdale, NJ: Lawrence Erlbaum.

Corrections Compendium. 1992. Lincoln, NE: CEGA Publishing.

Crutchfield, Robert D., Michael R. Geerken, and Walter R. Gove. 1982. "Crime Rate and Social Integration." *Criminology* 20:467–478.

Daniel, Wayne. 1990. *Applied Nonparametric Statistics.* Boston: PWS-Kent Publishing.

Daly, Kathleen. 1994. *Gender, Crime and Punishment.* New Haven: Yale University Press.

DeFronzo, James. 1983. "Economic Assistance to Impoverished Americans." *Criminology* 21:119–136.

Doerner, W. G. 1978. "The Index of Southernness Revisited." *Criminology* 16:47–56.

Doerner, W. G. (1983). "Why Does Johnny Reb Die When Shot? The Impact of Medical Resources Upon Lethality" *Sociological Inquiry* 53:1–15.

Draper, N. R., and H. Smith. 1981. *Applied Regression Analysis, 2nd Ed.* New York: Wiley.

Elliott, Delbert, and Suzanne Ageton. 1980. "Reconciling Race and Class Differences in Self-Reported and Official Estimates of Delinquency." *American Sociological Review* 45:95–110.

Elliott, Delbert, David Huizinga, and Suzanne Ageton. 1985. *Explaining Delinquency and Drug Use.* Beverly Hills, CA: Sage.

Farnworth, Margaret, and Michael J. Leiber. 1989. "Strain Theory Revisited: Economic Goals, Educational Means, and Delinquency." *American Sociological Review* 54:263–274.

Farrington, David P. 1977. "The Effects of Public Labeling." *British Journal of Criminology* 17:112–125.

Farrington, David P. 1993. "Understanding and Preventing Bullying," in *Crime and Justice: A Review of Research,* Michael Tonry, Ed. Chicago: University of Chicago Press.

Federal Bureau of Investigation. 1983. *Uniform Crime Reports, 1982.* U.S. Department of Justice. Washington, DC: U.S. Government Printing Office.

Federal Bureau of Investigation. 1991. *Uniform Crime Reports, 1990.* U.S. Department of Justice. Washington, DC: U.S. Government Printing Office.

Federal Bureau of Investigation. 1992. *Uniform Crime Reports, 1991.* U.S. Department of Justice. Washington, DC: U.S. Government Printing Office.

Federal Bureau of Investigation. 1993. *Uniform Crime Reports, 1992.* U.S. Department of Justice. Washington, DC: U.S. Government Printing Office.

Fisher, Bonnie, and Jack L. Nasar. 1995. "Fear Spots in Relation to Microlevel Physical Cues: Exploring the Overlooked." *Journal of Research in Crime and Delinquency* 32:214–239.

Flanagan, Timothy J., and Kathleen Maguire (Eds.). 1991. *Sourcebook of Criminal Justice Statistics.* U.S. Department of Justice, Bureau of Justice Statistics. Washington, DC: U.S. Government Printing Office.

Gaes, Gerald G. 1985. "The Effects of Overcrowding in Prison." In *Crime and Justice: A Review of Research,* Michael Tonry and Norval Morris, Eds. Chicago: University of Chicago Press.

Galle, Omer R., Walter R. Gove, and J. Miller McPherson. 1972. "Population Density and Pathology: What Are the Relations for Man?" *Science* 176:23–29.

Gastil, R. D. 1971. "Homicide and a Regional Culture of Violence." *American Sociological Review* 36:412–437.

Gastil, R. D. 1975. *Cultural Regions of the United States.* Seattle: University of Washington Press.

Gilsinan, James F. 1989. "They is Clowning Tough: 911 and the Social Construction of Reality." *Criminology* 27:329–344.

Glueck, Sheldon, and Eleanor Glueck. 1950. *Unraveling Juvenile Delinquency.* New York: The Commonwealth Fund.

Gottfredson, Michael, and Travis Hirschi. 1990. *A General Theory of Crime.* Stanford, CA: Stanford University Press.

Gove, W. R., M. Hughes, and O. R. Galle. 1979. "Overcrowding in the Home: An Empirical Investigation of Its Possible Pathological Consequences." *American Sociological Review* 44:59–80.

Grasmick, Harold G., Charles R. Tittle, Robert J. Bursik, and Bruce J. Arneklev. 1993. "Testing the Core Implications of Gottfredson and Hirschi's General Theory of Crime." *Journal of Research in Crime and Delinquency* 30:5–29.

Grasmick, Harold G., and Anne L. McGill. 1994. "Religion, Attribution Style, and Punitiveness Toward Juvenile Offenders." *Criminology* 32:23–46.

Greene, William H. 1990. *Econometric Analysis.* New York: Macmillan.

Greenwood, Peter, and Susan Turner. 1993. "Evaluation of the Paint Creek Youth Center: A Residential Program for Serious Delinquents." *Criminology* 31:263–279.

Hackney, S. 1969. "Southern Violence." *American Historical Review* 74:906–925.

Hanushek, Eric A., and John E. Jackson. 1977. *Statistical Methods for Social Scientists.* New York: Academic Press.

Hays, William L. 1994. *Statistics, 4th Ed.* New York: Harcourt Brace College Publishers.

Hirschi, Travis, and Michael J. Hindelang. 1977. "Intelligence and Delinquency: A Revisionist View." *American Sociological Review* 42:571–587.

Hirschi, Travis. 1969. *Causes of Delinquency.* Berkeley, CA: University of California Press.

Hood, Roger, and Richard Sparks. 1970. *Key Issues in Criminology.* New York: McGraw-Hill.

Hook, E. B. 1973. "Behavior Implications of the Human XYY Genotype." *Science* 179:139–150.

Humphries, D., and D. Wallace. 1980. "Capitalist Accumulation and Urban Crime, 1950–1971." *Social Problems* 28:179–193.

Innes, C. A. 1986. *Profile of State Prison Inmates, 1986.* Special Report NCJ-109926. Department of Justice, Bureau of Justice Statistics. Washington, DC.: U.S. Government Printing Office.

Irwin, John. 1970. *The Felon.* Englewood Cliffs, NJ: Prentice-Hall.

Jaccard, James. 1983. *Statistics for the Behavioral Sciences.* Belmont, CA: Wadsworth.

Jung, R. S., and L. A. Jason. 1988. "Firearm Violence and the Effects of Gun Control Legislation." *American Journal of Community Psychology* 16:515–524.

Kantor, Glenda, and Murray A. Straus. 1987. "The 'Drunken Bum' Theory of Wife Beating." *Social Problems* 34:213–230.

Kelly, Katharine D., and Walter S. DeKeseredy. 1994. "Women's Fear of Crime and Abuse in College and University Dating Relationships." *Violence and Victims* 9:17–30.

Kirk, R. E. 1968. *Experimental Design: Procedures for the Behavioral Sciences.* Monterey, CA: Brooks-Cole.

Kleck, Gary. 1988. "Crime Control through the Private Use of Armed Force." *Social Problems* 35:1–21.

Kleck, Gary, and E. Britt Patterson. 1993. "The Impact of Gun Control and Gun Ownership on Violence Rates." *Journal of Quantitative Criminology* 9:249–287.

Kohfeld, Carol W., and John Sprague. 1990. "Demography, Police Behavior, and Deterrence." *Criminology* 28:111–136.

Lester, D. 1988. "Gun Control, Gun Ownership, and Suicide Prevention." *Suicide and Life Threatening Behavior* 18:176–180.

Lester, D., and M. E. Murrell. 1982. "The Preventive Effect of Strict Gun Control Laws on Suicide and Homicide." *Suicide and Life Threatening Behavior* 12:131–140.

Loftin, Colin, and R. H. Hill. 1974. "Regional Subculture and Homicide." *American Sociological Review* 39:714–724.

Loftin, Colin, Milton Heumann, and David McDowall. 1983. "Evaluating an Alternative to Gun Control." *Law and Society Review* 17:287–318.

Loftin, Colin, and David McDowall. 1984. "The Deterrent Effects of the Florida Felony Firearm Law." *Journal of Criminal Law and Criminology* 75:250–259.

Loftin, Colin, David McDowall, Brian Wiersema, and Talbert Cottey. 1991. "Effects of Restrictive Licensing of Handguns on Homicide and Suicide in the District of Columbia." *The New England Journal of Medicine* 325:1615–1620.

Lundsgarde, H. 1977. *Murder in Space City.* New York: Oxford University Press.

Magaddino, J. P., and M. H. Medoff. 1982. "Homicides, Robberies and State 'Cooling-Off' Schemes." In *Why Handgun Bans Can't Work,* D. B. Kates (ed.). Bellevue, WA: Second Amendment Foundation.

Magaddino, J. P., and M. H. Medoff. 1984. "An Empirical Analysis of Federal and State Firearm Controls." In *Firearms and Violence,* D. B. Kates (ed.). Cambridge, MA: Ballinger.

Maguire, Kathleen, and Ann L. Pastore (Eds.). 1993. *Sourcebook of Criminal Justice Statistics 1992.* U.S. Department of Justice, Bureau of Justice Statistics. Washington, DC: U.S. Government Printing Office.

Maguire, Kathleen, and Ann L. Pastore (Eds.). 1994. *Sourcebook of Criminal Justice Statistics 1993.* U.S. Department of Justice, Bureau of Justice Statistics. Washington, DC: U.S. Government Printing Office.

Maguire, Kathleen, and Ann L. Pastore (Eds.). 1995. *Sourcebook of Criminal Justice Statistics 1994.* U.S. Department of Justice, Bureau of Justice Statistics. Washington, DC: U.S. Government Printing Office.

McPheters, Lee R., Robert Mann, and Don Schlagenhauf. 1984. "Economic Response to a Crime Deterrence Program." *Economic Inquiry* 22:550–570.

Messner, Steven F. 1982. "Poverty, Inequality, and the Urban Homicide Rate." *Criminology* 20:103–114.

Messner, Steven F. 1983. "Regional and Racial Effects on the Urban Homicide Rate: The Subculture of Violence Revisited." *American Journal of Sociology* 88:997–1007.

Miller, B. A., T. H. Nochajski, K. E. Leonard, H. T. Blane, D. M. Gondoli, and P. M. Bowers. 1990. "Spousal Violence and Alcohol/Drug Problems among Parolees and Their Spouses." *Women & Criminal Justice* 1:55–72.

Moffitt, Terrie E. 1993. "Adolescence-Limited and Life Course Persistent Antisocial Behavior: A Developmental Taxonomy." *Psychological Review* 100:674–701.

Moos, Rudolf H. 1975. *Evaluating Correctional and Community Settings.* New York: Wiley.

Murray, D. R. 1975. "Handguns, Gun Control Laws and Firearm Violence." *Social Problems* 23:81–92.

Myers, Martha. 1988. "Social Background and the Sentencing of Judges." *Criminology* 26:649–676.

Nacci, P. L., H. E. Teitelbaum, and J. Prather. 1977. "Population Density and Inmate Misconduct Rates." *Federal Probation* 41:26–31.

Nicholson, R., and A. Garner. 1980. *The Analysis of the Firearms Control Act of 1975.* Washington, DC: U.S. Conference of Mayors.

Nurco, David N., Thomas E. Hanlon, Timothy W. Kinlock, and Karen R. Duszynski. 1988. "Differential Criminal Patterns of Narcotic Addicts over an Addiction Career." *Criminology* 26:407–424.

Ogle, Robin S., Daniel Maier-Katkin, and Thomas Bernard. 1995. "A Theory of Homicidal Behavior among Women." *Criminology* 33:173–194.

Peete, Thomas A., Trudie F. Milner, and Michael R. Welch. 1994. "Levels of Social Integration in Group Contexts and the Effects of Informal Sanction Threat on Deviance." *Criminology* 32:85–106.

Pierce, Glenn L., and William J. Bowers. 1981. "The Bartley-Fox Gun Law's Short-Term Impact on Crime in Boston." *The Annals* 455:120–137.

Quetelet, Lambert Adolphe. 1968 [1842]. *Treatise on Man.* Trans. R. Knox and T. Smibert. Edinburgh: William and Robert Chambers.

Raine, Adrian. 1993. *The Psychopathology of Crime.* San Diego: Academic Press.

Reed, John S. 1971. "To Live and Die in Dixie: A Contribution to the Study of Southern Violence." *Political Science Quarterly* 86:429–486.

*Report to the Nation on Crime and Justice,* 2nd Ed. 1988. Special Report NCJ-105506. U.S. Department of Justice, Bureau of Justice Statistics. Washington, DC: U.S. Government Printing Office.

Roncek, Dennis W. 1991. "Using Logit Coefficients to Obtain the Effects of Independent Variables on Changes in Probabilities." *Social Forces* 70:509–518.

Sampson, Robert J., and John H. Laub. 1993. *Crime in the Making: Pathways and Turning Points through Life.* Cambridge: Harvard University Press.

Scheffe, H. 1959. *The Analysis of Variance.* New York: Wiley.

Sechrest, D. K. 1991. "The Effects of Density on Jail Assaults." *Journal of Criminal Justice* 19:211–233.

Seitz, S. T. 1972. "Firearms, Homicides, and Gun Control Effectiveness." *Law and Society Review* 6:595–614.

Sherman, Lawrence W. 1992. *Policing Domestic Violence: Experiments and Dilemmas.* New York: Free Press.

Sherman, Lawrence W., Janell D. Schmidt, Dennis P. Rogan, Douglas A. Smith, Patrick R. Gartin, Ellen G. Cohn, and Anthony R. Bacich. 1991. "From Initial Deterrence to Long-Term Escalation: The Effects of Short-Custody Arrest for Poverty Ghetto Domestic Violence." *Criminology* 29:821–850.

Smith, H. W. 1975. *Strategies of Social Research.* Englewood Cliffs, NJ: Prentice-Hall.

Smith, M. D., and R. N. Parker. 1980. "Type of Homicide and Variation in Regional Rates." *Social Forces* 59:136–147.

Smith, P. Z. 1993. *Felony Defendants in Large Urban Counties, 1990.* Special Report NCJ-141872. Department of Justice, Bureau of Justice Statistics. Washington, DC: U.S. Government Printing Office.

*Statistical Abstract of the United States.* 1992. Washington, DC: U.S. Government Printing Office.

*Statistical Abstract of the United States.* 1993. Washington, DC: U.S. Government Printing Office.

Steffensmeier, Darrell, John Kramer, and Cathy Streifel. 1993. "Gender and Imprisonment Decisions." *Criminology* 31:411–446.

Straus, Murray A., and Richard J. Gelles. 1990. *Physical Violence in American Families.* Interuniversity Consortium for Political and Social Research, Codebook 7733. Ann Arbor: Institute for Social Research, University of Michigan.

Sutherland, Edwin. 1973. *On Analyzing Crime.* Chicago: University of Chicago Press.

Taylor, Ralph B., and Jeanette Covington. 1988. "Neighborhood Changes in Ecology and Violence." *Criminology* 26:553–590.

Tukey, J. W. 1953. "The Problem of Multiple Comparisons." Unpublished manuscript. Princeton University.

Tukey, J. W. 1977. *Exploratory Data Analysis.* Reading, MA: Addison-Wesley.

Uniform Crime Reports. 1972. *Crime in the United States.* Washington, DC: U.S. Government Printing Office.

Uniform Crime Reports. 1982. *Crime in the United States.* Washington, DC: U.S. Government Printing Office.

Uniform Crime Reports. 1991. *Crime in the United States.* Washington, DC: U.S. Government Printing Office.

Uniform Crime Reports. 1992. *Crime in the United States.* Washington, DC: U.S. Government Printing Office.

United States Sentencing Commission. 1992. *Annual Report.* Washington, DC: U.S. Sentencing Commission.

Weisburd, David, Stanton Wheeler, Elin Waring, and Nancy Bode. 1991. *Crimes of the Middle Class: White Collar Offenders in the Federal Courts.* New Haven: Yale University Press.

Wilkinson, K. P. 1984. "A Research Note on Homicide and Rurality." *Social Forces* 63:445–452.

Williams, Kirk R. 1984. "Economic Sources of Homicide: Reestimating the Effects of Poverty and Inequality." *American Sociological Review* 49:283–289.

Williams, Kirk R., and Robert L. Flewelling. 1988. "The Social Production of Criminal Homicide: A Comparative Study of Disaggregated Rates in American Cities." *American Sociological Review* 53:421–431.

Wilson, James Q., and Richard J. Herrnstein. 1985. *Crime and Human Nature.* New York: Simon & Schuster.

Wolfgang, Marvin E. 1958. *Patterns in Criminal Homicide.* Philadelphia: University of Pennsylvania Press.

Wolfgang, Marvin E., and Franco Ferracuti. 1967. *The Subculture of Violence.* London: Tavistock.

Worden, Alissa Pollitz. 1993. "The Attitudes of Women and Men in Policing: Testing Conventional and Contemporary Wisdom." *Criminology* 31:203–242.

Wright, Richard T., and Scott H. Decker. 1994. *Burglars on the Job.* Boston: Northeastern University Press.

Zimring, Franklin E. 1991. "Firearms, Violence and Public Policy." *Scientific American* November: 48–54.

# Index

*Difference Between Means T–Test* $= t_{obt} = \dfrac{\bar{x}_1 - \bar{x}_2}{\sqrt{\dfrac{(n_1 - 1)s_1^2 + (n_2 - 1)s_2^2}{n_1 + n_2 - 2}}\sqrt{\dfrac{n_1 + n_2}{n_1 n_2}}}$      (12.7)      p. 351

*T Test for Dependent Samples* $= t_{obt} = \dfrac{\bar{X}_D - \mu_D}{S_D / \sqrt{n - 1}}$      (12.11)      p. 366

**Computations for Analysis of Variance (ANOVA) – F Test**      p. 398

$SS_{Between} = \Sigma(\bar{X}_k - \bar{X}_G)^2 \quad df_{Between} = k - 1$

$SS_{Within} = \displaystyle\sum_i \sum_k (\bar{X}_{ik} - X_k)^2 \quad df_{Within} = N - k$

*Estimated variance between groups* $= \dfrac{SS_{Between}}{df_{Between}}$

*Estimated variance within groups* $= \dfrac{SS_{Within}}{df_{Within}}$

$F_{obt} = \dfrac{Estimated\ variance\ between\ groups}{Estimated\ variance\ within\ groups}$

*Ordinary Least Squares (OLS) Regression Line* $= y = a + bx$      (14.4)      p. 442

$where\ b = \dfrac{N\Sigma xy - (\Sigma x)(\Sigma y)}{N\Sigma x^2 - (\Sigma x)^2}$